TAKING SIDES

Clashing Views on

Economic Issues

TWELFTH EDITION

TAKING SIDES

Clashing Views on

Economic Issues

TWELFTH EDITION

Selected, Edited, and with Introductions by

Frank J. Bonello
University of Notre Dame

McGraw-Hill/Dushkin
A Division of The McGraw-Hill Companies

This book is dedicated to Thomas R. Swartz, my co-editor through the first eleven editions of this volume. His contributions are still evident in this edition, especially in the material carried over from the eleventh edition and in the Introduction. Perhaps he will find time to read the new portions of the twelfth edition as a part of his well-deserved retirement. It is also dedicated to my children and grandchildren. In order of their births, they are John Anthony, David Joseph, Michael Thomas, and Amanda Marie.

Cover image: Photos.com

Cover Acknowledgment
Maggie Lytle

Manufactured in the United States of America

Twelfth Edition

123456789DOCDOC98765

Library of Congress Cataloging-in-Publication Data
Main entry under title:
Taking sides: clashing views on controversial economic issues/selected, edited, and with introductions by Frank J. Bonello.—12th ed.
Includes bibliographical references and index.
1. United States—Economic policy—1971–1981. 2. United States—Economic policy—1981–1993.
3. United States—Economic policy—1993–.
I. Bonello, Frank J., *comp*.
338.9'22

0-07-312952-6
ISSN: 1094-7612

Printed on Recycled Paper

Preface

Where there is much desire to learn, there of necessity will be much arguing.

—John Milton (1608–1674), English poet and essayist

Presented here are 18 debates on important and compelling economic issues, which are designed to stimulate critical thinking skills and initiate lively and informed discussion. These debates take economic theory and show how it is applied to current, real-world public policy decisions, the outcomes of which will have an immediate and personal impact. How these debates are resolved will affect our taxes, jobs, wages, educational system, and so on; in short, they will shape the society in which we live.

It has been our intent throughout each of the 12 editions of *Taking Sides: Clashing Views on Controversial Economic Issues* to select issues that reveal something about the nature of economics itself and something about how economics relates to current, everyday newspaper headlines and television news stories on public policy concerns. To assist the reader, we begin each issue with an *issue introduction,* which sets the stage for the debate as it is argued in the "yes" and "no" selections. Each issue concludes with a *postscript* that briefly reviews the arguments and makes some final observations. The introduction and postscript do not preempt what is the reader's own task: to achieve a critical and informed view of the economic issue at stake. Certainly, the reader should not feel confined to adopt one or the other of the positions presented. The views presented should be used as starting points, and the suggestions for further reading that appear in each issue postscript offer additional resources on the topic. Internet site addresses (URLs) have been provided at the beginning of each part, which should also prove useful as resources for further research. At the back of the book is a listing of all the *contributors to this volume,* which provides information on the economists, policymakers, political leaders, and commentators whose views are debated here.

Changes to this edition This new edition of *Taking Sides* represents a considerable revision. Of the 18 issues, seven are completely new. Thus, as the journey into the new millennium continues, this substantially revised book will help us understand the implications of a changing set of economic issues that were not part of our world just a few years ago. The new issues are: "Should the Regulations Regarding Overtime Pay Be Changed?" (Issue 2); "Will the Medicare Modernization Act of 2003 and Its Drug Discount Cards Lower the Cost of Prescription Drugs for Seniors?" (Issue 4); "Is Wal-Mart Good for the Economy?" (Issue 7); "Should Social Security Be Changed to Include Personal Retirement Accounts?" (Issue 8); "Are Credit Card Companies Exploiting American Consumers?" (Issue 10); "Do Living Wage Laws Improve Economic Conditions in Cities?" (Issue 16); and "Is the No Child Left Behind Act Working?" (Issue 18).

As with all of the previous editions, the issues in the twelfth edition can be used in any sequence. Although the organization of the book loosely parallels the sequence of topics found in a standard introductory economics textbook, you can pick and choose which issues to read first, since they are designed to stand alone. The modification to Part 3 introduced in the seventh edition has been retained. That part, "The World Around Us," allows coverage of a broader set of problems society faces in an ever-changing world.

A word to the instructor *An Instructor's Manual With Test Questions* (multiple-choice and essay) is available through the publisher. A general guidebook, *Using Taking Sides in the Classroom,* which discusses methods and techniques for integrating the pro/con approach into any classroom setting, is also available. An online version of *Using Taking Sides in the Classroom* and a correspondence service for *Taking Sides* adopters can be found at `http://www.dushkin.com/usingts/`.

Taking Sides: Clashing Views on Controversial Economic Issues is only one title in the Taking Sides series. If you are interested in seeing the table of contents for any of the other titles, please visit the Taking Sides Web site at `http://www.dushkin.com/takingsides`.

Acknowledgments Friends and readers across the United States and Canada have offered helpful comments and suggestions. As always, their suggestions were welcomed and have markedly enhanced the quality of this edition of *Taking Sides*. If as you read this book you are reminded of an essay that could be included in a future edition, I hope that you will drop me a note at Bonello.1@nd.edu. I very much appreciate your interest and help, and I am always pleased to hear from you.

I am most appreciative of the encouragement and the effort that the staff of McGraw-Hill/Dushkin have expanded in expediting this edition of *Taking Sides*, especially Nichole Altman, Developmental Editor. To all those, I owe a huge debt, many thanks, and none of the blame for any shortcomings that remain in this edition of *Taking Sides*.

Frank J. Bonello
University of Notre Dame

Contents In Brief

Contents

Preface v

Introduction: Economics and Economists: The Basis for Controversy xvi

PART 1 MICROECONOMIC ISSUES 1

Issue 1. Are Profits the Only Business of Business? 2

YES: Milton Friedman, from "The Social Responsibility of Business Is to Increase Its Profits," *The New York Times Magazine* (September 13, 1970) *4*

NO: Robert Almeder, from "Morality in the Marketplace: Reflections on the Friedman Doctrine," in Milton Snoeyenbos, Robert Almeder, and James Humber, eds., *Business Ethics*, rev. ed. (Prometheus Press, 1998) *10*

Free-market economist Milton Friedman contends that the sole responsibility of business is to increase its profits. Philosopher Robert Almeder maintains that if capitalism is to survive, it must act in socially responsible ways that go beyond profit making.

Issue 2. Should the Regulations Regarding Overtime Pay Be Changed? 21

YES: Elaine Chao, from "Bush Administration Proposal," *Congressional Digest* (March 2004) *23*

NO: Ross Eisenbrey, from "On the Department of Labor's Final Overtime Regulations," Testimony before the Senate Subcommittee on Labor, Health and Human Services, and Education (May 4, 2004) *28*

Secretary of Labor Elaine Chao believes that today's workers are "severely disadvantaged" by current regulations regarding overtime pay, and she believes it is time to institute new rules that would "benefit more workers." Ross Eisenbrey, Economic Policy Institute vice president, believes that the Department of Labor's proposed changes will mean "longer hours and less pay for millions of workers—and more litigation for our entire economy."

Issue 3. Is There Discrimination in U.S. Labor Markets? 39

YES: William A. Darity, Jr., and Patrick L. Mason, from "Evidence on Discrimination in Employment: Codes of Color, Codes of Gender," *Journal of Economic Perspectives* (Spring 1998) *41*

NO: James J. Heckman, from "Detecting Discrimination," *Journal of Economic Perspectives* (Spring 1998) *57*

Professor of economics William A. Darity, Jr., and associate professor of economics Patrick L. Mason assert that the lack of progress made since the mid-1970s toward establishing equality in wages between the races is evidence of persistent discrimination in U.S. labor markets. Professor

NO: Evelyn Z. Brodkin, from "Requiem for Welfare," *Dissent* (Winter 2003) *276*

Cato Institute researcher Michael J. New presents statistical evidence that welfare reform, and not a growing economy, is the primary cause of the recent decline in welfare caseloads. This means that welfare reform has been a success. Evelyn Z. Brodkin, an associate professor in the School of Social Service Administration and lecturer at the University of Chicago Law School, contends that in assessing welfare reform, one must look beyond the decline in welfare caseloads and ask, What has happened to those who no longer receive welfare? Her answer to this question evokes in Brodkin nostalgia for the "bad old days" of unreformed welfare.

PART 3 THE WORLD AROUND US 289

Issue 13. Are Protectionist Policies Bad for America? 290

YES: Murray N. Rothbard, from "Protectionism and the Destruction of Prosperity," Ludwig von Mises Institute, `http://mises.org/fullarticle.asp?title=Protectionism&month=1` (July 13, 1998) *292*

NO: Patrick J. Buchanan, from "Free Trade Is Not Free," Address to the Chicago Council on Foreign Relations (November 18, 1998) *300*

Free-trade economist Murray N. Rothbard objects to the prospect of protectionism, which he sees as an attempt by the few who make up special interest groups "to repress and loot the rest of us" who make up the many. Social critic and three-time presidential hopeful Patrick J. Buchanan argues that America's "new corporate elite" is willing to sacrifice the country's best interests on "the altar of that golden calf, the global economy."

Issue 14. Should We Sweat About Sweatshops? 308

YES: Richard Appelbaum and Peter Dreier, from "The Campus Anti-Sweatshop Movement," *The American Prospect* (September–October 1999) *310*

NO: Nicholas D. Kristof and Sheryl WuDunn, from "Two Cheers for Sweatshops," *The New York Times Magazine* (September 24, 2000) *321*

Sociologist Richard Appelbaum and political scientist Peter Dreier chronicle the rise of student activism on American campuses over the issue of sweatshops abroad. Students demand that firms be held responsible for "sweatshop conditions" and warn that if conditions do not improve, American consumers will not "leave their consciences at home when they shop for clothes." News correspondents Nicholas D. Kristof and Sheryl WuDunn agree that the working conditions in many offshore plant sites "seem brutal from the vantage point of an American sitting in his living room." But they argue that these work opportunities are far superior to the alternatives that are currently available in many parts of the world and that what is needed are more sweatshops, not fewer sweatshops.

Issue 15. Are the Costs of Global Warming Too High to Ignore? 327

YES: Lester R. Brown, from *Eco-Economy: Building an Economy for the Earth* (W. W. Norton, 2001) *329*

NO: Lenny Bernstein, from "Climate Change and Ecosystems," A Report of the George C. Marshall Institute (August 2002) *342*

Lester R. Brown, founder and president of the Earth Policy Institute, describes his vision of an environmentally sustainable economy, which includes food supplies, population growth issues, water availability, climatic changes, and renewable energy. Lenny Bernstein, head of L. S. Bernstein & Associates, which advises companies and trade associations on political and scientific developments on global environmental issues, acknowledges that ecosystems are sensitive to climate change, but he argues that the change that we have seen repeated again and again over the course of history can lead to benefits for our children and our children's children.

Issue 16. Do Living Wage Laws Improve Economic Conditions in Cities? 357

YES: Chris Tilly, from "Next Steps for the Living-Wage Movement," *Dollars & Sense* (September–October 2001) *359*

NO: Steven Malanga, from "How the 'Living-Wage' Sneaks Socialism into Cities," *City Journal* (Winter 2003) *364*

Professor Chris Tilly supports the living wage for two basic reasons: (1) It is only fair to increase the incomes of those who earn the lowest wages, and (2) the living wage laws that have been passed "have not escalated costs, nor repelled businesses." Author Steven Malanga believes that the actions to pass living wage laws represent a "savvy left-wing political movement," and that living wage laws threaten the economic health of cities by increasing wage costs and "send businesses fleeing to other locales."

Issue 17. Has the North American Free Trade Agreement Hurt the American Economy? 375

YES: Robert E. Scott, from "NAFTA's Hidden Costs: Trade Agreement Results in Job Losses, Growing Inequality, and Wage Suppression for the United States," *EPI Briefing Paper* (April 2001) *377*

NO: Daniel T. Griswold, from "NAFTA at 10: An Economic and Foreign Policy Success," *Free Trade Bulletin* (December 2002) *384*

Economic Policy Institute director Robert E. Scott argues that besides the loss of a significant number of jobs, the North American Free Trade Agreement (NAFTA) has generated a number of less visible harmful effects on the American economy. These include increased income inequality and reduced fringe benefits. Daniel T. Griswold, associate director of the Cato Institute's Center for Trade Policy Studies, contends that NAFTA has helped the American economy by producing better-paying jobs and contributing to increased manufacturing output in the United States between 1993 and 2001.

Issue 18. Is the No Child Left Behind Act Working? 390

YES: House Education and the Workforce Committee, from "Fact Sheet: No Child Left Behind Is Working," `http://edworkforce.house.gov/issues/108th/recess/nclbworks.htm` (October 7, 2004) *392*

NO: Gerald W. Bracey, from "The Perfect Law: No Child Left Behind and the Assault on Public Schools," *Dissent* (Fall 2004) *398*

The House Education and the Workforce Committee lists a number of positive results for the No Child Left Behind Act, including higher reading and math test scores in several states as well as improved data and information for teachers and parents. Professor Gerald W. Bracey believes that the No Child Left Behind Act is, from the perspective of the Republican party, a perfect law because it will ultimately transfer billions from the public sector to the private sector, because it will reduce the size of government, and because it will "wound or kill" a large Democratic party power base.

Contributors 406
Index 414

Introduction

Economics and Economists: The Basis for Controversy

Frank J. Bonello and Thomas R. Swartz

> I think that Capitalism, wisely managed, can probably be more efficient for attaining economic ends than any alternative system yet in sight, but that in itself it is in many ways extremely objectionable.
>
> —Lord John Maynard Keynes, *The End of Laissez-Faire* (1926)

Although almost 80 years have passed since Lord Keynes penned these lines, many economists still struggle with the basic dilemma he outlined. The paradox rests in the fact that a free-market system is extremely efficient. It is purported to produce more at a lower cost than any other economic system. But in producing this wide array of low-cost goods and services, problems arise. These problems—most notably a lack of economic equity and economic stability—concern some economists.

If the problems raised and analyzed in this book were merely the product of intellectual gymnastics undertaken by "egg-headed" economists, then we could sit back and enjoy these confrontations as theoretical exercises. Unfortunately, we are not afforded that luxury. The essays contained in this book touch each and every one of us in tangible ways. They are real-world issues. Some focus upon "macroeconomic" topics such as the minimum wage. Another set of issues deals with "microeconomic" topics. (We refer to these issues as "micro" problems not because they are small problems, but because they deal with small economic units, such as households, firms, or individual industries. An example here is government assistance for seniors in their purchases of prescription drugs.) A third set of issues deals with matters that do not fall neatly into the macroeconomic or microeconomic classifications. This set includes three issues relating to the international aspects of economic activity including the effects of the North American Free Trade Agreement and the question of importing goods produced in sweatshops in foreign countries. The third set also includes issues dealing with education, the living wage, and pollution.

The range of issues and disagreements raises a fundamental question: Why do economists disagree? One explanation is suggested by Lord Keynes' 1926 remark. How various economists react to the strengths and weaknesses found in an economic system depends upon how they view the relative importance of efficiency, equity, and stability. These are central terms, and we will define them in detail in the following pages. For now, the important point is that some economists may view efficiency as overriding. In other cases, the same economists may be willing to sacrifice the efficiency generated by the market in order to ensure increased economic equity and/or increased economic stability.

Given the extent of conflict, controversy, and diversity, it might appear that economists rarely, if ever, agree on any economic issue. It would be most misleading if the reader were left with this impression. Economists rarely challenge the internal logic of the theoretical models that have been developed and articulated by their colleagues. Rather, they will challenge either the validity of the assumptions used in these models or the value of the ends these models seek to achieve. For example, it is most difficult to discredit the internal logic of the microeconomic models employed by the "free-market economist." These models are elegant, and their logical development is persuasive. However, these models are challenged. The challenges typically focus upon such issues as the assumption of functioning, competitive markets and the desirability of perpetuating the existing distribution of income. In this case, those who support and those who challenge the operation of the market agree on a large number of issues. But they disagree most assuredly on a few issues that have dramatic implications.

This same phenomenon of agreeing more often than disagreeing is also true in the area of economic policy. In this area, where the public is most acutely aware of differences among economists, these differences are not generally over the kinds of changes that will be brought about by a particular policy. Again, the differences more typically concern the timing of the change, the specific characteristics of the policy, and the size of the resulting effect or effects.

Economists: What Do They Represent?

Newspapers, magazines, and TV commentators all use handy labels to describe certain members of the economics profession. What do the headlines mean when they refer to the "Chicago School," the "Keynesians," the "Institutional Economists," or the "Radical Economists"? What do these individuals stand for? Since labels are used throughout this book, we feel obliged to identify the principal groups or camps in our profession. Let us warn you that this can be a misleading venture. Some economists—perhaps most economists—defy classification. They drift from one camp to another, selecting a gem of wisdom here and another there. These are practical men and women who believe that no one camp has all the answers to all the economic problems confronting society.

Recognizing this limitation, four major groups of economists can be identified. These groups are differentiated on the basis of two basic criteria: how they view efficiency relative to equity and stability, and what significance they attach to imperfectly competitive market structures. Before describing the views of the four groups on these criteria, it is essential to understand the meaning of certain terms to be used in this description.

Efficiency, equity, and stability represent goals for an economic system. An economy is efficient when it produces those goods and services that people want and does so without wasting scarce resources. Equity in an economic sense has several dimensions. It means that income and wealth are distributed according to accepted principles of fairness, that those who are unable to care for themselves receive adequate care, and that mainstream economic activity is open to all persons. Stability is viewed as the absence of sharp ups and downs in business activity, in prices, and in employment. In other words, stability is marked by steady increases in output, little inflation, and low unemployment.

When the term "market structures" is used, it refers to the number of buyers and sellers in the market and the amount of control they exercise over price. At one extreme is a perfectly competitive market where there are so many buyers and sellers that no one has any ability to influence market price. One seller or buyer obviously could have great control over price. This extreme market structure, which we call pure monopoly, and other market structures that result in some control over price are grouped under the broad label of imperfectly competitive markets. That is, imperfect competition is a situation where the number of market participants is limited and, as a consequence, the participants have the ability to influence price. With these terms in mind, we can begin to examine the various schools of economic thought.

Free-Market Economists

One of the most visible groups of economists and perhaps the easiest to identify and classify are the free-market economists. In general, this is also the group of economists that persons have in mind when they speak of conservative economists. These economists believe that the market, operating freely without interferences from government or labor unions, will generate the greatest amount of well-being for the greatest number of people.

Economic efficiency is one of the priorities for free-market economists. In their well-developed models, consumer sovereignty—consumer demand for goods and services—guides the system by directly influencing market prices. The distribution of economic resources caused by these market prices not only results in the production of an array of goods and services that are demanded by consumers, but this production is undertaken in the most cost-effective fashion. The free-market economists claim that, at any point, some individuals must earn incomes, which are substantially greater than other individuals. They contend that these higher incomes are a reward for greater efficiency or productivity and that this reward-induced efficiency will result in rapid economic growth that will benefit all persons in the society. They might also admit that a system driven by these freely operating markets will be subject to occasional bouts of instability (slow growth, inflation, and unemployment). However, they maintain that government action to eliminate or reduce this periodic instability will only make matters worse. Consequently, government, according to the free-market or conservative economist, should play a minor role in the economic affairs of society.

Although the models of free-market economists are dependent upon functioning, competitive markets, the lack of these competitive markets in the real world does not seriously jeopardize their position. First, they assert that large firms are necessary to achieve low per-unit costs; that is, a single large firm may be able to produce a given level of output with fewer scarce resources than a large number of small firms. Second, they suggest that the benefits associated with the free operation of markets are so great compared to government intervention that even a "second best solution" of imperfectly competitive markets still yields benefits far in excess of government intervention.

These advocates of the free market have been given various labels over time. The oldest and most persistent label is "classical economists." This is because the classical economists of the eighteenth century, particularly Adam Smith, were the first to point out the virtues of the market. Smith captured the essence of the system with the following words:

> Every individual endeavors to employ his capital so that its produce may be of greatest value. He generally neither intends to promote the public interest nor knows how much he is promoting it. He intends only his own security, only his own gain. And he is in this led by an invisible hand to promote an end that was no part of his intention. By pursuing his own interest he frequently promotes that of society more effectively than when he really intends to promote it.
>
> —Adam Smith, *The Wealth of Nations* (1776)

Liberal Economists

Another significant group of economists in the United States can be classified as liberal economists. "Liberal" in this instance refers to the willingness to intervene in the free operation of the market. These economists share with the free-market economists a great respect for the market. The liberal economist, however, does not believe that the explicit and implicit costs of a freely operating market should or can be ignored. Rather, the liberal maintains that the costs of an uncontrolled marketplace are often borne by those in society who are least capable of bearing them: the poor, the elderly, and the infirm. Additionally, liberal economists maintain that the freely operating market sometimes results in economic instability (that is, in bouts of inflation, unemployment, and slow or negative growth).

Consider for a moment the differences between free-market or conservative economists and liberal economists at the microeconomic level. Liberal economists take exception to the free market on two grounds. First, these economists find a basic problem with fairness in the marketplace. Since the market is driven by the forces of consumer spending, there are those who through no fault of their own (they may be aged, young, infirm, physically or mentally handicapped) may not have the wherewithal to participate in the economic system. Second, the unfettered marketplace does not and cannot handle spillover effects or what are known as "externalities." These are the third-party effects that may occur as a result of some action. Will a firm willingly compensate its neighbors for the pollutants it pours into the nearby lake? Will a truck driver willingly drive at a safe speed and in the process reduce the highway accident rate? Liberal economists think not. These economists are therefore willing to have the government intervene in these and other similar cases.

The liberal economists' role in macroeconomics is more readily apparent. Ever since the failure of free-market economics during the Great Depression of the 1930s, Keynesianism (still another label for liberal economics) has become widely known. In his 1935 book, *The General Theory of Employment, Interest, and Money,* Lord John Maynard Keynes laid the basic groundwork for this school of thought. Keynes argued that the history of freely operating market economies was marked by periods of recurring recessions, sometimes very deep recessions that are called depressions. He maintained that government intervention through its fiscal policy—government tax and spending power—could eliminate, or at least soften these sharp reductions in economic activity and as a result move the economy along a more stable growth path. Thus for the Keynesians, or liberal economists, one of the "extremely objectionable" aspects of a free-market economy is its inherent instability.

Liberal economists are also far more concerned about the existence of imperfections in the marketplace than are their free-market counterparts. They reject the notion that imperfect competition is an acceptable substitute for competitive markets. These economists may agree that the imperfectly competitive firms can achieve some savings because of their large size and efficiency, but they assert that since there is little or no competition, the firms are not forced to pass on these cost savings to consumers. Thus liberal economists, who in some circles are labeled "antitrusters," are willing to intervene in the market in two ways. They are prepared to allow some monopolies, such as public utilities, to exist, but they contend that government must regulate these monopolies. In other cases, they maintain that there is no justification for monopolies, and they are prepared to invoke the powers of antitrust legislation to break up existing monopolies, and/or prevent the formation of new ones.

The Mainstream Critics and Radical Reform Economists

There are two other groups of economists we must identify. One group can be called mainstream critics. Included in this group are individuals like Thorstein Veblen (1857–1929) with his critique of conspicuous consumption, and John Kenneth Galbraith (b. 1908), with his views on industrial structure. One reasonably cohesive subgroup of mainstream critics are the post-Keynesians, so-named because they believe that as the principal economic institutions have changed over time, they have remained closer to the spirit of Keynes than have the liberal economists. As some have suggested, the key aspect of Keynes as far as the post-Keynesians are concerned is his assertion that "expectations of the future are not necessarily certain." On a more practical level, post-Keynesians assert, among other things, that the productivity of the economic system is not significantly affected by changes in income distribution, that the system can still be efficient without competitive markets, that conventional fiscal policies cannot control inflation, and that "income policies" are the means to an effective and equitable answer to the inflationary dilemma. (This characterization of post-Keynesianism is drawn from Alfred S. Eichner's "Introduction" in *A Guide to Post-Keynesian Economics,* M.E. Sharpe, 1978).

The fourth and last group can be called radical reformist economists. Many in this group trace their ideas to the nineteenth-century philosopher-economist Karl Marx and his most impressive work, the three volumes of *Das Kapital*. As with the other three groups of economists, there are subgroups of radical reform economists. One subgroup, which may be labeled contemporary Marxists, is best represented by those who have published their research results over the years in the *Review of Radical Political Economy*. These economists examine issues that have been largely ignored by mainstream economists, such as war, sexism, racism, imperialism, and civil rights. In their analyses of these issues, they borrow from and refine the work of Marx. In the process, they emphasize the role of class in shaping society and the role of the economy in determining class structures. Moreover, they see a need to encourage explicitly the development of some form of democratic socialism, for only then will the greatest good for the greatest number be ensured.

In concluding this section, we must warn you to use these labels with extreme care. Our categories are not hard and fast. There is much grayness around the edges and little that is black and white in these classifications. This does not mean, however, that they have no value. It is important to understand the philosophical background of the individual authors. This background does indeed color or shade their work.

Summary

It is clear that there is no shortage of economic problems. These problems demand solutions. At the same time, there is no shortage of proposed solutions. In fact, there is often an oversupply supply of solutions. The 18 issues included in this volume will acquaint you or, more accurately, reacquaint you with some of these problems. And, of course, there are at least two proposed solutions for each of the problems. Here we hope to provide new insights regarding the alternatives available and the differences and similarities of these alternative remedies.

If this introduction has served its purpose, you will be able to identify common elements in the proposed solutions to the different problems. For example, you will be able to identify the reliance on the forces of the market advocated by free-market economists as the remedy for several economic ills. This introduction should also help you understand why there are at least two proposed solutions for every economic problem; each group of economists tends to interpret a problem from its own philosophical position and to advance a solution that is grounded in that same philosophical framework.

Our intention, of course, is not to connect persons to one philosophic position or another. We hope instead to generate discussion and promote understanding. To do this, not only must each of us see a proposed solution, we must also be aware of the foundation that supports that solution. With greater understanding, meaningful progress in addressing economic problems can be achieved.

On the Internet . . .

The Dismal Scientist

The Dismal Scientist provides free economic data, analysis, and forecasts on a variety of topics.

http://www.dismal.com

Economist.com

The Web edition of *The Economist* is available free to subscribers of the print edition or for an annual fee to those who wish to subscribe online. A selection of articles is available free to those who want to explore the journal.

http://www.economist.com

The Electronic Policy Network

This site offers timely information and analysis of national policy in the form of a virtual magazine.

http://epn.org

Resources for Economists on the Internet

This guide to economic resources on the Internet is sponsored by the American Economic Association. It is an excellent starting point for anyone who wants to do research on economic topics. It has many Web links.

http://rfe.org

Statistical Resources on the Web: Comprehensive Economics

This site provides links to a wide variety of economic data at the city, state, country, and global levels.

http://www.lib.umich.edu/govdocs/stecon.html

WebEc: WWW Resources In Economics

This site is a virtual library that categorizes free information in economics available on the World Wide Web.

http://www.helsinki.fi/WebEc

Internet Resources for Economists

This site offers a number of links to economic blogs, classic works, textbooks, data sources, journals, etc.

http://www.oswego.edu/~economic/econweb.htm

PART 1

Microeconomic Issues

Economic decisions made at the microeconomic level affect our lives in a variety of important ways. Public and private actions determine what goods and services are produced, as well as the prices we pay for them. The actions also affect our incomes and even our health. In this part, we examine the profit decisions of businesses, overtime pay for workers, discrimination, the cost of prescription drugs, the health care industry, and reform of medical malpractice litigation.

ISSUE 1

Are Profits the Only Business of Business?

YES: Milton Friedman, from "The Social Responsibility of Business Is to Increase Its Profits," *The New York Times Magazine* (September 13, 1970)

NO: Robert Almeder, from "Morality in the Marketplace: Reflections on the Friedman Doctrine," in Milton Snoeyenbos, Robert Almeder, and James Humber, eds., *Business Ethics,* rev. ed. (Prometheus Press, 1998)

ISSUE SUMMARY

YES: Free-market economist Milton Friedman contends that the sole responsibility of business is to increase its profits.

NO: Philosopher Robert Almeder maintains that if capitalism is to survive, it must act in socially responsible ways that go beyond profit making.

Every economic society—whether it is a traditional society in Central Africa, a fossilized planned economy such as Cuba's, or a wealthy capitalist society such as those found in North America, Western Europe, and the Pacific Rim—must address the basic economic problem of resource allocation. These societies must determine *what* goods and services they can and will produce, *how* these goods and services will be produced, and *for whom* these goods and services will be produced.

The *what, how,* and *for whom* questions must be answered because of the problem of scarcity. Even if a given society were indescribably rich, it would still confront the problem of scarcity—in the case of a rich society, "relative scarcity." It might have all the resources it needs to produce all the goods and services it would ever want, but it could not produce all these things simultaneously. Thus, even a very rich society must set priorities and produce first those goods and services with the highest priority and postpone the production of those goods and services with lower priorities. If time is of the essence, this society would determine *how* these goods and services should be produced.

And since this wealthy society cannot produce all it wants instantly, it must also determine *for whom* the first bundle of goods and services will be produced.

Few, if any, economic societies are indescribably rich. On the other hand, there are many examples of economic societies that face grinding deprivation daily. In these societies and in all the societies that fall between poverty and great affluence, the *what, how,* and *for whom* questions are immediately apparent. Somehow these questions must be answered.

In some societies, such as the Amish communities of North America, the answers to these questions are found in tradition: Sons and daughters follow in their parents' footsteps. Younger generations produce *what* older generations produced before them. The methods of production—the horsedrawn plow, the hand-held scythe, the use of natural fertilizers—remain unchanged; thus, the *how* question is answered in the same way that the *for whom* question is answered—by following historic patterns. In other societies, such as self-sustaining religious communities, there is a different pattern of responses to these questions. In these communities, the "elder" of the community determines *what* will be produced, *how* it will be produced, and *for whom* it will be produced. If there is a well-defined hierarchical system, it is similar to one of the former stereotypical command economies of Eastern Europe.

Although elements of tradition and command are found in the industrialized societies of Western Europe, North America, and Japan, the basic answers to the three questions of resource allocation in these countries are determined by profit. In these economic societies, *what* will be produced is determined by what will yield the greatest profit. Consumers, in their search for maximum satisfaction, will bid for those goods and services that they want most. This consumer action drives the prices of these goods and services up, which, in turn, increases producers' profits. The higher profits attract new firms into the industry and encourage existing firms to increase their output. Thus, profits are the mechanism that ensures that consumers get what they want. Similarly, the profit-seeking behavior of business firms determines *how* the goods and services that consumers want will be produced. Since firms attempt to maximize their profits, they select those means of production that are economically most efficient. Lastly, the *for whom* question is also linked to profits. Wherever there is a shortage of goods and services, profits will be high. In the producers' attempts to increase their output, they must attract factors of production (land, labor, and capital) away from other economic activities. This bidding increases factor prices or factor incomes and ensures that these factors will be able to buy goods and services in the open marketplace.

Both Milton Friedman and Robert Almeder recognize the merits of a profit-driven economic system. They do not quarrel over the importance of profits. But they do quarrel over whether or not business firms have obligations beyond making profits. In the following selection, Friedman holds that the *only* responsibility of business is to make profits and that anyone who maintains otherwise is "preaching pure and unadulterated socialism." In the second selection, Almeder, who is clearly not a "socialist," contends that business must act in socially responsible ways "if capitalism is to survive."

Milton Friedman

The Social Responsibility of Business Is to Increase Its Profits

When I hear businessmen speak eloquently about the "social responsibilities of business in a free-enterprise system," I am reminded of the wonderful line about the Frenchman who discovered at the age of 70 that he had been speaking prose all his life. The businessmen believe that they are defending free enterprise when they declaim that business is not concerned "merely" with profit but also with promoting desirable "social ends; that business has a social conscience" and takes seriously its responsibilities for providing employment, eliminating discrimination, avoiding pollution and whatever else may be the catchwords of the contemporary crop of reformers. In fact they are—or would be if they or anyone else took them seriously—preaching pure and unadulterated socialism. Businessmen who talk this way are unwitting puppets of the intellectual forces that have been undermining the basis of a free society these past decades.

The discussions of the "social responsibilities of business" are notable for their analytical looseness and lack of rigor. What does it mean to say that "business" has responsibilities? Only people can have responsibilities. A corporation is an artificial person and in this sense may have artificial responsibilities, but "business" as a whole cannot be said to have responsibilities, even in this vague sense. The first step toward clarity in examining the doctrine of the social responsibility of business is to ask precisely what it implies for whom.

Presumably, the individuals who are to be responsible are businessmen, which means individual proprietors or corporate executives. Most of the discussion of social responsibility is directed at corporations, so in what follows I shall mostly neglect the individual proprietor and speak of corporate executives.

In a free-enterprise, private-property system, a corporate executive is an employee of the owners of the business. He has direct responsibility to his employers. That responsibility is to conduct the business in accordance with their desires, which generally will be to make as much money as possible while conforming to the basic rules of the society, both those embodied in law and those embodied in ethical custom. Of course, in some cases his employers may have a different objective. A group of persons might establish a corporation for an eleemosynary purpose—for example, a hospital or a school. The

From Milton Friedman, "The Social Responsibility of Business Is to Increase Its Profits," *The New York Times Magazine* (September 13, 1970).

manager of such a corporation will not have money profit as his objective but the rendering of certain services.

In either case, the key point is that, in his capacity as a corporate executive, the manager is the agent of the individuals who own the corporation or establish the eleemosynary institution, and his primary responsibility is to them.

Needless to say, this does not mean that it is easy to judge how well he is performing his task. But at least the criterion of performance is straightforward, and the persons among whom a voluntary contractual arrangement exists are clearly defined.

Of course, the corporate executive is also a person in his own right. As a person, he may have many other responsibilities that he recognizes or assumes voluntarily—to his family, his conscience, his feelings of charity, his church, his clubs, his city, his country. He may feel impelled by these responsibilities to devote part of his income to causes he regards as worthy, to refuse to work for particular corporations, even to leave his job, for example, to join his country's armed forces. If we wish, we may refer to some of these responsibilities as "social responsibilities." But in these respects he is acting as a principal, not an agent; he is spending his own money or time or energy, not the money of his employers or the time or energy he has contracted to devote to their purposes. If these are "social responsibilities," they are the social responsibilities of individuals, not of business.

What does it mean to say that the corporate executive has a "social responsibility" in his capacity as businessman? If this statement is not pure rhetoric, it must mean that he is to act in some way that is not in the interest of his employers. For example, that he is to refrain from increasing the price of the product in order to contribute to the social objective of preventing inflation, even though a price increase would be in the best interests of the corporation. Or that he is to make expenditures on reducing pollution beyond the amount that is in the best interests of the corporation or that is required by law in order to contribute to the social objective of improving the environment. Or that, at the expense of corporate profits, he is to hire "hard-core" unemployed instead of better-qualified available workmen to contribute to the social objective of reducing poverty.

In each of these cases, the corporate executive would be spending someone else's money for a general social interest. Insofar as his actions in accord with his "social responsibility" reduce returns to stockholders, he is spending their money. Insofar as his actions raise the price to customers, he is spending the customers' money. Insofar as his actions lower the wages of some employees, he is spending their money.

The stockholders or the customers or the employees could separately spend their own money on the particular action if they wished to do so. The executive is exercising a distinct "social responsibility," rather than serving as an agent of the stockholders or the customers or the employees, only if he spends the money in a different way than they would have spent it.

But if he does this, he is in effect imposing taxes, on the one hand, and deciding how the tax proceeds shall be spent, on the other.

This process raises political questions on two levels: principle and consequences. On the level of political principle, the imposition of taxes and the expenditure of tax proceeds are governmental functions. We have established elaborate constitutional, parliamentary and judicial provisions to control these functions, to assure that taxes are imposed so far as possible in accordance with the preferences and desires of the public—after all, "taxation without representation" was one of the battle cries of the American Revolution. We have a system of checks and balances to separate the legislative function of imposing taxes and enacting expenditures from the executive function of collecting taxes and administering expenditure programs and from the judicial function of mediating disputes and interpreting the law.

Here the businessman—self-selected or appointed directly or indirectly by stockholders—is to be simultaneously legislator, executive and jurist. He is to decide whom to tax by how much and for what purpose, and he is to spend the proceeds—all this guided only by general exhortations from on high to restrain inflation, improve the environment, fight poverty and so on and on.

The whole justification for permitting the corporate executive to be selected by the stockholders is that the executive is an agent serving the interests of his principal. This justification disappears when the corporate executive imposes taxes and spends the proceeds for "social" purposes. He becomes in effect a public employee, a civil servant, even though he remains in name an employee of a private enterprise. On grounds of political principle, it is intolerable that such civil servants—insofar as their actions in the name of social responsibility are real and not just window-dressing—should be selected as they are now. If they are to be civil servants, then they must be selected through a political process. If they are to impose taxes and make expenditures to foster "social" objectives, then political machinery must be set up to guide the assessment of taxes and to determine through a political process the objectives to be served.

This is the basic reason why the doctrine of "social responsibility" involves the acceptance of the socialist view that political mechanisms, not market mechanisms, are the appropriate way to determine the allocation of scarce resources to alternative uses.

On the grounds of consequences, can the corporate executive in fact discharge his alleged "social responsibilities"? On the one hand, suppose he could get away with spending the stockholders' or customers' or employees' money. How is he to know how to spend it? He is told that he must contribute to fighting inflation. How is he to know what action of his will contribute to that end? He is presumably an expert in running his company—in producing a product or selling it or financing it. But nothing about his selection makes him an expert on inflation. Will his holding down the price of his product reduce inflationary pressure? Or, by leaving more spending power in the hands of his customers, simply divert it elsewhere? Or, by forcing him to produce less because of the lower price, will it simply contribute to shortages? Even if he could answer these questions, how much cost is he justified in imposing on his stockholders, customers and employees for this social purpose? What is the appropriate share and what is the appropriate share of others?

And, whether he wants to or not, can he get away with spending his stockholders', customers' or employees' money? Will not the stockholders fire him? (Either the present ones or those who take over when his actions in the name of social responsibility have reduced the corporation's profits and the price of its stock.) His customers and his employees can desert him for other producers and employers less scrupulous in exercising their social responsibilities.

This facet of "social responsibility" doctrine is brought into sharp relief when the doctrine is used to justify wage restraint by trade unions. The conflict of interest is naked and clear when union officials are asked to subordinate the interest of their members to some more general social purpose. If the union officials try to enforce wage restraint, the consequence is likely to be wildcat strikes, rank-and-file revolts and the emergence of strong competitors for their jobs. We thus have the ironic phenomenon that union leaders—at least in the U.S.—have objected to Government interference with the market far more consistently and courageously than have business leaders.

The difficulty of exercising "social responsibility" illustrates, of course, the great virtue of private competitive enterprise—it forces people to be responsible for their own actions and makes it difficult for them to "exploit" other people for either selfish or unselfish purposes. They can do good—but only at their own expense.

Many a reader who has followed the argument this far may be tempted to remonstrate that it is all well and good to speak of government's having the responsibility to impose taxes and determine expenditures for such "social" purposes as controlling pollution or training the hard-core unemployed, but that the problems are too urgent to wait on the slow course of political processes, that the exercise of social responsibility by businessmen is a quicker and surer way to solve pressing current problems.

Aside from the question of fact—I share Adam Smith's skepticism about the benefits that can be expected from "those who affected to trade for the public good"—this argument must be rejected on grounds of principle. What it amounts to is an assertion that those who favor the taxes and expenditures in question have failed to persuade a majority of their fellow citizens to be of like mind and that they are seeking to attain by undemocratic procedures what they cannot attain by democratic procedures. In a free society, it is hard for "good" people to do "good," but that is a small price to pay for making it hard for "evil" people to do "evil," especially since one man's good is another's evil.

I have, for simplicity, concentrated on the special case of the corporate executive, except only for the brief digression on trade unions. But precisely the same argument applies to the newer phenomenon of calling upon stockholders to require corporations to exercise social responsibility (the recent G.M. crusade, for example). In most of these cases, what is in effect involved is some stockholders trying to get other stockholders (or customers or employees) to contribute against their will to "social" causes favored by the activists. Insofar as they succeed, they are again imposing taxes and spending the proceeds.

The situation of the individual proprietor is somewhat different. If he acts to reduce the returns of his enterprise in order to exercise his "social responsibility," he is spending his own money, not someone else's. If he wishes to spend his money on such purposes, that is his right, and I cannot see that there is any objection to his doing so. In the process, he, too, may impose costs on employees and customers. However, because he is far less likely than a large corporation or union to have monopolistic power, any such side effects will tend to be minor.

Of course, in practice the doctrine of social responsibility is frequently a cloak for actions that are justified on other grounds rather than a reason for those actions.

To illustrate, it may well be in the long-run interest of a corporation that is a major employer in a small community to devote resources to providing amenities to that community or to improving its government. That may make it easier to attract desirable employees, it may reduce the wage bill or lessen losses from pilferage and sabotage or have other worthwhile effects. Or it may be that, given the laws about the deductibility of corporate charitable contributions, the stockholders can contribute more to charities they favor by having the corporation make the gift than by doing it themselves, since they can in that way contribute an amount that would otherwise have been paid as corporate taxes.

In each of these—and many similar—cases, there is a strong temptation to rationalize these actions as an exercise of "social responsibility." In the present climate of opinion, with its widespread aversion to "capitalism," "profits," the "soulless corporation" and so on, this is one way for a corporation to generate goodwill as a by-product of expenditures that are entirely justified in its own self-interest.

It would be inconsistent of me to call on corporate executives to refrain from this hypocritical window-dressing because it harms the foundations of a free society. That would be to call on them to exercise a "social responsibility"! If our institutions, and the attitudes of the public make it in their self-interest to cloak their actions in this way, I cannot summon much indignation to denounce them. At the same time, I can express admiration for those individual proprietors or owners of closely held corporations or stockholders of more broadly held corporations who disdain such tactics as approaching fraud.

Whether blameworthy or not, the use of the cloak of social responsibility, and the nonsense spoken in its name by influential and prestigious businessmen, does clearly harm the foundations of a free society. I have been impressed time and again by the schizophrenic character of many businessmen. They are capable of being extremely far-sighted and clear-headed in matters that are internal to their businesses. They are incredibly short-sighted and muddleheaded in matters that are outside their businesses but affect the possible survival of business in general. This short-sightedness is strikingly exemplified in the calls from many businessmen for wage and price guidelines or controls or income policies. There is nothing that could do more in a brief period to destroy a market system and replace it by a centrally controlled system than effective governmental control of prices and wages.

The short-sightedness is also exemplified in speeches by businessmen on social responsibility. This may gain them kudos in the short run. But it helps to strengthen the already too prevalent view that the pursuit of profits is wicked and immoral and must be curbed and controlled by external forces. Once this view is adopted, the external forces that curb the market will not be the social consciences, however highly developed, of the pontificating executives; it will be the iron fist of Government bureaucrats. Here, as with price and wage controls, businessmen seem to me to reveal a suicidal impulse.

The political principle that underlies the market mechanism is unanimity. In an ideal free market resting on private property, no individual can coerce any other, all cooperation is voluntary, all parties to such cooperation benefit or they need not participate. There are no "social" values, no "social" responsibilities in any sense other than the shared values and responsibilities of individuals. Society is a collection of individuals and of the various groups they voluntarily form.

The political principle that underlies the political mechanism is conformity. The individual must serve a more general social interest—whether that be determined by a church or a dictator or a majority. The individual may have a vote and a say in what is to be done, but if he is overruled, he must conform. It is appropriate for some to require others to contribute to a general social purpose whether they wish to or not.

Unfortunately, unanimity is not always feasible. There are some respects in which conformity appears unavoidable, so I do not see how one can avoid the use of the political mechanism altogether.

But the doctrine of "social responsibility" taken seriously would extend the scope of the political mechanism to every human activity. It does not differ in philosophy from the most explicitly collectivist doctrine. It differs only by professing to believe that collectivist ends can be attained without collectivist means. That is why, in my book "Capitalism and Freedom," I have called it a "fundamentally subversive doctrine" in a free society, and have said that in such a society, "there is one and only one social responsibility of business—to use its resources and engage in activities designed to increase its profits so long as it stays within the rules of the game, which is to say, engages in open and free competition without deception or fraud."

Robert Almeder

Morality in the Marketplace: Reflections on the Friedman Doctrine

Introduction

In seeking to create a climate more favorable for corporate activity, International Telephone and Telegraph allegedly contributed large sums of money to "destabilize" the duly elected government of Chile. Even though advised by the scientific community that the practice is lethal, major chemical companies reportedly continue to dump large amounts of carcinogens and mutagens into the water supply of various areas and, at the same time, lobby strongly to prevent legislation against such practices. General Motors Corporation, other automobile manufacturers, and Firestone Tire and Rubber Corporation have frequently defended themselves against the charge that they knowingly and willingly marketed a product that, owing to defective design, had been reliably predicted to kill a certain percentage of its users and, moreover, refused to recall promptly the product even when government agencies documented the large incidence of death as a result of the defective product. Finally, people often say that numerous advertising companies happily accept, and earnestly solicit, accounts to advertise cigarettes knowing full well that as a direct result of their advertising activities a certain number of people will die considerably prematurely and painfully. Most recently, of course, American Tobacco Companies have been charged with knowingly marketing a very addictive product known to kill untold numbers in slow, painful and costly deaths while the price of the stock of these companies has made fortunes for the shareholders. We need not concern ourselves with whether these and other similar charges are true because our primary concern here is with what might count as a justification for such corporate conduct were it to occur. There can be no question that such corporate behavior sometimes occurs and is frequently legal, or at least not illegal. The question is whether corporate behavior should be constrained by non-legal or moral considerations. If so, to what extent and how could it be done? As things presently stand, it seems to be a dogma of contemporary capitalism rapidly emerging throughout the world that the sole responsibility of business is to make as much money as is *legally* possible. But the interesting question is whether this view is rationally defensible.

Sometimes, although not very frequently, corporate executives will admit to the sort of behavior depicted above and then proceed proximately to justify such behavior in the name of their responsibility to the shareholders or owners (if the shareholders are not the owners) to make as much profit as is legally possible. Thereafter, less proximately and more generally, they will proceed to urge the more general utilitarian point that the increase in profit engendered by such corporate behavior begets such an unquestionable overall good for society that the behavior in question is morally acceptable if not quite praiseworthy. More specifically, the justification in question can, and usually does, take two forms.

The first and most common form of justification consists in urging that, as long as one's corporate behavior is not illegal, the behavior will be morally acceptable because the sole purpose of being in business is to make a profit; and the rules of the marketplace are somewhat different from those in other places and must be followed if one is to make a profit. Moreover, proponents of this view hasten to add that, as Adam Smith has claimed, the greatest good for society in the long run is achieved not by corporations seeking to act morally, or with a sense of social responsibility in their pursuit of profit, but rather by each corporation seeking to maximize its own profit, unregulated in that endeavor except by the laws of supply and demand along with whatever other laws are inherent to the competition process. This, they say, is what has made capitalist societies the envy of the world while ideological socialisms sooner or later fail miserably to meet deep human needs. Smith's view, that there is an invisible hand, as it were, directing an economy governed solely by the profit motive to the greatest good for society in the long run,[1] is still the dominant motivation and justification for those who would want an economy unregulated by any moral concern that would, or could, tend to decrease profits for some *alleged* social or moral good.

Milton Friedman, for example, has frequently asserted that the sole moral responsibility of business is to make as much profit as is legally possible; and by that he means to assert that attempts to regulate or restrain the pursuit of profit in accordance with what some people believe to be socially desirable ends are in fact *subversive* of the common good because the greatest good for the greatest number is achieved by an economy maximally competitive and unregulated by moral rules in its pursuit of profit.[2] So, on Friedman's view, the greatest good for society is achieved by corporations acting legally, but with no further regard for what may be morally desirable; and this view begets the paradox that, *in business,* the greatest good for society can be achieved only by acting without regard for morality, at least in so far as moral rules are not reflected in the legal code. Moreover, adoption of this position constitutes a fairly conscious commitment to the view that while one's personal life may well need moral governance beyond the law, when pursuing profit, it is necessary that one's corporate behavior be unregulated by any moral concern other than that of making as much money as is legally possible; curiously enough, it is only in this way that society achieves the greatest good. So viewed, it is not difficult to see how a corporate executive could sincerely and consistently adopt rigorous standards of morality in his or her personal life and yet feel quite comfortable in abandoning those standards in the pursuit of profit. Albert Carr, for example, likens the conduct of business to that of playing poker.[3] As Carr would have it, moral busybodies who insist on corporations acting morally might do just as well to censure a good bluffer in poker for being deceitful. Society, of course, lacking a perspective such as Friedman's and Carr's is only too willing to view such behavior as strongly hypocritical and fostered by an unwholesome avarice.

The second way of justifying, or defending, corporate practices that may appear morally questionable consists in urging that even if corporations were to take seriously the idea of limiting profits because of a desire to be moral or more responsible to social needs, then corporations would be involved in the unwholesome business of selecting and implementing moral values that may not be shared by a large number of people. Besides, there is the overwhelming question of whether there can be any non-questionable moral values or non-controversial list of social priorities for corporations to adopt. After all, if ethical relativism is true, or if ethical nihilism is true (and philosophers can be counted upon to argue agressively for both positions), then it would be fairly silly of corporations to limit profits for what may be a quite dubious reason, namely, for being moral, when there are no clear grounds for doing it, and when it is not too clear what would count for doing it. In short, business corporations could argue (as Friedman has done)[4] that corporate actions in behalf of society's interests would require of corporations an ability to clearly determine and rank in noncontroversial ways the major needs of society; and it would not appear that this could be done successfully.

Perhaps another, and somewhat easier, way of formulating this second argument consists in urging that because moralists and philosophers generally fail to agree on what are the proper moral rules (if any), as well as on whether we should be moral, it would be imprudent to sacrifice a clear profit for a dubious or controversial moral gain. To authorize such a sacrifice would be to abandon a clear responsibility for one that is unclear or questionable.

If there are any other basic ways of justifying the sort of corporate behavior noted at the outset, I cannot imagine what they might be. So, let us examine these two modes of justification. In doing this, I hope to show that neither argument is sound and, moreover, that corporate behavior of the sort in question is clearly immoral if anything is immoral—and if nothing is immoral, then such corporate behavior is clearly contrary to the long-term interest of a corporation. In the end, we will reflect on ways to prevent such behavior, and on what is philosophically implied by corporate willingness to act in clearly immoral ways.

The "Invisible Hand"

Essentially, the first argument is that the greatest good for the greatest number will be, and can only be, achieved by corporations acting legally but unregulated by any moral concern in the pursuit of profit. As we saw earlier, the evidence for this argument rests on a fairly classical and unquestioning acceptance of Adam Smith's view that society achieves a greater good when each person is allowed to pursue her or his own self-interested ends than when each person's pursuit of self-interested ends is regulated in some way or another by moral rules or concern. But I know of no evidence Smith ever offered for this latter claim, although it seems clear that those who adopt it generally do so out of respect for the perceived good that has emerged for various modern societies as a direct result of the free enterprise system and its ability to raise the overall standard of living of all those under it.

However, there is nothing inevitable about the greatest good occurring in an unregulated economy. Indeed, we have good inductive evidence from the age of the Robber Barons that unless the profit motive is regulated in various ways (by statute or otherwise) untold social evil can, and *will,* occur because of the natural tendency of the system to place ever-increasing sums of money in ever-decreasing numbers of hands as a result of the nature of competition unregulated. If all this is so, then so much the worse for all philosophical attempts to justify what would appear to be morally questionable corporate behavior on the grounds that corporate behavior, unregulated by moral concern, is necessarily or even probably productive of the greatest good for the greatest number. Moreover, a rule utilitarian would not be very hard pressed to show the many unsavory implications to society as a whole if society were to take seriously a rule to the effect that, if one acts legally, it is morally permissible to do whatever one wants to do to achieve a profit. We shall discuss some of those implications of this rule below before drawing a conclusion.

The second argument cited above asserts that even if we were to grant, for the sake of argument, that corporations have social responsibilities beyond that of making as much money as is legally possible for the shareholders, there would be no noncontroversial way for corporations to discover just what these responsibilities are in the order of their importance. Owing to the fact that even distinguished moral philosophers predictably disagree on what one's moral responsibilities are, if any, it would seem irresponsible to limit profits to satisfy dubious moral responsibilities.

For one thing, this argument unduly exaggerates our potential for moral disagreement. Admittedly, there might well be important disagreements among corporations (just as there could be among philosophers) as to a priority ranking of major social needs; but that does not mean that most of us could not, or would not, agree that certain things ought not be done in the name of profit even when there is no law prohibiting such acts. Doubtless, there will always be a few who would do most anything for a profit; but that is hardly a good argument in favor of their having the moral right to do so rather than a good argument showing that they refuse to be moral. In sum, it is difficult to see how this second argument favoring corporate moral nihilism is any better than the general argument for ethical nihilism based on the variability of ethical judgments or practices; and apart from the fact that it tacitly presupposes that morality is a matter of what we all in fact would, or should, accept, the argument is maximally counterintuitive (as I shall show) by way of suggesting that we cannot generally agree that corporations have certain clear social responsibilities to avoid certain practices. Accordingly, I would now like to argue that if anything is immoral, a certain kind of corporate behavior is quite immoral although it may not be illegal.

Murder for Profit

Without caring to enter into the reasons for the belief, I assume we all believe that it is wrong to kill an innocent human being for no other reason than that doing so would be more financially rewarding for the killer than if he were to earn his livelihood in some other way. Nor, I assume, should our moral feeling on this matter change depending on the amount of money involved. Killing an innocent baby for fifteen million dollars would not seem to be any less objectionable than killing it for twenty cents. It is possible, however, that a self-professing utilitarian might be tempted to argue that the killing of an innocent baby for fifteen million dollars would not be objectionable if the money were to be given to the poor; under these circumstances, greater good would be achieved by the killing of the innocent baby. But, I submit, if anybody were to argue in this fashion, his argument would be quite deficient because he has not established what he needs to establish to make his argument sound. What he needs is a clear, convincing argument that raising the standard of living of an indefinite number of poor persons by the killing of an innocent person is a greater good for all those affected by the act than if the standard of living were not raised by the killing of an innocent person. This is needed because part of what we mean by having a basic right to life is that a person's life cannot be taken from him or her without a good reason. If our utilitarian cannot provide a convincing justification for his claim that a greater good is served by killing an innocent person in order to raise the standard of living for a large number of poor people, then it is hard to see how he can have the good reason that he needs to deprive an innocent person of his or her life. Now, it seems clear that there will be anything but unanimity in the moral community on the question of whether there is a greater good achieved in raising the standard of living by killing an innocent baby than in leaving the standard of living alone and not killing an innocent baby. Moreover, even if everybody were to agree that the greater good is achieved by the killing of the innocent baby, how could that be shown to be true? How does one compare the moral value of a human life with the moral value of raising the standard of living by the taking of that life? Indeed, the more one thinks about it, the more difficult it is to see just what would count as objective evidence for the claim that the greater good is achieved by the killing of the innocent baby. Accordingly, I can see nothing that would justify the utilitarian who might be tempted to argue that if the sum is large enough, and if the sum were to be used for raising the standard of living for an indefinite number of poor people, then it would be morally acceptable to kill an innocent person for money.

These reflections should not be taken to imply, however, that no utilitarian argument could justify the killing of an innocent person for money. After all, if the sum were large enough to save the lives of a large number of people who would surely die if the innocent baby were not killed, then one would as a rule be justified in killing the innocent baby for the sum in question. But this situation is obviously quite different from the situation in which one would attempt to justify the killing of an innocent person in order to raise the standard of living for an indefinite number of poor people. It makes sense to kill one innocent person in order to save, say, twenty innocent persons; but it makes no sense at all to kill one innocent person to raise the standard of living of an indefinite number of people. In the latter case, but not in the former, a comparison is made between things that are incomparable.

Given these considerations, it is remarkable and somewhat perplexing that certain corporations should seek to defend practices that are in fact instances of killing innocent persons for profit. Take, for example, the corporate practice of dumping known carcinogens into rivers. On Milton Friedman's view, we should not regulate or prevent such companies from dumping their effluents into the environment. Rather we should, if we like, tax the company after the effluents are in the water and then have the tax money used to clean up the environment.[5] For Friedman, and others, the fact that so many people will die as a result of this practice seems to be just part of the cost of doing business and making a profit. If there is any moral difference between such corporate practices and murdering innocent human beings for money, it is hard to see what it is. It is even more difficult to see how anyone could justify the practice and see it as no more than a business practice not to be regulated by moral concern. And there are a host of other corporate activities that are morally equivalent to deliberate killing of innocent persons for money. Such practices number among them contributing funds to "destabilize" a foreign government, selling cigarettes while knowing that they are highly addictive killers of innocent people, advertising cigarettes, knowingly marketing children's clothing having a known cancer-causing agent, and refusing to recall (for fear of financial loss) goods known to be sufficiently defective to directly maim or kill a certain percentage of their unsuspecting users because of the defect. On this latter item, we are all familiar, for example, with convincingly documented charges that certain prominent automobile and tire manufacturers will knowingly market equipment sufficiently defective to increase the likelihood of death as a direct result of the defect, and yet refuse to recall the product because the cost of recalling and repairing would have a greater adverse impact on profit than if the product were not recalled and the company paid the projected number of predictably successful suits. Of course, if the projected cost of the predictably successful suits were to outweigh the cost of recall and repair, then the product would be recalled and repaired, but not otherwise.

In cases of this sort, the companies involved may admit to having certain marketing problems or a design problem, and they may even admit to having made a mistake; but, interestingly enough, they do not view themselves as immoral or as murderers for keeping their product in the market place when they know people are dying from it, people who would not die if the defect were corrected.

The important point is not whether in fact these practices have occurred in the past, or occur even now; there can be no doubt that such practices have occurred and continue to occur. Rather the point is that when companies act in such ways as a matter of policy, they must either not know what they do is murder (i.e., unjustifiable killing of an innocent person), or knowing that it is murder, seek to justify it in terms of profit. And I have been arguing that it is difficult to see how any corporate manager could fail to see that these policies amount to murder for money, although there may be no civil statute against such corporate behavior. If so, then where such policies exist, we can only assume that they are designed and implemented by corporate managers who either see nothing wrong with murder for money (which is implausible) or recognize that what they do is wrong but simply refuse to act morally because it is more financially rewarding to act immorally.

Of course, it is possible that corporate executives would not recognize such acts as murder. They may, after all, view murder as a legal concept involving one non-corporate person or persons deliberately killing another noncorporate person or persons and prosecutable only under existing criminal statute. If so, it is somewhat understandable how corporate executives might fail, at least psychologically, to see such corporate policies as murder rather than as, say, calculated risks, tradeoffs, or design errors. Still, for all that, the logic of the situation seems clear enough.

Conclusion

In addition to the fact that the only two plausible arguments favoring the Friedman doctrine are unsatisfactory, a strong case can be made for the claim that corporations *do* have a clear and noncontroversial moral responsibility not to design or implement, for reasons of profit, policies that they know, or have good reason to believe, will kill or otherwise seriously injure innocent persons affected by those policies. Moreover, we have said nothing about wage discrimination, sexism, discrimination in hiring, price fixing, price gouging, questionable but not unlawful competition, or other similar practices that some will think businesses should avoid by virtue of responsibility to society. My main concern has been to show that because we all agree that murder for money is generally wrong, and since there is no discernible difference between that and certain corporate policies that are not in fact illegal, then these corporate practices are clearly immoral (that is, they ought not to be done) and incapable of being morally justified by appeal to the Friedman doctrine since that doctrine does not admit of adequate evidential support. In itself, it seems sad that this argument needs to be made and, if it were not for what appears to be a fairly strong commitment within the business community to the Friedman doctrine in the name of the unquestionable success of the free enterprise system, the argument would not need to be stated.

The fact that such practices do exist—designed and implemented by corporate managers who, for all intents and purposes appear to be upright members of the moral community—only heightens the need for effective social prevention. Presumably, of course, any company willing to put human lives into the profit and loss column is not likely to respond to moral censure. Accordingly, I submit that perhaps the most effective way to deal with the problem of preventing such corporate behavior would consist in structuring legislation such that senior corporate managers who knowingly concur in practices of the sort listed above can effectively be tried, at their own expense, for murder, rather than censured and fined a sum to be paid out of corporate profits. This may seem a somewhat extreme or unrealistic proposal. However, it seems more unrealistic to think that aggressively competitive corporations will respond to what is morally necessary if failure to do so could be very or even minimally profitable. In short, unless we take strong and appropriate steps to prevent such practices, society will be reinforcing a destructive mode of behavior that is maximally disrespectful of human life, just as society will be reinforcing a value system that so emphasizes monetary gain as a standard of human success that murder for profit could be a corporate policy if the penalty for being caught at it were not too dear.

Fortunately, a number of states in America have enacted legislation that makes corporations subject to the criminal code of that state. This practice began to emerge quite strongly after the famous Pinto case in which an Indiana superior court judge refused to dismiss a homicide indictment against the Ford Motor Company. The company was indicted on charges of reckless homicide stemming from a 1978 accident involving a 1973 Pinto in which three girls died when the car burst into flames after being slammed in the rear. This was the first case in which Ford, or any other automobile manufacturer, had been charged with a criminal offense. The indictment went forward because the state of Indiana adopted in 1977 a criminal code provision permitting corporations to be charged with criminal acts. At the time, incidentally, twenty-two other states had similar codes. At any rate, the judge, in refusing to set aside the indictment, agreed with the prosecutor's argument that the charge was based not on the Pinto design fault, but rather on the fact that Ford had permitted the car "to remain on Indiana highways knowing full well its defects." The fact that the Ford Motor company was ultimately found innocent of the charges by the jury is incidental to the point that the increasing number of states that allow corporations to fall under the criminal code is an example of social regulation that could have been avoided had corporations and corporate managers not followed so ardently the Friedman doctrine.

In the long run, of course, corporate and individual willingness to do what is clearly immoral for the sake of monetary gain is a patent commitment of a certain view about the nature of human happiness and success, a view that needs to be placed in the balance with Aristotle's reasoned argument and reflections to the effect that money and all that it brings is a means to an end, and not the sort of end in itself that will justify acting immorally to attain it. What that beautiful end is and why being moral allows us to achieve it, may well be the most rewarding and profitable subject a human being can think about. Properly understood and placed in perspective, Aristotle's view on the nature and attainment of human happiness could go a long way toward alleviating the temptation to kill for money.

In the meantime, any ardent supporter of the capitalistic system will want to see the system thrive and flourish; and this it cannot do if it invites and demands government regulation in the name of the public interest. A *strong* ideological commitment to what I have described above as the Friedman doctrine is counterproductive and not in anyone's long-range interest because it is most likely to beget an ever-increasing regulatory climate. The only way to avoid such encroaching regulation is to find ways to move the business community into the long-term view of what is in its interest, and effect ways of both determining and responding to social needs before society moves to regulate business to that end. To so move the business community is to ask business to regulate its own modes of competition in ways that may seem very difficult to achieve. Indeed, if what I have been suggesting is correct, the only kind of enduring capitalism is humane capitalism, one that is at least as socially responsible as society needs. By the same token, contrary to what is sometimes felt in the business community, the Friedman doctrine, ardently adopted for the dubious reasons generally given, will most likely undermine capitalism and motivate an economic socialism by assuring an erosive regulatory climate in a society that expects the business community to be socially responsible in ways that go beyond just making legal profits.

In sum, being socially responsible in ways that go beyond legal profit making is by no means a dubious luxury for the capitalist in today's world. It is a necessity if capitalism is to survive at all; and, presumably, we shall all profit with the survival of a vibrant capitalism. If anything, then, rigid adherence to the Friedman doctrine is not only philosophically unjustified, and unjustifiable, it is also unprofitable in the long run, and therefore, downright subversive of the long-term common good. Unfortunately, taking the long-run view is difficult for everyone. After all, for each of us, tomorrow may not come. But living for today only does not seem to make much sense either, if that deprives us of any reasonable and happy tomorrow. Living for the future may not be the healthiest thing to do; but do it we must, if we have good reason to think that we will have a future. The trick is to provide for the future without living in it, and that just requires being moral.[6]

This paper is a revised and expanded version of "Morality in the Marketplace," which appears in Business Ethics *(revised edition) eds. Milton Snoeyenbos, Robert Almeder and James Humber (Buffalo, N.Y.: Prometheus Press, 1992) 82–90, and, as such, it is a revised and expanded version of an earlier piece "The Ethics of Profit: Reflections on Corporate Responsibility," which originally appeared in* Business and Society *(Winter 1980, 7–15).*

Notes

1. Adam Smith, *The Wealth of Nations,* ed. Edwin Canaan (New York: Modern Library, 1937), p. 423.
2. See Milton Friedman, "The Social Responsibility of Business Is to Increase Its Profits," in *The New York Times Magazine* (September 13, 1970), pp. 33, 122–126 and "Milton Friedman Responds," in *Business and Society Review* no. 1 (Spring 1972), p. 5ff.

3. Albert Z. Carr, "Is Business Bluffing Ethical?" *Harvard Business Review* (January–February 1968).
4. Milton Friedman in "Milton Friedman Responds," in *Business and Society Review* no. 1 (Spring 1972), p. 10.
5. Ibid.
6. I would like to thank J. Humber and M. Snoeyenbos for their comments and criticisms of an earlier draft.

POSTSCRIPT

Are Profits the Only Business of Business?

Friedman dismisses the pleas of those who argue for socially responsible business action on the grounds that these individuals do not understand the role of the corporate executive in modern society. Friedman points out that the executives are responsible to the corporate owners, and if the corporate executives take a "socially responsible" action that reduces the return on the owners' investment, they have spent the owners' money. This, Friedman maintains, violates the very foundation of the American political-economic system: individual freedom. If the corporate executives wish to take socially responsible actions, they should use their own money; they should not prevent the owners from spending their money on whatever social actions they might wish to support.

Almeder argues that some corporate behavior is immoral and that defense of this immoral behavior imposes great costs on society. He likens corporate acts such as advertising cigarettes, marketing automobiles that cannot sustain moderate rear-end collisions, and contributing funds to destabilize foreign governments to murdering innocent children for profit. He argues that society must not condone this behavior but, instead, through federal and state legislation, must continue to impose regulations upon businesses until businesses begin to regulate themselves.

Perhaps no single topic is more fundamental to microeconomics than the issue of profits. Many pages have been written in defense of profits; see, for example, Milton and Rose Friedman's *Free to Choose: A Personal Statement* (Harcourt Brace Jovanovich, 1980). A classic reference is Frank H. Knight's *Risk, Uncertainty, and Profits* (Kelly Press, 1921). Friedrich A. Hayek, the author of many journal articles and books, is a guru for many current free marketers. There are a number of other books and articles, however, that are highly critical of the Friedman-Knight-Hayek position, including Christopher D. Stone's *Where the Law Ends: Social Control of Corporate Behavior* (Harper & Row, 1975). Others who challenge the legitimacy of the notion that markets are morally free zones include Thomas Mulligan, "A Critique of Milton Friedman's Essay 'The Social Responsibility of Business Is to Increase Its Profits,'" *Journal of Business Ethics* (1986); Daniel M. Hausman, "Are Markets Morally Free Zones?" *Philosophy and Public Affairs* (Fall 1989); and Andrew Henley, "Economic Orthodoxy and the Free Market System: A Christian Critique," *International Journal of Social Economics* (vol. 14, no. 10, 1987).

ISSUE 2

Should the Regulations Regarding Overtime Pay Be Changed?

YES: Elaine Chao, from "Bush Administration Proposal," *Congressional Digest* (March 2004)

NO: Ross Eisenbrey, from "On the Department of Labor's Final Overtime Regulations," Testimony before the Senate Subcommittee on Labor, Health and Human Services, and Education (May 4, 2004)

ISSUE SUMMARY

YES: Secretary of Labor Elaine Chao believes that today's workers are "severely disadvantaged" by current regulations regarding overtime pay, and she believes it is time to institute new rules that would "benefit more workers."

NO: Ross Eisenbrey, Economic Policy Institute vice president, believes that the Department of Labor's proposed changes will mean "longer hours and less pay for millions of workers—and more litigation for our entire economy."

The Fair Labor Standards Act (FLSA) became law in 1938. The purpose of this legislation was to, as far as possible, eliminate "labor conditions detrimental to the maintenance of the minimum standard of living necessary for the health, efficiency, and the general well being of workers." There were three major elements in this effort. The first involved setting standards for minimum wages (see Issue 11). Control of child labor constituted the second element. The last element concerned the maximum number of hours an individual could be employed in a week before that individual become eligible for overtime (premium) pay.

The FLSA was possible only because of a change in thinking by the U.S. Supreme Court. Up through 1937, the Court opposed laws that regulated work; this position was based on the view that such laws violated the Constitution's commerce clause. For example, by 1923, 17 states had passed minimum wage laws. But in that year, the Court held that these laws were unconstitutional.

Continuing in this tradition, the Court struck down the national minimum wage provision of the National Recovery Act in 1935. But changes in Court membership led to the Court's acceptance of a Washington State minimum wage law in 1937. This reversal set the stage for the passage of the FLSA a year later.

Focusing on the overtime provisions of the FLSA, 44 hours was the length of the standard workweek. This was subsequently lowered to 40 hours per week two years later. FLSA also established "time and a half" as the legal remuneration for each hour worked beyond 40 in a week. But this new law did not cover all workers. Because the law was federal, it covered only workers involved in interstate commerce. But the law also excluded a significant number of workers involved in interstate commerce, such as workers in so-called white-collar occupations or those engaged in executive, administrative, or professional activities.

The problem then became one of defining more specifically what constituted executive, administrative, or professional activities. To answer this question, three tests were devised. The first test was relatively straightforward; it required that an exempt worker be paid a salary rather than on an hourly basis. The second test required that the exempt worker have a certain minimum level of earnings. Before the proposed changes, the minimum earnings salary level was set at $155 per week for certain executive and administrative employees and $170 per week for certain professional employees. The third test required that the exempt worker have work responsibilities that are associated with executive, administrative, and professional positions. This third test was called "the duties test." Generally speaking, the duties test required that exempt administrator or professional employees exercise "independent judgment and discretion" in carrying out their job responsibilities, while exempt executives are those who supervise two or more employees and have management as their primary responsibility.

The push for modification of the FLSA's overtime pay regulation came from both employees and employers. For employees, their concern was that the earnings test had not been revised since 1975. Thus as wages increased, even if increases simply offset inflation, the number of exempt workers could increase. But employers wanted changes as well, arguing that the regulations were too complex and did not fit the modern workforce. Here the employers noted that the definitions of executive, administrative, and professional duties had not undergone any significant changes since 1954.

Responding to the demands for change, Labor Secretary Elaine Chao and the Bush administration proposed a set of revisions, increasing the minimum level of earnings and establishing new definitions for the duties test. The proposed changes were controversial, supported by employers but generally opposed by workers. New regulations went into effect on August 23, 2004 and remain controversial.

YES 

Elaine Chao

Bush Administration Proposal

I am pleased to appear before you today to discuss the Department of Labor's proposed revision of the Fair Labor Standards Act's (FLSA) "white-collar" regulations. These regulations set forth the criteria for determining who is excluded from the Act's minimum wage and overtime requirements as an executive, administrative, or professional employee. The regulations that the Department is revising appear in Title 29 of the Code of Federal Regulations, at Part 541.

Employee Definitions

When Congress passed the Fair Labor Standards Act in 1938, it chose not to provide definitions for many of the terms used, including who is an "executive, administrative, or professional" employee. Rather, in Section 13(a) of the Act, Congress expressly granted to the Secretary of Labor the authority and responsibility to "define and delimit" these terms "from time to time by regulations."

As you are aware, there has been an enormous amount of press coverage since the proposed rule was published in March 2003. Given the importance of this issue, the amount of press coverage has been deserved. However, much of the reported information has been misleading and inaccurate. I welcome the opportunity today to set the record straight regarding the intentions of the Department in issuing an update to the Part 541 regulations. I also welcome the opportunity to re-emphasize the Department's goals in undertaking this important task.

There are many reasons for updating this half-century-old rule. The primary goal is to have better rules in place that will benefit more workers. Because the rules have not been updated in decades, changes are necessary now to provide hardworking Americans who currently do not automatically have that right with the opportunity to receive overtime pay.

Had these changes been made 10 years ago, lower-wage workers would have had an additional $8 billion in their paychecks. The proposed rule would lead to guaranteed overtime for an additional 1.3 million low-wage workers.

The main purpose of this effort is to restore the intent of the FLSA—to restore overtime protections, especially to low-wage, vulnerable workers who have little bargaining power with employers. Of the 1.3 million workers who would be guaranteed overtime pay under the Department's proposal, all earn less than $22,100 per year; nearly 55 percent are women; more than 40 percent are minorities; nearly 25 percent are Hispanic; and nearly 70 percent have only a high school education or less.

The job "duties" tests have not been updated since 1949 and are plainly written for an economy that has long passed us by. As I have pointed out many times, the existing regulations identify occupations such as leg men, straw bosses, and key-punch operators—all occupations which no longer exist in the twenty-first century workplace. The salary-basis test was set in 1954. The minimum salary levels were last updated in 1975, some 29 years ago. Under the salary rates that are still in effect today, an employee earning only $8,060 a year may qualify as an exempt "executive."

Rule Clarification

Another important goal is to create rules that can be more easily read and understood. Greater certainty and clarity will allow workers to be paid properly. Under the current rules, burdensome and costly class action lawsuits are often necessary to sort out the rights of employees and the obligations of employers. This is harmful to workers who often must wait years to realize their rights, and burdensome to employers who otherwise could use litigation costs to grow and expand their businesses and create new jobs. Indeed, overtime is the fastest growing area of employment litigation in America. Overtime litigation costs are currently draining an estimated $2 billion a year out of resources that could be better used to grow the economy and create jobs.

Clear, concise, and updated rules will better protect workers and strengthen the Department's ability to enforce the law. With more clearly defined rules in place, the Department will be able to more quickly and efficiently settle overtime pay disputes, and build upon its strong enforcement record on behalf of workers.

Exemption Provisions

The existing regulations require three basic tests for each exemption:

- A minimum salary level, now set at $155 per week for executive and administrative employees and $170 per week for professionals under the basic "long" duties tests for exemption, whereas a higher salary level of $250 per week triggers a shorter duties test in each category.
- A salary-basis test, requiring payment of a fixed, predetermined salary amount that is not subject to reduction because of variations in the quality or quantity of work performed.
- A duties test, specifying the particular types of job duties that qualify for each exemption.

Our proposal would increase the minimum salary level required for exemption as a "white-collar" employee to $425 per week, or $22,100 per year. This is a $270 per week increase, and the largest increase since the Congress passed the Fair Labor Standards Act in 1938. Under this change, all employees earning less than $22,100 a year automatically would be entitled to the overtime protections of the FLSA. Under the existing rules, even a worker earning minimum wage would not be automatically entitled to overtime protections.

We believe that this change would result in an estimated 1.3 million additional workers becoming eligible for overtime pay for the first time, sharing up to $895 million in additional wages every year.

As in the current regulations, the Department's proposal also includes a streamlined test for higher-compensated "white-collar" employees. To qualify for exemption under this section of the proposed rule, an employee must:

- Be guaranteed total annual compensation of at least $65,000, regardless of the quality or quantity of work performed.
- Perform office or nonmanual work.
- Meet at least one of the exempt duties or responsibilities specified for an executive, administrative, or professional employee.

This is the same concept found in the current rule's Special Proviso for High Salaried Executive, commonly referred to as the "short test." The test for these "highly compensated" workers has been the subject of many of the comments we have received.

HIGHLIGHTS OF THE PROPOSED RULE

Minimum Salary Level

Under current rules, an employee earning only $155 a week can qualify as a "white-collar" employee not entitled to overtime pay. The proposal would raise this minimum salary to $425 a week, an increase of $270 a week.

Duties Tests

The proposed rule retains the current "short test" reliance on an employee's primary duty. The proposal would eliminate the "long test" rule restricting exempt employees from devoting more than 20 percent of time in a work week performing nonexempt duties.

Executive Duties—The proposed executive duties test has three requirements: managing the enterprise, directing the work of two or more employees, and having authority to hire or fire.

Administrative Duties—The proposal would replace the "discretion and independent judgment" test with a new test that employees must hold a "position of responsibility."

Professional Duties—The proposal recognizes as exempt "learned professionals" certain employees who gain equivalent knowledge and skills through a combination of job experience, military training, attending a technical school, or attending community college.

The Department's proposal would simplify, clarify, and update the duties tests to ensure that the regulations are easy for employees and employers to understand and for the Department to enforce.

The current rule provides two sets of duties tests for each of the three exemption categories. There is both a "short" duties test and a "long" duties test for each of the executive, administrative, and professional exemptions. The current long duties tests only apply to employees earning between $8,000 and $13,000 a year. Given these low levels, these tests essentially have been inoperative for a decade.

Accordingly, to simplify this complex process the Department's proposal would eliminate the long duties test and instead rely on the existing "primary duty" approach found in the current short tests. To be exempt, an employee must receive the required minimum salary amount and have a primary duty of performing the duties specified for an executive, administrative, or professional employee.

Under the Department's proposal, the executive exemption adds a third requirement to the current short test that makes it more difficult to qualify as an exempt executive. In other words, fewer workers would qualify as exempt executives under the proposal than qualify for the exemption under the current regulations.

Under the proposal, an exempt executive must:

- Have a primary duty of managing the entire enterprise or a customarily recognized department or subdivision thereof.
- Direct the work of two or more other workers.
- Have authority to hire or fire other employees or have recommendations as to the hiring and firing be given particular weight. This third requirement is from the long duties test, and its addition makes the exemption more difficult to achieve.

The Department did not propose substantial changes to the professional exemption. To the extent debate in Congress and comments submitted expressed concern that the Department was upsetting the law in this area, let me say that the Department intends to clarify that this is not the case.

In any rulemaking process, certain areas receive more public comment than others. The Department's proposed revision to the administrative exemption is one such area. The major proposed change to the duties test for the administrative exemption is replacing the "discretion and independent judgment" requirement, which has been a source of much confusion and litigation, with a new standard that exempt administrative employees must hold a "position of responsibility with the employer."

To meet this requirement, an employee must either customarily and regularly perform work of substantial importance or perform work requiring a high level of skill or training. In our proposal, the Department specifically sought comment about replacing the "discretion and independent judgment" element of the test. Both proponents and opponents of this proposed change submitted lengthy and helpful comments that the Department very carefully and deliberately is considering.

Background on the Proposed Regulations

Despite what has appeared in the press, let me emphasize that it has never been the intent of the Department to upset the overtime rights of hardworking American workers. The recent debates in the Senate and House have helped the Department identify areas in which the intent of these revisions needs to be made clearer. For example, it is not, nor has it been, the intent of the Department to change the overtime status of police, firefighters, paramedics, EMTs [emergency medical technicians], and other first responders.

Similarly, it is not, nor has it been, the intent of the department to change the overtime rights of registered nurses, licensed practical nurses, and other similar health care employees. The department also did not intend to substantially change the educational requirements for the professional exemption.

Furthermore, the overtime status of "blue-collar" workers will not change. Blue-collar employees in production, maintenance, construction, and similar occupations such as carpenters, electricians, mechanics, plumbers, iron workers, craftsmen, operating engineers, longshoremen, and construction workers will not see their right to overtime change. This regulation will not affect workers subject to a collective bargaining agreement. These and other critical issues will be addressed in the final rule.

Updating the Part 541 regulations is a bipartisan issue. This is not a Republican or Democratic issue, and it is not a new idea. The Carter Administration recognized in 1979 that the rules were antiquated and placed Part 541 reform on the Department's regulatory agenda. This issue has been on the Department's regulatory agenda for more than two decades. The last administration before this one to suggest that these regulations be modernized was the Clinton Administration.

In conclusion, the Department continues to work on developing a final rule that is based on the comments we have received and the debate we have heard. We are working diligently to achieve a rule that takes into consideration the concerns that have been expressed and that makes sense for the twenty-first century workplace. It will also protect the overtime rights of American workers far better than the half-century-old regulation now on the books.

Today's workers are not protected at all—they are severely disadvantaged by rules that few can understand in the context of the modern workplace. They are disadvantaged if they have to go to court to get overtime wages they have rightfully earned. And, they are disadvantaged if they have to wait years for that money to find its way into their pockets. It is time to update this rule.

Ross Eisenbrey

On the Department of Labor's Final Overtime Regulations: Preliminary Analysis of DOL's Final Rule on Overtime Exemptions

Introduction

The U.S. Department of Labor has issued a final rule that changes the legal exemptions from the right to overtime pay for executives, professionals and administrative employees. Many in Congress, the press, and the public have asked EPI to estimate how many employees will lose overtime pay or the right to receive it as a result of this new rule. However, such an estimate will take time and it is too soon to give a complete answer to that question. The rule and its explanatory text and regulatory analysis are more than 500 pages long and differ in unexpected ways from the proposed rule the DOL issued last year. The final rule and its preamble are also rife with ambiguity. Many regulatory provisions have been changed without real explanation, even while the Department claims—contrary to the plain language of the rule—that it is not changing the law.

All in all, the rule means longer hours and less pay for millions of workers—and more litigation for our entire economy. A number of things about the rule are immediately clear:

First, the Department has created new exemptions that jeopardize the overtime rights of millions of employees who earn between $23,660 and $100,000 a year. The overtime rights of the nation's 367,000 nursery school and pre-school teachers are weakened. Low-level working supervisors all throughout American industry will be reclassified as "executives" and will lose overtime rights; just as fast food assistant managers already have in some jurisdictions, even though they spend 90% or more of their time doing routine, production-line work such as flipping burgers and taking customer orders.

Despite its claims to the contrary, the new rule's treatment of cooks, chefs, and sous chefs, for example, of whom 2.4 million are employed in the

From Testimony Before the Senate Committee on Labor, Health, and Human Services and Education, May 2004.

United States, will cause hundreds of thousands to lose their right to overtime pay. Funeral directors and embalmers will be treated as exempt learned professional employees by the Labor Department for the first time, and large numbers of employees in the financial services industry will be adversely affected by a new blanket exemption.

Second, the rule will lead to an explosion of litigation because the Department chose to adopt new definitions that are unclear and new tests for exemption that require a case-by-case analysis that will be almost impossible for Wage and Hour's enforcement staff. Most notably, the new rule encourages employers to treat non-degreed employees as professionals, as long as they have "substantially similar" knowledge and do substantially similar work. The best possible objective criterion is missing: there is no requirement that they receive substantially similar pay. How will the Department know whether a non-degreed sous chef has substantially the same knowledge as a college grad? By making him prepare a soufflé, or taste-testing his Caesar salad? The rule also reduces the requirement that an exempt executive manage "the enterprise in which he is employed or of a customarily recognized department or subdivision thereof," to a new and embarrassing level of absurdity. Rather than the enterprise or a department or subdivision, it will be enough to be in charge of a "grouping or team." Unhelpfully, the Department suggests that a "case-by-case analysis is required"—a guaranteed recipe for litigation. Department stores will argue that an employee "in charge of" the perfume counter is an exempt executive because she has the "authority" to suggest shift assignments for two other employees.

Third, contrary to the Bush Administration's claims, it is not the case that 1.3 million low-wage workers who are not getting overtime pay now will. The Administration is engaged in consumer fraud, selling this new regulation on the promise of benefits it knows full well will not materialize. Part of the problem is that the Department's estimate assumes that every employee among these 1.3 million low-wage workers actually worked overtime during the year, even though the evidence is that they did not, and even though only about one employee in seven generally works overtime. If the Department had made this same assumption with respect to the proposed rule, it would have found that almost 5 million employees would have lost overtime pay, rather than the 644,000 it claimed. Moreover, the number of employees who will be guaranteed coverage by the $23,660 threshold will diminish over time because it is not indexed for inflation. An administration that cared about low-wage workers would have raised the threshold to at least keep pace with inflation since 1975, in other words, to at least $28,075.

Fourth, by the Department's own estimates, more than 100,000 employees who earn $100,000 a year or more will lose their right to overtime pay. As inflation and rising productivity increase the pay of American workers, the number of employees adversely affected by this new test will grow each year.

Fifth, a bizarre and poorly explained new exemption for "team leaders" creates the potential for hundreds of thousands of currently exempt nonsupervisory workers to lose their overtime rights. The use of self-managed teams of non-managerial, non-supervisory, front-line employees is widespread in American industry, and millions of employees are routinely involved in them. The regulations provide no definition of "team leader," it has never been defined in FLSA case law, and the Department's assertion that it is clarifying current law is patently false.

Sixth, the Department's claims that it has clarified and expanded the overtime rights of police officers and other first responders are untrue. The ambiguities in the rule make their rights more uncertain than ever.

Seventh, despite the Department's claims in power point presentations to public officials that blue-collar workers are entitled to overtime, the rule limits overtime rights to "**non-management** blue-collar employees," begging the question of who gets classified as a **management** blue-collar worker, a seemingly new class of exempt workers that will grow significantly under these new rules.

Eighth, by reducing the penalties for employers who illegally dock the pay of salaried workers, the Department removes an important deterrent and makes it more likely that hourly employees will lose overtime pay.

Analysis

Chefs and Cooks

The treatment of cooks and chefs is a good example of the artful deception of the final rule and the magnitude of the rule's potential harm. Under current law, chefs, sous chefs, and other cooks can be found exempt and denied overtime pay *only* if they manage a kitchen, supervise, hire and fire other employees, and have executive duties as their primary duty. They are not, however, learned professionals, because cooking is not a learned profession (it is not "a field of science or learning" and does not involve "work that is primarily intellectual in nature"), and most chefs learn through on-the-job training and apprenticeship, not formal education at a college or school of culinary arts. Nevertheless, the final rule expands the exemption to treat "chefs and sous chefs" with a four-year degree as exempt learned professionals. In addition, the rule for the first time extends the exemption for creative professionals to chefs and sous chefs even though cooking has never been found by a court to meet the test of being "a recognized field of artistic or creative endeavor," as required by new 541.302(a) or the current law's test for artistic professionals— "a recognized field of artistic endeavor." 541.302(b)

The effect of these two new avenues of exemption for chefs and cooks will be a significant loss of overtime coverage. Now that the Department has created the "learned profession" of being a chef or cook[1] with a four-year culinary arts degree, 541.301(d) of the final rule permits employers to deny overtime pay to any of the hundreds of thousands of chefs or cooks who have "substantially the same knowledge level and perform substantially the same work as the degreed employees, but who attained the advanced knowledge through a combination of work experience and intellectual instruction." As the Department of Labor's Occupational Outlook Handbook points out, "many chefs are trained on the job," "others may receive formal training in independent cooking schools," and still others get two-year degrees or learn through apprenticeships sponsored by industry associations and trade unions. The new creative professional exemption legalizes the denial of overtime to non-degreed chefs who do not have executive duties, effectively catching any chef the other exemptions missed, since every chef creates unique new recipes—the criterion identified at a hearing before a House committee by Secretary Chao and Administrator McCutchen for distinguishing between a creative chef and a non-exempt chef or cook.

There are about 2.4 million cooks and chefs in the United States, about 60% of whom are fast food cooks, institution and cafeteria cooks, or short order cooks, and are unlikely to be exempted, whatever their skills might be. The other 850,000 chefs, head cooks, and restaurant cooks are fair game for the three exemptions, depending on their skills and creativity—and the creativity of their employers.

Nursery School Teachers

According to the testimony of Karen Dulaney Smith, a management consultant on FLSA issues who for 12 years was a federal Wage Hour Division investigator, nursery school teachers who devoted most of their day to custodial care were always considered non-exempt employees, regardless of their educational attainment, because their work did not require the consistent exercise of discretion and independent judgment. A Wage Hour Division opinion letter written in 2000 is consistent with Ms. Smith's testimony that most preschool teachers are non-exempt and entitled to overtime under current law.

> Based on the information provided, it is our opinion that while "childhood education settings" (for ages 0-5), commonly referred to as preschools may engage in some basic educational activities for the children attending, preschool employees whose primary duty is to protect and care for the needs of the children would not ordinarily meet the requirements for exemption as teachers. 2000 DOLWH Lexis 14 (September 20, 2000).

The final rule removes the discretion and judgment requirement from the current regulation's definition of a professional employee in current section 541.3(b) and places it in the definition of "work requiring advanced knowledge" at 541.301(b)—a provision that applies only to learned professionals. Thus, under the final rule, all nursery teachers will be exempt, and all of those who have been found to be entitled to overtime in the past will lose that entitlement.

Funeral Directors and Embalmers

With the exception of two federal judicial circuits, funeral directors and embalmers have never been held to be exempt learned professionals. As the Department admits in the preamble to the final rule, "In the past, the Department has taken the position that licensed funeral directors and embalmers are not exempt learned professionals." Moreover, for at least the past six years, Congress has considered legislation to exempt funeral directors and embalmers but has chosen not to do so. Nevertheless, the Department has chosen to create a new exemption requiring only four years of post-secondary education, including a year of mortuary science school (which includes courses in cosmetology, according to the court in *Rutlin v. Prime Succession, Inc.*). In most of the nation, the final rule takes away the overtime rights of funeral directors and embalmers, yet the Department's economic analysis does not account for any change in coverage.

Working Foremen and Working Supervisors

The final rule turns current law on its head and eliminates the right to overtime pay for low-level supervisors who spend the vast majority of their time performing routine, manual, non-exempt production, as long as their most important duty is managerial. Relying on poorly reasoned cases interpreting the current regulations, most notably the *Burger King* cases from the First and Second Circuits, the final rule completely reverses those regulations, which set a limit of 20% on the amount of non-exempt work a supervisor can do and still be found an exempt executive.

Section 541.115(b) of current law provides:

> Clearly, the work of the same nature as that performed by the employee's subordinates must be counted as nonexempt work, and if the amount of such work performed is substantial the exemption does not apply. ("Substantial" as used in this section means more than 20 percent.")

Section 541.115(c) of current law applies the same rule to a supervisor whose work is different from his subordinates':

> Another type of working foreman or working supervisor who cannot be classed as a bona fide executive is one who spends a substantial amount of time in work which, although not performed by his subordinates, consists of ordinary production work or other routine, recurrent, repetitive tasks which are a regular part of his duties. Such an employee is in effect holding a dual job.

The current rule is simple common sense. An employee who spends 90% of his time frying French fries and flipping burgers is not a bona fide executive, even if he is simultaneously responsible for supervising the other two employees on his shift. An employee who works on a sewing machine six or seven hours a day is not a bona fide executive, even if he does supervise other employees.

Nevertheless, the final rule rejects common sense and adopts the position that an employee can spend 100% of his time performing ordinary, routine, repetitive, non-exempt production tasks and yet still be a bona fide executive by concurrently or simultaneously performing "executive" duties such as supervision of two other employees. New section 541.106(b) provides:

> For example, an assistant manager in a retail establishment may perform work such as serving customers, cooking food, stocking shelves, and

> cleaning the establishment, but performance of such nonexempt work does not preclude the exemption if the assistant manager's primary duty is management. An assistant manager can supervise employees and serve customers at the same time without losing the exemption. An exempt employee can also simultaneously direct the work of other employees and stock shelves.

The implications of this change in the law are far greater than the Department admits. While claiming to conform the regulations to current case law, in fact the Department is rejecting the better-reasoned cases and extending the worst case law beyond retail to the rest of American industry. *Burger King* and the other cases that have permitted employees to do unlimited amounts of menial work while still being held to be exempt executives are not the law in every judicial circuit, and they have not been extended outside of the fast food and retail industries. New section 541.106 applies the notion of concurrent duties to every industry, including construction, manufacturing, and other "blue collar" work. Employees who spend the vast majority of their time doing blue-collar, manual labor will now be subject to exemption as "bona fide executives" as long as the employer can establish that their most important duty is supervisory.

Because the Department treats this sweeping new rule as established law, its economic analysis does not account for any loss of overtime rights or pay. One can get a sense of how damaging this change will be, however, by examining the Department's estimate that 346,000 low-income "managers and administrators not elsewhere classified" and "supervisors and proprietors of sales occupations" will have their overtime rights restored by the new $23,660 salary test. In the Department's view, all of those low-income employees would otherwise qualify as "bona fide executives" or administrators, despite their abysmal pay.

Clarity and Litigation

The new concurrent duties test in 541.106 is a good example of how the final rule increases confusion and makes increased litigation a certainty. The final rule abandons the bright line test that an employee who spends more than 80% of his time doing nonexempt work cannot be a bona fide executive and replaces it with language that forces the employer and employee to make a determination on a "case-by-case basis and based on the factors in section 541.700."

The learned professional exemption, which has required, except in rare instances, that any bona fide exempt professional must have a specialized academic degree (a clear, objective test), is expanded in the final rule to permit non-degreed employees to be exempted and denied overtime pay if they have "substantially the same knowledge and do substantially the same work" as the degreed professionals. This one provision will generate thousands of unnecessary cases and devour the resources of the Wage and Hour Division as it tries to weigh the knowledge of thousands of non-degreed employees working in dozens of different professional occupations. The Department failed to add any sensible objective measure of equivalence, such as a market test: is the non-degreed employee receiving substantially the same pay?

Even when the Department claims to be bringing clarity to difficult issues, it isn't. New 541.3 provides that the "exemptions do not apply to manual laborers or other 'blue-collar' workers who perform work involving repetitive operations with their hands, physical skill and energy." Anyone doing any such work would seem to be exempt under the final rule, but the Department has thrown in a qualifier that destroys any illusion of clarity. Section 541.3 goes on to say that "*non-management* production-line employees and *non-management* employees in maintenance, construction and similar occupations . . . are not exempt under the regulations." This raises the question: What is a *management* blue-collar employee? What is a *management* production line worker? We have already seen the answer in 541.106: an employee can spend all day doing production work or construction work—manual, blue-collar work—and be exempt as a bona fide executive as long as he simultaneously supervises two other employees. Construction and utility crews all over America work without any manager higher than a working foreman to supervise them, a more senior employee charged with ensuring the safety and quality of the work, even as he works side-by-side with the other laborers. If his most important duty is managing the other employees, his employer will exempt him as a bona fide executive who concurrently does exempt and non-exempt work. As the preamble of the final rule makes clear, the Department now believes that an executive can be in charge of a unit no more substantial than "a grouping or a team."

Team Leaders

There are many other examples of the Department changing the law to weaken overtime protection while simultaneously increasing the law's confusion and the likelihood of litigation. None is more glaring than the new exemption for "team leaders" in 541.203(c). Current law has no equivalent provision, and I have found no case that holds "team leaders" to be exempt even if they have no supervisory duties. The term "team leader" is widely used in American industry, and usually describes a non-management employee responsible for calling meetings and directing a group of front-line employees who have been given an important task of a kind that historically was reserved to management, such as improving efficiency and productivity, improving customer service, researching and implementing IT improvements, identifying safety problems and recommending solutions, or improving employee morale. According to an expert in the field, Professor Thomas Kochan of the MIT Sloan School of Management, there are somewhere between 750,000 and 2.3 million currently non-exempt team leaders who could lose their right to overtime because of this new exemption. It appears that the management of a team would transform a manual laborer or other blue-collar employee into a "management blue-collar employee," leading to exemption and loss of overtime pay.

The Department has opened an enormous loophole, but does almost nothing to explain it in the preamble of the final rule. Administrator

McCutchen has suggested that current section 541.205(c) also allows the exemption of team leaders, but that language bears no resemblance to new 541.203(c):

> Employees whose work is "directly related" to management policies or to general business operations include those whose work affects policy or whose responsibility it is to carry it out. The phrase also includes a wide variety of persons who either carry out major assignments in conducting the operations of the business, or whose work affects business operations to a substantial degree.

New 541.203(c) has created a significant new exemption and a significant new source of confusion and litigation.

Police Officers

New section 541.3 seems to deny the application of the exemptions to most law enforcement personnel, and the preamble specifically addresses the case of police sergeants, normally the lowest level of front-line supervision on a police force. The treatment of sergeants is instructive. The preamble explains that sergeants are entitled to overtime "because their primary duty is not management or directly related to management or general business operations; neither do they work in a field of science or learning where a specialized academic degree is a standard prerequisite for employment." This raises the question, what if a sergeant had so much management responsibility that it did constitute his primary duty? When asked in a public forum whether a sergeant is exempt regardless of his duties, just by virtue of his rank, Solicitor of Labor Howard Radzeley refused to respond. This is not surprising, since the Fair Labor Standards Act does not permit the DOL to exempt employees by title or rank: their duties must be examined to determine whether they are executive, administrative, or professional. Nor does the statute justify treating one kind of manager differently from another based on whether one is a first responder. Congress could change the statute to accomplish such distinctions, but it has not.

The bottom line is that the rights of police officers are still at risk. The final rule makes it easier to find that an employee's primary duty is an exempt duty, because it allows employees to spend unlimited amounts of their time doing non-exempt work (work such as investigating crime scenes, making arrests, etc.) and yet still be found exempt. Police officers could also be exempt if they are deemed "team leaders," whose primary duty is presumed by the final rule to be administrative.

Low-Income Workers

There is no basis in fact for the Department's estimate that 1.3 million low-income workers will receive overtime pay that they are not receiving now. There are only 1.2 million salaried white collar employees who work overtime and make less than $23,660 a year. Using the Department's own estimates of the likelihood of exemption for such low-paid employees, fewer than one-fifth—about 250,000—are likely to be exempt. As the Department admits, the lower paid an employee is, the less likely it is that she is exempt as a bona fide executive, professional or administrator. The Department actually admits that it has fabricated its estimate. Even though the BLS Current Population Survey data show that a minority of the employees the Department considers likely to be exempt actually reported working any overtime, the Department assumed for the purpose of its estimate that 100% of them did.

Notes

1. The American Heritage Dictionary defines chef as "A cook, especially the chief cook of a large kitchen staff." According to the Department of Labor's Occupational Outlook Handbook, "The terms chef and cook are often used interchangeably. . . ." "Chefs and cooks create recipes and prepare meals. . . ." "A sous chef, or sub chef, is the second-in command and runs the kitchen in the absence of the chef."

POSTSCRIPT

Should the Regulations Regarding Overtime Pay Be Changed?

Labor Secretary Chao believes that the time has come for revision of the regulations that determine who is eligible for overtime pay. She begins by noting that the original FLSA explicitly gave the Secretary of Labor "the authority and responsibility to 'define and delimit'" the notions of white-collar occupations that are exempt from the FLSA's overtime pay regulations. She asserts that the main reason for the proposed changes is to benefit more workers, in particular "to restore overtime protections, especially to low-wage vulnerable workers who have little bargaining power with employers." She notes that some of the regulations have not changed since 1949. She then reviews the existing regulations and how she purposes to change these rules. In particular, she proposes that to be exempt, "an employee must receive the required minimum salary amount and have a primary duty of performing duties specified for an executive, administrative or professional employee." She concludes by declaring that the proposed changes will do a much better job of protecting the overtime rights of workers than the set of rules that are 50 years old.

Policy analyst Eisenbrey begins with a summary statement of his evaluation of the proposed changes in the overtime pay regulations of FLSA: They mean "longer hours and less pay for millions of workers—and more litigation for our entire economy." He then offers a set of eight specific conclusions that he has drawn from his analysis of the proposed changes. For example, he believes litigation will increase because the proposed changes involve ambiguous definitions. Moreover, he finds that the proposed reductions in the penalties faced by employers for violations of FLSA is likely to make violations more likely. Eisenbrey proceeds to evaluate the impact of the proposed changes on various sets of workers including chefs and cooks, nursery school teachers, police officers, and low-income workers. With respect to the last group, he argues that the Department of Labor's estimate that its proposed changes would increase the number of workers receiving overtime pay by 1.3 million is grossly overestimated.

For the current regulations regarding exemptions from overtime pay under FLSA, see the Department of Labor's "Fair Pay Fact Sheet by Exemption under the Fair Labor Standards Act (FLSA)" at `http://www.dol.gov/esa/regs/compliance/whd/fairpay/fs17a_overview.htm`. For articles that support the proposed changes in FLSA, see "The New Overtime Regulations: Clearer Rules, Fewer Conflicts," by Paul Kersy (The Heritage Foundation Web Memo #485, `http://www.hertigage.org/Research/Labor/wm485.cfm`)

and "Who Benefits from the New Overtime Regulations? A Data Analysis of the U.S. Department of Labor's Assessment," from Kirk A. Johnson (The Heritage Foundation, Center for Data Analysis Report #04-08, http://www.hertigage.org/Research/Labor/cda-08cfm). Eisenbrey, in collaboration with Jared Bernstein, presents a more detailed analysis in "Eliminating the Right to Overtime Pay: Department of Labor Proposal Means Lower Pay, Longer Hours for Millions of Workers," Economic Policy Institute Briefing Paper (June 26, 2003). Finally, the entire March 2004 issue of *Congressional Digest* is devoted to this topic.

ISSUE 3

Is There Discrimination in U.S. Labor Markets?

YES: William A. Darity, Jr., and Patrick L. Mason, from "Evidence on Discrimination in Employment: Codes of Color, Codes of Gender," *Journal of Economic Perspectives* (Spring 1998)

NO: James J. Heckman, from "Detecting Discrimination," *Journal of Economic Perspectives* (Spring 1998)

ISSUE SUMMARY

YES: Professor of economics William A. Darity, Jr., and associate professor of economics Patrick L. Mason assert that the lack of progress made since the mid-1970s toward establishing equality in wages between the races is evidence of persistent discrimination in U.S. labor markets.

NO: Professor of economics James J. Heckman argues that markets—driven by the profit motive of employers—will compete away any wage differentials that are not justified by differences in human capital.

Over 45 years have passed since Rosa Parks refused to give up her seat on a segregated Montgomery, Alabama, bus. America has had these years to finally overcome discrimination, but has it? Have the domestic programs of Presidents John F. Kennedy and Lyndon Johnson that were enacted after those turbulent years following Parks's act of defiance made it possible for African Americans to succeed within the powerful economic engine that drives American society? Or does racism still stain the Declaration of Independence, with its promise of equality for all?

Before we examine the economics of discrimination, perhaps we should look backward to see where America has been, what progress has been made, and what is left—if anything—to accomplish. American history, some say, reveals a world of legalized apartheid where African Americans were denied access to the social, political, and economic institutions that are the mainstays of America. Without this access, millions of American citizens were doomed to live lives on the fringes of the mainstream. Thus, the Kennedy/Johnson programs left one legacy, which few now dispute: These programs effectively dismantled the system of legalized discrimination and, for the first time since the end of slavery, allowed blacks to dream of a better life.

The dream became a reality for many. Consider the success stories that are buried in the poverty statistics that were collected and reported in the 1960s. Poverty scarred the lives of one out of every five Americans in 1959. But poverty was part of the lives of fully one-half of all African American families. Over time fewer and fewer Americans, black and white, suffered the effects of poverty; however, even though the incidence of poverty has been cut in half for black Americans, more than 25 percent of African American families still live in poverty. Even more distressing is the reality that African American children bear the brunt of this economic deprivation. In 1997, 37.2 percent of the "next generation" of African Americans lived in families whose total family income was insufficient to lift them out of poverty. (Note that although black Americans suffer the effects of poverty disproportionately, white-not-Hispanic families are the single largest identifiable group who live in poverty: white-not-Hispanic people make up 46.4 percent of the entire poor population; white-Hispanic, 22.2 percent; and black, 25.6 percent.)

The issue for economists is why so many African Americans failed to prosper and share in the great prosperity of the 1990s. Few would deny that in part the lack of success for black Americans is directly associated with a lack of "human capital": schooling, work experiences, and occupational choices. The real question, however, is whether differences between blacks and whites in terms of human capital can explain most of the current wage differentials or whether a significant portion of these wage differentials can be traced to labor market discrimination.

In the following selections, William A. Darity, Jr., and Patrick L. Mason argue that a significant part of the reason for black Americans' lack of economic success is discrimination, while James J. Heckman maintains that the issue is all human capital differences.

YES 

William A. Darity, Jr., and Patrick L. Mason

Evidence on Discrimination in Employment

There is substantial racial and gender disparity in the American economy. As we will demonstrate, discriminatory treatment within the labor market is a major cause of this inequality. The evidence is ubiquitous: careful research studies which estimate wage and employment regressions, help-wanted advertisements, audit and correspondence studies, and discrimination suits which are often reported by the news media. Yet, there appear to have been periods of substantial reductions in economic disparity and discrimination. For example, Donohue and Heckman (1991) provide evidence that racial discrimination declined during the interval 1965–1975. Gottschalk (1997) has produced statistical estimates that indicate that discrimination against black males dropped most sharply between 1965 and 1975, and that discrimination against women declined during the interval 1973–1994. But some unanswered questions remain. Why did the movement toward racial equality stagnate after the mid-1970s? What factors are most responsible for the remaining gender inequality? What is the role of the competitive process in elimination or reproduction of discrimination in employment?

The Civil Rights Act of 1964 is the signal event associated with abrupt changes in the black-white earnings differential (Bound and Freeman, 1989; Card and Krueger, 1992; Donohue and Heckman, 1991; Freeman, 1973). Along with other important pieces of federal legislation, the Civil Rights Act also played a major role in reducing discrimination against women (Leonard, 1989). Prior to passage of the federal civil rights legislation of the 1960s, racial exclusion and gender-typing of employment was blatant. The adverse effects of discriminatory practices on the life chances of African Americans, in particular, during that period have been well-documented (Wilson, 1980; Myers and Spriggs, 1997, pp. 32–42; Lieberson, 1980). Cordero-Guzman (1990, p. 1) observes that "up until the early 1960s, and particularly in the south, most blacks were systematically denied equal access to opportunities [and] in many instances, individuals with adequate credentials or skills were not, legally, allowed to apply to certain positions in firms." Competitive market forces certainly did not eliminate these discriminatory practices in the decades leading

From William A. Darity, Jr., and Patrick L. Mason, "Evidence on Discrimination in Employment: Codes of Color, Codes of Gender," *Journal of Economic Perspectives,* vol. 12, no. 2 (Spring 1998). References and some notes omitted.

up to the 1960s. They remained until the federal adoption of antidiscrimination laws.

Newspaper help-wanted advertisements provide vivid illustrations of the openness and visibility of such practices. We did an informal survey of the employment section of major daily newspapers from three northern cities, the *Chicago Tribune,* the *Los Angeles Times* and the *New York Times,* and from the nation's capital, *The Washington Post,* at five-year intervals from 1945 to 1965. (Examples from southern newspapers are even more dramatic.) . . .

With respect to gender-typing of occupations, help-wanted advertisements were structured so that whole sections of the classifieds offered job opportunities separately and explicitly for men and women. Men were requested for positions that included restaurant cooks, managers, assistant managers, auto salesmen, sales in general, accountants and junior accountants, design engineers, detailers, diemakers, drivers, and welders. Women were requested for positions that included household and domestic workers, stenographers, secretaries, typists, bookkeepers, occasionally accountants (for "girls good at figures"), and waitresses.[1] The *Washington Post* of January 3, 1960, had the most examples of racial preference, again largely for whites, in help-wanted ads of any newspaper edition we examined. Nancy Lee's employment service even ran an advertisement for a switchboard operator—presumably never actually seen by callers—requesting that all *women* applying be white! Advertisements also frequently included details about the age range desired from applicants, like men 21–30 or women 18–25. Moreover, employers also showed little compunction about specifying precise physical attributes desired in applicants.[2]

Following the passage of the Civil Rights Act of 1964, none of the newspapers carried help-wanted ads that included any explicit preference for "white" or "colored" applicants in January 1965. However, it became very common to see advertisements for "European" housekeepers (a trend that was already visible as early as 1960). While race no longer entered the help-wanted pages explicitly, national origin or ancestry seemed to function as a substitute. Especially revealing is an advertisement run by the Amity Agency in the *New York Times* on January 3, 1965, informing potential employers that "Amity Has Domestics": "Scottish Gals" at $150 a month as "mothers' helpers and housekeepers," "German Gals" at $175 a month on one-year contracts, and "Haitian Gals" at $130 a month who are "French speaking." Moreover, in the "Situations Wanted" section of the newspaper, prospective female employees still were indicating their own race in January 1965.

The case of the help-wanted pages of the *New York Times* is of special note because New York was one of the states that had a state law against discrimination and a State Commission Against Discrimination in place, long prior to the passage of the federal Civil Rights Act of 1964. However, the toothlessness of New York's State Commission Against Discrimination is well-demonstrated by the fact that employers continued to indicate their racial preferences for new hires in help-wanted ads, as well as by descriptions of personal experience like that of John A. Williams in his semi-autobiographical novel, *The Angry Ones* (1960 [1996], pp. 30–1).

Help-wanted ads were only the tip of the iceberg of the process of racial exclusion in employment. After all, there is no reason to believe that the employers who did not indicate a racial preference were entirely open-minded about their applicant pool. How successful has the passage of federal antidiscrimination legislation in the 1960s been in producing an equal opportunity environment where job applicants are now evaluated on their qualifications? To give away the answer at the outset, our response is that discrimination by race has diminished somewhat, and discrimination by gender has diminished substantially. However, neither employment discrimination by race or by gender is close to ending. The Civil Rights Act of 1964 and subsequent related legislation has purged American society of the most overt forms of discrimination. However, discriminatory practices have continued in more covert and subtle forms. Furthermore, racial discrimination is masked and rationalized by widely-held presumptions of black inferiority.

Statistical Research on Employment Discrimination

Economic research on the presence of discrimination in employment has focused largely on black-white and male-female earnings and occupational disparities. The position typically taken by economists is that some part of the racial or gender gap in earnings or occupations is due to average group differences in productivity-linked characteristics (a human capital gap) and some part is due to average group differences in treatment (a discrimination gap). The more of the gap that can be explained by human capital differences, the easier it becomes to assert that labor markets function in a nondiscriminatory manner; any remaining racial or gender inequality in employment outcomes must be due to differences between blacks and whites or between men and women that arose outside the labor market. . . .

Regression Evidence on Racial Discrimination

When we consider economic disparities by race, a difference emerges by gender. Using a Blinder-Oaxaca approach in which women are compared by their various racial and ethnic subgroups, Darity, Guilkey and Winfrey (1996) find little systematic evidence of wage discrimination based on U.S. Census data for 1980 and 1990.[3] However, when males are examined using the same Census data a standard result emerges. A significant portion of the wage gap between black and white males in the United States cannot be explained by the variables included to control for productivity differences across members of the two racial groups.

Black women are likely to have the same school quality and omitted family background characteristics as black men (the same is true for white women and men). Hence, it strains credibility to argue that the black-white earnings gap for men is due to an omitted labor quality variable unless one also argues that black women are paid more than white women conditional on the unobservables. The findings of Darity, Guilkey and Winfrey (1996), Rodgers and Spriggs (1996) and Gottschalk (1997) indicate that in 1980 and 1990 black men in the United States were suffering a 12 to 15 percent loss in earnings due to labor market discrimination.

There is a growing body of evidence that uses color or "skin shade" as a natural experiment to detect discrimination. The approach of these studies has been to look at different skin shades within a particular ethnic group at a particular place and time, which should help to control for factors of culture and ethnicity other than pure skin color. Johnson, Bienenstock, and Stoloff (1995) looked at dark-skinned and light-skinned black males from the same neighborhoods in Los Angeles, and found that the combination of a black racial identity and a dark skin tone reduces an individual's odds of working by 52 percent, after controlling for education, age, and criminal record! Since both dark-skinned and light-skinned black males in the sample were from the same neighborhoods, the study *de facto* controlled for school quality. Further evidence that lighter-complexioned blacks tend to have superior incomes and life chances than darker-skinned blacks in the United States comes from studies by Ransford (1970), Keith and Herring (1991) and Johnson and Farrell (1995).

Similar results are found by looking at skin color among Hispanics. Research conducted by Arce, Murguia, and Frisbie (1987) utilizing the University of Michigan's 1979 National Chicano Survey involved partitioning the sample along two phenotypical dimensions: skin color, ranging from Very Light to Very Dark on a five-point scale; and physical features, ranging from Very European to Very Indian on a five-point scale. Chicanos with lighter skin color and more European features had higher socioeconomic status. Using the same data set, Telles and Murguia (1990) found that 79 percent of $1,262 of the earnings differences between the dark phenotypic group and other Mexican Americans was *not* explained by the traditional variables affecting income included in their earnings regression. Further support for this finding comes from Cotton (1993) and Darity, Guilkey, and Winfrey (1996) who find using 1980 and 1990 Census data that black Hispanics suffer close to ten times the proportionate income loss due to differential treatment of given characteristics than white Hispanics. Evidently, skin shade plays a critical role in structuring social class position and life chances in American society, even between comparable individuals within minority groups.

Cross-national evidence from Brazil also is relevant here. Despite conventional beliefs in Brazil that race is irrelevant and class is the primary index for social stratification, Silva (1985) found using the 1976 national household survey that blacks and mulattos (or "browns") shared closely in a relatively depressed economic condition relative to whites, with mulattos earning slightly more than blacks. Silva estimated that the cost of being nonwhite in Brazil in 1976 was about 566 cruzeiros per month (or $104 U.S.). But Silva found slightly greater unexplained income differences for mulattos, rather than blacks vis-à-vis whites, unexplained differences he viewed as evidence of discrimination. A new study by Telles and Lim (1997), based upon a random national survey of 5000 persons conducted by the Data Folha Institute des Pesquisas, compares economic outcomes based upon whether race is self-identified or interviewer-identified. Telles and Lim view interviewer-identification as more useful for establishing social classification and treatment. They find that self-identification underestimates white income and over-estimates brown and black incomes relative to interviewer-classification.

Despite the powerful results on skin shade, some continue to argue that the extent of discrimination is overestimated by regression techniques because of missing variables. After all, it seems likely that the general pattern of unobserved variables—for example, educational quality or labor force attachment—would tend to follow the observed variables in indicating reasons for the lower productivity of black males (Ruhm, 1989, p. 157). As a result, adjusting for these factors would reduce the remaining black-white earnings differential.[4]

As one might imagine, given the framework in which economists tackle the issue of discrimination, considerable effort has been made to find measures of all imaginable dimensions of human capital that could be used to test the presence of labor market discrimination. This effort has uncovered one variable in one data set which, if inserted in an earnings regression, produces the outcome that nearly all of the black-white male wage gap is explained by human capital and none by labor market discrimination. (However, thus far no one has suggested a reasonable missing variable for the skin shade effect.) The particular variable that eliminates evidence of discrimination in earnings against black men as a group is the Armed Forces Qualifying Test (AFQT) score in the National Longitudinal Survey of Youth (NLSY).

A number of researchers have confirmed with somewhat different sample sizes and methodologies that including AFQT scores in an earnings equation virtually will eliminate racial differences in wages. . . .

The conclusion of this body of work is that labor market discrimination against blacks is negligible or nonexistent. Using Neal and Johnson's (1996) language, the key to explaining differences in black and white labor market outcomes must instead rest with "premarket factors." These studies have led Abigail and Stephan Thernstrom (1997) in a prominent *Wall Street Journal* editorial to proclaim that "what may look like persistent employment discrimination is better described as employers rewarding workers with relatively strong cognitive skills."

But matters are not so straightforward. The essential problem is what the AFQT scores are actually measuring, and therefore what precisely is being controlled for. There is no consensus on this point. AFQT scores have been interpreted variously as providing information about school quality or academic achievement (O'Neill, 1990), about previously unmeasured skills (Ferguson, 1995; Maxwell, 1994; Neal and Johnson 1996), and even about intelligence (Herrnstein and Murray, 1994)—although the military did not design AFQT as an intelligence test (Rodgers and Spriggs, 1996).[5] The results obtained by O'Neill (1990), Maxwell (1994), Ferguson (1995), and Neal and Johnson (1996) after using the AFQT as an explanatory variable are, upon closer examination, not robust to alternative specifications and are quite difficult to interpret.

The lack of robustness can be illustrated by looking at how AFQT scores interact with other variables in the earnings equation. Neal and Johnson (1996), for example, adjust for age and AFQT score in an earnings equation, but not for years of schooling, presumably on the assumption that same-age individuals would have the same years of schooling, regardless of race. However, this assumption does not appear to be true. Rodgers, Spriggs and Waaler (1997) find that white youths had accumulated more schooling at a given age than black or Hispanic youths. When AFQT scores are both age and education-adjusted, a black-white wage gap reemerges, as the authors report (p. 3):[6]

> . . . estimates from models that use our proposed age and education adjusted AFQT score [show] that sharp differences in racial and ethnic wage gaps exist. Instead of explaining three-quarters of the male black-white wage gap, the age and education adjusted score explains 40 percent of the gap. Instead of explaining the entire male Hispanic-white gap, the new score explains 50 percent of the gap . . . [B]lack women no longer earn more than white women do, and . . . Hispanic women's wage premium relative to white women is reduced by one-half.

Another specification problem arises when wage equations are estimated using both AFQT scores and the part of the NLSY sample that includes measures of psychological well-being (for "self-esteem" and "locus of control") as explanatory variables. The presence of the psychological variables restores a negative effect on wages of being African-American (Goldsmith, Veum and Darity, 1997).[7]

Yet another specification problem becomes relevant if one interprets AFQT scores as providing information about school quality. But since there is a school survey module of the NLSY which can be used to provide direct evidence on school quality, using variables like the books/pupil ratio, the percent of students classified as disadvantaged, and teacher salaries, it would surely be more helpful to use this direct data on school quality rather than the AFQT scores. In another method of controlling for school quality, Harrison (1972) compared employment and earnings outcomes for blacks and whites living in the same black ghetto communities, on grounds that school quality would not be very different between them. Harrison found sharp differences in earnings favoring whites.[8]

One severe difficulty in interpreting what differences in the AFQT actually mean is demonstrated by Rodgers and Spriggs (1996) who show that AFQT scores appear to be biased in a specific sense. . . . [They] create a hypothetical set of "unbiased" black scores by running the mean black characteristics through the equation with the white coefficients. When those scores replace the actual AFQT scores in a wage equation, then the adjusted AFQT scores no longer explain black-white wage differences. A similar result can be obtained if actual white scores are replaced by hypothetical scores produced by running white characteristics through the equation with black coefficients.[9] Apparently, the AFQT scores themselves are a consequence of bias in the underlying processes that generate AFQT scores for blacks and whites. Perhaps AFQT scores are a proxy for skills that do not capture all skills, and thus leave behind a bias of uncertain direction. Or there may be other predictors of the test that are correlated with race but which are left out of the AFQT explanatory equation.

To muddy the waters further, focusing on the math and verbal subcomponents of AFQT leads to inconsistent implications for discriminatory differentials. For example, while a higher performance on the verbal portion of the AFQT contributes to higher wages for black women versus black men, it apparently has little or no effect on the wages of white women versus white men (Currie and Thomas, 1995). However, white women gain in wages from higher scores on the math portion of the AFQT, but black women do not. Perhaps this says that white women are screened (directly or indirectly) for employment and pay on the basis of their math performance, while black women are screened based upon their verbal skills. Perhaps this is because white employers have a greater "comfort zone" with black women who have a greater verbal similarity to whites. Or perhaps something not fully understood and potentially quirky is going on with the link between these test results and wages.

Finally, since skill differentials have received such widespread discussion in recent years as an underlying cause of growing wage inequality in the U.S. economy—see, for example, the discussion in the Spring 1997 issue of *The Journal of Economic Perspectives*—it should be pointed out that growth in the rewards to skill does not mean that the effects of race have diminished. If the importance of race and skill increase simultaneously, then a rising skill premium will explain more of the changes in *intraracial* wage inequality, which may well leave a larger unexplained portion of interracial wage inequality. For example, when Murnane et al. (1995) ask whether test scores in math, reading, and vocabulary skills for respondents in the National Longitudinal Study of the High School Class of 1972 and High School and Beyond datasets have more explanatory power in wage equations for 1980 graduates than 1972 graduates, their answer is "yes"—the rate of return to cognitive skill (test scores) increased between 1978 and 1986. However, in these same regressions, the absolute value of the negative race coefficient is larger for the 1980 graduates than it is for the 1972 graduates! These results confirm that there are increasing returns to skills measured by standardized tests, but do not indicate that the rise in returns to skills can explain changes in the black-white earnings gap very well.

The upshot is the following. There is no doubt that blacks suffer reduced earnings in part due to inferior productivity-linked characteristics, like skill gaps or school quality gaps, relative to nonblack groups. However, evidence based on the AFQT should be treated with extreme caution. Given that this one variable in one particular data set is the only one that suggests racial discrimination is no longer operative in U.S. employment practices, it should be taken as far from convincing evidence. Blacks, especially black men, continue to suffer significantly reduced earnings due to discrimination and the extent of discrimination.

Direct Evidence on Discrimination: Court Cases and Audit Studies

One direct body of evidence of the persistence of employment discrimination, despite the presence of antidiscrimination laws, comes from the scope and dispensation of job discrimination lawsuits. A sampling of such cases from recent years . . . reveals [that] discriminatory practices have occurred at highly visible U.S. corporations often having multinational operations. The suits reveal racial and gender discrimination in employment, training, promotion, tenure, layoff policies, and work environment, as well as occupational segregation.

Perhaps the most notorious recent case is the $176 million settlement reached between Texaco and black employees after disclosure of taped comments of white corporate officials making demeaning remarks about blacks, remarks that revealed an outlook that translated into corresponding antiblack employment practices. Clearly, neither federal antidiscrimination laws nor the pressures of competitive markets have prevented the occurrence of discriminatory practices that have resulted in significant awards or settlements for the plaintiffs.

Another important source of direct evidence are the audit studies of the type conducted in the early 1990s by the Urban Institute (Mincy, 1993). The Urban Institute audit studies sought to examine employment outcomes for young black, Hispanic, and white males, ages 19–25, looking for entry-level jobs. Pairs of black and white males and pairs of Hispanic and non-Hispanic white males were matched as testers and sent out to apply for jobs at businesses advertising openings. Prior to application for the positions, the testers were trained for interviews to minimize dissimilarity in the quality of their self-presentation, and they were given manufactured résumés designed to put their credentials on a par. The black/white tests were conducted in Chicago and in Washington, D.C., while the Hispanic/non Hispanic tests were conducted in Chicago and in San Diego.

A finding of discrimination was confirmed if one member of the pair was offered the position and the other was not. No discrimination was confirmed if both received an offer (sequentially, since both were instructed to turn the position down) or neither received an offer. This is a fairly stringent test for discrimination, since, in the case where no offer was made to either party, there is no way to determine whether employers were open to the prospect of hiring a black or an Hispanic male, what the overall applicant pool looked like, or who was actually hired. However, the Urban Institute audits found that black males were three times as likely to be turned down for a job as white males, and Hispanic males also were three times as likely as non-Hispanic white males to experience discrimination in employment (Fix, Galster and Struyk, 1993, pp. 21–22).

Bendick, Jackson and Reinoso (1994) also report on 149 race-based (black, white) and ethnicity-based (Hispanic, non-Hispanic) job audits conducted by the Fair Employment Council of Greater Washington, Inc. in the D.C. metropolitan area in 1990 and 1991. Testers were paired by gender. The audit findings are striking. White testers were close to 10 percent more likely to receive interviews than blacks. Among those interviewed, half of the white testers received job offers versus a mere 11 percent of the black testers. When both testers received the same job offers, white testers were offered 15 cents per hour more than black testers. Black testers also were disproportionately "steered" toward lower level positions after the job offer was made, and white testers were disproportionately considered for unadvertised positions at higher levels than the originally advertised job.

Overall, the Fair Employment Council study found rates of discrimination in excess of 20 percent against blacks (in the black/white tests) and against Hispanics (in the Hispanic/non-Hispanic tests). In the Hispanic/non-Hispanic tests, Hispanic male job seekers were three times as likely to experience discrimination as Hispanic females. But, surprisingly, in the black/white tests, black females were three times as likely to encounter discrimination as black males. The racial results for women in this particular audit stand in sharp contrast with the results in the statistical studies described above.

The most severe criticisms of the audit technique have come from Heckman and Siegelman (1993). At base, their central worry is that testers cannot be paired in such a way that they will not signal a difference that legitimately can be interpreted by the prospective employer as a difference in potential to perform the job, despite interview training and doctored résumés.[10] For example, what about intangibles like a person's ability to make a first impression or the fact that certain résumés may be unintentionally superior to others?

In an audit study consciously designed to address many of the Heckman and Siegelman (1993) methodological complaints, Neumark, Bank, and Van Nort (1995) examined sex discrimination in restaurant hiring practices. Four testers (all college students, two men and two women) applied for jobs waiting tables at 65 restaurants in Philadelphia. The restaurants were separated into high, medium, and low price, according to average cost of a meal. Waiters at the high price restaurants tend to receive greater wages and tips than their counterparts in low price restaurants; specifically, the authors find that average hourly earnings for waiters were 47 and 68 percent higher in the high price restaurant than the medium and low price restaurant, respectively. One man and one woman applied for a job at each restaurant, so there were 130 attempts to obtain employment. Thirty-nine job offers were received.

One interesting twist to this methodology is that three reasonably comparable résumés were constructed, and over a three-week period each tester used a different résumé for a period of one week. This résumé-switching mitigates any differences that may have occurred because one résumé was better than another. To reduce other sources of unobserved ability—for example, the ability to make a good first impression—the testers were instructed to give their applications to the first employee they encountered when visiting a restaurant. That employee was then asked to forward the résumé to the manager. In effect, personality and appearance were eliminated as relevant variables for the interview decision, if not for the job offer decision.

Neumark et al. (1995) find that in the low-priced restaurants, the man received an offer while the woman did not 29 percent of the time. A woman never received an offer when the man did not. In the high-priced restaurants, the man received an offer while the woman did not in 43 percent of the tests, while the woman received an offer while the man did not in just 4 percent of the tests. Also, at high-priced restaurants, women had roughly a 40 percent lower probability of being interviewed and 50 percent lower probability of obtaining a job offer, and this difference is statistically significant. Hence, this audit study shows that within-occupation employment discrimination may be a contributing source to wage discrimination between men and women. . . .

The Theoretical Backdrop

Standard neoclassical competitive models are forced by their own assumptions to the conclusion that discrimination only can be temporary. Perhaps the best-known statement of this position emerges from Becker's (1957) famous "taste for discrimination" model. If two groups share similar productivity profiles under competitive conditions where at least some employers prefer profits to prejudice, eventually all workers must be paid the same wage. The eventual result may involve segregated workforces—say, with some businesses hiring only white men and others hiring only black women—but as long as both groups have the same average productivity, they will receive the same pay. Thus, in this view, discrimination only can produce temporary racial or gender earnings gaps. Moreover, alternative forms of discrimination are separable processes; wage discrimination and employment segregation are unrelated in Becker's model.

Despite the theoretical implications of standard neoclassical competitive models, we have considerable evidence that it took the Civil Rights Act of 1964 to alter the discriminatory climate in America. It did not, by any means, eliminate either form of discrimination. Indeed, the impact of the law itself may have been temporary, since there is some evidence that the trend toward racial inequality came to a halt in the mid-1970s (even though interracial differences in human capital were continuing to close) and the momentum toward gender equality may have begun to lose steam in the early 1990s. Moreover, we believe that the forms of discrimination have altered in response to the act. Therefore, it is not useful to argue that either racial or gender discrimination is inconsistent with the operation of competitive markets, especially when it has taken antidiscrimination laws to reduce the impact of discrimination in the market. Instead, it is beneficial to uncover the market mechanisms which permit or encourage discriminatory practices.

Since Becker's work, orthodox microeconomics has been massaged in various ways to produce stories of how discrimination might sustain itself against pressures of the competitive market. The tacit assumption of these approaches has been to find a way in which discrimination can increase business profits, or to identify conditions where choosing not to discriminate might reduce profits.

In the customer discrimination story, for example, businesses discriminate not because they themselves are bigoted but because their clients are bigoted. This story works especially well where the product in question must be delivered via face-to-face contact, but it obviously does not work well when the hands that made the product are not visible to the customer possessing the "taste for discrimination." Moreover, as Madden (1975, p. 150) has pointed out, sex-typing of jobs can work in both directions: "While service occupations are more contact-oriented, sexual preference can work both ways: for example, women are preferred as Playboy bunnies, airline stewardesses, and lingerie salespeople, while men seem to be preferred as tire salespeople, stockbrokers, and truck drivers."

Obviously, group-typing of employment will lead to a different occupational distributions between group A and B, but will it lead to different earnings as well? Madden (1975, p. 150, emphasis in original) suggests not necessarily:

> . . . consumer discrimination causes occupational segregation rather than wage differentials. If the female wage decreases as the amount of consumer contact required by a job increases, women seek employment in jobs where consumer contact is minimal and wages are higher. Only if there are not enough non-consumer contact jobs for working women, forcing them to seek employment in consumer-contact jobs, would consumer discrimination be responsible for wage differentials. Since most jobs do not require consumer contact, consumer discrimination would segregate women into these jobs, but not *cause* wage differentials.

Perhaps the best attempt to explain how discrimination might persist in a neoclassical framework is the statistical discrimination story, which, at base, is a story about imperfect information. The notion is that potential employers cannot observe everything they wish to know about job candidates, and in this environment, they have an incentive to seize group membership as a signal that allows them to improve their predictions of a prospective candidate's ability to perform.

However, this model of prejudicial beliefs does not ultimately wash well as a theory of why discrimination should be long-lasting. If average group differences are perceived but not real, then employers should *learn* that their beliefs are mistaken. If average group differences are real, then in a world with antidiscrimination laws, employers are likely to find methods of predicting the future performance of potential employees with sufficient accuracy that there is no need to use the additional "signal" of race or gender. It seems implausible that with all the resources that corporations put into hiring decisions, the remaining differentials are due to an inability to come up with a suitable set of questions or qualifications for potential employees.

Moreover, models of imperfect competition as explanations of discrimination do not solve the problem completely either. The reason for the immutability of the imperfection is rarely satisfactorily explained—and often not addressed at all—in models of this type (Darity and Williams, 1985). Struggle as it may, orthodox microeconomics keeps returning to the position that sustained observed differences in economic outcomes between groups must be due to an induced or inherent deficiency in the group that experiences the inferior outcomes. In the jargon, this is referred to as a deficiency in human capital. Sometimes this deficiency is associated with poor schooling opportunities, other times with culture (Sowell, 1981).[11] But the thrust of the argument is to absolve market processes, at least in a putative long run, of a role in producing the differential outcome; the induced or inherent deficiency occurs in premarket or extra-market processes.

Certainly years of schooling, quality of education, years of work experiences and even culture can have a role in explaining racial and gender earnings differences. However, the evidence marshaled above indicates that these factors do not come close to explaining wage differentials and employment patterns observed in the economy. Instead, discrimination has been sustained both in the United States and elsewhere, for generations at a time. Such discrimination does not always even need direct legal support nor has it been eliminated by market pressures. Instead, changes in social and legal institutions have been needed to reduce it.

James Heckman (1997, p. 406) draws a similar conclusion in his examination of a specific sector of employment, the textile industry:

> . . . substantial growth in Southern manufacturing had little effect on the labor-market position of blacks in Southern textiles prior to 1965. Through tight and slack labor markets, the proportion of blacks was small and stable. After 1964, and in synchronization with the 1964 Civil Rights Act, black economic progress was rapid. Only South Carolina had a Jim Crow law prohibiting employment of blacks as textile workers, and the law was never used after the 1920s. Yet the pattern of exclusion of blacks was prevalent throughout Southern textiles, and the breakthrough in black employment in the industry came in all states at the same time. Informally enforced codes and private practices, and not formally enforced apartheid, kept segregation in place, and market forces did not break them down.

Nontraditional alternatives to orthodox microeconomic analysis can lead to a logically consistent basis for a persistent gap in wage outcomes. These alternatives typically break down the line between in-market and pre-market discrimination so often drawn in conventional economics. The first of these involves a self-fulfilling prophecy mechanism. Suppose employers believe that members of group A are more productive than members of group B on average. Suppose further that they act upon their beliefs, thereby exhibiting a stronger demand for A workers, hiring them more frequently and paying them more.

Next, suppose that members of group B become less motivated and less emotionally healthy as a consequence of the employment rebuff. Notice that the original decision not to hire may have been completely unjustified on productivity grounds; nonetheless, the decision made *in* the labor market—a decision not to hire or to hire at low pay—alters the human capital characteristics of the members of group B so that they become inferior candidates for jobs. The employers' initially held mistaken beliefs become realized over time as a consequence of the employers' initial discriminatory decisions. As Elmslie and Sedo (1996, p. 474) observe in their development of this argument, "One initial bout of unemployment that is not productivity based can lay the foundation for continued future unemployment and persistently lower job status even if no future discrimination occurs."

More broadly, depressed expectations of employment opportunities also can have an adverse effect on members of group B's inclination to acquire additional human capital—say, through additional schooling or training. The effects of the past could be passed along by the disadvantaged group from generation to generation, another possibility ignored by orthodox theory. For example, Borjas (1994) writes of the ethnic intergenerational transmission of economic advantage or disadvantage. He makes no mention of discrimination in his work but a potential interpretation is that the effects of past discrimination, both negative and positive, are passed on to subsequent generations. Other evidence along these lines includes Tyree's (1991) findings on the relationship between an ethnic group's status and performance in the past and the present, and Darity's (1989) development of "the lateral mobility" hypothesis based upon ethnic group case histories.

More narrowly, the group-typed beliefs held by employers/selectors also can have a strong effect on the performance of the candidate at the interview stage. In an experiment performed in the early 1970s, psychologists Word, Zanna and Cooper (1974, pp. 109–120) found that when interviewed by "naïve" whites, trained black applicants "received (a) less immediacy, (b) higher rates of speech error, and (c) shorter amounts of interview time" than white applicants. They then trained white interviewers to replicate the behavior received by the black applicants in the first phase of their experiment, and found that "naïve" white candidates performed poorly during interviews when they were "treated like blacks." Such self-fulfilling prophecies are familiar in the psychology literature (Sibicky and Dovidio, 1986).

A second nontraditional theory that can lead to a permanent gap in intergroup outcomes is the noncompeting groups hypothesis advanced by the late W. Arthur Lewis (1979). Related arguments emerge from Krueger's (1963) extension of the trade-based version of the Becker model, Swinton's (1978) "labor force competition" model for racial differences, and Madden's (1975) male monopoly model for gender differences, but Lewis's presentation is the most straightforward. Lewis starts with an intergroup rivalry for the preferred positions in a hierarchical occupational structure. Say that group A is able to control access to the preferred positions by influencing the required credentials, manipulating opportunities to obtain the credentials, and serving a gatekeeping function over entry and promotion along job ladders. Group B is then rendered "noncompeting."

One theoretical difficulty with this argument that its proponents rarely address is that it requires group A to maintain group solidarity even when it may have subgroups with differing interests. In Krueger's (1963) model, for example, white capitalists must value racial group solidarity sufficiently to accept a lower return on their capital as the price they pay for a generally higher level of income for all whites (and higher wages for white workers). In Madden's (1975) model, male capitalists must make a similar decision on behalf of male workers.

This noncompeting group hypothesis blurs the orthodox distinction between in-market and pre-market discrimination, by inserting matters of power and social control directly into the analysis. This approach then links discrimination to racism or sexism, rather than to simple bigotry or prejudice. It leads to the proposition that discrimination—in the sense of differential treatment of those members of each group with similar productivity-linked characteristics—is an endogenous phenomenon. "In-market" discrimination need only occur when all the earlier attempts to control access to jobs, credentials, and qualifications are quavering.

One interesting implication here is that growth in skills for what we have been calling group B, the disadvantaged group, may be accompanied by a surge of in-market discrimination, because that form of discrimination has become more necessary to preserve the position of group A. There are several instances of cross-national evidence to support this notion. Darity, Dietrich and Guilkey (1997) find that while black males were making dramatic strides in acquiring literacy between 1880 and 1910 in the United States, simultaneously they were suffering increasing proportionate losses in occupational status due to disadvantageous treatment of their measured characteristics. Geographer Peggy Lovell (1993) finds very little evidence of discrimination in earnings against blacks in northern Brazil, where blacks are more numerous, but substantial evidence of discrimination against them in southern Brazil. Northern Brazil is considerably poorer than southern Brazil and the educational levels of northern black Brazilians are more depressed than in the south.[12] It is easy to argue that the exercise of discrimination is not "needed" in the north, since blacks are not generally going to compete with whites for the same sets of jobs. Indeed, there is relatively more evidence of discrimination against mulattos than blacks, the former more likely to compete directly with whites for employment. A third example, in a study using data for males based upon a survey taken in Delhi in 1970, Desi and Singh (1989) find that the most dramatic instance of discriminatory differentials in earnings was evident for Sikh men vis-à-vis Hindu high caste men. On the other hand, most of the earnings gap for Hindu middle caste, lower caste and scheduled caste men was due to inferior observed characteristics. Since these latter groups could be excluded from preferred positions because of an inadequate educational background, it would not be necessary for the upper castes to exercise discrimination against them. Sikh males, on the other hand, possessed the types of credentials that would make them viable contestants for the positions desired by the Hindu higher castes.

A final alternative approach at construction of a consistent economic theory of persistent discrimination evolves from a reconsideration of the neoclassical theory of competition. Darity and Williams (1985) argued that replacement of neoclassical competition with either classical or Marxist approaches to competition—where competition is defined by a tendency toward equalization of rates of profit and where monopoly positions are the consequence of competition rather than the antithesis of competition—eliminates the anomalies associated with the orthodox approach (Botwinick, 1993; Mason, 1995, forthcoming-b). A labor market implication of this approach is that wage diversity, different pay across firms and industries for workers within the same occupation, is the norm for competitive labor markets. In these models, remuneration is a function of the characteristics of the individual and the job. The racial-gender composition of the job affects worker bargaining power and thereby wage differentials. In turn, race and gender exclusion are used to make some workers less competitive for the higher paying positions. This approach emphasizes that the major elements for the persistence of discrimination are racial or gender differences in the access to better paying jobs within and between occupations.

Whatever alternative approach is preferred, the strong evidence of the persistence of discrimination in labor markets calls into question any theoretical apparatus that implies that the discrimination must inevitably diminish or disappear.

Notes

1. The only significant exception to the help-wanted ads pattern of maintaining a fairly strict sexual division of labor that we could detect was evident in the *Los Angeles Times* employment section of early January 1945, where we found women being sought as aircraft riveters, assemblers, and army photographers. Of course, World War II was ongoing at that stage, and the comparative absence of men produced the "Rosie the Riveter" phenomenon. However, despite wartime conditions, even this temporary breakdown in gender-typing of occupations was not evident in the help-wanted ads for the *Chicago Tribune,* the *New York Times,* or the *Washington Post* at the same time. Moreover, racial preferences also remained strongly pronounced in wartime advertisements of each of the four newspapers.
2. The C.W. Agency, advertising in the *Los Angeles Times* on January, 1, 1950, wanted a "Girl Model 38 bust, 25 waist, 36 hips"; "Several Other Types" with physical characteristics unspecified in the advertisement apparently also were acceptable.
3. The 1980 and 1990 Censuses provide only self-reported information on interviewees' race and their ancestry, which makes it possible to partition the American population into 50 different detailed ethnic and racial groups, like Asian Indian ancestry women, Mexican ancestry women, Polish ancestry women, French Canadian ancestry women, and so on. The explanatory variables were years of school, years of college, number of children, married spouse present, years of work experience, years of work experience squared, very good or fluent English, disabled, born in the United States, assimilated (that is either married to a person with a different ethnicity or having claimed two different ethnic groups in the census), location, region, and occupation. Annual earnings was the dependent variable. There was no control for the difference between potential and actual experience; hence, to the extent that the gap between potential and actual experience and the rate of return to actual experience varies by race, the results for the female regressions may be less reliable than the results for the male regression.
4. For a view that unobservable factors might favor black male productivity, thereby meaning that the regression coefficients are underestimating the degree of discrimination, see Mason (forthcoming-a).
5. Indeed, if one uses a measure that, unlike the AFQT, was explicitly designed as a measure of intelligence, it does not explain the black-white gap in wages. Mason (forthcoming-b; 1996) demonstrates this by using in a wage equation an explanatory variable that comes from a sentence completion test given to 1972 respondents to the Panel Study of Income Dynamics (PSID)—a test which was designed to assess "g," so-called general intelligence. Mason finds that the significant, negative sign on the coefficient for the race variable is unaffected by inclusion of the PSID sentence completion test score as an explanatory variable. Indeed, Mason (1997) finds that although discrimination declined during 1968 to 1973, discrimination grew by 2.0 percent annually during 1973–1991. On the other hand, the rate of return to cognitive skill (IQ) was relatively constant during 1968–1979, but had an annual growth rate of 1.6 percent during 1979–1991.
6. Mason (1997) finds a similar result when age and education-adjusted IQ scores are used.

7. Attention to the psychological measures also provides mild evidence that blacks put forth more effort than whites, a finding consistent with Mason's (forthcoming-a) speculation that there may be unobservables that favor black productivity. Mason argues that effort or motivation is a productivity-linked variable that favors blacks, based upon his finding that blacks acquire more schooling than whites for a comparable set of resources.
8. Card and Krueger (1992) also directly control for school quality. They find that there is still a substantial wage gap left after controlling for school quality.
9. Systematic racial differences in the structural equations for the determination of standardized test scores also are evident in the General Social Survey data. Fitting equations for Wordsum scores separately for blacks and whites also yields statistically distinct structures (White, 1997).
10. Although some of their criticisms along these lines frankly strike us as ridiculous; for example, concerns about facial hair on the Hispanic male testers used by the Urban Institute.
11. To address the effects of culture, following Woodbury (1993), Darity, Guilkey, and Winfrey (1996) held color constant and varied culture by examining outcomes among blacks of differing ancestries. Unlike Sowell's expectation, black males of West Indian and non-West Indian ancestry were being confronted with the same racial penalty in U.S. labor markets by 1990.
12. The portion of the gap that can be explained by discrimination is much lower in the high black region of Brazil, the Northeast, than the rest of Brazil. We know of no evidence which suggests that this is or is not true for the U.S. south.

NO 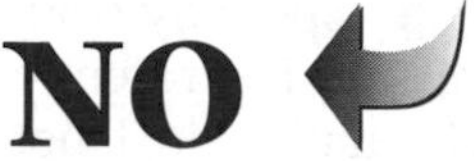

James J. Heckman

Detecting Discrimination

In the current atmosphere of race relations in America, the authors of the three main papers presented in this symposium are like persons crying "fire" in a crowded theater. They apparently vindicate the point of view that American society is riddled with racism and that discrimination by employers may account for much of the well-documented economic disparity between blacks and whites. In my judgement, this conclusion is not sustained by a careful reading of the evidence.

In this article, I make three major points. First, I want to distinguish market discrimination from the discrimination encountered by a randomly selected person or pair of persons at a randomly selected firm as identified from audit studies.

Second, I consider the evidence presented by the authors in the symposium, focusing for brevity and specificity on labor markets. It is far less decisive on the issue of market discrimination than it is claimed to be. Disparity in market outcomes does not prove discrimination in the market. A careful reading of the entire body of available evidence confirms that most of the disparity in earnings between blacks and whites in the labor market of the 1990s is due to the differences in skills they bring to the market, and not to discrimination within the labor market. This interpretation of the evidence has important consequences for social policy. While undoubtedly there are still employers and employees with discriminatory intentions, labor market discrimination is no longer a first-order quantitative problem in American society. At this time, the goal of achieving black economic progress is better served by policies that promote skill formation, like improving family environments, schools and neighborhoods, not by strengthening the content and enforcement of civil rights laws—the solution to the problem of an earlier era.

Third, I want to examine the logic and limitations of the audit pair method. All of the papers in this symposium use evidence from this version of pair matching. However, the evidence acquired from it is less compelling than is often assumed. Inferences from such studies are quite fragile to alternative assumptions about unobservable variables and the way labor markets work. The audit method can find discrimination when in fact none exists; it can also

From James J. Heckman, "Detecting Discrimination," *Journal of Economic Perspectives,* vol. 12, no. 2 (Spring 1998).

disguise discrimination when it is present. These findings are especially troubling because the Equal Employment Opportunity Commission has recently authorized the use of audit pair methods to detect discrimination in labor markets (Seelye, 1997).

Discrimination Definition and Measurement

The authors of these papers focus on the question of whether society is color blind, not on the specific question of whether there is market discrimination in realized transactions. But discrimination at the individual level is different from discrimination at the group level, although these concepts are often confused in the literature on the economics of discrimination.

At the level of a potential worker or credit applicant dealing with a firm, racial discrimination is said to arise if an otherwise identical person is treated differently by virtue of that person's race or gender, and race and gender by themselves have no direct effect on productivity. Discrimination is a causal effect defined by a hypothetical *ceteris paribus* conceptual experiment—varying race but keeping all else constant. Audit studies attempt to identify racial and gender discrimination so defined for the set of firms sampled by the auditors by approximating the *ceteris paribus* condition.

It was Becker's (1957) insight to observe that finding a discriminatory effect of race or gender at a randomly selected firm does not provide an accurate measure of the discrimination that takes place in the market as a whole. At the level of the market, the causal effect of race is defined by the marginal firm or set of firms with which the marginal minority member deals. The impact of market discrimination is not determined by the most discriminatory participants in the market, or even by the average level of discrimination among firms, but rather by the level of discrimination at the firms where ethnic minorities or women actually end up buying, working and borrowing. It is at the margin that economic values are set. This point is largely ignored in the papers in this symposium.

This confusion between individual firm and market discrimination arises in particular in the audit studies. A well-designed audit study could uncover many individual firms that discriminate, while at the same time the marginal effect of discrimination on the wages of employed workers could be zero. . . . Purposive sorting within markets eliminates the worst forms of discrimination. There may be evil lurking in the hearts of firms that is never manifest in consummated market transactions.

Estimating the extent and degree of distribution, whether at the individual or the market level, is a difficult matter. In the labor market, for example, a worker's productivity is rarely observed directly, so the analyst must instead use available data as a proxy in controlling for the relevant productivity characteristics. The major controversies arise over whether relevant omitted characteristics differ between races and between genders, and whether certain included characteristics systematically capture productivity differences or instead are a proxy for race or gender.

How Substantial Is Labor Market Discrimination Against Blacks?

In their paper in this symposium, [William A.] Darity [Jr.] and [Patrick L.] Mason present a bleak picture of the labor market position of African-Americans in which market discrimination is ubiquitous. They present a quantitative estimate of the magnitude of estimated discrimination: 12 to 15 percent in both 1980 and 1990 using standard regressions fit on Current Population Survey and Census data. Similar regressions show that the black/white wage gap has diminished sharply over the last half century. Comparable estimates for 1940 show a black/white wage gap ranging from 30 percentage points, for men age 25–34 to 42 percentage points, men age 55–64. In 1960, the corresponding numbers would have been 21 percent and 32 percent, for the same two age groups; in 1970, 18 and 25 percent (U.S. Commission on Civil Rights, 1986, Table 6.1, p. 191). The progress was greatest in Southern states where a blatantly discriminatory system was successfully challenged by an external legal intervention (Donohue and Heckman, 1991; Heckman, 1990).

How should the residual wage gap be interpreted? As is typical of much of the literature on measuring racial wage gaps, Darity and Mason never precisely define the concept of discrimination they use. As is also typical of this literature, the phrase "human capital variable" is thrown around without a clear operational definition. The implicit definition of these terms varies across the studies they discuss. In practice, human capital in these studies has come to mean education and various combinations of age and education, based on the available Census and Current Population Survey (CPS) data. However, there is a staggering gap between the list of productivity characteristics available to economic analysts in standard data sources and what is available to personnel departments of firms. Regressions based on the Census and/or CPS data can typically explain 20 to 30 percent of the variation in wages. However, regressions based on personnel data can explain a substantially higher share of the variation in wages; 60–80 percent in professional labor markets (for example, see Abowd and Killingsworth, 1983). It is not idle speculation to claim that the standard data sets used to estimate discrimination omit many relevant characteristics actually used by firms in their hiring and promotion decisions. Nor is it idle speculation to conjecture that disparity in family, neighborhood and schooling environments may account for systematic differences in unmeasured characteristics between race groups.

Consider just one well-documented source of discrepancy between Census variables and the productivity concepts that they proxy: the measurement of high school credentials. The standard Census and CPS data sources equate recipients of a General Equivalence Degree, or GED, with high school graduates. However, black high school certificate holders are much more likely than whites to receive GEDs (Cameron and Heckman, 1993), and a substantial portion of the widely trumpeted "convergence" in measured black educational attainment has come through GED certification. Thus, in 1987 in the NLSY data that Darity and Mason discuss, and Neal and Johnson (1996) analyze, 79 percent of black males age 25 were high school certified, and 14 percent of the credential holders were GED recipients. Among white males, 88 percent were high school certified, and only 8 percent of the white credential holders were GED certified. Given the evidence from Cameron and Heckman that GED recipients earn the same as high school dropouts, it is plausible that standard Census-based studies that use high school credentials to control for "education" will find that the wages of black high school "graduates" are lower than those of whites.

Most of the empirical literature cited by Darity and Mason takes Census variables literally and ignores these issues. The GED factor alone accounts for 1–2 percentage points of the current 12–15 percent black-white hourly wage gap. An enormous body of solid evidence on inferior inner city schools and poor neighborhoods makes the ritual of the measurement of "discrimination" using the unadjusted Census or Current Population Survey data a questionable exercise.

Darity and Mason bolster their case for rampant discrimination by appealing to audit pair evidence. They do not point out that audit pair studies have primarily been conducted for hiring in entry level jobs in certain low skill occupations using overqualified college students during summer vacations. They do not sample subsequent promotion decisions. They fail to point out that the audits undersample the main avenues through which youth get jobs, since only job openings advertised in newspapers are audited, and not jobs found through networks and friends (Heckman and Siegelman, 1993, pp. 213–215). Auditors are sometimes instructed on the "problem of discrimination in American society" prior to sampling firms, so they may have been coached to find what the audit agencies wanted to find. I have already noted that audit evidence does not translate into actual employment experiences and wages obtained by actors who purposively search markets.

Putting these objections to the side, what do the audits actually show for this unrepresentative snapshot of the American labor market? Table 1 presents evidence from three major audits in Washington, D.C., Chicago and Denver. The most remarkable feature of this evidence is the a + b column which records the percentage of audit attempts where black and white auditors were treated symmetrically (both got a job; neither got a job). In Chicago and Denver this happened about 86 percent of the time. The evidence of disparity in hiring presented in the last two columns of the table suggests only a slight preference for whites over minorities, in several pairs, minorities are favored. Only a zealot can see evidence in these data of pervasive discrimination in the U.S. labor market. And, as I will show in the next section, even this evidence on disparity has to be taken with a grain of salt, because it is based on the implicit assumption that the distribution of unobserved productivity is the same in both race groups.

Darity and Mason go on to dismiss the research of Neal and Johnson (1996) who analyze a sample of males who took an achievement or ability test in their early teens—specifically, the Armed Forces Qualifications Test (AFQT)—and ask how much of the gap in black-white wages measured a decade or so after the test was taken can be explained by the differences in the test scores.[1] It is remarkable and important that this early "premarket" measure of ability

Table 1

Outcomes From Major Audit Studies for Blacks
(outcome: get job or not)

Number of Audits	Pair	(a) Both Get Job	(b) Neither Gets a Job	Equal Treatment a + b	White Yes, Black No	White No, Black Yes
Chicago*						
35	1	(5) 14.3%	(23) 65.7%	80.0%	(5) 14.3%	(2) 5.7%
40	2	(5) 12.5%	(25) 62.5%	75.0%	(4) 10.0%	(2) 15.0%
44	3	(3) 6.8%	(37) 84.1%	90.9%	(3) 6.8%	(1) 2.3%
36	4	(6) 16.7%	(24) 66.7%	83.4%	(6) 16.7%	(0) 0.0%
42	5	(3) 7.1%	(38) 90.5%	97.6%	(1) 2.4%	(2) 0.0%
197	Total	(22) 11.2%	(147) 74.6%	85.8%	(19) 9.6%	(9) 4.5%
Washington*						
46	1	(5) 10.9%	(26) 56.5%	67.4%	(12) 26.1%	(3) 6.5%
54	2	(11) 20.4%	(31) 57.4%	77.8%	(9) 16.7%	(3) 5.6%
62	3	(11) 17.7%	(36) 58.1%	75.8%	(11) 17.7%	(4) 6.5%
37	4	(6) 16.2%	(22) 59.5%	75.7%	(7) 18.9%	(2) 5.4%
42	5	(7) 16.7%	(26) 61.9%	77.6%	(7) 16.7%	(2) 4.8%
241	Total	(40) 16.6%	(141) 58.5%	75.1%	(46) 19.1%	(14) 5.8%
Denver**						
18	1	(2) 11.1%	(11) 61.1%	72.1%	(5) 27.8%	(0) 0.0%
53	2	(2) 3.8%	(41) 77.4%	81.2%	(0) 0.0%	(10) 18.9%
33	3	(7) 21.2%	(25) 75.8%	97.0%	(1) 3.0%	(0) 0.0%
15	4	(9) 60.0%	(3) 20.0%	80.0%	(2) 6.7%	(2) 13.3%
265	9	(3) 11.5%	(23) 88.5%	100.0%	(0) 0.0%	(0) 0.0%
145	Total	(23) 15.8%	(103) 71.1%	86.9%	(7) 4.8%	(12) 8.3%

Note: Results are percentages; figures in parentheses are the relevant number of audits.

*This study was conducted by the Urban Institute.

**Denver pair numbers are for both black and Hispanic audits. For the sake of brevity, I only consider the black audits. The Denver study was not conducted by the Urban Institute but it was conducted to conform to Urban Institute practice.

Sources: Heckman and Siegelman (1993).

plays such a strong role in explaining wages measured a decade after the test is taken. This is as true for studies of white outcomes taken in isolation as it is for blackwhite comparisons. Their findings are important for interpreting the sources of black-white disparity in labor market outcomes. . . .

The Neal-Johnson story is not about genetic determination. They demonstrate that schooling and environment can affect their measured test score. A huge body of evidence, to which the Neal-Johnson study contributes, documents that human abilities and motivations are formed early and have a decisive effect on lifetime outcomes; the evidence is summarized in Heckman

(1995) and in Heckman, Lochner, Taber, and Smith (1997). Not only is early ability an important predictor of later success for blacks or whites, it can be manipulated. Early interventions are far more effective than late ones because early skills and motivation beget later skills and motivation. As Heckman, Lochner. Taber and Smith document, however, successful early interventions can be quite costly.

The objections raised by Darity and Mason against the Neal-Johnson study are largely specious. For example, Rodgers and Spriggs (1996) miss the point of the Neal-Johnson article by "adjusting" the test score by a later variable, such as schooling. But ability is known to be an important determinant of schooling (Cawley, Heckman and Vtylacil, 1998), so it should be no surprise that "adjusting" the score for later schooling eliminates an important component of ability and that adjusted scores play a much weaker role in explaining black-white differentials.[2]

Only one point raised by Darity and Mason concerning Neal and Johnson is potentially valid—and this is a point made by Neal and Johnson in their original article. Black achievement scores may be lower than white scores not because of the inferior environments encountered by many poor blacks, but because of expectations of discrimination in the market. If black children and their parents face a world in which they receive lower rewards for obtaining skills, they will invest less if they face the same tuition costs as whites. Poor performance in schools and low achievement test scores may thus be a proxy for discrimination to be experienced in the future.

There is solid empirical evidence that expectations about rewards in the labor market influence human capital investment decisions; for example, the reward to skills held by black workers increased following the passage of the 1964 Civil Rights Act, and a rapid rise in college enrollment of blacks followed (Donohue and Heckman, 1991). But the difficulty with the argument in this context is that it presumes that black parents and children operate under mistaken expectations about the present labor market. Although it was once true that the returns to college education were lower for blacks than for whites (Becker, 1957; U.S. Civil Rights Commission, 1986), the return to college education for blacks was higher than the return for whites by the mid-1970s, and continues to be higher today. Some parallel evidence presented by Johnson and Neal (1998) shows that the returns to (coefficient on) AFQT scores for black males in an earnings equation are now as high or higher than those for whites, although they used to be lower in the pre–Civil Rights era. Given the greater return for blacks to college education and ability, it seems implausible to argue that a rational fear of lower future returns is currently discouraging black formation of skills.

Ability as it crystallizes at an early age accounts for most of the measured gap in black and white labor market outcomes. Stricter enforcement of civil rights laws is a tenuous way to improve early childhood skills and ability.[3] The weight of the evidence suggests that this ability and early motivation is most easily influenced by enriching family and preschool learning environments and by improving the quality of the early years of schooling.

The Implicit Assumptions Behind the Audit Method

The method of audit pairs operates by controlling for systematic observed differences across pairs. It does this by attempting to create two candidates for jobs or loans who are "essentially" the same in their paper qualifications and personal characteristics, and then comparing their outcomes in their dealings with the same firm. Averaging over the outcomes at all firms for the same audit pair produces an estimate of the discrimination effect. An average is often taken over audit pairs as well to report an "overall" estimate of discrimination. More sophisticated versions of the method will allow for some heterogeneity in treatment among firms and workers or firms and applicants.

One set of difficulties arise, however, because there are sure to be many unobserved variables. As noted by Heckman and Siegelman (1993), given the current limited state of knowledge of the determinants of productivity within firms, and given the small pools of applicants from which matched pairs are constructed that are characteristic of most audit studies, it is unlikely that all characteristics that might affect productivity will be perfectly matched. Thus, the implicit assumption in the audit pair method is that controlling for some components of productivity and sending people to the same firm will reduce the bias below what it would be if random pairs of, say, whites and blacks were compared using, for example, Census data. The implicit assumption that justifies this method is that the effect of the unobserved characteristics averages out to zero across firms for the same audit pair.

However, the mean of the differences in the unobserved components need not be zero and assuming that it is begs the problem. Nowhere in the published literature on the audit pair method will you find a demonstration that matching one subset of observable variables necessarily implies that the resulting difference in audit-adjusted treatment between blacks and whites is an unbiased measure of discrimination—or indeed, that it is even necessarily a better measure of discrimination than comparing random pairs of whites and blacks applying at the same firm or even applying to different firms. . . .

Consider the following example. Suppose that the market productivity of persons is determined by the sum of two productivity components. These two productivity components are distributed independently in the population so their values are not correlated with each other. Both factors affect employer assessments of employee productivity.[4] Suppose further that average productivity of the sum is the same for both whites and blacks; however, blacks are more productive on average on one component while whites are more productive on average on the other. Now consider an audit pair study that equates only the first component of productivity and equates firm effects by sending the audit pair to the same firm. Under these conditions, the audit estimator is biased toward a finding of discrimination, since in this example, only the characteristic which makes black productivity look relatively high is being used to standardize the audit pair. The condition of zero mean of unobservable productivity differences across race groups is not especially compelling and requires a priori knowledge that is typically not available.

Now consider the case in which the observed and unobserved components of productivity are dependent. In this case, making the included components as alike as possible may accentuate the differences in the unobserved components. As a result, it can increase the bias over the case where the measured components are not aligned.

. . . [T]hink of pairing up black and white high jumpers to see if they can clear a bar set at a certain height. There is no discrimination, in the sense that they both use the same equipment and have the bar set at the same level. Suppose now that the chance of a jumper (of any race) clearing the bar depends on two additive factors: the person's height and their jumping technique. We can pair up black and white jumpers so that they have identical heights, but we can't directly observe their technique. Let us make the generous assumption, implicit in the entire audit literature, that the mean jumping technique is equal for the two groups. Then, if the variance of technique is also the same for white and black high-jumpers, we would find that the two racial groups are equally likely to clear the bar. On the other hand, if the variance differs, then whether the black or white pair is more likely to clear the bar will depend on how the bar is set, relative to their common height, and which racial group has a higher variance in jumping technique. If the bar is set at a low level so that most people of the given height are likely to clear the bar, then the group with the lower variance will be more likely to clear the bar. If the bar is set at a very high level relative to the given height, then the group with a higher variance in jumping technique will be more likely to clear the bar. A limitation of the audit method is readily apparent from this analogy: there is no discrimination, yet the two groups have different probabilities of clearing the bar.[5] And if there is discrimination—that is, the bar is being set higher for blacks—the differential dispersion in the unobserved component could still cause the minority group to clear the bar more often. The method could fail to detect discrimination when it does exist.

Thus, depending on the distribution of unobserved characteristics for each race group and the audit standardization level, the audit method can show reverse discrimination, or equal treatment, or discrimination, even though blacks and whites in this example are subject to the same cutoff and face no discrimination. The apparent bias depends on whether the level of qualifications set by the audit designer makes it more or less likely that the applicant will receive the job, and the distribution of variables that are unobservable to the audit design. The apparent disparity favoring Washington whites in Table 1 may be a consequence of differences in unobserved characteristics between blacks and whites when there is no discrimination.

Even more disturbing, suppose that there is discrimination against blacks, so the productivity cutoff used by firms is higher for blacks than whites. Depending on the audit designer's choice of what level of qualifications are given to the auditors, the audit study can find no discrimination at all. However, whether the qualifications make it relatively likely or unlikely to get the job is a fact rarely reported in audit studies. . . .

Making audit pairs as alike as possible may seem an obviously useful step, but it can greatly bias the inference about average discrimination or discrimination at the margin. Intuitively, by taking out the common components that are most easily measured, differences in hiring rates as monitored by audits arise from the idiosyncratic factors, and not the main factors, that drive actual labor markets. These examples highlight the fragility of the audit method to untested and unverifiable assumptions about the distributions of unobservables. Similar points arise in more general nonlinear models that characterize other employment decision rules.

The Becker Model

The papers in this symposium make the erroneous claim that in Becker's (1957) model, market discrimination disappears in the long run. It need not. Entrepreneurs can consume their income in any way they see fit. If a bigoted employer prefers whites, the employer can indulge that taste as long as income is received from entrepreneurial activity just as a person who favors an exotic ice cream can indulge that preference by being willing to pay the price. Only if the supply of entrepreneurship is perfectly elastic in the long run at a zero price, so entrepreneurs have no income to spend to indulge their tastes, or if there are enough nonprejudiced employers to hire all blacks, will discrimination disappear from Becker's model.

However, even if the common misinterpretation of Becker's model is accepted, it is far from clear that the prediction of no or little discrimination in the U.S. labor market in the long run is false. The substantial decline over the past 50 years in wage differentials between blacks and whites may well be a manifestation of the dynamics of the Becker model. It may take decades for the effects of past discrimination in employment and schooling as it affects current endowments of workers to fade out of the labor market. But the evidence from the current U.S. labor market is that discrimination by employers alone does *not* generate large economic disparities between blacks and whites.

Appendix

Implicit Identifying Assumptions in the Audit Method

Define the productivity of a person of race $r \in \{1, 0\}$ at firm f, with characteristics $\underset{\sim}{X} = (X_1, X_2)$ as $P(\underset{\sim}{X}, r, f)$. $r = 1$ corresponds to black; $r = 0$ corresponds to white. Assume that race does not affect productivity so we may write $P = P(\underset{\sim}{X}, f)$. The treatment at the firm f for a person of race r and productivity P is $T(P(\underset{\sim}{X}, f), r)$. Racial discrimination exists at firm f if

$$T(P(\underset{\sim}{X}, f), r = 1) \neq T(P(\underset{\sim}{X}, f), r = 0).$$

As noted in the text, audit methods monitor discrimination at randomly selected firms within the universe designated for sampling, not the firms where blacks are employed.

The most favorable case for auditing assumes that T (or some transformation of it) is linear in f and X. Assume for simplicity that $P = X_1 + X_2 + f$

and $T(P, r) = P + \gamma r$. When $\gamma < 0$ there is discrimination against blacks. γ may vary among firms as in Heckman and Siegelman (1993). For simplicity suppose that all firms are alike. Audit methods pair racially dissimilar workers in the following way: they match some components of $\underset{\sim}{X}$ and they sample the same firms. Let P_1^* be the standardized productivity for the black member of the pair; P_0^* is the standardized productivity for the white member. If $P_0^* = P_1^*$,

$$T(P_1^*, 1) - T(P_0^*, 0) = \gamma.$$

When averaged over firms, the average treatment estimates the average γ.

Suppose that standardization is incomplete. We can align the first coordinate of X at $\{X_1 = X_1^*\}$ but not the second coordinate, X_2, which is unobserved by the auditor but acted on by the firm. $P_1^* = X_1^* + X_2^1$ where X_2^1 is the value of X_2 for the $r = 1$ member and $P_0^* = X_1^* + X_2^1$. In this case

$$T(P_1^*, 1) - T(P_0^*, 0) = X_2^1 - X_2^0 + \gamma.$$

For averages over pairs to estimate γ without bias, it must be assumed that $E(X_2^1) = E(X_2^0)$; i.e., that the mean of the unobserved productivity traits is the same. This is the crucial identifying assumption in the conventional audit method. Suppose that this is true so $E(X_2^1) = E(X_2^0) = \mu$. Then the pair matching as in the audit method does not increase bias and in general reduces it over comparisons of two X_1-identical persons at two randomly selected firms. Under these conditions, bias is lower than if two randomly chosen auditors are selected at the same firm if $E(X_1^1) \neq E(X_1^0)$.

However, the decision rule to offer a job or extend credit often depends on whether or not the perceived productivity P exceeds a threshold c:

$$T = 1 \text{ if } P \geq T = c$$
$$T = 0 \text{ otherwise}$$

In this case, the audit pair method will still produce bias even when it does not when T is linear in $\underset{\sim}{X}$ and f unless the *distributions* of the omitted characteristics are identical in the two race groups. Suppose that $P = X_1 + X_2$. X_2 is uncontrolled. Then assuming no discrimination ($\gamma = 0$)

$$T(P_1^*\ 1) = 1 \text{ if } X_1^* + X_2^1 + f \geq c = 0 \text{ otherwise}$$
$$T(P_{0,}^*\ 0) = 1 \text{ if } X_1^* + X_2^0 + f \geq c = 0 \text{ otherwise.}$$

Even if the distributions of f are identical across pairs, and f is independent of X, unless the *distributions* of X_2^1 and X_2^0 are identical, $\Pr(T(P_1^*, 1) = 1) \neq \Pr(T(P_0^*) = 1)$ for most values of the standardization level X_1^*. The right tail area of the distribution governs the behavior of these probabilities. This implies that even if blacks and whites face the same cutoff value, and in this sense are treated without discrimination in the labor market, even if the means of the distributions of unobservables are the same across race group, if the distributions of the unobservables are different, their probabilities of being hired will differ and will depend on the level of standardization used in the audit study—something that is rarely reported. The pattern of racial disparity in Table 1 may simply be a consequence of the choice of the level of standardization in those audits, and not discrimination.

Worse yet, suppose that the cutoff $c = c_1$ for blacks is larger than the cutoff $c = c_0$ for whites so that blacks are held to a higher standard. Then depending on the right tail area of X_2^1 and X_2^0, the values of c_1 and c_0, and the level of standardization X_1^*,

$$\Pr(T(P_1^*) = 1) \gtreqless P(T(P_0^*, 0) = 1).$$

In general, only if the *distributions* of X_2^1 and X_2^0 are the same for each race group, will the evidence reported in Table 1 be informative on the level of discrimination in the universe of sampled firms.

Figures 1 and 2 illustrate these two cases for X_2^1 and X_2^0 normally distributed (and independent of each other) where X_1^* is the level of audit standardization and firms are standardized to have $f = 0$. In Figure 1 there is no discrimination in the market. Yet the black hire rate falls short of the white rate if the standardization rate is $X_1^* < 0$, and the lower the value of X_1^*, the greater the shortfall. In Figure 2, which is constructed for a hypothetical economy where there is discrimination against blacks, for high standardization rates, audits would appear to reveal discrimination *in favor* of blacks when in fact blacks are being held to a higher standard. The evidence in Table 1 is intrinsically ambiguous about the extent of discrimination in the market. For further discussion, see Heckman and Siegelman (1993).

Figure 1

Relative Hiring Rate as a Function of the Level of Standardization. Blacks Have More Dispersion. Threshold Hiring Rule: No Discrimination Against Blacks Normally Distributed Unobservables

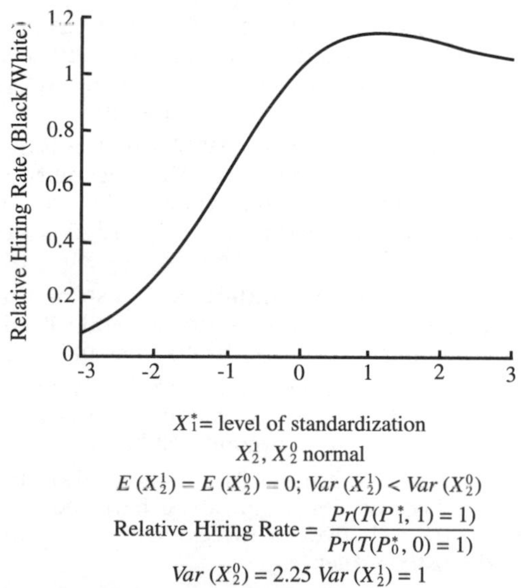

X_1^* = level of standardization

X_2^1, X_2^0 normal

$E(X_2^1) = E(X_2^0) = 0$; $Var(X_2^1) < Var(X_2^0)$

$$\text{Relative Hiring Rate} = \frac{Pr(T(P_1^*, 1) = 1)}{Pr(T(P_0^*, 0) = 1)}$$

$Var(X_2^0) = 2.25\ Var(X_2^1) = 1$

$c_1 = c_0 = 0$

Figure 2

Relative Hiring Rate as a Function of the Level of Standardization. Blacks Held to Higher Standard; Blacks Have More Dispersion. Threshold Hiring Rule: No Discrimination Against Blacks Normally Distributed Unobservables

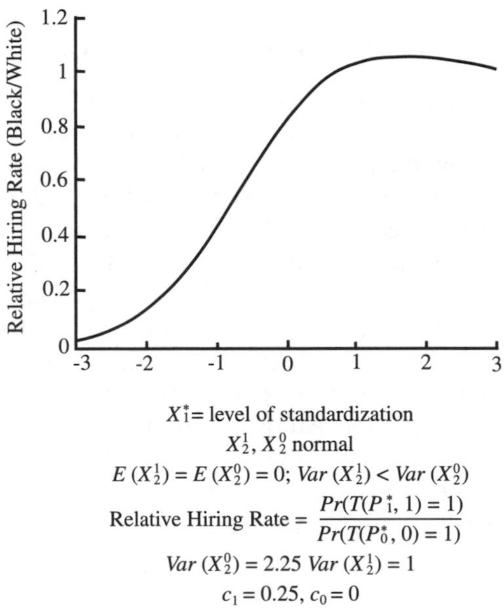

Notes

1. Specifically, Darity and Mason write: "This effort has uncovered one variable in one data set which, if inserted in an earnings regression, produces the outcome that nearly all of the black male-white male wage gap is explained by human capital and none by labor market discrimination."
2. The Rodgers and Spriggs comment (1997) on Neal-Johnson raises other red herrings. Their confused discussion of endogeneity of AFQT, and their "solution" to the problem end up with an "adjusted" AFQT measure that is poorly correlated with the measured AFQT, and so is a poor proxy for black ability.
3. However, nothing I have said vindicates abolishing these laws. They have important symbolic value and they addressed and solved an important problem of blatant discrimination in the American South.
4. They need not be perfectly observed by employers but may only be proxied. However, it is easiest to think of both components as fully observed by the employer, but that the observing economist has less information.
5. I owe this analogy to Alan Krueger. This analogy also shows how artificial the audit studies are because one would expect to find athletes choosing their sports based on their chances of success, as in the purposive search in the labor market discussed earlier.
6. For simplicity, assume that γ is the same across all firms. Alternatively, assume that it is distributed independently of $\underset{\sim}{X}$ and f.

7. Allowing f to vary but assuming it is normal mean zero and variance σ_f^2 does not change the qualitive character of these calculations assuming tnat f is distributed independently of the characteristics.

References

Abowd, John, and Mark Killingsworth, "Sex, Discrimination, Atrophy, and the Male-Female Wage Differential," *Industrial And Labor Relations Review,* Fall 1983, *22*:3, 387–402.

Becker, Gary, *The Economics of Discrimination.* Chicago: University of Chicago Press, 1957.

Cameron, Stephen, and James Heckman, "The Nonequivalence of High School Equivalents," *Journal of Labor Economics, 1993, 11*:1, pt1, 1–47.

Cawley, John, James Heckman, and Edward Vytlacil, "Cognitive Ability and the Rising Return to Education," NBER working paper 6388, January 1998.

Donohue, John, and James Heckman, "Continuous vs. Episodic Change: The Impact of Affirmative Action and Civil Rights Policy on The Economic Status of Blacks," *Journal of Economic Literature,* December 1991. *29*:4, 1603–43.

Heckman, James, "The Central Role of the South in Accounting For The Economic Progress of Black Americans," Papers and Proceedings of The American Economic Association, May 1990.

Heckman, James, "Lessons From the Bell Curve," *Journal of Political Economy,* 1995, *103*:5, 1091–1120.

Heckman, James, and Peter Siegelman, "The Urban Institute Audit Studies: Their Methods and Findings." In M. Fix and R. Struyk, eds. *Clear and Convincing Evidence: Measurement of Discrimination in America.* Urban Institute, Fall 1993.

Heckman, James, Lance Lochner, Christopher Taber, and Jeffrey Smith, "The Effects of Government Policy on Human Capital Investment and Wage Inequality," *Chicago Policy Review,* Spring 1997, *1*:2, 1–40.

Johnson, William R., and Derek Neal, "Basic Skills and the Black-White Earnings Gaps." In Jencks, Christopher and Meredith Phillips, eds. *The Black-White Test Score Gap.* Washington, D.C. Brookings, 1998.

Neal, Derek, and William Johnson, "The Role of Premarket Factors in Black-White Wage Differences," *Journal of Political Economy, 1996, 104:5,* 869–95.

Rodgers III, William, and William Spriggs, "What Does AFQT Really Measure: Race, Wages, Schooling and the AFQT Score," *The Review of Black Political Economy,* Spring 1996, *24*:4, 13–46.

Rodgers III, William, William E. Spriggs, and Elizabeth Waaler, "The Role of Premarket Factors in Black-White Differences: Comment," Unpublished Manuscript, College of William and Mary, May 25, 1997.

Seelye, Katherine, "Employment Panel To Send People Undercover to Detect Bias in Hiring," *New York Times,* Sunday, December 7, 1997, p. 22.

U.S. Commission on Civil Rights, *The Economic Progress of Black Men in America,* Clearinghouse Publication 91, 1986.

POSTSCRIPT

Is There Discrimination in U.S. Labor Markets?

Economists assume that markets are anonymous; that is, they assume that rational economic actors would not take race, sex, religious affiliation, or any other personal characteristic into consideration when buying or selling. Consumers are trying to maximize their consumer satisfaction, while producers are in the same marketplace trying to maximize their profits. Just as the often paraphrased axiom of Adam Smith suggests: Each acting for his or her own self-interest advances the well-being of the whole. In the world of neoclassical economics, there is simply no room for discrimination.

Yet the appearance of discrimination, if not the reality of discrimination, is all around us. Why are unemployment rates for African Americans twice those for white Americans? Why, on the average, do African American households earn 60 cents for every dollar earned by white households? Why do U.S. corporations, universities, courthouses, and even military officers' clubs have so many whites? And, more important, why do nearly 40 percent of African American children suffer the life-altering effects of poverty? Is this the product of market discrimination, or is it the consequence of deficient skill levels among African Americans?

In addition to Heckman's many contributions—he is perhaps the most prolific contributor to this debate from the neoclassical position—we suggest that you return to the source of his position, the work of Gary Becker, who in 1957 wrote *The Economics of Discrimination* (University of Chicago Press). Some of Heckman's other work is also highly recommended. See, for example, his essay "Lessons From the Bell Curve," *Journal of Political Economy* (vol. 103, 1995), pp. 1091–1120, and the book chapter he wrote with Peter Siegelman, "The Urban Institute Audit Studies: Their Methods," which appears in Michael Fix and Raymond Struyk, eds., *Clear and Convincing Evidence: Measurement of Discrimination in America* (Urban Institute Press, 1993). Finally, you might read Heckman's paper "The Value of Quantitative Evidence on the Effect of the Past on the Present," *American Economic Review* (May 1997).

Darity and Mason have also contributed extensively to this literature. See, for example, Mason's "Male Interracial Wage Differentials: Competing Explanations," *Cambridge Journal of Economics* (May 1999). You might also look for Darity and Samuel L. Myers, Jr.'s book *Persistent Disparity* (Edward Edgar, 1999). Lastly, we suggest a coauthored essay by Darity, Jason Dietrich, and David K. Guilkey, "Racial and Ethnic Inequality in the United States: A Secular Perspective," *American Economic Review* (May 1997).

ISSUE 4

Will the Medicare Modernization Act of 2003 and Its Drug Discount Cards Lower the Cost of Prescription Drugs for Seniors?

YES: Mark Merritt, from Testimony before the Senate Committee on Finance (June 8, 2004)

NO: Robert M. Hayes, from Testimony before the Senate Committee on Finance (June 8, 2004)

ISSUE SUMMARY

YES: Pharmaceutical Care Management Association President Mark Merritt believes that the introduction of drug discount cards has stimulated competition among drug card sponsors, retail pharmacies, and drug manufacturers, and this competition will generate drug discounts for the elderly of about 17 percent on brand name drugs and 35 percent on generic drugs.

NO: Medicare Rights Center President Robert M. Hayes asserts that drug discount cards "will do some people some important good, but the discount cards are leaving the overwhelming majority of people with Medicare without help and angry."

Medicare came into existence on July 30, 1965, when President Lyndon B. Johnson signed Public Law 98-97. This law amended the Social Security Act by adding Title XVIII, which created Medicare, best described as a program to provide health care to the elderly. Generally speaking, people who are over age 65 and getting Social Security benefits automatically qualify for Medicare. Public Law 98-97 also added Title XIX or Medicaid, a program designed to help the poor obtain health care. Thus this public law, by extending the ability of the elderly and the poor to obtain medical care, constituted a critical component of President Johnson's Great Society program.

At its creation, Medicare consisted of two major parts. Part A is a hospital insurance program that covers inpatient hospital care, skilled nursing care, and other services. Part B is described as a medial services insurance program and covers physician services, outpatient hospital services, certain home health services, and durable medical equipment. At the end of 2003, Medicare covered 41 million persons with annual costs of approximately $280 billion, or about 2.7 percent of gross domestic product.

The financing of expenditures differs between Part A and Part B. Part A is financed by a portion of the Social Security tax on people still working. For 2005, the combined employer-employee tax is 15.3 percent of wages. This is divided into an Old Age, Survivors, and Disability Insurance (OASDI) component of 12.4 percent on wages up to $90,000 and a Medicare component of 2.9 percent on all wages. Part B is financed by monthly premiums of those who are enrolled and by transfers from the general fund of the U.S. Treasury. For 2005, the Part B premium is $78.20 per month.

On December 8, 2003, President George W. Bush signed the Medicare Modernization Act (MMA). This legislation has been described as the most significant change in Medicare since its creation in 1965. In particular, it established Part D of Medicare, which was intended to fill an important gap in Medicare's coverage by providing some assistance to seniors for their purchases of prescription drugs.

This assistance involved two programs. The first extends over the period June 1, 2004 to January 1, 2006. During this period, Medicare enrollees can acquire Medicare Prescription Drug Discount Cards (MPDDC). These cards will be offered by private organizations, but are approved by Medicare. The issuers of the cards can charge an annual fee up to $30, and the MPDDC will provide discounts of 10 to 25 percent on selected drugs at selected pharmacies. Because the program is voluntary, the Medicare enrollee must compare the costs and benefits of a particular card with the costs and benefits of other cards as well as other avenues that can be used to reduce the cost of prescription drugs (buying the drugs from abroad, use of mail order, etc.).

On January 1, 2006, the Medicare Prescription Drug Coverage (MPDC), the second program, will replace the MPDDC. Like the MPDDC, MPDC will also be voluntary. The enrollee will pay a monthly premium (currently estimated at about $35 a month) for a basic benefit package. In addition, the individual will also pay an annual deductible of $250. There will be coinsurance as well: 25 percent of the cost of covered drugs between $251 and $2,250; 100 percent of the cost of covered drugs between $2,251 and $5,100; and 5 percent of the cost of covered drugs above $5,101. A drug plan can be obtained from a private company or from the government, and a private company can alter the monthly premium, deductible, and coinsurance so long as the package (costs and benefits) are at least as good as the basic package just described. But regardless of which plan is purchased, if the individual's annual drug costs are at least $5,100 and he/she has spent $3,600 on covered drugs, then the individual will only have to pay the 5 percent coinsurance for each covered drug during the remainder of the year.

YES 

Mark Merritt

Medicare Drug Card: Delivering Savings for Participating Seniors

I. Introduction

Good morning Chairman Grassley, Ranking Member Senator Baucus, and Members of the Committee. I am Mark Merritt, President and CEO of the Pharmaceutical Care Management Association (PCMA). I am pleased to be here today to discuss the role pharmacy benefit managers are playing to make the Medicare drug discount card program a success for senior and disabled beneficiaries.

PCMA is the national association representing America's pharmacy benefit managers (PBMs). PCMA represents both independent, stand-alone PBMs and health plans' PBM subsidiaries. Together, PCMA member companies administer prescription drug plans that provide access to safe, effective, and affordable prescription drugs for more than 200 million Americans in private and public health care programs. PCMA appreciates the opportunity to testify before the Senate Finance Committee regarding the recently enacted Medicare prescription drug discount card program. I applaud you, Chairman Grassley, Ranking Member Senator Baucus and all the other committee Members who worked so hard to bring the promise of more affordable medicines to millions of America's seniors and disabled beneficiaries.

The bipartisan Medicare Modernization Act (MMA) provides a historic opportunity for the private sector to work in partnership with government to make prescription drugs more affordable to our nation's elderly and disabled, particularly those most in need. PCMA and its member companies have long supported efforts to provide Medicare beneficiaries with the benefit of drug discounts made available through competitive price negotiation and quality drug management services. We believe PBMs will play a pivotal role in the overall success of the drug discount card program and many of our member companies have made a considerable investment to that end.

Today, I would like to focus my testimony on four key areas:

- How vertical and horizontal competition among drug card sponsors, retail pharmacies, and drug manufacturers is driving down drug prices and providing savings and value to beneficiaries, particularly those with low incomes;

From Testimony before the Senate Committee on Finance, June 8, 2004.

- How PBM-sponsored drug cards are providing beneficiaries with more than just discounts on drugs, but also valuable care management services that can lead to additional cost savings and enhance the quality of care for seniors and the disabled;
- Highlight steps PBMs have taken to prepare for the launch of the discount card; and
- The challenges and opportunities we see in educating seniors and the disabled about the drug card program's benefits.

II. Competition Works to Benefit Consumers

The Medicare drug discount card program is providing seniors and the disabled with a maximum choice of medications and flexibility in how and where they get their medications filled. Beneficiaries have access to virtually all classes of outpatient drugs available by prescription at discounted rates. Moreover, they have been provided an important new option: the mail-service pharmacy option, which adds further cost-savings, quality and safety protections, and convenience. This freedom of choice and flexibility for seniors and the disabled is what drives card sponsors to compete for their business and is critical to the government's effort to make prescription drugs more affordable.

Preliminary estimates by the Centers for Medicare & Medicaid Services (CMS) indicate that as many as 2.87 million eligible beneficiaries have enrolled in the program, with the majority being automatically enrolled by managed care plans. It is still too soon to tell how many seniors will ultimately enroll in the drug card program or how deep the savings will be for beneficiaries. That said, PCMA member companies believe that enrollment is continuing at a brisk pace and that there are several positive signs that point to the program's long-term success.

The Discounts are Real

There is ample evidence to suggest that the discounts provided to beneficiaries participating in the program are meaningful and making a difference. The savings are real, particularly for the estimated over 4 million Medicare beneficiaries who qualify for the $600 transitional assistance. Low-income seniors who can now avail themselves of PBMs' cost-management tools can make their $1200 subsidy go even further because PBMs can help them stretch those dollars.

- Based on a survey of PCMA member companies conducted prior to the launch of the card program, PCMA estimates that seniors with the Medicare drug card will see discounts averaging 17 percent for brand-name drugs and 35 percent for generics, compared to consumers paying retail pharmacy prices with no prescription drug coverage. These data are in keeping with CMS' own data which shows that drug cards are offering savings of up to 18 percent on brand name drugs and 30 to 60 percent on generics.
- Furthermore, according to CMS preliminary estimates, card sponsors are passing over 90 percent of the discounts they receive on to seniors

participating in the program. This shows that competition is working to deliver savings for seniors, and it proves that the rebate and discount disclosure requirements included in the MMA are working to benefit beneficiaries as Congress intended.[1]

- Savings are even greater for low-income beneficiaries who need the help the most. Take, for example, a hypothetical 66 year-old man living in Brooklyn, NY, with high cholesterol, high blood pressure, diabetes, and impotence. His drug needs can be met with a combination of two brand-name drugs and two generics. Without the Medicare discount card, he could get these drugs through AARP's drug program (available to all AARP members at an average discount of 16 percent off retail) for $195 per-month at retail and $182 per-month through mail order. With the Medicare card, the $600 dollar subsidy, and additional discounts offered directly by drug manufacturers for low-income seniors, he can get the same drugs for $71 per month retail and $60 per month mail order. This is an overall savings of 63 percent and 67 percent respectively.[2]

Competition Among Card Sponsors Yields Further Discounts

Since the first publication of drug prices offered by the different card programs in early May, there has been considerable competition among card sponsors to provide the most affordable drugs. PCMA's own internal analysis of price changes from May 11 through June 1 shows the following:

- Overall, for a large basket of commonly prescribed drugs[3] with no generics yet available, prices declined for retail—and particularly mail service—in the three weeks they were monitored.
- The following chart compares the top five drug discount cards offering the best mail service (90-day supply) prices for this basket of brand-name drugs.

Card Sponsor[4]	5/11/04	6/01/04	*Difference ($)	Difference (%)
Card #1	$1697.27	$1559.41	$137.86	–8%
Card #2	$1829.21	$1661.15	$168.06	–9%
Card #3	$2082.04	$1673.14	$408.90	–20%
Card #4	$2094.03	$1829.21	$264.82	–13%
Card #5	$2215.35	$1829.21	$386.14	–17%

- As this chart shows, the average reduction to already discounted prices for the top 5 cards over the three week period was 13 percent.
- It is also worth noting that not only did prices decline within each of the top 5 slots during the three week period, but that the price differential between the Card #1 and Card #5 was also halved during this time. On 5/11/04, the difference in price between Card #1 and Card #5 was $518. On 6/01/04, the difference was $269. This shows that card sponsors jockeying for a spot in the top five made even more significant reductions in prices in order to compete.

Direct Government Purchasing Schemes Offer a False Hope of More Access, Affordability

Some have proposed reopening the Medicare law to permit the federal government to negotiate directly with drug manufacturers and purchase prescription drugs on seniors' behalf, similar to the Veterans' Administration (VA). However, there is considerable evidence to suggest that direct negotiation of drug prices by the federal government may actually *limit* seniors' access to prescriptions and will not necessarily yield the savings predicted by proponents. First, to replicate the VA model would mean adoption of a national formulary, something Members of this Committee fought hard to avoid during negotiations on the Medicare drug benefit. The VA formulary restricts access to prescription drugs to 31 classes. In contrast, most commercial plans offer a much broader selection of therapeutic classes. Moreover, an August 2000 US General Accounting Office (GAO) report concluded that if the federal government was to provide other purchasers access to the VA's government-mandated discounts, those discounts will disappear as drug manufacturers raise the wholesale price of their drugs to make up for the loss in revenue.[5] Finally, in January 2003, the GAO has reported that PBMs have been able to get better discounts than some state Medicaid programs. In a review of five state Medicaid programs, the GAO found that Medicaid was only getting an 11 percent discount off of cash-paying retail prices versus PBMs' 18 percent discount.[6]

PBMs are Better Able to Deliver Value to Seniors

Because PBMs are neither retail pharmacies nor drug manufacturers, they are generally able to achieve discounts at both ends of the pharmaceutical chain—from the manufacturer and from the retail pharmacy. PBMs are uniquely capable in securing these discounts, managing pharmacy care, and delivering savings to consumers. PBMs are able to achieve these important goals because PBMs represent significant volume in their customer base; are able to leverage inherent efficiencies in their electronic claims processing technology; are able to provide a mail-service pharmacy option; and because of their commitment to the use of generic drugs where appropriate and available.

That PBMs deliver value to their current customers in both private industry and government is well documented. In its 2003 report, the GAO found that PBMs contributed to an 18 percent reduction in the average price for brand-name drugs for, among others, Members of Congress and their staffs in the Federal Employees Health Benefit Program (FEHBP). This, in turn, caused a total annual reduction in drug spending of between 3 and 9 percent for FEHBP plans.[7]

One area that PBMs can provide unmatched value for seniors is through the mail-service pharmacy option. Mail-service pharmacies typically fill prescriptions for maintenance medications; i.e., prescriptions that are used on a continuing basis for individuals managing complex or chronic illnesses. For seniors with limited mobility or disabled beneficiaries living in rural or urban under-served areas, the mail-service pharmacy option can be a vital lifeline to maintaining their health and well-being. Plan designs often allow consumers to obtain a 90-day supply of medication instead of the usual 30- or 60-day scripts that are filled by retail pharmacies. Consumers save money as well by paying only one co-payment for the 90-day supply of medication filled by a mail-service pharmacy, rather than the three separate co-payments required for 30-day supplies filled at a retail pharmacy. A 2002 industry survey of 14,000 mail-service pharmacy consumers found that more than 95 percent were satisfied with the condition of the drugs they received; the accuracy of the drugs that were delivered; with the professionalism of customer service; and the cost savings provided by mail-service pharmacies.

These savings would not be possible without the right market conditions. One such condition is keeping the terms of a contract confidential. Competition for market share drives drug manufacturers to negotiate discounts and rebates with PBMs. It is competition for retail customers that drives retail pharmacies to negotiate discounts with PBMs. If efforts to force disclosure of proprietary contract pricing information are successful, drug manufacturers will have little incentive to negotiate deeper discounts because they will know the competition got a better deal. Last year during the Medicare prescription drug debate, Congress considered—and ultimately rejected—a proposal that would have undermined the competitive marketplace under the guise of "transparency" and "disclosure." The Congressional Budget Office estimated that the proposal would have cost the Medicare program $40 billion over ten years because PBMs' ability to drive discounts for beneficiaries would be undermined.[8] Moreover, as already noted, such public disclosure is not necessary. CMS is already utilizing the transparency requirements in the new law and has found that PBMs and other card sponsors are passing more than 90 percent of the discounts they secure on prescription drugs on to beneficiaries in the drug card program.

III. PBM Drug Discount Card Benefits Provide Quality Protections

Seniors need ***more*** than just discounted drugs. We believe that the funded drug benefit that will be made available in 2006 will go a long way towards meeting those needs. In the interim, however, our focus should not solely be on the cost of drugs. We must also look at how those drugs are being utilized and if they are being used safely and appropriately.

Here again, PBMs have and will continue to prove their value. When a senior enrolls in a Medicare-approved PBM drug discount card, he or she is not only receiving discounts, he or she is getting the benefit of certain care management services PBMs provide to help ensure good health outcomes. We expect that when the fully funded drug benefit begins in 2006, seniors and the disabled will have access to the full range of tools and techniques that PBMs rely upon to improve drug safety and quality. Preserving PBMs' proven tools and techniques should be a top priority as policymakers work to implement the new Medicare drug benefit.

One of the most important functions PBMs perform is drug utilization review. Consider: one in four seniors sees four or more physicians; however nearly one in 10 seniors was prescribed medications by six or more different doctors in 2002. One in three seniors used four or more different pharmacies and one in seven seniors used five or more pharmacies to fill prescriptions in 2002.[9] As these data suggest, it can be difficult for any one physician or pharmacist to know all the drugs a senior is taking at one time. PBMs, however, are able to keep a patient's prescription drug history in one central file, with appropriate privacy protections. When a senior enrolls in a PBM-sponsored drug discount card, that senior receives the added protection of having their drug utilization continuously monitored for dangerous interactions and/or for under- or over-medicating. A real-time alert will be sent from the PBM to the pharmacy if a potentially dangerous drug interaction is about to take place.

IV. PBMs Will Play Pivotal Role in Drug Card's Success for Beneficiaries

As already noted, PBMs have a proven track record in bringing high quality, affordable medicines to beneficiaries in public programs and to the under-65 population with prescription drug coverage provided by employers, Taft-Hartley trustee plans, state and federal-employee benefit plans, and health plans. Now the Medicare drug discount card program has challenged PBMs to step up to the plate and prove their value to millions of Medicare beneficiaries, particularly those with low incomes, who today pay full retail prices for their prescription drugs. PBMs are meeting this challenge.

Since the Medicare Modernization Act was signed into law last December, PCMA member companies have worked countless hours and spent millions of dollars to develop and market their drug cards. This effort includes 1) submitting proposals for drug cards to CMS for approval; 2) once approved, working with CMS on marketing, disclosure, compliance and drug price submission requirements; 3) engaging in new contract negotiations with network pharmacies and drug manufacturers for thousands of drugs covered by the program; and 4) rolling out the new cards through marketing and enrollment campaigns which have required sponsors to increase call center staff by up to 15 percent.

The information reporting requirements alone are staggering. These requirements include not only providing a complete inventory of covered drugs, but also a weekly updated list of the retail and mail-service pricing for each dosage of each drug. In addition, each card sponsor must provide a list of the retail pharmacies where seniors can go to get their drugs. Furthermore, each card sponsor is required to inform CMS the extent to which negotiated price concessions with manufacturers are being passed on to beneficiaries through pharmacies. If adequate discounts are not being passed on, or card sponsors attempt to "bait and switch" beneficiaries by luring them with artificially low drug prices only to raise those prices once they have enrolled, CMS has broad auditing authority—backed by tough sanctions and civil monetary penalties—to protect beneficiaries.

Some critics' assertion that drug card sponsors will game the system are unfounded. The flexibility included in the MMA with regard to drug pricing and drug lists stands primarily to benefit Medicare beneficiaries.

- In the commercial marketplace, prescription drugs are rarely, if ever, removed from a formulary during a contract period unless the FDA determines a drug to be unsafe. With respect to the drug discount card program, we do not anticipate a drug being withdrawn from a list unless the FDA determines it to be unsafe.
- To the extent that there are changes to the drug list in the discount card program, they are likely to occur because a drug card sponsor is adding a new brand name or generic drug to the drug list. Adding a drug to the drug list would presumably further drive down drug prices because of increased competition within a therapeutic class.
- If a drug manufacturer *does* raise the price of a drug, the card sponsor must submit pricing changes to CMS, with supporting rationale. In reviewing price increases, CMS has the authority to impose penalties or expel a card sponsor from the program if they deem the price increase to be excessive or unwarranted. Given the potential penalties, it is unlikely that card sponsors will raise drug prices without compelling data.

V. Consumer Education Is Greatest Challenge and Opportunity Going Forward

Without a doubt, the greatest challenge to making the drug card a success for beneficiaries is informing them about how to enroll and to choose the drug card that best meets their needs and provides the maximum benefit. The `www.medicare.gov` website is a crucial tool—the near and long-term benefits of making available retail pricing on thousands of drugs cannot be overstated.

Of course, seniors need to be able to rely on the accuracy of the information. There have been a few kinks in the system since the website was launched over a month ago, but CMS is working collaboratively with Medicare drug card sponsors to make the information better and more usable for seniors and the disabled. CMS should be commended for its effort in this endeavor.

In many ways, the Medicare price comparison web site lets the genie out of the bottle. Not only are retail drug prices available on one site, but information about the availability of generics and home delivery of medicines may provide seniors with new options they previously did not know existed. This information is helping to provide greater savings and enhanced convenience for seniors and provides all consumers—not just seniors—with a valuable tool for understanding and gauging competing drug prices. As a result, we expect consumers to demand more information so that they may make more informed choices. The Medicare price comparison website may well become the engine that drives quality and sparks greater transparency throughout the entire health system.

VI. Conclusion

PCMA and its member companies stand committed to do what we can to ensure the Medicare Modernization Act makes good on its promise to deliver more affordable prescription drugs to our nation's elderly and disabled, particularly those most in need. While the Medicare drug discount card program was conceived as an interim first step in this effort, we believe the program holds the potential to change the way beneficiaries access and use prescription drugs and may well have ramifications beyond the life of the program and into other parts of the system.

In time, we expect to learn more about the lessons these experiences will provide as we prepare for 2006. PCMA and its member companies will continue to work hard to conduct outreach and enroll beneficiaries in the drug card program because we believe in the tangible value it represents to Medicare beneficiaries.

Mr. Chairman and Members of the Committee, thank you for the opportunity to testify today and I look forward to answering any questions you might have.

Notes

1. "Medicare Rx Card Sponsors Are Passing On 'More than 90%' of Discounts," The Pink Sheet, May 24, 2004.
2. Joe Antos, "The Truth About the Medicare Drug Discount Card," American Enterprise Institute, May 27, 2004. Statistics are based on a 7-month cost estimate (May–December 2004) of price information available on May 3 at `www.medicare.gov` and assumption of use of the $600 subsidy available to low income seniors on June 1.
3. The following drugs and their strengths were included in this basket of drugs: Cozaar (100mg) for angina; Viagra (50mg) for impotence; Lipitor (40mg) for high cholesterol; Fosamax (40mg) for osteoporosis; Celebrex (200mg) for arthritis; Nexium (20mg) for gastric reflux disease; Lexapro (10mg) for anxiety; and Norvasc (5mg) for high blood pressure.
4. Note that the top five drug cards on 5/11/04 may not necessarily be the same top five cards on 6/01/04.
5. US General Accounting Office, "Prescription Drugs: Expanding Access to Federal Prices Could Cause Other Price Changes," GAO/HEHS-00-118. August 2000.
6. US General Accounting Office, "Effects of Using Pharmacy Benefit Managers on Health Plans, Enrollees and Pharmacies," GAO-03-196, January 2003, p. 10.
7. *Ibid*, p. 4.
8. Congressional Budget Office, "Cost Estimate of HR 1, Medicare Prescription Drug and Modernization Act, and S 1, Prescription Drug and Medicare Improvement Act of 2003," July 22, 2003.
9. Medco Health Solutions, 2003 Drug Trend Report.

NO 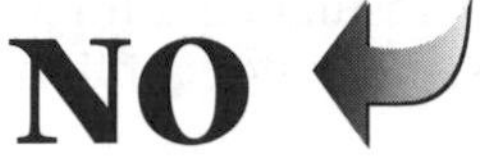

Robert M. Hayes

Medicare Drug Card: Delivering Savings for Participating Beneficiaries

Good morning, Mr. Chairman, Senator Baucus, Committee members. My name is Robert M. Hayes, and I am the President of the Medicare Rights Center. We appreciate the opportunity to bring to this Committee the real life experiences of men and women with Medicare who are grappling with the opportunities, and with the frustrations, of the new Medicare discount drug card program.

The context of today's hearing is important. Drug pricing and discount cards need not be the subject of partisan rancor. The focus must be on the humanitarian life and death crises that older and disabled Americans face because they cannot afford the medicine that their doctors prescribe.

Without doubt, the greatest and gravest unmet need of older and disabled Americans is the unavailability of affordable prescription medicine. From the trenches in which we work, Mr. Chairman, the unaffordability of prescription medicine is a national emergency. It is within that reality that we approach the Medicare discount card program, and it is the needs of men and women who cannot afford needed medicine that we bring to you.

The Medicare Rights Center

The Medicare Rights Center ("MRC") is the largest independent source of Medicare information and assistance in the United States. Founded in 1989, MRC helps older adults and people with disabilities get good affordable health care. Day in and day out we work to assist people with Medicare access needed health care. Tens of thousands of callers use our help-lines annually, and we reach out to assist people with Medicare enroll in programs that can help them.

The Medicare Rights Center is a not-for-profit consumer service organization, with offices in New York, Washington and Baltimore. It is supported by foundation grants, individual donations and contracts with both the public and private sectors. We are consumer driven and independent. We are not

From Testimony before the Senate Committee on Finance, June 8, 2004.

supported by the pharmaceutical industry, drug companies, insurance companies or any other special interest group. Our mission is to serve the 41 million men, women and children with Medicare. . . .

Our counselors are trained to assist consumers with complex problems and we complement the basic services offered by the 1-800-MEDICARE hotline operated by the Centers for Medicare and Medicaid Services (CMS). 1-800-MEDICARE is the largest source of referrals to our hotline, and CMS provides about 25 percent of the financial support for the MRC hotline: the rest we raise privately. To date, we have received no new support from CMS, or any other public agency, in the wake of the widespread and desperate demand for information triggered by the Medicare prescription drug discount card program.

Needless Pain, Lost Lives

For many, many years this Committee, this Congress, our nation have been numbed by the overwhelming data documenting the human hardship, the needless pain, the lost lives caused by the unaffordability of prescription medicine. I cannot shake from my memory the elderly woman who tearfully told me that she lies to her husband whenever her doctor gives her a prescription. If she told him about the prescription, she said, her husband would insist that she fill it. She wants him to keep taking his heart medicine, and she knows they could not afford another prescription. That is an obscenity in America in the 21st Century, and I know that is why we are here today.

I will take just a few minutes to outline what consumers are experiencing in the wake of the Medicare discount card roll out. This evidence already has been widely reported and well established.

One, the men and women who turn to us for help are in a state of high anxiety: they are confused or frustrated or angry—or all three.

Two, most people with Medicare will receive little if any benefit from the Medicare discount card program. This is not a political statement and it is not a point in dispute. As you know, CMS itself is aiming to enroll about seven million people, 17 percent of people with Medicare into the discount card program over the next 17 months.

Three, some people—those with low incomes, those without any drug coverage and those who learn about and sign up for the Medicare discount card program—will be able to afford some medicine thanks to the Medicare discount program's transitional assistance. This is far too important a point to lose.

In many ways we are critics of a hopelessly complex and wasteful program because all it would take to help everyone at much less cost is for the government to negotiate fair drug prices with the pharmaceutical industry. Yet some people will have improved health and a better life once they enroll in the discount program's transitional assistance. We join with groups like the National Council on Aging, and other groups more critical of the Medicare Modernization Act, in meeting our responsibility to help enroll as many people as possible, and to push this Administration into making enrollment as feasible as possible.

How can that be done?

First, recognize that web sites and voice automated phone systems are—even when they work—a sliver of a solution. We know that, despite hearings like this, news coverage, tens of millions of dollars in advertising by CMS, most people with Medicare do not even know about the discount cards. Confused and frustrated seniors are among the most knowledgeable.

The need to understand the discount card program is most important for low income people who have the most to gain—$600 annually from transitional assistance. But last week's survey by the Kaiser Family Foundation found that only 15 percent of seniors—that's one in seven—with incomes below $20,000 have ever used the internet. Twenty-six million seniors with Medicare have incomes below $20,000.

A "Wild West" Marketplace

Here's how complicated the drug market is for an actual consumer, including the most sophisticated consumers with the best of support. Last month I sat at a witness table like this with Stan Baumhofer, a gentleman from Portland, Oregon, while we were testifying before the Health Subcommittee of the House Energy and Commerce Committee. Mr. Baumhofer testified quite enthusiastically about the savings he would enjoy using his Medicare Approved Drug Discount Card. At the Medicare Rights Center we are really more social workers than political analysts, so I gave Mr. Baumhofer my card and offered our help in reviewing his drug needs as time goes forward. In fact, had Mr. Baumhofer been prudently counseled to look beyond the Medicare approved drug discount cards for help, he would have found much deeper savings.

If you look at Table A attached to this testimony, you will see the results of our analysis showing that Mr. Baumhofer could save over $2,700 more using existing drug assistance programs than he could using the best Medicare approved discount card for his prescription drug needs. Of course Mr. Baumhofer is correct in appreciating the value of the discount card that, he said, would save him $1,750 a year. But when existing drug programs can save him over $4,500 annually, he needs to know that as well. After all, those savings are over 25 percent of his $16,000 annual income.

The point of Mr. Baumhofer's tale is not to diminish the value of any program that helps a single person afford a single prescription. And of course we intend no criticism of the House members who assisted Mr. Baumhofer in his testimony. Our own experts at the Medicare Rights Center are struggling mightily to assist people in the best way possible.

The point of this analysis is to show just how complex the prescription drug marketplace has become, how Byzantine the process of finding discounts can be, and how utterly helpless the savviest of consumers—including those assisted by the best intentioned professionals—become in the face of layer upon layer of pricing changes, discount programs and assistance programs. This is not a marketplace where willing buyers meet willing sellers to establish price. It's the Wild West, and the consumer is without ammunition.

The Baumhofer tale also raises another interesting point: if the Administration could use its influence with the pharmaceutical industry to maintain its patient assistance programs, would it not better serve the American public to promote these assistance programs and enroll eligible Americans in them? As the chart shows, Mr. Baumhofer is far better served by assistance programs than by any Medicare approved card. And all people eligible for transitional assistance are eligible for each of the major drug companies' assistance programs.

No Surprise

Absolutely no one should be surprised that very few people have signed up for Medicare-approved discount cards to date. The program's structure is hopelessly complex, and for most people the benefit is meager. Permit me to spend a moment reviewing the structure of the program.

The design of the discount benefit, and even worse the design of the 2006 Part D drug benefit, draws all the wrong lessons from decades of experience with existing income-tested programs, especially the Medicare Savings Programs known by their acronyms QMB, SLMB and QI-1. It is well established that the design of the enrollment process for any public benefit will determine whether more than a small percentage of eligible individuals enroll in and benefit from the program.

"A Dirty Secret"

It is a dirty secret to most of the American people that the design of most low-income programs excludes about half of the people eligible for the benefit. It's common knowledge to all of us experts. But when political leaders speak of the safety net for poor Americans—be it in health care, housing, food—they only rarely acknowledge that half the people in need go unassisted. Tragically, in many ways the people in greatest need—that is those least aware of government programs that can help and least able to navigate bureaucratic hurdles to assistance—most frequently lose out. We thank Senator Bingaman and other members of this Committee who have been leaders in working aggressively to correct this.

The good news is that if we want full enrollment in public benefit programs, we know how to do it. Since 1966, enrollment in the voluntary Part B Medicare program has hovered between 95 and 97 percent. Automatic enrollment, with voluntary opt-out is the simple but magic solution. . . .

In North Dakota, only one in four people are receiving the assistance to which they are entitled. Even in the relatively high enrollment states of Senator Lott, Senator Frist, Senator Grassley and Senator Snowe (Mississippi, Tennessee, Iowa and Maine, respectively), where enrollment is above 70 percent, thousands of poor people are going without needed health care because of their inability to enroll in Medicare Savings Programs. Senator Baucus, the story in Montana pretty much tracks national data—only about half of the people eligible for assistance receive it.

For today's discount card enrollment effort, here's a modest prescription: The single most useful step to assist people access the $1200 transitional benefit—as it is now designed—is to require automatic enrollment of anyone who has established eligibility through an existing program, principally the Medicare Savings Programs. That alone could bring nearly a million very low income Americans into the discount card program. It is a humanitarian act, and it is a prudent political act. It will do what the Administration repeatedly says it wants to do: help bring affordable prescription drugs now to the neediest men and women with Medicare.

We understand, but hardly appreciate, that there is a debate within the Administration about the wisdom of automatic enrollment. We have heard from some in the Administration that auto-enrollment would undermine the voluntary nature of the drug card. To that, from the perspective of the real world, we say, "Come on." Neither the White House nor the Internal Revenue Service forced Americans to jump through hoops to claim their tax refunds two summers ago. The checks were just mailed to you. People with Medicare eligible for the $1200 in transitional assistance should be treated similarly.

While there are a million Americans who will benefit from automatic enrollment in transitional assistance, there are an additional 18 million people with Medicare who have incomes under $20,000 a year who will not be helped by automatic enrollment and who remain largely without assistance in affording the medicines their doctors prescribe. The push to enroll eligible Americans in transitional assistance is a noble one. But that push cannot obscure the reality that many, many medically needy Americans will be unable to afford prescription drugs until this Congress requires the federal government to bargain for best prices with the major pharmaceutical companies.

The CMS Website and 1-800-MEDICARE

I won't speak about the difficulties of the CMS web site or the 800-MEDICARE phone line now; we have quietly provided CMS with a good deal of feedback since late last month, and we will continue to do so as partners in the effort to maximize consumer understanding of the discount card program.

We recognize that CMS is trying, but CMS—just like people with Medicare—has been dealt a cruel hand by the structure of this discount card program. At the end of the day, a reasonably informed choice for most people with Medicare will be impossible. It is wasteful to spend tens of millions of tax dollars in futile attempts to explain nuanced choices involving scores of plans offering hundreds of medical products and services. Rather than offering multiple card choices with scant benefits, a useful drug assistance program would provide a truly meaningful benefit with multiple medication and pharmacy choices. The structure of the discount program, and we expect the 2006 benefit as currently designed, does not work and no magic by a CMS webmaster can change that.

It is not premature to look ahead to 2006. As currently designed, we fear that the Part D Medicare drug benefit will be so complex to navigate that today's drug card program will look like child's play. If the 2006 Medicare drug benefit is to be both a humanitarian and political victory, Congress and the Administration must revamp the structure of the benefit with three words in mind: simplify, simplify, simplify.

To that end, I will conclude with six points of essential reform so that the 2006 drug benefit can meet its stated purpose—to assist the neediest older Americans secure medicine that they can afford.

- **Automatically enroll all eligible persons in the low-income drug benefit.** The MMA already provides that full benefit Medicaid recipients be enrolled in the low-income subsidy and a prescription drug plan if they fail to enroll themselves. Persons can then opt-out of the program so the benefit is still voluntary. Likewise, automatic enrollment procedures should be applied to all state pharmacy assistance program and Medicare Savings Programs recipients. (CMS has permitted states to automatically enroll state pharmacy assistance recipients in transitional assistance and is now considering extending automatic enrollment to Medicare Savings Programs enrollees.)

Automatic enrollment procedures, such as those used for Medicare Part B, are the best way to maximize enrollment in health insurance programs.[1] Persons automatically receive Part B when they turn 65 and sign up for Social Security[2] unless they affirmatively decline Part B enrollment. As a result, Part B has a 95.5 percent participation rate. In contrast, national participation in the Medicare Savings Programs stands at about 50 percent because persons must affirmatively apply for benefits.[3] This is despite fifteen years of efforts by the federal government, states, and community organizations to increase awareness of the programs and to ease application and eligibility requirements.

- **Remove the asset tests, which represent a leading barrier to enrollment in low-income programs.** The onerous task of verifying the worth of certain items (including burial accounts, life insurance policies, bank accounts, and vehicles) prevents many eligible older Americans and Americans with disabilities from completing applications for the Medicare Savings Programs.[4] Additionally, people who would qualify for the low-income assistance programs based on income, but not assets, are hardly well-off. The median value of assets for persons with incomes between 100 and 135 percent of poverty is 8,000.[5]
- **Require the use of simplified application procedures and allow self-certification of income and assets.** Cumbersome enrollment processes represent a leading barrier to participation in low-income assistance programs. In particular, face-to-face interviews and income and asset verifications pose insurmountable hurdles for many older people, especially those with low literacy, limited English-speaking skills, and cognitive impairments.[6] Simplified enrollment should include easy-to-complete mail-in and online application forms, prohibit requirements for in-person interviews, allow applicants to self declare the value of their income, and minimize verifications for

assets. CMS should also use presumptive eligibility to allow persons who appear to be eligible to apply in pharmacies and doctor's offices and receive benefits immediately. Persons are more likely to enroll in benefits if they can access them immediately.

- **Streamline the renewal process.** Burdensome renewal procedures, like complicated enrollment procedures, can undermine participation in low-income assistance programs.[7] Easing renewal requirements also makes sense because most persons with Medicare have fixed incomes, and most persons remain eligible for the programs from year to year.[8] Streamlined renewal should involve:
  - Yearly, rather than quarterly or semi-annual renewals and
  - Passive renewal procedures whereby states send enrolled individuals a recertification form with all of their eligibility information filled in and ask them to return the form only if some of their information is incorrect. Persons who do not return the form would be automatically retained in the program.
- **Increase SHIP funding so eligible persons can cut through the red tape and receive benefits.** Even when application processes are simplified, many older persons and persons with disabilities need personalized assistance to complete the application process.[9] Moreover, a recent study commissioned by CMS identifies personalized assistance as a key factor in getting persons enrolled in the Medicare Savings Programs.[10] SHIPs are uniquely equipped to provide this personalized help.[11]
- **Federalize enrollment in the low income drug benefit and the Medicare Savings Programs.** The MMA requires that Medicaid offices and the Social Security Administration determine eligibility for the new low income drug benefit. The Medicare Savings Programs are now administered by Medicaid offices. But applying through Medicaid offices presents multiple obstacles, including Byzantine documentation requirements, traveling to often inaccessible offices, and long waits for service once persons get arrive.[12] Federalizing both administration of the low-income drug benefit and the Medicare Savings Programs would improve participation in both programs because Social Security is generally more user-friendly and accessible for older persons and persons with disabilities. Also, having enrollment administered by one agency will promote accountability and reduce confusion.

These modest steps, even standing alone, can play a significant role in fulfilling the legislative purpose behind the MMA creation of the Part D drug benefit.

In sum, the discount cards will do some people some important good, but the discount cards are leaving the overwhelming majority of people with Medicare without help and angry. There are lessons to be learned from the frustrations of this spring:

- humanitarian and political goals converge when a drug benefit provides meaningful relief in a structure that most people with Medicare can understand;
- if there is the will, there are straight forward ways to increase substantially enrollment in low income benefit programs; and

Table A

Prescription Drug Cost Comparison for Stan Baumhofer, Portland, OR; Annual Income: $16,000; All prices are for a month's supply

	Current[13]	Retail[14]	Medicare-Approved Card[15]	Manufacturer Pharm. Asst
Lipitor[16]		$105.73	$97.01	$0[17]
Lisinopril[18]		$45.16	$19.23	$0[19]
Plavix[20]		$127.34	$112.97	$0[21]
Toprol xl[22]		$26.87	$21.39	$6.00[23]
Total Costs	$403.31	$305.10	$250.60[24]	$6.00
Total Savings[25]		$98.00	$152.71	$397.31

We found that Mr. Baumhofer could get his drugs for just $6 if he took advantage of the drug companies' assistance programs. In contrast, he would pay $250.60 using the best of the Medicare-approved drug discount card programs.

- until the federal government is willing to use its market power to drive down drug prices for all Americans, most people with Medicare will not see a drug benefit that provides them with what they need—the ability to afford the medicines that their doctors prescribe.

Notes

1. Dahlia K. Remler and Sherry A. Glied, "What Other Programs Can Teach Us: Increasing Participation in Health Insurance Programs." *American Journal of Public Health*, January 2003.
2. Persons who qualify for Medicare based on a disability are automatically enrolled in Part B when they sign up for Medicare after r two year waiting period.
3. In 2001, CMS found that 40.5 percent of those eligible for the QMB and SLMB programs were not enrolled. Actuarial Research Corporation, *Dual Eligible Buy-In Status*, prepared for the Centers for Medicare and Medicaid Services, May 2001. Nationally, only about 145,000 (10%) of the estimated 1.4 million eligible individuals are enrolled in the QI-1 program. 68 Fed. Reg. 50792 (Aug. 22, 2003).
4. Kim Glaun, *Medicaid Programs to Assist Low-Income Medicare Beneficiaries: Medicare Savings Programs: Case Study Findings* (Washington, Kaiser Commission on Medicaid and the Uninsured, December 2002) [Hereafter *Glaun Medicare Savings Programs*]
5. Laura Summer and Lee Thompson, *How Asset Tests Block Low-Income Medicare Beneficiaries from Needed Benefits* (Commonwealth Fund, May 2004) [Hereafter: *Summer Asset Tests*]. About 30 percent of persons with incomes at or below poverty are disqualified for the Qualified Medicare Beneficiary Program because they have a modest life insurance policy or vehicle valued at more than $4,500. Seventy-five percent of these persons have assets that exceed the life insurance limit by $8,500 or less. *Id.*
6. Glaun *Medicare Savings Programs.*
7. Glaun *Medicare Savings Programs;* Michael J. Perry, Susan Kannel, and Adrianne Dulio, *Barriers to Medicaid Enrollment for Seniors: Findings From 10 Focus Groups*

With Low-Income Seniors (Washington, the Kaiser Commission on Medicaid and the Uninsured, January 2002).

8. *See* Summer *Asset Tests*; Susan Haber, et. al, Evaluation of Qualified Medicare Beneficiary (QMB) and Specified Low-Income Medicare Beneficiary (SLMB) Programs (commissioned by the Centers for Medicare and Medicaid Services, October 2003) [Hereafter *Haber Evaluation of QMB*]
9. *See* Glaun *Medicare Savings Programs.*
10. Haber *Evaluation of QMB.*
11. In a 2002 report on the effectiveness of SHIPs, the Health and Human Services Office of Inspector General (HHS OIG) wrote, "The SHIPs are uniquely positioned to provide personal locally-oriented counseling and assistance services with trained counselors who often have similar backgrounds, cultures, and experiences as the beneficiaries they serve." HHS OIG, February 2002.
12. Medicare Rights Center, *An Investigative Report on Medicare Savings Programs in New York City: Local Involvement in Federal Programs Impedes Access for People with Low Incomes*, December 2001.
13. This is the amount, according to Mr. Baumhofer's May 20, 2004 testimony to the House Energy and Commerce Committee, that he spent for his prescription drugs without a Medicare-approved drug discount card or other assistance. His testimony did not include the prices for individual drugs.
14. Prices on June 2, 2004 including a 10% senior discount available at Bowman's Hillsdale Pharmacy, 6256 SW Capitol Hwy Portland, OR 97201.
15. Using Envision Rx Plus Medicare-Approved Drug Discount Card at Bowman's Hillsdale Pharmacy
16. 20 MG 30 TABS
17. Pfizer Connection to Care (Annual income cap is $16,000 (single)).
18. 30 MG 30 TABS
19. Merck Patient Assistance Program. Merck produces Prinivil, which is the trade name for the generic drug Lisinopril. Mr. Baumhofer could receive Prinivil, in place of Lisinopril, for no cost. (Annual income cap is $18,000 (single))
20. 75 MG 30 TABS
21. Bristol-Myers Squibb Patient Assistance Program. Bristol-Myers has not set down the qualifications for its Patient Assistance Program in writing. However, in a personal conversation with Medicare Rights Center staff on June 2, 2004, a Bristol-Myers Squibb representative indicated that based upon her experience with similar applications, Mr. Baumhofer would qualify to receive Plavix for free through the company's patient assistance program.
22. 50 MG 30 TABS
23. AstraZeneca Together Rx Program (Annual income cap is $28,000 (single)). See: Freudenheim, Milt and Robert Pear. "Drug Discounts Beginning Tuesday, but Sign-Ups Lag." *New York Times* 1 June 2004.
24. See Mr. Baumhofer's testimony.
25. Total savings are calculated in comparison to Mr. Baumhofer's current prescription drug cost expenditure.

POSTSCRIPT

Will the Medicare Modernization Act of 2003 and Its Drug Discount Cards Lower the Cost of Prescription Drugs for Seniors?

Merritt begins with a description of the organization he represents: The Pharmaceutical Care Management Association consists of organizations that manage pharmacy benefit programs. These organizations administer plans that provide access to prescription drugs for more than 200 million Americans. He then addresses four issues in the context of the Medicare Modernization Act (MMA) and drug discount cards. First, he details how competition between drug card issuers, retail pharmacies, and drug manufacturers benefits consumers. He links the drug discount cards to greater competition and offers several examples to demonstrate the cost savings that seniors can experience in their prescription drug purchases. Second, he describes how drug discount cards, by providing "valuable care management services," can generate even more cost savings and better quality care for the elderly. Third, he highlights the actions that his association members have taken to improve their drug discount cards. Finally, he discusses the challenges and opportunities of educating the public about drug discount cards.

Like Merritt, Hayes begins by describing the organization he represents: the Medicare Rights Center. It is a non-profit organization that "helps older adults and people with disabilities get good affordable health care." He then offers three observations about the environment that has existed since the passage of the MMA. Central to that environment are the feeling of the persons who come to the Medicare Rights Center: "they are confused or frustrated or angry—or all three." He documents that few people have signed up for Medicare-approved drug discount cards, in large part because the program's structure is "hopelessly complex, and for most people the benefit is meager." He then offers a series of six essential reforms that he believes must be enacted if the MMA's drug provisions are to meet their stated purpose of helping the elderly purchase prescription drugs. He proposes, for example, automatic enrollment for eligible persons in the low-income drug benefit and that other application procedures be simplified.

In a search for addition material on the MMA and drug discount cards, a good place to start would be the references that both Merritt and Hayes provide in the footnotes in their papers. Besides the Senate hearings from which the Merritt and Hayes articles are taken, there were also House hearings on the MMA and drug discount cards. These hearings can be accessed at http://waysandmeans.house.gov/hearings.asp?formmode=detail&hearing=139&comm=1. For the Bush administration's views on the MMA, see chapter 10 in the *2004 Economic Report of the President.* Additional information on Medicare, the MMA, and drug discount cards can be obtained directly from the Social Security Administration at http://www.medicare.gov/.

ISSUE 5

Should Markets Be Allowed to Solve the Shortage in Body Parts?

YES: Charles T. Carlstrom and Christy D. Rollow, from "The Rationing of Transplantable Organs: A Troubled Lineup," *The Cato Journal* (Fall 1997)

NO: Nancy Scheper-Hughes, from "The End of the Body: The Global Traffic in Organs for Transplant Surgery," Organs Watch, `http://sunsite.berkeley.edu/biotech/organswatch/pages/cadraft.html` (May 14, 1998)

ISSUE SUMMARY

YES: Free-market economists Charles T. Carlstrom and Christy D. Rollow argue that the simple use of market incentives can go a long way to solving the shortage of transplantable organs. They contend that although some people may have "qualms about the buying and selling of organs, the cost of our current approach is that shortages will remain endemic, and ultimately, more lives will be lost."

NO: Professor of anthropology Nancy Scheper-Hughes acknowledges that markets in and of themselves are not evil. But she asserts that "by their very nature markets are indiscriminate, promiscuous and inclined to reduce everything, including human beings, their labor and even their reproductive capacity to the status of commodities, to things that can be bought, sold, traded, and stolen."

The first human heart transplant in the United States took place a surprisingly short time ago. Dr. Michael DeBakey performed the first successful coronary artery bypass graft in 1964, and less than four years later, on May 3, 1968, Dr. Denton Cooley and his team of surgeons shocked the world by announcing that they had successfully transplanted a heart in Everett Thomas, who lived for 204 days with a heart donated by a 15-year-old girl. Until Cooley and DeBakey achieved this revolutionary medical breakthrough, those with progressive heart failure were doomed to die. There was simply no hope of reversing the process that destroys this vital organ.

Cooley and his team performed their second operation, which was quickly followed by a series of other transplants in their Houston, Texas, operating theater. At first there was no real shortage of transplantable organs; the carnage on U.S. highways alone was enough to supply the limited number of healthy hearts that these teams of surgeons could reasonably expect to transplant. But as the word spread among those who were dying of various heart conditions, the demand for this radical surgery skyrocketed.

Any time that a shortage appears, there are several ways to mediate between those who demand and those who control the supply. In a market economy, price performs the role of the "grand allocater." In brief, whoever is willing to pay the highest price moves to the top of the waiting list. Applying this model to body parts, those who are less fortunate in terms of their resource holdings become less fortunate in terms of access to the limited supply of organs. This seemingly "cold-blooded" solution is quick to bring a chorus of protests. But what are the alternatives? Can lessons be learned from parallel situations? Should a shortage of human hearts and other transplantable organs that are needed to save lives be treated like a shortage of gasoline, which fuels our cars, or a shortage of electricity, which runs air conditioners and traffic signals? In the cases of gasoline and electricity, price controls have been used to address the shortages.

How did these market interventions work? The gasoline shortages that arose in the 1970s were a result of the Organization of Petroleum Exporting Countries' (OPEC) successful attempts to artificially restrict the world's supply of crude oil. As a result, the price of gasoline skyrocketed. Both the Nixon administration in the early 1970s and the Carter administration at the end of the 1970s responded by imposing "ceiling prices." The price of regular grade gasoline was not allowed to rise above $1.75 a gallon. Since the equilibrium price of gasoline was well above this level, a shortage resulted. A serious question arose: Who would get the limited supply? In a market arrangement, those who were willing to pay the highest price would get the gasoline. In the case of the price-controlled world of the 1970s, those who were willing to wait in long lines got the limited supply. Whoever was in line first got a chance to buy the limited quantity that was available. Is that any more "just" or "fair" than a market solution?

In the following selection, Charles T. Carlstrom and Christy D. Rollow suggest that a price-controlled world is no more just or fair than a controlled system and that, worse, this world of market controls is inefficient. They advocate the use of market incentives to solve the shortage. In their view, markets are not only a more efficient solution but a solution that will actually save more lives than the current system. In the second selection, Nancy Scheper-Hughes takes serious exception to Carlstrom and Rollow's position. She asks, Which lives will be saved? Will those who are poor be condemned to death simply because they are poor? Will the organs that are needed for transplants be "harvested" from both rich and poor equally, or will only the poor be economically blackmailed into selling their organs so that they can survive in our market-dominated world?

Charles T. Carlstrom and Christy D. Rollow

The Rationing of Transplantable Organs: A Troubled Lineup

On June 6, 1995, baseball legend Mickey Mantle was placed on the transplant waiting list after being diagnosed with end-stage liver disease caused by hepatitis, liver cancer, and years of alcohol abuse. Two days later, he underwent surgery, despite the fact that the average liver transplant patient waits 67 days. His doctors claimed that Mantle received no preferential treatment; rather, his gravely ill status placed him at the top of the list. Yet, because of Mantle's original liver cancer, he died two months later. Given that 804 patients died in 1995 while awaiting a liver transplant, Mantle's case and others like his raise questions about which of the 7,400 liver patients on the waiting list should have received the 3,900 livers that became available that year. Society has to confront this and similar questions because of the severe shortage of transplantable organs.

Organs are not the only goods rationed in the United States—they are just the most controversial. Hunting permits, oil drilling leases, cellular telephone licenses, and radio frequencies are other examples of rationed resources. The distinguishing feature of these goods is that prices alone are not permitted to allocate the commodity; as a result, someone must determine how they will be distributed.

There are many ways that goods can be rationed, such as lotteries, first-come, first-served, and coupons. As a consequence of price controls, gasoline was rationed in the 1970s, largely on a first-come, first-served basis.[1] The result was long lines at the pumps and an effective price of gasoline that included both the direct cost of purchasing gas plus the indirect cost of queuing. Although some view such a system as equitable, its inefficiencies are obvious once we factor in the time and even the gas wasted as people waited in line. Rationing also played a role during World War II, when the government issued coupons for purchasing staples such as meat and butter. This solution was also seen as equitable in many quarters, although, like lotteries, it did not ensure that those who most needed or valued a good received it.

This conflict between equity and efficiency arises whenever goods are rationed. Determining the most equitable way to allocate gasoline and food is difficult, but deciding how to allocate transplantable organs is infinitely more

From Charles T. Carlstrom and Christy D. Rollow, "The Rationing of Transplantable Organs: A Troubled Lineup," *The Cato Journal*, vol. 17, no. 2 (Fall 1997). References omitted.

complex. The complexity stems from the fact that someone must choose who receives lifesaving transplants—a decision that impacts efficiency through the number of lives lost over time. Since both equity and efficiency are paramount when rationing goods, the market for transplantable organs is an ideal case to illustrate this conflict.

Ten Americans die each day while awaiting an organ transplant, and the problem is becoming more severe. Between 1988 and 1994, the median waiting time nearly doubled (see Figure 1). It is imperative, then, that society find ways to increase the supply of organs, even through buying and selling. For most goods, prices are allowed to adjust to provide incentives, thus ensuring their most efficient allocation. While some people would understandably have qualms about the buying and selling of organs, the cost of our current approach is that shortages will remain endemic, and ultimately, more lives will be lost. Allowing monetary payments may not completely eliminate this shortage, but it will undoubtedly increase the number of organs available.

This paper examines the inherent difficulties of rationing by analyzing the market for transplantable organs. We look at the current procurement and

Figure 1

Median Waiting Times, 1988–94

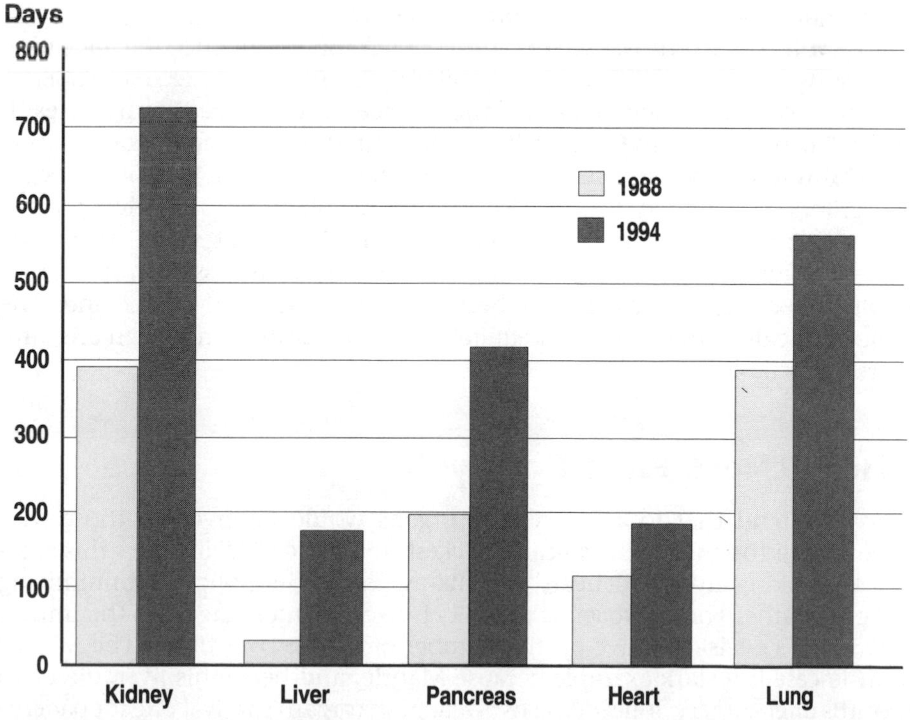

Source: UNOS (1995)

allocation system and discuss various proposals to increase the efficiency of the market. Although the particulars of this market are unique to organ transplantation, society faces similar choices whenever prices are regulated and shortages occur. As Dr. Arthur L. Caplan, director of the Center for Bioethics at the University of Pennsylvania, notes, "It [organ transplantation] is a case study of rationing. It is of fundamental interest to every American. All of us will have to confront the decision of what is fair in the allocation of scarce resources. This is a canary in a mine that all of us will have to enter."

Rationing Organs: The Current System

In 1984, Congress passed the National Organ Transplant Act, which outlawed the buying and selling of internal organs.[2] The National Task Force on Organ Transplantation recommended to Congress in 1986 that organ donation remain purely voluntary, governed by the altruism of the donor or the donor's family. Additionally, it suggested that the "selection of patients for transplant not be subject to favoritism, discrimination on the basis of race or sex, or ability to pay" (U.S. House of Representatives 1991: 44). This nondiscriminatory clause is crucial, because when prices are regulated and shortages occur, goods must be rationed. Since discrimination is one form of rationing, it is costless when markets are not allowed to operate freely.[3] In contrast, in an unregulated market, individuals and firms must forgo profits if they wish to discriminate—that is, engage in nonprice rationing.

Another concern was that political clout would influence the allocation process; hence, an independent nonprofit organization was selected to operate the Transplantation Network under the auspices of the Department of Health and Human Services. In October 1986, the United Network for Organ Sharing (UNOS) was awarded this federal contract. The group's task is twofold: establish criteria that match donors with waiting recipients, and develop policies that facilitate the procurement of organs. Figure 2 illustrates that within the current voluntary system, UNOS has been largely unsuccessful in increasing donations; supply increases have been minimal compared to demand. The major difficulties in devising an equitable organ distribution system are summarized in Table 1.

The Sickest-First Policy

Many contend that in a fair system, organs would be given to those who "need them the most—the so-called sickest-first policy." UNOS uses this strategy in ranking liver and heart patients as part of its policy of minimizing patient deaths. The approach is myopic, however, since it ignores the impact that today's decisions have on the number of deaths over time.[4] The Mickey Mantle case is a stark example because Mantle, and hence his liver, died two months after surgery. Indeed, the two-year graft (organ) survival rate for patients who are in intensive care prior to their liver transplant is approximately 50 percent, compared to 75 percent for those who are still relatively healthy.

Figure 2

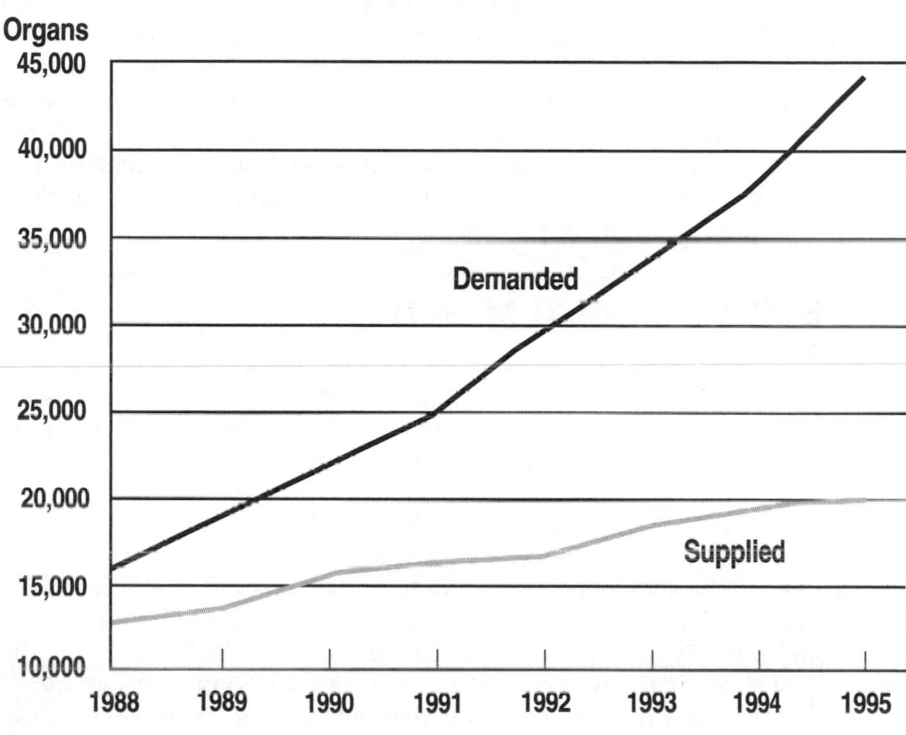

Source: UNOS (1996)

Table 1

Organ Rationing Schemes

Allocation Methods	Benefits	Costs
Waiting time	Equitable	Inappropriate matching; organ wastage; no consideration of urgency
Priority to sickest first	Equitable	Higher retransplantation and death rates; less benefit overall
Priority to sickest last	Higher overall survival; less retransplantation	Sickest patients die
Best biological match	Higher overall survival; less retransplantation	Fewer transplants for certain groups, including highly sensitized patients and some minorities

Source: UNOS (1977)

These groups' individual two-year survival rates differ by 10 to 15 percentage points.

Given the differences in two-year survival rates, the cost of transplanting 100 fewer livers into intensive-care patients today would be a loss of 85 to 90 lives versus 100 over a two-year period.[5] Since graft survival rates are higher for healthier patients, the number needing retransplantation would decline. Thus, another benefit of this one-time policy change would be to free organs for others. Another advantage is that by transplanting livers into healthier individuals, the number of critically ill patients would decrease, thereby saving additional lives. On net, this policy change would be more efficient because it would save more lives.

The Best Biological Match

Another allocation method (the one emphasized for kidneys) is biological matching, which is measured by the quality of the antigen match between donor and patient.[6] Once a kidney becomes available, UNOS searches among waiting-list patients and ranks them according to their biological match with that organ. When four of the six most critical antigens match, the one-year graft survival rate is 13 percentage points higher than for a total antigen mismatch. Four years later, that difference increases to 20 percent.

Instead of biological matching, waiting time alone could be emphasized—the first-come, first-served approach.[7] While this may seem more equitable, the cost of such a policy change would be enormous. In the first year alone, the average biological match would decrease by nearly three antigens, and graft survival rates would fall by about 6 percentage points. Even discounting subsequent declines in graft survival rates, the number of kidney transplant candidates eventually would increase by nearly 5,600, translating into approximately 202 more waiting-list deaths each year.[8] The importance of graft survival is obvious, given that nearly one-quarter of those on the kidney waiting list have received a transplant previously.

Despite their emphasis on biological matching, UNOS distributes kidneys on a regional basis, mandating that kidneys procured within a region stay local.[9] If, on the other hand, kidneys were distributed nationally, the pool of potential recipients would increase, thereby increasing the likelihood of finding a patient with a good antigen match. Thus, distributing kidneys nationally would expand the average biological match. This policy change not only would save lives, but also would eliminate inequities caused by regional variations in waiting times.[10]

Discrimination in Kidney Allocation

Certain groups of patients wait longer than others for kidney transplants and, because of equity concerns, are given special consideration. For example, highly sensitized patients are much more likely to reject an organ transplant because of antibodies acquired from multiple blood transfusions or from rejecting a previous transplant. UNOS gives them preference when a kidney is found that will not necessarily be rejected; otherwise, they may never be transplanted. Giving highly sensitized patients preference can be extremely costly, however, because it reduces the size of the waiting-recipient pool searched. In effect, UNOS limits its search to the prioritized group unless a match outside the group is considerably higher. Thus, the likelihood of finding a well-matched kidney decreases, along with patient and graft survival rates. Since highly sensitized patients make up less than 3 percent of all kidney patients awaiting transplants, discriminating for them is likely to cost more than if the group receiving preference were larger.

An even greater preference is given to patients with type-O blood. Although organs from donors with type-O blood can potentially be transplanted into patients with any blood type, transplant candidates with O blood can receive only an organ of the same type. Thus, to ensure that these patients' waits are not substantially longer, UNOS mandates that kidneys from O donors will go only to O patients, with the exception of perfectly matched kidneys. The cost of this policy is that potentially good matches are forgone.

Other groups, such as blacks, also spend a disproportionate amount of time awaiting transplants. The median waiting time for black kidney patients is twice as long as it is for whites. This has led many to conclude that UNOS's policies are inherently racist and that blacks should receive preference similar to that given to highly sensitized patients. The longer waiting time, however, is not due to discrimination but to a disproportionate number of blacks who suffer from hypertension and diabetes—the two major causes of kidney failure.

Blacks represent 29 percent of all patients with end-stage renal disease, while they make up only 12 percent of the population and donate less than 12 percent of all kidneys. These numbers are important because the quality of the biological match is usually better when both the donor and the recipient are of the same race. The fact that blacks demand more kidney transplants as a share of their population and that the supply of kidneys from blacks is, if anything, slightly less than this figure explains the wide discrepancy between black and white waiting times.[11] Thus, a policy change giving preference to blacks not only would be more inefficient, costing additional lives, but also would violate UNOS's directive not to discriminate.

Encouraged Volunteerism: The Need for Incentives

Changes in the way UNOS rations organs can potentially decrease waiting times and save lives, but major reductions in waiting-list deaths, and thus improvements in efficiency, will require a substantial increase in organ donations. Table 2 shows the gap between the number of available organs and the number of people who need a kidney, liver, pancreas, heart, or lung transplant. Although the shortages vary, most of them are critical and have shown little response to public awareness programs, professional education efforts, or legislation. "Routine inquiry laws, for example, require hospital personnel to inform the families of potential donors about their option to donate. In fact, doctors still mention this opportunity only two-thirds of the time.[12]

Table 2

U.S. Organ Waiting List and Transplant Statistics

Organ	Quantity Demand (as of 12/25/96)	Quantity Supply (January–December 1996)
Total kidney	36,013	11,949
Cadaveric		8,560
Living		3,389
Liver	7,467	4,058
Pancreas	1,786	1,022
Heart	3,935	2,381
Lung	2,546	844

Note: Multiple organ transplants are counted as more than one organ.
Source: UNOS (1997)

Trading Organs

The only way to increase the supply of organs is to increase the number of cadaveric organs, with the exception of kidneys, for which there is also the possibility of living donations.[13] More than one-quarter of the 11,700 kidneys donated each year come from living related individuals—an impressive number considering that kidney removal requires the donor to be hospitalized for five to seven days and to spend two to three months convalescing.[14]

What can be done to further increase the supply of kidneys from living donors? Currently, only 7 percent of these donations are from nonrelated individuals (primarily spouses), mainly because kidneys from nonrelated donors are usually poor matches or of the wrong blood type. To increase donations, UNOS could facilitate the trading of kidneys, allowing patients to receive a well-matched kidney in exchange for a kidney from a spouse or close friend. This policy would increase kidney donations from both related and nonrelated sources. For instance, a patient's relative or spouse may be willing to donate a kidney, but because they have the wrong blood type, they are not suitable donors for that individual.[15]

Financial Incentives

Although altruism can be a powerful factor in motivating organ donations, it works best within families and cannot be expected to function as efficiently in the market for cadaveric organs. Individuals may sign anatomical donor cards indicating their wishes, but in practice, procurement agencies will remove organs only with familial consent. Thus, to increase supply, it is necessary to provide families with additional incentives. This is especially true given the relatively few deaths (10,000 to 12,000 annually) that occur in such a way that the deceased's organs are suitable for transplantation.

To increase donations, we need to consider financial incentives mimicking those that prices provide in a market economy. Perhaps the simplest approach is to give tax incentives to families who agree to donation. Donated organs already go to UNOS, a nonprofit organization; therefore, a monetary value would need to be assigned to organs only for tax purposes. To significantly increase the donor pool, society should also reconsider its position against the buying and selling of cadaveric organs. Allowing payments to surviving family members is another way of providing market incentives.[16]

To operate efficiently, the structure of this market would still require a centralized agency like UNOS to facilitate the matching process. Donor and recipient information is critical, since an individual's willingness to pay would depend on the quality of the antigen match with the available organ. One possible market structure would be to grant authority to buy and sell organs exclusively to the federal government, an approach suggested by Nobel laureate Gary S. Becker.

Shifting Rents

A common misperception about situations in which goods are not allowed to be bought and sold is that their market value is zero. An unintended consequence of price restrictions, however, is that the quantity supplied falls and the good becomes extremely valuable. To take advantage of the difference between the regulated price and the market's valuation, black markets tend to develop. Even if the price of the good does not rise, the actual cost may increase because of queuing costs, as in the case of gasoline price controls.

Black markets for transplantable organs have not developed in the United States, but it is possible that the price of transplants is higher, because organs cannot be legally sold. The law allows for "reasonable payments to all who participate in the organ donation process." The ambiguity of this term provides an opportunity for organ procurement organizations (OPOs) to artificially inflate prices. Currently, they receive approximately $25,000 for retrieving just the kidneys from a cadaver. An interesting, but as yet unresolved, question is how much of this $25,000 includes an implicit market price for the organ.

Other medical personnel (transplant surgeons, hospitals, etc.) also benefit financially from the organ procurement process, and are probably collecting some of these profits, also known as rents. Rents accrue whenever the quantity of a good is artificially restricted, thereby giving organizations monopolistic power. In the case of organs, the price, not the quantity per se, is restricted; however, the net effect is the same. Because of this, the shadow price (value) and hence the amount collected are likely to depend on the relative scarcity of the organ. Liver transplants are among the most expensive transplant surgeries—$300,000 on average—and as Table 2 indicates, livers are in especially short supply.

Figure 3 illustrates this concept in the market for transplantable organs, where S_c represents the supply of organs under the current system, and P_H represents the price that would clear the market.[17] This is the highest price, over and above normal fees, that a hospital can potentially charge for a transplant. Area OP_HaO_c shows the maximum rents that would be collected.

Figure 3

The Market for Transplantable Organs

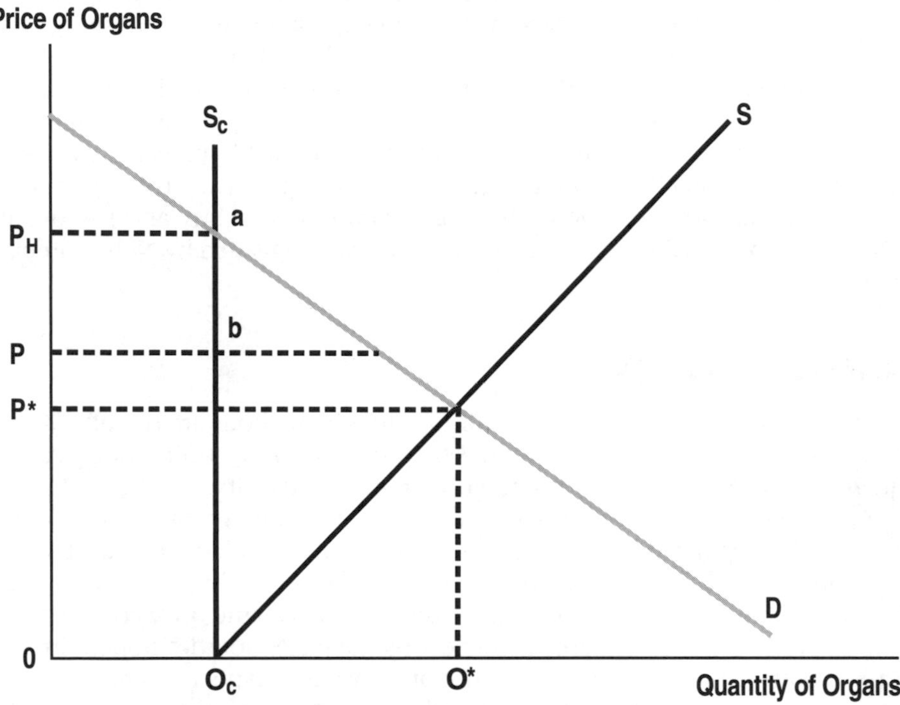

It is clear, however, that all of these rents are not being collected, given current shortages. Yet, it is equally clear that some rents are being collected. For example, it is particularly telling that OPOs keep procured organs in their local area, even though UNOS's policies sometimes dictate otherwise. This is frequently true when OPOs are affiliated with hospitals' transplant centers, in which case the potential profits of keeping organs in-house can be substantial. Thus, there is an implicit market price, *P*, between zero and P_H that is being charged. At that price, the value of rents would be area $OPbO_c$. If *P* is above *P**, as shown, then selling organs would actually lower the total price of a transplant (including the equilibrium price of the organ, *P**). Similarly, if *P* is below the market-clearing price, the total price of a transplant would increase by less than *P**. Thus, allowing organs to be sold would increase their supply, lower their market value, and shift payments from OPOs, hospitals, and surgeons to family members.

Even if the price of transplantation did rise by the full amount of *P**, the money going to donors' families ("death benefits") would likely pale in comparison to the overall price of the operation. Consider the case where the family benefit is $5,000 and rent shifting does not occur. When allocated among two kidneys, a heart, liver, and pancreas, the extra cost per organ is probably closer to $1,000, an insignificant amount compared to the price of a transplant.

Equity Issues

Selling organs would not favor the rich at the expense of the poor, as many argue, since those receiving organ payments would likely have lower average incomes. Organ recipients, both rich and poor, would also benefit from the increased supply of organs. Currently, Medicare pays for kidney transplants, while 90 percent of liver and heart transplants are covered by Medicare, Medicaid, and private insurance.[18] Each additional organ supplied benefits everyone, regardless of wealth.

Repealing the prohibition against the buying and selling of organs could lessen the disparity between black and white waiting times for kidneys. Because the antigen match is usually higher for individuals of the same race, any policy change that increases the percentage of black donors from its present level of 12 percent will decrease their waiting time. Thus, organ payments are more likely to persuade people of lower average income, including blacks, to donate, even if the payment amount is the same across all groups.

Given the higher demand for kidneys from black donors, in the absence of nondiscriminatory laws, payments to individual black families would likely be higher than payments to whites. But even without government assistance, this would not aggravate income inequality, since the extra amount paid by blacks would largely go to blacks. Given that Medicare (and frequently Medicaid) pays for kidney transplants, if anything, income inequality would be reduced by allowing organs to be sold.

Budgetary Concerns

Budgetary concerns are also misplaced. As previously noted, buying and selling organs may not increase transplantation costs at all, and even if it does, this policy change would still save Medicare money. It costs Medicare more than $40,000 annually to dialyze each kidney patient, while the cost of a transplant and subsequent medication is about $100,000 the first year and $12,000 per year thereafter. Because of this, the Health Care Financing Administration estimates that transplantation is considerably more cost effective than continued dialysis.

For example, if the average life of a transplanted kidney were only three years, the budgetary impact of organ payments would be neutral. The median graft survival rate, however, is closer to six years. Therefore, as long as the family benefit is less than $180,000 ($90,000 per kidney), the government will save money. Since the vast majority (nearly 70 percent) of all waiting-list patients are waiting for kidneys, each additional dollar spent encouraging families to donate will save taxpayer money.

Conclusion

Rationing is considered anathema to most Americans, yet it is necessary when prices are regulated. Goods are frequently rationed by simplistic methods such as lotteries or first-come, first-served. These may be more "equitable" approaches, but they are also among the most inefficient and can ultimately harm everyone involved. The inefficiencies are particularly pronounced in the market for transplantable organs, where costs are measured in human lives.

Deciding what is fair and who should be first in line for organ transplants is especially troubling and difficult. Dr. Mark Siegler, who directs the University of Chicago clinical ethics program, has stated that "all alcoholics should go to the bottom of the transplant list . . . yet Dr. Siegler [also] said he would exempt Mickey Mantle from his rule because the baseball legend is 'a real American hero' . . . [W]e have got to take them with all their warts and failures and treat them differently." It is especially important that UNOS resolve these issues given the current prohibition against the buying and selling of organs.

The cost of this prohibition is that lives are being lost. Additional incentives, including monetary, are required if cadaveric organ donations are to increase substantially. Even if these incentives do not eliminate the need for rationing, each additional organ procured will reduce the difficult, and sometimes arbitrary, decisions that UNOS must make. While many feel that the distribution of organs is too important to be left to market forces, ultimately, it is too important not to be.

Notes

1. Some states developed other rationing schemes based on license plate numbers and birthdays. These were largely ineffective in reducing queuing.
2. Specifically, the law prohibits the selling of organs if the transfer affects interstate commerce. Therefore, states may allow payments for organs, as long as the organs stay within state boundaries. However, given the current distribution system, states find it problematic to allow the selling of organs. Thus, the 1984 law has effectively prohibited a market in transplantable organs.
3. There may be social costs associated with discrimination, but it is costless for the individual firm.
4. A similar tradeoff exists during wartime with the triage of combat victims. This system maximizes overall survival by allowing the most critically ill soldiers to die.
5. This assumes that all intensive-care patients would die within two years without a transplant.
6. Biological matching is not considered for livers and hearts because of time constraints. Ordinarily, when transplanting kidneys, a patient's health status is not considered given the alternative of dialysis.
7. Currently, UNOS gives only slight priority to waiting time.
8. Estimate is based on authors' calculations.
9. The exception is if an individual with a perfect match is identified in another region.
10. There are costs involved in distributing organs nationally, because of increases in ischemic (preservation) time. These costs are small for kidneys, but large for other organs such as hearts. The feasibility of distributing livers nationally is currently being debated.
11. Nevertheless, many argue that steps should be taken to end "discrimination. As a result, the number of black transplant coordinators has been increased in

an effort to ensure that blacks have equal access to transplants. Not surprisingly, these efforts have failed.

12. One reason for the law's failure is lack of enforcement. There is a remarkable belief that monitoring is unnecessary. One staff member from Oregon's Health Department expresses it this way: "In a small state one does not need to coerce people to comply, especially with a requirement that is perceived as good policy."

13. Recently, however, doctors successfully transplanted a segment (lobe) of liver from a living donor.

14. A new laparoscopic procedure could reduce the recovery time from two to three months to two to three weeks. Doctors and ethicists are divided over the ethics of allowing living kidney donations.

15. UNOS's procedures do allow for the trading of cadaveric organs. For example, when one region receives a perfectly matched kidney from outside the area, UNOS requires that the receiving region eventually reimburse the sending region with a payback kidney.

16. The extent to which payments would elicit donations is unclear. The answer will likely come from pilot programs, such as the one recently introduced in Pennsylvania. Residents are offered the opportunity to contribute one dollar to a "Donor Awareness Trust Fund" when they renew their drivers' licenses or complete their state income tax forms. Up to 10 percent of this fund (a maximum of $3,000) can be redistributed to families of deceased donors for hospital, medical, and funeral costs.

17. Actually, the notion of market clearing in this market is ambiguous. By convention, an organ shortage is defined to occur when the quantity demanded (as measured by waiting-list patients) exceeds the annual supply. At any point in time, however, the quantity of organs demanded will exceed the available supply, even in a free market. Effectively, the relevant time frame for market clearing should be organ-specific and should depend on the mortality rate of those awaiting transplants.

18. Medicare covers almost all kidney recipients and pays 80 percent of expenses. The remaining 20 percent is picked up by either private insurance or Medicaid.

Nancy Scheper-Hughes  **NO**

The End of the Body

The Global Economy and Brute Life

In a recent issue of *Atlantic Monthly* (January 1998) George Soros, best known as a world-class billionaire financier, analyzed some of the deficiencies of the global capitalist economy. It is a fairly elementary exercise, but coming from a person in his position, one tends to sit up and take notice. The benefits of world capitalism, Mr. Soros notes, are unevenly distributed. Capital is in a better position than labor. And, surely it is better to be situated at the center of the global economy than at the peripheries. Given the inherent instability of the global financial system, *busts* will inevitably follow *booms,* like night the day, and capital tends to return to its centers leaving the minor players in faraway places high and dry. Meanwhile, the rapid growth of global monopolies have compromised the authority of states and weakened their regulatory functions.

But what bothers Mr. Soros most is the erosion of social values and social cohesion in the face of the increasing dominance of anti-social market values. Not that markets are to be blamed, of course. By their very nature markets are indiscriminate, promiscuous and inclined to reduce everything, including human beings, their labor and even their reproductive capacity to the status of commodities, to things that can be bought, sold, traded, and stolen. So, while, according to Mr. Soros, a Market Economy is generally a good thing, we cannot live by markets alone. "Open" and democratic societies require strong social institutions to serve such vital goals as social justice, political freedom, bodily integrity and other human rights. The real dilemma, as Mr. Soros sees it, is one of uneven development. The evolution of the global market has outstripped the development of a mediating global society.

Indeed, amidst the neo-liberal readjustments of virtually all contemporary societies, North and South, we are experiencing today a rapid depletion, an "emptying out" even, of the traditional modernist, humanist, and pastoral ideologies and practices. But meanwhile, new mediations between capital and work, between bodies and the state, belonging and extra-territoriality, and even between, social exclusion and medical-technological inclusion are taking shape. So, rather than a conventional story of the sad decline of humanistic social values and social relations, our discussion is tethered to a frank recognition that the conventional grounds on which those modernist values and practices were based have shifted beyond recognition.

Nowhere, perhaps, are these processes more transparent than in the rapid dissemination in the past decade of organ transplantation technologies and practices which under the ideal conditions of an "open," neo-liberal, global Market Economy has allowed for an unprecedented movement of, among other "things," mortally sick bodies moving in one direction and detached "healthy" organs (transported by commercial airlines in ordinary plastic beer coolers stored in the overhead luggage compartment of the economy section) in another direction, creating a bizarre "kula ring" of international trade. This essay critically explores—with particular reference to recent organ transplantation "developments" in Brazil, South Africa, India, the United States, and China—the new forms of bio-economics and bio-sociality (Rabinow 1996) that are now emerging in the wake of the internationalization of this immensely powerful, if crude, medical technology.

What is needed, then, is something akin to Donna Haraway's (1985) radical "manifesto" for the cyborg bodies and cyborg selves that we have, in fact, already become through the appearance of these strange markets, excess capital, advanced bio-technology, "surplus bodies" and human "spare parts." Together, these have allowed for a spectacularly lucrative world trade in organ transplantation which promises to certain, select individuals of reasonable economic "means" living almost anywhere in the world—from the Kalahari Desert in Botswana to the deserts of the Arab Emirate of Oman—a "miraculous" extension in what Giorgio Agamben (1998) refers to as "brute" or "bare" life, the elementary form of biological "species life." This, in turn, is made possible by the internal and domestic reorganization of neo-liberal, democratic states and their successful capture of the "cadaver" now redefined as the "state's body" and the concomitant politicization of death. By this we mean the increasing capacity of the post-transplantation State to define and determine the hour of death and to claim, unashamedly, the "first rights" (and first *rites*) to the disposal of the body's parts.

Until very recently, only highly deviant authoritarian and police states—Nazi Germany, Argentina in the late 1970s, Brazil in the 1960s and 1970s, and South Africa under apartheid—had assumed this capacity in the 20th century, this final word, as it were, over brute life, politicized death, and the creation and *maintenance* of a surplus population of "living dead," whether Black industrial workers kept in barbaric worker hostels in apartheid South Africa (see Ramphele 1994), the "disappeared" in Argentina, or those walking cadavers kept hostage in Nazi concentration camps. The "democratization" of practices bearing at least some family resemblances to these (i.e., the "living dead" maintained in intensive care units for the purpose of organ retrieval) in neo-liberal states has generally occurred in the absence of public outrage or resistance, with the possible exception of public unrest following democratic Brazils' passage of its authoritarian law of "presumed consent" to organ donation in 1997, which we shall discuss. . . .

In the face of this ultimate, late modern dilemma—this "end of the body" as we see it—the task of anthropology is relatively clear and straight forward:

the recovery of our discipline's unrealized radical epistemological promise and a commitment to the "primacy of the ethical" (Scheper-Hughes 1994) while daring to risk practical, even political, involvement in the dangerous topic[1] under consideration. The need to define new ethical standards for the international practice of organ donation—especially in light of the abuses that undermine the bodily integrity of socially disadvantaged members of society and the public trust that is necessary for voluntary organ donation to continue, brought together a small international task force. The "Bellagio Task Force on Transplantation, Bodily Integrity, and the International Traffic in Organs," led by social historian, David Rothman, is comprised of a dozen international transplant surgeons, organ procurement specialists, human rights activists, and a medical anthropologist (myself, NS-H) meeting in 1995 and again in 1996 in the Rockefeller Conference Center in Bellagio, Italy. The task force is examining the ethical, social, and medical ramifications of these problems and is considering various strategies to impact them, including the creation of an international human rights body—a "Human Organs Watch," if you like—to monitor reports of any gross violations in the procurement and distribution of human organs in transplant surgery. An initial report of the Task Force was published in *Transplantation Proceedings* (Rothman et al., 1997). At the 1996 meeting, I was "delegated" by the Task Force to launch a very exploratory, ethnographic, comparative study of the social and economic context of organ transplantation, including the global and domestic traffic in organs.

The field research on which this discussion is based, therefore, derives from this "mission." It represents the preliminary findings from the early stages of the collaborative "Selling Life" project. . . .

The focus on the "commodification" of the body and body parts within the new global economy owes a particular debt to the writings and thought of Sidney Mintz, particularly his magisterial book, *Sweetness and Power.* This article is offered as a "transplanted" surrogate for the 1996 Sidney Mintz lecture which I was extremely honored to present at Johns Hopkins University.[2]

The Organs Ring and the Commodified Body

Indeed, as Arjun Appadurai has noted (1986) there is nothing fixed, stable, or sacrosanct about the "commodity candidacy" of things. Nowhere is this more dramatically illustrated than in the "booming" global and domestic markets in human organs and tissues from both living and deceased donors to supply the transplant industry, a medical business driven by the simple market calculus of "supply and demand." The very idea of organ "scarcity" is what Ivan Illich would call an artificially created need, invented by transplant technicians and dangled before the eyes of an ever expanding sick, aging, and dying population. This market is part of an impressive development and refinement of transplant technologies. These developments were facilitated historically through the medical definition of irreversible coma (at the end of the 1950s) and the new legal status of "brain death" (at the end of the 1960s) in which, as Giorgio Agamben (1998:163) notes, death became an epiphenomenon of transplant technologies. These transformations reveal the extent to which the sovereign power of postmodern states, both "democratic" and authoritarian, is operationalized through the life sciences and medical practices. These apparatuses, sciences, and technologies are globally integrated in markets which, in turn, increasingly reconfigure local states and local "cultures."

Lawrence Cohen, for example, who has worked in rural towns in various regions of India, from north to south, now reports that in a very brief period of time the idea of trading "a kidney for a dowry" has caught on and become one strategy for poor parents desperate to arrange a comfortable marriage for an "extra" daughter. In other words, a spare kidney for a spare daughter. Cohen notes that ten years ago when villagers and townspeople first heard through newspaper reports of kidney sales occurring in the cities of Bombay and Madras they responded with predictable alarm and revulsion. Today, some of these same villagers speak *matter of factly* about just when in the course of a family cycle it might be necessary to sell a "spare" organ. Some village parents say they can no longer complain about the fate of a dowry-less daughter. "Haven't you got a spare kidney?" one or another unsympathetic neighbor is likely to respond.

And in rural Brazil, over a similarly short period and in response to demands to "donate" a kidney to a family member, working class people have begun to view their bodies and body parts as comprised of unessential redundancies. "Nanci," I was challenged by a forty year old woman who had "given" a kidney (for a small compensation) to a distant relation, "Wouldn't you feel compelled to give an organ of which you yourself had two and the other 'fellow' had none?" I pointed out, rather lamely, that the Good Lord had given us two of quite a few organs and I hated to think of myself as selfish (*egoista*) for wanting to hang on to as many of the pairs as I could! It was not so long ago—1986, in fact—and in this same community when I had been invited to accompany a small procession to the graveyard where we ceremoniously buried a "fellow's" amputated foot! The folk Catholic ideology of the sacredness of the body—and the integrity of its component parts—was still then the commanding ethos. And though I felt a bit silly giving that gangrenous foot the benefit of a decade of the rosary as a "send off," Rosalva's reconceptualization in the late 1990s of her body as a mere reservoir of spare parts struck me as a troublesome turn of events.

The particular and well documented case of organ selling and, more recently, of organ stealing (see *New York Times,* May 12, 1998) in Indian villages is but one small, if well documented, link in a "booming" world market in organs and human tissues (not to mention blood, semen, ova, and babies) that links east and west, north and south. Over the past 30 years, organ transplantation has been transformed from a rare and experimental procedure performed in a few advanced medical centers in the first world to a fairly common therapeutic procedure carried out in hospitals and clinics, not all of them certified and legitimate, throughout the world. Kidney transplantation, which is the most universal form of organ transplant, is now conducted in the U.S., in most European and Asian countries, in several South American and Middle Eastern countries, and in a few African countries (in North Africa and South Africa). Survival rates for kidney transplant have increased markedly over the past decade, although these still vary by country and by quality and type of organ (living or cadaveric).

Until recently the "best" medical option for kidney transplantation was using a genetically closely related living donor (Fischel 1991). Today, however, morbidity rates from infection and hepatitis are higher in countries like Brazil, India, and China, which still rely heavily on living kidney donors than in the U.S., Canada, and the countries of Western Europe which rely more on cadaveric donation. But within some poorer countries to the South, like Brazil, survival rates for kidney transplant are still better with a matched living donor than with an "anonymous" cadaveric organ which stands a good chance of not having been adequately tested or screened.

Organ transplantation now takes place in a trans-national space with both donors and recipients following the paths of capital and technology in the global economy. In general, the movement of donor organs follows modern routes of capital: *from South to North, from third world to first world, from poor to rich bodies, from black and brown to white bodies, from young to old bodies, productive to less productive, and female to male bodies.* Residents of the Gulf States (Kuwait, Saudi Arabia, Oman, United Arab Emirates) travel primarily to India to obtain kidneys, while residents of Taiwan, Hong Kong, Korea and Singapore travel to mainland China for transplant surgery, allegedly with organs removed from executed prisoners. Japanese patients travel to North America as well as to Taiwan and Singapore for organs retrieved from brain dead donors, a definition of death only very recently and reluctantly accepted in Japan.

And, a great many people—and by no means are all of them wealthy—have shown their willingness to travel great distances to secure a transplant using both legal and illegal channels. This is so even when the survival rates in some of the more commercialized contexts is quite poor. Between 1983–1988, 131 patients from just three renal units in the United Arab Emirates and Oman traveled to Bombay, India where they purchased, through local brokers, kidneys from living donors. The donors, from urban shantytowns outside Bombay, were compensated between $2,000 and $3,000 for a kidney. News of the "organs bazaars" operating in the slums of Bombay, Calcutta and Madras appeared in Indian weeklies and in special reports by ABC and the BBC. Meanwhile, prestigious medical journals, (including *The Lancet* and *Transplant Proceedings*) published dozens of articles analyzing the medical risks and poor outcomes resulting from transplantation using "poor quality" kidneys from medically compromised "donors."[3]

A medically invented, artificial scarcity in human organs for transplantation has generated a kind of panic and a desperate international search for them and for new surgical possibilities. Bearing many similarities to the international market in adoption, those looking for transplant organs are so single minded in their quest that they are sometimes willing to put aside questions about how the organ [or "the baby" in the case of adoption] was obtained. In both instances the language of "gifts," "donations," "heroic rescues" and "saving lives" masks the extent to which ethically dubious and even illegal practices are used to obtain the desired "scarce" commodity, infant or kidney, for which foreigners (or "better off" nationals) are willing to pay what to ordinary people seems a king's ransom. With desperation built in on both sides of the equation—deathly ill "buyers" and desperately needy "sellers"—once seemingly "timeless" religious beliefs in the sanctity of the body and proscriptions against body mutilation have collapsed over night in some parts of the third world under the weight of these new market's demands. These new demands are driven by the rapid dissemination of the medical technology and expertise of transplant surgery and a new global social imagry about the possibilities of bodily rejuvenation and "repair" through organ replacement.

The gap between supply and demand that drives the new global trade in organs is exacerbated by religious sanctions and/or cultural inhibitions with respect to "brain death" and the proper handling of the dead body. Prohibitions in one country or region can stimulate an "organs market" in more secular or culturally pluralistic neighboring countries or regions. Meanwhile, the "scarcity" of organs produced in the wake of centralized "waiting lists" for transplantation has provided many incentives to physicians, hospital administrators, government officials, and blatantly commercial intermediaries to engage in ethically questionable tactics for obtaining organs. For example, heart transplantation is hardly performed at all in Japan due to deep reservations about the social definition of brain death, while most kidney transplants are gotten with living, related donors (see Lock 1996, 1997; Ohnuki-Tierney 1994).

For many years desperate Japanese nationals have resorted to intermediaries with connections to the underworld of organized crime (the so called "body mafia") to locate donor hearts or (when lacking related donors), paid unrelated kidney donors in other countries, including the United States. According to Lock (personal communication, 1997) who is engaged in a comparative study of transplant surgery in Japan and Canada (1996, 1997), a ring of Japanese *yakuza* gangsters, working on behalf of desperate Japanese transplant candidates through connections at a major medical center in Boston was uncovered by journalists and broken up by police there a decade ago. And, until recently, Japanese kidney patients also traveled to Taiwan and Singapore to purchase organs obtained (without consent) from executed prisoners, until this practice was roundly condemned by the World Medical Association in 1994 and was prohibited by new regulations.

The ban on the use of organs from executed prisoners in one part of "capitalist" Asia, opened up the possibilities for a similar practice in another part of "communist" Asia. The demand for hard currency by strapped governments recognizes no fixed ideological or political boundaries. Recently, the *New York Times* (February 24, 1998) reported on an FBI operation which led to the arrest of two Chinese citizens charged with conspiring to sell human organs of executed prisoners. The undercover "sting" operation was set up by the human rights activist, Harry Wu, who has been alerting the world since the 1980s to this alleged, covert practice in China. This particular case is still pending investigations, but its outcome may determine once and for all the veracity of Harry Wu's (and other human right activists') contested claims about the organs trade in China today, which we will discuss at greater length below.

Despite the publicity and attention to the more spectacular international traffic in human organs, an equally important though far less explored dimension of the organs trade is domestic, following the usual routes of social and economic cleavages and obeying domestic rules of class, race, gender, and geography. Dr. X, an elderly Brazilian surgeon and nephrologist, admitted during an interview in São Paulo in 1997 that "the commerce in organs has always been a reality in Brazil and among and between Brazilians.

"Those who suffer most," he said, are the usual "nobodies," mostly poor and uneducated, who are tricked into "donation" through illegal and unethical bodily transactions. The elderly doctor cited a transplantation scandal that occurred in Brazil in the late 1980s, one of several such cases exposed by local journalists and human rights activists. This particular one concerned a young accident victim, a mere girl of 12 years, from the interior town of Taubate, who while undergoing surgery on her broken leg, had a "spare" kidney removed by unscrupulous surgeons. Following a complaint lodged by her family who noticed a scar where none should have been, the local Public Defender began an investigation but it was interrupted by the Federal Police. Consequently, the Federal Board of Medicine was "compelled" to pass a verdict of "not guilty" due to lack of evidence.

But the poor and socially disadvantaged populations of Brazil and elsewhere in the world have not remained silent in the face of these threats and assaults to their health and to their bodily integrity, security, and dignity. For many years these marginal populations, living in urban shantytowns and hillside favelas, possessing little or no "symbolic capital" have announced their fears and their outrage through the idiom of seemingly "wild" rumors and urban legends . . . that warn of the existence and the dangerous proximity of markets in bodies and body parts (Scheper-Hughes 1996). The circulation of the rumors and "urban legends" of organ theft have produced in their wake a climate of hostile "civil" resistance toward even legitimate and altruistic organ donation and organ transplantation in some countries to the South (such as Brazil and Argentina) where voluntary donations began to drop precipitously in the 1980s. Medical associations and governments have tried, without success, to correct the "disinformation" being disseminated by the persistent organ stealing rumors.

And, in a curious reversal, these "illiterate" rumors originating in the periphery have migrated to the comfortable and affluent "core," the comfortable middle class communities of the U.S. Despite the appointment of a full-time USIA [United States Information Agency] disinformation specialist, Todd Leventhal (see USIA 1994) who has led a long and expensive U.S. government campaign to kill the "body parts" rumor, as recently as the late fall of 1997 a variant of the organ stealing rumor carrying dire warnings about the existence of seductive female (or, less often, male) medical "agents" involved in the body parts trade was circulated among thousands of Americans via an electronic mail "chain letter." One strand of the chain was passed among a network of progressive academics, and to my amusement I was one of the recipients. The warning was followed a few days later by an apology stating that the story may have been "just a rumor."

Indeed, it would seem from this that a great many people in the world, both North and South, are uneasy. Something seems amiss or profoundly wrong about the nature of the beast that medical technology has released in the name of transplant surgery. But why now, why so many years later? Has transplant surgery opened a Pandora's Box that has resulted in a long overdue, popular backlash? Or, is there something new about the current organization of transplant surgery that has turned a once proud and altruistic moment in medical history into something unseemly and grotesque?

Dr. B., a heart transplant surgeon in Cape Town, South Africa whom I interviewed in February 1998, said he has become very *"disheartened"* about his profession's recent decline in prestige, trust, and value: "Organ transplantation has moved from an era back in 1967 when the atmosphere and public attitude was very different. . . . You know, people then still spoke about organ donation as that fantastic gift. Our first organ donor, Denise Dawer, and her family, were very much hallowed here. They were given a lot of credit for what they did and their photos are displayed in our hospital's new Transplant Museum. Society at that stage was still very positive. Now that there have been hundreds of thousands of donors throughout the world, the idea of organ donation has lost some of its luster. And, donors' families throughout the world have been put under a lot more pressure. And there have been some incidents that were unfortunate. . . . So we've begun to all of a sudden to experience a sea of backlash. In Europe there has been a strong backlash because of the state's demand, the moral requirement even, to donate. Europeans have generally had a good social conscience, they tend to believe in the better good of society, and so up until now they supported organ transplantation as a social good. But, now, suddenly objections are beginning to be raised. The Lutheran Church in Germany, for example, has started to question the idea of brain death, long after it had been generally accepted there. And so we have seen a drop of about 20% in organ donations in Europe, but especially in Germany. This is entirely new. So we are experiencing a real backlash, and what happens in Germany, unfortunately, has repercussions for South Africa.". . .

The Right to Sell and Future Markets

Despite evidence of widespread moral panic about bodily integrity and organ stealing some transplant surgeons and bioethicists, like Dr. Abdullah Daar, a member of the Bellagio Task Force, [a working group set up by Columbia University to study the use of organs for transplantations] sees the commercialization and commodification of human organs, whether one likes it or not, as a fait accompli. Labor is sold, sex is sold, sperm and ova are sold, even babies are sold in international adoption. What makes kidneys so special, so exempt? Daar has asked repeatedly. What is needed, he insists, is rigorous oversight and regulation in addition to an official Donors Bill of Rights that would both inform and protect potential donors.

But other members of the Task Force argue with Daar's reliance on western notions of contract and individual "choice." They are mindful of the social and economic context that makes the "choice" to sell a kidney anything but a "free" and "autonomous" one in an urban slum of Calcutta or a shantytown of São Paulo. Similarly, the idea of "consent" is problematic in a prison with the executioner looking over one's shoulder. In response to Daar's critique of human rights "paternalism" and his defense of the autonomy of the individual and his or her right to sell an organ, Veena Das has countered that in all notions of contract there are certain exclusions—such as in family law, labor law, and anti-trust law. There are basic assumptions concerning protected areas of life—anything that would damage social or community relations—that should be taken outside of contract theory. A market price—even a fair one—on body parts exploits the desperation of the poor. In addition, many humanists and bioethicists hold it to be self-evident that certain objects (like irreplaceable, non renewable solid organs) are fundamentally "inalienable" from the person. To ask the law to negotiate, as Daar suggests, a fair and reasonable price for a live human kidney is asking the law to go against everything that contract theory (as well as society) stands for. In addition, one has to be concerned about the effects of organ sales on the coarsening of medical practice and on doctors who are forced to inflict physical harm on one person who is not viewed as a "patient" in order to save the life of another individual who is exclusively viewed as "the patient."

Nonetheless, the movement toward commercialization is gaining ground in the United States. The AMA (American Medical Association) is currently considering the possibility of financial incentives that would enable people to bequeath organs to their heirs or to charity for a price. Dr. L.R. Cohen (no relation to anthropologist Lawrence Cohen) has proposed a "futures market" in cadaveric organs that would operate through contracts offered to the general public. These contracts would provide that at the time of the seller's death, if organs are successfully transplanted from his body, a substantial sum would be paid to his designee. He suggests $5,000 per major organ utilized. Cohen's proposal is based on the idea that a market can exist side by side with and even supplement altruism. Pure gifting can always be expected among family members, but financial inducements might be necessary to provide organs for strangers.

Dr. Charles Plows, Chair of the AMA's Committee on Ethical and Judicial Affairs agrees in principle with Cohen's proposal: "The only one who doesn't get anything out of this whole transplant transaction is the person who's deceased. The hospital makes money out of furnishing the areas where this work is done. Certainly, transplant surgeons do well for themselves. The patient gets a life-saving organ. But the man or woman who's donating the organ receives nothing." At present the AMA is exploring several options. One is a fixed price per organ. Another is to let market forces—supply and demand—set the price. The idea still makes a lot of doctors in the U.S. uncomfortable, but Dr. Plows and his colleague hope to get a pilot project off the ground in 1998.

India: Kidney Bazaar

The first inklings of a commercial market in organ trafficking appeared in 1983 when an American physician, H. Barry Jacobs, established the International Kidney Exchange in an attempt to broker kidneys from living donors in the Third World, especially India. By the early 1990s upwards of 2,000 kidney *transplants with living donors* were performed each year in India, leading

Prakash Chandra (1991) and other investigative journalists to refer to their country as the "great organ bazaar of the world." Proponents of paid living donors, such as Dr. K.C. Reddy, an Indian urologist with a thriving practice of kidney transplantation in Madras, argued that legalizing the trade would eliminate middle men who profit by exploiting paid donors.

Meanwhile, the free market in kidneys that catered through the 1980s to wealthy patients from the Middle East was forced underground following the passage of a law in 1994 that criminalizes organ sales. Recent reports by human rights activists, journalists, and medical anthropologists, including Lawrence Cohen, indicate that the law has produced in its wake an even larger *domestic* black market in kidneys. In some areas this new business is controlled by organized, cash-rich crime gangs expanding out from the heroin trade (in some cases with the backing of local political leaders). In other areas the business are controlled by ever more wealthy owners of profit hospitals.

An investigative report (*Frontline* December 26, 1997) found that a doctor-broker nexus in Bangalore and Madras still profits from the sale of kidneys by poor Indian donors to rich Indians, and to a smaller number of absolutely desperate foreigners with end-stage renal disease. A loophole in the law allows unrelated donors related to recipients by "ties of affection" to give a kidney following approval by local Medical Authorization Committees. These committees have been readily corrupted in areas where kidney sales have become an important source of local income. The result is that sales are now conducted with official seals of approval by the local Authorization Committee.

Today, Lawrence Cohen reports from the field, only the very rich can get an unrelated kidney. In addition to paying the donor, the middle men, and the hospital, now they must bribe the Authorization Committee members as well. As for the kidney sellers, recruited by brokers who get half the cost of the sale, almost all are trapped in terrible cycles of debt and caught in the clutches of money lenders. The kidney trade is another link, Cohen suggests, in an older and earlier system of debt peonage which has been reinforced by neoliberal structural readjustment policies. Kidney sales are a key sign, says Cohen, of the sometimes bizarre effects of a global capitalism that seeks to turn everything into a commodity.

And there are hints and allegations of criminal practices within this climate of rampant commercialism. During the Berkeley conference on the commercialization of organs, Das told an NPR (National Public Radio, "Marketplace" program) reporter of a young woman she encountered in Delhi whose stomach pains were diagnosed as a bladder stone requiring surgery. But, in fact, the doctor, the woman charged, used the bladder stone as a pretext to operate and remove one of her kidneys which he delivered to a middleman for an undisclosed and confidential third party.

China: Collective Bodies

Today, China stands alone in continuing to use the organs of executed prisoners for transplant surgery. Although this practice has been documented by various international human rights organizations and investigated even by the FBI, Chinese public officials have impeded any form of inspection or verification of the executions. In October 1984, a Chinese government directive issued a document stating that "the use of corpses or organs of executed criminals *must be kept strictly secret,* and attention must be paid to avoid negative repercussions" (cited in *Human Rights Watch/Asia* 1994:7).

Following up on a report published by Human Rights Watch/Asia in August 1994 on "Organ Procurement and Judicial Execution in China," David Rothman visited major hospitals in Beijing and Shanghai in 1995 where he interviewed transplant surgeons and other medical officers about the technical and the social dimensions of transplant surgery as practiced at their respective units. While the surgeons and hospital administrators answered technical questions freely and accurately, they refused to respond to such questions as: Where do donated organs come from? How many foreigners come to the medical institutions seeking transplants? How much do the hospitals charge for various transplant operations?

While the "blank stares" of Chinese medical personnel that Rothman encountered in response to his questions are no proof of complicity or guilt, Dr. C.J. Lee, head of a transplant team in Taiwan, and member of the Bellagio Task Force, shared with the Task Force his personal knowledge and experience of transplant practices in Asia. The use of the organs of executed prisoners was practiced at his own unit in Taiwan until the country responded to the pressure of international human rights activists against it. China has held out, in part, Dr. Lee suggests, because of the need for foreign dollars and in part because there is less ethical soul-searching in China (as elsewhere in Asia) [or] "informed consent." And, an alternative social ethic interprets the practice as a kind of public service, an opportunity to pay the community back for wrongs committed and to gain merit for one's self.

Of course, not all Chinese embrace this collectivist ethos and some see the practice as a gross human rights abuse. Mr. Lin, a recent Chinese immigrant to California, reported a disturbing story (recorded for NPR's "Marketplace") during the Berkeley conference on the commercialization of organs, 1996. Just before arriving in California two years ago he visited a friend at a medical center in Shanghai. In the bed next to his friend was a wealthy and politically well situated professional man who told Mr. Lin that he was waiting for a kidney transplant later that day. His new kidney would arrive, he said, as soon as a prisoner was executed that morning. Minutes after the condemned prisoner was shot in the head, doctors present at the execution would quickly extract his kidneys and rush them to the hospital where two transplant surgery teams would be assembled and waiting. Reports by Human Rights Watch/Asia and by the Laogai Research Foundation (January 1995) have documented through Chinese informants and available medical and prison statistics that the state systematically takes kidneys, cornea, liver tissue and heart valves from executed prisoners. While these organs are sometimes given to reward politically well connected Chinese, often they are sold to medical "visitors" from Hong Kong, Taiwan, Singapore and other Pacific Rim nations who will pay as much as $30,000 for an organ.

Harry Wu, the human rights activist imprisoned in China until recently, was among the first to reveal the sale of prisoners' organs. At the Berkeley conference Wu said: "In 1992 I interviewed a doctor who routinely participated in removing kidneys from condemned prisoners. In one case she said, breaking down in the telling, that she had even participated in a surgery in which two kidneys were removed from a living, anesthetized prisoner late at night. The following morning the prisoner was executed by a bullet to the head." In this chilling case, brain death followed, rather than preceded, the harvesting of his vital organs.

Wu and other human rights activists claim that the Chinese Government takes organs from 2,000 executed prisoners each year. Moreover, that number is growing because the list of capital crimes in China has been expanded to accommodate the demand for organs. While the precise number of prisoners executed in China each year is unknown, Amnesty International has recently reported that a new "Strike Hard" anti-crime campaign has led to a sharp increase in the number of people executed, among them petty thieves and tax cheaters. In 1996 alone at least 6,100 death sentences were handed out and at least 4,367 confirmed executions took place. David Rothman, among others, is convinced that what lies behind the draconian anti-crime campaign is a "thriving medical business" that relies on prisoners' organs for raw materials. The state is sponsoring, he says, an "insatiable killing machine" driven by the rapacious "need" for fresh and healthy organs.

Recently, Wu's allegations have been bolstered following a sting operation he set up in New York City that led to the arrest of two Chinese citizens offering to sell cornea, kidneys, livers and other human organs to American doctors wanting them for transplant surgery. Posing in the undercover operation as a prospective customer from a dialysis center, Wu produced a video tape of the men, Mr. Wang Chenyong and Mr. Fu Xingqi in a Manhattan hotel room offering to sell him quality organs from a dependable source—fifty to two hundred prisoners executed on Hainan Island each year. Mr. Wang guaranteed this commitment by producing documents to Wu indicating that he had been deputy chief of criminal prosecutions in that prison. A pair of cornea would cost an exorbitant $5,000. In a taped telephone call, Wang boasted of making a 1000% profit (*Mail and Guardian* 2/27/1998; *San Jose Mercury News* 3/19/98; *New York Times* 2/24/98). Following their arrest by FBI agents the men were charged with conspiring to sell human organs and are being held without bond awaiting criminal proceedings. As a further fallout, a German company, Frenesius Medical Care A.G., based in a suburb of Frankfurt, announced that it was ending its half-interest in a kidney dialysis unit (next to a transplant clinic) in Guangzhou, China, citing the company's strong suspicions that foreign patients visiting the center may also be there to receive "kidneys harvested from executed Chinese criminals" (*New York Times* 3/7/98). [A] Frenesius spokesman stated that the company did not know anything about the "cover-up" role of the dialysis center and that the center was totally administered by Chinese medical personnel and controlled by military commands. . . .

The Move to Primary Care and Privatization of Organ Transplantation

. . . As organ transplantation moves into the private sector, a creeping commercialism has necessarily taken hold. In the absence of a national policy regulating transplant surgery, and no regional, let alone national, official waiting lists, the distribution of transplantable organs is appallingly informal and subject to corruption. Public and private hospitals can hire their own transplant coordinators who are under pressure from competing, even warring, factions to "drop" the usable heart or kidney in a bucket rather than give it to a competitor. The situation is grave. The temptation "to accommodate" patients who are able to pay is affecting both the public and private sector hospitals. At Groote-Schurr Hospital's kidney transplant unit, a steady trickle of donor "couples" arrive from Mauritius and Nimibia. Although they claim to be related, the nurses say that many are simply paid donors, but since they arrive from across the border, the doctors look the other way. While I was in Cape Town, a very ill older business man from the Cameroons arrived at the kidney transplant unit with a paid donor the man found in Johannesburg. The donor was a young university student from Burundi who agreed to part with one of his kidneys for his expenses and a bonus of 2,000 rand (about $400). The head of the kidney unit read the international medical codes against organ sales to the pair, explained the risks and dangers of living kidney donation, but as they persisted he agreed to order the blood matching tests. When they failed to match and were turned away, the symbiotic pair begged to be transplanted in any case. Such was their almost unimaginable desperation, that they were willing to face the eventuality of almost certain organ rejection. Of course, the doctors refused their plea. Will private hospitals be as conscientious as the public ones in refusing hopeless cases among those patients willing to pay regardless of the outcome?

Meanwhile, those who live at a distance, without easy means of communication and transportation, such as in the sprawling townships of Soweto outside Johannesburg and Khayalitsha outside Cape Town have a ghost of a chance of receiving a transplant. The rule of thumb among heart and kidney transplant surgeons in Johannesburg is: "No fixed home, no phone, no organ." The ironies are striking. At the famous Chris Hani Bara Hospital on the outskirts of Soweto, I met a sprightly and playful middle aged man, flirting with nurses, during his dialysis treatment. "He's very familiar with you!" I commented to the head nurse. "And well, he might be," she replied. "He's been on the waiting list for a kidney for more than 20 years." Not a single patient at the huge Bara Hospital's kidney unit had received a transplant in the past year.

The week before I was in the splendid, suburban community of Sun Valley outside Cape Town where, in a private, gated community protected by armed guards for the comfort and security of the wealthy, white, and mostly retired residents, I met with Mr. W. Breytanbach, Ex-Deputy Minister of Defense under President P.W. Botha, still recuperating from the heart transplant he had received on his government pension and health plan in less than a month's wait. At first he was distraught on learning that he was the recipient of the heart of a young, colored nurse, and at first he blamed his difficult recovery on his "inferior woman's heart." He has since softened, he says, and he has even tried to contact the family of his donor through the hospital network so that he could thank them. The family has not responded. As we chatted about his time served on South Africa's notorious Security Committee, I had to control my rising sense of outrage. The sub-heading, "State Killer Gets New Heart" came several times to mind during the interview, prompting me, finally, to ask Mr. Breytanbach if he thought he owed the new South African government something for having given him, of all people, a new lease on life. He replied:

> "To this day I still do not know why I was given a heart transplant. I know that at the time I had only 10 or 12 days at most to live and if I did not have [the operation] I would be dead. And it is great to be alive! I look at the country and I see that there may be more people more deserving than me of a heart transplant, and many who cannot get it because of a shortage of funds or of donors with so many people waiting for hearts. But by hook or by crook, I don't know how Dr. V. does it [in the private hospital] but I have been there and I can see that there are no questions asked about whether the person can really afford it or not. If need be, [heart transplant surgeon] just goes ahead and operates."

At the venerable Groote-Schuur Hospital, however, the waiting time for all major surgical procedures has increased and a virtual moratorium has brought heart transplantation to a standstill.

Concluding Remarks

Organ transplantation depends, as Cantarovitch (1990) suggests, on a social contract and social trust, the grounds for which must be explicit. This requires national and international laws protecting the rights of both organ donors and organ recipients. At a very rudimentary level, the practice of organ transplantation requires a reasonably fair and equitable health care system. For example, the Ministry of Health in Gauteng, South Africa proposed a temporary moratorium in late 1995 on heart transplants in an effort to sort out unreliable private sector doctors performing these operations under questionable medical circumstances. The present moratorium in Cape Town is more difficult to justify.

The social ethics of transplant surgery also require a reasonably democratic state in which basic human rights, especially bodily integrity, are protected and guaranteed. Organ transplantation occurring, even in elite medical centers by the most conscientious of physicians, within the milieu of a police state or authoritarian state—as the illustrations from China, and from pre-democratic transition in Brazil and South Africa exemplify—all too readily lead to gross human rights abuses of both living and dead bodies. Similarly, where vestiges of forced labor exist (especially in "debt peonage" systems which unfairly bind workers to their "owners"), and where unjust transactions keep being "legally" and "medically" covered-up (including trade in corneas, kidneys, children and facilitation of access to care) the panic and mistrust of medicine and transplant surgery in particular will persist.

Under conditions like these the most vulnerable will continue to fight back with the only resources they have—gossip, rumors, or rebuttals and resistance to "modern laws." In this way, they settle accounts, albeit obliquely, with the "situation of emergency" that continues to exist for them in this time of economic and democratic readjustments. These subaltern lives manifest their consciousness of the real and unjust processes of social exclusion/inclusion at work in the everyday, and articulate their own ethical categories and political stances in the face of the "consuming" demands which value their bodies most at the point they can be claimed by the State as "brain dead" and therefore as a reservoir of spare parts. While to transplant surgeons and to body dealers an organ is just an organ, a heart is just a pump, and a kidney is just a filter, a thing, a commodity better used than wasted, to vast numbers of ordinary people an organ is something else—a lively, animate, spiritualized part of the self that most would still like to take with them when they die.

Notes

1. I refer to this as a "dangerous" topic advisedly. The global "organs trade" is extensive, extremely lucrative, explicitly illegal in the legal codes of most countries, unethical according to every governing body of medical, professional life, and therefore, covert. The organs trade links elite surgeons and technicians from the upper reaches of bio-medical practice to "body mafia" from the lowest reaches of the criminal world. The practice involves complicity or, at least, by-stander "passivity" from within the ranks of police, mortuary workers, pathologists, civil servants, ambulance drivers, emergency room workers, eye bank and blood bank managers, and transplant coordinators. Although I have been harassed in the field before with respect to other research projects, this is the first time when in the course of my investigations into various aspects of global traffic (organs and babies) in the interior of Brazil I was warned by a close friend of being followed by a possible "hit man" representing a local (and deeply implicated) Judge, forcing me to leave the site earlier than intended.
2. The original Sidney Mintz lecture, "Small Wars: the End of Childhood," was based on my introduction to the co-edited (with Carolyn Sargent) volume, *Small Wars: the Cultural Politics of Childhood* (University of California Press) which is slated to appear in November 1998. I gratefully acknowledge the initial critical reading of that text by Richard Fox and Sidney Mintz.
3. Saalahudeen and his colleagues (1990) noted the poor medical outcomes for the large number of patients who travelled from the Gulf States to India for organ transplants in the 1980s.

POSTSCRIPT

Should Markets Be Allowed to Solve the Shortage in Body Parts?

As Carlstrom and Rollow suggest, there are some interesting parallels between the price controls and rationing that were used to contain the surge in fuel prices after OPEC flexed its muscles in the 1970s and the initial adjustments to the current shortage of body parts. As the price of fossil fuels increased and the lines outside of filling stations lengthened, alternative sources of energy began to appear in the marketplace.

If the price of kidneys, hearts, lungs, and other transplantable organs remains high, will the development of artificial organs continue? Will the practice of transplanting organs taken from other species, such as pig hearts, into humans be perfected and more generally accepted? Will the cloning of human body parts become as widespread as the raising of antibiotic cultures in laboratories?

But even if there is a universal acceptance of "human meat markets," existing law prohibits it. In 1987 Congress revised the National Organ Transplant Act to explicitly bar the sale of human organs. Should that ban be lifted, as Carlstrom and Rollow argue? They are not alone in their attempts to legalize the sale of transplantable organs; others also support the move to create a market for body parts. Indeed, the support is widespread in the Libertarian community. Perhaps the most vocal advocate is the Cato Institute (`www.cato.org`), but advocacy does not end there. Former Delaware governor Pete du Pont, who serves as policy chair of the National Center for Policy Analysis, has also endorsed this position. A number of Web sites support the views of Carlstrom and Rollow. See Organ Keeper (`http://www.organkeeper.com`); Organ Sales.com (`http://www.organsales.com`); and the Organ Selling Homepage (`http://web. pitt.edu/~htk/`).

Those who are opposed to selling organs cringe at the thought of replacing the donor system with a vendor system. In another essay by Scheper-Hughes, "Theft of Life: The Globalization of Organ Stealing Rumors," *Anthropology Today* (June 1996), the author explores the possibility of organ theft as the high price of organs and a market to sell them in become ever more present. Many people assert that the inequities that currently exist between whites and ethnic minorities would increase sharply if society moved to a market system for the allocation of human organs. H. Leon Hewitt provides an extensive bibliography on this subject at the Web site Negative Effects of Organ Transplants, sponsored by the Institute on Race, Health Care and the Law, at `http://www.udayton.edu/~health/03access/98hewitt.htm`.

ISSUE 6

Is It Time to Reform Medical Malpractice Litigation?

YES: U.S. Department of Health and Human Services, from "Confronting the New Health Care Crisis: Improving Health Care Quality and Lowering Costs by Fixing Our Medical Liability System" (July 24, 2002)

NO: Jackson Williams, from "Bush's Medical Malpractice Disinformation Campaign: A Rebuttal to the HHS Report on Medical Liability," A Report of Public Citizen's Congress Watch (January 2003)

ISSUE SUMMARY

YES: The U.S. Department of Health and Human Services (HHS) argues that although the United States has a health care system that "is the envy of the world," it is a system that is about to be brought to its knees by aggressive attorneys who force the medical community to practice costly "defensive medicine."

NO: Jackson Williams, legal counsel for the watchdog group Public Citizen, charges that the position taken by the HHS is factually "incorrect, incomplete, or misleading" and even contradicted by other governmental agencies.

The headline reads, "Princeton Senior Permanently Disabled." The newspaper story reveals that honor student John Francis slipped on the icy steps of the Harvey S. Firestone Memorial Library after the ice storm that swept through central New Jersey. Francis was rushed to Pokagon Hospital, where emergency surgery was required to repair his ruptured spleen. Unfortunately, Francis failed to recover his strength and vitality after the surgery. He visited the campus infirmary, where X-rays of the surgery site revealed a silhouette of a silver object in his abdominal cavity. When Francis took the X-rays to his surgeon, it was clear that a retractor had been left behind. That is not the end of this tragic story, however. During surgery to remove this foreign object, it was discovered that the retractor had caused the growth of flesh-eating bacteria: necrotizing faciitis. The damage was severe indeed; this once avid tennis player is now permanently disabled. He will be confined to a wheelchair for the rest of his life.

The question that this news article raises is the fundamental question addressed in this issue. Francis has been irreversibly damaged by a medical mistake. The liability seems clear: someone left the retractor behind, and the presence of this foreign object has caused flesh-eating bacteria to grow and invade an otherwise healthy body.

So what is owed to Francis? Few would challenge a demand to be compensated for the explicit costs he incurred: the additional medical expenditures, his wheelchair, and perhaps the costs associated with the extra semester he will spend earning his undergraduate degree. Then there is the "gray area." What of his future employment? Although Francis can be gainfully employed, are his options now limited? If his options are limited, should he be compensated for the fact that he cannot become the tennis pro he wanted to be but must now resign himself to being a stockbroker? Is he entitled to receive compensation for the pain and suffering he will endure for the rest of his life?

It is important to note that "medical misadventures" are few and far between, given the number of medical procedures that occur annually in the United States. The U.S. medical care industry is universally regarded as the best in the world. Thousands and thousands of individuals each year undergo medical procedures in the United States. Since physicians are human, however, mistakes are made. The number of people who suffer the consequences of these mistakes is a tiny fraction of those who seek medical relief, but that number is not inconsequential. Some estimate that in 2003 alone, nearly 100,000 will die of a medical misstep. A surprising number of other surgical procedures will result in some foreign object being left behind the sutures; in fact, it is estimated that in 2003, some 1,500 retractors, gauze pads, sponges, etc., will be left behind. Consequently, Francis is not alone in facing the lifelong aftereffects of a surgery gone wrong.

In light of rapidly rising medical insurance rates, it is fair to ask what underlies those rate increases. The medical community and the medical insurance industry, backed by the George W. Bush administration, allege that jury awards for "pain and suffering" are excessive and unreasonable and that they undermine the foundations of the medical industry. Attorneys for those who are impacted by alleged medical misadventures respond that the skyrocketing medical insurance rates are not the result of jury awards and court settlements; rather, they can be traced to insurance companies that have been mismanaged and the recent decline in interest rates in the U.S. economy at large.

The following selections exhibit vastly different views as to why medical malpractice insurance rates are increasing. The U.S. Department of Health and Human Services points a finger at extreme jury awards in medical malpractice cases, arguing that these awards drive the price of malpractice insurance beyond the reach of some practitioners. As a result, these doctors must either increase their fees, which reduces accessibility, or they must begin to practice "defensive medicine"—prescribing redundant medicines, making unnecessary referrals to specialists, and recommending too many invasive procedures. Jackson Williams accuses the HHS of disinformation, concluding that medical malpractice insurance rates are rising not because of jury awards but because of poor management decisions on the part of insurance companies.

U.S. Department of Health and Human Services

YES

Confronting the New Health Care Crisis

American health care is the envy of the world, but with rapidly rising health care costs, reforms are needed to make high-quality, affordable health care more widely available. These include new approaches to making employer-provided coverage more affordable, new initiatives to help states expand Medicaid and S-CHIP [State Children's Health Insurance Program] coverage for lower-income persons, and new policies including health insurance credits for persons who do not have access to employer or public health insurance. A critical element for enabling all of these reforms to provide real relief, and to help all Americans get access to better and more affordable health care, is curbing excessive litigation.

Americans spend proportionately far more per person on the costs of litigation than any other country in the world. The excesses of the litigation system are an important contributor to "defensive medicine"—the costly use of medical treatments by a doctor for the purpose of avoiding litigation. As multimillion-dollar jury awards have become more commonplace in recent years, these problems have reached crisis proportions. Insurance premiums for malpractice are increasing at a rapid rate, particularly in states that have not taken steps to make their legal systems function more predictably and effectively. Doctors are facing much higher costs of insurance, and some cannot obtain insurance despite having never lost a single malpractice judgment or even faced a claim.

This is a threat to health care quality for all Americans. Increasingly, Americans are at risk of not being able to find a doctor when they most need one because the doctor has given up practice, limited the practice to patients without health conditions that would increase the litigation risk, or moved to a state with a fairer legal system where insurance can be obtained at a lower price.

This broken system of litigation is also raising the cost of health care that all Americans pay, through out-of-pocket payments, insurance premiums, and federal taxes. Excessive litigation is impeding efforts to improve quality of care. Hospitals, doctors, and nurses are reluctant to report problems and participate in joint efforts to improve care because they fear being dragged into lawsuits, even if they did nothing wrong.

From U.S. Department of Health and Human Services, Office of the Assistant Secretary for Planning and Evaluation, "Confronting the New Health Care Crisis: Improving Health Care Quality and Lowering Costs by Fixing Our Medical Liability System" (July 24, 2002). Notes omitted.

Increasingly extreme judgments in a small proportion of cases and the settlements they influence are driving this litigation crisis. At the same time, most injured patients receive no compensation. Some states have already taken action to squeeze the excesses out of the litigation system. But federal action, in conjunction with further action by states, is essential to help Americans get high-quality care when they need it, at a more affordable cost.

Access to Care Is Threatened

There are a number of obstacles that limit access to affordable health care in this country, including lack of affordable insurance and an outdated Medicare program. We now face another—the litigation crisis that has made insurance premiums unaffordable or even unavailable for many doctors, through no fault of their own. This is making it more difficult for many Americans to find care, and threatening access for many more.

- Nevada is facing unprecedented problems in assuring quick access to urgently needed care. The University of Nevada Medical Center closed its trauma center in Las Vegas for ten days earlier this month [July 2002]. Its surgeons had quit because they could no longer afford malpractice insurance. Their premiums had increased sharply, some from $40,000 to $200,000. The trauma center was able to re-open only because some of the surgeons agreed to become county government employees for a limited time, which capped their liability for non-economic damages if they were sued. This is obviously only a temporary solution. If the Las Vegas trauma center closes again, the most severely injured patients will have to be transported to the next nearest Level 1 trauma center, five hours away. Access to trauma care is only one problem Nevada faces; access to obstetrics and many other types of care is also threatened.
- Overall, more than 10% of all doctors in Las Vegas are expected to retire, or relocate their practices by this summer. For example, Dr. Cheryl Edwards, 41, closed her decade-old obstetrics and gynecology practice in Las Vegas because her insurance premium jumped from $37,000 to $150,000 a year. She moved her practice to West Los Angeles, leaving 30 pregnant women to find new doctors.
- Dr. Frank Jordan, a vascular surgeon, in Las Vegas, left practice. "I did the math. If I were to stay in business for three years, it would cost me $1.2 million for insurance. I obviously can't afford that. I'd be bankrupt after the first year, and I'd just be working for the insurance company. What's the point?"
- Other states are facing the same problem. A doctor in a small town in North Carolina decided to take early retirement when his premiums skyrocketed from $7,500 to $37,000 per year. His partner, unable to afford the practice expenses by himself, may now close the practice, and work at a teaching hospital.
- Pennsylvania physicians are also leaving their practices. About 44 doctors at the height of their careers in Delaware County outside Philadelphia left the state in 2001 or stopped practicing medicine because of high malpractice insurance costs. . . .

Patient Safety Is Jeopardized

Because the litigation system does not accurately judge whether an error was committed in the course of medical care, physicians adjust their behavior to avoid being sued. A recent survey of physicians revealed that one-third shied away from going into a particular specialty because they feared it would subject them to greater liability exposure. When in practice, they engage in defensive medicine to protect themselves against suit. They perform tests and provide treatments that they would not otherwise perform merely to protect themselves against the risk of possible litigation. The survey revealed that over 76% are concerned that malpractice litigation has hurt their ability to provide quality care to patients.

Because of the resulting legal fear:

- 79% said that they had ordered more tests than they would, based only on professional judgment of what is medically needed, and 91% have noticed other physicians ordering more tests;
- 74% have referred patients to specialists more often than they belived was medically necessary;
- 51% have recommended invasive procedures such as biopsies to confirm diagnoses more often than they believed was medically necessary; and
- 41% said that they had prescribed more medications, such as antibiotics, than they would based only on their professional judgment, and 73% have noticed other doctors similarly prescribing excessive medications.

Every test and every treatment poses a risk to the patient, and takes away funds that could better be used to provide health care to those who need it.

Physicians' understandable fear of unwarranted litigation threatens patient safety in another way. It impedes efforts of physicians and researchers to improve the quality of care. As medical care becomes increasingly complex, there are many opportunities for improving the quality and safety of medical care, and reducing its costs, through better medical practices. According to some experts, these quality improvement opportunities hold the promise of not only significant improvements in patient health outcomes, but also reductions in medical costs of as much as 30%. . . .

However, these efforts and other efforts are impeded and discouraged by the lack of clear and comprehensive protection for collaborative quality efforts. Doctors are reluctant to collect quality-related information and work together to act on it for fear that it will be used against them or their colleagues in a lawsuit. Perhaps as many as 95% of adverse events are believed to go unreported. To make quality improvements, doctors must be able to exchange information about patient care and how it can be improved—what is the effect of care not just in one particular institution or of the care provided by one doctor—but how the patient fares in the system across all providers. These quality efforts require enhancements to information and reporting systems.

In its recent report, "To Err is Human," the Institute of Medicine (IOM) observed that, "[R]eporting systems are an important part of improving patient safety and should be encouraged. These voluntary reporting systems [should] periodically assess whether additional efforts are needed to address gaps in information to improve patient safety and to encourage health care organizations to participate in . . . reporting, and track the development of new reporting systems as they form."

However, as the IOM emphasized, fear that information from these reporting systems will be used to prepare a lawsuit against them, even if they are not negligent, deters doctors and hospitals from making reports. This fear, which is understandable in the current litigation climate, impedes quality improvement efforts. According to many experts, the "#1 barrier" to more effective quality improvement systems in health care organizations is fear of creating new avenues of liability by conducting earnest analyses of how health care can be improved. Without protection, quality discussions to improve health care provide fodder for litigants to find ways to assert that the status quo is deficient. Doctors are busy, and they face many pressures. They will be reluctant to engage in health care improvement efforts if they think that reports they make and recommendations they make will be thrown back at them or others in litigation. Quality improvement efforts must be protected if we are to obtain the full benefit of doctors' experience in improving the quality of health care.

The IOM Report emphasized the importance of shifting the inquiry from individuals to the systems in which they work: "The focus must shift from blaming individuals for past errors to a focus on preventing future errors by designing safety into the system." But the litigation system impedes this progress—not only because fear of litigation deters reporting but also because the scope of the litigation system's view is restricted. The litigation system looks at the past, not the future, and focuses on the individual in an effort to assess blame rather than considering how improvements can be made in the system. "Tort law's overly emotional and individualized approach . . . has been a tragic failure."

Health Care Costs Are Increased

The litigation and malpractice insurance problem raids the wallet of every American. Money spent on malpractice premiums (and the litigation costs that largely determine premiums) raises health care costs. Doctors alone spent $6.3 billion last year to obtain coverage. Hospitals and nursing homes spent additional billions of dollars.

The litigation system also imposes large indirect costs on the health care system. Defensive medicine that is caused by unlimited and unpredictable liability awards not only increases patients' risk but it also adds costs. The leading study estimates that limiting unreasonable awards for non-economic damages could reduce health care costs by 5–9% without adversely affecting quality of care. This would save $60–108 billion in health care costs each year. These savings would lower the cost of health insurance and permit an additional 2.4–4.3 million Americans to obtain insurance.

The costs of the runaway litigation system are paid by all Americans, through higher premiums for health insurance (which reduces workers' take home pay if the insurance is provided by an employer), higher out-of-pocket payments when they obtain care, and higher taxes.

The Federal Government—and thus every taxpayer who pays federal income and payroll taxes—also pays for health care, in a number of ways. It provides direct care, for instance, to members of the armed forces, veterans, and patients served by the Indian Health Service. It provides funding for the Medicare and Medicaid programs. It funds Community Health Centers. It also provides assistance, through the tax system, for workers who obtain insurance through their employment. The direct cost of malpractice coverage and the indirect cost of defensive medicine increases the amount the Federal Government must pay through these various channels, it is estimated, by $28.6–47.5 billion per year. If reasonable limits were placed on non-economic damages to reduce defensive medicine, it would reduce the amount of taxpayers' money the Federal Government spends by $25.3–44.3 billion per year. This is a very significant amount. It would more than fund a prescription drug benefit for Medicare beneficiaries *and* help uninsured Americans obtain coverage through a refundable health credit.

The Increasingly Unpredictable, Costly, and Slow Litigation System Is Responsible

Insurance premiums are largely determined by the expensive litigation system. The malpractice insurance system and the litigation system are inexorably linked. The litigation system is expensive, but, at the same time, it is slow and provides little benefit to patients who are injured by medical error. Its application is unpredictable, largely random, and standardless. It is traumatic for all involved.

Most victims of medical error do not file a claim—one comprehensive study found that only 1.53% of those who were injured by medical negligence even filed a claim. Most claims—57–70%—result in no payment to the patient. When a patient does decide to go into the litigation system, only a very small number recover anything. One study found that only 8–13% of cases filed went to trial; and only 1.2–1.9% resulted in a decision for the plaintiff.

Although most cases do not actually go to trial, it costs a significant amount of money to defend each claim—an average of $24,669. The most dramatic cost, however, is the cost of the few cases that result in huge jury awards. Even though few cases result in these awards, they encourage lawyers and plaintiffs in the hope that they can win this litigation lottery, and they influence every settlement that is entered into.

A large proportion of these awards is not to compensate injured patients for their economic loss—such as wage loss, health care costs, and replacing services the injured patient can longer perform (such as child care). Instead, much of the judgment (in some cases, particularly the largest judgments, perhaps 50% or more) is for non-economic damages. Awarded on top of compensation for the injured patient's actual economic loss, non-economic damages are said to be compensation for intangible losses, such as pain and suffering, loss of consortium, hedonic (loss of the enjoyment of life) damages, and various other theories that are imaginatively created by lawyers to increase the amount awarded.

Non-economic damages are an effort to compensate a plaintiff with money for what are in reality non-monetary considerations. The theories on which these awards are made however, are entirely subjective and without any standards. As one scholar has observed: "The perceived problem of pain and suffering awards is not simply the amount of money expended, but also the erratic nature of the process by which the size of the awards is determined. Juries are simply told to apply their 'enlightened conscience' in selecting a monetary figure they consider to be fair."

Unless a state has adopted limitations on non-economic damages, the system gives juries a blank check to award huge damages based on sympathy, attractiveness of the plaintiff, and the plaintiff's socio-economic status (educated, attractive patients recover more than others).

The cost of these awards for non-economic damages is paid by all other Americans through higher health care costs, higher health insurance premiums, higher taxes, reduced access to quality care, and threats to quality of care. The system permits a few plaintiffs and their lawyers to impose what is in effect a tax on the rest of the country to reward a very small number of patients who happen to win the litigation lottery. It is not a democratic process.

The number of mega-verdicts is increasing rapidly. The average award rose 76% from 1996–1999. The median award in 1999 was $800,000, a 6.7% increase over the 1998 figure of $750,000; and between 1999 and 2000, median malpractice awards increased nearly 43%. Specific physician specialties have seen disproportionate increases, especially those who deliver babies. In the small proportion of cases where damages were awarded, the median award in cases involving obstetricians and gynecologists jumped 43% in one year, from $700,000 in 1999 to $1,000,000 in 2000.

The number of million dollar plus awards has increased dramatically in recent years. In the period 1994–1996, 34% of all verdicts that specified damages assessed awards of $1 million or more. This increased by 50% in four years; in 1999-2000, 52% of all awards were in excess of $1 million. There have been 21 verdicts of $9 million or more in Mississippi since 1995—one of $100,000,000. Before 1995 there had been no awards in excess of $9,000,000.

These mega-awards for non-economic damages have occurred (as would be expected) in states that do not have limitations on the amounts that can be recovered. . . .

Mirroring the increase in jury awards, settlement payments have steadily risen over the last two decades. The average payment per paid claim increased from approximately $110,000 in 1987 to $250,000 in 1999. Defense expenses per paid claim increased by $24,000 over the same period.

The winning lottery ticket in litigation, however, is not as attractive as it may seem at first blush. A plaintiff who wins a judgment must pay the lawyer 30–40% of it, and sometimes even more. Lawyers, therefore, have an interest in finding the most attractive case. They develop a portfolio of cases and have an incentive to gamble on a big "win." If only one results in a huge verdict, they have had a good payday. Thus, they have incentives to pursue cases to the end in the hope of winning the lottery, even when their client would be satisfied by a settlement that would make them whole economically. The result of the contingency fee arrangement is that lawyers have few incentives to take on the more difficult cases or those of less attractive patients.

One prominent personal injury trial lawyer explained the secret of his success: "The appearance of the plaintiff [is] number one in attempting to evaluate a lawsuit because I think that a good healthy-appearing type, one who would be likeable and one that the jury is going to want to do something for, can make your case worth double at least for what it would be otherwise and a bad-appearing plaintiff could make the case worth perhaps half . . ."

For most injured patients, therefore, the litigation process, while offering the remote chance of a jackpot judgment, provides little real benefit, even for those who file claims and pursue them. Even successful claimants do not recover anything on average until five years after the injury, longer if the case goes to trial.

The friction generated by operating the system takes most of the money. When doctors and hospitals buy insurance (sometimes they are required to buy coverage that provides more "protection" than the total amount of their assets), it is intended to compensate victims of malpractice for their loss. However, only 28% of what they pay for insurance coverage actually goes to patients; 72% is spent on legal, administrative, and related costs. Less than half of the money that does go back to injured patients is used to compensate the patient for economic loss that is not compensated from other sources—the purpose of a compensation system. More than half of the amount the plaintiff receives duplicates other sources of compensation the patient may have (such as health insurance) and goes for subjective, non-economic damages (a large part of which, moreover, actually goes to the plaintiff's lawyer).

The malpractice system does not accurately identify negligence, deter bad conduct, or provide justice. The results it obtains are unpredictable, even random. The same study that found that only 1.53% of patients who were injured by medical error filed a claim also found, on the flip side, that most events for which claims were filed did not constitute negligence. Other studies show the same random results. "The evidence is growing that there is a poor correlation between injuries caused by negligent medical treatment and malpractice litigation."

Not surprisingly, most people involved in health care delivery on a day-to-day basis believe that the system does not accurately reflect the realities of health care or correctly identify malpractice. A recent survey indicated that 83% of physicians and 72% of hospital administrators do not believe the system achieves a reasonable result. . . .

Insurance Premiums Are Rising Rapidly

The cost of the excesses of the litigation system shows up in the cost of malpractice insurance coverage. Premiums have increased rapidly over the past several years. Experts believe we are seeing just the tip of what will happen this year and next. Rates have escalated rapidly for doctors who practice internal medicine, general surgery, and obstetrics/gynecology. The average increases ranged from 11% to 17% in 2000, were about 10% in 2001, but are accelerating rapidly. . . . A recent special report revealed that rate increases are averaging 20%.

However, these increases have varied widely across states, and some states have experienced increases of 30–75%, although there is no evidence that patient care had worsened. . . . [A] major contributing factor to the most enormous increases in liability premiums has been rapidly growing awards for non-economic damages in states that have not reformed their litigation system to put reasonable standards on these awards.

Among the states with the highest average medical malpractice insurance premiums are Florida, Illinois, Ohio, Nevada, New York, and West Virginia. These states have not reformed their litigation systems as others have. (Florida's caps apply only in limited circumstances. New York has prevented insurers from raising rates, and accordingly it is expected that substantial increases will be needed in 2003.) . . .

The effect of these premiums on what patients must pay for care can be seen from an example involving obstetrical care. The vast majority of awards against obstetricians involve poor outcomes at childbirth. As a result, payouts for poor infant outcomes account for the bulk of obstetricians' insurance costs. If an obstetrician delivers 100 babies per year (which is roughly the national average) and the malpractice premium is $200,000 annually (as it is in Florida), each mother (or the government or her employer who provides her health insurance) must pay approximately $2,000 merely to pay her share of her obstetrician's liability insurance. If a physician delivers 50 babies per year, the cost for malpractice premiums per baby is twice as high, about $4,000. It is not surprising that expectant mothers are finding their doctors have left states that support litigation systems imposing these costs.

In addition to premium increases for physicians, nursing home malpractice costs are rising rapidly because of dramatic increases in both the number of lawsuits and the size of awards. Nursing homes are a new target of the litigation system. Between 1995 and 2001, the national average of insurance costs increased from $240 per occupied skilled nursing bed per year to $2,360. From 1990 to 2001, the average size of claims tripled, and the number of claims increased from 3.6 to 11 per 1,000 beds.

These costs vary widely across states, again in relation to whether a state has implemented reforms that improve the predictability of the legal system. Florida ($11,000) had one of the highest per bed costs in 2001. Nursing homes in Mississippi have been faced with increases as great as 900% in the past two years. It has been recently reported that "nearly all companies that used to write nursing home liability [insurance] are getting out of the business." Since the costs of nursing home care are mainly paid by Medicaid and Medicare, these increased costs are borne by taxpayers, and consume resources that could otherwise be used to expand health (or other) programs.

Insurers Are Leaving the Market

The litigation crisis is affecting patients' ability to get care not only because many doctors find the increased premiums unaffordable but also because liability insurance is increasingly difficult to obtain at any price, particularly in nonreform states. Demonstrating and exacerbating the problem, several major carriers have stopped selling malpractice insurance.

- St. Paul Companies, which was the largest malpractice carrier in the United States, covering 9% of doctors, announced in December 2001 that it would no longer offer coverage to any doctor in the country.
- MIXX pulled out of every state; it will reorganize and sell only in New Jersey.
- PHICO and Frontier Insurance Group have also left the medical malpractice market.
- Doctors Insurance Reciprocal stopped writing group specialty coverage at the beginning of 2002.

States that had not enacted meaningful reforms (such as Nevada, Georgia, Oregon, Mississippi, Ohio, Pennsylvania, and Washington) were particularly affected. Fifteen insurers have left the Mississippi market in the past five years.

States With Realistic Limits on Non-Economic Damages Are Faring Better

The insurance crisis is less acute in states that have reformed their litigation systems. States with limits of $250,000 or $350,000 on non-economic damages have average combined highest premium increases of 12–15%, compared to 44% in states without caps on non-economic damages. . . .

As Table 1 shows, there is a substantial difference in the level of medical malpractice premiums in states with meaningful caps, such as California, Wisconsin, Montana, Utah and Hawaii, and states without meaningful caps.

In the early 1970s, California faced an access crisis like that facing many states now and threatening others. With bi-partisan support, including leadership from then Governor Jerry Brown and now Congressman Henry Waxman, then chairman of the Assembly's Select Committee on Medical Malpractice, California enacted comprehensive changes to make its medical liability system more predictable and rational. The Medical Injury Compensation Reform Act of 1975 (MICRA) made a number of reforms, including:

- Placing a $250,000 limit on non-economic damages while continuing unlimited compensation for economic damages.

Table 1

Malpractice Liability Rate Ranges by Specialty by Geography as of July 2001

	Cap in Non-Economic Damages	Low	High
INTERNISTS			
State Wide Data			
Wisconsin	$350,000	$5,000	$6,000
Montana	$250,000	5,300	7,000
Utah	$250,000	5,900	5,900
Hawaii	$350,000	6,800	6,800
Connecticut	No cap	6,200	15,800
Washington	No cap	7,100	9,000
Metropolitan Area Data			
California (Los Angeles area)	$250,000	$7,900	$13,000
Pennsylvania (Urban Philadelphia area)	No cap	10,700	11,800
Nevada (Las Vegas area)	No cap	11,600	15,800
Illinois (Chicagoland area)	No cap	16,500	28,100
Florida (Miami and Ft. Lauderdale areas)*	No cap	17,600	50,700
GENERAL SURGEONS			
State Wide Data			
Wisconsin (state wide)	$350,000	$16,000	$17,500
Montana (state wide)	$250,000	23,300	27,000
Utah (state wide)	$250,000	26,200	26,200
Hawaii (state wide)	$350,000	24,500	24,500
Connecticut (state wide)	No cap	26,200	45,800
Washington (state wide)	No cap	20,100	32,600
Metropolitan Area Data			
California (Los Angeles area)	$250,000	$23,700	$42,200
Pennsylvania (Urban Philadelphia area)	No cap	31,500	35,800
Nevada (Las Vegas area)	No cap	40,300	56,900
Illinois (Chicagoland area)	No cap	50,000	70,200
Florida (Miami and Ft. Lauderdale areas)*	No cap	63,200	126,600
OBSTETRICIANS/GYNECOLOGISTS			
State Wide Data			
Wisconsin (state wide)	$350,000	$23,800	$27,500
Montana (state wide)	$250,000	36,000	38,600
Hawaii (state wide)	$350,000	40,900	40,900
Utah (state wide)	$250,000	44,300	44,300
Connecticut (state wide)	No cap	45,400	64,800
Washington (state wide)	No cap	34,100	59,300

(continued)

Table 1 (Continued)

	Cap in Non-Economic Damages	Low	High
Metropolitan Area Data			
California (Los Angeles area)	$250,000	$46,900	$57,700
Pennsylvania (Urban Philadelphia area)	No cap	45,900	66,300
Nevada (Las Vegas area)	No cap	71,100	94,800
Illinois (Chicagoland area)	No cap	72,500	110,100
Florida (Miami and Ft. Lauderdale areas)*	No cap	108,000	208,900

Source: Medical Liability Monitor, Vol. 26, No. 10, October 2001: Shook, Hardy, Bacon, L.L.P., October 9, 2001.

*Florida imposes caps of $250,000–350,000 unless neither party demands binding arbitration or the defendant refuses to arbitrate.

- Shortening the time in which lawsuits could be brought to three years (thus ensuring that memories would still be fresh and providing some assurance to doctors that they would not be sued years after an event that they may well have forgotten).
- Providing for periodic payment of damages to ensure the money is available to the patient in the future.

California has more than 25 years of experience with this reform. It has been a success. Doctors are not leaving California. Insurance premiums have risen much more slowly than in the rest of the country without any effect on the quality of care received by residents of California. Insurance premiums in California have risen by 167% over this period while those in the rest of the country have increased 505%. This has saved California residents billions of dollars in health care costs and saved federal taxpayers billions of dollars in the Medicare and Medicaid programs.

The President's Framework for Improving the Medical Liability System

Federal and state action is needed to address the impact of the medical liability crisis on health care costs and the quality of care.

Achieving a Fair, Predictable, and Timely Medical Liability Process

As years of experience in many states have proven, reasonable limits on the amount of non-economic damages that are awarded significantly restrain increases in the cost of malpractice premiums. These reforms improve the predictability of the medical liability system, reducing incentives for filing frivolous suits and for prolonged litigation. Greater predictability and more timely resolution of cases means patients who are injured can get fair compensation more quickly. They also reduce health care costs, enabling Americans to get more from their health care spending and enabling federal health programs to provide more relief. They improve access to care, by making insurance more affordable and available. They also improve the quality of health care, by avoiding unnecessary "defensive" treatments and enabling doctors to spend significantly more time focusing on patient care. Congress needs to enact legislation that would give all Americans the benefit of these reforms, eliminate the excesses of the litigation system, and protect patients' ability to get care.

The President [George W. Bush] supports federal reforms in medical liability law that would implement these proven steps for improving our health care system:

- Improve the ability of all patients who are injured by negligence to get quicker, unlimited compensation for their "economic losses," including the loss of the ability to provide valuable unpaid services like care for children or a parent.
- Ensure that recoveries for non-economic damages could not exceed a reasonable amount ($250,000).
- Reserve punitive damages for cases that justify them—where there is clear and convincing proof that the defendant acted with malicious intent or deliberately failed to avoid unnecessary injury to the patient—and avoid unreasonable awards (anything in excess of the greater of two times economic damages or $250,000).
- Provide for payment of a judgment over time rather than in one lump sum—and thus ensure that the money is there for the injured patient when needed.
- Ensure that old cases cannot be brought years after an event when medical standards may have changed or witnesses' memories have faded, by providing that a case may not be brought more than three years following the date or injury or one year after the claimant discovers or, with reasonable diligence, should have discovered the injury.
- Informing the jury if a plaintiff also has another source of payment for the injury, such as health insurance.
- Provide that defendants pay any judgment in proportion to their fault, not on the basis of how deep their pockets are.

The success of the states that have adopted reforms like these shows that malpractice premiums could be reduced by 34% by adopting these reforms. The savings to the Federal Government resulting from reduced malpractice premiums would be $1.68 billion.

Legislation such as H.R. 4600—a bill introduced by Congressman Jim Greenwood [R-Pennsylvania] with almost 100 bipartisan cosponsors—is now pending in Congress. Enactment of this legislation with improvements to ensure that its meaningful standards will apply nationally, will be a significant step toward the goals of affordable, high-quality health care for all Americans, and a fair and predictable liability system for compensating injured patients.

In addition, there are other promising approaches for compensating patients injured by negligence fairly and without requiring them to go through full-scale, time-consuming, and expensive litigation. Just as states like California have demonstrated the effectiveness of litigation reforms, they should also adopt and evaluate the impact of alternatives to litigation.

Early Offers is one innovative approach. This would provide a new set of balanced incentives to encourage doctors to make offers, quickly after an injury, to compensate the patient for economic loss, and for patients to accept. It would make it possible for injured patients to receive fair compensation quickly, and over time if any further losses are incurred, without having to enter into the litigation fray. Because doctors and hospitals would have an incentive to discover adverse events quickly in order to make a qualifying offer, it would lead to prompt identification of quality problems. The money that otherwise would be spent in conducting litigation would be recycled so that more patients get additional recovery, more quickly, with savings left over to the benefit of all Americans. It may also be possible to implement an administrative form of Early Offers as an option for care provided under federal health programs.

A second innovative approach involves strengthening medical review boards. Boards with special expertise in the technical intricacies of health care can streamline the fact-gathering and hearing process, make decisions more accurately, and provide compensation more quickly and predictably than the current litigation process. As with Early Offers, incentives are necessary for patients and health care providers to submit cases to the boards and to accept their decisions.

The Administration intends to work with states on developing and implementing these alternatives to litigation, so that injured patients can be fairly compensated quickly and without the trauma and expense that litigation entails.

NO 

Jackson Williams

Bush's Medical Malpractice Disinformation Campaign

Introduction

The medical community continues to tout a report, *Confronting the New Health Care Crisis: Improving Health Care Quality and Lowering Costs by Fixing Our Medical Liability System,* issued by the Department of Health and Human Services [HHS] last summer [2002] as making an overwhelming case for medical liability "reform." In truth, a cursory examination of the report finds it to be a classic "clip job"—a collection of anecdotes, reports, and propaganda provided by lobbyists and stamped with the government's official imprimatur. The report cites such sources as Fox News Channel, Congressman Chip Pickering, and the Physician Insurers Association of America, the trade group leading the lobbying campaign. *It contains no new research nor any data generated by government health care experts or economists.*

A more intensive examination of the report shows that most of the "facts" it provides are incorrect, incomplete, or misleading; and that its conclusions are contradicted by those of other government agencies. . . .

The Bush Administration Says: "Access to Care Is Threatened"

> *"There are a number of obstacles that limit access to affordable health care in this country, including lack of affordable insurance and an outdated Medicare program. We now face another—the litigation crisis that has made insurance premiums unaffordable or even unavailable for many doctors, through no fault of their own. This is making it more difficult for many Americans to find care, and threatening access for many more. Dr. Cheryl Edwards, 41, closed her decade-old obstetrics and gynecology practice in Las Vegas because her insurance premium jumped from $37,000 to $150,000 a year. She moved her practice to West Los Angeles, leaving 30 pregnant women to find new doctors."*
>
> *The Facts: Malpractice insurance costs are a miniscule part of a doctor's expenses and don't affect decisions about where to practice medicine.*

From Jackson Williams, "Bush's Medical Malpractice Disinformation Campaign: A Rebuttal to the HHS Report on Medical Liability," A Report of Public Citizen's Congress Watch (January 2003).

- *There is a greater likelihood of doctors withdrawing from practice due to increases in their office rents or payroll costs than due to increases in malpractice insurance costs.* While there is a temporary spike in medical malpractice insurance rates due to insurance industry economics, it is necessary to look at the larger and longer-term picture. Specifically, while physicians spend about 3.2 percent of their gross income on medical malpractice costs, they spend 17 percent on payroll costs and 5.8 percent on office rent. According to the Medicare Payment Advisory Commission (MedPAC), the average increase in medical malpractice insurance rates last year was 4.4 percent. A doctor who stops practicing because of a malpractice insurance increase would be just as likely to retire due to increased health insurance costs for office staff, or because of increased rent for office space. If increased costs to doctors justify legislative action, they could also justify repeal of wages and hours laws or enactment of rent control laws.
- *Liability laws have no effect on a doctor's decision where to practice.* Even though damage awards are higher in more affluent states, those states still have more doctors. The District of Columbia has the highest average damage award and the most doctors. Idaho, with the fewest doctors, has the third lowest median damage award. While five of the states with the lowest per capita number of doctors have enacted caps on noneconomic damages, only three of the states with the highest number of doctors per capita have enacted them. According to the U.S. Chamber of Commerce, Iowa, Utah, and South Dakota rank 5th, 8th and 9th for "reasonable litigation environment," yet those states rank in the bottom ten in number of doctors. Only one state in the Chamber's legal climate top ten, Connecticut, also ranks in the top ten for doctors. California, whose damage caps supposedly drew Dr. Edwards from Las Vegas, did not add one additional doctor per 100,000 residents between 1990 and 1999, but the number of doctors per 100,000 residents increased in Nevada from 136 to 162 during that period.
- *Two factors explain almost all the variation in the number of doctors in a state: income level and urbanization.* Like anyone else, doctors want to live in places where they can earn high incomes, enjoy cultural and leisure activities, and send their children to good schools. Seven of the top ten states for doctors also rank in the top ten states in percentage of households earning $200,000 or more. Doctors want to live in areas with lots of affluent people—such areas are more likely to have the leafy suburbs, premium housing, clubs, and other amenities that doctors want. For every $1,000 increase in a state's median income for a four-person family, a state will have 2.3 more doctors per 100,000 residents. Doctors migrate to states on lists of "Best Places to Live": Forty of the top 100 cities with "strong arts, cultural programs, and higher education" were in the ten states with the highest per capita number of doctors, while there were none in the ten states with the lowest per capita number of doctors. Polled by the U.S. Chamber of Commerce, 41 percent of West Virginia doctors said that the inability of the state's poor resident to pay fees was responsible for the state's shortage of doctors, and 27 percent said that quality of life in the state was responsible.

- *There is no relationship between the level of increase in liability insurance premiums and the likelihood of discontinuing obstetric practice.* A recent study examined whether New York obstetricians facing higher premiums for obstetric liability insurance were more likely to discontinue practicing than physicians experiencing lower increases in premiums. The study found that the decrease in doctors practicing obstetrics was associated with the length of time since receiving a medical license in New York. This relationship "very likely represents the phenomenon of physicians retiring from practice or curtailing obstetrics as they age."

The Bush Administration Says: "Patient Safety Is Jeopardized"

"In its recent report, 'To Err is Human,' the Institute of Medicine (IOM) observed that, '[R]eporting systems are an important part of improving patient safety and should be encouraged. These voluntary reporting systems [should] periodically assess whether additional efforts are needed to address gaps in information to improve patient safety . . .' However, as the IOM emphasized, fear that information from these reporting systems will be used to prepare a lawsuit against them, even if they are not negligent, deters doctors and hospitals from making reports."

The Facts: Patient safety is enhanced by the tort system; it would be further enhanced by increased regulation of doctors.

- *The Administration's own Council of Economic Advisors said the opposite last year—the tort system increases patient safety.* Even the conservative appointees to the President's Council of Economic Advisors admit, "a patient purchasing a medical procedure, for example, may be unlikely to fully understand the complex risks, costs and benefits of that procedure relative to others. Such a patient must turn to a physician who serves as a 'learned intermediary,' though there remains the problem that the patient may also not be able to judge the skill of the physician from whom the procedure is 'purchased.' In such a case, the ability of the individual to pursue a liability lawsuit in the event of an improper treatment, for example, provides an additional incentive for the physician to follow good medical practice. Indeed, from a broad social perspective, this may be the least costly way to proceed—less costly than trying to educate every consumer fully. In a textbook example, recognition of the expected costs from the liability system causes the provider to undertake the extra effort or care that matches the customer's desire to avoid the risk of harm. This process is what economists refer to as 'internalizing externalities.' In other words, the liability system makes persons who injure others aware of their actions, and provides incentives for them to act appropriately."
- *Patient safety is at risk from medical providers' failure to commit to reducing medical errors.* In 1999 the Institute of Medicine released its report on patient safety in the U.S. The report estimated that between 44,000 and 98,000 Americans die annually as a result of preventable medical errors. The IOM recommended creation of a nationwide *mandatory* reporting system of serious errors—those that result in death or serious

harm—for hospitals, other institutional providers and ambulatory care systems. The IOM argued that such a system is necessary to hold providers accountable for maintaining safety and to implement safety systems that reduce the likelihood of such events occurring. IOM also recommended that health professional licensing conduct periodic re-examinations and re-licensing of doctors, nurses, and other key providers, based on both competence and knowledge of safety practices. Neither of these recommendations has been implemented, due to opposition from the medical community; nor are they mentioned in the HHS report.

- *Patient safety is also at risk from incompetent doctors.* Five percent of doctors are responsible for 54 percent of malpractice in the U.S., according to records in the National Practitioner Data Bank, maintained by HHS. An inquiry to this database, which covers malpractice judgments and settlements since September 1990, found that 5.1 percent of doctors (35,009) have paid two or more malpractice awards to patients. These doctors are responsible for 54 percent of all payouts reported to the Data Bank. Of these, only 7.6 percent have ever been disciplined by state medical boards. Even physicians who have made 5 payouts have been disciplined at only a 13.3 percent rate.

The Bush Administration Says: "Health Care Costs Are Increased"

"The litigation and malpractice insurance problem raids the wallet of every American. Money spent on malpractice premiums (and the litigation costs that largely determine premiums) raises health care costs. The litigation system also imposes large indirect costs on the health care system. Defensive medicine that is caused by unlimited and unpredictable liability awards not only increases patients' risk but it also adds cost . . . The leading study estimates that limiting unreasonable awards for noneconomic damages could reduce health care costs by 5–9% without adversely affecting quality of care. This would save $60–108 billion in health care costs each year."

The Facts: The Congressional Budget Office (CBO) says that limiting liability would have a negligible impact on health care costs.

- *In evaluating the impact of H.R. 4600, which would have severely limited the ability of patients to recover damages, the Congressional Budget Office projected only minimal savings.* This bill, which contained very stringent restrictions on patients' ability to recover damages, passed the U.S. House in 2002. CBO said: "The percentage effect of H.R. 4600 on overall health insurance premiums would be far smaller than the percentage impact on medical malpractice insurance premiums. Malpractice costs account for a very small fraction of total health care spending; even a very large reduction in malpractice costs would have a relatively small effect on total health plan premiums. In addition, some of the savings leading to lower medical malpractice premiums—those savings arising from changes in the treatment of collateral-source benefits—would represent a shift in costs from medical malpractice insurance to health insurance. Because providers of collateral-source benefits would be prevented from recovering their costs arising from the malpractice injury, some of the costs that would be borne by malpractice insurance under current law would instead be borne by the providers of collateral-source benefits. Most such providers are health insurers."

- *The Congressional Budget Office has rejected the "defensive medicine" theory.* CBO was asked to quantify the savings from reduced "defensive medicine" if Congress passed H.R. 4600. CBO declined, saying:

> Estimating the amount of health care spending attributable to defensive medicine is difficult. Most estimates are speculative in nature, relying, for the most part, on surveys of physicians' responses to hypothetical clinical situations, and clinical studies of the effectiveness of certain intensive treatments. Compounding the uncertainty about the magnitude of spending for defensive medicine, there is little empirical evidence on the effect of medical malpractice tort controls on spending for defensive medicine and, more generally, on overall health care spending.
>
> A small number of studies have observed reductions in health care spending correlated with changes in tort law, but that research was based largely on a narrow part of the population and considered only hospital spending for a small number of ailments that are disproportionately likely to experience malpractice claims. Using broader measures of spending, CBO's initial analysis could find no statistically significant connection between malpractice tort limits and overall health care spending. Although the provisions of H.R. 4600 could result in the initiation of fewer lawsuits, the economic incentives for individual physicians or hospitals to practice defensive medicine would appear to be little changed.

- *Overall tort expenditures are less than the cost of medical injuries.* Because so few medical injuries result in compensation to patients, the overall expenditures made for medical liability are far below the projected injury costs. The Institute of Medicine estimated the costs of preventable medical injuries in hospitals alone at between $17 billion and $29 billion a year. The Utah Colorado Medical Practice study estimated it at $20 billion. By contrast, the National Association of Insurance Commissioners reports that the total amount spent on medical malpractice insurance in 2000 was $6.4 billion. This is at least three to five times less than the cost of malpractice to society.
- *A leading actuary says the HHS report's numbers are "rubbish."* According to Robert Hunter, Director of Insurance for Consumer Federation of America, "The total cost of medical malpractice premiums is $6.4 billion (not just for doctors, as the report says, but for doctors, hospitals and other facilities). This represents about one-half of a percent of total health care expenses. In other words, if an outright ban were placed on medical malpractice lawsuits the total savings would be about $6 billion. The idea that a cap of any kind can save $60 to $108 billion is pure rubbish. How in the world could 'defensive medicine' possibly be more than equal to the total risk measured in premiums, much less 10 to 20 times the risk, as HHS assumes? This makes no economic sense at all."

The Bush Administration Says: "The Increasingly Unpredictable, Costly, and Slow Litigation System Is Responsible"

"Insurance premiums are largely determined by the expensive litigation system . . . Its application is unpredictable, largely random, and standardless . . . Although most cases do not actually go to trial, it costs a significant amount of money to defend each claim—an average of $24,669 . . . Awarded on top of compensation for the injured patient's actual economic loss, non-economic damages are said to be compensation for intangible losses, such as pain and suffering, loss of consortium, hedonic (loss of the enjoyment of life) damages, and various other theories that are imaginatively created by lawyers to increase the amount awarded . . . The average award rose 76% from 1996–1999. The median award in 1999 was $800,000, a 6.7% increase over the 1998 figure of $750,000; and between 1999 and 2000, median malpractice awards increased nearly 43%."

The Facts: The medical malpractice litigation process is logical, and awards are explained by income, cost of health care, and injury severity.

- *Government data show that medical malpractice awards have increased at a much slower pace than claimed by Jury Verdict Research.* According to the federal government's National Practitioner Data Bank (NPDB), the median medical malpractice payment by a physician to a patient rose 35 percent from 1997 to 2001, from $100,000 to $135,000. By contrast, data from Jury Verdict Research (JVR), a private research firm, which was cited in the HHS report shows that awards rose 100 percent from 1997 to 2000, from $503,000 to $1 million. The reason for the huge difference, which is explained in more detail below: JVR collects only jury *verdict* information that is reported to it by attorneys, court clerks and stringers. The NPDB is the most comprehensive source of information that exists because it includes both verdicts *and* settlements. Ninety-six percent of all medical malpractice cases are settled, as opposed to decided by a jury, and settlements result in much lower awards than jury verdicts. Jury verdicts are higher than the average settlement because cases involving severe injuries are more likely to go to trial, and the defendant has usually rejected a settlement offer for a much smaller amount. JVR reported that the median final plaintiff demand in 2000 was $562,000, and the median final settlement offer from the doctor was $80,000. Thus, in the twenty percent of trials that doctors lost, a conscious decision was made to risk a much higher jury verdict. The plaintiffs were usually willing to settle for about half of what the jury awarded. According to NPDB's database of all medical malpractice settlements and judgments, the median payment in a settlement in 2000 was $125,000, same as the median for all payments; but the median payment for a judgment was $235,000. This figure is lower than the jury verdict figure because the ultimate payment received by a successful plaintiff reflects remittiturs ordered by judges, and discounts agreed to by plaintiffs in order to avert appeals.
- *Government data show that medical malpractice awards have increased at a slower pace than health insurance premiums.* While NPDB data show that

the median medical malpractice payment rose 35 percent from 1997 to 2001 (an average of 8.5 percent a year), the average premium for single health insurance coverage increased 39 percent over that time period (9.5 percent a year). Payments for health care costs, which directly affect health insurance premiums, make up the lion's share of most medical malpractice awards.

- *"Non-economic" damages are not as easy to quantify as lost wages or medical bills, but they compensate real injuries.* So-called "non-economic" damages are awarded for the pain and suffering that accompany any loss of normal functions (e.g. blindness, paralysis, sexual dysfunction, lost bowel and bladder control) and inability to engage in daily activities or to pursue hobbies, such as hunting and fishing. This category also encompasses damages for disfigurement and loss of fertility. The fact that Americans spend a great deal of money to remedy these conditions (e.g. on pain relief medication, reconstructive surgery, etc.) belies any notion that such damages are "non-economic." According to Physician Insurer Association of America (PIAA), the average payment between 1985 and 2001 for a "grave injury," which encompasses paralysis, was only $454,454.
- *No evidence supports the claim that jury verdicts are random "jackpots."* Studies conducted in California, Florida, North Carolina, New York, and Ohio have found that jury verdicts bear a reasonable relationship to the severity of the harm suffered. In total the studies examined more than 3,500 medical malpractice jury verdicts and found a consistent relationship between the severity of the injury and the size of the verdict. Uniformly the authors concluded that their findings did not support the contention that jury verdicts are frequently unpredictable and irrational.
- *The insurance industry's own numbers demonstrate that awards are proportionate to injuries.* PIAA's Data Sharing Report also demonstrates the relationship between the severity of the injury and the size of the settlement or verdict. PIAA, as do most researchers, measures severity of injury according to the National Association of Insurance Commissioners' classifications. The average indemnity paid per file was $49,947 for the least severe category of injury and increased with severity, to $454,454 for grave injuries. All researchers found that the amount of jury verdicts fell off in cases of death, for which the average indemnity was $195,723. This is not surprising, as the costs of medical treatment for a grave injury are likely to be greater and pain and suffering would be experienced over a longer time period than in the case of death.
- *The contingency fee system discourages attorneys from bringing frivolous claims.* Medical malpractice cases are brought on a contingency fee basis, meaning the attorney receives payment only in the event there is a settlement or verdict. If the claim is closed without payment, the attorney does not receive a fee. Since attorneys must earn money to stay in business, it follows that they would not intentionally take on a non-meritorious case.
- *The high cost of preparing a medical malpractice case discourages frivolous claims—and meritorious claims as well.* Medical malpractice cases are very expensive for plaintiffs' attorneys to bring, with out-of-pocket

costs for cases settled at or near the time of trial (when most cases are settled) ranging from $15,000 to $25,000. If the case goes to trial, the costs can easily be doubled. These costs do not include the plaintiff's attorney's time, and an attorney pursuing a frivolous case incurs opportunity costs in not pursuing other cases. An attorney incurs expenses beginning with the determination of whether a case has merit. First, the attorney is required to obtain copies of the patient's medical records from all the providers for analysis by a competent medically trained person. If that initial consultation reveals a likelihood of medical negligence, the records must then be submitted to medical specialists, qualified to testify in court, for final review. Typically, the records must be sent to experts outside of the plaintiff's state, as physicians within the state will refuse to testify against local colleagues. As a result, the experts who agree to review records and testify can and do charge substantial fees. Fees from $1,000 per hour to several thousand dollars are not uncommon. Discovery involves taking the sworn testimony of witnesses and experts. Such depositions cost $300 and up, depending upon their length and complexity. If an expert witness is deposed, the plaintiff's attorney is charged for the witness' preparation time and time attending the deposition.

- *Plaintiffs drop 10 times more claims than they pursue.* PIAA reports that between 1985 and 2001 a total of 108,300 claims were "dropped, withdrawn or dismissed." This is 63 percent of the total number of claims (172,474) closed during the study period. It is unclear what portion constitutes involuntarily dismissed cases (dismissed after a motion was filed by the defendant) rather than cases voluntarily dismissed by plaintiffs. According to researchers at the University of Washington School of Medicine, about nine percent of claims files are closed after the defendant wins a contested motion. Based on this figure, Public Citizen estimates that about 54 percent of claims are being abandoned by patients. An attorney may send a statutorily-required notice of intent to claim or file a lawsuit in order to meet the requirements of the statute of limitations but, after collecting medical records and consulting with experts, decide not to pursue the claim. We estimate that the number of cases withdrawn voluntarily by plaintiffs was 92,621, *10 times* the number of cases that were taken to trial and lost during that period (9,293). The percentage of claims pursued by plaintiffs to final rejection by a jury is only *five percent.*
- *The small number of claims pursued to a defense verdict are not frivolous.* Researchers at the American Society of Anesthesiologists arranged for pairs of doctors to review 103 randomly selected medical negligence claims files. The doctors were asked to judge whether the anesthesiologist in question had acted reasonably and prudently. The doctors only agreed on the appropriateness of care in 62 percent of the cases; they disagreed in 38 percent of cases. The researchers concluded, "These observations indicate that neutral experts (the reviews were conducted in a situation that did not involve advocacy or financial compensation) commonly disagree in their assessments when using the accepted standard of reasonable and prudent care." The percentage of all medical malpractice claims that go to trial is only 6.6 percent, according to PIAA, meaning that the parties and their attorneys

ultimately reach agreement about liability five times more often than neutral doctors do. If truly frivolous lawsuits were being pursued, the proportion of claims going to trial would exceed the 38 percent of claims on which even doctors will disagree.

- *The costs of defending claims that are ultimately dropped are not unreasonable.* Medical liability insurers have complained about the costs of defending cases that are ultimately dropped. But the professional obligation of lawyers to exercise due diligence is essentially identical to the duty of physicians. The lawyer must rule out the possibility of proving medical negligence before terminating a claim, just as doctors must rule out the possibility of illnesses suggested by their patients' symptoms. The doctor performs his duty by administering tests; the lawyer performs hers by using discovery procedures. Both processes can lead to dead ends. But plaintiffs' lawyers have no financial incentive to abuse the litigation process: they are using their own time and money to pursue discovery activities, and are only paid for work on behalf of clients whose cases are successful.
- *Award amounts correlate to plaintiff's income and the cost of living in the plaintiff's home state.* Median malpractice awards vary from state to state. Much of the variation is explained by two factors—median family income and urbanization. Public Citizen's analysis of NPDB and census data found that for every $1,000 increase in a state's median family income, the median award amount increases by about $1,100. Our analysis also found that awards increase in relation to state population density—logical, since urbanized areas have a higher cost of living than rural areas.

The Bush Administration Says: "Insurance Premiums Are Rising Rapidly"

"The cost of the excesses of the litigation system shows up in the cost of malpractice insurance coverage. Premiums have increased rapidly over the past several years."

The Facts: The spike in medical liability premiums was caused by the insurance cycle, not by an "explosion" of lawsuits or "skyrocketing" jury verdicts.

- *There is no growth in the number of new medical malpractice claims.* According to the National Association of Insurance Commissioners (NAIC), the number of new medical malpractice claims declined by about four percent between 1995 and 2000. There were 90,212 claims filed in 1995; 84,741 in 1996; 85,613 in 1997; 86,211 in 1998; 89,311 in 1999; and 86,480 in 2000.
- *For much of the 1990s, doctors benefited from artificially lower premiums.* According to the International Risk Management Institute (IRMI), one of the leading analysts of commercial insurance issues, "What is happening to the market for medical malpractice insurance in 2001 is a direct result of trends and events present since the mid to late 1990s. Throughout the 1990s, and reaching a peak around 1997 and 1998, insurers were on a quest for market share, that is, they were driven

more by the amount of premium they could book rather than the adequacy of premiums to pay losses. In large part this emphasis on market share was driven by a desire to accumulate large amounts of capital with which to turn into investment income." IRMI also noted: "Clearly a business cannot continue operating in that fashion indefinitely."

- *West Virginia Insurance Commissioner blames the market.* According to the Office of the West Virginia Insurance Commission (one of the states in the throes of a medical malpractice "crisis"), "[T]he insurance industry is cyclical and necessarily competitive. We have witnessed these cycles in the Medical Malpractice line in the mid-'70's, the mid-'80's and the present situation. This particular cycle is, perhaps, worse than previous cycles as it was delayed by a booming economy in the '90's and is now experiencing not just a shortfall in rates due to competition, but a subdued economy, lower interest rates and investment yields, the withdrawal of a major medical malpractice writer and a strong hardening of the reinsurance market. Rates will, at some point, reach an acceptable level to insurers and capital will once again flow into the Medical Malpractice market."
- *Medical liability premiums track investment results.* J. Robert Hunter, one of the country's most knowledgeable insurance actuaries and director of insurance for the Consumer Federation of America, recently analyzed the growth in medical liability premiums. He found that premiums charged do not track losses paid, but instead rise and fall in concert with the state of the economy. When the economy is booming and investment returns are high, companies maintain premiums at modest levels; however, when the economy falters and interest rates fall, companies increase premiums in response.
- *The same trends are present in other lines of insurance.* Property/casualty refers to a large group of liability lines of insurance (30 in total) including medical malpractice, homeowners, commercial, and automobile. The property/casualty insurance industry has exhibited cyclical behavior for many years, as far back as the 1920s. These cycles are characterized by periods of rising rates leading to increased profitability. Following a period of solid but not spectacular rates of return, the industry enters a down phase where prices soften, supply of the insurance product becomes plentiful, and, eventually, profitability diminishes, or vanishes completely. In the down phase of the cycle, as results deteriorate, the basic ability of insurance companies to underwrite new business or, for some companies even to renew some existing policies, can be impaired. This is because the capital needed to support the underwriting of risk has been depleted through losses. The current market began to harden in 2001, following an unusually prolonged period of soft market conditions in the property-casualty section in the 1990s. The current hard market is unusual in that many lines of insurance are affected at the same time, including medical malpractice. As a result, premiums are rising for most types of insurance. The increases have taken policyholders by surprise given that they came after several years of relatively flat to decreasing prices.
- *Insurer mismanagement compounded the problems.* Compounding the impact of the cycle has been misleading accounting practices. As the

Wall Street Journal found in a front page investigative story on June 24, 2002, "[A] price war that began in the early 1990s led insurers to sell malpractice coverage to obstetrician-gynecologists at rates that proved inadequate to cover claims. Some of these carriers had rushed into malpractice coverage because an accounting practice widely used in the industry made the area seem more profitable in the early 1990s than it really was. A decade of short-sighted price slashing led to industry losses of nearly $3 billion last year." Moreover, "In at least one case, aggressive pricing allegedly crossed the line into fraud." According to Donald J. Zuk, chief executive of SCPIE Holdings Inc., a leading malpractice insurer in California, "Regardless of the level of . . . tort reform, the fact remains that if insurance policies are consistently under-priced, the insurer will lose money."

The Bush Administration Says: "Insurers Are Leaving the Market"

"The litigation crisis is affecting patients' ability to get care not only because many doctors find the increased premiums unaffordable but also because liability insurance is increasingly difficult to obtain at any price, particularly in non-reform states. Demonstrating and exacerbating the problem, several major carriers have stopped selling malpractice insurance."

The Facts: At least three of the four insurance companies identified by HHS as leaving the market had serious management problems during the past two years.

- *PHICO had been placed under the supervision of insurance regulators and was later sued by the state's Insurance Department.* The lawsuit alleged that PHICO directors ignored signs of financial trouble at the company and pressured the board to pay dividends at a time when the insurer's surplus "was declining drastically and significant strengthening of loss reserves was required."
- *St. Paul exited other insurance markets as well.* St. Paul Companies reported in December 2001 that it had $85 million in exposure as related to the Enron Corporation and that it held approximately $23 million in Enron Corporation senior unsecured debt. At the same time St. Paul announced it would exit its medical malpractice business, it also announced it would add reserves for claims related to the September 11 terrorist attacks, "exit certain reinsurance lines, exit countries where the company is not likely to achieve competitive scale, and reduce corporate overhead expenses, including staff reductions."
- *MIIX was found by Weiss Ratings to be the hardest hit by the property and casualty insurance industry's overall $6.6 billion decline in investment gains during the first half of 2002.* MIXX reported the largest capital losses. Weiss, a leading independent provider of ratings and analyses of financial services companies, downgraded MIIX from D- to E+, E being the lowest score possible. A former MIIX official has alleged conflicts of interest on the company's board that may have affected the situation.

The Bush Administration Says: "States With Realistic Limits on Non-Economic Damages Are Faring Better"

"The insurance crisis is less acute in states that have reformed their litigation systems. States with limits of $250,000 or $350,000 on non-economic damages have average combined highest premium increases of 12–15%, compared to 44% in states without caps on non-economic damages . . ."

The Facts: Neither the HHS report nor anyone else has presented a factual case that caps lower premiums; Public Citizen's analysis found that premiums are higher in states with caps.

- *The HHS report's "comparison" of premiums in ten states with caps to just ten states without caps is pure baloney.* HHS omitted data from other states without damage caps that did not have high premium increases. The Pennsylvania Medical Society . . . released a critique of another premium comparison, concluding that "Multivariate modeling must be used to control for outside influences . . . An issue as important as liability insurance reform deserves no less than a careful scientific approach to assessment of the impact of policy changes." While they did not prepare a multivariate model, Public Citizen did.
- *Public Citizen's analysis finds that, controlling for other factors, premiums are higher in states with caps than in states without caps.* Public Citizen entered U.S. Census, NPDB, and Medical Liability Monitor data into a multiple regression model to determine the effect that damage caps have on awards and on doctors' liability insurance premiums. Our preliminary finding is that a damage cap lowers the median payment made by doctors to plaintiffs by $29,000, in turn lowering a doctor's premium by about $11,000. Nevertheless, controlling for this and the rate of lawsuits against doctors in each state, states with caps still have premiums that are $14,000 higher than in states without caps, a $3,000 net increase. We believe that the cap encourages doctors to take more cases to trial, and the resulting higher defense attorney costs more than offset the lower indemnity payments.

POSTSCRIPT

Is It Time to Reform Medical Malpractice Litigation?

The question of medical malpractice litigation must be placed in context. No one disputes the fact that doctors make mistakes. Physicians are human and are therefore subject to human fallibilities. It should be noted that the large majority of these medical errors never result in legal action. But since the United States does not have in place a nationally mandated reporting system for medical mishaps and near mishaps, the public does not have certain knowledge of just how many medical mistakes are made annually. Doctors and their insurance carriers would have people believe that every medical mistake is litigated and that many other lawsuits are brought to the courts when there are no grounds for them. Lawyers, for their part, argue that they file lawsuits for only a small fraction of the medical mistakes that are made annually in the United States. Indeed, they contend that if it were not for the cases they did bring to light, the public would naively believe that doctors are infallible.

The truth of the matter may lie somewhere in the middle. Outside observers generally assume that about one out of every six "medical misadventures" results in a lawsuit. Of those who do seek legal redress, about half of these malpractice lawsuits are settled out of court or withdrawn before they go to trial. It is those that find their way through the court system and result in large financial settlements that are political lightning rods.

Those who litigate medical malpractice cases contend that their jury and settlement awards have little impact on medical malpractice insurance rates. They contend that the appearance of high insurance premiums can be traced to poor management decisions. When times were good and interest rates were high, these companies engaged in excessive competition, which drove the insurance rates down too far in the most competitive markets. When times were not as good and interest rates were low, insurance companies had no choice but to increase their rates. The increase, of course, was most severe in markets where the rates had been driven to the lowest levels.

This issue has been hotly debated in recent months; consequently, you might look to the press for background reading. The *New York Times* is a good source. The March 16, 2003, issue of the *New York Times Magazine* carried an article concerning four individuals who had foreign objects left in their bodies after surgeries. "The Biggest Mistake of Their Lives" discusses the case of Dan Jennings. If the miseries suffered by John Francis, as described in the introduction to this issue, seem remarkably like those of Jennings, that is because Francis is a fictional character based on Jennings.

Those who would limit malpractice awards have written widely. See, for example, "The Tort Mess," by Michael Freeman, *Forbes* (May 13, 2002). The American Medical Association has many such references, including "Medical Liability Reform Background and Talking Points." This summary, which was updated on May 8, 2002, incorporates many of the points found in the HHS report. To see how the medical community interprets history in this area, see James C. Mohr, "American Medical Malpractice Litigation in Historical Perspective," *JAMA* (April 3, 2000). Finally, to read firsthand how the insurance industry feels, see Doctor's Company chairman Richard E. Anderson's July 17, 2002, testimony before the Subcommittee on Health, Committee on Energy and Commerce, in "Harming Patient Access to Care: The Impact of Excessive Litigation."

For a good summary of President George W. Bush's statement on the medical malpractice issue and a panel discussion, see the January 16, 2003, segment of *The News Hour With Jim Lehrer*, which includes Larry Smarr, president of the Physicians Insurers Association of America; Ken Suggs, secretary to the Association of American Trial Lawyers; Donald Palmisano, president-elect of the American Medical Association; and Joanne Doroshow, executive director of the Center for Justice and Democracy.

On the Internet . . .

Financial Management Service

Besides reading a daily statement from the U.S. Department of the Treasury, one can also access this site to find information on the federal budget from the Office of Management and Budget and a variety of statistics on social and economic conditions in the United States.

http://www.fms.treas.gov

Joint Economic Committee

This site describes the work of the Joint Economic Committee of the U.S. Congress. It includes the research reports of the Committee on many topics including tax reform and government spending, monetary policy, and international economic policy.

http://www.house.gov/jec/

The Public Debt Online

This site provides "to the penny" information on the current debt of the U.S. federal government. It also provides historical information on the dollar size of the debt, on ownership of the debt, and the interest expense associated with the debt.

http://www.publicdebt.treas.gov/opd/opd.htm

U.S. Macroeconomic and Regional Data

Hosted by the State University of New York, Oswego, Department of Economics, this site contains the full text of recent *Economic Reports of the President* and links to various global and regional economic indicators.

http://www.oswego.edu/~economic/mac-data.htm

U.S. Department of the Treasury

In addition to information about the U.S. Treasury Department itself, this site features information on a variety of topics including the financing of the fight against terrorism, key initiatives of the Department, and money management.

http://www.ustreas.gov

PART 2

Macroeconomic Issues

Government policy and economics are tightly intertwined. Fiscal policy and monetary policy have a dramatic impact on the national economy, and the state of the economy can often lead to changes in tax revenues, government spending, and interest rates. Decisions regarding Social Security, taxes, the minimum wage, or welfare reform must be made in the context of broad macroeconomic goals, and the debates on these issues are more than theoretical. Each has a significant impact on our lives.

- Is Wal-Mart Good for the Economy?
- Should Social Security Be Changed to Include Personal Retirement Accounts?
- Should the Double Taxation of Corporate Dividends Be Eliminated?
- Are Credit Card Companies Exploiting American Consumers?
- Is It Time to Abolish the Minimum Wage?
- Are Declining Caseloads a Sign of Successful Welfare Reform?

ISSUE 7

Is Wal-Mart Good for the Economy?

YES: Los Angeles County Economic Development Corporation, from "Wal-Mart Supercenters: What's in Store for Southern California?" http://www.laedc.info/data/documents.asp (January 2004)

NO: Democratic Staff of the House Committee on Education and the Workforce, from "Everyday Low Wages: The Hidden Price We All Pay for Wal-Mart," http://www.mindfully.org/Industry/2004/wal-mart-labor-record16feb04.htm (February 16, 2004)

ISSUE SUMMARY

YES: The Los Angeles County Economic Development Corporation believes that the introduction of Wal-Mart supercenter stores into the Southern California market will generate significant savings for consumers on their grocery, apparel, and general merchandise spending, and the redirected spending from the savings will create over 35,000 new jobs.

NO: The Democratic Staff of the House Committee on Education and the Workforce believes that Wal-Mart, in its efforts to achieve and maintain low prices, has "come to represent the lowest common denominator in the treatment of working people."

Given the company's ubiquitous presence across the country, it would come as a great surprise to find an American who did not recognize the name "Wal-Mart" or find someone who had not shopped at a Wal-Mart store. Many people are familiar with the yellow smiley face that appears in Wal-Mart television ads, in its newspapers ads, and on its in-store promotions. While many people might not know of the persons who created other major retailers like Target, Home Depot, and Kmart, a fair number would be able to identify Sam Walton as Wal-Mart's founder. And, some of these would even be able to tell a short story about the company's history.

Such a short story would begin in 1962; this is the year Sam Walton opened the first Wal-Mart store in Rogers, Arkansas. Interestingly enough, 1962 also marked the first year of operations for Kmart and Target. All three retailers are similar in their devotion to discount retailing. Indeed, Sam Walton began his venture into discount retailing, in part because his chain of Arkansas and Kansas variety stores (what used to be called five- and ten-cent stores) had experienced competition from regional discount retailers. It was 1968 when Wal-Mart first ventured outside of Arkansas, establishing outlets in Missouri and Oklahoma.

By 1970 there were 38 Wal-Mart stores with annual sales of $44.2 million and 1,500 employees. By the end of the decade, sales had grown to $1.2 billion with 276 stores in 11 states and 21,000 employees. By its twenty-fifth anniversary in 1987, Wal-Mart had reached sales of $15.9 billion with 1,198 stores, and some 200,000 employees. Today, Wal-Mart stands as a "global colossus" with $256 billion in global revenue, 5,000 stores in 10 countries, and 1.3 million employees. It is said to be the largest private or non-government employer in the world.

What explains Wal-Mart's business success? According to the company's founder, "The secret of successful retailing is to give your customers what they want." And what do customers want? Sam Walton thought they wanted everything: "a wide assortment of good quality merchandise; the lowest possible prices; guaranteed satisfaction with what you buy; friendly, knowledgeable service; convenient hours; free parking; a pleasant shopping experience." Based on Wal-Mart's business success, Sam Walton's creation appears to give consumers what they want. And many, based on the growth figures previously cited, consider Wal-Mart to be the ultimate business success story.

But not everyone admires this business success. Rather, there are those who believe that Wal-Mart's business success has been built upon a series of abuses, with most of the abuses related to the company's goal of offering the lowest possible prices. These critics charge that in its drive to achieve its goal of lowest prices, Wal-Mart is driven to be anti-union, to pay low wages, to discriminates against women, to refuse to pay workers for some of their work, and to break child labor laws.

This issue examines the role of Wal-Mart in the economy. The first reading is a segment of an economic impact study prepared by the Los Angeles County Economic Development Corporation (LAEDC). In this study, paid for by Wal-Mart, the non-profit organization assesses what would happen if Wal-Mart began to open a series of so-called Supercenter stores in Southern California. The report concludes that Wal-Mart's entry into the Southern California market would be of major benefit to consumers and create a significant number of new jobs. The second reading, prepared by the Democratic Staff of the House Committee on Education and the Workforce, summarizes a series of reports prepared by others as well as a series of legal actions taken against Wal-Mart. The staff's conclusion from this summary is that Wal-Mart's business success has only been achieved at a very high social cost.

Los Angeles County Economic Development Corporation

Wal-Mart Supercenters: What's in Store for Southern California?

Executive Summary

Wal-Mart Stores, Inc. is now the largest grocery retailer in the country based on sales. It is preparing to introduce its Supercenters, which combine a large general merchandise store with a full service market, into Southern California. The City of Los Angeles, in particular, with its 3.61 million people, 1.28 million households, and annual food store spending of approximately $5.65 billion, is a very attractive market. Wal-Mart's planned expansion into the local grocery business creates both a challenge to the major grocery store chains in the region, and an opportunity for cities to encourage strategic reinvestment in underserved neighborhoods.

The LAEDC [Los Angeles County Economic Development Corporation] agreed to assess the economic implications of Wal-Mart's entry into the Southern California grocery market because existing studies, which tend to tally only the negative impacts of Wal-Mart's operations, miss half the story. Here we aim to provide a fair and balanced assessment of both the good and not so good impacts of Supercenters in Southern California. Thus, we include not only the potential effects on existing grocery chains and their employees, but also the potential savings to consumers, and the potential job creation outside the grocery industry.

Costs and Savings

Wal-Mart Supercenters have a substantial cost advantage relative to traditional supermarkets, based on careful supply chain and inventory management, volume discounts, and lower labor costs. Much of this can be attributed to Wal-Mart's willingness to invest in technology and business practices which make its operations more efficient. Wal-Mart passes the savings on to consumers, offering lower prices on groceries than traditional grocery market chains. If Wal-Mart Supercenters are introduced in Los Angeles, food prices should fall.

Wal-Mart shoppers would immediately save an estimated average of 15 percent relative to what they would have paid under the current status quo.

The savings could be higher, particularly in portions of the City of Los Angeles such as South Los Angeles and the northeast San Fernando Valley, which are underserved by traditional grocery stores. The corner stores where much of the food purchases in these areas take place offer uncompetitive prices relative to existing grocery stores, never mind Supercenters. As Wal-Mart gradually builds market share, major competitors will lower their prices as well, thus bringing additional savings to some consumers who will never set foot in a Wal-Mart store. Smaller stores will adjust by emphasizing specific market niches and specialty products which Wal-Mart does not provide.

The LAEDC conservatively calculated the potential savings to consumers in the City of Los Angeles to be *at least* $668 million, or $524 per household, annually, once Wal-Mart reaches 20 percent market share. The savings could be much higher, though the savings will not materialize overnight. They will increase gradually over many years in step with Wal-Mart's market share. These savings add to a household's discretionary *after tax dollars*—the portion of the income actually available for spending. This "found" money will be redirected to other items, including housing, savings, health, entertainment, and transportation. As households redeploy their savings, their spending will create jobs outside the grocery industry. In the City of Los Angeles, redirected grocery savings will create 6,500 additional jobs. The new jobs will be in a wide variety of occupations, reflecting the diverse spending patterns of Los Angeles households and the breadth of the regional economy.

The LAEDC also looked at the potential impact of Wal-Mart Supercenters on the entire Southern California market. In Los Angeles County, the aggregate annual savings to consumers would be at least $1.78 billion. When the savings are redirected to other purchases, the county-wide job creation will total 17,300 jobs. For consumers in Imperial, Los Angeles, Orange, Riverside, San Bernardino, San Diego and Riverside counties, the combined total annual savings will be at least $3.76 billion. The seven-county Southern California job creation total is 36,400 jobs.

Wal-Mart compensation, while lower than for the best-paid unionized grocery employees, is better than most people realize, particularly in its food business. Wal-Mart benefits include health care, a stakeholders' bonus, which is paid to employees at stores that perform well, profit-sharing, company contributions to 401(k) plans, which are the most common form of defined contribution retirement plan, a 15 percent discount on company stock, and a 10 percent discount on purchases of general merchandise. Wal-Mart's healthcare plan requires employees to share the upfront costs (Wal-Mart pays 2/3rd; the associates pay 1/3rd), but in return does not have single incident or lifetime caps on coverage.

Two important factors make Wal-Mart's wages appear lower than they might otherwise. First, Supercenters are a relatively new phenomenon. Most Supercenters have simply not been open long enough to have accumulated many employees with lengthy service records, and thus higher rates of pay. Second, and perhaps most important, Wal-Mart's pay among its front line grocery workers is skewed downwards because it promotes from within. Wal-Mart recruits its management primarily from within the ranks of its own employees.

This opens up career opportunities for associates, and crucially for wage comparisons, removes some of the most experienced and best paid Wal-Mart employees from the pool of workers typically being compared. In contrast to unionized grocery stores, where some of the most senior employees are cashiers, at Wal-Mart cashier is an entry level position.

Unionized grocery workers earn $2.50–$3.50 per hour more, on average, than Supercenter employees in Southern California could expect. Some union grocery workers are very well compensated, but the wages of the most highly compensated among them are frequently mistaken for *average* union wages, which are lower. The widely-cited Orange County Business Council (OCBC) study calculated the potential wage loss if all union workers in the Southern California grocery industry were to earn the same wages as Wal-Mart employees. Using more realistic assumptions of Wal-Mart Supercenter employee pay (and hence a narrower wage gap), we find the potential cumulative wage loss in Los Angeles County is $150 million to $258 million annually. For the 7-county Southern California region (including Los Angeles), the range is $307 million to $529 million. If all current unionized grocery employees were to eventually earn the equivalent of Wal-Mart Supercenter employees, the lost spending due to eroded household income could cost Los Angeles County alone 1,500 to 2,500 jobs and the 7-county region 3,000 to 5,100 jobs. Should these losses materialize, they would be offset by region-wide gains of 36,400 jobs, meaning that outside the grocery sector at least seven jobs would be added for every one lost.

Timing

Timing will be critical in determining the potential impact of Supercenters. Experience in other regions suggests that existing stores will have time to adjust. The potential benefits as well as the costs of Wal-Mart entering the Southern California grocery market described in this report assume that Wal-Mart will eventually gain a market share of 20 percent. Yet, gaining share will take a long time.

Wal-Mart will struggle to find suitable locations for its stores in many areas of heavily urbanized, built-out Southern California, including most of the City of Los Angeles. By comparison, in Fort Worth, Texas, it took Wal-Mart six years to achieve a 6.5 percent share in a market where stores can be built quickly. Unlike California, permitting, environmental regulation, and community opposition are not generally a factor in Texas, where growth has nonetheless proceeded at only a modest pace. Wal-Mart appears to be proceeding cautiously in California, with plans to build just 40 Supercenters in the state over the next three to five years. This represents just 4 percent of the 1,000 new Supercenters that will be added nationwide during the same period. Based solely on the state's share of the national population and the potential size of its market, the expected number of new Supercenters in California should be in the range of 100 to 150. If the distribution of existing Supercenters were factored in, the California number would be higher still. Again, by comparison, Texas, which is the nation's second most populous state, already has many Supercenters while California, the most populous state, has none.

The slow roll out of Supercenters in Southern California, compared to other regions, will delay the arrival of benefits for consumers, but it will also give Wal-Mart's competitors more time to adapt. With Southern California's rapidly growing population, Wal-Mart is likely to increase its presence by taking a greater share of overall market growth, rather than by luring existing customers from large supermarket chains. While a scenario in which Wal-Mart captures most of this growth may constitute a challenge for the major supermarket chains, their situation—aside from fierce price competition, which benefits consumers, and increased pressure on their balance sheets—is not likely to be significantly different than it is now.

Conclusion

All indicators suggest that Wal-Mart will gradually enter the grocery market in Southern California. A 20 percent market share may be achievable over time, but not in the near future. Unlike what has occurred in other parts of the country, Supercenters will be rolled out slowly here, delaying the arrival of benefits. Conversely, any negative impacts will also be delayed, and lessened, since competitors will have more time to adapt. Over the long term, Wal-Mart is likely to increase its market share by absorbing a larger share of overall market growth, rather than by attracting existing customers from the large grocery chains.

The real choice facing the City of Los Angeles is whether Wal-Mart will serve residents from within the city's boundaries or from without. If Wal-Mart decides to open Supercenters to serve demand in the region, the stores could conveniently serve customers residing in the City of Los Angeles from within the city, or from neighboring jurisdictions. In the former case, the city government would have the opportunity to influence Wal-Mart's presence. The City of Los Angeles could guide Wal-Mart and other large scale retailers to sites where their presence and spending would be a boon for local redevelopment. If, however, Wal-Mart builds in neighboring jurisdictions, the City of Los Angeles will have no control over the development. Wal-Mart customers in Los Angeles would leave the city to shop, taking their taxable spending (and any resulting local sales tax revenues) with them.

Study Highlights

Savings for Consumers and New Jobs Outside the Grocery Industry

- Supercenter customers will save an average of 15 percent on their groceries.
- Price competition will lead to reduced prices at existing grocery chains, providing customers who shop at stores other than Wal-Mart average savings of 10 percent.

- Increased competition in non-grocery items will lead to price reductions averaging 3 percent at general merchandise and apparel competitors.
- Money that people save on groceries will be redirected to other items, including housing, savings, health, entertainment, and transportation. This new spending will, in turn, create jobs outside the grocery industry.

Savings in the City of Los Angeles

- Consumers in the City of Los Angeles are conservatively estimated to save at least $668 million annually, or $524 per household, per year.
- Redirected grocery savings will create 6,500 additional full-time-equivalent jobs.

Savings in Los Angeles County

- Consumers in Los Angeles County are conservatively estimated to save at least $1.78 billion annually, or $569 per household, per year.
- Redirected grocery savings will create 17,300 new jobs County-wide.

Savings in Southern California

- Consumers in Imperial, Los Angeles, Orange, Riverside, San Bernardino, San Diego, and Ventura Counties are conservatively estimated to save at least $3.76 billion annually, or $589 per household, per year.
- In these seven counties, 36,400 new jobs will be created.

Potential Impacts to Major Grocery Chains

- Major grocery companies have used fear of intense competition to seek wage concessions from unionized employees, most likely by lowering the wages of new hires.
- Future foregone wages of unionized grocery employees in Los Angeles County could equal $150 million to $258 million annually, and could reach $307 to $529 million annually across the entire 7-county Southern California region.
- These foregone wages would reduce overall household spending, potentially costing Los Angeles County 1,500 to 2,500 jobs and the 7-county region (including Los Angeles) 3,000 to 5,100 jobs.
- These losses will be offset by region-wide gains of 36,400 jobs outside the grocery business, or a net gain of at least seven new jobs for every one lost.

Catalyst for Redevelopment

- Wal-Mart can be used as a catalyst for redevelopment, particularly in areas saddled with struggling (or failed) retail centers. In Panorama City, Wal-Mart replaced the Broadway department store, creating new jobs and revitalizing the mall and the surrounding neighborhood. Wal-Mart will open stores in an abandoned K-Mart in Canoga Park and in an abandoned AutoNation site in Harbor Gateway.
- Wal-Mart has demonstrated a willingness to enter communities that other businesses appear uninterested in serving. In Baldwin Hills,

Wal-Mart brought jobs and retail opportunities to an underserved community by opening a store in a former Macy's, which had sat vacant for five years.

- There are many parts of Los Angeles that are underserved by retail. The need is acute in the grocery sector and these communities stand to gain the most if Wal-Mart were to enter the market and offer lower prices.

Sales Tax Leakage

- Jurisdictions without Supercenters will lose taxable sales when their residents shop elsewhere. Supercenters have become an issue because they sell groceries, which are non-taxable. Sixty to seventy percent of the sales at Supercenters, however, are taxable. The appeal of Supercenters, for both Wal-Mart and the consumer, is that they allow shoppers to combine trips and do all of their purchasing in one location. If city residents choose to buy their groceries at Supercenters outside of the city, the City of L.A. will lose out on the local share of any taxable purchases shoppers make on those trips.
- Cities without Supercenters will also lose out on sales tax revenue when their residents combine trips to Wal-Mart with shopping at nearby stores.
- Overall sales taxes will increase to the extent that customers spend their savings generated from lower-priced groceries (which are not taxable) on goods which are taxable.
- The modest increase in overall taxable sales should not obscure the key issue—the distribution of taxable sales (and hence tax revenues) among Southern California jurisdictions based on where consumers choose to shop.

Democratic Staff of the House Committee on Education and the Workforce

Everyday Low Wages: The Hidden Price We All Pay for Wal-Mart

Introduction

The retail giant Wal-Mart has become the nation's largest private sector employer with an estimated 1.2 million employees.[1] The company's annual revenues now amount to 2 percent of the U.S. Gross Domestic Product.[2] Wal-Mart's success is attributed to its ability to charge low prices in mega-stores offering everything from toys and furniture to groceries. While charging low prices obviously has some consumer benefits, mounting evidence from across the country indicates that these benefits come at a steep price for American workers, U.S. labor laws, and community living standards.

Wal-Mart is undercutting labor standards at home and abroad, while those federal officials charged with protecting labor standards have been largely indifferent. Public outcry against Wal-Mart's labor practices has been answered by the company with a cosmetic response. Wal-Mart has attempted to offset its labor record with advertising campaigns utilizing employees (who are euphemistically called "associates") to attest to Wal-Mart's employment benefits and support of local communities. Nevertheless—whether the issue is basic organizing rights of workers, or wages, or health benefits, or working conditions, or trade policy—Wal-Mart has come to represent the lowest common denominator in the treatment of working people.

This report reviews Wal-Mart's labor practices across the country and around the world and provides an overview of how working Americans and their allies in Congress are seeking to address the gamut of issues raised by this new standard-bearer of American retail.

Wal-Mart's Labor Practices

Workers' Organizing Rights

The United States recognizes workers' right to organize unions. Government employers generally may not interfere with public sector employees' freedom of association. In the private sector, workers' right to organize is protected by

From the Democratic Staff of the House Committee on Education and the Workforce, February 16, 2004.

the National Labor Relations Act.[3] Internationally, this right is recognized as a core labor standard and a basic human right.[4]

Wal-Mart's record on the right to organize recently achieved international notoriety. On January 14, 2004, the International Confederation of Free Trade Unions (ICFTU), an organization representing 151 million workers in 233 affiliated unions around the world, issued a report on U.S. labor standards.[5] Wal-Mart's rampant violations of workers' rights figured prominently. In the last few years, well over 100 unfair labor practice charges have been lodged against Wal-Mart throughout the country, with 43 charges filed in 2002 alone. Since 1995, the U.S. government has been forced to issue at least 60 complaints against Wal-Mart at the National Labor Relations Board.[6] Wal-Mart's labor law violations range from illegally firing workers who attempt to organize a union to unlawful surveillance, threats, and intimidation of employees who dare to speak out.

With not a single Wal-Mart store in the United States represented by a union, the company takes a pro-active role in maintaining its union-free status. Wal-Mart has issued "A Manager's Toolbox to Remaining Union Free," which provides managers with lists of warning signs that workers might be organizing, including "frequent meetings at associates' homes" and "associates who are never seen together start talking or associating with each other."[7] The "Toolbox" gives managers a hotline to call so that company specialists can respond rapidly and head off any attempt by employees to organize.

When employees have managed to obtain a union election and vote for a union, Wal-Mart has taken sweeping action in response. In 2000, when a small meatcutting department successfully organized a union at a Wal-Mart store in Texas, Wal-Mart responded a week later by announcing the phase-out of its meatcutting departments entirely. Because of deficient labor laws, it took the meatcutters in Texas three years to win their jobs back with an order that Wal-Mart bargain with their union.[8] Rather than comply, Wal-Mart is appealing this decision.[9]

Wal-Mart's aggressive anti-union activity, along with the nation's weak labor laws, have kept the largest private sector employer in the U.S. union-free. Breaking the law that guarantees workers' right to organize has material consequences for both the workers and the company. According to data released by the Bureau of Labor Statistics in January 2004, union workers earn median weekly salaries of $760, compared to non-union workers' median weekly salaries of $599—a difference of over 26 percent.[10] In the supermarket industry, the union difference is even more pronounced, with union members making 30 percent more than non-union workers. Union representation also correlates with higher benefits.[11] For instance, 72 percent of union workers have guaranteed pensions with defined benefits, while only 15 percent of non-union workers enjoy such retirement security.[12] On the health care front, which will be explored in more detail later, 60 percent of union workers have medical care benefits on the job, compared to only 44 percent of non-union workers.[13] For companies like Wal-Mart seeking to maintain low labor costs, these statistics obviously provide an incentive to remain union-free.

Unfortunately, U.S. labor laws fail to provide a sufficient disincentive against violating workers' rights.

Low Wages

By keeping unions at bay, Wal-Mart keeps its wages low—even by general industry standards. The average supermarket employee makes $10.35 per hour.[14] Sales clerks at Wal-Mart, on the other hand, made only $8.23 per hour on average, or $13,861 per year, in 2001.[15] Some estimate that average "associate" salaries range from $7.50 to $8.50 per hour.[16] With an average on-the-clock workweek of 32 hours, many workers take home less than $1,000 per month.[17] Even the higher estimate of a $13,861 annual salary fell below the 2001 federal poverty line of $14,630 for a family of three.[18] About one-third of Wal-Mart's employees are part-time, restricting their access to benefits.[19] These low wages, to say the least, complicate employees' ability to obtain essential benefits, such as health care coverage, which will be explored in a later section.

The low pay stands in stark contrast to Wal-Mart's slogan, "Our people make the difference." Now-retired Senior Vice President Don Soderquist has explained: "'Our people make the difference' is not a meaningless slogan—it's a reality at Wal-Mart. We are a group of dedicated, hardworking, ordinary people who have teamed together to accomplish extraordinary things."[20] With 2002 company profits hitting $6.6 billion, Wal-Mart employees do indeed "accomplish extraordinary things."[21] But at poverty level wages, these workers are not sharing in the company's success.

Unequal Pay and Treatment

Title VII of the Civil Rights Act prohibits discrimination in employment based on employees' race, color, religion, sex, or national origin.[22] Additionally, the Equal Pay Act, an amendment to the Fair Labor Standards Act, prohibits unequal pay for equal work on the basis of sex.[23] These basic labor and civil rights laws have become an issue at Wal-Mart.

In 2001, six women sued Wal-Mart in California claiming the company discriminated against women by systematically denying them promotions and paying them less than men. The lawsuit has expanded to potentially the largest class action in U.S. history—on behalf of more than 1 million current and former female employees. While two-thirds of the company's hourly workers are female, women hold only one-third of managerial positions and constitute less than 15 percent of store managers.[24] The suit also claims that women are pushed into "female" departments and are demoted if they complain about unequal treatment. One plaintiff, a single mother of four, started at Wal-Mart in 1990 at a mere $3.85 an hour. Even with her persistent requests for training and promotions, it took her eight years to reach $7.32 an hour and seven years to reach management, while her male counterparts were given raises and promotions much more quickly. For this plaintiff, annual pay increases were as little as 10 cents and never more than 35 cents per hour.[25]

Off-the-Clock Work

While wages are low at Wal-Mart, too often employees are not paid at all. The Fair Labor Standards Act (FLSA), along with state wage and hour laws, requires hourly employees to be paid for all time actually worked at no less than a minimum wage and at time-and-a-half for all hours worked over 40 in a week.[26] These labor laws have posed a particular obstacle for Wal-Mart. As of December 2002, there were thirty-nine class-action lawsuits against the company in thirty states, claiming tens of millions of dollars in back pay for hundreds of thousands of Wal-Mart employees.[27]

In 2001, Wal-Mart forked over $50 million in unpaid wages to 69,000 workers in Colorado. These wages were paid only after the workers filed a class action lawsuit. Wal-Mart had been working the employees off-the-clock. The company also paid $500,000 to 120 workers in Gallup, New Mexico, who filed a lawsuit over unpaid work.[28]

In a Texas class-action certified in 2002 on behalf of 200,000 former and current Wal-Mart employees, statisticians estimated that the company short-changed its workers $150 million over four years—just based on the frequency of employees working through their daily 15 minute breaks.[29]

In Oregon, 400 employees in 27 stores sued the company for unpaid, off-the-clock overtime. In their suit, the workers explained that managers would delete hours from their time records and tell employees to clean the store after they clocked out. In December 2002, a jury found in favor of the workers.[30] One personnel manager claimed that, for six years, she was forced to delete hours from employee time sheets.[31]

In the latest class-action, filed in November 2003, noting evidence of systematic violations of the wage-and-hour law, a judge certified a lawsuit for 65,000 Wal-Mart employees in Minnesota. Reacting to the certification, a Wal-Mart spokesperson told the Minneapolis *Star Tribune:* "We have no reason to believe these isolated situations . . . represent a widespread problem with off-the clock work."[32]

Many observers blame the wage-and-hour problems at Wal-Mart on pressure placed on managers to keep labor costs down. In 2002, operating costs for Wal-Mart were just 16.6 percent of total sales, compared to a 20.7 percent average for the retail industry as a whole.[33] Wal-Mart reportedly awards bonuses to its employees based on earnings. With other operating and inventory costs set by higher level management, store managers must turn to wages to increase profits. While Wal-Mart expects those managers to increase sales each year, it expects the labor costs to be cut by two-tenths of a percentage point each year as well.[34]

Reports from former Wal-Mart managers seem to corroborate this dynamic. Joyce Moody, a former manager in Alabama and Mississippi, told the *New York Times* that Wal-Mart "threatened to write up managers if they didn't bring the payroll in low enough." Depositions in wage and hour lawsuits reveal that company headquarters leaned on management to keep their labor costs at 8 percent of sales or less, and managers in turn leaned on assistant managers to work their employees off-the-clock or simply delete time from employee time sheets.[35]

Child Labor and Work Breaks Violations

The Fair Labor Standards Act and state wage and hour laws also govern child labor and work breaks. These work time regulations have likewise posed a problem at Wal-Mart stores.

In January 2004, the *New York Times* reported on an internal Wal-Mart audit which found "extensive violations of child-labor laws and state regulations requiring time for breaks and meals."[36] One week of time records from 25,000 employees in July 2000 found 1,371 instances of minors working too late, during school hours, or for too many hours in a day. There were 60,767 missed breaks and 15,705 lost meal times.[37]

According to the *New York Times* report: "Verette Richardson, a former Wal-Mart cashier in Kansas City, Mo., said it was sometimes so hard to get a break that some cashiers urinated on themselves. Bella Blaubergs, a diabetic who worked at a Wal-Mart in Washington State, said she sometimes nearly fainted from low blood sugar because managers often would not give breaks."[38]

A store manager in Kentucky told the *New York Times* that, after the audit was issued, he received no word from company executives to try harder to cut down on violations: "There was no follow-up to that audit, there was nothing sent out I was aware of saying, 'We're bad. We screwed up. This is the remedy we're going to follow to correct the situation.'"[39]

Unaffordable or Unavailable Health Care

In 2002, 43 million non-elderly Americans lacked health insurance coverage—an increase of almost 2.5 million from the previous year. Most Americans receive their health insurance coverage through their employers. At the same time, most of the uninsured are working Americans and their families, with low to moderate incomes. Their employers, however, either do not offer health insurance at all or the health insurance offered is simply unaffordable.[40]

Among these uninsured working families are a significant number of Wal-Mart employees, many of whom instead secure their health care from publicly subsidized programs. Fewer than half—between 41 and 46 percent—of Wal-Mart's employees are insured by the company's health care plan, compared nationally to 66 percent of employees at large firms like Wal-Mart who receive health benefits from their employer.[41] In recent years, the company increased obstacles for its workers to access its health care plan.

In 2002, Wal-Mart increased the waiting period for enrollment eligibility from 90 days to 6 months for full-time employees. Part-time employees must wait 2 years before they may enroll in the plan, and they may not purchase coverage for their spouses or children. The definition of part-time was changed from 28 hours or less per week to less than 34 hours per week. At the time, approximately one-third of Wal-Mart's workforce was part-time. By comparison, nationally, the average waiting period for health coverage for employees at large firms like Wal-Mart was 1.3 months.[42]

The Wal-Mart plan itself shifts much of the health care costs onto employees. In 1999, employees paid 36 percent of the costs. In 2001, the employee burden rose to 42 percent. Nationally, large-firm employees pay on average 16 percent of the premium for health insurance. Unionized grocery workers typically pay nothing.[43] Studies show that much of the decline in employer-based health coverage is due to shifts of premium costs from employers to employees.[44]

Moreover, Wal-Mart employees who utilize their health care confront high deductibles and co-payments. A single worker could end up spending around $6,400 out-of-pocket—about 45 percent of her annual full-time salary—before seeing a single benefit from the health plan.[45]

According to an AFL-CIO report issued in October 2003, the employees' low wages and Wal-Mart's cost-shifting render health insurance unaffordable, particularly for those employees with families. Even under the Wal-Mart plan with the highest deductible ($1,000)—and therefore with the lowest employee premium contribution—it would take an $8 per hour employee, working 34 hours per week, almost one-and-a-half months of pre-tax earnings to pay for one year of family coverage.[46]

Wal-Mart's spending on health care for its employees falls well below industry and national employer-spending averages. A Harvard Business School case study on Wal-Mart found that, in 2002, Wal-Mart spent an average of $3,500 per employee. By comparison, the average spending per employee in the wholesale/retailing sector was $4,800. For U.S. employers in general, the average was $5,600 per employee.[47]

In the end, because they cannot afford the company health plan, many Wal-Mart workers must turn to public assistance for health care or forego their health care needs altogether. Effectively, Wal-Mart forces taxpayers to subsidize what should be a company-funded health plan. According to a study by the Institute for Labor and Employment at the University of California-Berkeley, **California taxpayers subsidized $20.5 million worth of medical care for Wal-Mart in that state alone.**[48] In fact, Wal-Mart personnel offices, knowing employees cannot afford the company health plan, actually encourage employees to apply for charitable and public assistance, according to a recent report by the PBS news program *Now With Bill Moyers*.[49]

When a giant like Wal-Mart shifts health insurance costs to employees, its competitors invariably come under pressure to do the same. Currently engaged in the largest ongoing labor dispute in the nation, unionized grocery workers in southern California have refused to accept higher health care costs resulting from cost-shifting on health insurance premiums by their grocery chain employers—cost-shifting, the grocers say, inspired by the threat of Wal-Mart competition. Beginning on October 11, 2003, 70,000 grocery employees of Vons, Pavilions, Ralphs, and Albertsons have either been on strike or locked out. The companies want to dramatically increase workers' share of health costs, claiming that the change is necessary in order to compete with Wal-Mart's incursion in the southern California market. E. Richard Brown, the director of the Center for Health Policy at the University of California, Los Angeles, told the *Sacramento Bee* that, if the grocery chains drastically reduce health benefits, the trends toward cost shifting and elimination of health coverage will accelerate. Following the grocers' lead, more employers would offer fewer benefits, would require their workers to pay more, and may even drop health benefits altogether.[50] Whether the current pressure from Wal-Mart is real or imagined or merely a convenient excuse for the grocers' cost-cutting bargaining position, Wal-Mart has sparked a new race to the bottom among American retail employers. Undeniably, such a race threatens to undermine the employer-based health insurance system.

Low Wages Mean High Costs to Taxpayers

Because Wal-Mart wages are generally not living wages, the company uses taxpayers to subsidize its labor costs. While the California study showed how much taxpayers were subsidizing Wal-Mart on health care alone, the total costs to taxpayers for Wal-Mart's labor policies are much greater.

The Democratic Staff of the Committee on Education and the Workforce estimates that one 200-person Wal-Mart store may result in a cost to federal taxpayers of $420,750 per year—about $2,103 per employee. Specifically, the low wages result in the following additional public costs being passed along to taxpayers:

- $36,000 a year for free and reduced lunches for just 50 qualifying Wal-Mart families.
- $42,000 a year for Section 8 housing assistance, assuming 3 percent of the store employees qualify for such assistance, at $6,700 per family.
- $125,000 a year for federal tax credits and deductions for low-income families, assuming 50 employees are heads of household with a child and 50 are married with two children.
- $100,000 a year for the additional Title I expenses, assuming 50 Wal-Mart families qualify with an average of 2 children.
- $108,000 a year for the additional federal health care costs of moving into state children's health insurance programs (S-CHIP), assuming 30 employees with an average of two children qualify.
- $9,750 a year for the additional costs for low income energy assistance.

Among Wal-Mart employees, some single workers may be able to make ends meet. Others may be forced to take on two or three jobs. Others may have a spouse with a better job. And others simply cannot make ends meet. Because Wal-Mart fails to pay sufficient wages, U.S. taxpayers are forced to pick up the tab. In this sense, Wal-Mart's profits are not made only on the backs of its employees—but on the backs of every U.S. taxpayer.

The ultimate costs are not limited to subsidies for underpaid Wal-Mart workers. When a Wal-Mart comes to town, the new competition has a ripple effect throughout the community. Other stores are forced out of business or forced to cut employees' wages and benefits in order to compete with Wal-Mart. The Los Angeles City Council commissioned a report in 2003 on the effects of allowing Wal-Mart Supercenters into their communities. The report, prepared by consulting firm Rodino and Associates, found that Supercenters drive down wages in the local retail industry, place a strain on public services, and damage small businesses. It recommended that the City Council refuse to allow any Supercenters to be built in Los Angeles without a promise from Wal-Mart to increase wages and benefits for its employees.[51]

The findings of the Rodino report are alarming. The labor impacts of a Wal-Mart Supercenter on low-income communities include:

- "Big box retailers and superstores may negatively impact the labor market in an area by the conversion of higher paying retail jobs to a fewer number of lower paying retail jobs. The difference in overall compensation (wages and benefits) may be as much as $8.00."
- "Lack of health care benefits of many big box and superstore employees can result in a greater public financial burden as workers utilize emergency rooms as a major component of their health care."
- "A study conducted by the San Diego Taxpayers Association (SDCTA), a nonprofit, nonpartisan organization, found that an influx of big-box stores into San Diego would result in an annual decline in wages and benefits between $105 million and $221 million, and an increase of $9 million in public health costs. SDCTA also estimated that the region would lose pensions and retirement benefits valued between $89 million and $170 million per year and that even increased sales and property tax revenues would not cover the extra costs of necessary public services."
- "[The threat of Wal-Mart's incursion into the southern California grocery market] is already triggering a dynamic in which the grocery stores are negotiating with workers for lowered compensation, in an attempt to re-level the 'playing field.'"
- "One study of superstores and their potential impact on grocery industry employees found that the entry of such stores into the Southern California regional grocery business was expected to depress industry wages and benefits at an estimated range from a low of $500 million to a high of almost $1.4 billion annually, potentially affecting 250,000 grocery industry employees . . . [T]he full impact of lost wages and benefits throughout Southern California could approach $2.8 billion per year."[52]

Reports such as these have provided supporting evidence to localities which seek to pass ordinances restricting "big box" or supercenter stores. Such ordinances were recently passed in Alameda and Contra Costa counties in California. Wal-Mart, however, has moved to overturn those ordinances. In Contra Costa, Wal-Mart launched a petition drive to challenge that county's ordinance in a referendum in March 2004. In Alameda, the company has filed a lawsuit to void an ordinance passed by the Board of Supervisors in January 2004.[53]

One of the most cited studies on Wal-Mart's impact on local communities was performed by economist Kenneth Stone at Iowa State University in 1993. Stone looked at the impact of Wal-Mart on small towns in Iowa. He found a 3 percent spike in total retail sales in communities immediately after a Wal-Mart opened. But the longer term effects of Wal-Mart were disastrous for nearby independent businesses. Over the course of the next several years, retailers' sales of mens' and boys' apparel dropped 44 percent on average, hardware sales fell by 31 percent, and lawn and garden sales fell by 26 percent. Likewise, a Congressional Research Service report in 1994 explained that Wal-Mart uses a saturation strategy with store development. In other words, it builds stores in nearby connected markets in order to stifle any competition in the targeted area by the size of its presence.[54]

By all accounts, Wal-Mart's development strategy has been working. Currently, Wal-Mart operates around 3,000 total stores and close to 1,400 Supercenters. It is the largest grocer in the U.S., with a 19 percent market share, and the third-largest pharmacy, with a 16 percent market share. According to Retail Forward, a global management consulting and research firm, for every one Supercenter that will open, two supermarkets will close.[55] Since 1992, the supermarket industry has experienced a net loss of 13,500 stores.[56] Over the next five years, Wal-Mart plans to open 1,000 more Supercenters in the U.S.[57] By 2007, Wal-Mart is expected to control 35 percent of food and drug sales in the U.S.[58]

Illegal Use of Undocumented Workers

Among the lowest paid workers in the U.S. economy are undocumented immigrants. As was reported in the fall of 2003, these workers are not foreign to the floors of Wal-Mart stores. On October 23, 2003, federal agents raided 61 Wal-Mart stores in 21 states. When they left, the agents had arrested 250 nightshift janitors who were undocumented workers.[59]

Following the arrests, a grand jury convened to consider charging Wal-Mart executives with labor racketeering crimes for knowingly allowing undocumented workers to work at their stores. The workers themselves were employed by agencies Wal-Mart contracted with for cheap cleaning services. While Wal-Mart executives have tried to lay the blame squarely with the contractors, federal investigators point to wiretapped conversations showing that executives knew the workers were undocumented.[60]

Additionally, some of the janitors have filed a class-action lawsuit against Wal-Mart alleging both racketeering and wage-and-hour violations. According to the janitors, Wal-Mart and its contractors failed to pay them overtime totaling, along with other damages, $200,000. One of the plaintiffs told the *New York Times* that he worked seven days per week for eight months, earning $325 for 60-hour weeks, and he never received overtime.[61] A legal question now being raised is whether these undocumented workers even have the right to sue their employers.[62]

Not surprisingly, this recent raid was not the first time Wal-Mart was caught using undocumented workers. In 1998 and 2001, federal agents arrested 102 undocumented workers at Wal-Marts around the country.[63]

President Bush's newly proposed temporary foreign worker plan would legalize such undocumented workers without granting them an opportunity for citizenship, creating a new class of indentured servants and a safer source of cheap labor for companies like Wal-Mart.

Trading Away Jobs

Since the recession began in March 2001, the United States has lost 2.4 million jobs. In every recession, since the Great Depression, jobs were recovered within the first 31 months after the recession began—until now. The latest recession began 34 months ago and officially ended in November 2001, but the jobs have not been recovered. For American working families, by all accounts, the "jobless recovery" has been of little benefit to them. While GDP growth was strong or solid in the third and fourth quarters of 2003, real wages for workers remained stagnant and even declined.[64]

Indeed, of the jobs that remain, the pay is low. The country has seen a dramatic shift from high-paying jobs to low-paying jobs. For instance, in New Hampshire, which still has not recovered the number of jobs it lost in the recession, new jobs pay 35 percent lower wages than lost jobs. In Delaware, those wages are 43 percent lower; in Colorado, 35 percent lower; in West Virginia, 33 percent lower. In fact, the low pay shift has hit all but two of the fifty states.[65]

Moreover, these changes in the labor market reveal themselves in a marked decline in living standards for low- and middle-income workers. The real weekly earnings for full-time workers age 25 and older fell for the bottom half of the workforce between the fourth quarters of 2002 and 2003. In particular, workers in the 10th percentile saw their weekly earnings fall 1.2 percent; in the 20th percentile, by 0.5 percent, in the 50th percentile, by 0.1 percent.[66] Conversely, earners in the top percentiles of income experienced growth. The 90th percentile, for instance, saw a 1.1 percent increase in weekly earnings. As the Economic Policy Institute points out: "This pattern of earnings growth suggests that while the economy is expanding, the benefits of growth are flowing to those at the top of the wage scale."[67]

These lower-paying jobs are largely service sector jobs, like retail, replacing traditionally higher-paying and unionized manufacturing jobs. Between January 1998 and August 2003, the nation experienced a net loss of 3 million manufacturing jobs.[68] During the "recovery," 1.3 million manufacturing jobs disappeared.[69] American manufacturers find it increasingly difficult to keep jobs in the U.S., given the availability of cheap labor abroad. In 2003, the U.S. trade deficit hit a record high of $551 billion, increasing 15 percent from 2002 and exceeding 5 percent of GDP.[70]

Wal-Mart plays a curiously illustrative role in this jobs phenomenon—not just in the creation of low-paying jobs and the downward pressure on wages and benefits, but also in the export of existing manufacturing jobs to foreign countries offering cheap labor. Wal-Mart markets itself with a patriotic, small-town, red-white-and-blue advertising motif. But Wal-Mart's trade practices are anything but small-town. Indeed, Wal-Mart conducts international trade in manufactured goods on a scale that can bring down entire nations' economies.

While the red-white-and-blue banners remain, long-gone are the days when Wal-Mart abided by the mottos of "Buy American" and "Bring It Home to the USA." In 1995, Wal-Mart claimed only 6 percent of its merchandise was imported. Today an estimated 50-60 percent of its products come from overseas.[71] In the past five years, Wal-Mart has doubled its imports from China. In 2002, the company bought 14 percent of the $1.9 billion of clothes exported by Bangladesh to the United States. Also in 2002, the company purchased $12 billion in merchandise from China, or 10 percent of China's total

U.S.-bound exports, a 20 percent increase from the previous year. In 2003, these Chinese purchases jumped to $15 billion, or almost one-eighth of all Chinese exports to the United States.[72] Today, more than 3,000 supplier factories in China produce for Wal-Mart.[73]

Wal-Mart maintains an extensive global network of 10,000 suppliers.[74] Whether American, Bangladeshi, Chinese, or Honduran, Wal-Mart plays these producers against one another in search of lower and lower prices. American suppliers have been forced to relocate their businesses overseas to maintain Wal-Mart contracts.[75] Overseas manufacturers are forced to engage in cut-throat competition that further erodes wages and working conditions of what often already are sweatshops. To keep up with the pressure to produce ever cheaper goods, factories force employees to work overtime or work for weeks without a day off. A Bangladeshi factory worker told the *Los Angeles Times* that employees at her factory worked from 8 a.m. to 3 a.m. for 10 and 15 day stretches just to meet Wal-Mart price demands. And still, Wal-Mart's general manager for Bangladesh complained of his country's factories, telling the *Los Angeles Times,* "I think they need to improve. When I entered a factory in China, it seemed they are very fast."[76]

While low-wage jobs displace higher-paid manufacturing jobs in the United States, undercutting living standards at home, living standards abroad are not reaping the benefits one might expect. Reports indicate that Wal-Mart's bargaining power is able to maintain low wages and poor working conditions among its foreign suppliers. The *Washington Post* has explained: "As capital scours the globe for cheaper and more malleable workers, and as poor countries seek multinational companies to provide jobs, lift production, and open export markets, Wal-Mart and China have forged themselves into the ultimate joint venture, their symbiosis influencing the terms of labor and consumption the world over."[77] Thanks to a ban on independent trade unions and a lack of other basic human rights, China offers Wal-Mart a highly-disciplined and cheap workforce. A Chinese labor official who asked to remain anonymous for fear of punishment told the *Washington Post* that "Wal-Mart pressures the factory to cut its price, and the factory responds with longer hours or lower pay. And the workers have no options."[78]

One employee of a Chinese supplier described the difficulties of surviving on $75 per month. She could rarely afford to buy meat, and her family largely subsisted on vegetables. Over four years, she had not received a single salary increase.[79]

Wal-Mart has countered that it insists that its suppliers enforce labor standards and comply with Chinese law. One-hundred Wal-Mart auditors inspect Chinese plants, and the company has suspended contracts with about 400 suppliers, mainly for violating overtime limits. An additional 72 factories were permanently blacklisted in 2003 for violating child labor standards. Still, critics point out that the Wal-Mart does not regularly inspect smaller factories that use middlemen to sell to the company. Nor does it inspect the factories of subcontractors. A Chinese labor organizer explained that the inspections are "ineffective," since Wal-Mart usually notifies the factories in advance. The factories "often prepare by cleaning up, creating fake time sheets and briefing workers on what to say."[80]

The factories themselves complain that, because Wal-Mart demands such low prices, they have slim profit margins—if any. A manager of one Chinese supplier told the *Washington Post,* "In the beginning, we made money . . . But when Wal-Mart started to launch nationwide distribution, they pressured us for a special price below our cost. Now, we're losing money on every box, while Wal-Mart is making more money."[81] Obviously, one way to regain a profit for such suppliers would be to begin cutting back on labor costs.

Finally, as testament to Wal-Mart's stalwart anti-union policy, none of its 31 stores in China are unionized, despite the fact that the Communist Party-controlled official union has told the company that it would not help workers fight for higher pay.[82] Oddly enough, Article 10 of China's Trade Union Law requires that any establishment with 25 or more workers must have a union. Wal-Mart, however, claims that it has received assurances from the central government that it need not allow unions in any of its stores.[83] As one reporter has explained, "The explanation for the apparent contradiction may be that the government's desire for foreign investment and jobs trumps any concern for workers' rights. That wouldn't be surprising in the Chinese environment, where strikes are forbidden and the official labor grouping actively supports the government's efforts to block the rise of independent unions."[84] With China, any company in search of pliant and cheap labor has found a perfect mix of cooperative government officials and workers made submissive through fear.

Disability Discrimination

The Americans with Disabilities Act (ADA) prohibits discrimination against persons with disabilities in employment matters. In particular, an employer may not discriminate against an employee or prospective employee who is otherwise qualified to perform the job if given reasonable accommodations.[85]

In addition to lawsuits over lost wages or unequal pay, Wal-Mart has faced a barrage of lawsuits alleging that the company discriminates against workers with disabilities. In 2001, Wal-Mart paid over $6 million to settle 13 such lawsuits. These cases were brought by the U.S. Equal Employment Opportunity Commission (EEOC) on behalf of disabled persons whom Wal-Mart failed to hire. The settlement also required Wal-Mart to change its procedures in dealing with disabled job applicants and provide more training for its employees on anti-discrimination laws.[86]

Yet, on January 20, 2004, the EEOC filed another lawsuit against the retail giant on behalf of a job applicant who claims he was not hired because he needed a wheelchair. The lawsuit was filed in Kansas City after the EEOC failed to obtain a settlement with Wal-Mart.[87]

Worker Safety

The Occupational Safety and Health Act (OSHA) is designed to protect workers from workplace injuries and illnesses.[88] OSHA is enforced by the Department of Labor's Occupational Safety and Health Administration. Regulations issued by that agency lay out clear rules for such safety matters as the provision of exits for employees.[89]

The latest Wal-Mart scandal to hit the news is its reported lockdown of its nighttime shift various stores around the country. According to a January 18, 2004, *New York Times* report, the company institutes a "lock-in" policy at some of its Wal-Mart and Sam's Club stores.[90] The stores lock their doors at night so that no one can enter or leave the building, leaving workers inside trapped. Some workers are then threatened that, if they ever use the fire exit to leave the building, they will be fired. Instead, a manager is supposed to have a key that will unlock doors to allow employees to escape. Many workers have found themselves locked in without a manager who has a key, as the *New York Times* story detailed.[91]

The company has claimed that the policy is designed to protect stores and employees from crime. Former store managers, however, have claimed the real reason behind the lockdown is to prevent "shrinkage"—i.e., theft by either employees or outsiders. It is also designed to eliminate unauthorized cigarette breaks or quick trips home.[92]

Locked-in workers have had to wait for hours off-the-clock for a manager to show up to let them go home after they completed their shift. One worker claims to have broken his foot on the job and had to wait four hours for someone to open the door. Another worker alleges she cut her hand with box cutters one night and was forced to wait until morning to go to the hospital, where she received thirteen stitches.[93]

In the history of American worker safety, some of the worst tragedies have involved employees locked in their workplaces in an emergency, including the Triangle Waist Company fire of 1911 in which 146 women died in a fire because the garment factory's doors were locked. As recently as 1991, 25 workers perished in a fire at a chicken processing plant in North Carolina. The plant's owner had locked the doors for fear of employee theft and unauthorized breaks. According to recent reports, ten percent of Wal-Mart's stores are subjected to the nighttime lockdown.[94]

In 2002, in a telling junction of alleged labor law violations, the National Labor Relations Board (NLRB) issued a complaint against a Wal-Mart in Texas regarding health and safety threats made by management against employees. According to the complaint, a company official told workers that, after a worker filed complaints regarding unsafe conditions with the Occupational Safety and Health Administration (OSHA), any fines imposed upon the company would come out of employee bonuses.[95] . . .

Conclusion

Wal-Mart's success has meant downward pressures on wages and benefits, rampant violations of basic workers' rights, and threats to the standard of living in communities across the country. The success of a business need not come at the expense of workers and their families. Such short-sighted profit-making strategies ultimately undermine our economy.

In the past few years, Wal-Mart has been subjected to dozens of class-action suits seeking backpay for hundreds of thousands of shortchanged workers, dozens of unfair labor practice complaints by the U.S. government for violations of workers' right to organize, and other legal actions stemming from the company's employment practices. At the same time, it has managed to keep its wages low and put suppliers on a downward spiral to cut their own wages. To keep up with Wal-Mart's low-cost demands, U.S. manufacturers have found it increasingly difficult to remain in the U.S. Cuts in health care benefits to Wal-Mart employees are pushing other U.S. grocers to do the same.

Wal-Mart's current behavior must not be allowed to set the standard for American labor practices. Standing together, America's working families, including Wal-Mart employees, and their allies in Congress can reverse this race to the bottom in the fast-expanding service industry. The promise that every American can work an honest day's work, receive an honest day's wages, raise a family, own a home, have decent health care, and send their children to college is a promise that is not easily abandoned. It is, in short, the American Dream.

Notes

1. Anthony Bianco and Wendy Zellner, "Is Wal-Mart Too Powerful?" *Business Week* 100 (October 6, 2003).
2. Charles Stein, "Wal-Mart Finds Success, Image Breed Contempt," *Boston Globe* H1 (November 30, 2003).
3. 29 U.S.C. § 141 *et seq.*
4. International Labor Organization, Convention No. 87, Freedom of Association and Protection of the Right to Organize (1948), and No. 98, Right to Organize and Collective Bargaining (1949).
5. International Confederation of Free Trade Unions (ICFTU), *Internationally Recognised Core Labour Standards in the United States: Report for the WTO General Council Review of the Trade Policies of the United States* (Geneva, January 14-16, 2004).
6. *Id.* at 3-4.
7. Wal-Mart, *A Manager's Toolbox to Remaining Union Free* at 20-21 (no date). Available online at `http://www.ufcw.org/issues_and_actions/walmart_workers_campaign_info/relevant_links/anti_union_manuals.cfm`.
8. Pan Demetrakakes, "Is Wal-Mart Wrapped in Union Phobia?" *Food & Packaging* 76 (August 1, 2003).
9. Dan Kasler, "Labor Dispute Has Historical Precedent," *Scripps Howard News Service* (November 3, 2003).
10. Bureau of Labor Statistics, Department of Labor, "Union Members in 2003," Table 1 (January 21, 2004).
11. Stephen Franklin and Delroy Alexander, "Grocery Walkouts Have Broad Reach," *Chicago Tribune* C1 (November 12, 2003).
12. Bureau of Labor Statistics, Department of Labor, "Employee Benefits in Private Industry, 2003," Table 1 (September 17, 2003).
13. *Id.*

14. Charles Williams, "Supermarket Sweepstakes: Traditional Grocery Chains Mull Responses to Wal-Mart's Growing Dominance," *The Post and Courier* (Charleston, SC) 16E (November 10, 2003).

15. *Id.*

16. "Unaffordable Health Care, Low Wages, Sexual Discrimination—the Wal-Mart Way of Life," http://www.ufcw.org/workplace_connections/retail/industry_news/index.cfm (January 26, 2004).

17. Doug Dority, "The People's Campaign: Justice@Wal-Mart," *Air Line Pilot* 55 (February 2003).

18. Bianco and Zellner, *supra* note 1.

19. PBS, "Store Wars: When Wal-Mart Comes to Town," http://www.pbs.org/itvs/storewars/stores3.html (February 2, 2004). This percentage of part-time employees was based on the earlier Wal-Mart definition of part-time as working 28 hours or less per week. In 2002, Wal-Mart changed the definition to less than 34 hours per week, which likely increased the company's number of part-time workers.

20. Wal-Mart.com, "3 Basic Beliefs," http://www.walmartstores.com/wmstore/wmstores/Mainabout.jsp?pagetype=about&categoryOID=-8242&catID=-8242&template=ContentLanding.jsp (January 26, 2004).

21. Karen Olsson, "Up Against Wal-Mart," *Mother Jones* 54 (March/April 2003).

22. 42 U.S.C. § 2000e *et seq.*

23. 29 U.S.C. § 206.

24. Neil Buckley and Caroline Daniel, "Wal-Mart vs. the Workers: Labour Grievances Are Stacking Up Against the World's Biggest Company," *Financial Times* 11 (November 20, 2003).

25. Sheryl McCarthy, "Wal-Mart—Always Low Wages for Women!" *Newsday* (May 1, 2003).

26. 29 U.S.C. § 201 *et seq.*

27. Associated Press, "Federal Jury Finds Wal-Mart Guilty in Overtime Pay Case," *Chicago Tribune*, Business 3 (December 20, 2003).

28. *Id.*

29. Steven Greenhouse, "Suits Say Wal-Mart Forces Workers to Toil Off the Clock," *New York Times* A1 (June 25, 2002).

30. Associated press, *supra* note 27.

31. Kristian Foden-Vencil, "Multiple Lawsuits Accuse Wal-Mart of Violating Workplace Regulations," *NPR Morning Edition* (January 14, 2004).

32. Gwendolyn Freed and John Reenan, "Wal-Mart Suit Gets Class Status," *Star Tribune* 1D (November 6, 2003).

33. Greenhouse, *supra* note 29.

34. United Food & Commercial Workers (UFCW), "Wal-Mart's War on Workers' Wages and Overtime Pay," http://www.ufcw.org/press_room/fact_sheets_and_backgrounder/walmart/wages.cfm (January 26, 2004).

35. Greenhouse, *supra* note 29.

36. Steven Greenhouse, "In-House Audit Says Wal-Mart Violated Labor Laws," *New York Times* 16A (January 13, 2004).

37. *Id.*

38. *Id.*

39. *Id.*

40. Kaiser Family Foundation, *The Uninsured: A Primer—Key Facts About Americans Without Health Insurance,* at 1 (December 2003).
41. AFL-CIO, *Wal-Mart: An Example of Why Workers Remain Uninsured and Underinsured,* at 1 (October 2003).
42. *Id.* at 11.
43. *Id.*
44. John Holahan, "Changes in Employer-Sponsored Health Insurance Coverage," *Snapshots of America's Families III,* Urban Institute (September 17, 2003).
45. AFL-CIO, *supra* note 41, at 16.
46. *Id.* at 12.
47. Panjak Ghemawat, Ken Mark, and Stephen Bradley, "Wal-Mart Stores in 2003," case study, Harvard Business School (revised January 30, 2004).
48. Sylvia Chase, "The True Cost of Shopping at Wal-Mart," *Now with Bill Moyers,* Transcript (December 19, 2003).
49. *Id.*
50. Laura Mecoy, "Health Benefits Fight Heats Up: South State Grocery Strike Spotlights a Contentious Trend in Contract Talks," *Sacramento Bee* A1 (January 19, 2004).
51. Nancy Cleeland, "City Report is Critical of Wal-Mart Supercenters," *Los Angeles Times* C1 (December 6, 2003).
52. Rodino Associates, *Final Report on Research for Big Box Retail/Superstore Ordinance,* prepared for Industrial and Commercial Development Division, Community Development Department, at 18–20 (October 28, 2003).
53. Michelle Maitre, "Wal-Mart is Suing Alameda County: Retail Giant Challenges Law that Bars Supercenters in Unincorporated Areas," *Alameda Times-Star* (Alameda, CA) at More Local News (January 27, 2004).
54. Jessica Hall and Jim Troy, "Wal-Mart Go Home! Wal-Mart's Expansion Juggernaut Stumbles as Towns Turn Thumbs Down and Noses Up," *Warfield's Business Record* 1 (July 22, 1994).
55. Bianco and Zellner, *supra* note 1.
56. Matthew Swibel, "How to Outsmart Wal-Mart," `Forbes.com` (November 24, 2003).
57. Bianco and Zellner, *supra* note 1.
58. Williams, supra note 14.
59. Steven Greenhouse, "Suit by Wal-Mart Cleaners Asserts Rackets Violation," *New York Times,* 12A (November 11, 2003).
60. Greg Schneider and Dina ElBoghdady, "Wal-Mart Confirms Probe of Hiring," *Washington Post* E1 (November 5, 2003).
61. Greenhouse, *supra* note 59.
62. Sarah Paoletti, "Q: Should illegal aliens be able to sue U.S. employers for labor racketeering?; Yes: Employees who have suffered discrimination or exploitation in the workplace are entitled to sue, regardless of their immigration status," *Insight Magazine* 46 (January 19, 2004).
63. Steven Greenhouse, "Illegally in the U.S., and Never a Day Off at Wal-Mart," *International Herald Tribune* 2 (November 6, 2003).
64. `Jobwatch.org`, Economic Policy Institute, `http://www.jobwatch.org/` (January 26, 2004).

65. Economic Policy Institute, "Jobs Shift from Higher-Paying to Lower-Paying Industries," *Economic Snapshots* (January 21, 2004).

66. Economic Policy Institute, "Economic Growth Not Reaching Middle- and Lower Wage Earners," *Economic Snapshots* (January 28, 2004).

67. *Id.*

68. Josh Bivens, Robert Scott, and Christian Weller, "Mending Manufacturing: Reversing poor policy decisions is the only way to end current crisis," *EPI Briefing Paper #44* (September 2003).

69. Economic Policy Institute, "Job Growth Up, Job Quality Down," *Economic Snapshots* (December 17, 2003).

70. Economic Policy Institute, "Souring Trade Deficit Threatens to Destabilize U.S. Financial Markets," *Economic Snapshots* (January 7, 2004).

71. Nancy Cleeland, Evelyn Iritani, and Tyler Marshall, "The Wal-Mart Effect: Scouring the Globe to Give Shoppers an $8.63 Polo Shirt," *Los Angeles Times* A1 (November 24, 2003).

72. Peter S. Goodman and Philip P. Pan, "Chinese Workers Pay for Wal-Mart's Low Prices," *Washington Post* A1 (February 8, 2004).

73. Cleeland, Iritani, and Marshall, *supra* note 71.

74. *Id.*

75. Abigail Goodman and Nancy Cleeland, "The Wal-Mart Effect: An Empire Built on Bargains Remakes the Working World," *L.A. Times* 1 (November 23, 2003); Charles Fishman, "The Wal-Mart You Don't Know," *Fast Company* 68 (December 2003).

76. Cleeland, Iritani, and Marshall, *supra* note 71.

77. Goodman and Pan, *supra* note 72.

78. *Id.*

79. *Id.*

80. *Id.*

81. *Id.*

82. *Id.*

83. Carl Goldstein, "Wal-Mart in China," *The Nation* (November 20, 2003).

84. *Id.*

85. 29 U.S.C. § 706 *et seq.*

86. "Disabled Man Sues Wal-Mart," *Business Journal* (Kansas City) (January 20, 2004).

87. *Id.*

88. 29 U.S.C. § 651 *et seq.*

89. 29 C.F.R. 1910.35 *et seq.*

90. Steven Greenhouse, "Workers Assail Lock-Ins by Wal-Mart," *New York Times* 1 (January 18, 2004).

91. *Id.*

92. *Id.*

93. *Id.*

94. *Id.*

95. `Walmartwatch.org`, "Wal-Mart's War on Workers: Frontline Report from Texas and California," `http://www.walmartwatch.com/info/internal.cfm?subsection_id=130&internal_id=351` (May 2, 2002).

POSTSCRIPT

Is Wal-Mart Good for the Economy?

LAEDC believes that the entry of Wal-Mart Supercenter stores into Southern California would lead to lower prices for consumers on their grocery, general merchandise, and apparel purchases. The magnitude of the savings is estimated for the City of Los Angeles, for Los Angeles County, and for Southern California. For the latter, the establishment of Wal-Mart Supercenters would eventually lead to savings amounting to $3.76 billion per year. LAEDC believes that consumers would take these savings and spend them on other things and thereby create new jobs. For the City of Los Angeles, the redirected grocery savings alone would create some 6,500 new jobs.

The Democratic Staff of the House Committee on Education and the Workforce cites a number of deficiencies in Wal-Mart's behavior. It charges that Wal-Mart has violated workers' right to organize, maintained low wages, discriminated against women and the disabled, failed to pay employees for all the hours they worked, violated child labor laws, provided inadequate health care insurance, used undocumented workers, and traded away jobs. When all these deficiencies are considered, the Democratic Staff concludes that the costs of Wal-Mart's low prices are just too high.

Perhaps the best place to start with additional readings on this issue is the complete versions of the LAEDC and the Democratic Staff reports. The former can be found at `http://www.google.com/search?q=cache:k2x3GeYdFOgJ:www.mayocommunications.com/2003LAEDCIMAGES/Wal-Mart%2520Supercenters%2520%2520What's%2520in%2520store%2520for%2520Southern%2520California.pdf+Wal-mart+economic+impact+study&hl=en&ie=UTF-8`, while the latter can be found at `http://edworkforce.house.gov/demcrats/WALMARTREPORT.pdf`. There are a number of additional studies on the effects of Wal-Mart, including "The New Colossus" by Jay Nordlinger in the *National Review* (April 19, 2004); *The Case Against Wal-Mart* by Al Norman in *Raphel Marketing* (2004); "The Case for Wal-Mart" by Karen DeCoster and Brad Edmonds (January 31, 2003), `http://www.mises.org/fullstory.aspx?control=1151`; "Declaring War on Wal-Mart" by Aaron Bernstein in *Business Week* (February 7, 2005); "Rejuvenating Wal-Mart's Reputation" by Thomas A. Hemphill in *Business Horizons* (January/February 2005); "Just Say No" by Julian E. Barnes and Tim Appenzeller in *U.S., News & World Report* (April 19, 2004); and "Up Against Wal-Mart" by Karen Olsson in *Mother Jones* (March/April 2003).

ISSUE 8

Should Social Security Be Changed to Include Personal Retirement Accounts?

YES: The White House, from "Strengthening Social Security for the 21st Century," `http://www.whitehouse.gov/infocus/socialsecurity/200501/strengtheningsocialsecurity.html` (February 2005)

NO: Dean Baker, from "Bush's Numbers Racket: Why Social Security Privatization Is a Phony Solution to a Phony Problem," *The American Prospect Online Edition* (January 14, 2005)

ISSUE SUMMARY

YES: The White House identifies a number of problems with the present structure of the Social Security system and proposes personal retirement accounts as a way of resolving these problems, and "dramatically reduce the costs of permanently fixing the system."

NO: Dean Baker, co-director of the Center for Economic and Policy Research, argues that President Bush's plan for personal retirement accounts would not fix Social Security; instead, it would "undermine a system that has provided security for ten of millions of workers, and their families, for seven decades, and which can continue to do so long into the future if it is just left alone."

In retrospect, it is not surprising that an event as catastrophic as the Great Depression of the 1930s would produce fundamental change in the American economy. The reality of the human suffering generated by the collapse of one-third of the nation's banks, an unemployment rate of 25 percent, and a 30 percent decline in the production of goods and services as well as household net worth led to a rush of legislation. The legislation, in general terms, was intended to achieve two objectives: to restore confidence in the economy and to provide greater economic security. Today the institutions and programs created by this legislative avalanche are familiar to almost all Americans, including the Federal Deposit Insurance Corporation, the Securities and Exchange Commission, and Social Security.

Social Security, more formally the Old Age, Survivors, and Disability Insurance Program (OASDI), was signed into law on August 14, 1935, by President Franklin D. Roosevelt. As originally designed, OASDI provided three types of benefits: retirement benefits to the elderly who were no longer working, survivor benefits to the spouses and children of persons who had died, and disability benefits to persons who experienced nonwork-related illness or injury. The Medicare portion of Social Security, which provides benefits for hospital, doctor, and medical expenses, was created in 1965 (see Issue 4).

There are many terms used to describe OASDI. It is an entitlement program in the sense that everyone who satisfies the eligibility requirements receives benefits. Eligibility is established by employment and contributions to the system (in the form of payroll taxes) for a minimum period of time. It is also a defined benefits program; that is, the level of benefits is determined by legislation. The opposite of a defined benefits program is a defined contributions program, where benefits are determined by contributions and whatever investment income is generated by those contributions. OASDI is also described as a pay-as-you-go system; this means that payments received by recipients are financed primarily by the contributions of current workers. Still another description of OASDI is that it is an income security program. In this context, the reference is to a whole set of government programs designed to provide minimum levels of income to various persons. Finally, OASDI is described as a social insurance program to distinguish it from private insurance programs. The insurance feature rests on the fact that OASDI protects against certain unforeseen events like disability or early death. The social feature arises from the fact that contributions and the level of benefits are determined by legislation as well as the fact that the contributions are mandatory (payroll taxes that must be paid). In a private insurance program, the beneficiary and the insurance issuer voluntarily negotiate the level of contributions and the level of benefits.

The Social Security "crisis" refers to the fact that with the currently legislated structure of revenues and benefits, the system will eventually be unable to meet its financial obligations. Presently revenues are greater than out-payments, and the excess is accumulated in a trust fund. Around the year 2019, out-payments will exceed revenues, and drawing down the trust fund will cover the difference. Eventually the trust fund will be exhausted, and revenues will only be sufficient to cover a portion of scheduled benefits. According to the most recent report from the Social Security Trustees, that year is 2042, and at that point revenues will be equal to 73 percent of scheduled benefits.

The White House

Strengthening Social Security for the 21st Century

The Problems Facing Social Security

- **A Social Security System designed for a 1935 world does not fit the needs of the 21st Century.** Social Security was designed in 1935 for a world that is very different from today. In 1935, most women did not work outside the home. Today, about 60% of women work outside the home. In 1935, the average American did not live long enough to collect retirement benefits. Today, life expectancy is 77 years. . . .
- **Social Security will not be changed for those 55 or older (born before 1950).** Today, more than 45 million Americans receive Social Security benefits and millions more are nearing retirement. For these Americans, Social Security benefits are secure and will not change in any way.
- **Social Security is making empty promises to our children and grandchildren.** For our younger workers, Social Security has serious problems that will grow worse over time. Social Security cannot afford to pay promised benefits to future generations because it was designed for a 1935 world in which benefits were much lower, life-spans were shorter, there were more workers per retiree, and fewer retirees were drawing from the system.
- **With each passing year, there are fewer workers paying ever-higher benefits to an ever-larger number of retirees.** Social Security is a pay-as-you-go system, which means taxes on today's workers pay the benefits for today's retirees. A worker's payroll taxes are not saved in an account with his or her name on it for the worker's retirement.
    - **There are fewer workers to support our retirees.** When Social Security was first created, there were 40 workers to support every one retiree, and most workers did not live long enough to collect retirement benefits from the system. Since then, the demographics of our society have changed dramatically. People are living longer and having fewer children. As a result we have seen a dramatic

From Strengthening Social Security for the 21st Century, February 2005. http://www.whitehouse.gov/infocus/socialsecurity/200501/strengtheningsocialsecurity.html. References omitted.

change in the number of workers supporting each retiree's benefits. According to the 2004 Report of the Social Security Trustees (page 47):

- In 1950, there were 16 workers to support every one beneficiary of Social Security.
- Today, there are only 3.3 workers supporting every Social Security beneficiary.
- And, by the time our youngest workers turn 65, there will be only 2 workers supporting each beneficiary.

- **Benefits are scheduled to rise dramatically over the next few decades.** Because benefits are tied to wage growth rather than inflation, benefits are growing faster than the rest of the economy. This benefit formula was established in 1977. As a result, today's 20-year old is promised benefits that are 40% higher, in real terms, than are paid to seniors who retire this year. But the current system does not have the money to pay these promised benefits.
- **The retirement of the Baby Boomers will accelerate the problem.** In just 3 years, the first of the Baby Boom generation will begin to retire, putting added strain on a system that was not designed to meet the needs of the 21st century. By 2031, there will be almost twice as many older Americans as today—from 37 million today to 71 million. . . .

- **Social Security is heading toward bankruptcy.** According to the Social Security Trustees, thirteen years from now, in 2018, Social Security will be paying out more than it takes in and every year afterward will bring a new shortfall, bigger than the year before. And, when today's young workers begin to retire in 2042, the system will be exhausted and bankrupt. . . . If we do not act now to save it, the only solution will be drastically higher taxes, massive new borrowing, or sudden and severe cuts in Social Security benefits or other government programs.
- **As of 2004, the cost of doing nothing to fix our Social Security system had hit an estimated $10.4 trillion, according to the Social Security Trustees.** . . . The longer we wait to take action, the more difficult and expensive the changes will be.
  - $10.4 trillion is almost twice the combined wages and salaries of every working American in 2004.
  - Every year we wait costs an additional $600 billion. . . .
  - Today's 30-year-old worker can expect a 27% benefit cut from the current system when he or she reaches normal retirement age. . . . And, without action, these benefit cuts will only get worse.

Personal Retirement Accounts

- **The President believes personal retirement accounts must be part of a comprehensive solution to strengthen Social Security for the 21st century.**
- **Under the President's plan, personal retirement accounts would start gradually. Yearly contribution limits would be raised over**

time, eventually permitting all workers to set aside 4 percentage points of their payroll taxes in their accounts. Annual contributions to personal retirement accounts initially would be capped, at $1,000 per year in 2009. The cap would rise gradually over time, growing $100 per year, plus growth in average wages.

- **Personal retirement accounts offer younger workers the opportunity to build a "nest egg" for retirement that the government cannot take away.**
  - **Personal retirement accounts provide ownership and control.** Personal retirement accounts give younger workers the opportunity to own an asset and watch it grow over time.
  - **Personal retirement accounts could be passed on to children and grandchildren.** The money in these accounts would be available for retirement expenses. Any unused portion could be passed on to loved ones. Permitting individuals to pass on their personal retirement accounts to loved ones will be particularly beneficial to widows, widowers, and other survivors. According to the non-partisan analysis by the Social Security Administration's Office of Retirement Policy, the ability to inherit personal accounts provides the largest gains to widows and other survivors.
  - **Personal retirement accounts help make Social Security better for younger workers.** A personal retirement account gives a younger worker the chance to save a portion of his or her money in an account and watch it grow over time at a greater rate than anything the current system can deliver. The account will provide money for the worker's retirement in addition to the check he or she receives from Social Security. Personal retirement accounts give younger workers the chance to receive a higher rate of return from sound, long-term investing of a portion of their payroll taxes than they receive under the current system.
- **Personal retirement accounts would be voluntary.** At any time, a worker could "opt in" by making a *one-time* election to put a portion of his or her payroll taxes into a personal retirement account.
  - Workers would have the flexibility to choose from several different low-cost, broad-based investment funds and would have the opportunity to adjust investment allocations periodically, but would not be allowed to move back and forth between personal retirement accounts and the traditional system. If, after workers choose the account, they decide they want only the benefits the current system would give them, they can leave their money invested in government bonds like those the Social Security system invests in now.
  - Those workers who do not elect to create a personal retirement account would continue to draw benefits from the traditional Social Security system, reformed to be permanently sustainable.
- **Personal retirement account options and management would be similar to that of the Federal employee retirement program, known as the Thrift Savings Plan (TSP).** A centralized administrative structure would be created to collect personal retirement account contributions, manage investments, maintain records, and facilitate withdrawals at retirement. The structure would be designed to facilitate

low costs, ease of use for new investors, and timely crediting of contributions. This centralized investment structure would help minimize compliance costs for employers.

- Contributions would be collected and records maintained by a central administrator. Similar to the TSP, private investment managers would be chosen through a competitive bidding process to manage the pooled account contributions.
- The central administrator would answer questions from account participants and distribute periodic account statements.
- The central administrator would also facilitate withdrawals and the purchase of annuities with account balances.
- Like TSP, we expect participants to have easy access to investment information and to their accounts. Participants could easily check account balances and adjust investment allocations.

- **Personal retirement accounts would be invested in a mix of conservative bonds and stock funds.** Guidelines and restrictions would be put in place to provide sound investment choices and prevent individuals from spending the money in these accounts on the lottery or at the race track. Workers would be permitted to allocate their personal retirement account contributions among a small number of very broadly diversified index funds patterned after the current TSP funds.
  - Like TSP, personal retirement accounts could be invested in a safe government securities fund; an investment-grade corporate bond index fund; a small-cap stock index fund; a large-cap stock index fund; and an international stock index fund.
  - In addition to these TSP-type funds, workers could choose a government bond fund with a guaranteed rate of return above inflation.
  - Workers could also choose a "life cycle portfolio" that would automatically adjust the level of risk of the investments as the worker aged. The life cycle fund would automatically and gradually shift the allocation of investment funds as the individual neared retirement age so that it was weighted more heavily toward secure bonds.
- **Personal retirement accounts would be protected from sudden market swings on the eve of retirement.** To protect near-retirees from sudden market swings on the eve of retirement, personal retirement accounts would be automatically invested in the "life cycle portfolio" when a worker reaches age 47, unless the worker and his or her spouse specifically opted out by signing a waiver form stating they are aware of the risks involved. The waiver form would explain in clear, easily understandable terms the benefits of the life cycle portfolio and the risks of opting out. By shifting investment allocations from high growth funds to secure bonds as the individual nears retirement, the life cycle portfolio would provide greater protections from sudden market swings.
- **Personal retirement accounts would not be eaten up by hidden Wall Street fees.** Personal retirement accounts would be low-cost. The Social Security Administration's actuaries project that the ongoing administrative costs for a TSP-style personal account structure would be roughly 30 basis points or 0.3 percentage points, compared to an

average of 125 basis points for investments in stock mutual funds and 88 basis points in bond mutual funds in 2003. . . .

- The low costs are made possible by the economies of scale of a centralized administrative structure, as well as limiting investment options to a small number of prudent, broadly diversified funds.
- Most of these administrative costs are for recordkeeping which would be done by the government, not investment management done by Wall Street. . . .

- **Personal retirement accounts would not be accessible prior to retirement.** American workers who choose personal retirement accounts would not be allowed to make withdrawals from, take loans from, or borrow against their accounts prior to retirement.
- **Personal retirement accounts would not be emptied out all at once, but rather paid out over time, as an addition to traditional Social Security benefits.** Under a system of personal retirement accounts, procedures would be established to govern how account balances would be withdrawn at retirement. This would involve some combination of annuities to ensure a stream of monthly income over the worker's life expectancy, phased withdrawals indexed to life expectancy, and lump sum withdrawals. Individuals would not be permitted to withdraw funds from their personal retirement accounts as lump sums, if doing so would result in their moving below the poverty line. Account balances in excess of the poverty-protection threshold requirement could be withdrawn as a lump sum for any purpose or left in the account to accumulate interest. Any unused portion of the account could be passed on to loved ones.
- **Personal retirement accounts would be phased in.** To ease the transition to a personal retirement account system, participation would be phased in according to the age of the worker. In the first year of implementation, workers currently between age 40 and 54 (born 1950 through 1965 inclusive) would have the option of establishing personal retirement accounts. In the second year, workers currently between age 26 and 54 (born 1950 through 1978 inclusive) would be given the option and by the end of the third year, all workers born in 1950 or later who want to participate in personal retirement accounts would be able to do so.
- **The President's personal retirement account proposal is fiscally responsible.** The President's proposal is consistent with his overall goal of cutting the deficit in half by 2009. Based on analysis by the Social Security Administration Actuary, the Office of Management and Budget estimates that the President's personal retirement account proposal will require transition financing of $664 billion over the next ten years ($754 billion including interest). This transition financing will not have the same effect on national savings, and thus the economy, as traditional government borrowing. Personal retirement accounts will not reduce the pool of savings available to the markets because every dollar borrowed by the Federal government to fund the transition is fully offset by an increase in savings represented by the accounts themselves. Moreover, the transition financing for personal retirement accounts should be viewed as part of a comprehensive plan to make the Social Security system permanently sustainable. Publicly released

analysis by the Social Security Administration has found that several comprehensive proposals including personal accounts would dramatically reduce the costs of permanently fixing the system. . . .

- **Establishing personal retirement accounts does not add to the total costs that Social Security faces.** Personal retirement accounts effectively pre-fund Social Security benefits already promised to today's workers and do not represent a net increase in Federal obligations. The obligation to pay Social Security benefits is already there. While personal retirement accounts affect the timing of these costs, they do not add to the total amount obligated through Social Security.

Dean Baker

Bush's Numbers Racket: Why Social Security Privatization Is a Phony Solution to a Phony Problem

The word from President Bush and his minions is that Social Security is on its last legs, facing imminent danger of bankruptcy. Fortunately, Bush is prepared to rescue this antiquated program by offering workers the opportunity to invest a portion of their Social Security taxes in private accounts. He would like us to believe that this plan will both get the government out from under a crushing debt burden, in the form of future Social Security obligations, and provide younger workers with a more secure retirement.

Almost every part of this story is untrue. First, Social Security does not face any crisis in the normal meaning of the term. Second, private accounts would not give workers a more secure retirement; they reduce security. And third, the basic logic of the story is faulty; it is impossible to both reduce government spending on Social Security and increase benefits, unless the plan somehow increases growth. And no economist seriously contends that putting Social Security money in the stock market will increase growth.

The Basic Numbers

Starting with the crisis story, the first place to look is the Social Security trustees' projections, the standard basis for analysis of the program. The most recent projections show that the program, with no changes whatsoever, can pay all benefits through the year 2042. Even after 2042, Social Security would always be able to pay a higher benefit (adjusted for inflation) than what current retirees receive, although the payment would only be about 73 percent of scheduled benefits.

The Social Security trustees' projections are based on extremely pessimistic assumptions about the future. (Four of the six trustees are political appointees of President Bush: the treasury, labor, and health and human services secretaries, plus the Social Security commissioner.) For example, the trustees assume that economic growth over the 75-year planning period will be less than half as fast as over the last 75 years. While most of this difference is due to the assumption of slower labor-force growth following the retirement of the baby-boomer generation, the trustees also assume that productivity growth will revert back to the rate of productivity growth during the slowdown years of 1973–95. Even so, the trustees themselves have begun using slightly more realistic assumptions. In 1997, they placed the year that Social Security would begin facing a shortfall at 2029. By 2003, they had revised that projection to 2042. Any system that gains 13 years of health in six years is hardly bankrupt.

The nonpartisan Congressional Budget Office (CBO) did its own analysis of the program last summer. Using only slightly more optimistic assumptions, the CBO found that the program, with no changes at all, could pay all benefits through the year 2052 and more than 80 percent of scheduled benefits in subsequent years.

On the face of it, the fact that Social Security may face a shortfall in just under 40 years (according to the trustees' report) or 50 years (according to the CBO) hardly sounds like a crisis. After all, the program faced projected shortfalls in the 1950s, '60s, '70s, and '80s. Each of these shortfalls was dealt with—usually with modest tax increases, and in the case of the '80s shortfall, a phased increase in the retirement age beginning in 2003. In the past, no one seemed to feel the need to begin whining about a looming crisis 40 or 50 years ahead of time.

But the proponents of the crisis story have been largely successful in spreading fear. Part of this success is due to the use of deceptive language in framing the issue. The promoters of the crisis routinely speak of an $11 trillion "unfunded liability" for Social Security. But most of the people who hear the $11 trillion figure or use it (including reporters) probably have no idea what it means.

The $11 trillion is obtained by projecting Social Security taxes and spending for the infinite future. The gap between projected spending and taxes for all time is then summed up (using a 3-percent real-discount rate) to get a projection of $11 trillion of debt.

However, more than two-thirds of this projected debt is due to spending beyond the 75-year planning period for Social Security. This means that the debt is not something that we are imposing on our children or grandchildren. Rather, it is a debt that we are projecting that our great-grandchildren would impose on their grandchildren—assuming pessimistic economic projections.

The basic story is that life expectancies are projected to increase through time. This raises the cost of the program through time. If taxes are never raised and benefits are never reduced, the shortfall would eventually be very large.

But serious people don't worry about designing Social Security for the 22nd century. (The secret here is that we don't actually get to design Social Security for the 22nd century anyhow—the people who are alive in 50, 60, and 70 years will design the program in a way that makes sense to them. They will not care at all about what we thought was a good system in 2005.)

If we just confine ourselves to the already lengthy 75-year planning period, the projected shortfall comes to $3 trillion. This may still sound very large. However, the Social Security trustees calculate that this shortfall is 0.7 percent of national income over the planning period. The CBO projects an even smaller number, just 0.4 percent of income over the next 75 years.

By comparison, the increase in annual defense spending since 2001 has been more than 1 percent of the gross domestic product, twice the size of the Social Security shortfall projected by the CBO. And Bush's tax increases equal about 2 percent of the GDP. In fact, rolling back Bush's tax cuts on the very wealthiest would raise sufficient revenue to cover the shortfall for 75 years.

The Trust-Fund Scare Stories

The promoters of privatization have one other standard trick to promote fear about Social Security's future: They point out that, beginning in 2018, Social Security will be forced to rely on income from the trust fund to pay benefits. But this was deliberate. The 1983 Social Security Commission, chaired by Alan Greenspan, deliberately designed a system that would build up a surplus—taxing more than was necessary to pay benefits—so that the income from this surplus could be used help pay the costs of the baby boomers' retirement. Drawing on the trust fund is no more of a problem for Social Security than it is for any pension fund to use some of its accumulated assets to pay benefits to retirees. Indeed, that is exactly what is supposed to happen.

Some conservatives have even derided the Social Security trust fund as an "accounting fiction." Like most claims to wealth in a modern economy, it exists primarily as an accounting entry (how much gold does Bill Gates have in his basement?), but it is hardly fiction. Under the law, the federal government is obligated to repay the government bonds held by the Social Security trust fund, just as it is obligated to repay other government bonds. While tax revenue will be needed to repay these bonds, it is slated to come from personal and corporate income taxes, both very progressive forms of taxation. By contrast, the Social Security tax is a highly regressive wage tax. The meaning of the trust fund is that workers effectively prepaid their Social Security taxes. Now, the government is obligated to tax the Bill Gates and Pete Petersons of the world to repay this debt.

Funny Numbers on Private Accounts

After telling people that Social Security poses the risk of economic disaster, the privatizers promise that individual accounts would provide everyone with a secure retirement. The basic argument is that high returns in the stock market would allow workers to get more money from their Social Security taxes than what they can get through the current system.

There is a simple and obvious problem with this logic. When they project rates of return in the stock market, the privatizers routinely assume that the returns in the future will be equal to the returns in the past, 6.5 percent to 7 percent above the rate of inflation. But the whole basis for projecting a Social Security shortfall is the assumption that the future will have far slower growth than in the past.

Given the much slower projected rate of profit growth, and the fact that price-to-earnings ratios in the stock market continue to be far higher than the historic average, it will be impossible for stock returns to be as high in the future as they were in the past. Projections of stock returns that are consistent with projections of profit growth and current price-to-earnings ratios are approximately 5 percent above the rate of inflation. Because most projections assume a 50-50 mix of stocks and bonds, the implied return on private accounts, after deducting administrative costs, would be about 3.5 percent. This is not much different than the 3-percent return projected for the government bonds held by the trust fund.

In short, there is no untapped bonanza to be claimed by putting Social Security money in the stock market. This step would add little, if anything, to average returns. It would simply add risk. Individual workers may do worse than the average because they make bad investment choices or they happen to retire during a downturn in the stock market. Going in this direction makes sense if the purpose is to increase fees for the financial industry, but it is not a step toward increasing workers' retirement security. Moreover, with individual accounts, retirees would have to worry about living too long, whereas Social Security is guaranteed for life.

Even with individual accounts, most workers would still see large benefit cuts under the second plan produced by President Bush's Social Security Commission, the one that Bush indicated would be the model for his proposal. An average wage earner who is age 20 at the time the plan is implemented could expect his or her basic Social Security benefit to be cut by $200,000, or more than 30 percent, over the course of his or her retirement. He or she could expect to make back less than $70,000, or about one-third of this cut, through his or her private account.

But it is not just the retirement security of individual workers that would be threatened by privatization. President Bush's plan would also lead to transition costs that could be as high as $200 billion a year (almost 2 percent of the GDP) for more than 30 years. The transition problem stems from the fact that workers would begin placing their money in private accounts immediately, leading to large losses of revenue to the government. However, the commission's plan proposes phasing in cuts to new retirees, beginning five years after the plan takes effect. These cuts would not get large enough to offset the lost revenue (and resulting interest burden) for more than three decades, which would lead to a substantial deficit increase in the intervening years.

In order to avoid the appearance that his plan would lead to record-breaking deficits (measured as a share of the GDP), President Bush wants to take this transition by not counting this borrowing as part of the budget. The argument is that we would pay this money back (with benefit cuts) 40 or 50 years in the future, so the current borrowing should not be viewed as adding to the deficit.

The question of whether the transition borrowing could be taken off the books is a political one, but politics won't determine the impact of this borrowing on the nation's economy. There is little evidence that financial markets look 40 and 50 years into the future (and it's not clear what they would see if they did). But every other country that has privatized its Social Security system has felt the need to offset the immediate loss of tax revenue with some spending cuts and/or tax increases. And none of them started with deficits that are as large as those the United States is currently running.

There were already grounds for believing that the Bush deficits were too large and would lead to a substantial increase in interest rates if not reduced quickly. Adding $200 billion a year to these deficits makes it far more likely that the country would face considerably higher interest rates in the near future.

There is also a good example of what can happen when a country tries the Bush approach to Social Security privatization (even if it didn't go quite as far). In 1994, Argentina partially privatized its social-security system. While there were some cuts included in this package, it cost the government an amount of tax revenue equal to approximately 0.9 percent of the GDP, equivalent to $100 billion a year in the United States. In 2001, Argentina went into bankruptcy and defaulted on its debt. If the social-security revenue had still been coming to the government over the period between 1994 and the default, Argentina would have been running a balanced budget in 2001.

The United States is obviously very different from Argentina, but this example is not encouraging for proponents of privatization. The financial markets were not impressed with the fact that Argentina's social-security payments would be lower 20 years in the future. The markets focused on the deficits the country was running in the present. It is likely that they would also focus on the $600 billion (plus deficits) that would result from President Bush's Social Security plan.

In short, Bush's plan would undermine a system that has provided security for tens of millions of workers, and their families, for seven decades, and which can continue to do so long into the future if it is just left alone. His private accounts would provide far less security, while hugely raising costs in the form of fees to the financial industry. Finally, the cost of transitioning to this new system could throw the country into an economic crisis. It's small wonder that Bush is facing increasing skepticism.

POSTSCRIPT

Should Social Security Be Changed to Include Personal Retirement Accounts?

The White House begins by describing what it believes are the problems facing Social Security. One central problem is that there are "fewer workers paying ever-higher benefits to an ever-larger number of retirees." Consequently, Social Security is facing critical financing problems; it is heading toward "bankruptcy." The White House refers to an estimate from the Social Security Trustees: "As of 2004 the cost of doing nothing to fix our Social Security system had hit an estimated $10.4 trillion." The White House lists the advantages of personal retirement accounts. One advantage is that ownership and control of the account would rest with the individual. Another advantage is that an individual could pass the account on to his or her children and grandchildren. Perhaps most importantly, the White House believes that the creation of these accounts would "would dramatically reduce the costs of permanently fixing the system."

Baker begins his analysis by denying the claims that he says the Bush administration makes about Social Security and personal retirement accounts. Baker argues (1) there is no Social Security "crisis," (2) the retirement accounts would not make retirement "more secure," and (3) "it is impossible to both reduce government spending on Social Security and increase benefits, unless the plan somehow increases growth." Baker then turns to the numbers that are used to support the claims of those who believe that there is a Social Security crisis. He finds fault with these numbers on a variety of criteria. For example, he disputes the forecast by the Social Security Trustees that by 2042 The Social Security trust fund will be exhausted; he believes this prediction is based on "extremely pessimistic assumptions about the future." He cites an alternative forecast by the nonpartisan Congressional Budget Office that sets 2052 as the corresponding date. He then proceeds to discuss the Social Security trust fund in more detail; in particular, he disputes the charge that it is an "accounting fiction." In the last part of his analysis, Baker discusses the numbers associated with private accounts. He asserts that these accounts would add little to average returns but would add risk. He concludes that the burdens of moving to the system proposed by the Bush administration "could throw the country into an economic crisis."

The Social Security "crisis" has been a major concern to economists and policymakers for at least the last 10 years. As a consequence, a vast amount of information is available about the "crisis" and personal retirement accounts, and there are several Web sites devoted exclusively to the issue. They include

The Social Security Network, available at `http://www.socsec.org/`, and the Cato Institute Project on Social Security Choice, available at `http://www.socialsecurity.org/`. A visit to the Social Security Administration's official Web site at `http://www.ssa.gov/` provides access to an array of useful information including the latest Trustees Report. Another batch of studies regarding Social Security can be found at the research center of the American Association of Retired Persons (AARP) at `http://search.aarp.org/cgi-bin/htsearch?config=htdig_research_aarp_org&method=and&restrict=research.aarp.org%2Fecon&words=social+security`. Several additional readings on Social Security are available from the Century Foundation at `http://www.tcf.org/about.asp`. Several specific plans for Social Security reform been developed. For example, see the description of The Ryan-Sununu Social Security reform bill by Peter Ferrara: "Personal Social Security Accounts that Work" Policy Report 185 Institute for Policy Innovation (November 2004). Another plan is offered by Michael Tanner, "The 6.2 Percent Solution: A Plan for Reforming Social Security," Cato Project on Social Security Choice SSP No. 32 (February 17, 2004). A third plan is offered by Peter A. Diamond and Peter R. Orszag in *Saving Social Security: A Balanced Approach* (Brookings Institution Press, 2003).

ISSUE 9

Should the Double Taxation of Corporate Dividends Be Eliminated?

YES: Norbert J. Michel, Alfredo Goyburu, and Ralph A. Rector, from "The Economic and Fiscal Effects of Ending the Federal Double Taxation of Dividends," A Working Paper of the Heritage Center for Data Analysis (January 27, 2003)

NO: Joel Friedman and Robert Greenstein, from "Exempting Corporate Dividends From Individual Income Taxes," A Report of the Center on Budget and Policy Priorities (January 11, 2003)

ISSUE SUMMARY

YES: Free-market economists Norbert J. Michel, Alfredo Goyburu, and Ralph A. Rector applaud the George W. Bush administration's initiative to eliminate the double taxation of corporate dividends. They assert that this action will improve economic efficiency and that, in the long run, this tax cut will pay for itself because it will stimulate economic growth.

NO: Economic policy analysts Joel Friedman and Robert Greenstein argue that there are no valid economic justifications to propose the elimination of the tax on dividends. All that cutting dividend taxes will really do, they say, is reduce the tax burden of high-income individuals.

The U.S. federal government engages in a wide variety of economic and noneconomic activities. In the United States these activities range from the provision of national and domestic security to the construction and maintenance of public and private transportation systems. Additionally, the government provides economic security in the form of income transfers to the elderly, the unemployed, and the poor. Finally, it creates institutions that allow markets to flourish, since markets are the engines that drive the economic system. All of these efforts are taken for granted, are costly, and must be paid for. To finance these activities, governments have three options: they can create money, they can tax, or they can borrow. The United States does not create money, but the government certainly does tax and borrow.

Consider, for example, federal government total outlays and receipts for fiscal year 2002. That year alone the federal government spent $2.01 trillion. This was financed by $1.85 trillion in receipts or taxes, and since taxes were less than expenditures, America incurred $160 billion in new federal debt. The bulk of this tax revenue came from income-related taxes: the individual income tax raised $858 billion; payroll taxes—largely social security contributions—generated $701 billion; and last, as well as a distant third, corporate income taxes accounted for another $148 billion. All the other federal taxes combined—federal excise taxes, customs duties, estate/gift taxes, and a dozen or so miscellaneous taxes—summed to a total of $146 billion in tax revenue.

The unvarnished truth is that no one likes to pay taxes. However, making deep cuts in the tax system is not always practical, given that there is a widespread belief that all or most of the expenditures and transfers that are generally taken for granted are demanded by a majority of taxpayers. Although "taxes, like death" are inevitable, the displeasure with taxes can be minimized if the tax system meets two basic criteria: equity and efficiency.

The first criterion of equity, or fairness, from the economist's perspective, requires looking horizontally and vertically. That is, for a tax to be horizontally equitable, that tax must treat individuals in identical circumstances identically. In this case, those with the same economic characteristics should pay the same amount in taxes. Vertical equity is a bit more complicated. It assumes that unlike individuals will be treated unequally; that is, a person with greater tax-paying capacity should not pay the same amount of taxes as someone with a lower income. At a minimum, those with higher incomes should pay proportionally the same as those with lower incomes and, in some cases, share a larger percentage of the tax burden than those of more moderate means.

Besides being equitable, a tax system needs to satisfy a second general criterion. Taxes should not interfere significantly with the efficient operation of a market economy. Consider the case of an extreme tax that took all of an individual's income. Economists would argue that this tax is inefficient because it would undermine work incentives. In technical terms, since work and leisure are substitutes for one another, a 100 percent tax would make the price of an additional hour of leisure equal to zero. Why work if you are not going to be better off from working? In this case one would expect folks to work far less and therefore increase their consumption of leisure. If no one works, the size of the economic pie has to decline because resources are wasted.

Most would conclude that taxes are necessary and that policymakers should do all they can to impose taxes that take into account equitable and efficient consequences of these taxes. Unfortunately, sometimes in order to get equity, one must sacrifice efficiency. In other cases, in order to get efficiency, one has to sacrifice equity. The importance that is placed on one or the other of these two considerations helps shape which taxes we support and which we take issue with. In the following selections, Norbert J. Michel, Alfredo Goyburu, and Ralph A. Rector argue that, above all, policymakers should maximize efficiency. Joel Friedman and Robert Greenstein, on the other hand, plead the case for equity.

YES Norbert J. Michel, Alfredo Goyburu, and Ralph A. Rector

The Economic and Fiscal Effects of Ending the Federal Double Taxation of Dividends

On January 7, 2003, President George W. Bush unveiled a multi-faceted proposal to improve the nation's economic growth. One of the most important features of his plan calls for abolition of the current federal double taxation of corporate dividends paid to individual shareholders. Economic analysts at the Center for Data Analysis (CDA) at The Heritage Foundation found, in a study of a dividend reform proposal similar to President Bush's, that ending the double taxation of dividends would improve the nation's economic growth, employment level, and other economic indicators over the next 10 years.

For example, CDA estimates indicate that the employment level would average 285,000 additional jobs from 2003 to 2012. In addition, CDA analysis has found that ending this double taxation would reduce federal revenue by $64 billion over ten years, or 79 percent less than an estimate that does not account for the effects of greater economic activity following the proposal's implementation. The CDA's $64 billion estimate is slightly more than one-fifth of the $364 billion cost estimated by the United States Department of the Treasury for President Bush's proposal.[1] The CDA and Treasury analyses consider slightly different proposals, but this cost difference is largely due to the more realistic estimation method used by the CDA.

The Treasury Department employs an erroneous "static" approach to estimate the revenue effect of tax law changes, while the CDA uses dynamic simulation, a method that accounts for the impact that federal tax policy may exert on economic growth.[2] Figure 1 shows that the estimation method chosen can make a large difference in the projected revenue loss. The figure compares the CDA's own static and dynamic projections of the federal revenue change resulting from a particular plan to end the double taxation of dividends.

This double taxation[3] has two stages. The first stage occurs when the federal government taxes shareholders on corporate income through corporate taxes. The second occurs after the corporation has distributed part of the post-tax profits to the shareholders in the form of dividends. In this second

Figure 1

Dynamic vs. Erroneous Static Revenue Cost Estimates of Ending Double Dividend Taxation

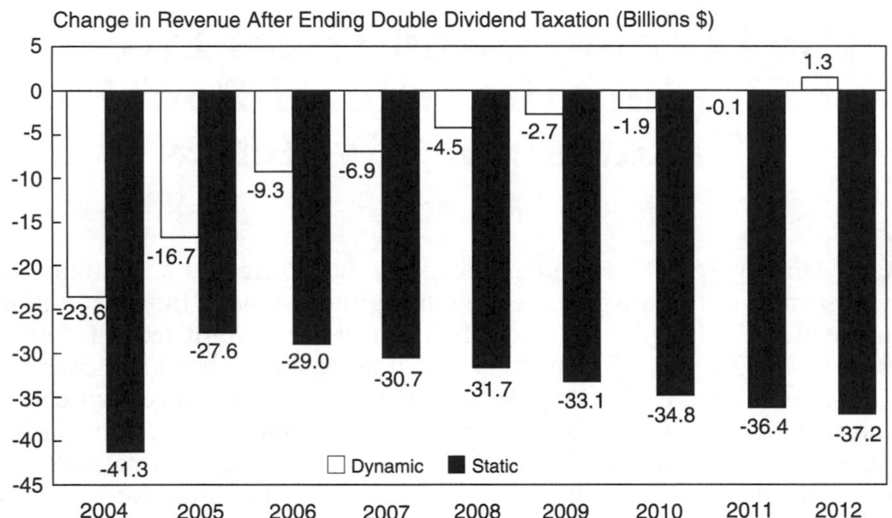

Note: Assumes legislative enactment on September 30, 2003.

Source: Estimates by the Center for Data Analysis at The Heritage Foundation, using August 2002 Congressional Budget Office projections and the DRI–WEFA U.S. Macroeconomic Model.

stage, the federal government taxes shareholders on their dividend income through the personal income tax.

Economists have long argued that the double taxation of dividends reduces the after-tax return on capital in the nation's economy and thus discourages investment—in other words, purchases of new business equipment and machinery.[4] This reduced investment in turn weakens economic growth. Consequently, eliminating the double taxation would spur investment and improve the economy's long-term growth. Recognizing these economic benefits, several nations, including Australia, France, Italy, Canada, Germany, Japan, and the United Kingdom, have abolished or reduced their double taxation of corporate dividends.[5]

One recent legislative proposal to abolish this double taxation in the United States was sponsored by Representative Christopher Cox (R–CA).[6] The Heritage Foundation's CDA used this proposal to illustrate the economic and federal fiscal effects of ending the double taxation of dividends.[7] To estimate these effects, Heritage analysts employed the DRI–WEFA U.S. Macroeconomic Model and the Center's own Individual Income Tax Model. Assuming the reform becomes law in September 2003, the investigation found that:[8]

- *GDP increases.* During the period from 2003 through 2012, the Cox proposal would increase the nation's gross domestic product (GDP) by an inflation-adjusted[9] $32 billion per year on average, compared to

Figure 2

Ending Double Taxation of Dividends Bolsters Economic Growth, Gross Domestic Product Compared to Baseline

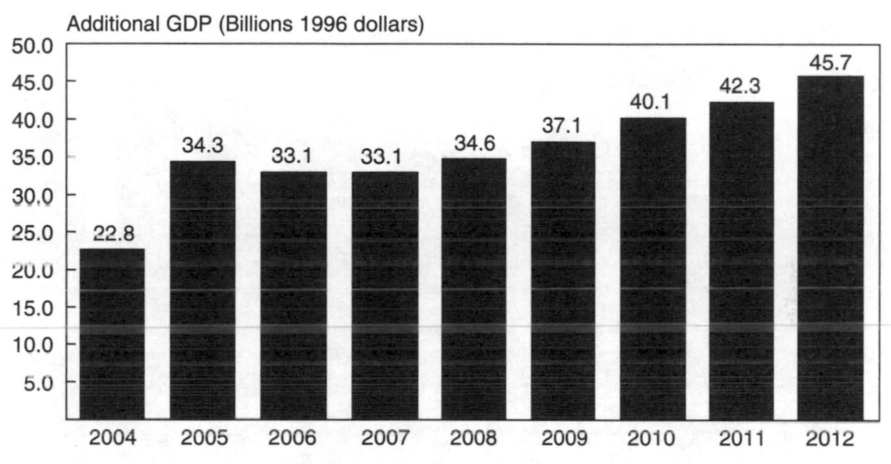

Note: Assumes legislative enactment on September 30, 2003.

Source: Estimates by the Center for Data Analysis at The Heritage Foundation, using August 2002 Congressional Budget Office projections and the DRI–WEFA U.S. Macroeconomic Model.

what it would otherwise have been. GDP would be at least $22 billion higher in 2004 and no less than $45 billion higher in 2012 if the proposal were to be implemented. (See Figure 2.)

- *Employment grows.* The provisions in the Cox bill would enable the economy to support 325,000 more jobs by 2012. (See Figure 3.) With these additional jobs in the economy, the unemployment rate would be 0.2 percent lower throughout the period 2005–2012 than current projections indicate.
- *Investment strengthens.* Over the 10-year period from 2003 through 2012, the proposal would result in an aggregate increase of at least $253 billion (adjusted for inflation) in non-residential investment. Because of this higher level of investment, the nation's non-residential capital stock would be $175 billion higher in 2012. (See Figure 4.)
- *Disposable income picks up.* Under the Cox legislation, disposable personal income would average an inflation-adjusted $56 billion higher from 2003 through 2012. (See Figure 5.) This higher level would raise annual disposable personal income by $192 per person on average during the period. For a family of four, this increase would correspond to $768 more in disposable income on average each year.
- *Personal savings increases.* The proposal would increase personal savings by an inflation-adjusted average of $18 billion per year from 2003 through 2012.
- *Higher economic growth reduces the "cost" to the Treasury by over 70 percent.* The CDA's own static estimates suggest the proposal would reduce federal revenue by about $300 billion from 2003 through 2012. However, the CDA's more realistic *dynamic* estimates show that the proposal

Figure 3

Ending Double Taxation of Dividends Strengthens Job Growth Compared to Baseline

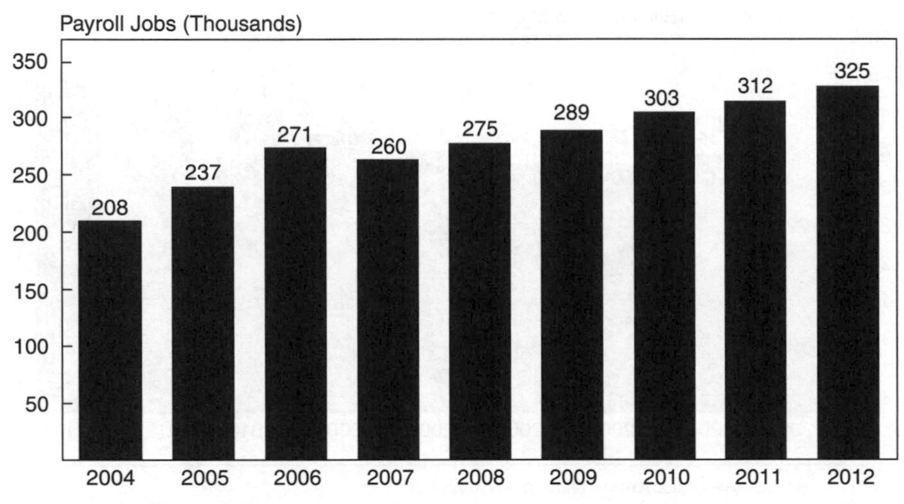

Note: Assumes legislative enactment on September 30, 2003.

Source: Estimates by the Center for Data Analysis at The Heritage Foundation, using August 2002 Congressional Budget Office projections and the DRI–WEFA U.S. Macroeconomic Model.

Figure 4

Ending Double Taxation of Dividends Raises Net Capital Stock Compared to Baseline

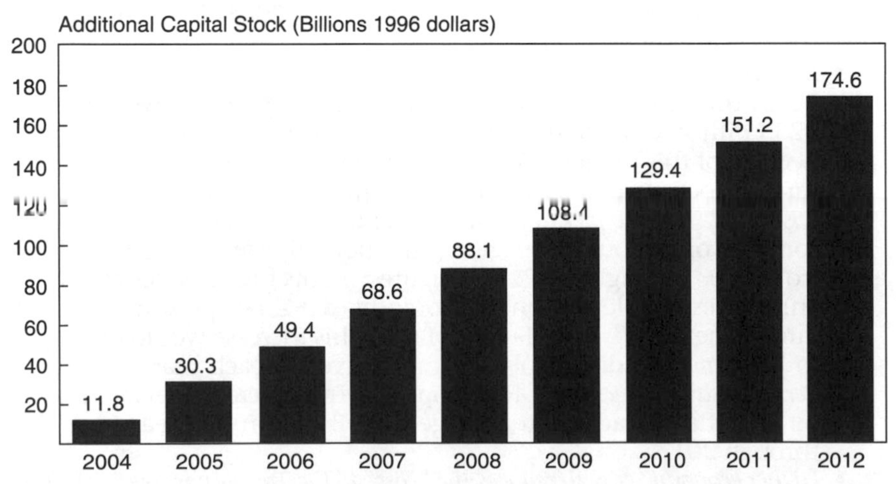

Note: Assumes legislative enactment on September 30, 2003.

Source: Estimates by the Center for Data Analysis at The Heritage Foundation, using August 2002 Congressional Budget Office projections and the DRI–WEFA U.S. Macroeconomic Model.

Figure 5

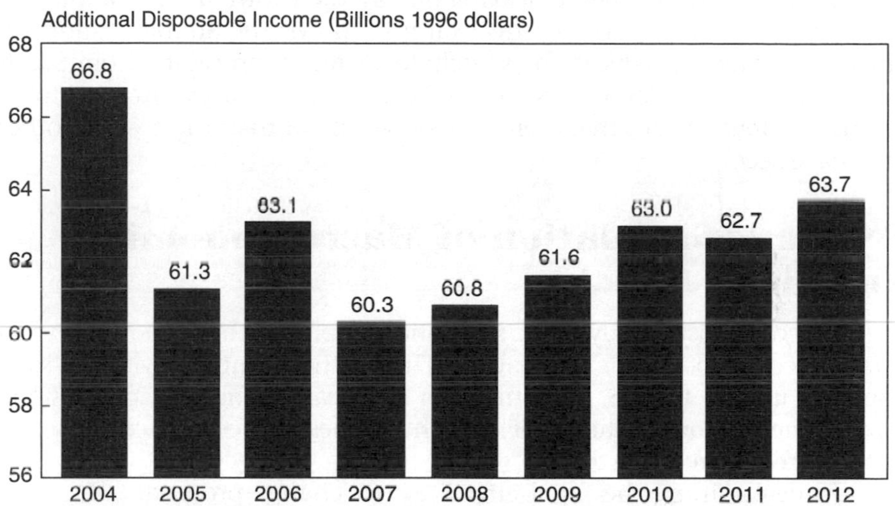

Note: Assumes legislative enactment on September 30, 2003.

Source: Estimates by the Center for Data Analysis at The Heritage Foundation, using August 2002 Congressional Budget Office projections and the DRI–WEFA U.S. Macroeconomic Model.

would reduce federal revenue during the period by a total of $64 billion. (See Figure 1.) During the last five years, the proposal would be nearly revenue neutral, since the improved economic growth caused by the legislation would, in turn, increase tax collections. For reasons discussed below, these estimates do not take into account the way in which the proposal's effect on capital gains tax collections would change federal tax revenue.

How the Double Taxation of Dividends Works

The double taxation of dividends[10] is one of the clearest examples of the way the nation's current tax law reduces the return on capital and, therefore, the incentive to invest. The following example illustrates the effect of this double taxation.

Consider $100 in pre-tax profit earned by a corporation in the flat 35 percent bracket. Suppose that, after paying the $35 in federal corporate taxes, the firm distributed the remaining $65 to a shareholder. Suppose, further, that this individual was in the 27 percent personal income tax bracket. This shareholder would pay $17.55 in personal income taxes on these dividends. This second round of taxation would leave only $47.45 of the original $100 in corporate profits. In other words, for every $100 in pre-tax profits, the federal government would absorb approximately $52.55 in taxes.

In contrast, consider the taxes the shareholder might have paid if that person could have received the dividend before the firm paid corporate taxes. In this case, the corporation would have paid the shareholder all $100 in the form of a dividend. The shareholder would then have paid $27 in personal income taxes on the dividends, leaving that investor with $73 out of the $100 in pre-tax corporate profit. As this example shows, the double taxation of corporate dividends reduced the shareholder's return on capital from $73 to $47.45—a reduction of 35 percent (or $25.55). In the aggregate, this lower return on capital means that there is less investment than there would otherwise have been.

Dynamic Simulation of Macroeconomic and Fiscal Effects

Heritage economists use dynamic simulation to project the economic and fiscal effects of proposals for tax changes. This method contrasts with the static approach used by the U.S. Department of the Treasury and the Congressional Joint Committee on Taxation (JCT), which assumes that federal tax policy does not affect economic growth.

In determining the fiscal effects of tax change proposals, the static approach does take into account some of the ways taxpayers alter their tax reporting and filing in response to changes in tax law. For example, the static approach takes into account that taxpayers could increase their itemized deductions or shift compensation from taxable to tax-exempt (or tax-deferred) forms in response to certain changes in the tax laws. However, the static approach does not take into account the way investors and workers alter their consumption, investment, saving, and work effort in response to changes in tax policy. This is a major shortcoming of the static approach because economic theory suggests that tax policy changes bring about such alterations.[11]

Such changes in taxpayers' behavior could affect important macroeconomic variables, including employment, personal income, and GDP. Thus, changes in tax law often exert an impact on the nation's economy. The static approach necessarily ignores these impacts, leading to systematic inaccuracies in the estimates of the fiscal effects of tax policy changes.

In contrast, The Heritage Foundation uses dynamic simulation in evaluating the fiscal and economic effects of tax policy proposals. Dynamic simulation takes into account the impact that tax policy legislation can exert on taxpayers' economic decisions, such as consumption, investment, saving, and work effort. Dynamic simulation, therefore, can reflect changes in macroeconomic variables that new tax policies can cause.

For example, if a tax rate reduction were to strengthen national economic growth and therefore increase the tax base, a resultant increase in tax collections could partially offset the federal revenue losses caused by the rate reduction. Static analysis would not take such an offset into account and therefore would overestimate the net decline in federal tax collections resulting from the tax rate reduction. Dynamic analysis would include this offset because it would take full account of the economic benefits that the tax rate reduction could cause.

It would also capture the ways in which these benefits could strengthen the economy, bolster the tax base, and ameliorate the reduction in tax collections.

In analyzing the economic and fiscal impact of the Cox proposal, CDA analysts made a number of assumptions regarding the alternative minimum tax, capital gains taxation, federal spending, and the date the bill would be enacted. These assumptions were as follows.

- *Alternative minimum tax.* The form of the bill submitted for consideration in the 107th Congress does not clearly state how the dividend tax credit should be handled under those parts of the tax code that establish the alternative minimum tax (AMT). Heritage Foundation analysts assumed that taxpayers required to file under the AMT rules would be able to take advantage of the dividend tax credit. If this were not the case, the dividend tax relief for those taxpayers would be negated.
- *Capital gains tax.* The Cox proposal would be expected to cause an increase in equity prices. This increase would likely cause investors to adjust their portfolios, perhaps triggering increased capital gains tax liability. Estimating the total increase in capital gains tax collections would require both distributional and basis data that are not readily available to Heritage economists. Therefore, CDA analysts assumed that such collections would remain unchanged relative to the baseline forecast.
- *Federal spending.* Heritage Foundation analysts assumed that Congress would make no government program spending reductions to offset federal revenue cuts expected with the Cox proposal. As a result, any changes in federal spending observed in the simulation are attributable solely to the Cox proposal's effect on the national economy and, in turn, the economy's effect on federal spending.
- *Dividend increase.* Heritage analysts assumed that ending the double taxation of dividends would increase dividend payouts by 10 percent. A portion of this increase would be caused by higher shareholder demand for dividends. In response to this higher demand, corporations would increase their payouts of dividends out of after-tax profits. The remainder of this 10 percent increase would be explained by a reduction in the user cost of capital and a corresponding increase in profits. Some of these higher profits would then be returned to shareholders as higher dividends. The combined result of these two effects was assumed to be a 10 percent increase in dividends.[12]
- *Date of enactment.* Heritage economists assumed that the tax reform would become law on September 30, 2003, and apply retroactively to dividends received after January 1, 2003. Assuming an earlier date of enactment would have resulted in the proposal's benefits being realized sooner.

Macroeconomic and Fiscal Effects of the Cox Proposal

Heritage economists used a modified version of the DRI–WEFA U.S. Macroeconomic Model to conduct a dynamic simulation of the effects of Representative Cox's bill.[13] Specifically, Heritage economists developed a baseline by adapting the DRI–WEFA macroeconomic forecast from September 2002 to yield the same economic and budget projections as those of the Congressional Budget Office (CBO) in August 2002.[14] Thus, the economic baseline employed in this analysis should be comparable to baselines used by the CBO and JCT in analyzing this legislation. . . .

Specifically, the dynamic analysis projects that the Cox proposal would:

- *Increase economic growth.* GDP would increase by an average of at least $32 billion per year (adjusted for inflation) within the period from 2003 through 2012. GDP would be an inflation-adjusted $22 billion higher in 2004 and $45 billion higher in 2012. (See Figure 2.)
- *Create more job opportunities.* The proposal would increase the number of jobs by at least 325,000 in 2012. (See Figure 3.) This increase in jobs would correspond to a decline in the unemployment rate of no less than 0.2 percent per year over the next 10 years. (See Figure 3.)
- *Increase investment.* Non-residential investment would average nearly $25 billion per year (adjusted for inflation) higher between 2003 and 2012. By the end of fiscal year 2012, the net capital stock would be at least an inflation-adjusted $174 billion higher. (See Figure 4.) The user cost of capital would be about 5.4 percent lower in 2012.
- *Increase disposable personal income.* Disposable personal income would increase by an inflation-adjusted average of $56 billion or more per year from 2003 through 2012. For a family of four, this increase in disposable income would correspond to an average of at least $768 per year. (See Figure 5.)
- *Increase personal savings and personal consumption.* Personal savings would average an inflation-adjusted $18 billion higher during the 10-year period. Personal consumption expenditures would average an inflation-adjusted $36 billion higher than current projections.
- *Slightly increase consumer prices.* Under the Cox proposal, growth in the consumer price index would average 0.1 percent higher from 2004 through 2008. Over the final four years of the forecast period, increases in the price level would be virtually unchanged in comparison with those of the baseline.
- *Decrease federal tax revenue.* The Cox dividend proposal would reduce total federal tax revenues by a total of $64 billion during its first 10 years. Close to $56 billion of this reduction would take place during the first five years, for an average of $11 billion per year. During the final five years of the simulation period, the tax cut would be virtually revenue neutral, reducing federal revenue by an average of less then $2 billion per year. During this latter five-year period, increases mostly in corporate and Social Security tax collections would offset expected declines in personal income taxes. Corporate tax collections would rise because of higher pre-tax corporate profits. Payroll taxes would increase because of higher employment levels.
- *Increase federal spending.* If Congress were not to reduce federal program spending to offset the tax revenue reductions caused by this proposal, overall federal spending would rise. Spending would average about $13 billion higher after ending the double taxation of dividends. About two-thirds of this increase would result from additional federal interest payments. The rest would be caused by increases in federal expenditures

on income-maintenance programs for federal and Social Security retirees. These increases in federal income maintenance spending would be caused mainly by higher consumer prices observed during the years from 2004 through 2008.

Conclusion

President Bush has proposed reforming the U.S. tax code to abolish the federal double taxation on corporate dividends. Economists have long argued that this double taxation exerts a harmful effect on the nation's economy because it increases the user cost of capital and therefore reduces investment in the United States. Last fall [2002], Representative Christopher Cox introduced legislation that would end this double taxation.

This Heritage Foundation working paper investigates the 10-year economic and fiscal impact of Representative Cox's proposal to abolish this double taxation. It finds that the proposal would, by the year 2012, improve growth in the nation's GDP, add hundreds of thousands of jobs to the economy, increase investment, strengthen growth in disposable income, and add to the nation's capital stock.

Notes

1. United States Department of the Treasury, Office of Public Affairs, "Tax Provisions of the President's Growth Package," at `http://www.treas.gov/press/releases/kd3739.htm`.
2. Forthcoming sections of this paper further discuss the differences between static and dynamic analysis.
3. The term "double taxation" refers only to the federal taxation of dividends. When state and local taxes and estate taxes are considered, there are more than two layers of taxation on dividend income. However, this working paper limits its discussion to federal tax policy, so its language refers only to federal double taxation. Consequently, the examples discussed herein set aside the effect of state and local taxation on corporate shareholder return and the user cost of capital.
4. For more on the economic effects of federal double taxation of dividends, see James M. Poterba, "Tax Policy and Corporate Saving," *Brookings Papers on Economic Activity* No. 2, 1987, pp. 455–515; Peter Birch Sorensen, "Changing Views of the Corporate Income Tax," *National Tax Journal,* Vol. 48, Issue 2 (June 1995), pp. 279–294; James M. Poterba and Lawrence H. Summers, "The Economic Effects of Dividend Taxation," National Bureau of Economic Research *Working Paper* No. 1353, 1984; and James M. Poterba and Lawrence H. Summers, "New Evidence that Taxes Affect the Valuation of Dividends," *The Journal of Finance,* Vol. 39, Issue 5 (December 1984), pp. 1397–1415.
5. Deborah Thomas and Keith Sellers, "Eliminate the Double Tax on Dividends," *Journal of Accountancy,* November 1994, and Ervin L. Black, Joseph Legoria, and Keith F. Sellers, "Capital Investment Effects of Dividend Imputation," *The Journal of the American Taxation Association,* Vol. 22, Issue 2 (2000), pp. 40–59.
6. H.R. 5323, 107th Congress.
7. The Center for Data Analysis was asked to evaluate this proposal in September 2002 and plans to evaluate the "exclusion method" in President Bush's proposal in a forthcoming study.

8. CDA analysts assumed that the reform would be enacted on September 30, 2003, and applicable retroactively to dividends paid after January 1, 2003.
9. All dollar values listed as "inflation-adjusted" are indexed to the general 1996 price level.
10. The Bureau of Economic Analysis (BEA) and the Internal Revenue Service (IRS) define the word "dividend" differently. This paper uses the BEA definition. There are at least two major differences between the BEA and IRS definitions. For example, the IRS defines as "dividend income" interest earned by mutual funds on the funds' non-equity holdings, while the BEA does not count this as dividend income. In contrast, the BEA counts as dividend income flows from S-Corporations, while the IRS does not. The numerical differences between the two definitions can be quite large. For example, during calendar year 2000, IRS dividends were $142.2 billion, while BEA dividends were $375.7 billion. See Thae S. Park, "Comparison of BEA Estimates of Personal Income and IRS Estimates of Adjusted Gross Income," Bureau of Economic Analysis, *Survey of Current Business,* November 2002, Table 2, at `http://www.bea.gov/bea/ARTICLES/2002/11November/1102irs&agi.pdf`.
11. For a discussion of the shortcomings of static analysis of the effects of tax policy changes, see Daniel J. Mitchell, "The Correct Way to Measure the Revenue Impact of Changes in Tax Rates," Heritage Foundation *Backgrounder* No. 1544, May 3, 2002, at `http://www.heritage.org/Research/Taxes/BG1544.cfm`. See also "The Argument for Reality-Based Scoring," Heritage Foundation *Web Memo* No. 92, March 29, 2002, at `http://www.heritage.org/Research/Taxes/WM92.cfm`, and Daniel R. Burton, "Reforming the Federal Tax Policy Process," Cato Institute, *Cato Policy Analysis* No. 463, December 17, 2002, at `http://www.cato.org/pubs/pas/pa-463es.html`.
12. Based on empirical evidence, this 10 percent increase in dividends appears to be a low-end estimate. See Martin Feldstein, "Corporate Taxation and Dividend Behavior," *The Review of Economic Studies,* Vol. 37, Issue 1 (January 1970), pp. 57–72, and Poterba, "Tax Policy and Corporate Saving." Assuming a larger increase in dividends would have resulted in a higher estimated growth in GDP.
13. The Center for Data Analysis used the Mark 11 U.S. Macroeconomic Model of DRI–WEFA, Inc., to conduct this analysis. The model was developed in the late 1960s by Nobel Prize–winning economist Lawrence Klein and several colleagues at the University of Pennsylvania. It is widely used by *Fortune* 500 companies, prominent federal agencies, and economic forecasting departments. The methodologies, assumptions, conclusions, and opinions herein are entirely the work of Heritage Foundation analysts. They have not been endorsed by, and do not necessarily reflect the views of, the owners of the model.
14. Congressional Budget Office, "The Budget and Economic Outlook: An Update," August 2002, at `http://www.cbo.gov/showdoc.cfm?index=3735&sequence=0`.
15. To maintain comparability with published CBO long-term projections, projections of changes in federal spending and revenue are not adjusted for inflation in this paper.

NO 

Joel Friedman and Robert Greenstein

Exempting Corporate Dividends From Individual Income Taxes

As the centerpiece of its "growth package," the [George W.] Bush Administration proposes a large reduction in the taxes that individuals pay on dividend payments they receive from corporations. According to Administration estimates, this tax cut reduces revenues by $364 billion, representing more than half of the package's $674 billion cost through 2013. This proposal to eliminate the taxes on dividends raises a number of questions. It would do little to stimulate the economy in the near term. In addition, its high cost over the next decade and beyond would result in further damage to the federal budget, increasing deficits and thereby reducing national savings and imposing long-term costs on the economy. . . .

Proposal Likely to Have Little Effect as Economic Stimulus

Even though the current weakness in the economy is used as justification for the proposal, reducing or eliminating the taxation of dividends would be ineffective at stimulating the economy now while it is weak. Indeed, most investors would not receive a tax cut from this proposal until *well over one year from now,* when they file their 2003 taxes in early 2004.

According to the Administration's estimates, exempting certain dividends from individual income taxes would cost $364 billion over the next decade. About 95 percent of this hefty cost would not occur until after 2003, by which time the economy is expected to have recovered from the current downturn.

Adding to the proposal's inefficiency as a stimulus mechanism is the fact that it would put cash primarily into the hands of high-income individuals, a group that is likely to save rather than spend a larger portion of any additional funds it receives than middle- and lower-income families. Yet only if funds are spent will they have the desired effect of stimulating the economy now. The Congressional Research Service found that "dividends are concentrated among higher income individuals who tend to save more" and that overall "using dividend tax reductions to stimulate the economy is unlikely to be very effective."[1]

Benefits Would Be Heavily Concentrated at the Top

It should also be noted that any claims that the benefits of this tax cut would be spread broadly across a growing "investor class" would be misleading. Many middle-income families are more likely to do their investing in the context of tax-deferred retirement accounts, such as 401(k)s and Individual Retirement Accounts. Yet only dividends paid from stocks held in taxable accounts would be affected by this proposal.

According to estimates by the Urban Institute-Brookings Institution Tax Policy Center:

- Nearly two-thirds of the benefits of exempting corporate dividends from the individual income tax would flow to the top five percent of the population, because these taxpayers own the lion's share of stocks. (The top five percent includes tax filers with incomes over $140,000; these filers have average income of $350,000.)
- The top one percent of tax filers—a group whose incomes start at $330,000 and that has average income of about $1 million—would receive 42 percent of the benefits.
- Those with incomes over $1 million—the top 0.2 percent of tax filers, with an average income that exceeds $3 million—would receive nearly one-quarter of the tax-cut benefits.
- In fact, the group with incomes over $1 million—which consists of about 226,000 tax filers in 2003—would receive roughly as much in benefits as the 120 million tax filers with incomes below $100,000. Stated another way, the top 0.2 percent of tax filers would receive nearly as much from this tax cut as the bottom 90 percent of filers combined.

The dollar value of the benefits of this tax cut for different income groups is also illustrative. Exempting corporate dividends from the individual income tax would yield an average annual tax savings of $27,100 for tax filers with incomes over $1 million, according to preliminary Tax Policy Center estimates. In contrast, those with incomes between $30,000 and $40,000 would see an average annual benefit of $42. Those with incomes between $40,000 and $50,000 would see an average annual benefit of $84.

The high-income taxpayers who would reap the vast majority of these tax-cut benefits have experienced far more substantial income gains over the past two decades than families lower down on the economic spectrum. Moreover, this high-income group is also the primary beneficiary of the tax-cut package enacted in 2001. Those with incomes over $1 million can expect an annual tax cut of *over $130,000* when all of the income-tax changes enacted in 2001 are fully in effect, and this figure does not even include the benefits this group would receive from repeal of the estate tax. The benefits of a dividend tax cut would come on top of this amount.

State Budget Deficits Would Be Enlarged

Exempting dividends from the individual income tax also would undercut other federal efforts to bolster the economy by worsening the dire fiscal situation in the states, which are facing a $60 billion to $85 billion budget gap in

IMPACT OF A DIVIDEND EXEMPTION ON THE ELDERLY

Supporters of exempting dividends from individual taxation are stressing the impact of this tax cut on the elderly. And indeed, preliminary Tax Policy Center estimates indicate that about 41 percent of the benefits of a dividend exemption would go to those over age 65. But while the elderly as a group would receive a large relative share of the tax cut, these benefits would flow predominately to those elderly individuals who have high incomes.

- Nearly 40 percent of the benefits of the dividend exemption that would accrue to elderly individuals would flow to the 2.5 percent of elderly people with incomes exceeding $200,000.
- Nearly three-quarters of the benefits that would go to the elderly from this tax cut would flow to the 19 percent of elderly with incomes above $75,000.
- Elderly people with incomes below $50,000—a group that represents two-thirds of all of the elderly in the nation—would receive only 13 percent of the tax cut going to the elderly and *less than 6 percent* of the total tax cut.

By citing a statistic showing that a large share of the benefits from the dividend exemption would go to the elderly, some proponents of this tax cut appear to be trying to foster the impression that it would benefit the average or typical elderly person. This is not the case. Most elderly have fairly low incomes and would receive little or nothing from this tax cut.

The benefits of the proposal would flow predominately to a small group of individuals with high incomes, and a disproportionate share of these high-income taxpayers happen to be elderly. That this is so does not alter the fact that most elderly people would not benefit significantly from it. In fact, many elderly could be adversely affected if the tax cut resulted in fewer resources being available for programs upon which ordinary elderly people rely.

the next fiscal year, the largest shortfall in the last half-century. As states cut spending and raise taxes to meet their balanced budget requirements, they are placing a drag on the economy. Cutting the individual tax on dividends would reduce state revenues, because of the linkages between state and federal tax codes. Eliminating the tax could reduce state revenues by approximately $4 billion a year.[2] In general, states will have to raise taxes or cut expenditures by one dollar for each dollar of revenue loss, further undermining the proposal's effectiveness as economic stimulus.

States would also be hard hit by the anticipated increase in interest rates expected to result from this proposal. The proposal will draw funds away from the bond market, as corporate stocks become more attractive investments following the tax cut. To compete for investor dollars with stocks paying dividends that are fully or partially exempt from taxation, entities that issue bonds—including state and local governments—would have to offer higher interest rates. In addition, the cost of reducing or eliminating taxes on dividends for individuals would enlarge the deficit and increase government borrowing. As government borrowing needs crowd out other borrowers, interest rates can rise. Overall, higher interest rates increase the cost of borrowing for states, putting further strain on their budgets.

Positive Effects on the Stock Market Appear to Be Exaggerated

Claims that this tax cut, by making stocks more valuable, would significantly buoy the stock market and thereby bolster consumer confidence and help the economy are likely to be exaggerated. A more muted response seems more likely than a strong reaction when one considers that over half of dividends would not be directly affected by the proposal (because they are paid to tax-exempt accounts, such as pension funds). Moreover, corporate investments would be negatively affected by the higher interest rates that would likely result from this tax cut.

Furthermore, trying to induce an increase in the stock market is an indirect and rather inefficient way to encourage consumers to spend more and thus stimulate the economy. The Congressional Research Service concluded that the link between a stock market increase and consumer spending "is weaker, more uncertain, and perhaps more delayed, than a direct stimulus to the economy via spending increases or cuts in taxes aimed at lower income individuals."[3] In addition, cutting dividends taxes to manipulate the market in an effort to aid investors hurt by the recent downturn is questionable public policy. As Brookings Institution economists Gale and Orszag have noted, "having the government bail out investors who voluntarily accepted risks by investing in the stock market would set a dangerous precedent."[4]

Potential Negative Impact on Certain Sectors of the Economy, Including Small Businesses

As the economy adjusted to lower taxes for corporate dividends, some sectors of the economy would likely be disadvantaged, at least in the short run. This tax cut would make stocks a more attractive investment in terms of their after-tax returns, prompting investors to pull funds out of some other investments and shift these dollars to corporate stocks.

As noted above, the tax cut would draw funds away from the bond market, which would result in higher interest rates. These higher rates not only raise costs for state and local governments and business investment but also for home mortgages and car loans. Similarly, one would also expect the non-corporate sector, which is comprised primarily of small businesses, to be affected adversely, as investment dollars shift into corporate stocks.

Effect on Economy Over the Long Run

The high cost of ending the taxation of dividends would likely mitigate any beneficial long-term impact the proposal might have on the economy. Supporters tout the positive effects of cutting dividend taxes on encouraging more investment in corporations. They often ignore the negative effects associated with the tax cut's long-term cost, however, and the resulting increase in the federal deficit. Although a one-time increase in the current deficit to pay for stimulus can be good economic medicine, permanently increasing future deficits as this proposal would do would have a corrosive effect on the economy. The preponderance of economic research indicates that sustained budget deficits reduce national savings, which results in less investment and ultimately lowers the nation's income in the future. So while the proposal may improve the efficiency of the allocation of investment dollars, it would also shrink the pool of investment dollars available by increasing the deficit. In the end, it is the combination of these positive and negative effects that will determine the overall impact on the economy.

Other Proposals Would Be More Effective Stimulus and Do Less Fiscal Damage Over the Long Run

Other proposals would be far more effective at providing immediate economic stimulus by directing funds to individuals and businesses that would spend the money—and thereby bolster the economy now when it is weak. A generous extension of unemployment benefits, for instance, would put money into the hands of families who are out of work and likely facing cash-flow constraints. Similarly, fiscal assistance to the states would pump money directly into the economy by helping states avoid making deep program cuts or increasing taxes, which would otherwise place a drag on the economy. A tax cut aimed at lower- and moderate-income working families would also offer considerably more stimulus for each dollar of cost in the ten-year budget window—than a cut in taxes on dividends.

Although a temporary increase in the deficit can be justified as providing economic stimulus in the short run, a permanent increase in the deficit is much harder to defend given the deterioration in the fiscal outlook and the knowledge that, just over the horizon, the retirement of the baby boomers will place a huge burden on the federal budget. Despite the need to begin to take steps now to reduce, or certainly not to worsen, future deficits—as well as the need to pay for the ongoing fight against terrorism at home and abroad and the generally agreed-upon need for a prescription drug benefit for seniors—this proposal would produce a substantial drain on the Treasury. These revenue losses would come on top of the massive revenue losses the 2001 tax cut will cause when it is fully in effect. Overall, a costly proposal to eliminate or reduce sharply individual taxes on corporate dividends seems particularly inappropriate.

Supporters of this tax cut are pushing for it to be part of an economic stimulus package, despite its being ineffective and inefficient as stimulus. By doing so, they may seek to create a belief that its high, permanent cost does not have to be offset. Including this proposal in a stimulus package that is said to warrant rapid congressional action avoids linking the proposal to broader consideration of corporate tax reforms that would address the "zero taxation" of much corporate income resulting from the proliferation of corporate tax avoidance and tax sheltering schemes. Any proposal to lighten the tax burden on corporate dividends should be considered, however, only in the context of a deficit-neutral package of corporate reforms, where the range of issues related to corporate taxation can be addressed together.

This analysis is divided into three sections. The first section looks at the cost and distribution of proposals to reduce or eliminate the tax on corporate dividends. The second assesses the impact on the economy of such a tax change. The final section examines the concept of the "double taxation" of corporate dividends and its relevance to the current debate.

Reducing or Eliminating the Tax on Corporate Dividends

A corporation can use dividends as a way to distribute earnings to its shareholders, with dividends being paid out of its after-tax income.[5] In other words, a corporation makes dividend payments to its shareholders out of the earnings that remain after corporate income taxes have been paid. Shareholders include these dividend payments in their income for tax purposes. To the extent that shareholders are subject to the individual income tax, they pay tax on their dividend income.

The Urban Institute-Brookings Institution Tax Policy Center estimates that in 2000, corporations paid $201 billion in dividends out of their after-tax incomes. More than half of these dividends were paid to tax-exempt entities—such as pension funds, individual retirement accounts, and non-profit foundations—or to individuals that owed no income tax. As a result, only about 46 percent of the dividends paid by corporations to individuals (or $93 billion in dividends) were subject to the individual income tax in 2000.[6]

Over the years, various options to eliminate the taxation of corporate dividends have been proposed. Some proposals would exempt from the *corporate* income tax all earnings paid out in dividends. Such proposals would be more costly than making dividends tax free for individuals, because of the large share of dividends flowing to tax-exempt accounts not currently subject to individual income taxes. . . .

Economic Impact of Eliminating the Individual Taxation of Dividends

The Treasury Department released a comprehensive report on various options to reduce the taxation of dividends in 1992.[7] Although the different options had varying effects, the Treasury Department concluded that all of the options—including ending taxes on dividends at the individual level—would have a positive impact on the economy. It concluded such a tax change "will encourage capital to shift into the corporate sector" and "stimulate improvements in overall economic well-being." But the Treasury report was able to reach these positive conclusions in large part because *it assumed that the cost of the tax cuts would be fully offset*. That is, the Treasury options were assessed assuming they had no net impact on the deficit. This assumption is in sharp contrast to the Bush Administration's tax-cut proposal, which is not expected to be offset and would result in higher deficits. These different assumptions are crucial to understanding the long-term effects of the proposals on the economy, because of the negative impact of budget deficits on future economic growth.

The Long-Term Effect—More Efficient Investments but Less Invested

Brookings Institution economists William Gale and Peter Orszag recently undertook an exhaustive review of the available economics literature on the impact of budget deficits on the economy.[8] They found a broad consensus among economists that "declines in budget surpluses (or increases in budget deficits) reduce national savings and thus reduce future national income." They also found that a wide variety of perspectives, from empirical research and leading macroeconomic models to the views of numerous leading academics and policy institutions, "all indicate that increases in expected future deficits raise long-term interest rates." Although the link between future deficits and long-term interest rates has received the most attention in the media, their paper makes the important point that because sustained budget deficits reduce national savings, they have a negative impact on the economy regardless of their effect on interest rates.[9]

As Gale and Orszag point out in their paper, an increase in the budget deficit and the resulting reduction in national savings mean the nation has less to invest. Lower investment leads to a smaller stock of capital assets and lower economic growth in the future. Exempting dividends from individual taxation may encourage a more efficient allocation of resources—that is, it may encourage more investments in those areas that will yield the highest returns for economic growth. But if the revenue losses generated by the tax cut are not offset and result in larger deficits, there will be lower national savings and thus less to invest. So even though the proposal may promote more efficient investment of the capital that is available, there will be a lower level of investment overall. It is the combined effect of these factors—more efficient investments, but less invested—that ultimately will determine the long-term impact of the proposal on the economy.

In Short Run, Tax Cut Offers Little to Boost Economy

Although the long-term impact of the proposal would be modest at best, its effects in the short term are clearer. The proposal is particularly ineffective economic stimulus, offering little "bang for the buck."

- The benefits of eliminating individual taxes on corporate dividends would flow primarily to those with higher incomes. This higher-income group, however, is likely to save more and spend less of any additional funds it receives than low- and moderate-income families would. Funds must be spent if they are to stimulate the economy in the near term.

- Despite the hefty ten-year cost of the proposal, only a small portion of the revenue losses would result in an immediate increase in spending. This undermines the proposal's effectiveness as a mechanism to deliver immediate stimulus to the economy. More than 90 percent of the revenue losses over the next ten years would occur after 2003, in years when the economy is expected to have recovered.
- The tax cut also is poorly designed to put money into the hands of consumers quickly, because most tax-cut recipients would not begin receiving the bulk of their annual tax-cut benefits until they filed their 2003 tax returns in early 2004. To receive the benefits earlier, taxpayers would have to adjust their withholding or estimated payments for the remainder of this year, a step that few—particularly those with only modest levels of dividends—would be likely to take, given the difficulty individuals would have estimating the impact of the tax cut and their fear of penalties in the event of underpayment.
- A tax cut for dividends would reduce state revenues because of the linkages between state and federal tax codes, worsening the state fiscal crisis that is imposing a drag on the economy. Preliminary estimates by the Center on Budget and Policy Priorities indicate that exempting dividends from individual income tax could cost states about $4 billion a year. Given the large budget deficits that states face and the requirements that they balance their budgets, states would be forced to make up for these revenue losses with dollar-for-dollar expenditure reductions or tax increases. Such actions by the states counteract federal efforts to stimulate the economy.[10]
- The proposal also could have a negative impact on the economy in the near-term because of its effects on long-term interest rates. As Gale and Orszag explain in their analysis, financial markets are forward looking and take into account today changes that are expected to occur in the future. Thus, a costly proposal to eliminate or substantially reduce the taxation of dividends would create the expectation of higher future deficits, which in turn could exert upward pressure on long-term interest rates today. These higher long-term rates could dampen prospects for current economic growth, because individuals and businesses make fewer large purchases when the long-term interest rates they pay on the funds they borrow to make the purchases rise to higher levels.

It also is worth noting that in the short run, a proposal to eliminate or reduce substantially the individual taxation of corporate dividends would create winners and losers—that is, it would benefit some sectors of the economy and some firms at the expense of others.

- With a tax cut for corporate stocks that pay dividends, the after-tax returns of this type of investment would rise. While more money would flow to these stocks, these funds would be drawn away from other sectors.
- Funds would likely flow out of the non-corporate sector and into corporate stocks. In the analysis it conducted in 1992, the Treasury

Department concluded that the proposal would result in "the reallocation of physical capital (and other real resources) from the rest of the economy into the corporate sector." Thus, the non-corporate sector—typically comprised of small businesses, including sole proprietors—would likely experience a loss of investment funds.

- Similarly, by making equities a more attractive investment, the proposal would make bonds relatively less attractive. Interest rates on bonds would rise under these circumstances, as the bond market would have to offer higher interest rates to attract investors. This result, plus the effect on interest rates stemming from the increase in the deficit the tax cut would engender, could place significant upward pressure on rates. Higher interest rates would not only affect business investment and borrowing by state and local governments, but would also impact consumers by increasing rates on home mortgages and car loans, for instance.

Positive Impact on the Stock Market Likely Exaggerated

Eliminating individual taxes on dividends would make dividend-paying stocks more valuable in terms of their after-tax return. Supporters of this tax cut maintain that investors would seek out these higher returns, thereby bidding up the price of these stocks and boosting the stock market as a whole. This improvement in the stock market would, in turn, have a salutary effect on the economy, they argue, as consumers, heartened by the increase in their portfolios, would react by increasing their spending. This analysis is flawed in a number of respects.

It is far from clear that the proposal would lead to a significant rise in the stock market. As noted previously, about half of all dividends are not subject to individual income tax, primarily because they flow to tax-exempt pension funds, retirement accounts, and non-profit foundations. None of the investment decisions made by these groups would be directly affected by the elimination of the individual tax on corporate dividends, because they are not subject to the tax. Further, corporate investments would be negatively affected by the higher interest rates that likely would follow from this deficit-increasing tax cut.

While one might expect to see stock prices rise modestly in reaction to the proposed tax cut, it would likely be a one-time increase that primarily yielded a windfall for current holders of dividend-paying stocks, who purchased their stocks at prices that reflected the current tax treatment of dividends. University of Michigan tax expert Reuven Avi-Yonah recently wrote that "it is doubtful that cutting the tax on dividends will have a significant impact on the stock market. And even if it did, current holders of the stock, wealthy individuals who bought the stock at a discounted price anticipating that they would be taxed on future dividends, would get an unjustified windfall."[11] Similarly, the *Daily Tax Report* issued by the Bureau of National Affairs cites economists from the investment firm Credit Suisse First Boston as predicting that cutting dividend taxes would have only a "mildly positive" effect on stock prices.[12]

The key question in assessing the stimulative effect of such changes in stock prices is whether a modest increase in the market would be sufficient to increase consumer spending enough to have a meaningful impact on the economy; most estimates—including those of the Federal Reserve—indicate that consumers boost their spending by only a few cents for each dollar increase in their wealth. If the goal is to get consumers to spend more, encouraging such spending through a rise in the stock market consequently is an indirect and inefficient method of achieving that goal. Other proposals, such as extending and strengthening unemployment benefits and providing fiscal assistance for states, would have far more "bang for the buck" in terms of stimulating the economy. As the Congressional Research Service recently concluded, the link between higher stock prices and increased consumer spending "is weaker, more uncertain, and perhaps more delayed, than a direct stimulus to the economy via increases in spending or cuts in taxes aimed at lower income individuals."[13]

"Double Taxation" of Corporate Dividends

Supporters of eliminating the taxation of corporate dividends typically argue that such a change is necessary to end the "double taxation" of these dividends. Double taxation arises because, in theory, corporations pay dividends out of their after-tax earnings, and these payments are subsequently taxed as part of the shareholders' income. Thus, these corporate earnings are taxed twice—once at the corporate level and again at the individual level.

In reality, not all corporate dividends are taxed twice; some are only taxed once and some not at all. As noted above, on the individual side, more than half of all corporate dividends flow to entities, such as tax-exempt retirement funds, that are not subject to individual income tax. Further, some corporate earnings distributed to shareholders are not subject to the corporate income tax, as corporations make use of available tax preferences and other less scrupulous tax avoidance techniques to lower or eliminate their tax bills.

Significant Corporate Profits Escape Corporate Income Tax

To be taxed twice, corporate profits first have to be subjected to the corporate income tax. Yet there is significant evidence that corporations are aggressively employing tax avoidance strategies that have resulted in a growing share of corporate profits escaping corporate taxation altogether. In recent years, the Treasury Department, the congressional tax-writing committees, academics and journalists have raised concerns over the rise in corporate tax sheltering activities.

As evidence of this trend, recent studies have shown a growing divergence in the amount of profits that corporations report to their shareholders (known as book income) and the amounts that these companies report to the Internal Revenue Service for purposes of paying corporate income taxes.[14] Harvard economist Mihir Desai concludes that the traditional link between these two measures of corporate profits has "broken down" and that "the patterns of the deteriorating link between tax and book income are consistent with increased levels of sheltering over the decade." For instance, Desai found that $154 billion, or more than half of the gap between corporate book and tax income in 1998, the latest year covered in his study, could not be explained by the traditional accounting differences between these two measures.

On a related front, the Institute on Taxation and Economic Policy examined the books of 250 large companies between 1996 and 1998.[15] Together these companies pay about 30 percent of all federal corporate income taxes.

- Over that three-year period, ITEP found that 41 companies—or about one in six of the total sample—paid "less than zero" in federal corporate taxes in at least one year. Despite reporting nearly $26 billion in profits to their shareholders over the period, these companies not only paid no corporate income tax but actually received rebate checks from the federal government totaling $3 billion. This list includes companies such as General Motors, ChevronTexaco, Goodyear and CSX.
- Building on these findings, Citizens for Tax Justice currently estimates that in 2002, *less than half* of corporate profits were subject to the corporate income tax. As [a] result, CTJ concludes that only a little more than half of corporate profits were subject to tax at *any* level, corporate or individual.[16]

In a *New York Times* article on January 5, 2003, *Times* business columnist Gretchen Morgenson concluded that "companies are paying less and less in taxes each year, making the 35 percent corporate tax rate a fiction."[17] Morgenson reported, for example, that Bristol-Myers Squibb's effective tax rate fell to 15.4 percent in 2001 from 25.2 percent in the previous year. (A firm's effective tax rate is the percentage of the firm's profits paid in taxes.) Similarly, in a recent article, Robert McIntyre, executive director of Citizens for Tax Justice and an expert in corporate tax avoidance, points out that CSX, despite having U.S. profits of more than $930 million over the past four years, paid no federal corporate income taxes over the period and instead received refunds totaling $164 million.[18]

Taxing Dividends Twice Not Relevant Equity Issue

The moniker "double taxation" tends to raise the specter of some group—in this case, individuals who receive dividends—being treated unfairly by the tax system, because part of their income is being taxed twice. On its editorial page, for example, the *Wall Street Journal* has argued that the policy of taxing dividend income twice should be ended as a matter of equity.[19]

But for economists, whether this income is taxed once or twice is not the relevant equity issue. As McIntyre aptly noted, "Who wouldn't feel better, for instance, about paying two taxes of 10 percent each rather than a single tax of 40 percent?"[20] Moreover, many forms of income are taxed more than once. An obvious example is wages. While corporate dividends are theoretically double taxed first at the corporate level and then at the individual level, an individual's wages are immediately subject to both payroll and income taxes.

Equity, in the context of taxes, is about whether taxpayers in similar circumstance pay similar amounts of tax and about how the burden of taxes is borne by different income groups, not about the number of times a particular type of income is taxed. The current federal tax system as a whole (including the taxation of dividends, and also including payroll and excise taxes) is modestly progressive.[21] The most significant equity issue related to the taxation of dividends is whether eliminating the tax on dividends and thereby reducing the level of progressivity in the tax system is a desirable step.

Concerns That Dividend Taxation Distorts Investment Decisions

The more significant concern raised by many economists is that the current tax treatment of corporate dividends may interfere with the efficient allocation of the nation's resources by directing investments into less productive, but more lightly taxed, areas. In a dynamic market economy, such as in the United States, investment funds flow to those areas that yield the highest *after-tax* return—other factors, such as risk, being equal. Consequently, investors may be deterred from investing in the corporate sector because the after-tax return of a corporate investment would be lower than the after-tax return of a non-corporate investment that is taxed only as part of an individual's income tax return.[22] Although it might offer a higher after-tax return, the non-corporate investment could be a less productive use of investment dollars (as measured by its *pre-tax* return) and thus be less beneficial for overall economic growth.

Furthermore, within the corporate sector, some economists believe the current tax treatment of dividends can distort corporate financing decisions. Corporations raise funds to finance capital investment through essentially three methods: debt (i.e., issuing bonds); equity (i.e., issuing new shares of stock); and retained earnings (i.e., reinvesting after-tax earnings rather than distributing them to shareholders in the form of dividends). The concern is that current tax law biases corporate investment decisions against issuing new equity and toward debt financing and retaining earnings, which are both more lightly taxed than dividends.[23] As a result, corporations may not be using an optimal mix of these three financing mechanisms, which would ultimately be less efficient for the economy.

There is a large body of academic work examining the impact on the economy of having separate corporate and individual income taxes. Many of these studies conclude that, for the efficiency reasons discussed above, the economy would benefit if the corporate and individual taxes were integrated. The 1992 Treasury study reached this conclusion and, to that end, proposed *a deficit-neutral* dividend exclusion at the individual level. There is not unanimous agreement on this issue among economists, however, particularly when international economic issues are taken into account. As University of Michigan international tax expert Reuven Avi-Yonah recently wrote, the case for corporate tax integration in a globalizing world "is much shakier than is commonly thought," with many of our trading partners now moving away from the full exclusion of dividends from taxation.[24]

Conclusion

As short-term stimulus, exempting all or a portion of corporate dividends from individual income taxes is ill-conceived. It fails to meet the basic requirements of any stimulus proposal, which are that such a proposal be temporary and be targeted in a way that encourages as much new spending as possible in the short term. The proposal to reduce or eliminate the taxation of dividends is clearly intended to be permanent, and its benefits would flow primarily to those with the highest incomes, a group likely to save more of a tax cut than moderate- and lower-income families would.

Despite its shortcomings as stimulus, reducing or eliminating individual taxes on corporate dividends is expected to be the centerpiece of the Bush Administration's economic growth package. The Administration likely will use the continued uncertainty surrounding the state of the economy both to push for rapid consideration of its package and to argue that the package's large long-term costs need not be offset. This, however, is the wrong context for debating the dividend proposal, since it precludes consideration of other relevant corporate tax issues and thus virtually ensures this costly tax cut will impose a permanent drain on the Treasury.

Consideration of measures to reduce or eliminate the so-called "double taxation" of corporate dividends should be accompanied by consideration of measures to curb the "zero taxation" of a rising share of corporate profits as a result of the increasingly aggressive use of corporate tax shelters and other tax-avoidance techniques. A tax cut for dividends should be considered only as part of a more comprehensive, deficit-neutral package of corporate tax reforms.

Notes

1. Gregg A. Esenwein and Jane G. Gravelle, "The Taxation of Dividend Income: An Overview and Economic Analysis of the Issues," Congressional Research Service, October 7, 2002.
2. Iris J. Lav, "Bush 'Growth Plan' Would Worsen State Budget Crises," Center on Budget and Policy Priorities, January 9, 2002.
3. Esenwein and Gravelle.
4. William Gale and Peter Orszag, "A New Round of Tax Cuts," Center on Budget and Policy Priorities, August 23, 2002.
5. Dividend-paying firms tend to be large, well-established companies. For example, many of the highest-yielding stocks (i.e., pay the highest dividends relative to their share prices) tend to be familiar companies, such as Philip Morris, J.P. Morgan Chase, General Motors, Eastman-Kodak, Dow Chemical, Bristol-Myers Squibb, ConAgra Foods, Ford Motor, and ChevronTexaco. See Greg Bartalos, "New Tax Plan May Yield Sweet Dividends," *Barron's Online*, December 12, 2002.
6. William G. Gale, "About Half of Dividend Payments Do Not Face Double Taxation," *Tax Notes*, November 11, 2002.
7. "Integration of the Individual and Corporate Tax Systems: Taxing Business Income Once," U.S. Department of the Treasury, January 1992.

8. William G. Gale and Peter R. Orszag, "The Economic Effects of Long-Term Fiscal Discipline," Urban-Brookings Tax Policy Center Discussion Paper, December 17, 2002.
9. Gale and Orszag point out that if lower national savings leads to increased foreign borrowing, interest rates may not rise. But if foreign borrowing increases, then America's indebtedness to rest of the world increases. The returns to these investments flow overseas, rather than raising the future incomes of Americans. As a result, higher deficits lower the nation's income in the future, regardless of whether interest rates increase.
10. States would also be negatively affected by the proposal because it would likely result in higher interest rates and thus increase their cost of borrowing.
11. Reuven S. Avi-Yonah, "Back to the 1930s? The Shaky Case for Exempting Dividends," *Tax Notes*, December 23, 2002
12. Brett Ferguson, "Treasury Renews Push for Higher Debt Limit, Warns Ceiling Could be Hit in late February," *BNA Daily Tax Report*, December 27, 2002.
13. Esenwein and Gravelle.
14. See Mihir Desai, "The Corporate Profit Base, Tax Sheltering Activity, and the Changing Nature of Employee Compensation," NBER Working Paper 8866, April 2002, and George A. Plesko, "Reconciling Corporation Book and Tax Net Income, Tax Years 1996–1998," *Statistics of Income Bulletin*, Spring 2002.
15. Robert S. McIntyre and T.D. Coo Nguyen, "Corporate Income Taxes in the 1990s," Institute on Taxation and Economic Policy, October 2000.
16. Robert McIntyre, "New Gang, Old Myths," *The American Prospect*, January 13, 2003.
17. Gretchen Morgenson, "Waiting for the President to Pass the Tax-Cut Gravy," *The New York Times*, January 5, 2003.
18. McIntyre, "New Gang, Old Myths."
19. "Ending Double Tax Trouble," *The Wall Street Journal*, December 26, 2002.
20. McIntyre, "New Gang, Old Myths."
21. Joel Friedman and Isaac Shapiro, "Are Taxes Too Concentrated at the Top? Rapidly Rising Income at the Top Lie Behind Increase in Share of Taxes Paid by High-Income Taxpayers," Center on Budget and Policy Priorities, December 18, 2002.
22. Earnings in a non-corporate business are taxed only at the individual income tax rates. The majority of non-corporate businesses are sole proprietorships, earnings from which are taxed at the owner's individual income tax rates. Other non-corporate enterprises such as partnerships are often referred to as "passthrough" companies because the earnings pass through to the partners and shareholders and are taxed at their individual rates. See Jack H. Taylor, "Passthrough Organizations Not Taxed As Corporations," Congressional Research Service, August 20, 2002.
23. Of these three methods, debt receives the most favorable tax treatment. Although interest payments to bondholders are treated as income to the bondholder, just as dividend payments are treated as income to shareholders, interest payments are a deductible expense for a corporation. As a deductible expense, interest payments reduce the amount of corporate profits subject to tax; in contrast, dividends are paid out of after-tax funds. Thus, interest payments are taxed at most only once, at the individual level, and are more lightly taxed than dividends, which can face both corporate and individual taxes.

Retained earnings can also be subject to double taxation, but to a much lesser degree than dividends. When a corporation retains its earnings for investment purposes, it tends to push the firm's share prices higher. Thus, shareholders become subject to higher capital gains taxes when (or if) they decide to sell their shares. But capital gains are taxed at a lower rate than regular income taxes, and shareholders can control when they will sell shares, potentially deferring capital gains taxes indefinitely. As a result, retained earnings generate lower taxes at the individual level than dividend payments, which are subject to tax in the year in which the payment is made at individual income tax rates.

24. Avi-Yohan.

POSTSCRIPT

Should the Double Taxation of Corporate Dividends Be Eliminated?

Ignore for the moment whether or not eliminating the tax on dividend income will stimulate the economy, and focus on the issue of "double taxation." If one concludes that the efficiency concerns raised by Michel, Goyburu, and Rector outweigh the equity issues raised by Friedman and Greenstein, one should ask whether or not there really is double taxation in the first place.

Before considering that discussion, it is important to understand how double taxation allegedly comes into being. Those who favor the repeal of the dividend tax argue that every time a corporation has an excess profit of one dollar that they plan to distribute as a dividend, 35 cents of that potential dividend goes to the U.S. Treasury, assuming that the corporation is in the highest corporate income tax bracket of 35 percent. As the corporation "distributes" its excess profits to its shareholders, those 65 pennies are now subject to personal income taxes. Again, assuming the highest tax bracket, this time of the personal income tax, the 65 cents that is distributed would be taxed at 38.6 percent. That represents another 24 cents in taxes for a total of 59 cents for every dollar earned and distributed to shareholders.

There are some very big assumptions here that should be underscored. One could ask, for example, just how much of a corporation's net income is subject to the corporate income tax? The taxation of corporate income is too complex to detail, but it is important to note that over the past 40 years, the amount of corporate taxes paid as a percentage of all federal taxes from all sources has steadily decreased. On the other hand, in the 1960s corporate taxes were a close second to personal income taxes as a percentage of federal tax revenue; now corporate taxes are a distant third to social security taxes. This is the result of accelerated depreciation allowances and other tax preferences that have been granted to the corporate sector. Thus, a significant amount of corporate net income never passes through the corporate tax mill. That portion of corporate net income that is distributed in the form of dividends is only taxed once—as personal income.

One could also note the consequences of corporations' having two options for their net income: they can distribute their net earnings as dividends, or they can "retain" these corporate earnings and invest them in the corporate enterprise. Over time this should increase the value of the corporation, but that increased valuation is not fully taxed as personal income. This is because any asset that is held for more than one year and that appreciates in value is subject to special rates. The maximum tax that an individual must pay on these capital gains is 20 percent, and that is not paid until the gain is realized—that is, there is no capital gain income to tax until the appreciated asset is sold. In this extreme case, the total tax is 48 percent (35 cents of corporate taxes and another 13 cents of capital gains taxes). This is not an insignificant amount, even though it is not the 60 percent that is often cited.

Much has been written in support of eliminating the tax on corporate dividends. Alan Greenspan offered an interesting view on this topic in his February 12, 2003, testimony before the House Financial Services Committee. Greenspan concluded that, in the long run, "virtually everyone" benefits from the elimination of this tax. Greenspan is not alone in this view, particularly in the conservative "think tanks." See, for example, the March 6, 2003, testimony before the House Ways and Means Committee by John H. Makin, a resident scholar of the American Enterprise Institute, which can be found on the Internet at `http://www.aei.org/news/newsID.16393/news_detail.asp`, and "How the Tax Code Contributed to the Corporate Scandals and Bankruptcies," by Lawrence H. Whitman, *Heritage Backgrounder No. 1578* (August 27, 2002).

Many others take exception to the tax code. Their concerns take several forms. William G. Gale and Peter R. Orszag, for example, question the growth consequences of eliminating the dividend tax in "The Economic Effects of Long Term Fiscal Discipline," Urban-Brookings Tax Policy Center Discussion Paper (December 17, 2002), which can be found at `http://www.som.yale.edu/faculty/pks4/files/macro_readings/inv_gale_orszag_brookings_021217.pdf`. Avrum D. Lank agrees in "Forget the Plan to Stop Taxing Dividends," *JSOnline/Milwaukee Journal Sentinel*, `http://www.jsonline.com/bym/your/jan03/113334.asp`. In this essay, Lank raises the issue of the complexities that this will introduce into the tax code. Many agree, including Gregg A. Esenwein and Jane G. Gravelle in "The Taxation of Dividends: An Overview and Economic Analysis of the Issues," Congressional Research Service (October 7, 2002) and Dean Baker in "The Dividend Tax Break: Taxing Logic," Center for Economic and Policy Research Issue Brief (January 6, 2003).

ISSUE 10

Are Credit Card Companies Exploiting American Consumers?

YES: Robert D. Manning, from "Perpetual Debt, Predatory Plastic," *Southern Exposure* (Summer 2003)

NO: Michael F. McEneney, from "Written Statement of Michael F. McEneney on Behalf of the Consumer Bankers Association," Testimony before the House Subcommittee on Financial Institutions and Consumer Credit (September 15, 2004)

ISSUE SUMMARY

YES: Professor Robert D. Manning lists a number of problems with credit cards, including high interest rates, misrepresentation of the cost of debt consolidation loans, use of double billing cycles, use of "bait and switch" techniques, improper use of personal consumer credit information, and the proliferation of a number of practices that are of little or no benefit to consumers.

NO: Lawyer Michael F. McEneney stresses the benefits that consumers experience because of the "ever-expanding choices available to consumers," and he supports his claims by reporting that a Federal Reserve study found that "91% of credit card holders are satisfied with their credit card issuers."

When a consumer makes a purchase, he or she can "pay" for the item in a variety of ways. There is the old-fashioned way of paying with cash—exchanging Federal Reserve Notes and treasury currency for the item. A second option, also of fairly long standing, involves paying by check. The options then evolve to more recent creations—credit cards, debit cards, and even stored-value cards. There is even something called a smart card.

Concentrating on credit cards, the statistics regarding their use are almost mind-boggling. According to one account:

- There are over 641 million credit cards in circulation.
- Credit cards in circulation support some $1.5 trillion in consumer spending.

- Some 115 million Americans carry monthly credit card debt.
- The average household has a credit card balance of about $8,000.

Of course, credit cards are issued by profit-seeking financial institutions, and it appears to be a lucrative business; in 2003 the before-tax profits of the credit card industry exceeded $30 billion.

These numbers become more impressive when one realizes that the ubiquitous credit card has only been around for a little more than 50 years. The creation of the credit card is usually attributed to Frank X. McNamara. Legend has it that he conceived of the notion of a credit card when he had insufficient cash to pay for a "power lunch" at Major's Cabin Grill in New York. So in 1951 Diners Club credit cards were issued to some 200 customers who were then able to charge their meals at 27 participating New York restaurants.

Today, people are most familiar with what are called general-purpose credit cards: Visa, MasterCard, Discover, and American Express. Other credit cards carry the name of a particular retailer (for example, the credit cards issued by oil companies, large department stores, and so on). Bank of America usually gets the credit for creating the first general-purpose credit card in 1958; back then it was called BankAmericard. In 1965 Bank of America began licensing other banks to issue BankAmericards. In 1977 BankAmericard became Visa. MasterCard, on the other hand, traces its origins to 1967 when four California banks introduced MasterCharge to compete with BankAmericard. MasterCharge became MasterCard in 1979.

Besides the distinction between general-purpose and other kinds of credit cards, there are also several types of general purpose credit cards. A secured credit card is one that requires a security deposit. These cards are typically issued to individuals with a troubled credit history or who are just starting out. There are also premium cards (gold, platinum, etc.); these cards have higher borrowing limits and frequently have extra features.

Visa and MasterCard credit cards can be obtained from any number of financial institutions. Each issuer is free to set whatever terms it wishes; that is, a bank issuing a Visa card or MasterCard is free to set its own conditions. These conditions include the APR (annual percentage rate) that applies to unpaid credit card balances, various fees (annual membership fee, cash advance fee, late payment fee, etc.) and incentives (rebates, frequent flier miles, car rental insurance, etc.). Making matters even more complex, a single credit card may have multiple APRs: one for purchases, another for cash advances, and a third for balance transfers. There may also be a special penalty APR, an introductory APR, and a delayed APR.

But something else is associated with credit cards: controversy. This issue takes us to the heart of that controversy. No one denies that the general-purpose card was a marvelous invention, conferring all kinds of benefits to their holders. But, the argument goes, the costs that consumers pay for these advantages are too high. Indeed, credit card issuers have taken advantages of unsuspecting and naïve consumers.

Robert D. Manning

Perpetual Debt, Predatory Plastic

Last year John, a 55-year-old African American living on public assistance in Takoma Park, Maryland, a Washington, D.C., suburb, received an invitation in the mail promising him a chance to join millions of other Americans who enjoy the convenience and status of credit-card membership. In its direct mail solicitation, United Credit National Bank Visa declared, "ACE VISA GUARANTEED ISSUE or we'll send you $100.00! (See inside for details.)" For the unsuspecting, it might have sounded like a terrific opportunity to enter the credit mainstream. But a closer look inside showed that the primary beneficiary was the credit-card company:

> Initial credit line will be at least $400.00. By accepting this offer, you agree to subscribe to the American Credit Educator Financial and Credit Education Program. The ACE program costs $289.00 plus $11.95 for shipping and handling plus $19.00 Processing Fee, a small price to pay compared to the high cost of bad credit! The Annual Card Fee [is] $49.00. . . . For your convenience, we will charge these costs to your new ACE Affinity VISA card.

In other words, getting the card would cost John $369, leaving a net credit line of as little as $31—all financed at an annual percentage rate (APR) of 19.8 percent. As a poor, minority consumer, John's been gouged often enough to recognize a come-on: "Man, they just want to rip me off." He didn't go for the offer.

The credit card industry tries to whitewash such usurious and predatory practices by arguing that it is "democratizing" access to credit through its offers to households previously limited to "second-tier" lenders such as pawnshops and rent-to-own stores.

But not everyone has John's hard-earned savvy. Many impoverished consumers are blinded by financial desperation, low literacy skills, and a desire to part of what the TV commercials tell them is an exclusive club: the fellowship of consumers lucky enough to have earned bank credit cards. After all, exclaim the well-dressed actors, "You work hard for your money. Don't you deserve some credit?"

Not surprisingly, they sign up and become willing subjects of America's new credit economy, a brave new world where technology, marketing innovations, and deregulation have transformed old ways of lending and borrowing. The only thing that hasn't changed is this time-honored principle: The most profitable way to make money off the vulnerable is to keep them in debt at the highest rates for as long as possible.

In the 1940s, when folksinger Merle Travis was memorializing the harsh life of Southern coal miners in his famous ballad "Sixteen Tons," consumer debt served as an effective management tool for lowering both wages and worker turnover. Coal miners became indebted to the company store through high prices and excessive finance charges in an era when "*saving for a rainy day*" reflected the vagaries of the business cycle (unemployment) and the physical risks of the job (accidents). As a result, company scrip often replaced government currency, and miners' household debts bound them to their employers in a form of debt servitude.

You load sixteen tons what do you get
Another day older and deeper in debt
Saint Peter don't you call me 'cause I can't go
I owe my soul to the company store

As mail order retailers like Sears Roebuck expanded into the hamlets of the American South in the early 20th century, the growth of working class consumer markets became intertwined with access to credit. Unlike the company stores of Appalachia, where extending credit was a profitable business practice, the "open book" credit policies of local merchants (usually interest free), as well as credit lines at retail chains, were designed primarily to promote sales volume and customer loyalty. Although household incomes rose throughout the 1950s and 60s, the popular Sears credit card—the largest proprietary consumer credit system in the post-World War II era—featured an onerous finance charge of 1.5 percent per month on outstanding balances. Even so, the high costs of administering these low volume "revolving" accounts typically resulted in annual losses to the company; retail profits were made from selling rather than financing consumption in the golden age of U.S. manufacturing.

The recent revolution in consumer financial services dates to the 1970s and the increasingly successful assaults against Depression-era banking regulations. For example, the 1933 McFadden Act limited national banks from crossing state boundaries and competing with state-chartered banks. Until the 1980s, these restrictions protected the community banking system and its conservative installment lending policies. Significantly, the best customers of these local banks were those with the lowest outstanding debts—the borrowers who were most likely to repay their loans within an agreed period.

By the late 1970s, high inflation and declining real wages encouraged families to embrace debt as a strategy for coping with financial hardship. State usury laws and interstate banking restrictions, however, limited the growth of the "all-purpose" or "universal" national bank credit card until 1978, when the U.S. Supreme Court ruled that nationally chartered banks could charge the highest interest rate permitted by their "home" states and export these rates to their out-of-state credit card clients. Banks quickly relocated their "brick and mortar" offices to states without usury ceilings—Citibank, for example, moved from New York to South Dakota. In this way, the universal credit card (led by Visa and MasterCard) was transformed into a high profit product that could hurdle state banking regulatory barriers.

The universal bank credit card played a major role in the deregulation of the U.S. banking industry in the 1980s. National "money center" banks faced mounting losses on Third World, residential, and commercial real estate loans following the 1981–82 recession. Credit cards became the banks' means of profit salvation. Although Citibank's credit card division bled over $500 million in red ink between 1979 and 1981, the sharp reduction in inflation and advances in computer technology sparked a dramatic shift toward consumer financial services over the next two decades.

In the 1980s, an average of one million blue-collar workers lost their jobs each year, swelling the pool of families struggling to make ends meet and increasing the demand for quick, unsecured consumers loans. The consumer services revolution shifted into high gear. Soaring bank profits fueled unprecedented consolidation. In 1977, the top 50 banks accounted for about half of the credit card market. Twenty-five years later, the top ten banks controlled over 80 percent of the market. In the process, "net" revolving credit card debt climbed from about $51 billion in 1980 to over $610 billion in 2002. At the same time, more than half of all outstanding credit card debt is resold in the secondary financial markets as securitized bonds, at a typical premium of 15 to 18 percent in 2001. Many institutional investors such as pension funds purchase these bonds for their portfolios.

Today, the ascendance of credit cards marks the shift from installment lending to revolving loans, where the "best" bank customers will never repay their high interest credit card balances. In this new world of consumer finance, the most disadvantage (debtors) subsidize the low cost of credit for the most advantaged (convenience users). It is this moral divide that leads banks to refer to those clients who pay their charges in full each month (39 percent of all customers in 2002) as "deadbeats."

The other 61 percent are the ones who fuel the banks' profits, and for them the price is growing ever higher. The true cost of borrowing on bank credit cards has more than doubled since the advent of banking deregulation in 1980, thanks to painful interest rates and escalating penalty and user fees. The upward spiral began in 1996, when the U.S. Supreme Court invalidated state limits on credit card fees by ruling that fees are part of the cost of borrowing. This decision produced a striking change in the way card issuers do business, along with some striking numbers:

- The average late fee jumped from $13 in 1996 to $30 in 2002.
- Penalty fee revenue climbed from $1.7 billion in 1996 to $7.3 billion in 2001.
- Total fee income rose more than five times faster than overall credit card profits between 1995 and 2001.
- Together penalty ($7.3 billion) and cash advance ($3.8 billion) fees equaled the after-tax profits of the entire credit card industry ($11.1 billion) in 2001.

* Three out of five families (61%) now carry a balance on their credit cards each month. Their average card debt has risen from over $10,000 in 1998 to over $12,000 in 2002.

In response, banks argue that they provide an efficient service to consumers in urgent need of cash or a necessary purchase. Also, they emphasize the payment flexibility credit cards give their clients, many of whom face increasing financial demands and prefer to carry balances from month to month.

As profits have climbed, corporate retailers have become increasingly dependent on finance revenues to make up for shrinking margins on consumer sales. In 2001, for instance, Sears and Circuit City reported that more than half of their profits were due to finance-related revenues. This is not surprising since credit cards are the most profitable product of the financial services industry. Even during the current recession, pre-tax profits of the credit card industry (measured by Return on Assets) jumped 20 percent from 2000 to 2001. The industry pulled in record pre-tax profits of nearly $18 billion in 2001, or a whopping 4 percent of assets—three times greater than the average of the banking industry.

Not incidentally, the growing burden of high-cost credit card debt is borne by middle-income and working poor families. The current recession, which elicited President Bush's patriotic exhortations to spend more time and money in the malls, has highlighted the critical role of consumer spending to the vitality of the corporate economy. Although government policymakers have encouraged household spending by reducing interest rates (the Federal Funds rate was cut from 6.5 percent in 2000 to 1.75 percent at end of 2001), the sharp decline in the cost of borrowing by banks has not been passed on to consumers. For the major credit card companies, the Federal Reserve's low-interest rate policy has produced a windfall, given that they had reduced their rates only modestly—from an average of 18 percent in 2000 to about 16 percent in 2001.

The industry, meanwhile, has fought to stop or hinder any state regulation of credit card interest rate ceilings and fees—or requirements that consumers be given meaningful notice of rate hikes or other changes in their contract provisions. For example, Maryland-based Chevy Chase Bank promised its credit card clients not to raise the top interest rate above 24 percent. In 1996, however, it moved its credit card headquarters to Virginia and raised its interest rate to a high of 28.8 percent. It also changed the terms of its contract to include higher late fees, a new overlimit fee, and a more costly "daily" calculation of finance charges—all without the sort of effective notification that would give customers a chance to reject these unfavorable amendments to their existing contracts.

Real disclosure would cut into profits, so the industry has fought to keep customers in the dark. If credit card clients understood the long-term cost of their accounts, they might make higher monthly payments—something banks don't want. The American Bankers Association has sued to prevent the enactment of a 2002 California law that requires banks to use clients' monthly statements to inform them of the number of years necessary to pay off the outstanding balance, assuming there are no additional charges and only the minimum payment is remitted.

Although banks emphasize the availability of low-interest balance transfers, the most indebted rarely qualify for these promotional programs or benefit for only a short period of time (two to six months). More frequently, heavily indebted households encounter "bait and switch" offers, where low-interest promises are quickly replaced with high-interest realities. Furthermore, credit card companies have adopted a stringent policy of imposing penalties on promotional interest rates for minor payment infractions or simply due to high outstanding balances on other consumer loan accounts.

In Houston, Texas, for example, Doug received an enticing six-month, 1.9 percent balance transfer offer from Chase MasterCard and shifted $5,000 from his MBNA credit card account. Unfortunately, Doug's wife mistakenly sent $80 instead of the required $97 for the first month's minimum payment. Even though it was received two weeks before the due date, his next statement reported $17 past due plus a $35 late fee. More striking was the increase in the interest rate, from 1.9 percent to 22.99 percent, even though he had not had a late payment in over two years. A Chase customer service representative informed Doug he would have to document six months of on-time payments before the bank would consider his request for a lower interest rate. This followed a previous "bait and switch" from Chase on the same card in 2001, where the 4.9 percent promotional rate was raised without warning—simply because the bank had decided that the balances on his other credit cards were "too high."

The passage of the Financial Services Modernization Act of 1997, which authorized the Citibank and Traveler's Group merger, marks the end of Depression-era regulation of retail banking as separate from commercial banking/insurance services. Moreover, the ability to acquire companies across financial services sectors and share client information with corporate subsidiaries underlies the rise of "cross-selling" financial products such as investment services to credit card clients. This explains Citibank's 1997 purchase, at a substantial premium, of AT&T's unprofitable credit card company (eighth largest), with its disproportionate number of high-income customers. For Citigroup, this corporate synergy produces multiple revenue flows by originating high interest loans through credit card and subprime lending, which are then resold through its Salomon Smith Barney division to individual and institutional investors.

Not incidentally, access to personal consumer credit information enables predatory lenders to identify highly indebted households that are susceptible to slippery solicitations for "debt consolidation." According to a 2002 California lawsuit, Household Finance obtained lists of prospective clients from Best Buy, K-Mart, Costco, and other retailers. Homeowners with high debts were identified from these lists and contacted by account executives at nearby-branches. Household promised these potential customers that their debt consolidation loans would save them money after the refinancing of their credit card, consumer loan, and mortgage debts into a single monthly payment. In the process, the lawsuit alleged, Household deliberately sought to "upsell," or persuade their clients to accept consolidated loans in amounts so high in relation to the value of their homes that it would be nearly impossible to sell or refinance in the future.

By misrepresenting the total cost of these debt consolidation loans (origination fees, mandatory insurance, high interest rates), the suit claims, Household Finance Corporation generates high profits from the initiation of these loans as well as from their resale in secondary mortgage and securitized bond markets.

Today, high credit card interest rates are no longer sufficient to satisfy the financial services industry's voracious appetite for profits. Penalty and transaction fees continue to rise while new fees are imposed, such as overdraft transactions, foreign currency conversion, and "double billing" cycles which reduce the payment "grace" period. In addition, banks have begun aggressively marketing financial-related services that offer little practical benefits for their clients. These include credit protection programs ($9.99 per month from Citibank) that cannot prevent identity fraud, and unemployment and injury insurance (typically 0.5 percent of outstanding monthly balance) with premium costs that usually exceed the minimum credit card payments provided by the insurance. The proliferation of these products yields big profits for the banks and only modest benefits for consumers.

For American families and consumer advocates, fighting back isn't easy. The industry has thwarted state and local attempts to create better consumer protections by invoking the principle of federal preemption—the U.S. Constitution's provision that public efforts to regulate the national banking system can be legislated only by Congress. The influence of the banking industry on both the U.S. Congress and the executive branch (MBNA was the largest contributor to George Bush's Presidential campaign) seemingly ensures that no significant pro-consumer bills will see the light of day in the next couple of years. At the same time, the industry has reduced its vulnerability to class-action lawsuits by specifying arbitration agreements in their credit card contracts that deny consumers their right to a day in court.

Now, with the threat of regulation and litigation diminished, the credit card industry is focusing its efforts on passing the Bankruptcy Reform Act. President Clinton vetoed the measure at the end of 2000, but other versions of this industry-written bill were passed by both houses of Congress in 2002, and again by the U.S. House of Representatives in April 2003. The aim of the bill is to increase the amount of unsecured consumer loans (especially credit card debts) that must be repaid before the approval of a bankruptcy petition. If this bill is enacted into law, it will expand the U.S. government's role as a *de facto* debt collector and increase the costs assumed by the public in extending consumer credit to the most risky credit card clients. In doing so, it will provide banks even greater incentive to push high-cost credit to their most marginal clients. For an industry whose motto is "Greed is Good," this legislative distortion of the free market system could enable it to top even its current record profits and spiraling executive bonuses.

Michael F. McEneney

Written Statement of Michael F. McEneney on Behalf of the Consumer Bankers Association

Before the Subcommittee on Financial Institutions and Consumer Credit

Good morning Chairman Bachus, Ranking Member Sanders, and Members of the Subcommittee. My name is Michael F. McEneney. I am a partner in the law firm of Sidley Austin Brown & Wood LLP. It is my pleasure to appear before you this morning on behalf of the Consumer Bankers Association ("CBA"). The CBA is the recognized voice on retail banking issues in the nation's capital. Member institutions are the leaders in consumer financial services, including auto finance, home equity lending, card products, education loans, small business services, community development, investments, deposits, and delivery. CBA was founded in 1919 and provides leadership, education, research, and federal representation on retail banking issues such as privacy, fair lending, consumer protection legislation, and regulation. CBA members include most of the nation's largest bank holding companies, as well as regional and super community banks that collectively hold two-thirds of the industry's total assets.

Today's hearing is focused on financial products and services from the consumer's perspective. There is no doubt that today's financial marketplace looks quite good from the consumer's perspective. The financial services marketplace offers consumers a wider variety of financial products and services than ever before. This includes loans, deposit products, checking accounts, investment options and a growing variety of payment and remittance services. Not only can consumers choose from a wide range of products, but they can obtain them over the phone, using the Internet, or through personal interaction at the financial institutions' offices.

Our financial marketplace is truly a success story. However, the success did not develop overnight, or by accident. There was a time when consumers did not enjoy all of the conveniences they are offered today. In fact, it was not too long ago when retail banking services looked much different than they do today. Back then many people had to carry cash or checks at all times because

From Testimony before the House Subcommittee on Financial Institute of Consumer Credit, September 15, 2004.

credit cards as we know them did not exist. And to get that cash people had to spend time going to the bank branch and standing in line for a teller. Why? There was no such thing as an ATM. Visiting the bank branch in person was also necessary to get a loan, and, in many instances, you had to have an account with the bank. The opportunities to shop around for a loan that are available today really did not exist. Most people were just happy if their bank approved them and accepted the rate the bank was offering at the time. The approval process could last weeks, and fewer people qualified for loans than would qualify today.

There are obviously a number of reasons for the spectacular evolution of the financial services industry and the ever-expanding choices available to consumers. However, I believe that most of these reasons relate to providing financial institutions with the flexibility to compete fiercely with one another to provide a better product to consumers at lower costs. I would like to use a few examples to illustrate my point.

First, the process by which consumers obtain home mortgages has been simplified and made more efficient through increased competition in the marketplace. Hopeful homebuyers at one time submitted their mortgage application to their bank and waited on pins and needles for several days, or even a few weeks, while their application was considered. Those who did not have a relationship with a bank, or those who did not have many local banks from which to choose, obviously had a more challenging time obtaining a mortgage. However, today, consumers benefit from lenders across the country competing with one another to provide consumers with home loan opportunities wherever they may reside. Decisions are oftentimes made almost instantaneously, and lenders are able to offer loans that meet a variety of consumer needs. Given the number of lenders and types of mortgages available, creditworthy borrowers are likely to have several choices when choosing how to finance their homeownership.

Second, we take for granted that a consumer today can obtain a credit card that suits his or her individual needs. The credit card may offer frequent flyer miles, or the logo of the consumer's charity. It may offer the consumer a rebate on some or all purchases the consumer makes with the credit card. The consumer can also shop for low interest rates, and credit cards that do not have any annual fees. I believe that all of these benefits can be traced in great part to the ease with which credit card issuers can compete with one another through a variety of mechanisms, including a process known as "prescreening."

It is hard to imagine, but there once was a time when annual fees were common and consumers obtained few "fringe" benefits for using their credit cards. Today, most people can find an offer for a card without an annual fee or that offers other benefits simply by reading their mail. Before large numbers of card issuers engaged in prescreening, a consumer obtained a credit card from his or her local bank. Although local banks competed with one another to provide retail banking services to consumers, including credit card products, the competition was nothing like we see today. Some time ago, credit card issuers began to prescreen consumers in order to offer them credit cards. This process, combined with uniform rules for interest rates and fees, allowed banks in any location to offer credit cards to consumers *nationwide* through the mail. Basically, prescreening allows a creditor to obtain a limited amount of credit information in order to offer consumers a "firm offer of credit." With the advent of prescreening, suddenly the consumer did not need to be satisfied with the credit card from his or her local bank—a card that likely had an annual fee and comparatively higher interest rates. In fact, as more card issuers made more credit card offers to consumers, consumers could pick from a variety of credit cards. Naturally, this competition fostered lower prices and improved features on credit cards. Perhaps these developments help explain why the staff of the Federal Reserve Board recently found that 91% of cardholders are satisfied with their credit card issuers.

Third, the ability of financial institutions to price their products in a more precise manner has resulted in enormous benefits to all consumers—most notably the extraordinary homeownership rate. This Subcommittee has gathered large amounts of information pertaining to our national credit system as part of its deliberations on the FACT Act just last year. However, a few of the key points are worth repeating today. The consumer reporting process has developed into a very sophisticated information delivery mechanism that allows lenders to evaluate large amounts of objective and accurate information about consumers. Successful lenders have used this information to evaluate and manage risk in a way that allows them to lower the costs of credit to those consumers who have good credit histories. Yet, consumers with good credit histories are not the only primary beneficiaries of the benefits resulting from the developments fostered by our national credit system. In fact, as lenders obtain more information about potential borrowers through applications and credit reports, for example, they can offer credit to consumers who at one time could not qualify for credit. Now, instead of a bank offering a "one size fits all" loan product to only those consumers with above average credit histories, the bank can use risk-based pricing to offer more consumers access to credit at a variety of risk-based prices. Indeed, many reputable lenders have developed successful lines of business making prudent loans to lower- and moderate-income families that have been traditionally underserved. The more competition there is from reputable lenders making responsible lending decisions to consumers, the less opportunity there will be for bad actors to prey on the vulnerable. That means more home mortgages, more college education loans, and more auto loans for safe transportation for consumers of all walks of life—not just the wealthy or those with perfect credit histories.

Competition in the market place also means an expanding pie where those who have been traditionally underserved can enter the mainstream of our economy. For example, CBA's members continue to develop and expand product offerings to satisfy the demands of an increasingly diverse market. This includes efforts to bank the so-called "unbanked" through use of payroll cards, stored value products, and remittance services in addition to offering low-cost traditional banking products, such as checking accounts. For example, CBA is hosting a Hispanic Banking Forum later this month to highlight bank activities in this area and provide an opportunity for banks to share their knowledge and experience.

Mr. Chairman, current law ensures that consumers receive valuable information with respect to financial products. Laws such as the Truth in Lending Act, the Truth in Savings Act, the Electronic Fund Transfer Act, and the Real Estate Settlement Procedures Act establish frameworks under which consumers are provided important disclosures with respect to the price of financial services, and the terms on which they are offered. Consumers receive a variety of disclosures in other contexts, such as under the Equal Credit Opportunity Act and the Fair Credit Reporting Act. In short, it is clear that consumers do not lack for disclosures of information in connection with financial transactions.

It is also important to note that our financial marketplace is a complex system that relies on providing consumers with choice. Any system that offers choices requires consumers to understand the relative benefits and costs of those choices. Disclosure laws like Truth in Lending are important, but they can only do so much in the absence of fundamental financial literacy on the part of consumers. Banks have long understood that the most innovative and beneficial financial products in the world are likely of no use to the consumer who lacks basic knowledge of how to participate in our financial system, and unsophisticated consumers are more easily targeted by the unscrupulous. That is why banks have been in the forefront of efforts to expand financial education.

In April 2004, CBA published a survey regarding the progress made in the financial literacy of consumers as a result of banks' educational efforts. The report focuses on eight areas including credit counseling, mortgage and homeownership, predatory lending, public school programs, college programs and small business training. The results of the survey evidence an increase in banks that participate in consumer financial literacy education. Of those that responded, 100% of the institutions participate in at least one of the eight areas of concentration. Most notably, approximately 89% of the 54 responding institutions offer public school financial literacy programs (this is a 16% increase from the survey conducted one year ago), and financial literacy efforts of banks in colleges almost doubled. A portion of CBA's 2004 Survey of Bank Sponsored Financial Literacy Programs has been submitted with this testimony. The entire survey may be found at `www.cbanet.org`.

In conclusion Mr. Chairman, I would like to highlight that consumers of all income levels in the United States have financial opportunities that are the envy of the world. Virtually any creditworthy consumer can obtain credit when they need it. Retail banking and other financial services are widely available and can be obtained by walking down the street to the local financial institution, or by using phone, mail or the Internet. Continued improvements in technology and risk control allow more financial institutions to improve their financial products, to offer them to broader groups of consumers, and to develop new financial products altogether. Naturally, we face the challenge of ensuring that consumers understand the opportunities they have available to them. But I can assure you that CBA's members are committed to ensuring that consumers receive the information they need, including through information disclosures and financial education materials and opportunities.

Thank you again for inviting me to appear before you today. I would be pleased to answer any questions.

POSTSCRIPT

Are Credit Card Companies Exploiting American Consumers?

Manning begins his critique of the credit card industry by relating the story of John, who was offered an effective credit line of $31 at a cost of $369. Manning believes that the new credit economy embodies what he calls a time-honored principle: "The most profitable way to make money off the vulnerable is to keep them in debt at the highest interest rate for as long as possible." Manning describes a number of changes that have led to the new credit economy, including two U.S. Supreme Court decisions. One was in 1978, allowing national banks to "charge the highest interest rate permitted by their 'home' states and export these rates to their out-of state-credit card clients." The second was in 1996, eliminating state-imposed limits on credit card fees. He proceeds to review a number of credit card company practices that produce "big profits for the banks and only modest benefits for consumers." Manning concludes by stating his opposition to a reform of bankruptcy law, supported by the credit card industry, that would allow the industry to "top even its current record profits and spiraling executive bonuses."

McEneney begins by identifying himself: He is appearing before the subcommittee on behalf of the Consumer Bankers Association, an organization that includes "most of the nation's largest bank holding companies, as well as regional and super community banks that collectively hold two-thirds of the industry's total assets." His assessment of the market for consumer financial products and services is positive; from the consumer perspective, it is "quite good." This assessment is based on the fact that consumers have lots of products that can be accessed in a variety of ways. McEneney believes this positive environment was created because financial institutions had the flexibility to compete with one another. He offers several examples. With respect to credit cards, he states "most people can find an offer for a card without an annual fee or that offers other benefits simply by reading their mail." This is the case because the competition for credit cards is national, and this national competition became possible because of prescreening. That is, before prescreening, consumers could only get a credit card from their local bank. McEneney cites a recent Federal Reserve survey that reported that 91 percent of credit card holders were "satisfied with their credit card issuers." He concludes his testimony by asserting, "consumers of all income levels in the United States have financial opportunities that are the envy of the world."

A good place to start for additional perspective on this issue is additional testimony before the House Subcommittee on Financial Institutions and Consumer Credit. During the September 15, 2004, hearings, Jean Ann Fox of the Consumer Federation of America and Tamara Draut of Demos offer more criticism of the credit card industry while Randy Lively of the American Financial Services Association extols the positives associated with credit cards: http://financialservices.house.gov/hearings.asp?formmode=detail&hearing=333. Manning has two books related to this issue: *Credit Card Nation: The Consequences of America's Addiction to Credit* (Basic Book, 2000) and *Give Yourself Credit!* (Alta Mira, 2004). General information on credit cards is available from the Federal Reserve at http://www.federalreserve.gov/pubs/shop/. The Federal Reserve also makes information available from its survey of banks that issue credit cards; the information includes, among other things, the name of the bank, the types of credit cards it issues, the APRs, annual fees, and other features: http://www.federalreserve.gov/pubs/shop/survey.htm. To find more information regarding Visa and MasterCard, visit their home sites.

ISSUE 11

Is It Time to Abolish the Minimum Wage?

YES: Thomas Rustici, from "A Public Choice View of the Minimum Wage," *The Cato Journal* (Spring/Summer 1985)

NO: Charles Craypo, from "In Defense of Minimum Wages," An Original Essay Written for This Volume (2002)

ISSUE SUMMARY

YES: Orthodox neoclassical economist Thomas Rustici asserts that the effects of the minimum wage are clear: It creates unemployment among the least-skilled workers.

NO: Labor economist Charles Craypo argues that a high minimum wage is good for workers, employers, and consumers alike and that it is therefore good for the economy as a whole.

In the midst of the Great Depression, Congress passed the Fair Labor Standards Act (FLSA) of 1938. In one bold stroke, it established a minimum wage rate of $.25 an hour, placed controls on the use of child labor, designated 44 hours as the normal workweek, and mandated that time and a half be paid to anyone working longer than the normal workweek. Fifty years later the debates concerning child labor, length of the workweek, and overtime pay have long subsided, but the debate over the minimum wage rages on.

The immediate and continued concern over the minimum wage component of the FLSA should surprise few people. Although $.25 an hour is a paltry sum compared to today's wage rates, in 1938 it was a princely reward for work. It must be remembered that jobs were hard to come by and unemployment rates at times reached as high as 25 percent of the workforce. When work was found, any wage seemed acceptable to those who roamed the streets with no safety net to protect their families. Indeed, consider the fact that $.25 an hour was 40.3 percent of the average manufacturing wage rate for 1938.

Little wonder, then, that the business community in the 1930s was up in arms. Business leaders argued that if wages went up, prices would rise. This would choke off the little demand for goods and services that existed in the marketplace, and the demand for workers would be sure to fall. The end result would be a return to the depths of the depression, where there was little or no hope of employment for the very people who were supposed to benefit from the Fair Labor Standards Act.

This dire forecast was demonstrated by simple supply-and-demand analysis. First, as modern-day introductory textbooks in economics invariably show, unemployment occurs when a minimum wage greater than the equilibrium wage is mandated by law. This simplistic analysis, which assumes competitive conditions in both the product and factor markets, is predicated upon the assumptions that as wages are pushed above the equilibrium level, the quantity of labor demanded will fall and the quantity of labor supplied will increase. This wage rigidity prevents the market from clearing. The end result is an excess in the quantity of labor supplied relative to the quantity of labor demanded.

The question that should be addressed in this debate is whether or not a simple supply-and-demand analysis is capable of adequately predicting what happens in real-world labor markets when a minimum wage is introduced or an existing minimum wage is raised. The significance of this is not based on idle curiosity. The minimum wage has been increased numerous times since its introduction in 1938. Most recently, effective September 1, 1997, legislation establishing the current minimum wage of $5.15 was signed into law by President Bill Clinton.

Did this minimum wage increase, and other increases before it, do irreparable harm to those who are least able to defend themselves in the labor market, the marginal worker? That is, if a minimum wage of $5.15 is imposed, what happens to all those marginal workers whose value to the firm is something less than $5.15? Are these workers fired? Do firms simply absorb this cost increase in the form of reduced corporate profits? What happens to productivity?

This is the crux of the following debate between Thomas Rustici and Charles Craypo. Rustici argues that the answer is obvious: there will be an excess in the quantity of labor supplied relative to the quantity demanded. In lay terms, there will be unemployment. Craypo rejects this neoclassical view. He recommends judging the minimum wage on the intent of the original legislation: increased aggregate demand and elimination of predatory labor market practices.

Thomas Rustici

A Public Choice View of the Minimum Wage

Why, when the economist gives advice to his society, is he so often cooly ignored? He never ceases to preach free trade . . . and protectionism is growing in the United States. He deplores the perverse effects of minimum wage laws, and the legal minimum is regularly raised each 3 to 5 years. He brands usury laws as a medieval superstition, but no state hurries to repeal its laws.

—George Stigler

Introduction

Much of public policy is allegedly based on the implications of economic theory. However, economic analysis of government policy is often disregarded for political reasons. The minimum wage law is one such example. Every politician openly deplores the spectacle of double-digit teenage unemployment pervading modern society. But, when economists claim that scientific proof, a priori and empirical, dictates that minimum wage laws cause such a regretful outcome, their statements generally fall on deaf congressional ears. Economists too often assume that policymakers are interested in obtaining all the existing economic knowledge before deciding on a specific policy course. This view of the policy-formation process, however, is naïve. In framing economic policy politicians will pay some attention to economists' advice, but such advice always will be rejected when it conflicts with the political reality of winning votes. . . .

Economic Effects of the Minimum Wage

Economic analysis has demonstrated few things as clearly as the effects of the minimum wage law. It is well known that the minimum wage creates unemployment among the least skilled workers by raising wage rates above free market levels. Eight major effects of the minimum wage can be discussed: unemployment effects, employment effects in uncovered sectors of the economy, reduction in nonwage benefits, labor substitution effects, capital substitution effects, racial discrimination in hiring practices, human capital

From Thomas Rustici, "A Public Choice View of the Minimum Wage," *The Cato Journal*, vol. 5, no. 1 (Spring/Summer 1985).

development, and distortion of the market process with respect to comparative advantage. Although the minimum wage has other effects, such as a reduction in hours of employment, these eight effects are the most significant ones for this paper.

Unemployment Effects

The first federal minimum wage laws were established under the provisions of the National Recovery Administration (NRA). The National Industrial Recovery Act, which became law on 16 June 1933, established industrial minimum wages for 515 classes of labor. Over 90 percent of the minimum wages were set at between 30 and 40 cents per hour.[1] Early empirical evidence attests to the unemployment effects of the minimum wage. Using the estimates of C. F. Roos, who was the director of research at the NRA, Benjamin Anderson states: "Roos estimates that, by reason of the minimum wage provisions of the codes, about 500,000 Negro workers were on relief in 1934. Roos adds that a minimum wage definitely causes the displacement of the young, inexperienced worker and the old worker."[2]

On 27 May 1935 the Supreme Court declared the NRA unconstitutional, burying the minimum wage codes with it. The minimum wage law reappeared at a later date, however, with the support of the Supreme Court. In what became the precedent for the constitutionality of future minimum wage legislation, the Court upheld the Washington State minimum wage law on 29 March 1937 in *West Coast Hotel v. Parrish*.[3] This declaration gave the Roosevelt administration and Labor Secretary Frances Perkins the green light to reestablish the federal minimum wage, which was achieved on 25 June 1938 when President Roosevelt signed into law the Fair Labor Standards Act (FLSA).

The FSLA included legislation affecting work-age requirements, the length of the workweek, pay rates for overtime work, as well as the national minimum wage provision. The law established minimum wage rates of 25 cents per hour the first year, 30 cents per hour for the next six years, and 40 cents per hour after seven years. The penalty for noncompliance was severe: violators faced a $10,000 fine, six months imprisonment, or both. In addition, an aggrieved employee could sue his employer for twice the difference between the statutory wage rate and his actual pay.[4]

With the passage of the FLSA, it became inevitable that major dislocations would result in labor markets, primarily those for low-skilled and low-wage workers. Although the act affected occupations covering only one-fifth of the labor force,[5] leaving a large uncovered sector to minimize the disemployment effects, the minimum wage was still extremely counterproductive. The Labor Department admitted that the new minimum wage had a disemployment effect, and one historian sympathetic to the minimum wage was forced to concede that "[t]he Department of Labor estimated that the 25-cents-an-hour minimum wage caused about 30,000 to 50,000 to lose their job. About 90% of these were in southern industries such as bagging, pecan shelling, and tobacco stemming."[6]

These estimates seriously understate the actual magnitude of the damage. Since only 300,000 workers received an increase as a result of the minimum wage,[7] estimates of 30,000–50,000 lost jobs reveal that 10–13 percent of those covered by the law lost their jobs. But it is highly dubious that only 30,000–50,000 low-wage earners lost their jobs in the entire country; that many unemployed could have been found in the state of Texas alone, where labor authorities saw devastation wrought via the minimum wage on the pecan trade. The *New York Times* reported the following on 24 October 1938:

> Information received today by State labor authorities indicated that more than 40,000 employees of the pecan nut shelling plants in Texas would be thrown out of work tomorrow by the closing down of that industry, due to the new Wages and Hours Law. In San Antonio, sixty plants, employing ten thousand men and women, mostly Mexicans, will close. . . . Plant owners assert that they cannot remain in business and pay the minimum wage of 25 cents an hour with a maximum working week of forty-four hours. Many garment factories in Texas will also close.[8]

It can reasonably be deduced that even if the Texas estimates had been wildly inaccurate, the national unemployment effect would still have exceeded the Department of Labor's estimates.

The greatest damage, however, did not come in Texas or in any other southern state, but in Puerto Rico. Since a minimum wage law has its greatest unemployment effect on low-wage earners, and since larger proportions of workers in poor regions such as Puerto Rico tend to be at the lower end of the wage scale, Puerto Rico was disproportionately hard-hit. Subject to the same national 25-cents-per-hour rate as workers on the mainland, Puerto Rican workers suffered much more hardship from the minimum wage law. According to Anderson:

> It was thought by many that, in the first year, the provision would not affect many industries outside the South, though the framers of the law apparently forgot about Puerto Rico, and very grave disturbances came in that island. . . . Immense unemployment resulted there through sheer inability of important industries to pay the 25 cents an hour.[9]

Simon Rottenberg likewise points out the tragic position in which Puerto Rico was placed by the enactment of the minimum wage:

> When the Congress established a minimum wage of 25 cents per hour in 1938, the average hourly wage in the U.S. was 62.7 cents. . . . It resulted in a mandatory increase for only some 300,000 workers out of a labor force of more than 54 million. In Puerto Rico, in contrast . . . the new Federal minimum far exceeded the prevailing average hourly wage of the major portion of Puerto Rican workers. If a continuing serious attempt at enforcement . . . had been made, it would have meant literal economic chaos for the island's economy.[10] . . .

After two years of economic disruption in Puerto Rico, Congress amended the minimum wage provisions.[11] The minimum wage was reduced to 12.5 cents per hour, but it was too late for many industries and for thousands of low-wage earners employed by them, who suddenly found unemployment the price they had to pay for the minimum wage.

In sum, the tragedy of the minimum wage laws during the NRA and the FLSA was not just textbook-theorizing by academic economists, but real-world disaster for the thousands who became the victims of the law. But these destructive effects have not caused the law to be repealed; to the contrary, it has been expanded in coverage and increased in amount.

. . . Evidence for the unemployment effects of the minimum wage continues to mount. Many empirical studies since the early 1950s—from early research by Marshall Colberg and Yale Brozen to more recent work by Jacob Mincer and James Ragan—have validated the predictions of economic theory regarding the unemployment effects of the minimum wage law. In virtually every case it was found that the net employment effects and labor-force participation rates were negatively related to changes in the minimum wage. In the face of 50 years of evidence, the question is no longer *if* the minimum wage law creates unemployment, but *how much* current or future increases in the minimum wage will adversely affect the labor market.

Employment in Uncovered Sectors

The labor market can be divided into two sectors: that covered by the minimum wage law, and that not covered. In a partially covered market, the effects of the minimum wage are somewhat disguised. Increasing it disemploys workers in the covered sector, prompting them to search for work in the uncovered sector if they are trainable and mobile. This then drives down the wage rate in the uncovered sector, making it lower than it otherwise would have been. Since perfect knowledge and flexibility is not observed in real-world labor markets, substantial unemployment can occur during the transition period.

Employees in the covered sector who do not lose their jobs get a wage-rate increase through the higher minimum wage. But this comes only at the expense of (1) the disemployed workers who lose their jobs and suffer unemployment during the transition to employment in the uncovered sector, and (2) everyone in the uncovered sector, as their wage rate falls due to the influx of unemployed workers from the covered sector. While increasing the incomes of some low-wage earners, increasing the minimum wage tends to make the lowest wage earners in the uncovered sector even poorer than they otherwise would have been.

Yale Brozen has found that the uncovered household sector served to absorb the minimum wage-induced disemployed in the past.[12] But the "safety valve" of the uncovered portion of the economy is rapidly vanishing with the continual elimination of various exemptions.[13] Because of this trend we can expect to see the level of structural unemployment increase with escalation of the minimum wage.[14]

Nonwage Benefits

Wage rates are not the only costs associated with the employment of workers by firms. The effective labor cost a firm incurs is usually a package of pecuniary and nonpecuniary benefits. As such, contends Richard McKenzie,

> employers can be expected to respond to a minimum wage law by cutting back or eliminating altogether those fringe benefits and conditions of work, like the company parties, that increase the supply of labor but which do not affect the productivity of labor. By reducing such non-money benefits of employment, the employer reduces his labor costs from what they otherwise would have been and loses nothing in the way of reduced labor productivity."[15]

If one takes the view that employees desire both pecuniary and nonpecuniary income, then anything forcing them to accept another mix of benefits would clearly make them worse off. For example, suppose worker A desires his income in the form of $3.00 per hour in wages, an air-conditioned workplace, carpeted floors, safety precautions, and stereo music. If he is *forced* by the minimum wage law to accept $3.25 per hour and fewer nonpecuniary benefits, he is worse off than at the preminimum wage and the *higher* level of nonpecuniary income. A priori, the enactment of minimum wage laws must place the worker and employer in a less-than-optimal state. Thus it may not be the case that only unemployed workers suffer from the minimum wage; even workers who receive a higher wage and retain employment may be net losers if their nonpecuniary benefits are reduced.

Labor Substitution Effects

The economic world is characterized by a plethora of substitutes. In the labor market low-skill, low-wage earners are substitutes for high-skill, high-wage earners. As Walter Williams points out:

> Suppose a fence can be produced by using either one high skilled worker or by using three low skilled workers. If the wage of high skilled workers is $38 per day, and that of a low skilled worker is $13 per day, the firm employs the high skilled worker because costs would be less and profits higher ($38 versus $39). The high skilled worker would soon recognize that one of the ways to increase his wealth would be to advocate a minimum wage of, say, $20 per day in the fencing industry. . . . After enactment of the minimum wage laws, the high skilled worker can now demand any wage up to $60 per day . . . and retain employment. Prior to the enactment of the minimum wage of $20 per day, a demand of $60 per day would have cost the high skilled worker his job. Thus the effect of the minimum wage is to price the high skilled worker's competition out of the market.[16]

Labor competes against labor, not against management. Since low-skill labor competes with high-skill labor, the minimum wage works against the lower-skill, lower-paid worker in favor of higher-paid workers. Hence, the consequences of the law are exactly opposite its alleged purpose.

Table 1

Value of the Minimum Wage, 1955–1995

Year	Value of the Minimum Wage, Nominal Dollars	Value of the Minimum Wage, 1995 Dollars†	Minimum Wage as a Percent of the Average Private Nonsupervisory Wage
1955	$0.75	$3.94	43.9%
1956	1.00	5.16	55.6
1957	1.00	5.01	52.9
1958	1.00	4.87	51.3
1959	1.00	4.84	49.5
1960	1.00	4.75	47.8
1961	1.15	5.41	53.7
1962	1.15	5.36	51.8
1963	1.25	5.74	54.8
1964	1.25	5.67	53.0
1965	1.25	5.59	50.8
1966	1.25	5.43	48.8
1967	1.40	5.90	52.2
1968	1.60	6.49	56.1
1969	1.60	6.21	52.6
1970	1.60	5.92	49.5
1971	1.60	5.67	46.4
1972	1.60	5.51	43.2
1973	1.60	5.18	40.6
1974	2.00	5.89	47.2
1975	2.10	5.71	46.4
1976	2.30	5.92	47.3
1977	2.30	5.56	43.8
1978	2.65	6.00	46.6
1979	2.90	5.99	47.1
1980	3.10	5.76	46.5
1981	3.35	5.68	46.2
1982	3.35	5.36	43.6
1983	3.35	5.14	41.8
1984	3.35	4.93	40.3
1985	3.35	4.76	39.1
1986	3.35	4.67	38.2
1987	3.35	4.51	37.3
1988	3.35	4.33	36.1
1989	3.35	4.13	34.7
1990	3.80	4.44	37.9
1991	4.25	4.77	41.1
1992	4.25	4.63	40.2
1993	4.25	4.50	39.2
1994	4.25	4.38	n/a
1995	4.25	4.25	n/a

†Adjusted for inflation using the CPI-U-X1.

Source: Center on Budget and Policy Priorities

Capital Substitution Effects

To produce a given quantity of goods, some bundle of inputs is required. The ratio of inputs used to produce the desired output is not fixed by natural law but by the relative prices of inputs, which change continuously with new demand and supply conditions. Based on relative input prices, producers attempt to minimize costs for a given output. Since many inputs are substitutes for one another in the production process, a given output can be achieved by increasing the use of one and diminishing the use of another. The optimal mix will depend on the relative supply and demand for competing substitute inputs.

As a production input, low-skill labor is often in direct competition with highly technical machinery. A Whirlpool dishwasher can be substituted for low-skill manual dishwashers in the dishwashing process, and an automatic elevator can take the place of a nonautomatic elevator and a manual operator. This [is] not to imply that automation "destroys jobs," a common Luddite myth. As Frederic Bastiat explained over a century ago, jobs are obstacles to be overcome.[17] Automation shifts the *kinds* of jobs to be done in society but does not reduce their total number. Low-skill jobs are done away with, but higher-skill jobs are created simultaneously. When the minimum wage raises the cost of employing low-skill workers, it makes the substitute of automated machinery an attractive option.

Racial Discrimination in Hiring Practices

At first glance the connection between the level of racial discrimination in hiring practices and the minimum wage may not seem evident. On closer examination, however, it is apparent that the minimum wage law gives employers strong incentives to exercise their existing racial preferences.[18] The minimum wage burdens minority groups in general and minority teenagers most specifically. Although outright racism has often been blamed as the sole cause of heavy minority teenage unemployment, it is clearly not the only factor. William Keyes informs us that

> In the late 1940's and early 1950's, young blacks had a lower unemployment rate than did whites of the same age group. But after the minimum wage increased significantly, especially in 1961, the black youth unemployment rate has increased to the extent that it is now a multiple of the white youth unemployment rate.[19]

To make the case that racism itself is the cause of the employment and unemployment disparity among blacks and whites, one would have to claim that America was more racially harmonious in the past than it is now. In fact, during the racially hostile times of the early 1900s 71 percent of blacks over nine years of age were employed, as compared with 51 percent for whites.[20] The minimum wage means that employers are not free to decide among low-wage workers on the basis of price differentials; hence, they face fewer disincentives to deciding according to some other (possibly racial) criteria.

To see the racial implications of minimum wage legislation, it is helpful to look at proponents of the law in a country where racial hostility is very strong, South Africa. Since minimum wage laws share characteristics in common with equal pay laws, white racist unions in South Africa continually support both minimum wage and equal-pay-for-equal-work laws for blacks. According to Williams:

> Right-wing white unions in the building trades have complained to the South African government that laws reserving skilled jobs for whites have been broken and should be abandoned in favor of equal pay for equal work laws. . . . The conservative building trades made it clear that they are not motivated by concern for black workers but had come to feel that legal job reservation had been so eroded by government exemptions that it no longer protected the white worker.[21]

The reason white trade unions are restless in South Africa is a $1.52-per-hour wage differential between black and white construction workers.[22] Although the owners of the construction firms are white, they cannot afford to restrict employment to whites when blacks are willing to work for $1.52 per hour less. As minimum wages eliminate the wage differential, the cost to employers of hiring workers with the skin color they prefer is reduced. As the cost of discrimination falls, and with all else remaining the same, the law of demand would dictate that more discrimination in employment practices will occur.

Markets frequently respond where they can, even to the obstacles the minimum wage presents minority groups. In fact, during the NRA blacks would frequently be advanced to the higher rank of "executives" in order to receive exemptions from the minimum wage.[23] The free market demands that firms remain color-blind in the conduct of business: profit, not racial preference, is the primary concern of the profit-maximizing firm. Those firms who fail the profit test get driven out of business by those who put prejudice aside to maximize profits. When markets are restricted by such laws as the minimum wage, the prospects for eliminating racial discrimination in hiring practices and the shocking 40–50 percent rate of black teenage unemployment in our cities are bleak.

Human Capital Development

Minimum wage laws restrict the employment of low-skill workers when the wage rate exceeds the workers' marginal productivity. By doing so, the law prevents workers with the least skills from acquiring the marketable skills necessary for increasing their future productivity, that is, it keeps them from receiving on-the-job training.

It is an observable fact, true across ethnic groups, that income rises with age.[24] As human capital accumulates over time, it makes teenagers more valuable to employers than workers with no labor-market experience. But when teenagers are priced out of the labor market by the minimum wage, they lose their first and most crucial opportunity to accumulate the human capital that would make them more valuable to future employers. This stunting reduces their lifetime potential earnings. As Martin Feldstein has commented:

> [F]or the disadvantaged young worker, with few skills and below average education, producing enough to earn the minimum wage is incompatible with the opportunity for adequate on-the-job learning. For this group, the minimum wage implies high short-run unemployment and the chronic poverty of a life of low wage jobs.[25]

Feldstein also finds a significant irony in the minimum wage: "It is unfortunate and ironic that we encourage and subsidize expenditure on formal education while blocking the opportunity for individuals to 'buy' on-the-job training."[26] This is especially hard on teenagers from the poorest minority groups, such as blacks and hispanics—a truly sad state of affairs, since the law is instituted in the name of the poor.

Distortion of the Market Process

Relative prices provide the transmission mechanism by which information is delivered to participants in the market about the underlying relative scarcities of competing factor inputs. They serve as signals for people to substitute relatively less scarce resources for relatively more scarce resources, in many cases without their even being aware of it.[27]

Whenever relative price differentials exist for input substitutes in the production process, entrepreneurs will switch from higher-priced inputs to lower-priced inputs. In a dynamically changing economy, this switching occurs continually. But when prices are not allowed to transmit market information accurately,

Table 2

Dates and Amounts of Minimum Wage Changes

Date	Amount	As a Percent of the Average Wage in Manufacturing (Old Minimum/New Minimum)
February 1967	$1.40	44.8%/50.2%
February 1968	$1.60	47.6%/54.4%
May 1974	$2.00	37.8%/47.3%
January 1975	$2.10	42.7%/44.9%
January 1976	$2.30	41.7%/45.6%
January 1978	$2.65	38.5%/44.4%
January 1979	$2.90	40.8%/44.6%
January 1980	$3.20	41.7%/44.5%
January 1981	$3.35	40.1%/43.3%
April 1990	$3.80	31.4%/35.6%
April 1991	$4.25	33.6%/37.6%

as in the case of prices artificially controlled by government, then distorted information skews the market and guides it to something clearly less than optimal.[28]

Minimum wages, being such a distortion of the price system, lead to the wrong factor input mix between labor and all other inputs. As a result, industry migrates to locations of greater labor supply more slowly, and labor-intensive industries tend to remain fixed in non-optimal areas, areas with greater labor scarcity. Large labor pools of labor-abundant geographical areas are not tapped because the controlled price of labor conveys the wrong information to all the parties involved. Thus, the existence of price differentials, as knowledge to be transmitted through relative prices, is hidden.[29] The slowdown of industrial migration keeps labor-abundant regions poorer than they otherwise would be because economic growth there is stifled. As Simon Rottenberg explains for the case of Puerto Rico:

> The aggregate effect of all these distortions was that Puerto Rico could be expected to produce fewer goods and services than would have otherwise been produced and that the rate at which insular per capita income rose toward mainland United States income standards could be expected to be dampened. In sum, the minimum wage law could be expected to reduce the rate of improvement in the standard of life of the Puerto Rican people and to intensify poverty in the island.[30]

In summary, the evidence is in on the minimum wage. All eight major effects of the minimum wage examined here make the poor, disadvantaged, or young in society worse off—the alleged beneficiaries turn out to be the law's major victims. . . .

Conclusion

George Stigler may have startled some economists in 1946 when he claimed that minimum wage laws create unemployment and make people who had been receiving less than the minimum poorer.[31] Fifty years of experience with the law has proven Stigler correct, leaving very few defenders in the economics profession.[32]

But economists have had little success in criticizing this very destructive law. Simon Rottenberg demonstrated the government's disregard for what most economists have to say about this issue in his investigation of the Minimum Wage Study Commission created by Congress in 1977. He noted the numerous studies presented to the commission that without exception found that the law had a negative impact on employment and intensified the poverty of low-income earners. The commission spent over $17 million to conduct the investigation and on the basis of the evidence should have eliminated the law. What was the outcome? The commission voted to *increase the minimum wage by indexing and expanding coverage.* As dissenting commissioner S. Warne Robinson commented about the investigation:

> The evidence is now in, and the findings of dozens of major economic studies show that the damage done by the minimum wage has been far

> more severe than even the critics of forty years ago predicted. Indeed, the evidence against the minimum wage is so overwhelming that the only way the Commission's majority was able to recommend it be retained was to ask us not to base any decisions on the facts.[33]

It cannot be that our elected representatives in Congress are just misinformed with respect to the minimum wage law. To the contrary, the *Congressional Record* demonstrates that they fully understand the law's effects and how the utilization of those effects can ensure reelection. Economists would do well to realize that governments have little interest in the truth when its implementation would contradict self-serving government policies. Rather than attempting to bring government the "facts," economists should educate the public. This is the only solution to the malaise created when people uncritically accept such governmental edicts as the minimum wage.

Notes

1. Leverett Lyon et al. *The National Recovery Administration: An Analysis and Appraisal* (New York: Da Capo Press, 1972), pp. 318–19.
2. Benjamin M. Anderson, *Economics and the Public Welfare: A Financial and Economic History of the United States, 1914–1946* (Indianapolis: Liberty Press, 1979), p. 336.
3. Jonathan Grossman, "Fair Labor Standards Act of 1938: Maximum Struggle for a Minimum Wage," *Monthly Labor Review* 101 (June 1978): 23.
4. "Wage and Hours Law," *New York Times,* 24 October 1938, p. 2.
5. Grossman, "Fair Labor Standards Act," p. 29.
6. Ibid., p. 28.
7. Ibid., p. 29.
8. "Report 40,000 Jobs Lost," *New York Times,* 24 October 1938, p. 2.
9. Anderson, *Economics and the Public Welfare,* p. 458.
10. Simon Rottenberg, "Minimum Wages in Puerto Rico," in *Economics of Legal Minimum Wages,* edited by Simon Rottenberg (Washington, D.C.: American Enterprise Institute, 1981), p. 330.
11. Rottenberg, "Minimum Wages in Puerto Rico," p. 333.
12. Yale Brozen, "Minimum Wage Rates and Household Workers," *Journal of Law and Economics* 5 (October 1962): 103–10.
13. Finis Welch, "Minimum Wage Legislation in the United States," *Economic Inquiry* 12 (September 1974): 286.
14. Brozen, "Minimum Wage Rates and Household Workers," pp. 107–08.
15. Richard McKenzie, "The Labor Market Effects of Minimum Wage Laws: A New Perspective," *Journal of Labor Research* 1 (Fall 1980): 258–59.
16. Walter Williams, *The State Against Blacks* (New York: McGraw-Hill, 1982), pp. 44–45.
17. Frederic Bastiat, *Economic Sophisms* (Irvington-on-Hudson, N.Y.: Foundation for Economic Education, 1946), pp. 16–19.
18. Walter Williams, "Government Sanctioned Restraints That Reduce the Economic Opportunities for Minorities," *Policy Review* 22 (Fall 1977): 15.

19. William Keyes," The Minimum Wage and the Davis Bacon Act: Employment Effects on Minorities and Youth," *Journal of Labor Research* 3 (Fall 1982): 402.
20. Williams, *State Against Blacks,* p. 41.
21. Ibid., p. 43.
22. Ibid., pp. 43–44.
23. Lyon, *National Recovery Administration,* p. 339.
24. U.S. Department of Commerce, Bureau of the Census, *Statistical Abstract of the United States 1982–83,* p. 431.
25. Martin Feldstein, "The Economics of the New Unemployment," *The Public Interest,* no. 33 (Fall 1973): 14–15.
26. Ibid., p. 15.
27. Thomas Sowell, *Knowledge and Decisions* (New York: Basic Books, 1980), p. 79.
28. Ibid.
29. Ibid., pp. 167–68.
30. Rottenberg, "Minimum Wages in Puerto Rico," p. 329.
31. George Stigler, "The Economies of Minimum Wage Legislation," *American Economic Review* 36 (June 1946): 358–65.
32. Although there are a few supporters left such as John K. Galbraith, many "liberal" economists such as Paul Samuelson and James Tobin have recently come out against the minimum wage. See Emerson Schmidt, *Union Power and the Public Interest* (Los Angeles: Nash, 1973).
33. Simon Rottenberg, "National Commissions: Preaching in the Garb of Analysis," *Policy Review* no. 23 (Winter 1983): 139.

Charles Craypo

In Defense of Minimum Wages

This article refutes the dominant view held by orthodox neoclassical economists such as Thomas Rustici. These economists assert that minimum wage laws should be abolished because they misallocate resources and cause production inefficiencies. I reject Rustici's conclusion and instead take the position that in most instances high minimum wages are good for workers, employers and consumers alike and hence are good for the economy as a whole.

Three things are wrong with Rustici's neoclassical view of things. It depends on an idealized world that by assumption favors more rather than less market competition as the solution to economic problems. Second, it ignores the reasons why governments enact minimum wage laws in the first place and instead interprets and judges them on inappropriate grounds. Third, the neoclassical argument against minimum wages is supported by contradictory empirical evidence that casts doubt on its theoretical validity and practical significance.

Critics of the orthodox neoclassical interpretation of minimum wages include both neoclassical and institutional applied labor economists. In fact, most of the contradictory empirical studies in recent years have [been] produced by neoclassical economists whose findings prompt them to question the dominant view. In addition to the research of mainstream economists, research critical of the orthodox position has come from the various institutional schools of thought which emphasize evolutionary change and systemic rather than deductive reasoning from an idealized model.

Most of the debate surrounds the federal minimum wage law contained in the Fair Labor Standards Act (FLSA) of 1938, which represented an essential part of President Roosevelt's agenda to get the nation out of the Great Depression. Labor law reformers had long advocated federal wage and hour laws in response to an historic pattern of low earnings among working families and intense wage competition among employers. The courts, however, struck down early attempts to establish federal standards on grounds the separate states had constitutional primacy in such matters. Individual states were reluctant to pass regulatory laws, however, because they feared industry would avoid locating there. The enormities of the depression nevertheless drove working people to strike employers and protest politically. Soon the Supreme

Court changed directions and ruled that the constitution does in fact allow Congress to regulate interstate commerce; Congress responded with numerous regulatory laws including the FLSA.

The inherent bias in neoclassical analysis. When polled, a large majority of American economists support Rustici in his opposition to minimum wage increases. This reflects their prior training in the neoclassical wage model, which generally rejects labor standards legislation on grounds that market outcomes are superior to anything government can achieve through regulation. Employers and others lobbying to abolish or weaken minimum wage laws therefore can count on the support of orthodox economists, despite widespread public approval of these laws. Indeed, in 1993, three-fourths of economists polled said that an increase in the minimum wage would increase unemployment, while a similar poll in 1996 found that 84% of the public favored an increase.

This vastly different view of the world underscores the first problem with Rustici's neoclassical analysis. The competitive market model it uses simply does not depict real labor markets accurately. It imagines all sorts of things that do not exist and ignores a great many other things that do. When this analysis is applied to particular labor market problems, such as declining real wages, it is likely to misdiagnose the ailment and to prescribe inappropriate public policy.

The problem is that in explaining how the interaction between worker skill and output determines wages the neoclassical model uses circular reasoning. It presumes that if we know the wage we also know the worth of the worker because market competition ensures that each worker is paid the value of his or her worth, as measured by the value of what each produces. It further presumes that the worker's productive value is determined by his or her level of skill and education, that is, by their accumulated "human capital." Therefore, if one worker is paid more than another worker, then the first worker must be worth more (that is, must have more skill and education) than the second; because the wage is, by definition, equal to output value, which in turn is determined by skill and education. Consequently, every worker must be worth what he or she is being paid, no more and no less. Workers who think they are not being paid enough must be wrong, because if they possessed more human capital they would be worth more therefore paid more.

This is tautological reasoning. It explains everything and nothing because it uses the thing it is trying to explain as the evidence with which to explain it. It does, however, allow neoclassical economists to reject any attempt to regulate wages on the grounds that the worker currently is being paid what he or she is worth. In the world of the neoclassical economist, forcing employers to pay a higher wage will simply place the individual employer at a competitive disadvantage and at the same time discriminate against workers who did not benefit from the regulated wage increase. As a result, neoclassical investigations of minimum wage effects usually ask a single question. How many workers will become unemployable following an increase in the minimum wage. The question derives from the competitive wage model, not from observed experiences or policy objectives.

With this mind-set, it is understandable that Rustici and other orthodox neoclassical economists see the solution to labor market problems, such as low earnings and unemployment, as more rather than less market determination and the elimination of existing regulations. If labor markets deliver less than ideal results it is because they are not free enough. Public policy must be to remove the imperfections. Unions and minimum wages are logical targets in this regard.

The problem with such deductive reasoning is that employers and employees seldom meet as equals in the labor market, although the model assumes that they do. In blue-collar settings, for example, the employment relationship favors employers, who typically offer jobs on a take-it-or-leave-it basis. Individual workers find there are far more workers than there are good jobs and they take what they can get on the terms that are offered. Employers simply have more options in the hiring process than do workers—except perhaps when unemployment is low and workers scarce in the lowest paying, least desirable occupations and industries, at which point employers turn to immigrant labor to fill job vacancies at the going wage levels. Additionally, employers know far more than hourly workers do about supply and demand conditions in local labor markets and are more mobile in terms of where and when to hire. They also can hold out much longer financially than can workers in the event of differences over wages and working conditions. Finally, and importantly, because they own the plant and equipment upon which the worker's livelihood depends, they can threaten to relocate the workplace or to replace the workers with machines or other workers.

In the absence of institutional protections such as union contracts and minimum wages, workers are in constant danger of having to compete with one another to see which of them will work for less pay and under the worst conditions. If one or a few employers are able to reduce labor standards by taking advantage of labor's inherent bargaining weakness, and in the process they expand markets and increase their profits, then the race is on among all employers to take down labor standards. The labor market degenerates into what institutional labor economists call destructive competition. As two institutional labor economists observed decades ago, "When an employer can hire workers for practically his own price, he can be slack and inefficient in his methods, and yet, by reducing wages, reduce his cost of production to the level of his more able competitor" (Commons and Andrews 1936:48).

The irrelevancy of the neoclassical analysis. This demonstrates the second thing wrong with Rustici's neoclassical interpretation. It examines and evaluates minimum wage laws only on the basis of what would result in a competitive market model. In doing so, it ignores the reasons why such laws are enacted in the first place and whether or not they solve the problems they were intended to solve. The problem with this approach is that it focuses on only one of the three forms of economic efficiency that are essential for a nation to sustain high-levels of production and consumption: a nation's need to provide high standards of living for its citizens.

Robert Kuttner (1997) argues that neoclassical preoccupation with allocative efficiency prevents an examination of macroefficiency and technical efficiency. Macroefficiency concerns a nation's ability to sustain or enhance total production, employment, and family living standards; whereas technical efficiency refers to the ability to generate new products and production methods through industrial invention and innovation. Allocative efficiency, on the other hand, is limited to looking after the immediate interests of the consumer by minimizing production costs and product prices. If only allocative efficiency is taken into account, the long-term interests of both producers and consumers is ignored as the nation neglects its overall economic growth, job and earnings performance, and progress in research/development.

It must be remembered that neither macro- nor technical efficiency necessarily results in optimal allocation efficiency in the short run, that is, in the lowest possible costs of production and consumer prices. Nor does optimal allocative efficiency necessarily help to maximize either macro- or technical efficiency. The postwar success of certain West European and Asian economies, led by Germany and Japan, testifies to the need to distinguish between alternative forms of economic efficiency and between short- and long-run goals and performance. Japanese industrial strategists made these distinctions for example when they targeted the global auto market in the late 1950s. They gave up shortrun cost efficiency in return for long-term product and workforce quality on their way to world supremacy in autos by the 1980s (Halberstam 1986).

Because neoclassical economists largely ignore macro- and technical efficiency in their analysis of competitive labor markets, their competitive model cannot estimate the macroeffects of incremental changes in prices and quantities in particular markets. The 1930s, for example, were characterized by the kind of intense wage and price competition that neoclassical economists associate with allocative efficiency. Consequently, the economy should have been performing at its best. But we still refer to what happened instead as the Great Depression.

Remember that the question deriving from the neoclassical market model is "How many workers are made unemployable because the new wage prices them out of competitive labor markets?" That is not, however, the question that advocates of the FLSA were concerned with in 1938, nor what people are concerned with today in view of the long-term decline in median real wages and the increase in unstable jobs. The problem then and now is not the ability to produce enough goods and services, but rather it is creating jobs at wages high enough to buy back what is produced and in the process sustain high living standards for everyone.

This was the task of the 1938 federal minimum wage. It was designed to do two things: (i) increase employment and purchasing power in order to stimulate the slumping economy; and (ii) drive out of the market employers who competed on the basis of cheap labor instead of through better products and state-of-the-art production methods. The country had been in economic crisis for the better part of a decade. It had become increasingly clear that much of the problem was due to low pay, long workweeks, and growing use of child rather than adult labor. Advocates of minimum wages were not the least dissuaded by neoclassical forecasts that some jobs would be lost and some employers driven out of business. That is precisely what they wanted to do, on grounds that a job that does not pay enough to support a family should not exist and an employer who cannot pay a living wage, even though other employers in that industry can and do pay the mandated living wage, should be driven from the marketplace.

In brief, if a job pays less than enough to sustain workers and their dependents at the customary standard of living, then that job is not paying its way in a productive economy because it is being subsidized by some household, charitable organization, or government transfer payment. The beneficiary of this subsidy is either the employer paying the low wage and making a profit by doing so, or the customer paying a low price for the good or service. Fast-food restaurant fare, for example, is cheap in part because fast-food workers earn poverty level wages. Home owners in wealthy suburbs can get their houses cleaned cheaply because the women who clean them live in low-income areas, need the money, and have few job options. A subsidy is a subsidy, whether the worker is part of a poor household or an affluent household and whether the employer is a large or a small business.

If you work for a fast-food restaurant why should your family subsidize the owners of that restaurant? In a like manner, why should taxpayers subsidize manufacturers that employ fathers and mothers who cannot support their families without receiving food stamps or a tax rebate from the government? Why should the large employer have to compete with a smaller rival that is being subsidized by low-income households and taxpayers?

This subsidization does not have to occur. In Australia, for example, restaurant workers, "bag boys" in grocery stores, bartenders in taverns, and other workers who are generally low paid in the United States are paid in excess of $12 an hour. Nevertheless, McDonalds hamburgers and Pizza Hut pizzas still abound in Australia. In the United States unionized waitresses in Las Vegas also earn $12 an hour, before tips, and Las Vegas is one of the fastest growing economic regions in America. Waitresses in other parts of the country commonly receive about half the level of the minimum wage, before tips, which forces them to show a certain amount of servitude in order to earn enough tips to make the job worthwhile (a subsidy to the employer from the customer) and leaves the worker unsure of her or his earnings from day-to-day and week-to-week. Such market outcomes reflect the low-status, devalued nature of these workers and occupations more than it does their value to both customers and employers.

Contradictory evidence for the neoclassical view. Rustici's neoclassical approach necessarily ignores the economic and social problems associated with low-wage jobs because it concentrates on workers rather than jobs. Such focus also shifts responsibility for low-wage incomes from jobs to workers by focusing on worker behavior rather than industrial strategies and government policies. Recall that the theory assumes the individual worker's wage is determined by his or her worth on the job; it further presumes that this worth is determined in large part by the amount of human capital the worker possesses in terms of formal education (college degrees) and occupational training (vocational and on-the-job training). Thus the job and its requirements are excluded from the analysis and low-wages are linked to the worker's efforts to acquire skill and education. When neoclassical researchers like Thomas Rustici want to verify their theory they study the earnings and employment experiences of groups of workers having low educational and vocational skills on grounds such workers are most likely to lose jobs as a result of minimum wage raises. Most neoclassical studies do indeed find greater unemployment among such groups following minimum wage increases.

But the findings of empirical studies themselves pose the third problem with Rustici's analysis. The results of far too many empirical studies—those conducted by neoclassical as well as institutional labor economists—have contradicted the neoclassical model for it to remain very convincing. During the Progressive Era prior to World War I, for example, government economists surveyed jobs before and after passage of state minimum wage laws covering women workers (Obenauer and von der Nienburg 1915). This and a later study conducted by Commons and Andrews (1936), found that mandated wages alleviated the degenerative effects of low wages and actually enhanced productivity by increasing worker desire and ability to produce. Only "parasitic" employers were threatened by minimum wages and relatively small numbers of jobs were eliminated.

Some years later, Princeton labor economist Richard Lester surveyed southern manufacturing employers after World War II and found they had not laid-off marginal workers in response to minimum wage increases, but instead had maintained their workforces and tried to offset the higher labor cost by increasing output and sales. This allowed them to take advantage of the economies of scale (lower per-unit costs of production) that accompany higher levels of plant and equipment utilization. Lester went on to note that workers doing the same jobs in different plants received different wages over long periods of time—another finding at odds with neoclassical reasoning—therefore, it was not possible to predict the employment effects of a minimum wage raise. His and other studies thus refuted the neoclassical notion of a single competitive wage. Workers with comparable skills often make quite different wages over long periods of time and those with different skills often earn the same wages. "Such matters are elementary and commonplace to a student of labor, but they seem to be largely overlooked by theorists of the [neoclassical] marginalist faith," he concluded (1947:148).

In the 1990s, another group of neoclassical revisionists using much the same investigative methods as Lester, but with more sophisticated equipment and techniques at their disposal, produced similar findings and came to much the same conclusion. Princeton economists David Card and Alan Krueger demonstrated that modest increases in minimum wage rates have little if any negative impact on the most exposed workers—teenagers. Instead of analyzing what happens to workers following minimum wage increases, they, like Lester before them, asked what happened to the jobs themselves. And like Lester, they discovered that employers did not respond as anticipated. Jobs in fast-food restaurants and other low-wage establishments did not decline, and in fact they even increased slightly in New Jersey when that state increased its minimum wage above the federal level. More surprising perhaps, in adjacent Pennsylvania, where no increase in the state minimum wage had occurred, fast-food employment actually fell slightly! Card and Krueger substantiated these findings in similar studies involving fast-food restaurant jobs in Texas and teenage workers in all industries in California (Card and Krueger 1995: Chapters 2 and 3).

These results, clearly at odds with the neoclassical literature, prompted one somewhat shaken but faithful neoclassical reviewer of Card and Krueger's work to conclude in 1995, just as the debate was getting underway on a proposal to raise the federal minimum wage to $5.15, that "we just don't know how many jobs would be lost if the minimum wage were increased to $5.15." Orthodox certainty was beginning to be eroded by the contradictory findings, but the basic model was not questioned. Many neoclassical economists hold doggedly to the view that jobs *must be* lost if minimum wages are increased. Consider, for example, a standard neoclassical labor economics text now in its sixth edition. The authors dismiss the Card-Krueger findings and insist instead that: "While the impact of the minimum wage on employment, especially that of young workers will undoubtedly continue to receive a great deal of research and public policy discussion, the best evidence remains that the overall impact of the law is to lower employment of unskilled workers while increasing the earnings of those who are able to get jobs" (Filer, Hamermesh, and Rees 1996:175).

In sum, neoclassical economists like Rustici find fault with the minimum wage because they contrast it with a theoretical system that is said to provide optimal results; but it is a system that ultimately is nonfalsifiable because of its tautological nature. They purport to refute the minimum wage on grounds it destroys low-wage jobs despite the fact that this is precisely what it is supposed to do. Finally, by limiting the inquiry to the dictates of a model that is inherently hostile to government regulation, they preclude serious debate on regulation as a policy tool.

Alternative analyses of minimum wage laws. The shortcomings of traditional neoclassical analysis become apparent when considered in terms of macro- and technical efficiency. Wage-based competition during the 1930s reduced already depressed earnings and worker purchasing power, which in turn decreased product demand and caused additional workers to be unemployed. The effect was to cut output, incomes, and profits. With no recovery in sight, large firms could not be expected to make more cars, radios, and appliances than they could sell, nor could they be expected to design and manufacture new products when consumers could afford neither old nor new models.

Economic recovery did not occur until total war production during 1940–45, when all the neoclassical rules of allocative efficiency were repealed: industry was cartelized, wages and prices were controlled, and productive decision making was centralized. Yet, despite the total violation of market rules, the defense plants were running day and night, workers were acquiring formal and informal education and training, incomes and profits were high. Then, from the late 1940s until the mid-1970s, industrial oligopolies and labor unions replaced government in administering the productive system, again in violation of allocative efficiency. But we look back fondly on those decades as the golden age of increased living standards and job security.

Since then, however, the economy has been deregulated in keeping with neoclassical doctrine and both product and labor markets made more competitive by domestic and global changes in industrial structure and behavior. Labor productivity has been increasing, albeit modestly, and labor resources probably have been allocated more efficiently than in the postwar decades, but real earnings are falling, job security declining, and living standards stagnating (Mishel, et al. 1997).

As a society we have three broad policy responses. One, we can remove a certain portion of the population from the productive system by offering social insurance and welfare benefits to able-bodied individuals including laid-off or displaced males and single mothers. This should raise wages by reducing the supply of workers. Two, we can "reform welfare," so to speak, and force welfare recipients to take jobs work under the terms offered by cutting off their welfare support and giving them no alternative. This should lower wages by putting the new low-wage workers in competition with existing ones. Finally, we can raise minimum wages enough to ensure that the lowest paid workers and households are self-sufficient. This would raise wages directly rather than indirectly, eliminate wage and price subsidies to employers and consumers and raise prices, that is, to the extent that higher labor costs are not offset by productivity gains or profit reductions.

Although liberal economists might consider the first remedy better than none, they, like economists generally, resist policies that allow and presumably encourage able-bodied persons to be consumers but not producers in a market-based economy. Other liberal social scientists, however, are more likely to prefer the welfare alternative on ethical and humanitarian grounds. Wealthy societies like the U.S. should, they argue, be willing to provide sustenance for their disadvantaged individuals and families, regardless of any economic inefficiencies that might result. Moreover, they say, all of society benefits when public assistance makes these families more stable and functioning than otherwise.

Surprisingly perhaps, some conservative economists have supported direct welfare payments. They did so, however, as a second best solution. Milton Friedman, for example, once argued that if the political majority is determined to assist the disadvantaged—as it was in the 1960s—then the least interventionist method is to send them government checks and be done with it, rather than pursue minimum wage or other interventionist labor market policies.

It is the second alternative, abolishing financial support, that conservative economists find most consistent with conventional theory. Others agree mainly for moral and ethical reasons. This has been true since industrial poverty first appeared in 1830s Britain (Persky 1997). Free market advocates urged the abolition of welfare support and wage supplements on grounds their elimination would increase the number of laborers and worker productivity while also lowering taxes and birth rates. As a secondary benefit, they and others claimed, it would enhance family stability and values by making parents responsible for their children and both children and wives dependent on and therefore respectful of and obedient to male wage earners. Conservatives are still moved by such thinking.

The third alternative is preferred by liberal economists and policy makers. It seeks to assure low-wage workers self-sufficiency by supplementing their inadequate earnings through the Earned Income Tax Credit, a tax rebate of up to several thousand dollars a year to the employee based on his or her Social Security payments. Advocates favor this approach because it effectively increases the employee's real wage rate and at the same time offsets the undesirable market outcomes of low wages without distorting wage and employment structures and obstructing allocative efficiency. They also believe that the long-run solution is worker training and education to enhance human capital.

Conservative and liberal economists tend to agree on the latter point, although they differ on whether such efforts should be publicly financed and broadly available or individuals should be primarily responsible for their own human capital enhancement.

In view of the bipartisan support for more education—which can accompany any of the three alternative policy responses—a word of caution is in order. More education is always laudable, but by itself cannot solve the problem of low wages. This is because employers use formal educational credentials, especially college degrees, to screen applicants for good jobs. Therefore, as the overall educational level of the work force rises, the amount of education needed to get a given job also increases. This jeopardizes the effectiveness of education as the justification for high pay. For if a college degree were to be conferred magically upon the entire working population tomorrow, who would bus and wait tables the day after? Most likely, employers would find and apply other screening criteria, perhaps relative college rankings or graduate degrees, in order to determine which college grads became managers and which servers.

Moreover, the supply of educated workers does not automatically create the demand for them. American engineering students, for instance, may wonder exactly what it is they are going to engineer when they read about U.S. companies hiring pools of low-wage but college trained information technologists in developing countries to work on computer software projects using high-speed satellite information links, or when they hear about domestic aerospace companies transferring technology overseas in exchange for sales contracts, or of NASA purchasing rocketry equipment from other industrialized countries in order to get the lowest possible price (Barlett and Steele 1996: 49–52, 93–9).

The third alternative is the best. It goes directly to the problem of low-wage jobs by increasing pre-tax earnings and incomes rather than depend on welfare and other transfer payments, let alone on market forces to do so. It is reasonable to presume that with rare exceptions people want the dignity and independence that comes with gainful employment. Society should expect and enable them to work. Doing so makes them participating stakeholders in the productive system, affords them the purchasing power to be effective consumers and fosters the stability and purpose to be involved citizens. But such outcomes depend on the availability of jobs paying enough to afford a decent living.

In addition, the high wage economy is most consistent over time with the three economic efficiencies. High minimum wages are to be preferred because they contribute to sustained economic growth (macroefficiency) and industrial capitalization and innovation (technical efficiency). It is true that minimum wage are inconsistent with neoclassical allocative efficiency in the short-run; but it is the long-run that we should be concerned. High-paid workers stay with their employers, which encourages the latter to invest in worker human capital, which in turn encourages the employers to adopt state-of-the-art production methods and sophisticated product design and performance. High paid workers also have the purchasing power to buy the goods and services that they and other high-paid workers produce.

A high wage policy is the best hope for a bright future for the American economy. It ensures a proficient labor force in a stable macroeconomy and encourages steady technological advancement. The larger society is only as prosperous as its individual parts. When labor standards are high the larger society prospers.

References

Barlett, Donald L., and James B. Steele. 1996. *America: Who Stole the Dream?* Kansas City: Andrews & McMeel.

Card, David Edward, and Alan B. Krueger. 1995. *Myth and Measurement: The New Economics of the Minimum Wage*. Princeton, NJ: Princeton University Press.

Commons, John R., and John B. Andrews. 1936. *Principles of Labor Legislation* (fourth edition). New York: Augustus M. Kelley (1967 Reprint).

Filer, Randall K., Daniel S. Hamermesh, and Albert Rees. 1996. *The Economics of Work and Pay*, sixth edition. New York: Harper Collins.

Halberstam, David. 1986. *The Reckoning*. New York: Morrow.

Kuttner, Robert. 1997. *Everything For Sale: The Virtues and Limits of Markets*. New York: Alfred A. Knopf.

Lester, Richard A. 1947. "Marginalism, Minimum Wages, and Labor Markets." *American Economic Review* 37 (March) pp. 135–48.

Mishel, Lawrence, Jared Bernstein, and John Schmitt. 1997. *The State of Working America, 1996–97*. Armonk, NY: M. E. Sharpe.

Obenauer, Marie L., and Bertha von der Nienburg. 1915. *Effect of Minimum Wage Determinations in Oregon*. Bureau of Labor Statistics, Bulletin No. 176. Washington: GPO.

Persky, Joseph. 1997. "Classical Family Values: Ending the Poor Laws as They Knew Them." *Journal of Economic Perspectives* 11 (Winter) pp. 179–89.

POSTSCRIPT

Is It Time to Abolish the Minimum Wage?

The impact of the minimum wage can be expressed in many ways. Two particularly rewarding ways of looking at such legislative initiatives are to examine minimum wages over time in real dollars and as a percentage of manufacturing wages.

A clear pattern should emerge from an examination of this data. The 1965–1970 period saw the highest level of the minimum wage in real terms. In constant 1982–1984 dollars, the minimum wage for these years was approximately $4.00 an hour and reached nearly 50 percent of the prevailing manufacturing wage. For the next 20 years, however, the value of the minimum wage in real terms and as a percentage of the manufacturing wage fell. It is only in recent years that it has begun to recover.

The renewed interest in the minimum wage can be traced in part to the research findings of David Card and Alan Krueger. These economists, as Craypo points out, have shaken the economics profession with their empirical research findings that moderate increases in the minimum wage have few negative effects on employment patterns and in some cases are associated with increases in employment. Their work has been published widely in professional journals: *Industrial and Labor Relations Review* (October 1992 and April 1994) and the *American Economic Review* (September 1994 and May 1995). They have also detailed their findings in a book entitled *Myth and Measurement: The New Economics of the Minimum Wage* (Princeton University Press, 1995).

Two vocal critics of Card and Krueger's research are David Neumark and William Wascher. Their empirical studies are supportive of the traditional neoclassical findings that the minimum wage causes unemployment, particularly among teenagers and young adults. See their work published in *Industrial and Labor Relations Review* (September 1992 and April 1994); NBER Working Paper No. 4617 (1994); *Journal of Business and Economic Statistics* (April 1995); and *American Economic Review Papers and Proceedings* (May 1995). Still often considered the best anti–minimum wage statement, however, is George J. Stigler's 1946 essay "The Economics of Minimum Wage Legislation," *American Economic Review.*

ISSUE 12

Are Declining Caseloads a Sign of Successful Welfare Reform?

YES: Michael J. New, from "Welfare Reform That Works: Explaining the Welfare Caseload Decline, 1996–2000," *Policy Analysis No. 435* (May 7, 2002)

NO: Evelyn Z. Brodkin, from "Requiem for Welfare," *Dissent* (Winter 2003)

ISSUE SUMMARY

YES: Cato Institute researcher Michael J. New presents statistical evidence that welfare reform, and not a growing economy, is the primary cause of the recent decline in welfare caseloads. This means that welfare reform has been a success.

NO: Evelyn Z. Brodkin, an associate professor in the School of Social Service Administration and lecturer at the University of Chicago Law School, contends that in assessing welfare reform, one must look beyond the decline in welfare caseloads and ask, What has happened to those who no longer receive welfare? Her answer to this question evokes in Brodkin nostalgia for the "bad old days" of unreformed welfare.

Given American society's traditional commitment to a market system and its fundamental belief in self-determination, Americans are uncomfortable enacting social welfare legislation that appears to give someone "something for nothing," even if that individual is clearly in need. Thus, when tracing the roots of the existing U.S. social welfare system back to its origins in the New Deal legislation of President Franklin D. Roosevelt during the Great Depression of the 1930s, one sees that many of the earliest programs linked jobs to public assistance. One exception was Aid to Families with Dependent Children (AFDC), which was established as part of the 1935 Social Security Act. This program provided money to families in which there were children but no breadwinner. In 1935, and for many years thereafter, this program was not particularly controversial. Two reasons explain this acceptance of AFDC: the number of beneficiaries was relatively small, and the popular image of an

AFDC family was that of a white woman with young children whose husband had died as a result of an illness or industrial accident.

In the early 1960s, as the U.S. economy prospered, poverty and what to do about it captured the attention of the nation. The Kennedy and Johnson administrations focused their social welfare programs on poor individuals—a minority of the population, especially, but not exclusively, a black minority—left behind as the general economy reached record levels of income and employment. Their policies were designed to address the needs of those who were trapped in "pockets of poverty," a description popularized in the early 1960s in the writings of Michael Harrington (1929–1989), a political theorist and prominent socialist. Between 1964 and 1969 the number of AFDC recipients increased by more than 60 percent, and the costs of the program more than doubled. The number of AFDC families continued to grow throughout the 1970s and the 1980s, and the program became increasingly controversial.

The controversy grew for several reasons: an increase in the number of recipients, an increase in costs, and a change in perceptions. The image of the welfare mother changed; she was increasingly perceived as a woman living in an urban public housing project whose children had been deserted by their father or as an unmarried woman who bore more children only to get more welfare.

In the 1980s social critics began to attack AFDC. They charged AFDC with encouraging welfare dependency and teenage pregnancies, dissolving the traditional family, and eroding the basic American work ethic. Welfare reform became an issue in the 1992 and 1996 presidential campaigns. In both of these campaigns, Bill Clinton promised, if elected, to "end welfare as we know it." Welfare reform became a reality eight months into the start of Clinton's second term with the enactment of the Personal Responsibility and Work Opportunity Reconciliation Act (PRWORA). This act abolished the AFDC entitlement that had guaranteed poor families a standardized set of welfare benefits for 60 years and replaced AFDC with a new block program entitled Temporary Assistance for Needy Families (TANF). The new legislation allowed states far more discretion in determining which families would be supported and how much support each of these families would receive.

The question addressed in this issue is whether or not welfare reform is working. Michael J. New presents evidence that the decline in welfare caseloads can be attributed to welfare reform. Evelyn Z. Brodkin looks beyond the caseload decline and its causes, arguing that to evaluate welfare reform it is necessary to determine what has happened to those who no longer receive government assistance.

YES 

Michael J. New

Welfare Reform That Works

Introduction

[In 1996] President [Bill] Clinton signed landmark welfare reform legislation into law. While previous attempts at reform resulted in only cosmetic changes, the Personal Responsibility and Work Opportunity Reconciliation Act of 1996 [PRWORA] has had a meaningful and lasting impact on the federal welfare regime. PRWORA ended the entitlement status of Aid to Families with Dependent Children [AFDC] and replaced it with a time-limited assistance and work requirement program called Temporary Assistance to Needy Families [TANF]. Most important, however, PROWRA gave states more leeway to structure their welfare administrations.

Under PROWRA, states receive federal block grant allocations totaling $16.5 billion a year until September 30, 2002. That allocation allows states to use TANF funding in any manner reasonably calculated to accomplish the purposes of TANF so long as the states maintain historical levels of spending agreed to in "maintenance of effort" plans. To continue receiving their full federal TANF allocations, states must also conform to specific requirements regarding current recipients' work participation rates and length of time on the rolls.[1]

Although PROWRA passed by wide margins in the House and Senate in 1996, it was still politically controversial. Then–senate minority leader Tom Daschle (D-S.D.) opposed the bill, calling the work requirements "extremist." Likewise, House Minority Leader Richard Gephardt (D-Mo.) voted against the bill, citing an Urban Institute study that predicted that welfare reform would force more than 1 million children into poverty. Sen. Daniel Patrick Moynihan (D-N.Y.) was even more strident. He proclaimed that the new law "was the most brutal act of social policy since reconstruction." He predicted: "Those involved will take this disgrace to their graves."[2]

Contrary to those alarming predictions, welfare reform went more smoothly than critics expected. A great deal of evidence has demonstrated that welfare reform has been effective at reducing dependence on welfare, reducing poverty, and lowering the rate of out-of-wedlock births:

- By 1999 overall poverty and child poverty had substantially declined. Some 4.2 million fewer people, including 2.3 million children, live in poverty today than did in 1996.[3]

- Hunger among children has been reduced by almost 50 percent since the passage of welfare reform.[4]
- By 2001 welfare caseloads had been reduced by 58 percent since welfare reform was enacted.[5]
- During the past six years, there has been a reduction in the rate of increase in out-of-wedlock childbearing.[6]

Even some opponents of PROWRA have acknowledged the success of welfare reform. Wendell Primus, a deputy assistant secretary in the Department of Health and Human Services, who resigned in protest after President Clinton signed the reform bill, remarked last year, "In many ways welfare reform is working better than I thought it would." He added, "The sky is not falling anymore. Whatever we have been doing during the past five years we ought to keep doing."[7]

However, a number of opponents of welfare reform still stubbornly refuse to acknowledge its progress, crediting instead the booming economy. Donna Shalala, who as secretary of Health and Human Services urged President Clinton to veto the welfare reform bill, said, "What happened on welfare reform was this combination of an economic boom and a political push to get people off the welfare rolls."[8] Others who argue that the economy deserves most of the credit for the decline in caseloads, including Marian Wright Edelman of the Children's Defense Fund, expressed concern about what would happen during the most recent economic slowdown.[9]

Their arguments in favor of an "economics" explanation of welfare caseload changes do not hold up to empirical scrutiny. While the strength of the economy does have an effect on the number of people receiving welfare, other economic expansions did not generate welfare caseload declines of similar magnitude. For instance, the economy expanded by 10.63 percent between 1993 and 1996, but the number of individuals receiving welfare declined by only 8.8 percent. Moreover, the economic expansion that took place during the 1980s failed to reduce the total number of individuals receiving AFDC.[10] Finally, welfare caseloads dramatically increased during the economic boom that took place during the mid to late 1960s largely because benefits became more generous.[11]

Existing Research

What, if not the booming economy, is responsible for the decline in welfare caseloads? A great deal of research has been carried out to analyze this question. In 1999 the Council of Economic Advisers analyzed the decline in welfare caseloads and concluded that the economy was responsible for 10 percent of the decline in registrants between 1996 and 1998. The authors argued that welfare reforms were responsible for approximately one-third of the decline and the remainder was the consequence of other, unnamed factors.[12]

In 1999 the Heritage Foundation released a more detailed study on welfare caseload declines. . . . They found that there were substantial differences among the states in their policies toward welfare recipients who were not performing mandated work activities. In some states, recipients would lose their entire TANF check at the first instance of nonperformance. In other states, however, recipients could be assured of keeping almost their entire benefit check regardless of their conduct.[13]

The Heritage analysts found that the strength of state sanctioning policies had a major impact on the magnitude of state welfare caseload declines. In general, the larger caseload reductions occurred in states with more stringent sanctions, and more modest declines took place in states with weaker sanctioning policies. The Heritage study also found that immediate work requirements also led to declines in the number of individuals receiving welfare. Interestingly, however, the authors found that the strength of the economy, as measured by each state's average unemployment rate, did not have a statistically significant impact on caseload declines.[14]

In the summer of 2001 the Manhattan Institute released a study by June O'Neill and M. Anne Hill titled "Gaining Ground? Measuring the Impact on Welfare and Work." . . . The authors concluded that welfare reform is responsible for more than half of the decline in the welfare population since 1996.[15]

However, O'Neill and Hill neglected to consider other factors that likely played a role in the caseload declines. For instance, they did not consider the effect of the relative strength of state sanctions on the number of welfare recipients. In addition, while the authors held benefit levels constant in their regression analysis, they did not elaborate on their findings. They also did not state whether they considered only benefits available through TANF or included benefits available to welfare recipients from other programs including the Women, Infants, and Children program, food stamps, and Medicare.

A final study that provides useful insights about welfare caseloads is William A. Niskanen's 1996 *Cato Journal* article "Welfare and the Culture of Poverty." Niskanen used 1992 data to examine the specific impact of welfare benefits on a variety of social pathologies. Holding a variety of demographic, cultural, and economic factors constant, he found that increases in AFDC benefits led to statistically significant increases in the numbers of welfare recipients, people in poverty, births to single mothers, abortions, and violent crimes.[16] That article is useful to this analysis because it provides evidence that higher levels of benefits lead to higher welfare caseloads.

Historically, benefit levels have been a politically salient issue. In his 1984 book *Losing Ground,* Charles Murray convincingly argued that increases in welfare benefits, which were legislated during the Great Society period, were largely responsible for the welfare caseload expansion that took place during the mid to late 1960s. According to Murray, before the increase in benefits, a woman facing an unplanned pregnancy had three basic choices. She could give the child up for adoption, get married, or fend for herself. However, when welfare benefits were increased, staying on welfare suddenly became an economically viable option for many unwed mothers.[17] Not surprisingly, welfare caseloads and the number of single-parent families soared.[18] Since the evidence suggests that high welfare benefits led to an increase in welfare caseloads during the 1960s, it seems reasonable that an analysis of benefit levels might help to explain the decline in caseloads during the 1990s.

Overall, previous and current research has identified three major factors that appear to affect fluctuations in welfare caseloads: the strength of sanctions, the performance of the economy, and the level of benefits. In order to determine the impact of each of those factors on welfare caseloads, I use state-level data to examine the effects of each of the foregoing determinants. A comparison of the states should prove fruitful because, during the past five years, states have experienced varying amounts of success in reducing their welfare caseloads. For instance, between August 1996 and August 2000, Wyoming reduced its welfare caseload by 91 percent. Conversely, Rhode Island reduced its caseload by a comparatively modest 22 percent over the same period. In addition, there are variations in the strength of state economies, the level of benefits states offer, and the stringency of state sanctioning policies. Because different state policies have resulted in different outcomes, a proper analysis of these variables across the states should be able to identify the policies that are the most responsible for the substantial declines in welfare caseloads.

Findings

Previous studies have indicated that the strength of state sanctions may be the most reliable predictor of welfare caseload declines at the state level. Even though the Heritage Foundation dealt with this issue extensively in its 1999 study, the topic is worth revisiting for several reasons. First, the Heritage study examined caseload declines up to June 1998,[19] and more data have been released since that time. Second, data from the U.S. Department of Health and Human Services and the U.S. General Accounting Office indicate that some states have changed their sanctioning policies.[20]

Sanctioning Policies

There are three types of state sanctioning policies:

1. Full family sanctioning: Some states sanction the entire TANF check at the first instance of nonperformance of required work or other activities. This is the strongest sanction a state can apply.
2. Graduated sanctioning: States that do not sanction the entire TANF check at the first instance of nonperformance but will sanction the full TANF check after multiple infractions.
3. Partial sanctioning: Some states sanction only the adult portion of the TANF check, even after repeated infractions. This enables recipients to retain the bulk of their TANF benefits even if they fail to perform workfare or other required activities.[21]

[Table 1] lists the sanctioning policies, the years they were in effect, and the monthly TANF benefit for the 50 states and the District of Columbia. Table 2 gives the average decline in caseload under the three types of sanctioning policies, as well as variations of those three types.

The results indicate that states with full family sanctions have, on average, experienced larger caseload declines than states with graduated sanctions. In

Table 1

State Sanctioning Policies and TANF Benefits

State	Years With Full Family Sanction	Years With Graduated Sanction	Years With Partial Sanction	Monthly TANF Benefit
Alabama		1996–2000		$164
Alaska			1996–2000	$923
Arizona		1996–2000		$347
Arkansas	1996–1998		1998–2000	$204
California			1996–2000	$565
Colorado		1996–2000		$356
Connecticut		1996–2000		$636
District of Columbia			1996–2000	$379
Delaware		1996–2000		$338
Florida	1996–2000			$303
Georgia		1996–2000		$280
Hawaii	1998–2000		1996–2000	$570
Idaho	1996–2000			$276
Illinois		1996–2000		$377
Indiana			1996–1998	$288
Iowa	1998–2000	1996–1998		$426
Kansas	1996–2000			$429
Kentucky		1996–2000		$262
Louisiana		1996–2000		$190
Maine			1996–2000	$418
Maryland	1996–2000			$388
Massachusetts		1996–2000		$565
Michigan		1996–2000		$459
Minnesota			1996–2000	$532
Mississippi	1996–2000			$120
Missouri			1996–2000	$292
Montana			1996–2000	$450
Nebraska	1996–2000			$364
Nevada		1996–2000		$348
New Hampshire			1996–2000	$550
New Jersey		1996–2000		$424
New Mexico		1996–2000		$389
New York			1996–2000	$577
North Carolina		1998–2000	1996–1998	$272
North Dakota		1996–2000		$490
Ohio	1996–2000			$362
Oklahoma	1996–2000			$292

(continued)

Table 1 (Continued)

State	Years With Full Family Sanction	Years With Graduated Sanction	Years With Partial Sanction	Monthly TANF Benefit
Oregon		1996–2000		$460
Pennsylvania		1996–2000		$421
Rhode Island			1996–2000	$554
South Carolina	1996–2000			$201
South Dakota		1996–2000		$430
Tennessee	1996–2000			$185
Texas			1996–2000	$188
Utah		1996–2000		$426
Vermont		1996–1999	2000	$656
Virginia	1996–2000			$354
Washington			1996–2000	$546
West Virginia		1996–2000		$253
Wisconsin	1996–2000			$628
Wyoming	1998–2000	1996–1998		$340

Sources: Data on sanctioning policies are from U.S. Department of Health and Human Services, "State Implementation of Major Changes to Welfare Policies 1992–1998," aspe.hhs.gov/hsp/Waiver-Policies99/W3JOBSsnct.htm; U.S. General Accounting Office, "Welfare Reform: State Sanction Policies and Number of Families Affected," March 2000, pp. 44–47; and State Policy Documentation Project, "Summary of State Sanction Policies," www.spdp.org/tanf/sanctions.htm. Data on TANF benefits are from U.S. House of Representatives, Committee on Ways and Means, *2000 Green Book: Background Material and Data on Programs within the Jurisdiction of the Committee on Ways and Means*, aspe.hhs.gov/2000gb/sec7.txt.

Table 2

Average Welfare Caseload Decline

Type of Sanction	Decline
Full family sanction for 4 years (12 states)	60.85%
Graduated sanction for 4 years (20 states)	52.17%
Partial sanctions for 4 years (13 states)	40.56%
Full family sanctions for 2 years, partial sanctions for 2 years (2 states)	43.62%
Full family sanctions for 2 years, graduated sanctions for 2 years (2 states)	65.75%
Graduated sanctions for 3 years, partial sanctions for 1 year (1 state)	36.32%
Overall average	51.36%

Sources: Data on sanctioning policies are from U.S. Department of Health and Human Services, "State Implementation of Major Changes to Welfare Policies 1992–1998," http://aspe.hhs.gov/hsp/Waiver-Policies99/W3JOBSsnct.htm; U.S. General Accounting Office, "Welfare Reform: State Sanction Policies and Number of Families Affected," March 2000, pp. 44–47; and State Policy Documentation Project, "Summary of State Sanction Policies," www.spdp.org/tanf/sanctions.htm. Data on caseloads are from Administration for Children and Families, www.acf.dhhs.gov/news/stats/caseload.htm.

addition, states with partial sanctions have had the least success in lowering their caseloads. Surprisingly, some of the states that changed their sanctioning policies actually showed the largest average caseload declines. However, this particular finding should be discounted because of the small size of the sample.

An analysis of variance test was run to determine whether the differences in mean caseload decline between the categories are statistically significant. The results . . . indicate that the differences in mean caseload decline between the categories do in fact achieve conventional standards of statistical significance. All of these findings are consistent with previous research on this topic.

Regression Analysis

Previous analysis has shown that other factors, including benefit levels and the strength of the economy, can also affect fluctuations in welfare caseloads. A multivariate regression analysis was used to determine the combined impact of sanctions, benefits, and the economy on the decline of state welfare caseloads. The regression analysis makes it possible to sort out the effects of each individual variable by holding constant the effects of all other variables.

Interpreting the Results

The regression results indicate that each state's ability to sanction welfare recipients not performing mandated work activities plays the most important role in determining how much welfare caseloads decline. This finding is consistent with the foregoing analysis. For each year that a state has a full family sanction in place, the regression model shows that the decline in its welfare caseload will be more than 5 percentage points greater than the decline in a state with a partial sanction. Similarly, for each year a state has a graduated sanction in place, the regression model shows that its caseload decline is more than 2.7 percentage points greater than that of a state with a partial sanction. Both of these findings are statistically significant.

These results are again broadly consistent with the results of the Heritage Foundation's 1999 study, which examined caseload fluctuations for a year and a half and demonstrated that more stringent sanctions resulted in larger caseload declines. The results of this regression also strengthen Heritage's original finding in two important ways. First, this study shows that the relationship between sanctions and caseload declines is not a short-term phenomenon. Examination of caseload declines for four years demonstrates that the relationship between caseload declines and sanctions is stable over a longer time period. Second, this study is able to take into account the fact that some states changed their sanctioning policies in 1998 and 1999, which adds strength to the analysis.

Figure 1 shows the impact of sanctions. It shows how the various sanctioning policies influence the percentage decline in state welfare caseloads in a hypothetical state with average real income growth (9.18 percent) and average TANF benefits as a percentage of state per capita personal income (16.81 percent). Figure 1 also indicates that the caseload will decline 61.54 percent in four years under a strong sanction, 52.04 percent under a medium sanction, and 40.62 percent under a weak sanction.

Sanctions are not the only variable that has an impact on welfare caseload declines. The economy also has an effect, though its impact is considerably less. The regression model estimates that, for each percentage point increase in

Figure 1

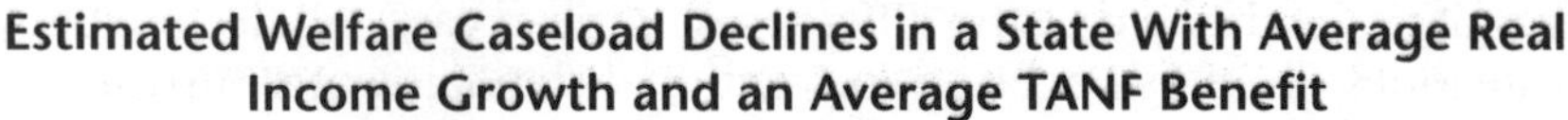

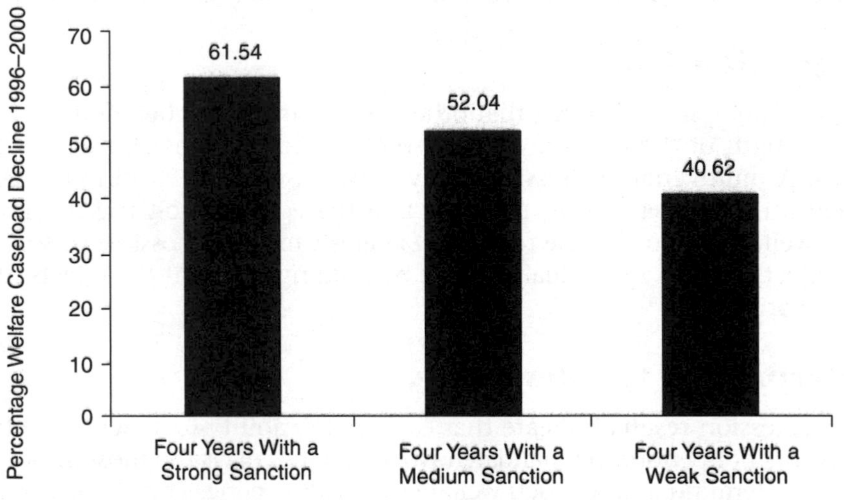

real per capita personal income between 1996 and 2000, welfare caseloads declined by an additional 1.166 percentage points. Those results are generally consistent with the Council of Economic Advisers' study, which found that the economy was responsible for part of the decline in welfare caseloads. Conversely, the results are at odds with the Heritage Foundation's findings that the economy had no statistically significant impact on caseload fluctuations. However, since most states experienced fairly similar rates of economic growth between 1996 and 2000, little of the actual variation in caseload declines can be attributed to the economy. In fact, the real per capita income growth rate for the state at the 25th percentile is only four percentage points less than the real per capita income growth rate for the state at the 75th percentile.

Figure 2 shows the impact of different rates of per capita personal income growth on welfare caseloads. The regression equation was used to show how fluctuations in personal income growth influence the percentage decline in the welfare caseload in a hypothetical state with a medium sanction and average TANF benefits. Caseloads in states with below-average economic growth (25th percentile, 7.00 percent) decline 49.50 percent; in states with average economic growth (50th percentile, 8.63 percent) they decline 51.40 percent; in states with above-average economic growth (75th percentile, 11.23 percent) they decline 54.43 percent.

Figure 2 indicates that the economy had only a marginal impact on welfare caseload declines. The difference in caseload decline between a state with a strong economy and a state with a weak economy was less than five percentage points. Conversely, Figure 1 indicates that differences in sanctioning policy could lead to differences in caseload decline that exceeded 20 percentage

Figure 2

Estimated Welfare Caseload Declines in a State With a Medium Sanction for Four Years and an Average TANF Benefit

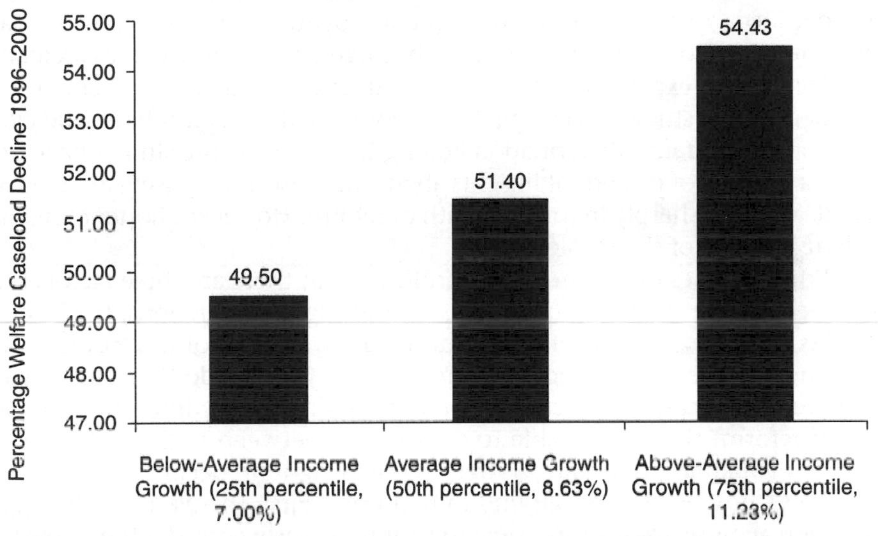

points. That indicates that other factors besides the economy are largely responsible for the dramatic decline in welfare caseloads that has taken place over the past five years.

The final factor that the regression model considers is the level of TANF benefits. Although benefits did not have as strong an impact as sanctions, they had an impact nonetheless. The results indicate that states that offered relatively low TANF benefits enjoyed more success in reducing their welfare caseloads. Specifically, if TANF benefits were reduced by 1 percent of state per capita personal income, the regression model estimates that welfare caseloads would decline by .480 percent. That finding approaches conventional standards of statistical significance. This result is consistent with expectations. High cash benefits increase the attractiveness of welfare and create a disincentive to leave the welfare rolls, even with the sanctions and work requirements of TANF. Conversely, low benefits increase the attractiveness of work relative to welfare and give welfare recipients a greater incentive to leave the welfare rolls.

Surprisingly, however, benefit levels have gone largely unexamined in the policy literature on caseload declines. Niskanen demonstrated that benefit levels have an effect on caseloads. Unfortunately, the Heritage Foundation and the Council of Economic Advisers all but ignored TANF benefit levels in their studies. O'Neill and Hill held benefit levels constant in their regression analysis, but they did not report their findings. Even though benefit levels have received little attention from policy analysts in recent years, they merit serious attention in future debates about welfare reform.

Conclusion

Welfare reform was one of the leading public policy stories of the 1990s. Since Congress enacted welfare reform in 1996, the number of people who are receiving welfare has been cut by nearly 60 percent, and both poverty and hunger have declined.[22] That has attracted a great deal of attention, and many scholars have attempted to explain the cause of the large declines in welfare caseloads.

Some states experienced considerably larger caseload declines than others. As a result, many studies analyzing the success of welfare reform have paid close attention to program differentiation among the states. Those studies have presented a number of important insights about the reasons why welfare caseloads have declined so sharply in the aftermath of reform. However, shortcomings are evident in many of the studies.

Prior analyses of welfare reform indicate that there are three factors that influence welfare caseload fluctuations: the strength of sanctions, the level of benefits, and the strength of the economy. However, all of the studies cited omit one or more of those factors from their analysis. In addition, since many studies consider caseload declines over a limited period of time since the passage of reform, they are unable to distinguish between policies that cause short-term fluctuations and those that lead to long-term declines.

This study breaks new ground in two ways. First, the use of multivariate regression analysis makes it possible to simultaneously consider the impact of the economy, sanctions, and TANF benefits and to determine which of those factors has had the most impact. Second, although many other studies consider caseload declines for a short period of time after reform, this study tracks declines for four years. Using a longer time frame increases the certainty that the various factors are having a long-term impact on caseloads and are not simply causing a temporary decline.

The most important finding is that the strength of state sanctioning policies had the largest impact on caseload declines between 1996 and 2000. The other variables that are considered, the strength of the economy and TANF benefit levels, achieve statistical significance, but their impact on caseload declines is considerably less than the impact of sanctioning policies. To demonstrate, the regression model estimates that differences in sanctioning policies could result in a 20 percentage point difference in caseload declines. Conversely, holding other factors constant, the model estimates that the difference in caseload decline between a state with a strong economy and a state with a weak economy is only about five percentage points.

Notes

1. Lisa Oliphant, "Four Years of Welfare Reform: A Progress Report," Cato Institute Policy Analysis no. 378, August 22, 2000, p. 2.
2. "Welfare As They Know It," Editorial, *Wall Street Journal,* August 29, 2001, p. A14.
3. U.S. Bureau of the Census, *Poverty in the United States 1999,* Current Population Reports Series P60-210 (Washington: U.S. Government Printing Office, 2000), p. B2.

4. Margaret Andrews et al., "Household Food Security in the United States, 1999," U.S. Department of Agriculture, Economic Research Service, 2000, p. 3.
5. Data on caseloads obtained from Administration for Children and Families, `www.acf.dhhs.gov/news/stats/aug-dec.htm`.
6. Stephanie Ventura and Christine Bachrach, "Nonmarital Childbearing in the United States 1940–1999," *National Vital Statistics Reports* 48, no. 16 (October 18, 2000): 1–2.
7. Quoted in Blaine Harden, "Two Parent Families Rise after Change in Welfare Laws," *New York Times,* August 12, 2001.
8. "Welfare As They Know It."
9. Ibid.
10. In 1983, 10.9 million individuals were receiving AFDC; by 1989, 12.1 million individuals were receiving AFDC. That is a caseload increase of 11 percent. U.S. Bureau of the Census, *Statistical Abstract of the United States: 1992* (Washington: Government Printing Office, 1992).
11. "Welfare As They Know It."
12. Council of Economic Advisers, "The Effects of Welfare Policy and the Economic Expansion on Welfare Caseloads: An Update," August 3, 1999, executive summary, p. 1.
13. Robert E. Rector and Sarah E. Youssef, *The Determinants of Welfare Caseload Decline* (Washington: Heritage Foundation, 1999), pp. 1–3.
14. Ibid., p. 6.
15. June O'Neill and M. Anne Hill, "Gaining Ground: Measuring the Impact of Welfare Reform on Welfare and Work," Manhattan Institute Civic Report 17, July 17, 2001.
16. William Niskanen, "Welfare and the Culture of Poverty," *Cato Journal* 16, no. 1 (Spring–Summer 1996).
17. Charles Murray, *Losing Ground* (New York: Basic Books, 1984), pp. 154–66.
18. Ibid., pp. 244, 263
19. Rector and Youssef, p. 1.
20. U.S. Department of Health and Human Services, "State Implementation of Major Changes to Welfare Policies 1992–1998," `http://aspe.hhs.gov/hsp/Waiver-Policies99/W3JOBSsnct.htm`; and U.S. General Accounting Office, "Welfare Reform: State Sanction Policies and Number of Families Affected," March 2000, pp. 44–47.
21. The names of the categories of sanctions are taken from ibid.
22. However, many of the people who have left the welfare rolls are still dependent on various transfer programs; the challenge of transition to self-sufficiency has not yet been met. See Oliphant.

Evelyn Z. Brodkin

NO

Requiem for Welfare

There were few mourners at welfare's funeral. In fact, its demise was widely celebrated when congressional Republicans teamed up with a majority of their Democratic colleagues and then-president Bill Clinton to enact a new welfare law in 1996. The law ended the sixty-one-year old federal commitment to aid poor families and ushered in a commitment to lower welfare rolls and put recipients to work.

To many politicians and the public, anything seemed preferable to the widely discredited program known as Aid to Families with Dependent Children (AFDC). Conservatives were sure that the new welfare would pull up the poor by their bootstraps and redeem them through the virtues of work. Liberals set aside their misgivings, hoping that work would redeem the poor politically and open opportunities to advance economic equality.

More than six years later, the demise of the old welfare remains largely unlamented. But what to make of the changes that have occurred in the name of reform? Often, laws produce more smoke than fire, intimating big change, but producing little. Not this time. In ways both apparent and not fully appreciated, welfare reform has reconfigured both the policy and political landscape. Some of these changes can evoke nostalgia for the bad old days of welfare unreformed.

Reconsidering Welfare's Fate

An immediate consequence of the new law was to defuse welfare as a hot political issue. There's little attention to it these days—apart from some five million parents and children who rely on welfare to alleviate their poverty (and the policy analysts who pore over mountains of data to calculate how it "works"). Legislators have shown no appetite for restarting the welfare wars of prior years. And is it any wonder? The news about welfare has looked good—at least, superficially. Caseloads have plummeted since implementation of the new welfare, dropping 57 percent between 1997 and 2001. Some smaller states essentially cleared their caseloads, with Wyoming and Idaho proudly announcing reductions of 88.9 percent and 85.1 percent, respectively. Even states with large, urban populations have cut caseloads by one-half to three quarters. . . .

Out With the "Old" Welfare

Reforming welfare assumed new urgency in the 1990s, an urgency grounded less in policy realities than in electoral politics. Alarms were sounded about a crisis of cost, although for three decades, spending on AFDC amounted to less than 2 percent of the federal budget. The $16 billion the federal government allocated to AFDC was dwarfed by spending on Social Security and defense, each costing more than $300 billion per year. Public opinion polls, however, indicated a different perception. Forty percent of respondents believed that welfare was one of the most expensive national programs, even larger than Social Security or defense.

Polls also indicated that much of the public believed welfare recipients had it too easy, although few knew what welfare really provided. In fact, AFDC gave only meager support to poor families. In 1996, the median monthly benefit for a family of three was $366. Even when combined with food stamps, welfare lifted few poor families above the federal poverty line. Even the much-touted crisis of dependency ("dependent" being a term loosely applied to anyone receiving welfare) was not reflected in the evidence. The share of families receiving welfare for extended periods declined between 1970 and 1985 and leveled off after that. Families that received welfare for more than six years constituted only a small minority of the welfare caseload at any point in time.

Although the hue and cry over a supposed welfare crisis was greatly overblown, Bill Clinton clearly appreciated welfare's potent political symbolism. As a presidential candidate, he famously pledged to "end welfare as we know it," a turn of phrase useful in demonstrating that he was a "new Democrat" unburdened by the liberalism of his predecessors. His proposals for reform emphasized neoliberal themes of work and individual responsibility, but coupled demands for work with provision of social services intended to improve individual employment prospects. The Clinton administration's plans also assumed the enactment of universal health insurance that would help underwrite the well-being of the working poor. But that did not happen. . . .

Clinton became the first elected Democratic President since Franklin Roosevelt to win a second term. But Clinton was no Roosevelt. In fact, he redeemed his pledge to "end welfare" by presiding over the destruction of a pillar of the New Deal welfare state.

Enter the "New" Welfare

The Personal Responsibility and Work Opportunity Reconciliation Act of 1996 replaced AFDC with a program aptly named Temporary Assistance to Needy Families (TANF). AFDC had provided an open-ended entitlement of federal funds to states based on the amount of benefits they distributed to poor families. TANF ended that entitlement, establishing a five-year block grant fixed at $16.5 billion annually (based on the amount allocated to AFDC in its last year) that states could draw down to subsidize welfare and related expenditures.

Mistrusting the states' willingness to be tough enough on work, Congress incorporated detailed and coercive provisions. First, it set time limits for assistance, restricting federal aid to a lifetime maximum of sixty months. If states wanted to exceed those limits, they would have to pay for most of it themselves. Second, parents were required to work or participate in so-called work activities after a maximum of two years of welfare receipt. Third, TANF established escalating work quotas. States that wanted to collect their full portion of federal dollars would have to show, by 2002, that 50 percent of adults heading single-parent households were working thirty hours per week. Fourth, it meticulously specified those work "activities" that would enable states to meet their quotas, among them paid work, job search, and unpaid workfare (in which recipients "worked off" their welfare benefits at minimum wage or provided child care for other welfare recipients). It limited the use of education and vocational training as countable activities.

Although the "work" side of TANF was clearly pre-eminent, there were some modest provisions on the "opportunity" side, with Congress providing $2.3 billion to help subsidize child care for working mothers and $3 billion in a block grant for welfare-to-work programs.

Beyond these prominent features, the new welfare also packed some hidden punches. It rewarded states for cutting welfare caseloads, largely without regard to how they did it. States that reduced their caseloads (whether those losing welfare found work or not) received credit against officially mandated quotas. If Congress was worried about states' slacking off from its tough work demands, the law indicated no concern that they might go too far in restricting access to benefits or pushing people off the welfare rolls. Only caseload reductions counted.

Under the banner of devolution, the law also gave states new authority to design their own welfare programs. While the welfare debate highlighted the professed virtues of innovation, less obvious was the license it gave states to craft policies even tougher and more restrictive than those allowed by federal law.

Pushing welfare decision making to the state and local level has never been good for the poor. In many states, poor families and their allies have little political influence. Moreover, constitutional balanced-budget requirements make states structurally unsuited to the task of protecting vulnerable residents against economic slumps. When unemployment goes up and state tax revenue goes down, the downward pressure on social spending intensifies.

The secret triumph of devolution lay, not in the opportunities for innovation, but in the opportunity for a quiet unraveling of the safety net.

The Unfolding Story of Welfare Transformed[1]

What has happened since 1996? For one thing, the new welfare changed a national program of income assistance to an array of state programs, each with its own assortment of benefits, services, restrictions, and requirements. There has always been wide variation in the amount of cash aid states provided, and federal waivers allowed states to deviate from some national rules. But devolution spurred far greater policy inconsistency by allowing states, essentially, to make their own rules. Consequently, what you get (or whether you get anything at all) depends on where you live.

In addition, devolution set off a state "race to the bottom," not by reducing benefit levels as some had predicted, but by imposing new restrictions that limited access to benefits. States across the nation have taken advantage of devolution to impose restrictions tougher than those required by federal law.

For example, although federal law required recipients to work within two years, most states require work within one year, some require immediate work, and others demand a month of job search before they even begin to process an application for assistance. No longer required to exempt mothers with children under three years old from work requirements, most states permit an exemption only for mothers with babies under one year old, and some have eliminated exemptions altogether. In nineteen states, lifetime limits for welfare receipt are set below the federal maximum of sixty months. Other states have imposed so-called family caps that preclude benefits for babies born to mothers already receiving welfare. If federal policymakers secretly hoped that states would do part of the dirty work of cutting welfare for them, they must be pleased with these results.

However, the picture from the states is anything but consistent or uniformly punitive. Many help those recipients accepting low-wage jobs by subsidizing the costs of transportation, child care, and medical insurance (although often only for one year). Twenty-two states try to keep low-wage workers afloat by using welfare benefits to supplement their incomes, "stopping the clock" on time limits for working parents. Significantly, the federal clock keeps ticking, and states adopting this strategy must use their own funds to support working families reaching the five-year lifetime limit. With state budgets increasingly squeezed by recession, it is hard to predict how strong the state commitment to preserve these supports will be.

Many state and local agencies have already cut back work preparation and placement programs funded under a $3 billion federal welfare-to-work block grant. Those funds spurred a short-term boom in contracting to private agencies. But the block grant expired leaving little evidence that states were able to build new systems for supporting work over the long term. In fact, no one knows exactly what all of this contracting produced, as state and local agencies kept limited records and conducted few careful evaluations. A close look at contracting in Illinois, for example, revealed the creation of a diffuse array of short-term programs operating under contract requirements that left many agencies unable to build anything of lasting value.

There is another strange twist to the convoluted welfare story: in their zest for services over support, states actually shifted government funds from the pockets of poor families to the pockets of private service providers. They distributed 76 percent of their AFDC funds in cash aid to the poor in 1996, but gave poor families only 41 percent of their TANF funds in 2000. Substantial portions of the TANF budget were consumed by child care costs, although it is difficult to say exactly how all the TANF funds were used. The General Accounting Office suggests that there is a fair amount of "supplantation" of services previously funded from other budget lines but now paid for by TANF.

Beyond the Caseload Count

The picture becomes still more complicated when one attempts to peer behind the head count in order to assess what actually happened in the purge of welfare caseloads. Exactly how did states push those caseloads down? What has happened to poor families that no longer have recourse to welfare? What kind of opportunities does the lower wage labor market really offer? Research has only begun to illuminate these crucial questions, but the evidence is disheartening.

Finding good jobs There are three ways to lower welfare caseloads. One is by successfully moving recipients into good jobs with stable employment where they can earn enough to maintain their families above poverty (or, at least, above what they could get on welfare). Recipients may find jobs on their own, which many do, or with connections facilitated by welfare agencies and service providers.

Financial supports provided by TANF have allowed some recipients to take jobs where they earn too little to make ends meet on their own. Child-care and transportation subsidies make a difference for those workers. They also benefit from federally funded food stamps that stretch the grocery budget. But food stamp use fell off 40 percent after 1994, although fewer families were receiving welfare and more had joined the ranks of the working poor. Absent external pressures, most states made no effort to assure access to food stamps for those losing welfare. In fact, government studies indicate that administrative hassles and misinformation discouraged low-income families from obtaining benefits.

Taking bad jobs A second way to lower welfare caseloads is to pressure recipients into taking bad jobs. Not all lower wage jobs are bad, but many of those most readily available to former recipients undermine their best efforts to make it as working parents. These jobs are characterized by unstable schedules, limited access to health insurance or pensions, no sick leave, and job insecurity. Because high turnover is a feature of these jobs, at any given moment, many are apt to be available. Indeed, employers seeking to fill these undesirable "high-velocity" jobs, where there is continuous churning of the workforce, are all too eager to use welfare agencies as a hiring hall.

This may partially explain why more than a fifth of those leaving welfare for work return within a year or two. Proponents of the new welfare conveniently blame individual work behavior or attitudes for job churning, but ignore the role of employers who structure jobs in ways that make job loss inevitable. What's a supermarket clerk to do when her manager makes frequent schedule changes, periodically shortens her hours, or asks her to work in a store across town? What happens is that carefully constructed child care arrangements break down, lost pay days break the family budget, and the hours it takes to commute on public transportation become unmanageable. The family-friendly workplace that more sought-after workers demand couldn't be farther from the hard reality of lower wage jobs.

One of the little appreciated virtues of the old welfare is that it served as a sort of unemployment insurance for these lower wage workers excluded from regular unemployment insurance by their irregular jobs. Welfare cushioned the layoffs, turnover, and contingencies that go with the territory. Under the new welfare, these workers face a hard landing because welfare is more difficult to get and offers little leeway to acquire either the time or skills that might yield a job with a future. Over the longer term, low-wage workers may find their access to welfare blocked by time limits. Although the five-year lifetime limit ostensibly targets sustained reliance on welfare, this limit could come back to bite those who cycle in and out of the lower wage labor force. At this point, no one knows how this will play out.

Creating barriers to access A third way to reduce welfare caseloads is by reducing access—making benefits harder to acquire and keep. Some states explicitly try to divert applicants by imposing advance job-search requirements, demanding multiple trips to the welfare office in order to complete the application process, or informally advising applicants that it may not be worth the hassle. In some welfare offices, caseworkers routinely encourage applicants to forgo cash aid and apply only for Medicaid and food stamps.

Benefits are also harder to keep, as caseworkers require recipients to attend frequent meetings either to discuss seemingly endless demands for documentation or to press them on issues involving work. Everyday life in an urban welfare office is difficult to describe and, for many, even harder to believe. There are the hours of waiting in rows of plastic chairs, the repeated requests for paperwork, the ritualized weekly job club lectures about how to smile, shake hands, and show a good attitude to employers. As inspiration, caseworkers leading job club sessions often tell stories from their own lives of rising from poverty to become welfare workers (positions likely to be cut back as caseloads decline). When clients tell their own tales of cycling from bad jobs to worse and ask for help getting a good job, caseworkers are apt to admonish them for indulging in a "pity party."

Access to welfare may also be constrained through a profoundly mundane array of administrative barriers that simply make benefits harder to keep. A missed appointment, misplaced documents (often lost by the agency), delayed entry of personal data—these common and otherwise trivial mishaps can result in a loss of benefits for "non-cooperation."

The Public Benefits Hotline, a call-in center that provides both advice and intervention for Chicago residents, received some ten thousand calls in the four years after welfare reform, most of them involving hassles of this sort.[2] In other parts of the country, these types of problems show up in administrative hearing records and court cases, where judges have criticized welfare agencies for making "excessive" demands for verification documents, conducting "sham assessments" leading to inappropriate imposition of work requirements, and sanctioning clients for missing appointments when they should have helped them deal with child care or medical difficulties.

Is There a Bottom Line?

The new welfare has produced neither the immediate cataclysm its opponents threatened nor the economic and social redemption its proponents anticipated. Opponents had warned that welfare reform would plunge one million children into poverty. In the midst of an unprecedented economic boom, that didn't happen. But, even in the best of times, prospects were not auspicious for those leaving welfare.

According to the Urban Institute, about half of those leaving welfare for work between 1997 and 1999 obtained jobs where they earned a median hourly wage of only $7.15. If the jobs offered a steady forty hours of work a week (which lower wage jobs usually don't), that would provide a gross annual income of $14,872. That places a mother with two children a precarious $1,000 above the formal poverty line for the year 2000 and a two-parent family with two children nearly $3,000 *below* that line. But more than one-fifth of those leaving welfare for work didn't make it through the year—either because they lost their jobs, got sick, or just couldn't make ends meet. The only thing surprising about these figures is that the numbers weren't higher. Others left or lost welfare, but did not find work, with one in seven adults losing welfare reporting no alternative means of support. Their specific fate is unknown, but most big cities have been reporting worrisome increases in homelessness and hunger.

If there is any bottom line, it is that caseloads have been purged. But neither the market for lower wage workers nor the policies put into practice in the name of welfare reform have purged poverty from the lives of the poor. Even in the last years of the economic boom, between 1996 and 1998, the Urban Institute found that three hundred thousand more individuals in single-parent families slipped into extreme poverty. Although they qualified for food stamps that might have stretched their resources a bit further, many did not get them. Government figures indicate that families leaving welfare for work often lose access to other benefits, which states do not automatically continue irrespective of eligibility.

More recently, census figures have begun to show the effects of recession coupled with an eroded safety net. The nation's poverty rate rose to 11.7 percent in 2001, up from 11.3 percent the prior year. More troubling still, inequality is growing and poverty is deepening. In 2001, the "poverty gap," the gap between the official poverty line and the income of poor individuals, reached its highest level since measurements were first taken in 1979. In California, often a harbinger of larger social trends, a startling two in three poor children now live in families where at least one adult is employed. Can the families of lower wage workers live without access to welfare and other government supports? Apparently, they can live, but not very well.

Slouching Toward Reauthorization

"We have to remember that the goal of the reform program was not to get people out of poverty, but to achieve financial independence, to get off welfare." This statement by a senior Connecticut welfare official quoted in the *New York Times* is more candid than most. But it illustrates the kind of political rationale that policymakers use to inoculate themselves against factual evidence of the new welfare's failure to relieve poverty.

With TANF facing reauthorization in the fall of 2002, it was clear that reconsideration of welfare policy would take place on a new playing field.

Tough work rules, time limits, and devolution were just the starting point. The Bush administration advanced a reauthorization plan that increased work requirements, cut opportunities for education and training, added new doses of moralism, and extended devolution.

The Republican-controlled House passed a TANF reauthorization bill (later deferred by the Senate) requiring recipients to work forty hours a week and demanding that states enforce these requirements for 70 percent of families receiving welfare by 2007. The bill also created incentives for states to require work within a month of granting welfare benefits and continued to credit states for caseload reductions, regardless of whether families losing welfare had jobs that could sustain them.

Families would face harsh new penalties, simply for running afoul of administrative rules. The House-passed measure required states to impose full family sanctions if caseworkers find a recipient in violation of those rules for sixty days. This makes entire families vulnerable to losing aid if a parent misses a couple of appointments or gets tangled in demands to supply documents verifying eligibility, just the type of problem that crops up routinely in states with complicated rules and outdated record-keeping systems.

One of the least mentioned but most dangerous features of the House bill was a "superwaiver" that would allow the executive branch to release states from social welfare obligations contained in more than a dozen federal poverty programs, including not only TANF, but also food stamps and Medicaid. This stealth provision would allow the Bush administration to override existing legislation by fiat. The nominal justification for the superwaiver is that it would ease the path of state innovation and experimentation. It would also ease the path for state cuts in social programs beyond all previous experience.

A more visibly contentious feature of the House bill was a provision to spend $300 million dollars per year on programs to induce welfare recipients to marry. This provision is one of the favorites of the religious right, along with the administration's funding for faith-based social services. These moral redemption provisions may be more important for what they signify to the Republican Party's conservative base than for what they do, as many states have resisted these types of things in the past. However, on this point, it is irresistible to quote America's favorite president, the fictional President Josiah Bartlet of the television series *West Wing*, who quipped: "When did the government get into the yenta [matchmaker] business?"

Of Poverty, Democracy, and Welfare

The demise of the old welfare marked more than an end to a policy that many believed had outlived its usefulness. It also marked the end of welfare *politics* as we knew it. In the tepid debate over reauthorization in the fall of 2002, the bitter conflicts of earlier years over government's role in addressing poverty were replaced by half-hearted tinkering. Even provisions with the potential to induce hand-to-hand combat—such as those on marriage or the superwaiver—elicited relatively low-intensity challenges.

Is this because the new welfare yielded the benefits that liberals had hoped for, removing a contentious issue from the table and conferring legitimation on the poor, not as recipients, but as workers? Did it satisfy conservatives by clearing caseloads and demanding work? That does not seem to be the case.

If the poor have benefited from a new legitimacy, it is hard to see the rewards. Congress has not rushed to offer extensive new work supports. In fact, the House bill contained $8 to $10 billion less for work supports than the Congressional Budget Office estimated would be needed. In 2002, Congress couldn't even agree to extend unemployment insurance for those outside the welfare system who were felled by recession, corporate collapses, and the hightech slide. While conservatives celebrated the caseload count, they also savored the opportunity to raise the ante with more onerous work requirements and marriage inducements, and even made a bid to eliminate other social protections through the superwaiver. . . .

Some congressional Democrats did take tentative steps against the tide, suggesting provisions that would fund new welfare-to-work services, provide additional job subsidies, increase the child care allotment, provide alternatives to work for recipients categorized as having work "barriers," and restore benefits to legal immigrants who were cut from welfare in 1996. Maryland Representative Benjamin Cardin was chief sponsor of a bill suggesting that states should be held accountable, not only for caseload reduction, but for poverty reduction. This notion had little traction in the 107th Congress and is likely to have even less in the next. Without the foundation of a politics of poverty to build on, such laudable ideas seem strangely irrelevant, even to the Democrats' agenda.

If welfare is a bellwether of broader political developments, there's little mistaking which way the wind is blowing. It has a decidedly Dickensian chill. The politics of poverty that gave birth to the old welfare has been supplanted by the politics of personal piety that gave birth to the new. This reflects a convergence between a neoliberal agenda of market dominance and a neoconservative agenda of middle-class moralism. In this reconfigured politics, personal responsibility is code for enforcement of the market. The new Calvinism advanced by welfare policy treats inequality as a natural consequence of personal behavior and attitude in an impartial marketplace. It is consistent with a shift in the role of the state from defender of the vulnerable and buffer against the market to one of protector-in-chief of both market and morals. This shift does not favor a small state, but a different state, one capable of enforcing market demands on workers, responding to corporate demands for capital (through public subsidies, bailouts, and tax breaks), and, perhaps more symbolically, regulating morality.

Welfare policy neither created, nor could prevent, these developments. Nor is it a foregone conclusion that government will shirk its social responsibilities. After all, America's growing economic inequality is fundamentally at odds with its commitment to political equality.

In contrast to the United States, the policies of Western European countries suggest that there need not be an absolute conflict between the welfare state and the market. Despite their allegiance to the latter, other nations continue to offer greater social protection to their citizens and worry about the democratic consequences of excluding the disadvantaged from the economy and the polity. U.S. policymakers need to move past stale debates pitting work against welfare and the poor against the nonpoor, if they are to advance policies that promote both social inclusion and economic opportunity.

Welfare, though small in scope, is large in relevance because it is a place where economic, social, and political issues converge. The old welfare acknowledged, in principle, a political commitment to relieve poverty and lessen inequality, even if, in practice, that commitment was limited, benefits were ungenerous, and access uneven. The new welfare dramatically changed the terms of the relationship between disadvantaged citizens and their state. It devolved choices about social protection from the State to the states, and it placed the value of work over the values of family well-being and social equity. As bad as the old welfare may have been, there is reason to lament its demise after all.

Notes

1. The discussion in this section draws, in part, on research conducted for the Project on the Public Economy of Work at the University of Chicago, supported by the Ford Foundation, the National Science Foundation, and the Open Society Institute. The author and Susan Lambert are co-directors.
2. The Hotline is a collaborative effort of the Legal Assistance Foundation of Chicago and community antipoverty advocates.

POSTSCRIPT

Are Declining Caseloads a Sign of Successful Welfare Reform?

New offers a brief description of the 1996 welfare reform, particularly that part of the PRWORA called TANF. He presents data that suggest that welfare reform is working, including a 58 percent decline in welfare caseloads over the 1996–2001 period. He isolates three factors that can explain the decline in caseloads: the strength of sanctions (sanctions refer to the amount of reduction in TANF checks a state imposes for the nonperformance of mandated work activities), the performance of the economy, and the level of benefits. Including these three explanations in his empirical analysis, New finds that all three have contributed to the decline in caseloads but that the state sanctioning policies have had considerably more of an impact than the other two factors. Thus, he concludes that welfare reform is indeed working.

Like New, Brodkin details what she considers to be the main provisions of PRWORA and TANF. She provides data indicating what has happened since 1996, including the nearly 60 percent decline in welfare caseloads over the 1996–2001 period. But she interprets the data differently than New, arguing that a true assessment of welfare reform must address three basic questions: What are the methods used by the states to reduce their caseloads? What is the condition of poor families when they no longer are able to receive welfare? and, What kind of opportunities are provided by the low-wage job market? She finds the answers to these questions disappointing. Brodkin concludes her evaluation by asserting that "the new welfare has placed the value of work over the values of family well being and social equity."

The analyses cited by New are a good place to begin further investigation of the welfare reform issue. Information on the government's definition and measurement of poverty can be found in the U.S. Department of Commerce's publication *Poverty in the United States: 2001,* `http://www.census.gov/hhes/www/poverty01.html`. Other studies of welfare reform include "Welfare Research Perspectives: Past, Present, and Future, 2002 Edition," by Barbara B. Blum and Jennifer Farnsworth Francis (National Center for Children in Poverty, 2002); "Gaining Ground: Women, Welfare Reform and Work," by June E. O'Neill and M. Anne Hill, *NCPA Policy Report No. 251* (February 2002); "Don't Tamper With Welfare Success," by Chris Schafer, *Society's Welfare/Fraser Forum* (July 2002); and "How Exisiting Welfare Reform Distorts Welfare Reality," which can be found on the Applied Research Center Web site at `http://www.arc.org/welfare/welfareresearch.html` (January 2001). Finally, there are a number of welfare analyses available on the Urban Institute's Web site, which can be found at `http://www.urban.org`.

On the Internet . . .

European Union in the United States

This European Union (EU) site provides access to information regarding EU membership and its basic organization and structure, to lists of EU publications, and to overviews of EU law and policy.

http://www.eurunion.org

OECD Online

The Organization for Economic Co-operation and Development (OECD) resulted from the need to rebuild Europe after World War II, but it expanded to become truly international, with policies designed to expand world trade on a multilateral, nondiscriminatory basis. At this site, one can find information regarding member countries, publications, statistics, and news releases.

http://www.oecd.org

International Monetary Fund (IMF)

The home page of the International Monetary Fund provides links to information about its purposes and activities, its news releases, and its publications including the most recent World Economic Outlook.

http://www.imf.org

International Trade Administration (ITA)

The U.S. Department of Commerce's International Trade Administration is dedicated to helping U.S. businesses compete in the global marketplace. This site offers assistance through many Web links under such headings as Trade Statistics, Tariffs and Taxes, Market Research, and Export Documentation. It also provides information regarding recent actions taken to promote trade.

http://www.ita.doc.gov

Social Science Information Gateway (SOSIG)

The Social Science Information Gateway catalogs 17 subjects and lists more URL addresses from European and developing countries than many U.S. sources do.

http://sosig.esrc.bris.ac.uk

The World Bank

The home page of the World Bank offers links to a vast array of information regarding developing countries. Of special interest is the link to World Development Indicators.

http://www.worldbank.org

PART 3

The World Around Us

For many years America held a position of dominance in international trade. That position has been changed by time, events, and the emergence of other economic powers in the world. Decisions that are made in the international arena will, with increasing frequency, influence our lives. Along with globalization, concern with the environment has grown over the years. This raises questions of sustaining the ecosystem in the face of both population and economic growth. America's place in the global economy is also related to our educational system, helping to determine the productivity of our workers.

ISSUE 13

Are Protectionist Policies Bad for America?

YES: Murray N. Rothbard, from "Protectionism and the Destruction of Prosperity," Ludwig von Mises Institute, `http://mises.org/fullarticle.asp?title=Protectionism&month=1` (July 13, 1998)

NO: Patrick J. Buchanan, from "Free Trade Is Not Free," Address to the Chicago Council on Foreign Relations (November 18, 1998)

ISSUE SUMMARY

YES: Free-trade economist Murray N. Rothbard objects to the prospect of protectionism, which he sees as an attempt by the few who make up special interest groups "to repress and loot the rest of us" who make up the many.

NO: Social critic and three-time presidential hopeful Patrick J. Buchanan argues that America's "new corporate elite" is willing to sacrifice the country's best interests on "the altar of that golden calf, the global economy."

The economic logic that supports international trade has changed little since David Ricardo provided us with his basic insight that the patterns and the gains of trade depend on relative factor prices. More correctly stated, Ricardo argued nearly 200 years ago that if there were differences in the "opportunity costs" of producing goods and services, trade will occur between countries and that, more important, the countries that engage in trade will all benefit.

Although the large majority of economists accept the logic and the policy conclusions of Ricardo's theory, the debate rages on. The debate between "free traders" and those who plead for protection is timeless. The basic logic of international trade is indistinguishable from the basic logic of purely domestic trade. That is, both domestic and international trade must answer the fundamental economic questions: *what* to produce, *how* to produce it, and *for whom* to produce it. The distinction is that the international trade questions are posed in an international arena. This is an arena filled with producers and consumers who speak different languages, use different currencies, and are often suspicious of the actions and reactions of foreigners.

If markets work the way they are expected to work, free trade simply increases the size or the extent of a purely domestic market and, therefore, increases the advantages of specialization. Market participants should be able to buy and consume a greater variety of inexpensive goods and services after the establishment of free trade than they could before free trade. One might ask, then, why some wish to close U.S. borders and deny Americans the benefits of free trade. The answer to this question is straightforward—these benefits do not come without a cost.

There are two sets of winners and two sets of losers in the game of free trade. The most obvious winners are the consumers of the less expensive imported goods. These consumers are able to buy the low-priced color television sets, automobiles, or steel that is made abroad. Another set of winners is the producers of the exported goods. All the factors in the export industry, as well as those in industries that supply the export industry, experience an increase in market demand. Therefore, their income increases. In the United States, agriculture is one such export industry. As new foreign markets are opened, farmers' incomes increase, as do the incomes of those who supply the farmers with fertilizer, farm equipment, gasoline, and other basic inputs.

On the other side of this coin are the losers. The obvious losers are those who own the factors of production that are employed in the import-competing industries. These factors include the land, labor, and capital that are devoted to the production of such U.S.-made items as color television sets, automobiles, and steel. The less expensive foreign imports displace the demand for these products. The consumers of exported goods are also the losers. For example, as U.S. farmers sell more of their products abroad, less of this output is available domestically. As a result, the domestic prices of these farm products and other export goods and services rise.

The bottom line is that there is nothing really "free" in a market system. Competition—whether it is domestic or foreign—creates winners and losers. Historically, we have sympathized with the losers when they suffer at the hands of foreign competitors. However, we have not let our sympathies seriously curtail free trade.

The "free" that Murray N. Rothbard and Patrick J. Buchanan debate in the following selections goes beyond the notion of winners and losers in a marketplace. Rothbard asserts that protectionism is a restraint of trade, which imposes severe losses on foreign and domestic consumers alike. Buchanan argues that we have to think of "America first, and not only first, but also second and third as well" when considering international trade issues.

Murray N. Rothbard

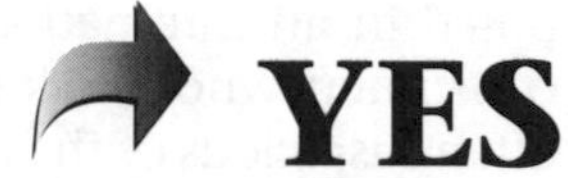

Protectionism and the Destruction of Prosperity

Protectionism, often refuted and seemingly abandoned, has returned, and with a vengeance. The Japanese, who bounced back from grievous losses in World War II to astound the world by producing innovative, high-quality products at low prices, are serving as the convenient butt of protectionist propaganda. Memories of wartime myths prove a heady brew, as protectionists warn about this new "Japanese imperialism," even "worse than Pearl Harbor." This "imperialism" turns out to consist of selling Americans wonderful TV sets, autos, microchips, etc., at prices more than competitive with American firms.

Is this "flood" of Japanese products really a menace, to be combated by the U.S. government? Or is the new Japan a godsend to American consumers?

In taking our stand on this issue, we should recognize that all government action means coercion, so that calling upon the U.S. government to intervene means urging it to use force and violence to restrain peaceful trade. One trusts that the protectionists are not willing to pursue their logic of force to the ultimate in the form of another Hiroshima and Nagasaki [Japanese cities destroyed by the first atomic bombs used in warfare].

Keep Your Eye on the Consumer

As we unravel the tangled web of protectionist argument, we should keep our eye on two essential points: (1) protectionism means force in restraint of trade; and (2) the key is what happens to the consumer. Invariably, we will find that the protectionists are out to cripple, exploit, and impose severe losses not only on foreign consumers but especially on Americans. And since each and every one of us is a consumer, this means that protectionism is out to mulct [swindle] all of us for the benefit of a specially privileged, subsidized few—and an inefficient few at that: people who cannot make it in a free and unhampered market.

Take, for example, the alleged Japanese menace. All trade is mutually beneficial to both parties—in this case Japanese producers and American consumers—otherwise they would not engage in the exchange. In trying to

From Murray N. Rothbard, "Protectionism and the Destruction of Prosperity," Ludwig von Mises Institute, `http://mises.org/fullarticle.asp?title=Protectionism&month=1` (July 13, 1998).

stop this trade, protectionists are trying to stop American consumers from enjoying high living standards by buying cheap and high-quality Japanese products. Instead, we are to be forced by government to return to the inefficient, higher-priced products we have already rejected. In short, inefficient producers are trying to deprive all of us of products we desire so that we will have to turn to inefficient firms. American consumers are to be plundered.

How to Look at Tariffs and Quotas

The best way to look at tariffs or import quotas or other protectionist restraints is to forget about political boundaries. Political boundaries of nations may be important for other reasons, but they have no economic meaning whatever. Suppose, for example, that each of the United States were a separate nation. Then we would hear a lot of protectionist bellyaching that we are now fortunately spared. Think of the howls by high-priced New York or Rhode Island textile manufacturers who would then be complaining about the "unfair," "cheap labor" competition from various low-type "foreigners" from Tennessee or North Carolina, or vice versa.

Fortunately, the absurdity of worrying about the balance of payments is made evident by focusing on inter-state trade. For nobody worries about the balance of payments between New York and New Jersey, or, for that matter, between Manhattan and Brooklyn, because there are no customs officials recording such trade and such balances.

If we think about it, it is clear that a call by New York firms for a tariff against North Carolina is a pure ripoff of New York (as well as North Carolina) consumers, a naked grab for coerced special privilege by less efficient business firms. If the 50 states were separate nations, the protectionists would then be able to use the trappings of patriotism, and distrust of foreigners, to camouflage and get away with their looting the consumers of their own region.

Fortunately, inter-state tariffs are unconstitutional. But even with this clear barrier, and even without being able to wrap themselves in the cloak of nationalism, protectionists have been able to impose inter-state tariffs in another guise. Part of the drive for continuing increases in the federal minimum-wage law is to impose a protectionist devise against lower-wage, lower-labor-cost competition from North Carolina and other southern states against their New England and New York competitors.

During the 1966 Congressional battle over a higher federal minimum wage, for example, the late Senator Jacob Javits (R-NY) freely admitted that one of his main reasons for supporting the bill was to cripple the southern competitors of New York textile firms. Since southern wages are generally lower than in the north, the business firms hardest hit by an increased minimum wage (and the workers struck by unemployment) will be located in the south.

Another way in which interstate trade restrictions have been imposed has been in the fashionable name of "safety." Government-organized state milk cartels in New York, for example, have prevented importation of milk from nearby New Jersey under the patently spurious grounds that the trip across the Hudson would render New Jersey milk "unsafe."

If tariffs and restraints on trade are good for a country, then why not indeed for a state or region? The principle is precisely the same. In America's first great depression, the Panic of 1819, Detroit was a tiny frontier town of only a few hundred people. Yet protectionist cries arose—fortunately not fulfilled—to prohibit all "imports" from outside of Detroit, and citizens were exhorted to buy only Detroit. If this nonsense had been put into effect, general starvation and death would have ended all other economic problems for Detroiters.

So why not restrict and even prohibit trade, i.e., "imports," into a city, or a neighborhood, or even on a block, or, to boil it down to its logical conclusion, to one family? Why shouldn't the Jones family issue a decree that from now on, no member of the family can buy any goods or services produced outside the family house? Starvation would quickly wipe out this ludicrous drive for self-sufficiency.

And yet we must realize that this absurdity is inherent in the logic of protectionism. Standard protectionism is just as preposterous, but the rhetoric of nationalism and national boundaries has been able to obscure this vital fact.

The upshot is that protectionism is not only nonsense, but dangerous nonsense, destructive of all economic prosperity. We are not, if we were ever, a world of self-sufficient farmers. The market economy is one vast latticework throughout the world, in which each individual, each region, each country, produces what he or it is best at, most relatively efficient in, and exchanges that product for the goods and services of others. Without the division of labor and the trade based upon that division, the entire world would starve. Coerced restraints on trade—such as protectionism—cripple, hobble, and destroy trade, the source of life and prosperity. Protectionism is simply a plea that consumers, as well as general prosperity, be hurt so as to confer permanent special privilege upon groups of less efficient producers, at the expense of more competent firms and of consumers. But it is a peculiarly destructive kind of bailout, because it permanently shackles trade under the cloak of patriotism.

The Negative Railroad

Protectionism is also peculiarly destructive because it acts as a coerced and artificial increase in the cost of transportation between regions. One of the great features of the Industrial Revolution, one of the ways in which it brought prosperity to the starving masses, was by reducing drastically the cost of transportation. The development of railroads in the early 19th century, for example, meant that for the first time in the history of the human race, goods could be transported cheaply over land. Before that, water—rivers and oceans—was the only economically viable means of transport. By making land transport accessible and cheap, railroads allowed interregional land transportation to break up expensive inefficient local monopolies. The result was an enormous improvement in living standards for all consumers. And what the protectionists want to do is lay an axe to this wondrous principle of progress.

It is no wonder that Frederic Bastiat, the great French laissez-faire economist of the mid-19th century, called a tariff a "negative railroad." Protectionists are just as economically destructive as if they were physically chopping up railroads, or planes, or ships, and forcing us to revert to the costly transport of the past—mountain trails, rafts, or sailing ships.

"Fair" Trade

Let us now turn to some of the leading protectionist arguments. Take, for example, the standard complaint that while the protectionist "welcomes competition," this competition must be "fair." Whenever someone starts talking about "fair competition" or indeed, about "fairness" in general, it is time to keep a sharp eye on your wallet, for it is about to be picked. For the genuinely "fair" is simply the voluntary terms of exchange, mutually agreed upon by buyer and seller. As most of the medieval scholastics were able to figure out, there is no "just" (or "fair") price outside of the market price.

So what could be "unfair" about the free-market price? One common protectionist charge is that it is "unfair" for an American firm to compete with, say, a Taiwanese firm which needs to pay only one-half the wages of the American competitor. The U.S. government is called upon to step in and "equalize" the wage rates by imposing an equivalent tariff upon the Taiwanese. But does this mean that consumers can never patronize low-cost firms because it is "unfair" for them to have lower costs than inefficient competitors? This is the same argument that would be used by a New York firm trying to cripple its North Carolina competitor.

What the protectionists don't bother to explain is why U.S. wage rates are so much higher than Taiwan. They are not imposed by Providence. Wage rates are high in the U.S. because American employers have bid these rates up. Like all other prices on the market, wage rates are determined by supply and demand, and the increased demand by U.S. employers has bid wages up. What determines this demand? The "marginal productivity" of labor.

The demand for any factor of production, including labor, is constituted by the productivity of that factor, the amount of revenue that the worker, or the pound of cement or acre of land, is expected to bring to the brim. The more productive the factory, the greater the demand by employers, and the higher its price or wage rate. American labor is more costly than Taiwanese because it is far more productive. What makes it productive? To some extent, the comparative qualities of labor, skill, and education. But most of the difference is not due to the personal qualities of the laborers themselves, but to the fact that the American laborer, on the whole, is equipped with more and better capital equipment than his Taiwanese counterparts. The more and better the capital investment per worker, the greater the worker's productivity, and therefore the higher the wage rate.

In short, if the American wage rate is twice that of the Taiwanese, it is because the American laborer is more heavily capitalized, is equipped with more and better tools, and is therefore, on the average, twice as productive. In a sense, I suppose, it is not "fair" for the American worker to make more than the Taiwanese, not because of his personal qualities, but because savers and investors have supplied him with more tools. But a wage rate is determined not just by personal quality but also by relative scarcity, and in the United States the worker is far scarcer compared to capital than he is in Taiwan.

Putting it another way, the fact that American wage rates are on the average twice that of the Taiwanese, does not make the cost of labor in the U.S. twice that of Taiwan. Since U.S. labor is twice as productive, this means that the double wage rate in the U.S. is offset by the double productivity, so that the cost of labor per unit product in the U.S. and Taiwan tends, on the average, to be the same. One of the major protectionist fallacies is to confuse the price of labor (wage rates) with its cost, which also depends on its relative productivity.

Thus, the problem faced by American employers is not really with the "cheap labor" in Taiwan, because "expensive labor" in the U.S. is precisely the result of the bidding for scarce labor by U.S. employers. The problem faced by less efficient U.S. textile or auto firms is not so much cheap labor in Taiwan or Japan, but the fact that other U.S. industries are efficient enough to afford it, because they bid wages that high in the first place.

So, by imposing protective tariffs and quotas to save, bail out, and keep in place less efficient U.S. textile or auto or microchip firms, the protectionists are not only injuring the American consumer. They are also harming efficient U.S. firms and industries, which are prevented from employing resources now locked into incompetent firms, and who could otherwise be able to expand and sell their efficient products at home and abroad.

"Dumping"

Another contradictory line of protectionist assault on the free market asserts that the problem is not so much the low costs enjoyed by foreign firms, as the "unfairness" of selling their products "below costs" to American consumers, and thereby engaging in the pernicious and sinful practice of "dumping." By such dumping they are able to exert unfair advantage over American firms who presumably never engage in such practices and make sure that their prices are always high enough to cover costs. But if selling below costs is such a powerful weapon, why isn't it ever pursued by business firms within a country?

Our first response to this charge is, once again, to keep our eye on consumers in general and on American consumers in particular. Why should it be a matter of complaint when consumers so clearly benefit? Suppose, for example, that Sony is willing to injure American competitors by selling TV sets to Americans for a penny apiece. Shouldn't we rejoice at such an absurd policy of suffering severe losses by subsidizing us, the American consumers? And shouldn't our response be: "Come on, Sony, subsidize us some more!" As far as consumers are concerned, the more "dumping" that takes place, the better.

But what of the poor American TV firms, whose sales will suffer so long as Sony is willing to virtually give their sets away? Well, surely, the sensible policy for RCA, Zenith, etc. would be to hold back production and sales until Sony drives itself into bankruptcy. But suppose that the worst happens, and RCA, Zenith, etc. are themselves driven into bankruptcy by the Sony price war? Well, in that case, we the consumers will still be better off, since the plants of the bankrupt firms, which would still be in existence, would be picked up for a song at auction, and the American buyers at auction would be able to enter the TV business and outcompete Sony because they now enjoy far lower capital costs.

For decades, indeed, opponents of the free market have claimed that many businesses gained their powerful status on the market by what is called "predatory price-cutting," that is, by driving their smaller competitors into bankruptcy by selling their goods below cost, and then reaping the reward of their unfair methods by raising their prices and thereby charging "monopoly prices" to the consumers. The claim is that while consumers may gain in the short run by price wars, "dumping," and selling below costs, they lose in the long run from the alleged monopoly. But, as we have seen, economic theory shows that this would be a mug's [fool's] game, losing money for the "dumping" firms, and never really achieving a monopoly price. And sure enough, historical investigation has not turned up a single case where predatory pricing, when tried, was successful, and there are actually very few cases where it has even been tried.

Another charge claims that Japanese or other foreign firms can afford to engage in dumping because their governments are willing to subsidize their losses. But again, we should still welcome such an absurd policy. If the Japanese government is really willing to waste scarce resources subsidizing American purchases of Sony's, so much the better! Their policy would be just as self-defeating as if the losses were private.

There is yet another problem with the charge of "dumping," even when it is made by economists or other alleged "experts" sitting on impartial tariff commissions and government bureaus. There is no way whatever that outside observers, be they economists, businessmen, or other experts, can decide what some other firm's "costs" may be. "Costs" are not objective entities that can be gauged or measured. Costs are subjective to the businessman himself, and they vary continually, depending on the businessman's time horizon or the stage of production or selling process he happens to be dealing with at any given time.

Suppose, for example, a fruit dealer has purchased a case of pears for $20, amounting to $1 a pound. He hopes and expects to sell those pears for $1.50 a pound. But something has happened to the pear market, and he finds it impossible to sell most of the pears at anything near that price. In fact, he finds that he must sell the pears at whatever price he can get before they become overripe. Suppose he finds that he can only sell his stock of pears at 70 cents a pound. The outside observer might say that the fruit dealer has, perhaps "unfairly," sold his pears "below costs," figuring that the dealer's costs were $1 a pound.

"Infant" Industries

Another protectionist fallacy held that the government should provide a temporary protective tariff to aid, or to bring into being, an "infant industry." Then, when the industry was well-established, the government would and should remove the tariff and toss the now "mature" industry into the competitive swim.

The theory is fallacious, and the policy has proved disastrous in practice. For there is no more need for government to protect a new, young, industry from foreign competition than there is to protect it from domestic competition.

In the last few decades, the "infant" plastics, television, and computer industries made out very well without such protection. Any government subsidizing of a new industry will funnel too many resources into that industry as compared to older firms, and will also inaugurate distortions that may persist and render the firm or industry permanently inefficient and vulnerable to competition. As a result, "infant-industry" tariffs have tended to become permanent, regardless of the "maturity" of the industry. The proponents were carried away by a misleading biological analogy to "infants" who need adult care. But a business firm is not a person, young or old.

Older Industries

Indeed, in recent years, older industries that are notoriously inefficient have been using what might be called a "senile-industry" argument for protectionism. Steel, auto, and other outcompeted industries have been complaining that they "need a breathing space" to retool and become competitive with foreign rivals, and that this breather could be provided by several years of tariffs or import quotas. This argument is just as full of holes as the hoary infant-industry approach, except that it will be even more difficult to figure out when the "senile" industry will have become magically rejuvenated. In fact, the steel industry has been inefficient ever since its inception, and its chronological age seems to make no difference. The first protectionist movement in the U.S. was launched in 1820, headed by the Pennsylvania iron (later iron and steel) industry, artificially force-fed by the War of 1812 and already in grave danger from far more efficient foreign competitors.

The Non-Problem of the Balance of Payments

A final set of arguments, or rather alarms, center on the mysteries of the balance of payments. Protectionists focus on the horrors of imports being greater than exports, implying that if market forces continued unchecked, Americans might wind up buying everything from abroad, while selling foreigners nothing, so that American consumers will have engorged themselves to the permanent ruin of American business firms. But if the exports really fell to somewhere near zero, where in the world would Americans still find the money to purchase foreign products? The balance of payments, as we said earlier, is a pseudo-problem created by the existence of customs statistics.

During the day of the gold standard, a deficit in the national balance of payments was a problem, but only because of the nature of the fractional-reserve banking system. If U.S. banks, spurred on by the Fed or previous forms of central banks, inflated money and credit, the American inflation would lead to higher prices in the U.S., and this would discourage exports and encourage imports. The resulting deficit had to be paid for in some way, and during the gold standard era this meant being paid for in gold, the international money. So as bank credit expanded, gold began to flow out of the country, which put the fractional-reserve banks in even shakier shape. To meet the threat to their solvency posed by the gold outflow, the banks eventually were forced to contract credit, precipitating a recession and reversing the balance of payment deficits, thus bringing gold back into the country.

But now, in the fiat-money era, balance of payments deficits are truly meaningless. For gold is no longer a "balancing item." In effect, there is no deficit in the balance of payments. It is true that in the last few years, imports have been greater than exports by $150 billion or so per year. But no gold flowed out of the country. Neither did dollars "leak" out. The alleged "deficit" was paid for by foreigners investing the equivalent amount of money in American dollars: in real estate, capital goods, U.S. securities, and bank accounts.

In effect, in the last couple of years, foreigners have been investing enough of their own funds in dollars to keep the dollar high, enabling us to purchase cheap imports. Instead of worrying and complaining about this development, we should rejoice that foreign investors are willing to finance our cheap imports. The only problem is that this bonanza is already coming to an end, with the dollar becoming cheaper and exports more expensive.

We conclude that the sheaf of protectionist arguments, many plausible at first glance, are really a tissue of egregious fallacies. They betray a complete ignorance of the most basic economic analysis. Indeed, some of the arguments are almost embarrassing replicas of the most ridiculous claims of 17th-century mercantilism: for example, that it is somehow a calamitous problem that the U.S. has a balance of trade deficit, not overall, but merely with one specific country, e.g., Japan.

Must we even relearn the rebuttals of the more sophisticated mercantilists of the 18th century: namely, that balances with individual countries will cancel each other out, and therefore that we should only concern ourselves with the overall balance? (Let alone realize that the overall balance is no problem either.) But we need not reread the economic literature to realize that the impetus for protectionism comes not from preposterous theories, but from the quest for coerced special privilege and restraint of trade at the expense of efficient competitors and consumers. In the host of special interests using the political process to repress and loot the rest of us, the protectionists are among the most venerable. It is high time that we get them, once and for all, off our backs, and treat them with the righteous indignation they so richly deserve.

Patrick J. Buchanan

Free Trade Is Not Free

This is a prestigious forum; and I appreciate the opportunity to address it. As my subject, I have chosen what I believe is the coming and irrepressible conflict between the claims of a new American nationalism and the commands of the Global Economy.

As you may have heard in my last [presidential] campaign, I am called by many names. "Protectionist" is one of the nicer ones; but it is inexact. I am an economic nationalist. To me, the country comes before the economy; and the economy exists for the people. I believe in free markets, but I do not worship them. In the proper hierarchy of things, it is the market that must be harnessed to work for man—and not the other way around.

As for the Global Economy, like the unicorn, it is a mythical beast that exists only in the imagination. In the real world, there are only national economies—Japan's that has lost its animal spirits, South Korea's that is deep in recession, China's which is headed for trouble, Brazil's which is falling, Indonesia and Russia's which are in collapse.

In these unique national economies, critical decisions are based on what is best for the nation. Only in America do leaders sacrifice the interests of their own country on the altar of that golden calf, the Global Economy.

What is Economic Nationalism? Is it some right-wing or radical idea? By no means. Economic nationalism was the idea and cause that brought [George] Washington, [Alexander] Hamilton and [James] Madison to Philadelphia. These men dreamed of creating here in America the greatest free market on earth, by elimination all internal barriers to trade among the 13 states, and taxing imports to finance the turnpikes and canals of the new nation and end America's dependence on Europe. It was called the American System.

The ideology of free trade is the alien import, an invention of European academics and scribblers, not one of whom ever built a great nation, and all of whom were repudiated by America's greatest statesmen, including all four presidents on Mount Rushmore.

The second bill that Washington signed into law was the Tariff Act of 1789. Madison saved the nation's infant industries from being buried by the dumping of British manufactures, with the first truly protective tariff, the Tariff Act of 1816. "Give me a tariff and I will give you the greatest

From Patrick J. Buchanan, "Free Trade Is Not Free," Address to the Chicago Council on Foreign Relations (November 18, 1998).

nation on earth," said [Abraham] Lincoln. "I thank God I am not a free trader," Theodore Roosevelt wrote to Henry Cabot Lodge.

Under economic nationalism, there was no income tax in the United States, except during the Civil War and Reconstruction. Tariffs produced fifty to ninety percent of federal revenue. And how did America prosper? From 1865 to 1913, U.S. growth averaged 4% a year. We began the era with half Britain's production, but ended with twice Britain's production.

Yet, this era is now disparaged in history books and public schools as the time of the Robber Barons, a Gilded Age best forgotten.

Not only did America rise to greatness through the economic nationalism so did every other first-rank power in history—from Britain in the 18th century, to [Otto von] Bismarck's Germany in the 19th, to post-war Japan. Economic nationalism has been the policy of rising nations, free trade the practice of nations that have commenced their historic decline. Today, this idea may be mocked by the talking heads, but it is going to prevail again in America, for it alone comports with the national interests of the United States. And this is the subject of my remarks.

. . . These are good times in America. . . .

Is this our reward for free trade? My answer is no. Though these are good times in America, our growth today is anemic, compared to what it was in the Protectionist Era, and the Roaring Twenties, when growth rates hit seven percent. Free trade does not explain our prosperity; free trade explains the economic insecurity that is the worm in the apple of our prosperity.

The great free-market economist Milton Friedman is credited with the line, "there is no free lunch." Let me amend to Friedman's Law with Buchanan's Corollary: Free trade is no free lunch.

And it is time its costs were calculated.

Back in 1848, another economist wrote that if free trade were ever adopted, societies would be torn apart. His name was Karl Marx, and he wrote: ". . . the Free Trade system works destructively. It breaks up old nationalities and carries antagonism of proletariat and bourgeoisie to the uttermost point . . . the Free trade system hastens the Social Revolution. In this revolutionary sense alone . . . I am in favor of Free Trade."

Marx was right. Here, then, is the first cost of open-borders free trade. It exacerbates the divisions between capital and labor. It separates societies into contending classes, and deepens the division between rich and poor. Under free trade, economic and social elites, whose jobs and incomes are not adversely impacted by imports or immigration, do well. For them, these have been the best of times. Since 1990, the stock market has tripled in value; corporate profits have doubled since 1992; there has been a population explosion among millionaires. America's richest one percent controlled 21 percent of the national wealth in 1949; in 1997 it was 40 percent. Top CEO salaries were 44 times the average wage of their workers in 1965; by 1996 they were 212 times an average worker's pay.

How has Middle America fared? Between 1972 and 1994, the real wages of working Americans fell 19 percent. In 1970, the price of a new house was twice a young couple's income; it is now four times. In 1960, 18 percent of women with children under six were in the work force; by 1995 it had risen 63 percent. The U.S. has a larger percentage of women in its work force than any industrial nation, yet median family income fell 6 percent in the first six years of the 1990s.

Something is wrong when wage earners work harder and longer just to stay in the same place. Under the free trade regime, economic insecurity has become a preexisting condition of life.

A second cost of global free trade is a loss of independence and national sovereignty. America was once a self-reliant nation; trade amounted to only 10 percent of GNP [gross national product]; imports only 4 percent. Now, trade is equal to 25% of GNP; and the trade surpluses we ran every year from 1900–1970 have turned into trade deficits for all of the last 27 years.

Since 1980 our total merchandise trade deficit adds up to $2 trillion. This year's [1998's] trade deficit is approaching $300 billion. Year in and year out, we consume more than we produce. This cannot last.

Look at what this is doing to an industrial plant that once produced 40 percent of all that the world produced. In 1965, 31 percent of the U.S. labor force had manufacturing equivalent jobs. By 1997, it was down to 15 percent, smallest share in 100 years.

More Americans now work in government than in manufacturing. We Americans no longer make our own cameras, shoes, radios, TV's, toys. A fourth of our steel, a third of our autos, half our machine tools, two-thirds of our textiles are foreign made. We used to be the world's greatest creditor nation; now, we are its greatest debtor.

Friends, this is the read-out of the electrocardiogram of a nation in decline. Writes author-economist Pat Choate, "a peek behind the glitter of record stock prices and high corporate profits reveals a deepening economic dry rot—a nation that is eating its seed corn and squandering its economic leadership position, here and abroad."

And American sovereignty is being eroded. In 1994, for the first time, the U.S. joined a global institution, the World Trade Organization, where America has no veto power and the one-nation, one-vote rule applies. Where are we headed? Look at the nations of Europe that are today surrendering control of their money, their immigration policy, their environmental policy, even defense policy—to a giant socialist superstate called the EU [European Union].

For America to continue down this road of global interdependence is a betrayal of our history and our heritage of liberty. What does it profit a man if he gain the whole world, and suffer the loss of his own country?

A third cost of the Global Economy is America's vulnerability to a financial collapse caused by events beyond our control. Never has this country been so exposed. When Mexico, with an economy no larger than Illinois', threatened a default in 1994, the U.S. cobbled together a $50 billion bailout, lest Mexico's default bring on what Michel Camdessus of the IMF [International Monetary Fund] called "global financial catastrophe."

When tiny Asian dominoes began to fall [in 1997], the IMF had to put together $117 billion in bailouts of Thailand, Indonesia, South Korea, lest the Asian crisis bring down all of Latin America and the rest of the world with it.

In the Global Economy, the world is always just one default away from disaster. What in heaven's name does the vaunted Global Economy give us—besides all that made-in-China junk down at the mall—to justify having the U.S. financial system at permanent risk of collapse—if some incompetent foreign regime decides to walk on its debts?

A fourth cost of this Global Economy is the de-industrialization of America and the de-Americanization of our industries. Many of our Fortune 500 corporations have already shed their American identity.

When Gilbert Williamson, then president of NCR [National Cash Register Company, now known as NCR Corporation], was asked about U.S. workers being unable to compete in a global economy, he dismissed the question with this remark: "I was asked the other day about U.S. competitiveness, and I replied that I don't think about it at all. We at NCR think of ourselves as a globally competitive company that happens to be headquartered in the United States."

Many companies still carry fine old American names, but their work forces are becoming less and less American. In 1985, GE employed 243,000 Americans; ten years later, it was down to 150,000. IBM has lopped off half of its U.S. workers in the past decade. Here is author William Greider:

"By 1995, Big Blue had become a truly global firm—with more employees abroad than at home . . . Intel . . . shrank U.S. employment last year from 22,000 to 17,000. Motorola's . . . work force is now only 56 percent American. . . . Ma Bell once made all its home telephones in the U.S. and now makes none here."

Boeing's Philip Condit says he would be happy if, twenty years from now, no one thought of Boeing as an American company.

Here is Carl A. Gerstacker of Dow Chemical: "I have long dreamed of buying an island owned by no nation and of establishing the World Headquarters of the Dow Company on the truly neutral ground of such an island, beholden to no nation or society." A Union Carbide spokesman agreed: "It is not proper for an international corporation to put the welfare of any country in which it does business above that of any other."

To this new corporate elite, putting America first betrays a lack of loyalty to the company. Some among our political elite share this view. Here is Strobe Talbott, [Bill] Clinton's roommate at Oxford and architect of his Russian policy: "All countries," said Talbott in 1991, "are basically social arrangements . . . No matter how permanent and even sacred they may seem at any one time, in fact they are all artificial and temporary . . . within the next hundred years . . . nationhood as we know it will be obsolete; all states will recognize a single, global authority."

This is the transnational elite, our new Masters of the Universe.

The Cold War has been succeeded by a new struggle. "The real divisions of our time," writes scholar Christisan Kopff, "are not between left and right, but between nations and the globalist delusion." That struggle will shape the politics of the new century; and a familiar question is being asked again across America: When the commands of the Global Economy conflict with call of patriotism, whose side are you on?

If you would see the consequences of free trade ideology, go to Detroit. In the 1950s this was the forge and furnace of the Arsenal of Democracy, with 2 million of the most productive people on earth. Compare Detroit then to Detroit now. Free trade is not free.

Forty years ago, Japan exported 6000 cars. Today, Japan has as large a share of the U.S. auto and truck market as GM.

How did Japan do it? Yes, they built fine cars; but the Japanese did not leave the outcome of this struggle for dominance in the world's first industry to the vagaries of the market place. The Japanese fixed the game.

Japan virtually sealed off its market to U.S. auto imports, subsidized its auto industry and exports, and paid its workers 15% of U.S. wages in factories that would have had to be shut down in the United States. Tokyo's political and industrial elite did not let [economist] Adam Smith [1723–1790] dictate how they would play the game.

In short, Tokyo in the 1970s and 1980s looked on our auto market the way their grandfathers looked on China in the 1920s and 30s—as an inviting target for conquest. They did not read Richard Cobden on free trade; they read Alexander Hamilton, who would never have allowed Japan to overrun our auto industry, our radio industry, or our television industry.

Remember NAFTA. This treaty was going to open Mexico to U.S. auto exports. Well, in 1996, we shipped 46,000 cars to Mexico; and Mexico sent 550,000 cars back to us. Where did Mexico get its booming auto industry? From Michigan, Ohio, and Missouri.

In the 1950s, "Engine Charlie" Wilson immortalized himself with the remark, "What's good for America is good for General Motors, and vice versa." What Engine Charlie said was true, when he said it. We see that now as we watch GM closing factories here and opening up abroad. GM's four newest plants are going up in Argentina, Poland, China, and Thailand. "GM's days of building new plants in North America may be over," says the *Wall Street Journal*.

GM used to be the largest employer in the United States; today, it is the largest employer in Mexico where it has built 50 plants in 20 years. In Juarez alone, there are 18 plants of Delphi Automotive, a GM subsidiary. Across from Juarez, El Paso is becoming a glorified truck stop, as Texans watch their manufacturing jobs go south.

Volkswagen has closed its U.S. plant in the Mon Valley and moved production of its new Beetle into Mexico, where it will produce 450,000 vehicles this year. Wages at Volkswagen's plant in Puebla average $1.69 an hour, one-third of the U.S. minimum wage.

Let me make a simple point here. If you remove all trade barriers between a Third World economy like Mexico and a First World country like the United States, First World manufacturers will head south, to the advantage of the lower wages, and the Third World workers will head north, to the advantage of the higher wages. Economics 101.

Since the free-trade era began, 4000 new factories have been built in northern Mexico, and 35 million immigrants, most of them poor, have come into the United States—among them five million illegal aliens, mostly from Mexico. Free trade is not free.

But the free traders respond: Who cares who makes what, where? What's important is that consumers get the best buy at the cheapest price. But this is Grasshopper Economics. Americans are not only consumers; we are producers and citizens. We have obligations to one another and to our country; and one of those obligations is not to behave like wastrel children squandering a family estate built up over generations. A family estate is something you can sell off—only once.

What is the wealth of nations? Is it stocks, bonds, derivatives—the pieces of paper traded on Wall Street that can be gone with in the wind? No, the true wealth of a nation lies in its factories, farms, fisheries, and mines, in the genius and capacities of its people. Industrial power is at the heart of economic power, and economic power is at the heart of strategic power. America won two world wars and the Cold War because our industrial power and technology proved beyond the ability of our enemies to match.

Is this steady attrition of America's independence in sovereignty irreversible? My answer is no. For the balance of power in America has begun to shift. In 1997, on the vote to give the president a blank check to negotiate trade treaties without Congressional amendment—so-called Fast Track authority, it went down to defeat. When Newt [Gingrich] brought up "fast track" this year [1998], it was crushed again, by 63 votes.

A majority of Americans no longer believe these trade deals are good for America, and a majority of the House now agrees with them. The force is with us. Neither NAFTA [North American Free Trade Agreement] nor GATT [General Agreement on Tariffs and Trade] would pass today.

The day is not too distant when economic nationalism will triumph. Several events will hasten that day. The first is the tidal wave of imports from Asia about to hit these shores. When all those manufactured goods pour in, taking down industries and killing jobs, there will arise a clamor from industry and labor for protection. If that cry goes unheeded, those who turn a stone face to the American workers will be turned out of power.

In the Democratic Party or the Republican Party or the Reform Party or some new party, economic nationalism will find its vehicle and its voice. Rely upon it.

It is already happening—with the crisis in the steel industry.

Here is a perfect example of the folly of free trade. Since the mid-1980s, fifty billion dollars was invested in modernization; a steel worker today is three times as productive as his father; and the industry has only a third as many workers as twenty-five years ago.

Yet, Russia, Japan, South Korea, Brazil and Indonesia—four of them being bailed out with our tax dollars—are dumping steel into our market, taking down our steel industry to save their own. Why do we allow subsidized foreign steel to be dumped into the U.S. to destroy the greatest private steel industry on earth?

Well, says the free trader: If we can get it cheaper, let our industry go, just as we let our televisions go, our textiles go, radios go, and the shoe industry go. Besides, these countries need to sell steel here to get the dollars to pay back their IMF loans. Thus, the United Steelworkers of America are being sacrificed—to make the world safe for Goldman Sachs.

There is another reason the free trade era is coming to a close. One day soon, Americans will wake up and discover that other nations do not believe in free trade, and do not practice our particular faith. China and Japan each run $60 billion in annual trade surpluses at America's expense, but each cordons off its own market to U.S. goods.

We must start looking out for America first. As Andrew Jackson once declared: "We have been too long subject to the policy of [foreign] merchants. We need to become more Americanized, and instead of feeding the paupers and laborers of Europe . . . feed our own, or in a short time . . . we shall all be rendered paupers ourselves."

America First, and not only first, but second and third as well.

POSTSCRIPT

Are Protectionist Policies Bad for America?

The desirability of free trade is an issue on which a large majority of professional economists agree. Survey after survey confirms this. Although economists are ardent supporters of free trade, they must grapple with the reality that the world that Ricardo modeled in 1807 is starkly different from the world we know in this new millennium.

The concern that Ricardo could ignore is the modern ability of capital and technology to cross national boundaries almost at will. This mobility of capital and technology suggests that a country's comparative advantages can radically change in a relatively short period of time. This is a far cry from Ricardo's world. In his world, comparative advantages were stable and predictable. Consider the example that Ricardo used to illustrate comparative advantage: the trade between England and Portugal in cloth and wine. In the nineteenth century, it was highly unlikely that agrarian Portugal would seriously challenge the manufacturing base of England and equally unlikely that dreary English weather would ever produce a wine to compete with the vineyards of sun-drenched Portugal. This kind of trade stability is rarely found in the modern world. Examples abound of comparative advantages won or lost overnight, as dollars and technology chase one another around the globe. Japan provides an interesting case study. Consider how quickly this country moved from dominance among Pacific Rim countries to fighting for its economic life as Korea, Malaysia, and their other Asian neighbors stole market after market from them.

The bottom line is clear. Comparative advantage does lead to economic efficiency, but, as with any market adjustment, there can be serious dislocations as less efficient producers must make way for more efficient producers. In the modern world this occurs quickly and sometimes quite unexpectedly. This does not mean that there is a shortage of advocates of free trade. Conservative "think tanks" provide ample support for Rothbard's position. For example, see the Reason Foundation, which sponsors *Reason Online* (`http://reason.com`). On October 25, 1999, it posted an article entitled "Buchanomics Rebuked," which is a frontal attack on Buchanan. To place the free trade argument in its historic context, see John V. C. Nye's essay "The Myth of Free-Trade Britain," The Library of Economics and Liberty, `http://www.econlib.org/library/Columns/y2003/Nyefreetrade.html` (March 3, 2003).

For more on Buchanan's position, see his book *The Great Betrayal: How American Sovereignty and Social Justice Are Being Sacrificed to the Gods of the Global Economy* (Little, Brown, 1998). Also read John Gray's *False Dawn: The Delusions of Global Capitalism* (New Press, 1999).

ISSUE 14

Should We Sweat About Sweatshops?

YES: Richard Appelbaum and Peter Dreier, from "The Campus Anti-Sweatshop Movement," *The American Prospect* (September–October 1999)

NO: Nicholas D. Kristof and Sheryl WuDunn, from "Two Cheers for Sweatshops," *The New York Times Magazine* (September 24, 2000)

ISSUE SUMMARY

YES: Sociologist Richard Appelbaum and political scientist Peter Dreier chronicle the rise of student activism on American campuses over the issue of sweatshops abroad. Students demand that firms be held responsible for "sweatshop conditions" and warn that if conditions do not improve, American consumers will not "leave their consciences at home when they shop for clothes."

NO: News correspondents Nicholas D. Kristof and Sheryl WuDunn agree that the working conditions in many offshore plant sites "seem brutal from the vantage point of an American sitting in his living room." But they argue that these work opportunities are far superior to the alternatives that are currently available in many parts of the world and that what is needed are more sweatshops, not fewer sweatshops.

The sleeping giant of student activism awoke in the late 1990s. This giant slumbered for nearly three decades. It was last heard from in the late 1960s and the early 1970s, when students on college campuses across the United States caused so much disruption that public awareness of the war in Vietnam slowly but surely came into focus. Prior to the antiwar activism, students were at the forefront of the civil rights movement. As in the case of the antiwar activists, the civil rights activists rebelled. They confronted their parents and grandparents but with less violent, less confrontational means than the antiwar activists.

Many argue that in both of these cases public policy might have eventually changed, but if it did change it would have taken much longer for that change to occur. In essence, these social historians maintain that without the idealism of college-aged students, society has a tendency to become inflexible and rigid. It is slower to change and more likely to assume that what exists today should always exist. The lack of student activism and the resulting return to more traditional values was the pattern throughout the late 1970s, the 1980s, and most of the 1990s. That peaceful atmosphere was shattered in the late 1990s.

It all began rather quietly on a talk show cohosted by Kathie Lee Gifford. In 1996 Charles Kernaghan, who is executive director of the National Labor Committee for Worker and Human Rights, charged that the Walmart apparel that bears Gifford's name was produced in offshore sweatshops that employed child labor. On air she roundly denied that charge. Kernaghan persisted. The media eventually covered the charges and the countercharges, and the more the story was denied, the more the media investigated. Kernaghan's allegations turned out to be true. Because of Gifford's high profile and the extensive coverage that this story received, college students soon learned of the widespread use of sweatshops to produce a wide range of items that they habitually wore.

Students were outraged; they wanted action immediately. Just as many of their uncles, aunts, fathers, and mothers had done 30 years earlier, the students staged sit-ins. University presidents could not duck the issue by simply assigning the problem to a study committee. Student activism had returned to college campuses. If university administrators did not want the situation to erupt into the widespread disruption and possible violence that marked the antiwar period, they had to act.

But how could these colleges and universities respond? More important, *should* they respond? They do not purchase their T-shirts and football jerseys directly from factories in China or Brazil; rather, they license firms who request the use of that university's logo to be sewn onto football jerseys or printed on T-shirts. Should colleges and universities require their licensees to guarantee that neither they nor their subcontractors will produce any items bearing the university's logo under sweatshop conditions? Is this wise? College T-shirts and football jerseys are cheap because they are produced in low-wage countries. If the same items were produced in the United States or another high-wage country, their prices would be substantially higher. Should universities deny their students the chance to buy these items at a low cost? If the answer is yes, what happens to the workers in El Salvador and other poor countries who will lose their jobs if the sweatshops are closed down? Is that what student activists want?

These and other questions are raised in the following selections. Richard Appelbaum and Peter Dreier detail the horrors of working in the sweatshops that allow Americans to pay less for their apparel and the student activism that has brought this issue to the attention of the public. Nicholas D. Kristof and Sheryl WuDunn argue that workers in sweatshops do not want to see them closed because they offer the best jobs many workers in poor countries have ever had.

Richard Appelbaum and
Peter Dreier

The Campus Anti-Sweatshop Movement

If University of Arizona activist Arne Ekstrom was aware of today's widely reported student apathy, he certainly was not deterred when he helped lead his campus anti-sweatshop sit-in. Nor, for that matter, were any of the other thousands of students across the United States who participated in anti-sweatshop activities during the past academic year, coordinating their activities on the United Students Against Sweatshops (USAS) listserv (a listserv is an online mailing list for the purpose of group discussion) and Web site.

Last year's student anti-sweatshop movement gained momentum as it swept westward, eventually encompassing more than 100 campuses across the country. Sparked by a sit-in at Duke University, students organized teach-ins, led demonstrations, and occupied buildings—first at Georgetown, then northeast to the Ivy League, then west to the Big Ten. After militant actions at Notre Dame, Wisconsin, and Michigan made the *New York Times, Business Week, Time,* National Public Radio, and almost every major daily newspaper, the growing student movement reached California, where schools from tiny Occidental College to the giant ten-campus University of California system agreed to limit the use of their names and logos to sweatshop-free apparel. Now the practical challenge is to devise a regime of monitoring and compliance.

The anti-sweatshop movement is the largest wave of student activism to hit campuses since students rallied to free Nelson Mandela by calling for a halt to university investments in South Africa more than a decade ago. This time around, the movement is electronically connected. Student activists bring their laptops and cell phones with them when they occupy administration buildings, sharing ideas and strategies with fellow activists from Boston to Berkeley. On the USAS listserv, victorious students from Wisconsin counsel neophytes from Arizona and Kentucky, and professors at Berkeley and Harvard explain how to calculate a living wage and guarantee independent monitoring in Honduras.

The target of this renewed activism is the $2.5 billion collegiate licensing industry—led by major companies like Nike, Gear, Champion, and Fruit of the Loom—which pays colleges and universities sizable royalties in exchange for the right to use the campus logo on caps, sweatshirts, jackets, and other items. Students are demanding that the workers who make these goods be paid a living wage, no matter where in the world industry operates. Students are also calling for an end to discrimination against women workers, public disclosure of the names and addresses of all factories involved in production, and independent monitoring in order to verify compliance.

These demands are opposed by the apparel industry, the White House, and most universities. Yet so far students have made significant progress in putting the industry on the defensive. A growing number of colleges and clothing companies have adopted "codes of conduct"—something unthinkable a decade ago—although student activists consider many of these standards inadequate.

In a world economy increasingly dominated by giant retailers and manufacturers who control global networks of independently owned factories, organizing consumers may prove to be a precondition for organizing production workers. And students are a potent group of consumers. If students next year succeed in building on this year's momentum, the collegiate licensing industry will be forced to change the way it does business. These changes, in turn, could affect the organization of the world's most globalized and exploitative industry—apparel manufacturing—along with the growing number of industries that, like apparel, outsource production in order to lower labor costs and blunt worker organizing.

The Global Sweatshop

In the apparel industry, so-called manufacturers—in reality, design and marketing firms—outsource the fabrication of clothing to independent contractors around the world. In this labor-intensive industry where capital requirements are minimal, it is relatively easy to open a clothing factory. This has contributed to a global race to the bottom, in which there is always someplace, somewhere, where clothing can be made still more cheaply. Low wages reflect not low productivity, but low bargaining power. A recent analysis in *Business Week* found that although Mexican apparel workers are 70 percent as productive as U.S. workers, they earn only 11 percent as much as their U.S. counterparts; Indonesian workers, who are 50 percent as productive, earn less than 2 percent as much.

The explosion of imports has proven devastating to once well-paid, unionized U.S. garment workers. The number of American garment workers has declined from peak levels of 1.4 million in the early 1970s to 800,000 today. The one exception to these trends is the expansion of garment employment, largely among immigrant and undocumented workers, in Los Angeles, which has more than 160,000 sweatshop workers. Recent U.S. Department of Labor surveys found that more than nine out of ten such firms violate legal health and safety standards, with more than half troubled by serious violations that could lead to severe injuries or death. Working conditions in New York City, the other major domestic garment center, are similar.

The very word "sweatshop" comes from the apparel industry, where profits were "sweated" out of workers by forcing them to work longer and faster at their sewing machines. Although significant advances have been made in such aspects of production as computer-assisted design, computerized marking, and computerized cutting, the industry still remains low-tech in its core production process, the sewing of garments. The basic unit of production continues to be a worker, usually a woman, sitting or standing at a sewing machine and sewing together pieces of limp cloth.

The structure of the garment industry fosters sweatshop production. During the past decade, retailing in the United States has become increasingly concentrated. Today, the four largest U.S. retailers—Wal-Mart, Kmart, Sears, and Dayton Hudson (owner of Target and Mervyns)—account for nearly two-thirds of U.S. retail sales. Retailers squeeze manufacturers, who in turn squeeze the contractors who actually make their products. Retailers and manufacturers preserve the fiction of being completely separate from contractors because they do not want to be held legally responsible for workplace violations of labor, health, and safety laws. Retailers and manufacturers alike insist that what happens in contractor factories is not their responsibility—even though their production managers and quality control officers are constantly checking up on the sewing shops that make their clothing.

The contracting system also allows retailers and manufacturers to eliminate much uncertainty and risk. When business is slow, the contract is simply not renewed; manufacturers need not worry about paying unemployment benefits or dealing with idle workers who might go on strike or otherwise make trouble. If a particular contractor becomes a problem, there are countless others to be found who will be only too happy to get their business. Workers, however, experience the flip side of the enormous flexibility enjoyed by retailers and manufacturers. They become contingent labor, employed and paid only when their work is needed.

Since profits are taken out at each level of the supply chain, labor costs are reduced to a tiny fraction of the retail price. Consider the economics of a dress that is sewn in Los Angeles and retails for $100. Half goes to the department store and half to the manufacturer, who keeps $12.50 to cover expenses and profit, spends $22.50 on textiles, and pays $15 to the contractor. The contractor keeps $9 to cover expenses and profits. That leaves just $6 of the $100 retail price for the workers who actually make the dress. Even if the cost of direct production labor were to increase by half, the dress would still only cost $103—a small increment that would make a world of difference to the seamstress in Los Angeles, whose $7,000 to $8,000 in annual wages are roughly two-thirds of the poverty level. A garment worker in Mexico would be lucky to earn $1,000 during a year of 48 to 60 hour workweeks; in China, $500.

At the other end of the apparel production chain, the heads of the 60 publicly traded U.S. apparel retailers earn an average $1.5 million a year. The heads of the 35 publicly traded apparel manufacturers average $2 million. In 1997, according to the *Los Angeles Business Journal,* five of the six highest-paid apparel executives in Los Angeles all came from a single firm: Guess?, Inc. They took home nearly $12.6 million—enough to double the yearly wages of 1,700 L.A. apparel workers.

Organizing workers at the point of production, the century-old strategy that built the power of labor in Europe and North America, is best suited to production processes where most of the work goes on in-house. In industries whose production can easily be shifted almost anywhere on the planet, organizing is extremely difficult. Someday, perhaps, a truly international labor movement will confront global manufacturers. But in the meantime, organized consumers may well be labor's best ally. Consumers, after all, are not as readily moved as factories. And among American consumers, college students represent an especially potent force.

Kathie Lee and Robert Reich

During the early 1990s, American human rights and labor groups protested the proliferation of sweatshops at home and abroad—with major campaigns focusing on Nike and Gap. These efforts largely fizzled. But then two exposés of sweatshop conditions captured public attention. In August 1995, state and federal officials raided a garment factory in El Monte, California a Los Angeles suburb—where 71 Thai immigrants had been held for several years in virtual slavery in an apartment complex ringed with barbed wire and spiked fences. They worked an average of 84 hours a week for $1.60 an hour, living eight to ten persons in a room. The garments they sewed ended up in major retail chains, including Macy's, Filene's and Robinsons-May, and for brand-name labels like B.U.M., Tomato, and High Sierra. Major daily papers and TV networks picked up on the story, leading to a flood of outraged editorials and columns calling for a clamp-down on domestic sweatshops. Then in April 1996, TV celebrity Kathie Lee Gifford tearfully acknowledged on national television that the Wal-Mart line of clothing that bore her name was made by children in Honduran sweatshops, even though tags on the garments promised that part of the profits would go to help children. Embarrassed by the publicity, Gifford soon became a crusader against sweatshop abuses.

For several years, then—Labor Secretary Robert Reich (now the *Prospect*'s senior editor) had been trying to inject the sweatshop issue onto the nation's agenda. The mounting publicity surrounding the El Monte and Kathie Lee scandals gave Reich new leverage. After all, what the apparel industry primarily sells is image, and the image of some of its major labels was getting a drubbing. He began pressing apparel executives, threatening to issue a report card on firms' behavior unless they agreed to help establish industry-wide standards.

In August 1996, the Clinton administration brought together representatives from the garment industry, labor unions, and consumer and human rights groups to grapple with sweatshops. The members of what they called the White House Apparel Industry Partnership (AIP) included apparel firms (Liz Claiborne, Reebok, L.L. Bean, Nike, Patagonia, Phillips-Van Heusen, Wal-Mart's Kathie Lee Gifford brand, and Nicole Miller), several nonprofit organizations (including the National Consumers League, Interfaith Center on Corporate Responsibility, International Labor Rights Fund, Lawyers Committee for Human Rights, Robert F. Kennedy Memorial Center for Human Rights, and Business for Social Responsibility), as well as the Union of Needletrades, Industrial and Textile Employees (UNITE), the Retail, Wholesale, and Department Store Union, and the AFL-CIO.

After intense negotiations, the Department of Labor issued an interim AIP report in April 1997 and the White House released the final 40-page report in November 1998, which included a proposed workplace code of conduct and a set of monitoring guidelines. By then, Reich had left the Clinton administration, replaced by Alexis Herman. The two labor representatives on the AIP, as well as the Interfaith Center on Corporate Responsibility, quit the group to protest the feeble recommendations, which had been crafted primarily by the garment industry delegates and which called, essentially, for the industry to police itself. This maneuvering would not have generated much attention except that a new factor—college activism—had been added to the equation.

A "Sweat-Free" Campus

The campus movement began in the fall of 1997 at Duke when a group called Students Against Sweatshops persuaded the university to require manufacturers of items with the Duke label to sign a pledge that they would not use sweatshop labor. Duke has 700 licensees (including Nike and other major labels) that make apparel at hundreds of plants in the U.S. and in more than 10 other countries, generating almost $25 million annually in sales. Following months of negotiations, in March 1998 Duke President Nannerl Keohane and the student activists jointly announced a detailed "code of conduct" that bars Duke licensees from using child labor, requires them to maintain safe workplaces, to pay the minimum wage, to recognize the right of workers to unionize, to disclose the locations of all factories making products with Duke's name, and to allow visits by independent monitors to inspect the factories.

The Duke victory quickly inspired students on other campuses. The level of activity on campuses accelerated, with students finding creative ways to dramatize the issue. At Yale, student activists staged a "knit-in" to draw attention to sweatshop abuses. At Holy Cross and the University of California at Santa Barbara, students sponsored mock fashion shows where they discussed the working conditions under which the garments were manufactured. Duke students published a coloring book explaining how (and where) the campus mascot, the Blue Devil, is stitched onto clothing by workers in sweatshops. Activists at the University of Wisconsin infiltrated a homecoming parade and, dressed like sweatshop workers in Indonesia, carried a giant Reebok shoe. They also held a press conference in front of the chancellor's office and presented him with an oversized check for 16 cents—the hourly wage paid to workers in China making Nike athletic shoes. At Georgetown, Wisconsin, Michigan, Arizona, and Duke, students occupied administration buildings to pressure their institutions to adopt (or, in Duke's case, strengthen) anti-sweatshop codes.

In the summer of 1998, disparate campus groups formed United Students Against Sweatshops (USAS). The USAS has weekly conference calls to discuss their negotiations with Nike, the Department of Labor, and others. It has sponsored training sessions for student leaders and conferences at several campuses where the sweatshop issue is only part of an agenda that also includes helping to build the labor movement, NAFTA, the World Trade Organization, women's rights, and other issues.

Last year, anti-sweatshop activists employed the USAS listserv to exchange ideas on negotiating tactics, discuss media strategies, swap songs to sing during rallies, and debate the technicalities of defining a "living wage" to incorporate in their campus codes of conduct. In May, the USAS listserv heated up after the popular Fox television series *Party of Five* included a scene in which one of the show's characters, Sarah (played by Jennifer Love Hewitt), helps organize a Students Against Sweatshops sit-in on her campus. A few real life activists worried that the mainstream media was trivializing the movement by skirting the key issues ("the importance of unionized labor, the globalization of the economy, etc.") as well as focusing most of that episode on the characters' love life. University of Michigan student Rachel Paster responded:

> Let's not forget that we ARE a student movement, and students do complain about boyfriends and fashion problems. One of the biggest reasons why USAS and local student groups opposing sweatshops have been as successful as we have been is that opposition to sweatshops ISN'T that radical. Although I'm sure lots of us are all for overthrowing the corporate power structure, the human rights issues involved are what make a lot of people get involved and put their energies into rallies, sit-ins, et cetera. If we were a 'radical' group, university administrations would have brushed us off. . . . The fact that they don't is testament to the fact that we have support, not just from students on the far left, but from students in the middle ground who don't consider themselves radicals. Without those people we would NEVER have gotten as far as we have.

Indeed, the anti-sweatshop movement has been able to mobilize wide support because it strikes several nerves among today's college students, including women's rights (most sweatshop workers are women and some factories have required women to use birth control pills as a condition of employment), immigrant rights, environmental concerns, and human rights. After University of Wisconsin administrators brushed aside anti-sweatshop protestors, claiming they didn't represent student opinion, the activists ran a slate of candidates for student government. Eric Brakken, a sociology major and anti-sweatshop leader, was elected student body president and last year used the organization's substantial resources to promote the activists' agenda. And Duke's student government unanimously passed a resolution supporting the anti-sweatshop group, calling for full public disclosure of the locations of companies that manufacture Duke clothing.

The Labor Connection

At the core of the movement is a strong bond with organized labor. The movement is an important by-product of the labor movement's recent efforts, under President John Sweeney, to repair the rift between students and unions that dates to the Vietnam War. Since 1996, the AFL-CIO's Union Summer has placed almost 2,000 college students in internships with local unions around the country, most of whom work on grassroots organizing campaigns with low-wage workers in hotels, agriculture, food processing, janitorial service, and other industries. The program has its own staff, mostly young organizers only a few years out of college themselves, who actively recruit on campuses, looking for the next generation of union organizers and researchers, particularly minorities, immigrants, and women. Union Summer graduates are among the key leadership of the campus anti-sweatshop movement.

UNITE has one full-time staff person assigned to work on sweatshop issues, which includes helping student groups. A number of small human rights watchdog organizations that operate on shoestring budgets—Global Exchange, Sweatshop Watch, and the National Labor Committee [NLC]—give student activists technical advice. (It was NLC's Charles Kernaghan, an energetic researcher and publicist, who exposed the Kathie Lee Gifford connection to sweatshops in testimony before Congress.) These groups have helped bring sweatshop workers on speaking tours of American campuses, and have organized delegations of student activists to investigate firsthand the conditions in Honduras, Guatemala, El Salvador, Mexico, and elsewhere under which workers produce their college's clothing.

Unions and several liberal foundations have provided modest funding for student anti-sweatshop groups. Until this summer USAS had no staff, nor did any of its local campus affiliates. In contrast, corporate-sponsored conservative foundations have, over the past two decades, funded dozens of conservative student publications, subsidized student organizations and conferences, and recruited conservative students for internships and jobs in right-wing think tanks and publications as well as positions in the Reagan and Bush administrations and Congress, seeking to groom the next generation of conservative activists. The Intercollegiate Studies Institute, the leading right-wing campus umbrella group, has an annual budget over $5 million. In comparison, the Center for Campus Organizing, a Boston-based group that works closely with anti-sweatshop groups and other progressive campus organizations, operates on a budget under $200,000.

This student movement even has some sympathizers among university administrators. "Thank God students are getting passionate about something other than basketball and bonfires," John Burness, a Duke administrator who helped negotiate the end of the 31-hour sit-in, told the *Boston Globe.* "But the tone is definitely different. In the old days, we used to have to scramble to cut off phone lines when they took over the president's office, but we didn't have to worry about that here. They just bring their laptops and they do work."

At every university where students organized a sit-in (Duke, Georgetown, Arizona, Michigan, and Wisconsin) they have wrested agreements to require licensees to disclose the specific location of their factory sites, which is necessary for independent monitoring. Students elsewhere (including Harvard, Illinois, Brown, the University of California, Princeton, Middlebury, and Occidental) won a public disclosure requirement without resorting to civil disobedience. A few institutions have agreed to require manufacturers to pay their employees a "living wage." Wisconsin agreed to organize an academic conference this fall to discuss how to calculate living-wage formulas for countries with widely disparate costs of living, and then to implement its own policy recommendations. [See Richard Rothstein, "The Global Hiring Hall: Why We Need Worldwide Labor Standards," *TAP,* Spring 1994.]

The Industry's New Clothes

Last November, the White House-initiated Apparel Industry Partnership created a monitoring arm, the Fair Labor Association (FLA), and a few months later invited universities to join. Colleges, however, have just one seat on FLA's 14-member board. Under the group's bylaws the garment firms control the board's decisionmaking. The bylaws require a "supermajority" to approve all key questions, thus any three companies can veto a proposal they don't like.

At this writing, FLA member companies agree to ban child and prison labor, to prohibit physical abuse by supervisors, and to allow workers the freedom to organize unions in their foreign factories, though independent enforcement has not yet been specified. FLA wants to assign this monitoring task to corporate accounting firms like PricewaterhouseCoopers and Ernst & Young, to allow companies to select which facilities will be inspected, and to keep factory locations and the monitoring reports secret. Student activists want human rights and labor groups to do the monitoring.

This is only a bare beginning, but it establishes the crucial moral precedent of companies taking responsibility for labor conditions beyond their shores. Seeing this foot in the door, several companies have bowed out because they consider these standards too tough. The FLA expects that by 2001, after its monitoring program has been in place for a year, participating firms will be able to use the FLA logo on their labels and advertising as evidence of their ethical corporate practices. [See Richard Rothstein, "The Starbucks Solution: Can Voluntary Codes Raise Global Living Standards?" *TAP,* July-August 1996.]

The original list of 17 FLA-affiliated universities grew to more than 100 by mid-summer of this year. And yet, some campus groups have dissuaded college administrations (including the Universities of Michigan, Minnesota, Oregon, Toronto, and California, as well as Oberlin, Bucknell, and Earlham

Colleges) from joining FLA, while others have persuaded their institutions (including Brown, Wisconsin, North Carolina, and Georgetown) to join only if the FLA adopts stronger standards. While FLA members are supposed to abide by each country's minimum-wage standards, these are typically far below the poverty level. In fact, no company has made a commitment to pay a living wage.

The campus movement has succeeded in raising awareness (both on campus and among the general public) about sweatshops as well as the global economy. It has contributed to industry acceptance of extraterritorial labor standards, something hitherto considered utopian. It has also given thousands of students experience in the nuts and bolts of social activism, many of whom are likely to carry their idealism and organizing experiences with them into jobs with unions, community and environmental groups, and other public interest crusades.

So far, however, the movement has had only minimal impact on the daily lives of sweatshop workers at home and abroad. Nike and Reebok, largely because of student protests, have raised wages and benefits in their Indonesian footwear factories—which employ more than 100,000 workers—to 43 percent above the minimum wage. But this translates to only 20 cents an hour in U.S. dollars, far below a "living wage" to raise a family and even below the 27 cents Nike paid before Indonesia's currency devaluation. Last spring Nike announced its willingness to disclose the location of its overseas plants that produce clothing for universities. This created an important split in industry ranks, since industry leaders have argued that disclosure would undermine each firm's competitive position. But Nike has opened itself up to the charge of having a double standard, since it still refuses to disclose the location of its non-university production sites.

Within a year, when FLA's monitoring system is fully operational, students at several large schools with major licensing contracts—including Duke, Wisconsin, Michigan, North Carolina, and Georgetown—will have lists of factories in the U.S. and overseas that produce university clothing and equipment. This information will be very useful to civic and labor organizations at home and abroad, providing more opportunities to expose working conditions. Student activists at each university will be able to visit these sites—bringing media and public officials with them—to expose working conditions (and, if necessary, challenge the findings of the FLA's own monitors) and support organizing efforts by local unions and women's groups.

If the student activists can help force a small but visible "ethical" niche of the apparel industry to adopt higher standards, it will divide the industry and give unions and consumer groups more leverage to challenge the sweatshop practices of the rest of the industry. The campus anti-sweatshop crusade is part of what might be called a "conscience constituency" among consumers who are willing to incorporate ethical principles into their buying habits, even if it means slightly higher prices. Environmentalists have done the same thing with the "buy green" campaign, as have various "socially responsible" investment firms.

Beyond Consumer Awareness

In a global production system characterized by powerful retailers and invisible contractors, consumer action has an important role to play. But ultimately it must be combined with worker organizing and legislative and regulatory remedies. Unionizing the global apparel industry is an organizer's nightmare. With globalization and the contracting system, any apparel factory with a union risks losing its business.

Domestically, UNITE represents fewer than 300,000 textile and garment industry workers, down from the 800,000 represented by its two predecessor unions in the late 1960s. In the low-income countries where most U.S. apparel is now made, the prospects for unionization are dimmer still. In Mexico, labor unions are controlled by the government. China outlaws independent unions, punishing organizers with prison terms. Building the capacity for unfettered union organizing must necessarily be a long-term strategy for union organizers throughout the world. Here, the student anti-sweatshop movement can help. The independent verification of anti-sweatshop standards that students want can also serve the goal of union organizing.

Public policy could also help. As part of our trade policy, Congress could require public disclosure of manufacturing sites and independent monitoring of firms that sell goods in the American market. It could enact legislation that requires U.S. companies to follow U.S. health and safety standards globally and to bar the import of clothing made in sweatshops or made by workers who are denied the basic right to organize unions. In addition, legislation sponsored by Representative William Clay could make retailers and manufacturers legally liable for the working conditions behind the goods they design and sell, thereby ending the fiction that contractors are completely independent of the manufacturers and retailers that hire them. Last spring the California Assembly passed a state version of this legislation. Student and union activists hope that the Democrat-controlled state senate and Democratic Governor Gray Davis—whose lopsided victory last November was largely attributed to organized labor's get-out-the-vote effort—will support the bill.

Thanks to the student movement, public opinion may be changing. And last spring, speaking both to the International Labor Organization in Geneva and at the commencement ceremonies at the University of Chicago (an institution founded by John D. Rockefeller and a stronghold of free market economics, but also a center of student anti-sweatshop activism), President Clinton called for an international campaign against child labor, including restrictions on government purchases of goods made by children.

A shift of much apparel production to developing countries may well be inevitable in a global economy. But when companies do move their production abroad, student activists are warning "you can run but you can't hide," demanding that they be held responsible for conditions in contractor factories no matter where they are. Students can't accomplish this on their own, but in a very short period of time they have made many Americans aware that they don't have to leave their consciences at home when they shop for clothes.

NO 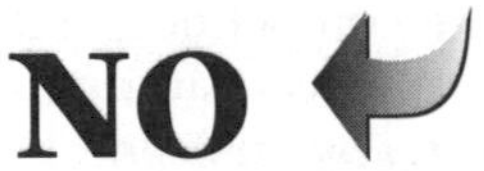

Nicholas D. Kristof and Sheryl WuDunn

Two Cheers for Sweatshops

It was breakfast time, and the food stand in the village in northeastern Thailand was crowded. Maesubin Sisoipha, the middle-aged woman cooking the food, was friendly, her portions large and the price right. For the equivalent of about 5 cents, she offered a huge green mango leaf filled with rice, fish paste and fried beetles. It was a hearty breakfast, if one didn't mind the odd antenna left sticking in one's teeth.

One of the half-dozen men and women sitting on a bench eating was a sinewy, bare-chested laborer in his late 30's named Mongkol Latlakorn. It was a hot, lazy day, and so we started chatting idly about the food and, eventually, our families. Mongkol mentioned that his daughter, Darin, was 15, and his voice softened as he spoke of her. She was beautiful and smart, and her father's hopes rested on her.

"Is she in school?" we asked.

"Oh, no," Mongkol said, his eyes sparkling with amusement. "She's working in a factory in Bangkok. She's making clothing for export to America." He explained that she was paid $2 a day for a nine-hour shift, six days a week.

"It's dangerous work," Mongkol added. "Twice the needles went right through her hands. But the managers bandaged up her hands, and both times she got better again and went back to work."

"How terrible," we murmured sympathetically.

Mongkol looked up, puzzled. "It's good pay," he said. "I hope she can keep that job. There's all this talk about factories closing now, and she said there are rumors that her factory might close. I hope that doesn't happen. I don't know what she would do then."

He was not, of course, indifferent to his daughter's suffering; he simply had a different perspective from ours—not only when it came to food but also when it came to what constituted desirable work.

Nothing captures the difference in mind-set between East and West more than attitudes toward sweatshops. Nike and other American companies have been hammered in the Western press over the last decade for producing shoes, toys and other products in grim little factories with dismal conditions. Protests against sweatshops and the dark forces of globalization that they seem to represent have become common at meetings of the World Bank and the World Trade Organization and, this month, at a World Economic Forum in Australia, livening up the scene for Olympic athletes arriving for the competition. Yet sweatshops that seem brutal from the vantage point of an American sitting in his living room can appear tantalizing to a Thai laborer getting by on beetles.

Fourteen years ago, we moved to Asia and began reporting there. Like most Westerners, we arrived in the region outraged at sweatshops. In time, though, we came to accept the view supported by most Asians: that the campaign against sweatshops risks harming the very people it is intended to help. For beneath their grime, sweatshops are a clear sign of the industrial revolution that is beginning to reshape Asia.

This is not to praise sweatshops. Some managers are brutal in the way they house workers in firetraps, expose children to dangerous chemicals, deny bathroom breaks, demand sexual favors, force people to work double shifts or dismiss anyone who tries to organize a union. Agitation for improved safety conditions can be helpful, just as it was in 19th-century Europe. But Asian workers would be aghast at the idea of American consumers boycotting certain toys or clothing in protest. The simplest way to help the poorest Asians would be to buy more from sweatshops, not less.

On our first extended trip to China, in 1987, we traveled to the Pearl River delta in the south of the country. There we visited several factories, including one in the boomtown of Dongguan, where about 100 female workers sat at workbenches stitching together bits of leather to make purses for a Hong Kong company. We chatted with several women as their fingers flew over their work and asked about their hours.

"I start at about 6:30, after breakfast, and go until about 7 p.m.," explained one shy teenage girl. "We break for lunch, and I take half an hour off then."

"You do this six days a week?"

"Oh, no. Every day."

"Seven days a week?"

"Yes." She laughed at our surprise. "But then I take a week or two off at Chinese New Year to go back to my village."

The others we talked to all seemed to regard it as a plus that the factory allowed them to work long hours. Indeed, some had sought out this factory precisely because it offered them the chance to earn more.

"It's actually pretty annoying how hard they want to work," said the factory manager, a Hong Kong man. "It means we have to worry about security and have a supervisor around almost constantly."

It sounded pretty dreadful, and it was. We and other journalists wrote about the problems of child labor and oppressive conditions in both China and South Korea. But, looking back, our worries were excessive. Those sweatshops tended to generate the wealth to solve the problems they created. If Americans had reacted to the horror stories in the 1980's by curbing imports of those sweatshop products, then neither southern China nor South Korea would have registered as much progress as they have today.

The truth is, those grim factories in Dongguan and the rest of southern China contributed to a remarkable explosion of wealth. In the years since our first conversations there, we've returned many times to Dongguan and the surrounding towns and seen the transformation. Wages have risen from about $50 a month to $250 a month or more today. Factory conditions have improved as businesses have scrambled to attract and keep the best laborers. A private housing market has emerged, and video arcades and computer schools have opened to cater to workers with rising incomes. A hint of a middle class has appeared—as has China's closest thing to a Western-style independent newspaper, Southern Weekend.

Partly because of these tens of thousands of sweatshops, China's economy has become one of the hottest in the world. Indeed, if China's 30 provinces were counted as individual countries, then the 20 fastest-growing countries in the world between 1978 and 1995 would all have been Chinese. When Britain launched the Industrial Revolution in the late 18th century, it took 58 years for per capita output to double. In China, per capita output has been doubling every 10 years.

In fact, the most vibrant parts of Asia are nearly all in what might be called the Sweatshop Belt, from China and South Korea to Malaysia, Indonesia and even Bangladesh and India. Today these sweatshop countries control about one-quarter of the global economy. As the industrial revolution spreads through China and India, there are good reasons to think that Asia will continue to pick up speed. Some World Bank forecasts show Asia's share of global gross domestic product rising to 55 to 60 percent by about 2025—roughly the West's share at its peak half a century ago. The sweatshops have helped lay the groundwork for a historic economic realignment that is putting Asia back on its feet. Countries are rebounding from the economic crisis of 1997–98 and the sweatshops—seen by Westerners as evidence of moribund economies—actually reflect an industrial revolution that is raising living standards in the East.

Of course, it may sound silly to say that sweatshops offer a route to prosperity, when wages in the poorest countries are sometimes less than $1 a day. Still, for an impoverished Indonesian or Bangladeshi woman with a handful of kids who would otherwise drop out of school and risk dying of mundane diseases like diarrhea, $1 or $2 a day can be a life-transforming wage.

This was made abundantly clear in Cambodia, when we met a 40-year-old woman named Nhem Yen, who told us why she moved to an area with particularly lethal malaria. "We needed to eat," she said. "And here there is wood, so we thought we could cut it and sell it."

But then Nhem Yen's daughter and son-in-law both died of malaria, leaving her with two grandchildren and five children of her own. With just one mosquito net, she had to choose which children would sleep protected and which would sleep exposed.

In Cambodia, a large mosquito net costs $5. If there had been a sweatshop in the area, however harsh or dangerous, Nhem Yen would have leapt at the chance to work in it, to earn enough to buy a net big enough to cover all her children.

For all the misery they can engender, sweatshops at least offer a precarious escape from the poverty that is the developing world's greatest problem. Over the past 50 years, countries like India resisted foreign exploitation, while countries that started at a similar economic level—like Taiwan and South Korea—accepted sweatshops as the price of development. Today there can be no doubt about which approach worked better. Taiwan and South Korea are modern countries with low rates of infant mortality and high levels of education; in contrast, every year 3.1 million Indian children die before the age of 5, mostly from diseases of poverty like diarrhea.

The effect of American pressure on sweatshops is complicated. While it clearly improves conditions at factories that produce branded merchandise for companies like Nike, it also raises labor costs across the board. That encourages less well established companies to mechanize and to reduce the number of employees needed. The upshot is to help people who currently have jobs in Nike plants but to risk jobs for others. The only thing a country like Cambodia has to offer is terribly cheap wages; if companies are scolded for paying those wages, they will shift their manufacturing to marginally richer areas like Malaysia or Mexico.

Sweatshop monitors do have a useful role. They can compel factories to improve safety. They can also call attention to the impact of sweatshops on the environment. The greatest downside of industrialization is not exploitation of workers but toxic air and water. In Asia each year, three million people die from the effects of pollution. The factories springing up throughout the region are far more likely to kill people through the chemicals they expel than through terrible working conditions.

By focusing on these issues, by working closely with organizations and news media in foreign countries, sweatshops can be improved. But refusing to buy sweatshop products risks making Americans feel good while harming those we are trying to help. As a Chinese proverb goes, "First comes the bitterness, then there is sweetness and wealth and honor for 10,000 years."

POSTSCRIPT

Should We Sweat About Sweatshops?

Economists have not remained mute as this debate has raged across college campuses. In a letter circulated across American campuses in September 2000, 90 academics, mostly economists, urged college and university presidents not to yield to student pressure demanding the adoption of strict codes of conduct for the manufacturers of university apparel that is produced in poor countries. There were many distinguished signers, including Nobel Laureate Robert Lucas, several former presidents of the American Economic Association, several former presidents of the Econometric Society, and Paul McCracken, former chairman of the President's Council of Economic Advisers. These market-oriented economists warned against codes of conduct that required offshore plants to pay wages that are above the prevailing wage rates. They asserted that these higher wages might result "in shifts in employment that will worsen the collective welfare of the very workers in poor countries who are supposed to be helped." This group is supported by the Academic Consortium on International Trade (ACIT), an organization of economists and lawyers dedicated to the establishment of free trade on a worldwide basis. Their Web site is at `http://www.spp.umich.edu/rsie/acit/`.

In "White Hats or Don Quixotes? Human Rights Vigilantes in the Global Economy," NBER Working Paper No. W8102 (January 2001), published by the National Bureau of Economic Research, Kimberly Ann Elliott and Richard Freeman examine the pros and cons of codes of conduct for multinationals working in poor countries. They analyze the incentives for corporations to respond to the demand for more equitable treatment of the workforce in these offshore facilities. They conclude that the pressure applied by student activist groups and others who are concerned about sweatshop conditions may be one of those cases "when 'doing good' actually does good." Elliott and Freeman also suggest that a counterpetition to the Academic Consortium on International Trade is being prepared by Robert Pollin of the University of Massachusetts at Amherst and James K. Galbraith of the University of Texas at Austin. As of April 2001 that petition had not appeared.

There is a wealth of antisweatshop literature to examine, much of which is produced by organized labor. The National Labor Committee, for example, provides a wellspring of data on this topic. They can be found on the Internet at `http://www.nlcnet.org`. In addition, there is an article on sweatshop abuses in nearly every issue of *Working USA,* a journal sponsored by organized labor. In addition to various organized labor groups, you might also check out the Global Alliance for Workers and Communities. This is an initiative of the International Youth Foundation in partnership with the

John D. and Catherine T. MacArthur Foundation. Their Web site is http://www.theglobalalliance.org. Other pro–worker rights organizations are the Campaign for Labor Rights, the Clean Clothes Campaign, the Collegiate Living Wage Association, the Ethical Trading Initiative, the Global Exchange, the International Labour Organisation, the International Labor Rights Fund, the Investor Responsibility Research Center, Sweatshop Watch, and the UNITE! Stop Sweatshops Campaign.

On the other side you will have no difficulty finding material to support globalization. Start with the National Retail Federation (NRF), which is the largest retail trade organization in the world. It represents 1.4 million U.S. retail establishments, which employ nearly 1 in every 5 American workers—about 20 million workers in all. See the NRF's Web site at http://www.nrf.com. The ACIT also provides an up-to-date list of articles that support globalization, which often entails acceptance of sweatshop use. Some of these articles are Daniel W. Drezner, "Bottom Feeders," *Foreign Policy* (November/December 2000); Michael Barkey, "Globalization, Social Justice and the Plight of the Poor," Acton Commentary, http://www.acton.org/ppolicy/comment/article.php?id=22 (August 2000); Philip Knight, "A Forum for Improving Globalisation," *Financial Times* (August 1, 2000); Thomas Friedman, "Knight Is Right," *The New York Times* (June 20, 2000); "Assessing Globalization," World Bank Briefing Papers (April 2000); "Globalization: Threat or Opportunity?" IMF Issues Brief (April 12, 2000); and "Trade and Poverty: Is There a Connection?" WTO Special Study No. 5 (March 2000).

ISSUE 15

Are the Costs of Global Warming Too High to Ignore?

YES: Lester R. Brown, from *Eco-Economy: Building an Economy for the Earth* (W. W. Norton, 2001)

NO: Lenny Bernstein, from "Climate Change and Ecosystems," A Report of the George C. Marshall Institute (August 2002)

ISSUE SUMMARY

YES: Lester R. Brown, founder and president of the Earth Policy Institute, describes his vision of an environmentally sustainable economy, which includes food supplies, population growth issues, water availability, climatic changes, and renewable energy.

NO: Lenny Bernstein, head of L. S. Bernstein & Associates, which advises companies and trade associations on political and scientific developments on global environmental issues, acknowledges that ecosystems are sensitive to climate change, but he argues that the change that we have seen repeated again and again over the course of history can lead to benefits for our children and our children's children.

The severe weather that has plagued much of the United States from the late 1980s to the present has offered some memorable events for Americans. National forests have burst into wildfires; electric bills have skyrocketed as air conditioners in homes and businesses have been run at full strength day and night; and local officials have banned car washing and lawn sprinkling to conserve precious water as lakes, streams, and reservoirs have fallen to critically low levels. Citizens and public policymakers alike have increasingly come to believe that the world has entered the long-predicted and much-feared period of global warming, which many associate with the "greenhouse effect."

In the past decade or so, stretching back to the 1992 United Nations Earth Summit in Rio de Janeiro, there have been a series of international agreements or attempted agreements to limit the amount of greenhouse gas emissions. The 1992 summit is worth noting in that regard. That summit produced a landmark treaty that suggested that stabilizing the world environment must be undertaken irrespective of costs. More than 180 countries, including the United States, ratified this treaty. It set the stage for a decade of international negotiations all aimed at rolling back toxic emissions—primarily in the industrialized world—to 1990 levels. In spite of these good intentions, there is little evidence that any measurable success was achieved. This might be attributed to the fact that the U.S. Senate has not ratified the implementing instrument—the 1997 Kyoto Protocol—which failed by a 95–0 vote in July 1997.

The Senate's concerns were that the treaty exempted developing countries and posed serious problems for the U.S. economy at large. Both of these problems can be traced to the fact that the only way to reduce greenhouse gas emissions, which are essentially carbon dioxide gases, would be to stop burning fossil fuels: coal, oil, natural gas, wood, and peat. Eliminating these emissions by taxing them or by imposing regulations comes at a high price. Poor countries cannot afford to do this, and the United States is unwilling to pay the high price. President George W. Bush, for his part, put the final coup de grace to the Kyoto Protocol in March 2001. He rejected the protocol, saying that it was "fatally flawed in fundamental ways." He went on to note that since climate change was a serious concern, he would ask the National Academy of Sciences to review the state of our understanding of global warming and to issue a report. That 2001 report is entitled *Climate Change Science: An Analysis of Some Key Questions* and can be accessed online at `http://www.nap.edu/books/0309075742/html/`.

This report and the debate over the Kyoto Protocol continue to be controversial. Most acknowledge that social and economic development has impacted the concentration levels of greenhouse gases in our atmosphere, but some people do challenge this widely held belief. Whatever the cause of the accumulated greenhouse gases in our atmosphere, what experts do know is that since the beginning of the Industrial Revolution, concentrations of these gases have increased by 30 percent. More worrisome, perhaps, is the fact that each year the world adds another 6 billion tons of carbon dioxide to the atmosphere.

At the crux of this debate are the consequences of the toxic wastes that we are dumping into the air—air that we depend upon for our very existence. No one seems to know for certain just how the environment will respond to these accumulated greenhouse gases. Many contend that in a very short period of time there will be a sharp rise in surface temperatures. If that turns out to be the case, modern civilization and the ecosystem will be in for dire consequences. Others believe that there might be a more gradual and more modest increase in global warming. This increase might be relatively easy to adjust to and perhaps even lead to benefits for the ecosystem and humankind.

In the following selections, Lester R. Brown argues that economic growth is generally incompatible with the environment but that by basing the economy in an ecological framework, environmentally sustainable economic development can be achieved. Lenny Bernstein maintains that human activities will not have a severe impact on ecosystems and that, in fact, ecosystems that adapt appropriately will benefit from human-induced climate change.

YES

Lester R. Brown

The Economy and the Earth

In 1543, Polish astronomer Nicolaus Copernicus published "On the Revolutions of the Celestial Spheres," in which he challenged the view that the Sun revolved around the earth, arguing instead that the earth revolved around the Sun. With his new model of the solar system, he began a wide-ranging debate among scientists, theologians, and others. His alternative to the earlier Ptolemaic model, which had the earth at the center of the universe, led to a revolution in thinking, to a new worldview.

Today we need a similar shift in our worldview, in how we think about the relationship between the earth and the economy. The issue now is not which celestial sphere revolves around the other but whether the environment is part of the economy or the economy is part of the environment. Economists see the environment as a subset of the economy. Ecologists, on the other hand, see the economy as a subset of the environment.

Like Ptolemy's view of the solar system, the economists' view is confusing efforts to understand our modern world. It has created an economy that is out of sync with the ecosystem on which it depends.

Economic theory and economic indicators do not explain how the economy is disrupting and destroying the earth's natural systems. Economic theory does not explain why Arctic Sea ice is melting. It does not explain why grasslands are turning into desert in northwestern China, why coral reefs are dying in the South Pacific, or why the Newfoundland cod fishery collapsed. Nor does it explain why we are in the early stages of the greatest extinction of plants and animals since the dinosaurs disappeared 65 million years ago. Yet economics is essential to measuring the cost to society of these excesses.

Evidence that the economy is in conflict with the earth's natural systems can be seen in the daily news reports of collapsing fisheries, shrinking forests, eroding soils, deteriorating rangelands, expanding deserts, rising carbon dioxide (CO_2) levels, falling water tables, rising temperatures, more destructive storms, melting glaciers, rising sea level, dying coral reefs, and disappearing species. These trends, which mark an increasingly stressed relationship between the economy and the earth's ecosystem, are taking a growing economic toll. At some point, this could overwhelm the worldwide forces of progress, leading to economic decline. The challenge for our generation is to

From Lester R. Brown, *Eco-Economy: Building an Economy for the Earth* (W. W. Norton, 2001), pp. 3–4, 6–23. Notes omitted.

reverse these trends before environmental deterioration leads to long-term economic decline, as it did for so many earlier civilizations.

These increasingly visible trends indicate that if the operation of the subsystem, the economy, is not compatible with the behavior of the larger system—the earth's ecosystem—both will eventually suffer. The larger the economy becomes relative to the ecosystem, and the more it presses against the earth's natural limits, the more destructive this incompatibility will be.

An environmentally sustainable economy—an eco-economy—requires that the principles of ecology establish the framework for the formulation of economic policy and that economists and ecologists work together to fashion the new economy. Ecologists understand that all economic activity, indeed all life, depends on the earth's ecosystem—the complex of individual species living together, interacting with each other and their physical habitat. These millions of species exist in an intricate balance, woven together by food chains, nutrient cycles, the hydrological cycle, and the climate system. Economists know how to translate goals into policy. Economists and ecologists working together can design and build an eco-economy, one that can sustain progress. . . .

Economists rely on the market to guide their decisionmaking. They respect the market because it can allocate resources with an efficiency that a central planner can never match (as the Soviets learned at great expense). Ecologists view the market with less reverence because they see a market that is not telling the truth. For example, when buying a gallon of gasoline, customers in effect pay to get the oil out of the ground, refine it into gasoline, and deliver it to the local service station. But they do not pay the health care costs of treating respiratory illness from air pollution or the costs of climate disruption.

Ecologists see the record economic growth of recent decades, but they also see an economy that is increasingly in conflict with its support systems, one that is fast depleting the earth's natural capital, moving the global economy onto an environmental path that will inevitably lead to economic decline. They see the need for a wholesale restructuring of the economy so that it meshes with the ecosystem. They know that a stable relationship between the economy and the earth's ecosystem is essential if economic progress is to be sustained.

We have created an economy that cannot sustain economic progress, an economy that cannot take us where we want to go. Just as Copernicus had to formulate a new astronomical worldview after several decades of celestial observations and mathematical calculations, we too must formulate a new economic worldview based on several decades of environmental observations and analyses.

Although the idea that economics must be integrated into ecology may seem radical to many, evidence is mounting that it is the only approach that reflects reality. When observations no longer support theory, it is time to change the theory—what science historian Thomas Kuhn calls a paradigm shift. If the economy is a subset of the earth's ecosystem, as [I contend], the only formulation of economic policy that will succeed is one that respects the principles of ecology.

The good news is that economists are becoming more ecologically aware, recognizing the inherent dependence of the economy on the earth's ecosystem. For example, some 2,500 economists—including eight Nobel laureates—have endorsed the introduction of a carbon tax to stabilize climate. More and more economists are looking for ways to get the market to tell the ecological truth. This spreading awareness is evident in the rapid growth of the International Society of Ecological Economics, which has 1,200 members and chapters in Australia/New Zealand, Brazil, Canada, India, Russia, China, and throughout Europe. Its goal is to integrate the thinking of ecologists and economists into a transdiscipline aimed at building a sustainable world.

Economy Self-Destructing

The economic indicators for the last half-century show remarkable progress. . . . [T]he economy expanded sevenfold between 1950 and 2000. International trade grew even more rapidly. The Dow Jones Index, a widely used indicator of the value of stocks traded on the New York Stock Exchange, climbed from 3,000 in 1990 to 11,000 in 2000. It was difficult not to be bullish about the long-term economic prospect as the new century began.

Difficult, that is, unless you look at the ecological indicators. Here, virtually every global indicator was headed in the wrong direction. The economic policies that have yielded the extraordinary growth in the world economy are the same ones that are destroying its support systems. By an conceivable ecological yardstick, these are failed policies. Mismanagement is destroying forests, rangelands, fisheries, and croplands—the four ecosystems that supply our food and, except for minerals, all our raw materials as well. Although many of us live in a high-tech urbanized society, we are as dependent on the earth's natural systems as our hunter-gatherer forebears were.

To put ecosystems in economic terms, a natural system, such as a fishery, functions like an endowment. The interest income from an endowment will continue in perpetuity as long as the endowment is maintained. If the endowment is drawn down, income declines. If the endowment is eventually depleted, the interest income disappears. And so it is with natural systems. If the sustainable yield of a fishery is exceeded, fish stocks begin to shrink. Eventually stocks are depleted and the fishery collapses. The cash flow from this endowment disappears as well.

As we begin the twenty-first century, our economy is slowly destroying its support systems, consuming its endowment of natural capital. Demands of the expanding economy, *as now structured,* are surpassing the sustainable yield of ecosystems. Easily a third of the world's cropland is losing topsoil at a rate that is undermining its long-term productivity. Fully 50 percent of the world's rangeland is overgrazed and deteriorating into desert. The world's forests have shrunk by about half since the dawn of agriculture and are still shrinking. Two thirds of oceanic fisheries are now being fished at or beyond their capacity; overfishing is now the rule, not the exception. And overpumping of underground water is common in key food-producing regions.

Over large areas of the world, the loss of topsoil from wind and water erosion now exceeds the natural formation of new soil, gradually draining the land of its fertility. In an effort to curb this, the United States is retiring highly erodible cropland that was earlier plowed in overly enthusiastic efforts to expand food production. This process began in 1985 with the Conservation Reserve Program that paid farmers to retire 15 million hectacres, roughly one tenth of U.S. cropland, converting it back to grassland or forest before it became wasteland.

In countries that lack such programs, farmers are being forced to abandon highly erodible land that has lost much of its topsoil. Nigeria is losing over 500 square kilometers of productive land to desert each year. In Kazakhstan, site of the 1950s Soviet Virgin Lands project, half the cropland has been abandoned since 1980 as soil erosion lowered its productivity. This has dropped Kazakhstan's wheat harvest from roughly 13 million tons in 1980 to 8 million tons in 2000—an economic loss of $900 million per year.

The rangelands that supply much of the world's animal protein are also under excessive pressure. As human populations grow, so do livestock numbers. With 180 million people worldwide now trying to make a living raising 3.3 billion cattle, sheep, and goats, grasslands are simply collapsing under the demand. As a result of overstocking, grasslands are now deteriorating in much of Africa, the Middle East, Central Asia, the northern part of the Indian subcontinent, and much of northwestern China. Overgrazing is now the principal cause of desertification, the conversion of productive land into desert. In Africa, the annual loss of livestock production from the cumulative degradation of rangeland is estimated at $7 billion, a sum almost equal to the gross domestic product of Ethiopia.

In China, the combination of overplowing and overgrazing to satisfy rapidly expanding food needs is creating a dust bowl reminiscent of the U.S. Dust Bowl of the 1930s—but much larger. In a desperate effort to maintain grain self-sufficiency, China has plowed large areas of the northwest, much of it land that is highly erodible and should never have been plowed.

As the country's demand for livestock products—meat, leather, and wool—has climbed, so have the numbers of livestock, far exceeding those of the United States, a country with comparable grazing capacity. In addition to the direct damage from overplowing and overgrazing, the northern half of China is literally drying out as aquifers are depleted by overpumping.

These trends are converging to form some of the largest dust storms ever recorded. The huge dust plumes, traveling eastward, affect the cities of northeast China—blotting out the sun and reducing visibility. Eastward-moving winds also carry soil from China's northwest to the Korean Peninsula and Japan, where people regularly complain about the dust clouds that filter out the sunlight and blanket everything with dust. Unless China can reverse the overplowing and overgrazing trends that are creating the dust bowl, these trends could spur massive migration into the already crowded cities of the northeast and undermine the country's economic future.

The world is also running up a water deficit. The overpumping of aquifers, now commonplace on every continent, has led to falling water tables as pumping exceeds aquifer recharge from precipitation. Irrigation problems are as old as irrigation itself, but this is a new threat, one that has evolved over the last half-century with the advent of diesel pumps and powerful electrically driven pumps.

Water tables are falling under large expanses of the three leading food-producing countries—China, India, and the United States. Under the North China Plan, which accounts for 25 percent of China's grain harvest, the water table is falling by roughly 1.5 meters (5 feet) per year. The same thing is happening under much of India, particularly the Punjab, the country's breadbasket. In the United States, water tables are falling under the grain-growing states of the southern Great Plains, shrinking the irrigated area. . . .

Economic demands on forests are also excessive. Trees are being cut or burned faster than they can regenerate or be planted. Overharvesting is common in many regions, including Southeast Asia, West Africa, and the Brazilian Amazon. Worldwide, forests are shrinking by over 9 million hectacres per year, an area equal to Portugal.

In addition to being overharvested, some rainforests are now being destroyed by fire. Healthy rainforests do not burn, but logging and the settlements that occur along logging roads have fragmented and dried out tropical rainforests to the point where they often will burn easily, ignited by a lightning strike or set afire by opportunistic plantation owners, farmers, and ranchers desiring more land.

In the late summer of 1997, during an El Niño–induced drought, tropical rainforests in Borneo and Sumatra burned out of control. This conflagration made the news because the smoke drifting over hundreds of kilometers affected people not only in Indonesia but also in Malaysia, Singapore, Viet Nam, Thailand, and the Philippines. A reported 1,100 airline flights in the region were canceled due to the smoke. Motorists drove with their headlights on during the day, trying to make their way through the thick haze. Millions of people became physically sick.

Deforestation can be costly. Record flooding in the Yangtze River basin during the summer of 1998 drove 120 million people from their homes. Although initially referred to as a "natural disaster," the removal of 85 percent of the original tree cover in the basin had left little vegetative cover to hold the heavy rainfall.

Deforestation also diminishes the recycling of water inland, thus reducing rainfall in the interior of continents. When rain falls on a healthy stand of dense forest, roughly one fourth runs off, returning to the sea, while three fourths evaporates, either directly or through transpiration. When land is cleared for farming or grazing or is clearcut by loggers, this ratio is reversed—three fourths of the water returns to the sea and one fourth evaporates to be carried further inland. As deforestation progresses, nature's mechanism for watering the interior of large continents such as Africa and Asia is weakening.

Evidence of excessive human demands can also be seen in the oceans. As the human demand for animal protein has climbed over the last several decades, it has begun to exceed the sustainable yield of oceanic fisheries. As a result, two thirds of oceanic fisheries are now being fished at their sustainable yield or beyond. Many are collapsing. In 1992, the rich Newfoundland cod fishery that had been supplying fish for several centuries collapsed abruptly, costing 40,000 Canadians their jobs. Despite a subsequent ban on fishing, nearly a decade later the fishery has yet to recover.

Farther to the south, the U.S. Chesapeake Bay has experienced a similar decline. A century ago, this extraordinarily productive estuary produced over 100 million pounds of oysters a year. In 1999, it produced barely 3 million pounds. The Gulf of Thailand fishery has suffered a similarly dramatic decline: depleted by overfishing, the catch has dropped by over 80 percent since 1963, prompting the Thai Fisheries Department to ban fishing in large areas.

The world is also losing its biological diversity as plant and animal species are destroyed faster than new species evolve. This biological impoverishment of the earth is the result of habitat destruction, pollution, climate alteration, and hunting. With each update of its *Red List of Threatened Species,* the World Conservation Union (IUCN) shows us moving farther into a period of mass extinction. In the latest assessment, released in 2000, IUCN reports that one out of eight of the world's 9,946 bird species is in danger of extinction, as is one in four of the 4,763 mammal species and nearly one third of all 25,000 fish species.

Some countries have already suffered extensive losses. Australia, for example, has lost 16 of 140 mammal species over the last two centuries. In the Colorado River system of the southwestern United States, 29 of 50 native species of fish have disappeared partly because their river habitats were drained dry. Species lost cannot be regained. As a popular bumper sticker aptly points out, "Extinction is forever."

The economic benefits of the earth's diverse array of life are countless. They include not only the role of each species in maintaining the particular ecosystem of which it is a part, but economic roles as well, such as providing drugs and germplasm. As diversity diminishes, nature's pharmacy shrinks, depriving future generations of new discoveries.

Even as expanding economic activity has been creating biological deficits, it has been upsetting some of nature's basic balances in other areas: With the huge growth in burning of fossil fuels since 1950, carbon emissions have overwhelmed the capacity of the earth's ecosystem to fix carbon dioxide. The resulting rise in atmospheric CO_2 levels is widely believed by atmospheric scientists to be responsible for the earth's rising temperature. The 14 warmest years since recordkeeping began in 1866 have all occurred since 1980.

One consequence of higher temperatures is more energy driving storm systems. Three powerful winter storms in France in December 1999 destroyed millions of trees, some of which had been standing for centuries. Thousands of buildings were demolished. These storms, the most violent on record in France, wreaked more than \$10 billion worth of damage—\$170 for each French citizen. Nature was levying a tax of its own on fossil fuel burning.

In October 1998, Hurricane Mitch—one of the most powerful storms ever to come out of the Atlantic—moved through the Caribbean and stalled for several days on the coast of Central America. While there, it acted as a huge pump pulling water from the ocean and dropping it over the land. Parts of Honduras received 2 meters of rainfall within a few days. So powerful was this storm and so vast the amount of water it dropped on Central America that it altered the topography, converting mountains and hills into vast mud flows that simply inundated whole villages, claiming an estimated 10,000 lives. Four fifths of the crops were destroyed. The huge flow of rushing water removed all the topsoil in many areas, ensuring that this land will not be farmed again during our lifetimes.

The overall economic effect of the storm was devastating. The wholesale destruction of roads, bridges, buildings, and other infrastructure set back the development of Honduras and Nicaragua by decades. The estimated $8.5 billion worth of damage in the region approached the gross domestic product of both countries combined. . . .

Perhaps the most disturbing consequence of rising temperature is ice melting. Over the last 35 years, the ice covering the Arctic Sea has thinned by 42 percent. A study by two Norwegian scientists projects that within 50 years there will be no summer ice left in the Arctic Sea. The discovery of open water at the North Pole by an ice breaker cruise ship in mid-August 2000 stunned many in the scientific community.

This particular thawing does not affect sea level because the ice that is melting is already in the ocean. But the Greenland ice sheet is also starting to melt. Greenland is three times the size of Texas and the ice sheet is up to 2 kilometers (1.2 miles) thick in some areas. An article in *Science* notes that if the entire ice sheet were to melt, it would raise sea level by some 7 meters (23 feet), inundating the world's coastal cities and Asia's rice-growing river floodplains. Even a 1-meter rise would cover half of Bangladesh's riceland, dropping food production below the survival level for millions of people.

As the twenty-first century begins, humanity is being squeezed between deserts expanding outward and rising seas encroaching inward. Civilization is being forced to retreat by forces it has created. Even as population continues to grow, the habitable portion of the planet is shrinking.

Aside from climate change, the economic effects of environmental destruction and disruption have been mostly local—collapsing fisheries, abandoned cropland, and shrinking forests. But if local damage keeps accumulating, it will eventually affect global economic trends. In an increasingly integrated global economy, local ecosystem collapse can have global economic consequences.

Lessons From the Past

In *The Collapse of Complex Civilizations,* Joseph Tainter describes the decline of early civilizations and speculates about the causes. Was it because of the degradation of their environment, climate change, civil conflict, foreign invaders? Or, he asks, "is there some mysterious internal dynamic to the rise and fall of civilizations?"

As he ponders the contrast between civilizations that once flourished and the desolation of the sites they occupied, he quotes archeologist Robert McAdams, who described the site of the ancient Sumerian civilization located on the central floodplain of the Euphrates River, an empty, desolate area now outside the frontiers of cultivation. Adams described how the "tangled dunes, long disused canal levees, and the rubble-strewn mounds of former settlement contribute only low, featureless relief. Vegetation is sparse, and in many areas it is almost wholly absent. . . . Yet at one time, here lay the core, the heartland, the oldest urban, literate civilization in the world."

The early Sumerian civilization of the fourth millennium BC was remarkable, advancing far beyond any that had existed before. Its irrigation system, based on sophisticated engineering concepts, created a highly productive agriculture, one that enabled farmers to produce a surplus of food that supported the formation of the first cities. Managing the irrigation system required a complex social organization, one that may have been more sophisticated than any that had gone before. The Sumerians had the first cities and the first written language, the cuneiform script. They were probably as excited about it as we are today about the Internet.

It was an extraordinary civilization, but there was an environmental flaw in the design of the irrigation system, one that would eventually undermine its agricultural economy. Water from behind dams was diverted onto the land, raising crop yields. Some of the water was used by the crops, some evaporated into the atmosphere, and some percolated downward. Over time, this percolation slowly raised the water table until eventually it approached the surface of the land. When it reached a few feet from the surface it began to restrict the growth of deep-rooted crops. Somewhat later, as the water climbed to within inches of the surface, it began to evaporate into the atmosphere. As this happened, the salt in the water was left behind. Over time, the accumulation of salt reduced the productivity of the land. The environmental flaw was that there was no provision for draining the water that percolated downward.

The initial response of the Sumerians to declining wheat yields was to shift to barley, a more salt-tolerant plant. But eventually the yields of barley also declined. The resultant shrinkage of the food supply undermined the economic foundation of this great civilization. . . .

One unanswerable question about these earlier civilizations was whether they knew what was causing their decline. Did the Sumerians understand that rising salt content in the soil was reducing their wheat yields? If they knew, were they simply unable to muster the political support needed to lower water tables, just as we today are struggling unsuccessfully to lower carbon emissions?

Learning From China

The flow of startling information from China helps us understand why our economy cannot take us where we want to go. Not only is China the world's most populous country, with nearly 1.3 billion people, but since 1980 it has been the world's fastest-growing economy—expanding more than fourfold. In effect, China is telescoping history, demonstrating what happens when large numbers of poor people rapidly become more affluent.

As incomes have climbed in China, so has consumption. The Chinese have already caught up with Americans in pork consumption per person and they are now concentrating their energies on increasing beef production. Raising per capita beef consumption in China to that of the average American would take 49 million additional tons of beef. If all this were to come from putting cattle in feedlots, American-style, it would require 343 million tons of grain a year, an amount equal to the entire U.S. grain harvest.

In Japan, as population pressures on the land mounted during a comparable stage of its economic development, the Japanese turned to the sea for their animal protein. Last year, Japan consumed nearly 10 million tons of seafood. If China, with 10 times as many people as Japan, were to try to move down this same path, it would need 100 million tons of seafood—the entire world fish catch.

In 1994, the Chinese government decided that the country would develop an automobile- centered transportation system and that the automobile industry would be one of the engines of future economic growth. Beijing invited major automobile manufacturers, such as Volkswagen, General Motors, and Toyota, to invest in China. But if Beijing's goal of an auto-centered transportation system were to materialize and the Chinese were to have one or two cars in every garage and were to consume oil at the U.S. rate, China would need over 80 million barrels of oil a day—slightly more than the 74 million barrels per day the world now produces. To provide the required roads and parking lots, it would also need to pave some 16 million hectacres of land, and area equal to half the size of the 31 million hectacres of land currently used to produce the country's 132-million-ton annual harvest of rice, its leading food staple.

Similarly, consider paper. As China modernizes, its paper consumption is rising. If annual paper use in China of 35 kilograms per person were to climb to the U.S. level of 342 kilograms, China would need more paper than the world currently produces. There go the world's forests.

We are learning that the western industrial development model is not viable for China, simply because there are not enough resources for it to work. Global land and water resources are not sufficient to satisfy the growing grain needs in China if it continues along the current economic development path. Nor will the existing fossil-fuel-based energy economy supply the needed energy, simply because world oil production is not projected to rise much above current levels in the years ahead. Apart from the availability of oil, if carbon emissions per person in China ever reach the U.S. level, this alone would roughly double global emissions, accelerating the rise in the atmospheric CO_2 level.

China faces a formidable challenge in fashioning a development strategy simply because of the density of its population. Although it has almost exactly the same amount of land as the United States, most of China's 1.3 billion people live in a 1,500-kilometer strip on the eastern and southern coasts. Reaching the equivalent population density in the United States would require squeezing the entire U.S. population into the area east of the Mississippi and then multiplying it by four.

Interestingly, the adoption of the western economic model for China is being challenged from within. A group of prominent scientists, including many in the Chinese Academy of Sciences, wrote a white paper questioning the government's decision to develop an automobile-centered transportation system. They pointed out that China does not have enough land both to feed its people and to provide the roads, highways, and parking lots needed to accommodate the automobile. They also noted the heavy dependence on imported oil that would be required and the potential air pollution and traffic congestion that would result if they followed the U.S. path.

If the fossil-fuel-based, automobile-centered, throwaway economy will not work for China, then it will not work for India with its 1 billion people, or for the other 2 billion people in the developing world. In a world with a shared ecosystem and an increasingly integrated global economy, it will ultimately not work for the industrial economies either.

China is showing that the world cannot remain for long on the current economic path. It is underlining the urgency of restructuring the global economy, of building a new economy—an economy designed for the earth.

The Acceleration of History

. . . Until recently, population growth was so slow that it aroused little concern. But since 1950 we have added more people to world population than during the preceding 4 million years since our early ancestors first stood upright. Economic expansion in earlier times was similarly slow. To illustrate, growth in the world economy during the year 2000 exceeded that during the entire nineteenth century.

Throughout most of human history, the growth of population, the rise in income, and the development of new technologies were so slow as to be imperceptible during an individual life span. For example, the climb in grainland productivity from 1.1 tons per hectare in 1950 to 2.8 tons per hectacre in 2000 exceeds that during the 11,000 years from the beginning of agriculture until 1950.

The population growth of today has no precedent. Throughout most of our existence as a species, our numbers were measured in the thousands. Today, they measure in the billions. Our evolution has prepared us to deal with many threats, but perhaps not with the threat we pose to ourselves with the uncontrolled growth in our own numbers.

The world economy is growing even faster. The sevenfold growth in global output of goods and services since 1950 dwarfs anything in history. In the earlier stages of the Industrial Revolution, economic expansion rarely exceeded 1 or 2 percent a year. Developing countries that are industrializing now are doing so much faster than their predecessors simply because they do not have to invent the technologies needed by a modern industrial society, such as power plants, automobiles, and refrigerators. They can simply draw on the experiences and technology of those that preceded them. . . .

The pace of history is also accelerating as soaring human demands collide with the earth's natural limits. National political leaders are spending more time dealing with the consequences of the collisions described earlier—collapsing fisheries, falling water tables, food shortages, and increasingly destructive storms—along with a steadily swelling international flow of environmental refugees and the many other effects of overshooting natural limits. As change has accelerated, the situation has evolved from one where individuals and societies change only rarely to one where they change continuously. They are changing not only in response to growth itself, but also to the consequences of growth.

The central question is whether the accelerating change that is an integral part of the modern landscape is beginning to exceed the capacity of our social institutions to cope with change. Change is particularly difficult for institutions dealing with international or global issues that require a concerted, cooperative effort by many countries with contrasting cultures if they are to succeed. For example, sustaining the existing oceanic fish catch may be possible only if numerous agreements are reached among countries on the limits to fishing in individual oceanic fisheries. And can governments, working together at the global level, move fast enough to stabilize climate before it disrupts economic progress?

The issue is not whether we know what needs to be done or whether we have the technologies to do it. The issue is whether our social institutions are capable of bringing about the change in the time available. As H.G. Wells wrote in *The Outline of History,* "Human history becomes more and more a race between education and catastrophe."

The Option: Restructure or Decline

Whether we study the environmental undermining of earlier civilizations or look at how adoption of the western industrial model by China would affect the earth's ecosystem, it is evident that the existing industrial economic model cannot sustain economic progress. In our shortsighted efforts to sustain the global economy, as currently structured, we are depleting the earth's natural capital. We spend a lot of time worrying about our economic deficits, but it is the ecological deficits that threaten our long-term economic future. Economic deficits are what we borrow from each other; ecological deficits are what we take from future generations.

Herman Daly, the intellectual pioneer of the fast-growing field of ecological economics, notes that the world "has passed from an era in which manmade capital represented the limiting factor in economic development (an 'empty' world) to an era in which increasingly scarce natural capital has taken its place (a 'full' world)." When our numbers were small relative to the size of the planet, it was humanmade capital that was scarce. Natural capital was abundant. Now that has changed. As the human enterprise continues to expand, the products and services provided by the earth's ecosystem are increasingly scarce, and natural capital is fast becoming the limiting factor while humanmade capital is increasingly abundant.

Transforming our environmentally destructive economy into one that can sustain progress depends on a Copernican shift in our economic mindset, a recognition that the economy is part of the earth's ecosystem and can sustain progress only if it is restructured so that it is compatible with it. The preeminent challenge for our generation is to design an eco-economy, one that respects the principles of ecology. A redesigned economy can be integrated into the ecosystem in a way that will stabilize the relationship between the two, enabling economic progress to continue.

Unfortunately, present-day economics does not provide the conceptual framework needed to build such an economy. It will have to be designed with an understanding of basic ecological concepts such as sustainable yield, carrying capacity, nutrient cycles, the hydrological cycle, and the climate system. Designers must also know that natural systems provide not only goods, but also services—services that are often more valuable than the goods.

We know the kind of restructuring that is needed. In simplest terms, our fossil-fuel-based, automobile-centered, throwaway economy is not a viable model for the world. The alternative is a solar/hydrogen energy economy, an urban transport system that is centered on advanced-design public rail systems and that relies more on the bicycle and less on the automobile, and a comprehensive reuse/recycle economy. And we need to stabilize population as soon as possible.

How do we achieve this economic transformation when all economic decisionmakers—whether political leaders, corporate planners, investment bankers, or individual consumers—are guided by market signals, not the principles of ecological sustainability? How do we integrate ecological awareness into economic decisionmaking? Is it possible for all of us who are making economic decisions to "think like ecologists," to understand the ecological consequences of our decisions? The answer is probably not. It simply may not be possible.

But there may be another approach, a simpler way of achieving our goal. Everyone making economic decisions relies on market signals for guidance. The problem is that the market often fails to tell the ecological truth. It regularly underprices products and services by failing to incorporate the environmental costs of providing them.

Compare, for example, the cost of wind-generated electricity with that from a coal-fired power plant. The cost of the wind-generated electricity reflects the costs of manufacturing the turbine, installing it, maintaining it, and delivering the electricity to consumers. The cost of the coal-fired electricity includes building the power plant, mining the coal, transporting it to the power plant, and distributing the electricity to consumers. What it does not include is the cost of climate disruption caused by carbon emissions from coal burning—whether it be more destructive storms, melting ice caps, rising sea level, or record heat waves. Nor does it include the damage to freshwater lakes and forests from acid rain, or the health care costs of treating respiratory illnesses caused by air pollution. Thus the market price of coal-fired electricity greatly understates its cost to society.

One way to remedy this situation would be to have environmental scientists and economists work together to calculate the cost of climate disruption, acid rain, and air pollution. This figure could then be incorporated as a tax on coal-fired electricity that, when added to the current price, would give the full cost of coal use. This procedure, followed across the board, would mean that all economic decisionmakers—governments and individual consumers—would have the information needed to make more intelligent, ecologically responsible decisions.

We can now see how to restructure the global economy so as to restore stability between the economy and the ecosystem on which it rests. When I helped to pioneer the concept of environmentally sustainable economic development some 27 years ago, at the newly formed Worldwatch Institute, I had a broad sense of what the new economy would look like. Now we can see much more of the detail. We can build an eco-economy with existing technologies. It is economically feasible if we can get the market to tell us the full cost of the products and services that we buy.

The question is not how much will it cost to make this transformation but how much it will cost if we fail to do it. Øystein Dahle, retired Vice President of Esso for Norway and the North Sea, observes, "Socialism collapsed because it did not allow prices to tell the economic truth. Capitalism may collapse because it does not allow prices to tell the ecological truth."

Lenny Bernstein

Climate Change and Ecosystems

Introduction

This report examines the basis for claims that projected human-induced climate change will have a severe impact on ecosystems. Past Marshall Institute Reports, most recently *Climate Science and Policy: Making the Connection,* have questioned the basis for projections that human activities will have a severe impact on the climate of the 21st century. This report does not repeat those arguments, but discusses the possible impact on ecosystems of different levels of climate change, as indicated by temperature rise, independent of time frame or cause.

There are many definitions of ecosystem. This report will use one developed by the Intergovernmental Panel on Climate Change (IPCC):

> A distinct system of interacting living organisms, together with their physical environment. The boundaries of what could be called an ecosystem are somewhat arbitrary, depending on the focus of interest or study. Thus the extent of an ecosystem may range from very small spatial scales to, ultimately, the entire Earth.

The ecosystems we discuss typically cover many thousand square miles, for example, the habitat of a bird species or a river's watershed.

Before considering specific claims of potential ecosystem damage, it is important to recognize that climate has always impacted on ecosystems and that human activities have been impacting on ecosystems for tens of thousands of years.

All of the plants and animals, including humans, that live on Earth are sensitive to climate and will respond to climate change. Climate is a key determinant of what crops can be grown in a particular area. Paleontologists argue that past climate changes were a factor, perhaps the major factor, in the extinction of the dinosaurs and many other species.

Human activities have had impacts on ecosystems since indigenous people, such as the Australian Aborigines, first used fire to clear underbrush to improve their hunting. Both primitive and modern people have caused the extinction of species, e.g. the moa in New Zealand and the passenger pigeon in North America.

The overwhelming majority of the Earth's ecosystems have been affected by human activities. Some of these activities have been planned, e.g., the conversion of forest to farmland. Others activities have been unplanned. For example, as documented in a recent issue of *Audubon*, the removal of wolves and other predators, and bans on hunting, have led to a dramatic increase in the U.S. deer population. This, in turn, has reduced the population of the plants deer like to eat, while increasing in the population of plants deer do not like to eat, thus changing the ecosystem.

Given the pervasive nature of human impacts, ecosystems can be divided into two categories:

- intensively-managed; farmland, managed forests and grasslands, and to a lesser extent, fisheries; and
- lightly-impacted; essentially unmanaged, natural wildlife areas and the oceans.

Concerns about intensely-managed ecosystems focus on the potential impact that climate change will have on the ability of these systems to produce the food and fiber they have traditionally supplied to the global economy. Concerns about lightly-impacted ecosystems focus on the potential for climate change to cause widespread species extinction.

This report examines the question: How sensitive are intensively-managed and lightly-impacted ecosystems to different levels of climate change? In the course of answering this question, it is necessary to consider the relative importance of climate change compared with other human impacts, such as habitat disruption and local or regional pollution, in determining the rate of species extinction.

Three climate changes are discussed in this report: higher atmospheric concentrations of CO_2, warmer temperatures, and increased precipitation. All IPCC projections are for higher CO_2. Based on projection of higher CO_2, climate models project increases in temperature for all parts of the world. They also project increases in average precipitation, but are less consistent in the projections of the regional distribution of precipitation. Most areas of the world are projected to get more precipitation than they now do, a few are projected to get less.

The IPCC Third Assessment Report includes projections of precipitation based on nine climate models using two emissions scenarios: high emissions and low emissions. The results were evaluated for 23 regions of the world, and for two seasons: winter and summer. This resulted in 92 comparisons (23 regions x 2 emissions scenarios x 2 seasons). IPCC reported that in a third (32) of the comparisons, the models gave inconsistent results. In 9 other comparisons they showed no significant change in precipitation. In 40 comparisons, they showed increases in precipitation, and in 11 comparisons they showed decreases. While these comparisons represent the best available modeling results, they hide large differences in the predictions of individual models. As the IPCC reports:

> The magnitude of regional precipitation changes varies considerably amongst models, with the typical range being around 0 to 50% where the direction of change is strongly indicated and around –30 to +30% where it is not.

Given the physical basis for assuming a wetter world, and the preponderance of modeling results, we will assume that most ecosystems will experience wetter conditions in the future.

Intensively-Managed Ecosystems

Society depends on ecosystems for a wide range of goods. Most of the food we eat, the wood we use for construction, and the natural fibers we use for clothing, are products of intensively-managed ecosystems. We also depend on both intensively-managed and lightly-impacted ecosystems for a wide variety of services including water purification and recreational opportunities. Since these ecosystems are sensitive to climate change, it is reasonable to ask whether changes in climate will diminish the ability of ecosystems to continue supplying these goods and services. The debate on the validity of this concern centers on the ability of human society to adapt intensively-managed ecosystems to climate change.

As climate changes, which it has and will in the future, human society will have to adapt to that change; adaptation is a necessity, not an option. But humanity's need to adapt to climate change is not a new phenomena, and both sides of the debate are succinctly captured by Brian Fagan, Professor of Archeology at the University of California, Santa Barbara, in his book, *The Little Ice Age:*

> Humanity has been at the mercy of climate change for its entire existence. Infinitely ingenious, we have lived through eight, perhaps nine, glacial episodes in the past 730,000 years. Our ancestors adapted to the universal but irregular global warming since the end of the Ice Age with dazzling opportunism. They developed strategies for surviving harsh drought cycles, decades of heavy rainfall or unaccustomed cold; adopted agriculture and stock-raising, which revolutionized human life; founded the world's first preindustrial civilization in Egypt, Mesopotamia, and the Americas. The price of sudden climate change, in famine, disease, and suffering, was often high.

Optimists point to the infinite ingenuity and dazzling opportunism Prof. Fagan refers to as evidence that humanity will be able to respond to any future climate change. Pessimists point to the high human costs of past climate changes. Which of these will shape the future?

The majority of studies of the impacts of climate change on intensively-managed ecosystems have the following characteristics:

- they assume today's technology with either no or limited adaptation;
- they use the impacts of severe weather events as predictors of the impacts of climate change; and
- they invariably show high negative impacts.

These studies are misleading. Severe weather events occur in the short-term, offering no opportunity for adaptation. But climate is the long-term average of weather, and climate change, whether natural or human-induced, will take decades to centuries to occur. During that time human society will continue to benefit from advances in knowledge and technology, and hence become more capable of adapting to different climate conditions.

The benefits of adaptation have been clearly demonstrated in the evolution of thinking about the potential impacts of climate change on agriculture. Early studies did not consider adaptation. They assumed no change in the behavior of farmers in response to changing climate. This was known as the "dumb farmer" hypothesis, and was at odds with all of human experience, which indicates that farmers and others whose livelihood is sensitive to climate are very attuned to climate change and adapt to it on a continuous basis.

Later studies considered adaptation by the individual farmer, i.e., planting species that were better matched to climate conditions. For example, wheat farmers have a wide variety of species to choose from, some of which are better adapted than others to the warmer, wetter conditions that are projected by climate models. Choosing these better adapted species would minimize the potential adverse impacts of climate change, and in many cases provide a net benefit. Still more sophisticated studies consider both farmer adaptation and marketplace adaptation. If climate changed sufficiently, wheat farmers might become corn farmers, and corn farmers might grow fruit and vegetables. Using a "smart farmer" assumption led to very different results, often showing that climate change yielded net benefits.

Benefits of Adaptation

The limited number of studies which take growth in adaptive capacity into account often show benefits for climate change. One such study by Adams *et al.* considers the impacts of climate change on U.S. agriculture in 2060, taking into account projected changes in the agricultural market to that time and allowing for the full range of adaptation. The authors considered the effects of changes in temperature, precipitation and atmospheric carbon dioxide (CO_2) content on agricultural yields. Photosynthesis, the process by which atmospheric CO_2 and water vapor are converted into plant matter, is enhanced by higher levels of atmospheric CO_2, though plants respond to increased CO_2 at different rates.

Adams, *et al.* looked at a series of cases in which atmospheric CO_2 concentration was increased from its 1999 level of about 365 ppm to 530 ppm, temperature increased by as much as 5°C, and precipitation increased by as much as 15%. These climate changes are larger than those typically projected by climate models for 2060. Farmers were allowed to adapt by either optimizing their current crops or by switching crops.

The authors found that for all cases studied, the U.S. benefited from improvements in the agricultural sector, with the benefits being split between consumers, who enjoyed lower food prices because of higher agricultural productivity, and the farmers who benefited from higher income. Not all cases resulted in benefits to both sides, nor were the benefits spread equally across all agricultural areas in the country, but the net effect for the U.S. economy was positive.

The physical basis for these benefits is fairly easy to understand. The benefits of higher CO_2 concentration have already been discussed. Warmer climates mean longer growing seasons and less chance of crop damage from frost. Much of the U.S. agricultural area suffers from periodic droughts, so increased precipitation also provides benefits.

A similar study by [Brent L.] Sohngen and [Robert] Mendelsohn for the U.S. timber industry projects benefits under the same range of climate change conditions. The authors conclude:

> Overall, the timber market is likely to adapt to climate change, thereby ameliorating the potential problem associated with ecological change. This work shows how harvest schedules will adjust from region to region and from moment to moment so as to use timber stocks efficiently during the transition period (to equilibrium climate change). These adjustments occur regardless of the specific climate and ecological scenario. This chapter also shows how timberland owners will adjust their replanting behavior by responding to future ecological and economic conditions. Despite the apparent severity of some ecological effects, market behavior offsets the potential damages through adaptation.

Overall, Mendelsohn and Neumann project that the benefits to managed ecosystems would result in a modest (+0.2%) benefit to the U.S. economy in 2060 for their moderate climate change case (+2.5°C, +7% precipitation). This result was generalized by the IPCC. In assessing these results, the IPCC concluded that there was medium confidence that small increases in temperature would have a net positive effect on the economies of developed nations.

The IPCC defines "small increases in temperature," as 0–2°C. This literature also indicates that most, if not all, of the benefit comes from gains in intensively-managed ecosystems.

While the IPCC agrees that moderate climate change would be beneficial to managed ecosystems in the developed world, it raises two concerns: first, that more than 2°C warming would have adverse effects, even in the developed world, and second, that even small amounts of climate change would have adverse effects in the developing world. Again, much of the basis for these concerns is the projected impact of climate change on intensely-managed ecosystems. The [following] paragraphs examine the validity of these concerns.

The basis for the IPCC's concerns about the inability of intensively-manage decosystems to adapt to large amounts of climate change appears to lie in the fact that the studies collected by Mendelsohn and Neumann, and other similar exercises, show declining benefits at large amounts of climate change. The extent to which these results are a function of model limitation or represent real limitations in the ability of intensively-managed ecosystems to adapt is unknown. As Mendelsohn and Neumann state:

> . . . it is important to recognize the significant limitations involved in projecting climate, biophysical, and economic conditions over the next century. Although this book seeks to improve the arsenal of methodologies

> to measure the economic impact of climate change, none of the existing methods are perfect replicas of the experience that society will face if climate gradually warms over the next century.

. . . For the US, which has been subjected to more analysis than any other part of the world, the benefits extend out to double the temperature level considered by the IPCC (5°C vs. 2.5°C). More scientific study and modeling will be needed to determine the extent to which this result can be generalized to other countries and regions. However, there is clearly room for more optimism than exhibited by the IPCC.

Adaptation in the Developing World

The question of whether adaptation can provide benefits for intensively-managed ecosystems in the developing world is more complex. The benefits of higher CO_2 concentration are equally applicable in developed and developing countries. However, most developing countries are in the tropics, and would see no benefit, but potential adverse effects, from rising temperature. The IPCC points out many cases in which extremely high temperatures will inhibit critical stages of plant growth for existing crop species. These studies often do not consider the potential for developing more heat resistant crops or opportunities for adaptation through crop switching. Also, it should be noted that climate models typically project less than global average warming in the tropics.

In many developing countries, the growing season is 365 days of the year and frost does not exist. Thus longer growing season and less potential frost damage are not considerations. Some of these countries also have generous rainfall, so additional rainfall will provide little additional benefit. Others are either arid or desert countries, in which case, additional rainfall is a major benefit. No single description fits all cases.

The IPCC recognizes that there is considerable opportunity for the agriculture and forestry sectors to adapt to climate change, and that there is evidence that they have done so in the past. But it then raises concerns that the poorest and most vulnerable countries will not have the ability to adapt. This conclusion overlooks two factors.

First, there is little reason to believe that developing nations cannot take advantage of improvements in agricultural technology and use them to adapt to any changes in climate. Some of the poorest countries in the world were the ones that benefited most in the 1950s and '60s from adopting the suite of agricultural technologies (improved plant varieties, increased used of fertilizer and irrigation) known as the "Green Revolution," which dramatically raised food production in much of the developing world. Countries with relatively stable governments benefited most. Democratic countries, such as India, were able to take quick advantage of these developments, but even dictatorships, such as Syria, which became self-sufficient in grain in 1991, saw improvements in food production. In today's world, despite a growing population, famine is a problem only in those countries which are at war or have unstable governments. . . .

Second, CO_2 emissions are the result of economic activity, which generates wealth, which in turn results in adaptive capacity. Since projected climate change and the ability to adapt to it are both the result of economic activity, we need to consider the future level of economic activity in developing nations.

The IPCC Special Report on Emissions Scenarios (SRES), published in 2000, provides a wide range of scenarios of the changes in CO_2 emissions and per capita income for both developed and developing nations from 1990 to 2100. As the IPCC is careful to point out, scenarios are not predictions, they are alternate images of how the future might unfold. This report does not address the analytical basis for these scenarios or whether any of them are likely. They are used solely as a basis for assessing the potential growth in the adaptive capacity of developing nations.

The IPCC scenarios all show a faster rate of economic growth in developing nations than in developed nations, resulting in a narrowing of the economic gap between the developed and developing worlds. This higher rate of economic growth also results in developing nations emitting a higher fraction of the world's CO_2 emissions in 2100 than they currently do. The emissions scenarios that lead to the highest level of projected temperature rise to 2100 are the scenarios that have the highest level of economic growth in the developing world.

The SRES does not give country-by-county projections but divides the world into four regions:

1. The countries that were OECD members in 1990,
2. Russia and Eastern Europe,
3. Asia, and
4. Africa and Latin America.

The first two regions are developed nations, the last two, the developing nations.

The SRES authors developed 40 baseline scenarios; none of these scenarios include overt actions to control greenhouse gas emissions. . . .

[Table 1] summarizes the SRES projections for population, total CO_2 emissions, CO_2 emissions per capita, and GDP [gross domestic product] per capita for 1990 and 2100 for the illustrative scenarios with the highest (A1FI) and lowest (B1) global CO_2 emissions.

What the numbers in Table 1 show is a dramatic narrowing of current differences between developed and developing nation per capita CO_2 emissions and GDP during the 21st century. Even in the IPCC's lowest economic growth illustrative scenario, A2 (not shown), developing nation GDP per capita increases more than ten-fold (2.3%/yr.) during the 21st century, and the ratio of developed nation to developing nation GDP per capita decreases to 4.2. It is reasonable to assume that this growth in the wealth of developing nations will be accompanied by a growth in their ability to adapt food production to climate variability and change. At a minimum, the adaptive capacity of developing nations should be roughly equivalent to that of developed nations today. In many cases it should exceed that level.

Table 1

SRES Projections: CO_2 Emissions and GDP per Capita

	1990	2100 Highest Emissions	2100 Lowest Emissions
Population, Billions			
Developed Nations	1.3	1.4	1.4
Developing Nations	4.0	5.7	5.7
Total CO_2 Emissions (GtC)*			
Developed Nations	4.1	10.0	1.1
Developing Nations	3.1	18.2	3.1
% Developing Nations	43	65	74
CO_2 per Capita (Tonnes C)			
Developed Nations	3.2	7.1	0.79
Developing Nations	0.78	3.2	0.54
Ratio	4.1	2.2	1.5
GDP per Capita (1990 US$)			
Developed Nations	13,800	109,500	71,700
Developing Nations	850	69,800	40,000
Ratio	16.1	1.6	1.8

*GtC = billion metric tonnes carbon

Pessimists argue that these broad averages hide pockets of poverty that will be resistant to economic growth. The evidence is overwhelming that poverty is caused by government corruption and the lack of rule of law, property rights and individual freedom. These problems dwarf the potential impacts of climate change and need to be addressed on an urgent basis, independent of concerns about potential climate change.

Lightly-Impacted Ecosystems

. . . Before discussing the potential impact of climate change on species extinction, we will consider the extent to which humans are and have been responsible for the extinction of other species. The most dramatic and well-known cases involve over-hunting, which led to the extinction of such species as the dodo, moa, and passenger pigeon, and almost led to the extinction of the American buffalo. But, habitat destruction has also been a major cause of species extinction. Conversion of natural habitats to intensive-managed farms and forests has caused the extinction of both plant and animal species.

More recently, the introduction of invasive species, non-native plants or animals that have no natural enemies, has been another factor contributing to the stress on endangered species. Some of these species have been purposely introduced (e.g. kudzu, which was introduced in the southeastern U.S.

for erosion control), while the introduction of others was inadvertent (e.g. zebra mussels, which entered the Great Lakes in the ballast water of ships).

While there is no debate that humans have been, and continue to be, responsible for the extinction of some species, there is an active debate as to how serious the problem is. We do not know how many species there are, nor what the background rate of species extinction is, nor how many species are becoming extinct as the result of human activities.

The current best estimate of the number of species on the Earth is between 10 and 80 million, of which only some 1.6 million have been identified. Such a wide range indicates deficiencies in the current estimating methodologies. Systematic studies invariably discover new species, even in intensively studied areas. For example, in 1998, about 12,000 species were known to exist in the Great Smoky Mountains National Park. In that year, the All Taxa (Species) Biodiversity Inventory project was started with the goal of raising the total number of species identified in the park to 100,000. Thus far, 1,480 new species have been identified in the park, 144 of which are new to science.

Background rates of extinction are similarly unknown. Fossil records indicate massive extinctions in the past, the most famous being the extinction of the dinosaurs 65,000,000 years ago. This extinction is now believed to have been caused when a massive asteroid hit the Earth creating a large, sudden change in climate. Fossil records also indicate that most of the species that existed over the Earth's history are now extinct. However, there is no accepted estimate for the number of species that would become extinct as the result of natural evolutionary processes during a "normal" year.

Estimates of the number of species becoming extinct because of human activities vary widely. One widely-quoted number is 40,000 per year, but as has been documented by Bjorn Lomborg in his book *The Skeptical Environmentalist,* this number can be traced to a speculation by Norman Myers, a well known environmentalist. Even critics of Lomborg's approach, such as Thomas Lovejoy, Chief Biodiversity Advisor to the President of the World Bank and a former Director of the World Wildlife Fund–US, agree that Myers provided no basis for his estimate. At the other extreme of the estimates for human-induced species extinction, documentary evidence exists for the extinction of only 1,033 species since 1600. Even those who believe that humans are not causing large-scale species extinction agree that this number is highly likely to be low, since undocumented extinctions as the result of human activities are certain to have occurred. . . .

Climate Change and Species Extinction

The starting point for concerns about the potential impacts of climate change on endangered species is indisputable: all plants and animals living on the Earth are sensitive to climate. All, with the possible exception of humans, have a preferred climate. These preferences are often shown as a plot of the type of ecosystem that will be prevalent as a function of average temperature and rainfall. Any change in climate will put stress on some plant or animal species. However, translating these generalities into threats to specific species is far from easy. The IPCC summarizes the problems involved as follows:

> Modeling changes in biodiversity in response to climate change presents some significant challenges. It requires projections of climate change at high spatial and temporal resolution and often depends on the balance between variables that are poorly handled by climate models (e.g., local precipitation and evaporative demand). It also requires an understanding of how species interact with each other and how these interactions affect the communities and ecosystems of which they are a part. In addition, the focus of attention in the results is often particular species that may be rare or show unusual biological behavior.

To address these knowledge gaps, the IPCC calls for:

> Improvement of regional scale models coupled with transient ecosystem models that deal with multiple pressures with appropriate spatial and temporal resolution and include spatial interactions between ecosystems within landscapes.

The term "landscape" refers to "groups of ecosystems (e.g., forests, rivers, lakes, etc.) that form a visible entity to humans.

Elsewhere the IPCC documents the huge difficulties involved in developing regional climate models. The challenges in developing transient ecosystem models are just as large, and coupling the two would be still another difficult task. Yet, the IPCC is correct in its conclusion that this is what would be needed for a predictive model of the effect of climate change on plant and animal species. Faced with the difficulty of developing predictive models and quantitative assessment tools, any discussion of the impacts of climate change on species is limited to qualitative statements. . . .

Any discussion of the role of climate change in future rates of species extinction must also consider the relative threats posed by climate change vs. habitat disruption and other human activities. Given the high level of uncertainty about both current and future rates of species extinction, we can only speculate about the relative importance of climate change vs. habitat disruption or other human activities.

One study has attempted such speculation and concluded that the dominant factors determining biodiversity decline will be climate change in polar regions and land-use change (habitat disruption) in the tropics. Temperate ecosystems were estimated to experience the least biodiversity change because major land-use changes have already occurred. There are far more plant and animal species, and apparently a far higher number of species becoming extinct, in the tropics than in polar regions. Therefore on a global basis, habitat disruption will continue to be the major impact on animal and plant species.

Not all of the impacts on ecosystems of projected climate change will be negative. As in the case of agriculture, a warmer, wetter, higher CO_2 world will be beneficial for uncultivated plants. Global ecosystem models project higher net biomass production, and observations of a variety of tree species indicate that they are already responding to higher atmospheric concentrations of CO_2 and higher temperatures with increased growth rates. Warmer, wetter conditions, and increased biomass production, also could be expected to benefit some animal species.

Animal and Plant Responses to Climate Change

There is agreement among experts that animals that are capable of moving will attempt to migrate in response to climate change. The movements of commercially important species, such as cod, in response to changes in ocean temperature, have been documented for centuries. More recent studies show that a variety of animal species have moved in response to the warming of the 20th century.

Individual plants cannot migrate, but plant species can and do migrate in response to changes in climate. All plants have seed dispersal mechanisms and therefore are constantly trying to establish seedlings in new areas. Seedlings thrive in a more desirable climate, but fail in a less desirable climate, moving the range of the plant as climate changes. The total change in range can be dramatic. Fossil evidence indicate that since the end of the last Ice Age, the balsam fir migrated from the southeastern U.S. to northern Canada, while the black spruce migrated from the central plains to Alaska.

While it is agreed that plants and animals could migrate in response to climate change, at least four further concerns are raised about the likelihood that this will occur to a sufficient degree to prevent large scale species extinction:

1. human activities, particularly habitat disruption, will block potential migration routes;
2. even if they can migrate, the members of a given ecosystem will migrate at different rates leading to imbalances that will result in species extinctions;
3. plants may not be able to migrate fast enough to keep up with projected rates of climate change; and
4. plants and animals that live in restricted niches, e.g., near mountain tops, will have no place to migrate.

These concerns assume no human intervention to help wild species to adapt to climate change. In light of the growing and successful effort to reintroduce species such as beaver and wolf to their former habitats, to replant native plants, and to remove invasive plant species, this assumption is overly conservative.

Can Species Migrate Given Habitat Disruption and Other Human Activities?

Human activities have fragmented the areas in which many plants and animals can thrive. The remaining habitats are often pictured as "islands," which climate change could make unattractive to the species that live there. Migration to other "islands" could be difficult or impossible because the paths for that migration would be blocked by farms, cities, etc. However, recent studies raise questions about this conceptual model. Many species have been shown to either make use of fairly limited habitats or use multiple habitats to provide the area they need.

A recent *New York Times* article quoted Dr. John Wiens, a professor of ecology at Colorado State University, as follows:

> "We need to shift our thinking away from isolated areas in the midst of inhospitable human development," he said. "They're not oceanic islands." Only if biologists think of fragments in the context of an overall landscape, he went on, can they help manage, conserve and restore these habitats.

The *New York Times* article went on to cite the work of Dr. Diane Debinski, a professor of animal ecology at Iowa State University. She found that even "habitat sensitive" species, which tend to stay in the interior of a particular "island," were present in greater number when those habitats were replicated in an attempt to provide a larger area of suitable habitat for these species. These results show that species are able to make use of all available suitable habitats, even if they are fragmented.

As noted above, habitat disruption is projected to be the largest contributor to human-induced species extinction in the 21st century. The steps that society will need to take to reverse this trend should also make it possible for plant and animal species to migrate in face of whatever climate change may occur in the future. . . .

Can Plants Migrate Fast Enough?

The IPCC summarizes the knowledge about the rate of plant species migration as follows:

> Many studies of past changes have estimated natural rates of migration of trees ranging from 40 to 500 meters per year. . . . Gear and Huntly calculated from several sites in Britain migration rates of Scot's pine of only 40–80 meters per year. However, for other species, such as white spruce, much faster dispersal rates of 1–2 kilometers per year have also been reported. It is not always clear whether observed past rates were maximal rates of migration or whether they were limited by the rate at which the climate changed.

The IPCC concludes that these rates of migration are slower than the 1.5–5.5 kilometers per year that trees would have to migrate to keep up with projected rates of warming. However, this analysis assumes that a tree's habitat is a fixed point. Viable trees have ranges that cover many kilometers. Climate change might reduce that range in the short-term, but climate change alone should not lead to significant rates of extinction. Adaptation, for example, by transplanting tree species, could be beneficial in speeding migration.

Can Species With Already Limited Habitats Survive?

If climate warms, the migration path for plants and animals that live on mountains will be upward. This option is limited, since the plant or animal will soon run out of mountain. Since soil conditions typically become poorer with increasing altitude, other factors may limit migration long before the top of the mountain is reached. For species that have very limited habitats, in the extreme, a single mountain, this could lead to extinction. No doubt some of the past climate-related extinctions occurred for this reason. However, most alpine species have broader habitats than a single mountain and would survive, albeit with a changed habitat.

Summary: Can Plants and Animals Adapt to Climate Change?

The answer to this question has to be yes, since plants and animals have been adapting to climate change for billions of years. However, not all plant and animal species will be successful in adapting. If biologists are correct that natural climate change has been a major factor in past species extinctions, any change in climate, whether natural or human-induced, will increase the risk that some marginal species will become extinct.

Despite the concern about climate change, habitat disruption will continue to be the largest threat posed by human activities to the survival of plant and animal species. Many innovative programs are being undertaken to help plants and animals counter the adverse effects of habitat disruption, and these programs will help make these species more resilient to climate change. However, understanding of ecosystem interactions and the potential impacts of climate change on those interactions is simply inadequate.

Migration is the major response that plants and animals can make to climate change. Many concerns have been raised about the ability of plants and animals to migrate given habitat disruption, scenarios involving high rates of climate change during the 21st century, etc. Societal efforts to counter adverse effects by relocating endangered plant and animal species to more favorable habitats could reduce the impact of these changes. . . .

Conclusions

The destruction of ecosystems and species extinction as a consequence of projected climate change have been reported widely by the media and drive much of the perception of the global warming debate. This study examined available scientific evidence to fairly evaluate the claim that anticipated changes in the Earth's climate will result in unacceptable ecosystem impacts.

There is no question that ecosystems are sensitive to climate change and that any significant change is likely to have detrimental consequences for some ecosystems and some species. However, the scope of these consequences is limited by the ability to adapt to an evolving climate.

With continued adaptation, intensively-managed ecosystems, such [as] farms and commercial forests, can benefit from the levels of climate change projected by the IPCC for the 21st century. Developed countries already have the necessary adaptive capacity, and developing countries will acquire the necessary adaptive capacity as their wealth increases.

Ecosystems, such as wildlife areas, which are currently lightly impacted by human activities, would also benefit from adaptation, but the understanding necessary to plan that adaptation is currently inadequate.

To address these questions in a manner that will provide information and analysis needed to evaluate risks and consequences, decision makers need better tools and better information. These include better models, more robust data collection, and better techniques for estimating species and effects on them.

POSTSCRIPT

Are the Costs of Global Warming Too High to Ignore?

It is reasonable to ask how the scientific community attempts to measure changes in the Earth's surface temperature. Certainly, written records only shed light on a tiny fraction of the Earth's long history, and even in the record books that we do have, written temperature records of more than 100 years ago are not available for large parts of the world.

In place of that written history the scientific community has turned to the physical records left by climatic changes. These appear in the growth rates of trees, sea sediment bore holes, pollen counts, the remains of coral colonies, ice cores, and mountain glacier deposits. They tell us that our world has undergone remarkable changes in the 10,000 years since the end of the last major ice age, which closed the Pleistocene epoch. It is important to examine two major climatic disturbances, which appear in more recent times—the past 1,000 years. Scientists call one of these disturbances the "Little Ice Age," which occurred approximately 1300–1900 A.D. The other anomaly occurred around 1000–1300 A.D. This relatively mild climatic period is called the Medieval Warm Period. It is remarkable in that in some regions radical increases in temperatures occurred. Some suggest that it may help explain the population explosion during the medieval period in Europe. This warm weather may also help explain why this period was marked by the construction of many European cathedrals. See H. H. Lamb, *Climate, History and the Modern World,* 2d ed. (Routledge, 1995).

An apparent conclusion is that global warming is not as clear-cut as some suggest. Simply because we can measure an increase in surface temperatures over a significant period of time may not in and of itself mean that we are experiencing global warming that can be traced to human activity. Rather, this warming may be the natural course of events—events that the world has experienced repeatedly over its long history. For more on that view, read Patrick J. Michaels and Robert Balling, Jr., *Satanic Gases: Clearing the Air About Global Warming* (Cato Institute, 2000). In it, the authors argue that those who warn of global warming have blown the issue all out of proportion and in the process have ignored all the evidence that suggests the contrary.

The other side is not mute on this issue. Indeed, there are many Web sites devoted to the issue of global warming. To read about the Kyoto Protocol, see `http://unfccc.int/resource/convkp.html`. Alternatively, visit the United Nations Industrial Development Organization's (UNIDO) Web site at `http://www.unido.org/doc/3941`. For a scholarly, balanced view, turn to Warwick J. McKibbin and Peter Wilcoxen's *Climate Change Policy After Kyoto: A Blueprint for a Realistic Approach* (Brookings Institution Press, 2002.)

ISSUE 16

Do Living Wage Laws Improve Economic Conditions in Cities?

YES: Chris Tilly, from "Next Steps for the Living-Wage Movement," *Dollars & Sense* (September–October 2001)

NO: Steven Malanga, from "How the 'Living-Wage' Sneaks Socialism into Cities," *City Journal* (Winter 2003)

ISSUE SUMMARY

YES: Professor Chris Tilly supports the living wage for two basic reasons: (1) It is only fair to increase the incomes of those who earn the lowest wages, and (2) the living wage laws that have been passed "have not escalated costs, nor repelled businesses."

NO: Author Steven Malanga believes that the actions to pass living wage laws represent a "savvy left-wing political movement," and that living wage laws threaten the economic health of cities by increasing wage costs and "send businesses fleeing to other locales."

The term "wages" is familiar to almost everyone; it refers to the income individuals generate for themselves by working. Economists accept this simple definition of wages but frequently add more perspective to the definition by also describing wages as the return to that factor of production known as labor. Economists then employ a whole slew of adjectives to distinguish between different kinds of wages.

One distinction concerns the differences in how wages are paid. Some wages are based on piece rates; that is, the worker is paid depending on his or her output—getting, say, a dollar for each program sold at a sporting event. Alternatively, wages can based on hours worked; here an individual is paid the same amount per hour regardless of how many units of output are produced in an hour. A third option is usually referred to as a salary; the individual earns a set amount per week or month regardless of how many hours are worked in that week or month (although there may be an understanding of how many hours will be worked during the pay period) or how much is to be produced in the week or month.

Perhaps the most important of the distinctions that economists make concerns the difference between nominal and real wages. The former simply refers to the number of dollars that a person earns per period of time by supplying services in the labor market. Real wages adjust nominal wages for changes in the prices of goods and services that workers buy and, thus, reflects the purchasing power of wages. More simply, the real wage is the ratio of the nominal wage to some appropriate price index. What is important in terms of changes in standards of living over time is the behavior of real wages.

Sometimes a distinction is made between wages that are paid in monetary form and those that are paid "in-kind." The latter represent compensation given to employees in the form of goods and services; for example, waiters and waitresses may be given free meals while faculty at some colleges get free tuition for their children. One advantage of in-kind wages is that they are typically not subject to income taxes. A disadvantage is that the employees may not necessarily want the goods or services that are given or available to them.

To complicate matters, there are terms that are linked to wages. Take for example the term "compensation." In the national income accounts, there is a distinction between wages and salaries on the one hand and compensation on the other. The latter is a broader term and in the national income accounts includes employer contributions for (1) employee pension and insurance funds and (2) government social insurance. As some would put it, the term "wages" excludes fringe benefits while the term "compensation" includes these items.

So having said all this, what is meant by the term "living wage," the subject of this issue? It is usually considered to be something that is greater than the minimum wage. A minimum wage is a floor set by the federal government or a state government (see Issue 11). That is, advocates of living wages believe that mandated minimum wages are not sufficient to keep a family out of poverty. For the past several years, the federally mandated minimum wage has been set at $5.15 per hour. A person working 40 hours a week for 50 weeks a year at this minimum wage would earn $10,300. But the federal government has set the poverty levels for 2004 at $19,157 for a family of four (with two children under 18 years of age). So to escape poverty in 2004, such a family with just one wage earner needed that wage earner to make $9.58 per hour.

The laws that have been passed establishing a living wage are local laws. That is, there is no federal living wage, and no state as yet has legislated a living wage. But, according to one source over 100 localities, including cities like Baltimore, Boston, Chicago, Cleveland, Detroit, Los Angeles, New York, San Antonio, and San Francisco, have passed living wage ordinances. So the question is: Have these various laws helped the low-wage workers they were intended to help as well as communities in which these workers live?

YES

Chris Tilly

Next Steps for the Living-Wage Movement

This past May, Harvard University students made national headlines by occupying a university building for three weeks to demand that Harvard and its contractors pay employees a living wage. While Harvard refused to grant the $10.25 wage that the students demanded, they did agree to form a study committee with ample student and union representation. In the days that followed, Harvard also ended a contract negotiation deadlock with food service workers by offering an unprecedented wage increase of over $1 per hour—a surprise move that many attributed to the feisty labor-student alliance built through the living-wage push.

Harvard's living-wage activists represent the tip of a much larger national iceberg, most of which has taken the form of attempts to pass local living-wage ordinances. Over 60 local governments have passed living-wage laws—almost all since a ground-breaking Baltimore ordinance passed in 1994—with more coming on board each month. Such ordinances typically require the local government, along with any businesses that supply it, to pay a wage well above the current federal minimum of $5.15. Living-wage coalitions originally set wage floors at the amount needed by a full-time, year-round worker to keep a family of four above the poverty line (currently about $8.40 per hour), but like the Harvard students, they are increasingly campaigning for higher figures based on area living costs. The community organization ACORN (Alliance of Community Organizations for Reform Now) has spearheaded many of the coalitions, and an up-to-date living-wage scorecard can be found on its web site. At the heart of the campaigns are low-wage workers like Celia Talavera, who joined Santa Monica's successful living-wage campaign last May. Referring to her job as a hotel housekeeper, she said, "I am fighting for a living wage because I want to work there for a long time."

The spread of living-wage laws reflects deep public concern about the unfairness of today's economy to those at the bottom of the paid workforce. A recent *USA Today* poll rated "lack of livable wage jobs" as Americans' top worry, even ahead of such perennial favorites as "decline of moral values." This sentiment makes living-wage laws eminently winnable. But it is worth pausing to ask: What, exactly, has the living-wage movement won? And how can we adapt this strategy to win more?

Limited Victories

Opponents of living-wage laws argue that they will increase costs to local taxpayers, and drive business away from the locality. Living-wage boosters have two responses. First, fairness is worth the cost. And second, studies have shown that such ordinances have not escalated costs, nor repelled businesses. But why not? After all, economic theory suggests that companies compelled to pay higher costs will either seek to pass them on, or move on to greener pastures.

One reason is that living-wage ordinances typically affect very few workers. At passage, an average of only about 1,000 per locality actually have their wages boosted (in part because many of those covered already earn the mandated wage or more). This number is stunningly small, given that living-wage adopters include Los Angeles, New York, Chicago, and numerous other large cities and counties.

But smallness cannot be the entire explanation. Johns Hopkins University economist Erica Schoenberger and others followed specific contracts to the City of Baltimore, looking at changes from before that city's living-wage law went into effect to two years after. They found that contract costs increased only about 1%, far less than inflation. One possibility, of course, is that the wage floor spurred contractors to find new ways to increase true efficiency—getting the same amount of work done with less labor and less effort. For instance, this can happen if higher wages allow employers to hold on to the same employees longer, shrinking employer expenditures on recruitment, hiring, and training. Or perhaps the businesses have simply accepted lower profit margins.

But there are three less pleasant possibilities as well. Contractors may have sped up their workers, extracting more work in return for the higher pay. They may have reduced the quality of goods or services they delivered. Or, they may simply have failed to comply with the law. The poor track record of many laws that declare labor rights without adequate enforcement mechanisms suggests that this last possibility may be quite real. Even the federal minimum wage is ignored by growing numbers of employers, says economist Howard Wial of the AFL-CIO's Working for America Institute.

Extend the Laws?

How should the living-wage movement respond to this evidence of limited impact? One possibility is to widen and sharpen living-wage laws' bite. Recent living-wage ordinances have set minimums as high as $12 per hour (in Santa Cruz, California). In Santa Monica, California, campaigners extended coverage to tourist-district businesses that had received city subsidies for redevelopment, and elsewhere coalitions aim to expand the law to include any business that receives substantial subsidies or tax abatements from the local government. Activists are also setting their sights on living-wage agreements with large private businesses—starting with those most vulnerable to political and public relations pressure, especially nonprofits such as Harvard. Even more ambitious are the advocates proposing state and federal living-wage laws; legislative proposals are pending in Hawaii, Vermont, and at the federal level. . . .

Others are pursuing area-wide minimum wages set at levels closer to a living wage. Washington, D.C., has long had a minimum wage $1 above the federal minimum. Similar referenda were defeated in Houston and Denver, but New Orleans citizens will vote on a local minimum wage this coming February.

These initiatives are important, because there is certainly room for significant wage increases before we can expect negative effects on employment. When adjusted for inflation, hourly wages for the lowest-paid tenth of the workforce jumped by 9% between 1995 and 1999, in large part due to living-wage laws and federal minimum-wage increases. Yet the unemployment rate at the end of the 1990s fell to its lowest level in 30 years. More fine-grained studies of state and federal minimum-wage increases yield the same result: Such increases have caused little or no worker displacement over the last ten years. One reason is that wages for the bottom tenth were beaten so far down over the 1980s and early 1990s—even after the recent wage surge, inflation-adjusted 1999 wages remained 10% below their 1979 level.

But if the movement succeeds in extending and increasing living wages, at some point economic theory is bound to be proven right: costs to taxpayers will climb, employment will decrease, or both. Even in the most positive scenario—that businesses find ways to increase productivity—remember that rising productivity typically means doing the same work with fewer workers. This was the experience of the Congress of Industrial Organizations (now part of the AFL-CIO), which unionized core manufacturing industries in the 1930s and 1940s. The CIO succeeded in hiking pay, and in the decades that followed, U.S. manufacturers avidly hunted for ways to boost productivity. The good news is that U.S. manufacturing became the most productive in the world for several decades. The bad news is that heightened efficiency shrank labor requirements dramatically. In fact, this is the main reason for declining U.S. manufacturing jobs, far overshadowing shifts in the global division of labor. Manufacturing is a slightly larger share of U.S. domestic output today than it was in 1960, but factory employment has dropped from 31% to 14% of the workforce.

If extending the living wage's impact will eventually either raise costs to taxpayers or diminish employment, it may be tempting to adopt the other major argument advocates use: fairness is worth the cost. And this answer makes a great deal of sense. Think for a moment about the federal *minimum wage's* effect. The average person who eats at McDonald's earns more than the average person who works at McDonald's, so if bumping up the minimum wage raises the cost of burgers, cash is shifting in more or less the right direction. By the same token, over the 1980s and 1990s, local and state privatization and tax cuts redistributed income from low-income workers to taxpayers who have higher incomes on average—so if living wages help to reverse this flow, that's a plus for equality.

What about job losses? Few would object to shutting down companies that rely on slavery or child labor. The same logic extends to exploitatively low wages. As with child labor laws, laws that bar low wages will put some workers out of a job. So it is important to view living-wage laws as part of a broader program that includes job creation, training, and income support for those unable to work. To achieve this broader program, we need a powerful movement. And the red-hot living-wage movement offers one of the strongest potential building blocks for such a broader movement.

Build the Movement?

That brings us to another response to the limited impact of living-wage laws to date: using the living wage as a movement-building tool. The living-wage issue encourages labor, community, and religious organizations to coalesce around genuine shared interests, creating an opportunity to open an even broader dialogue on wage fairness and inequality.

The goal should be to build movements that can address some of the weaknesses of current living-wage laws, including non-compliance and the potential for speed-up or job loss. Of course the U.S. institution that has been most effective in monitoring compliance with labor laws, curbing speed-up, and lobbying for job creation is the labor movement—and living-wage laws provide a golden opportunity for strengthening unions. Baltimore activists who won that city's 1994 living-wage ordinance, considered the spark of the current living-wage prairie fire, sought above all to slow down union-busting privatization. Living-wage laws close off low wages as a competitive strategy, dulling the edge of employer resistance to unions. Some coalitions have also won clauses requiring covered businesses to be neutral in union organizing campaigns or even to immediately recognize any union that signs up a majority of workers, foreclosing employers' usual anti-union tactics. A lower profile way to disarm anti-union employers is to ban retaliation against workers organizing for a living wage—which basically puts a local law against union-busting on the books to supplement weak federal laws.

In addition, living-wage advocates need to pay attention to winning laws that nurture the living-wage movement itself. For instance, some laws give living-wage coalition constituents the first crack at applying for jobs covered by the living wage, in some cases through coalition-controlled hiring halls. Patronage usually gets a bad name, but this kind of community control over hiring can help cement a living-wage movement's strength by giving it the ability to reward its members and supporters. Moreover, although advocates dream of short-cutting the process of passing hundreds of local laws by winning federal legislation, in reality the local mobilizations are the key to success with compliance. Any federal law is likely to remain a dead letter unless we have built those hundreds of robust place-based coalitions ready to monitor the law's implementation and use it as an organizing tool.

The biggest challenge in movement building is reaching beyond wages and jobs to the less obvious issues. For instance, how do we defend the quality of public services? Many nonprofits and community-based organizations have been drawn into the game of privatizing social services. Sometimes these agencies enter unholy alliances with private businesses and city officials to oppose living-wage laws, because they fear it will threaten their job programs for disadvantaged workers. Organizations representing workers, communities, service providers, and clients must search for common ground based on high wages and adequate services. In Massachusetts, for example, unions and service providers have campaigned jointly for a state-funded living wage for human-service workers employed by hundreds of state contractors.

Another tough nut to crack is how to win adequate income for those who are unable to work for pay, or who end up working on a very part-time or part-year basis. Unfortunately, some of the same public attitudes that make it easy to build coalitions around living wages—equating work with virtue, for example—make it hard to defend welfare for people not working for wages. The principals from the living-wage movement—unions, churches, and ACORN itself—have also joined efforts to demand more adequate and less restrictive welfare benefits, but so far with much less success.

More Than Just a Living

The sixty local living-wage laws to date represent a tremendous victory for working people, but one that is, so far, narrow in scope. The challenge now is to extend the reach of the laws, while building and broadening the living-wage movement at the same time. Extending the laws' reach means bringing more cities on board, but even more importantly, boosting the numbers and types of workers covered within each city. To the extent that advocates succeed in passing stronger laws, they will engender fiercer resistance—both direct challenges to the legislation and more covert attempts to flout the laws or shift the costs. To successfully counter this resistance, movement-building efforts must go beyond the boundaries of the current living-wage movement. The end result will look less like a living-wage movement, more like a broad insurgent movement to redistribute income and other resources.

Steven Malanga

How the "Living Wage" Sneaks Socialism into Cities

Over the last decade, a savvy left-wing political movement, supported by radical economic groups, liberal foundations, and urban activists, has lobbied for a government-guaranteed "living wage" for low-income workers, considerably higher than the current minimum wage. The movement has scored enormous success: 80 cities nationwide, from New York to San Francisco, now have living-wage legislation in place. Many of the earliest laws were narrowly focused on workers at companies with government contracts. But as the movement has grown, it has successfully imposed its mandate on a wider array of businesses; one city has even passed a citywide living wage.

This is bad news for cities. The living wage poses a big threat to their economic health, because the costs and restrictions it imposes on the private sector will destroy jobs—especially low-wage jobs—and send businesses fleeing to other locales. Worse still, the living-wage movement's agenda doesn't end with forcing private employers to increase wages. It includes opposing privatization schemes, strong-arming companies into unionizing, and other economic policies equally harmful to urban health.

The living-wage movement got its start in mid-1990s Baltimore, whose radical urban politics and anti-business ethos provided fertile ground. In 1993, a coalition of Baltimore's left-leaning church leaders, unionists, and community activists began to push for a "social compact" that included a hike in the minimum wage to $6.10—43 percent above the federal minimum wage at the time—for service workers in hotels and other businesses in the city's redeveloped Inner Harbor, a prime tourist area.

Baltimore's then-mayor Kurt Schmoke initially balked at the potential harm that such a wage increase would inflict on the city's already shrinking economy and budget. But he eventually signed a compromise bill that guaranteed the new $6.10 minimum for workers at any companies contracting with the city, on the principle that, unlike the Inner Harbor firms, these employers benefited directly from public funds and thus had an obligation to pay a higher minimum as a way of helping the city carry out its self-proclaimed mission of improving the lot of the urban poor.

Supporters hailed the increase as a costless victory for low-income workers. The labor-backed Preamble Center for Public Policy rushed out a study purporting to show that the legislation benefited Baltimore workers but did no harm to the local economy or to the city budget, because city contractors effortlessly absorbed the cost of the wage hike. The study's claims didn't withstand scrutiny—contracting costs *did* rise—but that was almost beside the point. Far from turning into a workers' paradise, Baltimore saw its economy crash and burn during the mid-1990s, with 58,000 jobs disappearing, even as the rest of Maryland added 120,000 jobs and other cities across the country prospered. The living-wage bill was just one expression of a fiercely anti-business climate that helped precipitate Baltimore's economic collapse.

Sensible observers would call Baltimore in the nineties an urban disaster, but to the nascent living-wage movement, the city became the poster child for future activism. Looking to the "success" of the living-wage campaign in Baltimore, a host of left-wing groups, including Ralph Nader's Citizens Action and the Association for Community Reform Now, or ACORN, joined forces in 1995 in a national "Campaign for an America That Works," which made the living wage central to its demands. The campaign was so radical that it had no impact on the national level. But on the local level, where the political environment is usually far to the left of Washington, it popularized the living-wage idea, which began to catch on in city after city.

As it spread beyond Baltimore, the living-wage movement at first purposely kept its aims narrow. Early legislative victories applied to just a few workers. In 1996, for example, Milwaukee County passed a law increasing the minimum wage only for city-contracted janitors and security guards to $6.25 an hour. New York City's law, passed over Mayor Giuliani's veto, applied only to government-contracted security personnel, cleaning workers, and temporary employees.

Soon, though, living-wage supporters began to win ever broader laws, covering ever more workers and businesses. Detroit's 1998 living wage applied to any business or nonprofit with a city contract or to any firm that had received $50,000 or more in economic development assistance—ranging from the Salvation Army to small manufacturers located in the city's economic development zones. San Francisco's law went beyond city contractors to cover workers at the city airport, on the grounds that businesses there leased land from the city; airlines, newsstands, fast-food restaurants—none was exempt. In early 2002, New Orleans, ACORN's national home, enacted the first city-wide living wage in the nation—something the movement would like to see replicated everywhere. Today, 42 states now have at least one municipality with living-wage legislation.

The movement owes much of its success to the model campaign—exportable anywhere, anytime, fast—that its proponents, above all ACORN's national living-wage center, have created. The prospective living-wage activist can find everything he needs to know in a step-by-step manual, concocted by ACORN director of living-wage campaigns Jed Kern and Wayne State University labor economist David Reynolds.

The manual echoes the organizational theories of legendary radical Saul Alinsky. Coalition building is key. Alinsky's *modus operandi* was to get diverse constituencies to support his various causes by emphasizing their shared interests. In the same way, ACORN urges local living-wage campaigns to build powerful coalitions of Hispanic workers, inner-city ministers, and various community advocacy groups.

To pull off such coalition building in practice, you need more than a manual, of course; you need money—and the movement has lots of it, thanks to the backing of leftist foundations. The Tides Foundation (currently lending financial support to groups opposing war in Iraq) has given hundreds of thousands of dollars to local and national living-wage groups. The Ford Foundation has been another big contributor.

The coalitions the movement has assembled have included hundreds of religious groups, allowing organizers to present their economic agenda as deeply moral—even divinely sanctioned. Labor groups have signed on, too, and some 60 coalitions of labor and interfaith religious groups have sprung up nationally since the mid-1990s to campaign for the living wage.

The Los Angeles–based Clergy and Laity United for Economic Justice (CLUE) is a prominent example. Formed during a successful living-wage campaign in Los Angeles, CLUE brought together an Episcopal priest who had worked to unionize Santa Monica's hotels, a Baptist minister who once invited a union local into Sunday services to get signatures for a hospital unionizing drive, and a rabbi who had campaigned against the Hollywood stereotyping of Palestinians as terrorists. To highlight the plight of "exploited" hotel service workers deprived of the living wage, the religious trio staged a dramatic procession through Beverly Hills to deposit bitter herbs at the doorstep of the Summit Hotel—evoking the Jewish tradition of using such herbs to recall the Israelites' deliverance from Egyptian bondage.

CLUE is only one of countless examples of the living-wage movement using religion to give it moral clout—in Providence, Rhode Island, churches even held a "living-wage Sunday." "It makes it hard to sound negative about a living-wage campaign when it's presented in those terms," says Jeffery Hunter, a government-affairs specialist with the Greater Detroit Chamber of Commerce, which fought in vain against one of the nation's earliest living-wage laws. Indeed, the very notion of a "living" wage makes anyone who opposes it seem like . . . well, an executioner.

Living-wage campaigns have repeatedly outflanked the business community by practicing what ACORN calls "legislative outmaneuver." Local groups work behind the scenes for months before going public. They draft partisan economists to release timely studies on the prospective benefits of the living wage before opponents can come up with any countering data, and they try to keep any actual legislation off the table until the very last minute, so that there's no fixed target for opponents to get a bead on. ACORN rationalizes these stealth campaigns by arguing that the business community will use, in the words of Kern and Reynolds's organizing manual, a "bag of dirty tricks" to fight the legislation. ACORN ominously—and ludicrously—warns: "Many companies today engage in tactics which hark back to the bloody [unionizing] battles of the 1930s."

ACORN's stealth tactics worked particularly well in Detroit. The Motor City business community had no idea that a living-wage ordinance was about to wallop them until just weeks before it showed up on a citywide referendum. "The organizers won," a labor newsletter observed, "by slipping quietly under Detroit's corporate and political radar." Same story in Boston: "The living-wage ordinance wasn't picked up on the radar until it was too late," complained a local business publication. The Boston law, the publication adds, "initially looked and sounded like yet another innocuous piece of feel-good legislation," but its small print included onerous provisions that required city contractors to work under the supervision of a living-wage enforcement committee and to prefer Boston residents for jobs over applicants from beyond the city limits.

These stealth campaigns can produce legislation so bad that it even turns earlier supporters of the living wage into enemies. In Detroit, then-mayor Dennis Archer, initially an ally of the living-wage proposal, excoriated its backers after it became law, because they "did not consult with business or with the [Detroit Regional] Chamber, [so that] the ordinance unfairly impacts on small business and non-profit groups." One hard-hit nonprofit, the Southeastern Michigan Salvation Army, chose not to renew several city contracts to provide housing services to the poor, because the living wage raised its costs too high. "We had a good working relationship with the city, but we ended that," says a spokesman. ACORN has since accused the Salvation Army—the *Salvation Army*—of "the big lie" for opposing its living-wage agenda.

Providing the intellectual muscle (such as it is) for the living-wage movement is a small group of Marxoid economists, led by University of Massachusetts–Amherst professor Robert Pollin, a longtime board member of the Union of Radical Political Economists, founded in the 1960s to bring Marxist economics to American universities. Pollin, a New School Ph.D., began serving as an advisor to living-wage campaigns in the mid-1990s, and in 1998 he co-authored (with Stephanie Luce) the book that has become the movement's bible: *The Living Wage: Building a Fair Economy.*

In *The Living Wage,* the class war rages on—and on. Businesses, assert Pollin and Luce, have grown increasingly hostile toward workers in recent years. Their sole evidence for this claim—that the unionization rate has plummeted over the last three decades—ignores the conventional explanations for union decline in the U.S.: more intense global competition, the shift to a service-oriented, knowledge-based economy, and more generous benefits at non-unionized companies. But never mind: to keep the ravenous capitalists under control, they argue, government clearly needs to impose a national living wage on the private sector. And that's just the beginning. Caps on profits, mandated benefits, rules to make unionization easier, massive taxation—government will manage the economy from top to bottom in *The Living Wage*'s warmed-over socialism.

Indeed, for Pollin and Luce, only one economic goal ultimately matters: raising worker salaries—no matter what the cost to the broader economy. Consider their discussion of prevailing wage laws, which set pay rates for public-sector construction projects. Pollin and Luce argue that these laws show what good living-wage legislation will achieve—and what damage the absence of government economic control inflicts on workers. The authors cite a study of nine states that repealed prevailing wage laws and then watched construction-worker annual salaries fall $1,500, or 6 percent. To the authors, this is entirely bad news. Nowhere do they try to estimate the savings for government (and thus for taxpayers) once the laws stopped demanding artificially high wages for construction contracts. Nor are the authors interested in the productivity gains for the construction industry—and hence for the economy as a whole—when wages settle at levels dictated by supply and demand, not government bureaucrats.

The complete rejection of a free-market economy by these living-wage gurus—and by the living-wage movement itself—is too much even for many liberal economists. One of the most telling critiques of *The Living Wage* came from self-professed liberal economist and *New York Times* columnist Paul Krugman. In an article archived on the "cranks" section of his website, Krugman observes that "what the living wage is really about is not living standards, or even economics, but morality. Its advocates are basically opposed to the idea that wages are a market price—determined by supply and demand."

But then, if living-wage advocates truly understood the free market, they'd know that it ultimately is far more moral than the centrally controlled economic system they endorse. If there is one thing that the last 50 years tell us, it is that the free market provides far greater economic opportunity and a decent standard of living for far more people than government-controlled markets. Pollin and Luce charge that the American economy is failing, because poverty levels in the United States aren't declining significantly. But the authors disregard the effect on the poverty level of the vast stream of immigrants—many of them poor and without skills—cascading into the country every year. What was remarkable about the American economy during the 1990s, when about 13 million low-skilled, low-wage immigrants arrived, is that poverty rates *didn't* soar, and actually declined slightly—showing the muscularity of our economy in lifting even many of these newcomers out of poverty. A recent Sphere Institute study of low-wage workers in California found that more than 80 percent moved up the economic ladder during the 1990s, their average income more than doubling, to $27,194. If that's not economic justice, nothing is. As for those Pollin (following the Census Bureau) calls poor: 40 percent own homes, 97 percent own color televisions, two-thirds have air conditioning, and about seven in ten own cars. This is hardly the poverty of a Vietnamese peasant or a 1930s sharecropper.

What's most appalling about Pollin and Luce's economic theorizing, however, is the cavalier way they talk about confiscating income from middle-income Americans to pay for their living-wage scheme. In a follow-up article to his book, published in the far-left *Nation* magazine, Pollin proposed a national living wage of $7.25 per hour, more than $2 above the current minimum. To achieve this, he says, would require a redistribution of income "equal to a reduction of only 6.6 percent in the incomes of the richest 20 percent of households, from roughly $106,600 to $100,000." *Only* 6.6 percent? Stripping $6,600 a year away from a family making $106,000 a year—a construction worker married to a secretary might well earn this much—is no insignificant levy (even though Pollin's math is wrong). Down more than $550 a month, such a middle-class family might have to forgo sending one of their kids to parochial school, or put off adding a room onto the house for the new baby—goals they may have worked very hard to achieve.

Not only is Pollin's national living wage wildly unfair; it wouldn't work. Numerous studies show that increasing the minimum wage produces no significant reduction in poverty levels and may even increase the number of families living in poverty by eliminating many low-wage jobs. A recent Congressional Budget Office report, for example, estimates that upping the minimum wage to $6.65 an hour (40 percent less than Pollin's proposal) would eradicate between 200,000 and 600,000 jobs. Moreover, it would wreak economic havoc, costing employers $7 billion a year in additional payroll costs. Nor, it's important to add, are minimum-wage earners necessarily struggling economically in the first place. About 64 percent of those receiving the minimum wage today aren't heads of households or sole earners. Many are children still living at home or second wage earners in their family. The average annual household income of a minimum-wage worker in the United States is nearly $44,000. And of course, almost no workers stay at the minimum for long.

Understandably, given these considerations, most economists today favor earned-income tax credits, not government-mandated wages, as a more effective way to aid the working poor. These tax credits, applied for when filing, provide thousands of dollars in cash rebates from federal and state governments, supplementing the income of low-wage workers without imposing direct new costs on businesses.

Pollin and his radical economist colleagues have regularly descended from the ivory tower to try to convince local elected officials around the country that living-wage laws will help low-wage workers without destroying jobs or significantly raising government expenses. In a 1997 study on a proposed living-wage law in Los Angeles, for instance, Pollin claimed that the legislation—doubling the minimum wage for government contractors—would increase the city's contracting costs by only $7.5 million. The wage hike, Pollin argued, would require just a $40 million increase in contractors' payrolls—something they could easily absorb, he held, given their total sales of $4 billion; little, if any, of the additional cost would be passed on to government.

In a later city-commissioned report, UCLA economist Richard Sander—who calls himself a "progressive Democrat" and a defender of narrowly drawn living-wage laws—demolished Pollin's rosy scenario. Sander estimated that the actual cost of the legislation to city government would be $42 million—six times Pollin's estimate. Moreover, Sander noted, adding $40 million to firms' salary costs, as the law proposed, was nothing to sneeze at—as is evident as soon as you compare the new costs not with companies' total revenues, as Pollin did, but with their very much smaller profits.

Los Angeles eventually enacted narrower living-wage legislation, and Sander has completed a study of it. He found that the city, and not its contractors, is bearing all the cost of its living wage. Hit with the legislation, L.A. vendors either raised prices or reduced services to the city. Adding in the expense of monitoring compliance with the law, the city bears "more than 100 percent of the cost," Sander says.

Joining the radical economists on the front lines of living-wage campaigns are the unions, which have their own reasons for supporting the legislation. For unions and their political allies, the threat of the living wage has become a powerful means to pressure firms to unionize. About two dozen current living-wage ordinances, and about a dozen more proposed laws, specifically exempt unionized companies from the legislation. So if a local city contractor paying $2 below the living wage unionizes, it won't have to raise salaries—at least in the short term.

No wonder that many living-wage campaigns erupt in places where unions are fighting tough organizing battles with local businesses. In Santa Monica, for example, a living-wage campaign got under way after a local hotel union had failed in a three-year effort to organize workers in the city's tourism district. The living-wage legislation that Santa Monica's left-leaning City Council then crafted and passed, with heavy union input all down the line, subjected every business in the tourism district to its terms—except unionized hotels. Santa Monica voters recently overturned the law in a referendum, though advocates are trying again.

These kinds of union-tailored living-wage laws are so blatantly pro-labor that they may be illegal. When a law forces employers to choose between paying higher wages and accepting a union, says Atlanta labor lawyer Arch Stokes, it amounts to a collective-bargaining ordinance. Municipalities don't have the legal right to supersede federal labor law and pass such legislation.

Municipal unions like living-wage laws, too, for a different reason. By raising the cost of city contracts, these laws make privatization efforts less appealing and thus protect the cushy jobs of city workers. After all, if cities can't save much money by contracting out work traditionally done by high-paid municipal workers, what is the point of privatizing? ACORN puts it bluntly in its manual: "The Living Wage undercuts the incentive to privatize."

Ironically, even as ACORN battles to make businesses and nonprofit contractors pay higher wages, the State of California is suing the group for paying its own workers below the minimum wage. ACORN argued that minimum-wage laws infringe on the group's First Amendment right of free speech. If it had to pay the minimum wage, the organization says—shamelessly echoing the arguments of the businesses that it is forever seeking to regulate—it would have to hire fewer people, making it harder to get its message out.

The living-wage movement's next steps are clear—and potentially devastating to urban prosperity. Activists are working hard to expand the number of those covered by existing living-wage legislation. In New York City, one of the first places to enact a living-wage law, the new City Council and Mayor Bloomberg recently extended it to 50,000 or so privately employed health-care workers. The powerful union SEIU/1199, representing some home health-care workers who fall under the extended legislation, lobbied heavily for the change. Thanks to Mayor Bloomberg, New York will now have the largest number of workers covered by any living-wage law in the nation. Other cities have expanded their laws, too. Oakland's initial edict, to take just one example, originally applied only to city contracts, but in early 2002 city lawmakers extended it to firms in the government-subsidized Port of Oakland.

It's not just the number of those covered that the movement wants to expand. ACORN activists have begun advocating more capacious living-wage laws that incorporate affirmative-action requirements, restrictions on employers' use of part-time workers, mandatory vacation time, and prohibitions on using revenues from public contracts to hire law firms to resist union-organizing efforts. San Francisco, already moving in this direction, amended its law a year after it passed to include certain health-care benefits on top of the wage boost.

As living-wage laws get broader and more expansive, supporters are also trying to offload some of the cost, increasingly burdensome to cities, onto state and federal government. The revision of the New York City law, for instance, zeroed in on health-care workers because many of them work in state-funded institutions. City Council members who sponsored the legislation justified it by saying that the state's share of the cost will be five or six times higher than the city's. And Detroit's law included contracts that the city simply administered but that were paid for by federal agencies, such as Housing and Urban Development.

Emboldened by their successes, living-wage advocates have gone on to help organize local coalitions to lobby for much broader left-wing economic programs, under the slogan "sustainable economics." ACORN's own organizing manual says it best: "[A]cross the country grassroots projects are using Living Wage as a campaign tool for building broad and comprehensive progressive agendas."

Sustainable economics covers a whole agenda of government social and fiscal policies to redistribute income and regulate business that add up to socialism by another name. The Milwaukee coalition responsible for that city's living-wage law, for example, is now pushing for an economic-development plan that includes more money for community job-training programs, laws that bolster union organizing and that require "socially responsible banking," government investment to create "environmentally friendly" jobs—and on and on. Its agenda even leaps beyond economics to require multicultural public school curricula, more ethnically diverse teaching staffs, and greater inclusion in curricula of topics such as workers' rights, the history of the labor movement, and family leave laws.

Lest this grand program sound like mere pie in the sky, note that living-wage advocates in California have already succeeded in getting the state's assembly to pass a sustainable economic plan for the greater Sacramento area. Startlingly, this plan forces growing suburban communities to share tax income with the city, and it restricts suburban growth, so that residents and businesses will find it more difficult to move just outside the city limits. Having created the policies on taxation, crime, and education that propelled the middle class out of urban America in the first place, the Left is now looking for a way to slow that flight by governmental fiat. It's yet more bad news for cities—especially since the rest of the country fortunately is still free and has plenty of room.

POSTSCRIPT

Do Living Wage Laws Improve Economic Conditions in Cities?

Tilly begins his discussion of the living wage by describing events at Harvard University during May 2001 when an alliance of students and labor pushed the University to adopt a living wage policy. He then indicates the spread of local living wage laws (LWL). He believes that the acceptance of LWL is rooted in the widespread belief that the modern economy is unfair to "those at the bottom of the paid workforce." The opponents of LWL argue that these laws increase the taxes that local residents have to pay, and they drive businesses away from the communities that adopt them. Tilly believes that the appropriate responses to these arguments are (1) fairness is worth any additional taxpayer cost, and (2) there is little evidence to suggest that business have fled the communities that have passed LWL. But Tilly recognizes that efforts to extend and increase living wages will eventually increase taxpayer costs, and/or employment will decrease. Therefore, the fairness argument is the ultimate defense for LWL. He also recommends that LWL be used as "a movement-building tool," transforming the LWL movement into a "broad insurgent movement to redistribute income and other resources."

Malanga opposes LWL because they threaten the economic health of communities by raising costs and imposing restrictions on business that lead to the loss of private-sector jobs and send business to communities that do not have LWL. In addition, he believes the LWL movement opposes "privatization schemes, strong-arming companies into unionizing, and other economic policies equally harmful to urban health." He offers several examples to support his claims including events in Baltimore, Detroit, Boston, and Los Angeles. He then examines the writings of those he believes provide the "intellectual muscle" for the LWL movement. Malanga argues that these writings suffer from a number of deficiencies including a misunderstanding of the free market.

Tilly suggests several additional readings at the end of his essay. A special edition of *Industrial Relations* (January 2005) is devoted to an examination of the consequences of living wage policies. The Economics Policy Institute has an *Issue Guide* to the living wage as well as several working papers on the living wage; these may be accessed at `http://www.epinet.org`. Other readings include *The Living Wage: Building a Fair Economy* by Robert Pollin and Stephanie Luce (The New Press, 1998); and "Living Wage, Live Action" by Robert Pollin in *The Nation* (November 23, 1998). An article by N. Gregory Mankiw, "The Cost of a Living Wage," which is critical of the living wage, can be found in the June 24, 2001 issue of the *Boston Globe*. Another critical study is Backgrounder #38 from The James Madison Institute entitled "The Living Wage Movement and Its Implications for Florida" (March 1, 2003). Several other critical studies may be accessed from the Web site of the Employment Policies Institute at http://www.epionline.org/study_lst.cfm. Finally, one can visit http://www;ivingwageresearch.org/.

ISSUE 17

Has the North American Free Trade Agreement Hurt the American Economy?

YES: Robert E. Scott, from "NAFTA's Hidden Costs: Trade Agreement Results in Job Losses, Growing Inequality, and Wage Suppression for the United States," *EPI Briefing Paper* (April 2001)

NO: Daniel T. Griswold, from "NAFTA at 10: An Economic and Foreign Policy Success," *Free Trade Bulletin* (December 2002)

ISSUE SUMMARY

YES: Economic Policy Institute director Robert E. Scott argues that besides the loss of a significant number of jobs, the North American Free Trade Agreement (NAFTA) has generated a number of less visible harmful effects on the American economy. These include increased income inequality and reduced fringe benefits.

NO: Daniel T. Griswold, associate director of the Cato Institute's Center for Trade Policy Studies, contends that NAFTA has helped the American economy by producing better-paying jobs and contributing to increased manufacturing output in the United States between 1993 and 2001.

The North American Free Trade Agreement (NAFTA) was signed into law in the fall of 1993. The passage of NAFTA was no simple matter. Although the basic agreement was negotiated by the Republican George Bush administration during the late 1980s and early 1990s, the Democratic Bill Clinton administration faced the challenge of convincing Congress and the American people that NAFTA would work to the benefit of the United States as well as Mexico and Canada. In meeting this challenge, President Clinton did not hesitate to use a bit of drama to press the case for NAFTA. He arranged for all former, then-living U.S. presidents (Bush, Ronald Reagan, Jimmy Carter, Gerald Ford, and Richard Nixon) to gather together and speak out in support of NAFTA. The public debate probably reached its zenith with a face-to-face confrontation between H. Ross Perot, a successful businessman who ran for president and was perhaps the most visible and outspoken opponent of NAFTA, and then–vice president Al Gore on the *Larry King Live* television show. The vote on NAFTA in the House of Representatives reflected the sharpness of the debate; it passed by only a slim margin.

In pressing the case for NAFTA, proponents in the United States raised two major arguments. The first argument was economic: NAFTA would produce real economic benefits. These benefits were purported to include increased employment in the United States and increased productivity. Note that these arguments were based on the economic notions of specialization and comparative advantage. The second argument was political: NAFTA would support the political and economic reforms being made in Mexico and promote further progress in these two domains. These reforms had made Mexico a "better" neighbor—that is, Mexico had taken steps to become more like the United States—and NAFTA would support further positive change. Here the links are between greater economic freedom and increased political freedom as well as greater economic stability and increased political stability.

In opposing NAFTA, critics in the United States countered both of these arguments, focusing mostly on U.S.-Mexican relations. They argued that freer trade between the United States and Mexico would mean a loss of jobs in the United States—Perot's reference to a "giant sucking sound" was the transfer of work and jobs from the United States to Mexico. They also argued that NAFTA did not do enough to protect the environment nor to improve working conditions in Mexico. They felt that the notion of passing NAFTA as a reward to the Mexican government was premature; the government had not done enough to improve economic and political conditions in Mexico.

Implementation of NAFTA began in 1994, and so evaluation at the point of its 10-year anniversary seems particularly timely. In assessing the impact of NAFTA, there are any number of different perspectives that can be employed. Should the focus be economic, political, or both? Should the evaluation concentrate on the benefits and costs to the United States, to Mexico, to Canada, or to all three countries? How much of the history that follows NAFTA can be attributed to NAFTA, and how much can be attributed to other factors? When is the appropriate time for an evaluation? In short, evaluation is no easy task.

But evaluation of NAFTA is important not only for its own sake. President George W. Bush supports an expansion of NAFTA to 34 countries in North, Central, and South America. This expansion is called the Free Trade Agreement of the Americas (FTAA). Clearly, whether or not a person is willing to support FTAA depends in part on whether that person believes that NAFTA has helped or hurt the American economy. Robert E. Scott, in the following criticism of NAFTA, explicitly connects NAFTA and FTAA. Because he believes NAFTA has had negative consequences for the U.S. economy, he is less than enthusiastic about FTAA. Although he does not directly address FTAA, Daniel T. Griswold maintains in the second selection that NAFTA has been a success, and he implies that almost all steps taken in the direction of freer trade will be beneficial to the U.S. economy.

YES 

Robert E. Scott

NAFTA's Hidden Costs

The North American Free Trade Agreement (NAFTA) eliminated 766,030 actual and potential U.S. jobs between 1994 and 2000 because of the rapid growth in the net U.S. export deficit with Mexico and Canada. The loss of these real and potential jobs[1] is just the most visible tip of NAFTA's impact on the U.S. economy. In fact, NAFTA has also contributed to rising income inequality, suppressed real wages for production workers, weakened collective bargaining powers and ability to organize unions, and reduced fringe benefits. . . .

Growing Trade Deficits and Job Losses

NAFTA supporters have frequently touted the benefits of exports while remaining silent on the impacts of rapid import growth (Scott 2000). But any evaluation of the impact of trade on the domestic economy must include *both* imports and exports. If the United States exports 1,000 cars to Mexico, many American workers are employed in their production. If, however, the U.S. imports 1,000 foreign-made cars rather than building them domestically, then a similar number of Americans who would have otherwise been employed in the auto industry will have to find other work. Ignoring imports and counting only exports is like trying to balance a checkbook by counting only deposits but not withdrawals.

The U.S. has experienced steadily growing global trade deficits for nearly three decades, and these deficits have accelerated rapidly since NAFTA took effect on January 1, 1994. Although gross U.S. exports to its NAFTA partners have increased dramatically—with real growth of 147% to Mexico and 66% to Canada—these increases have been overshadowed by the larger growth in imports, which have gone up by 248% from Mexico and 79% from Canada, as shown in Table 1. As a result, the $16.6 billion U.S. net export deficit with these countries in 1993 increased by 378% to $62.8 billion by 2000 (all figures in inflation-adjusted 1992 dollars). . . .

The growing U.S. trade deficit has been facilitated by substantial currency devaluations in Mexico and Canada, which have made both countries' exports to the United States cheaper while making imports from the United States more expensive in those markets. These devalued currencies have also encouraged

Table 1

U.S. Trade With Canada and Mexico, 1993–2000, Totals for All Commodities (Millions of Constant 1992 Dollars)

			Change since 1993		
	1993	2000	Dollars	Percent	Jobs lost or gained
Canada					
Domestic exports	$90,018	$149,214	$59,196	66%	563,539
Imports for consumption	108,087	193,725	85,638	79	962,376
Net exports	(18,068)	(44,511)	(26,443)	146	(398,837)
Mexico					
Domestic exports	$39,530	$97,509	$57,979	147%	574,326
Imports for consumption	38,074	132,439	94,364	248	941,520
Net exports	1,456	(34,930)	(36,386)	n.a	(367,193)
Mexico and Canada					
Domestic exports	$129,549	$246,723	$117,174	90%	1,137,865
Imports for consumption	146,161	326,164	180,003	123	1,903,896
Net exports	(16,612)	(79,441)	(62,828)	378	(766,030)

investors in Canada and Mexico to build new and expanded production capacity to export even more goods to the U.S. market.

The Mexican peso was highly overvalued in 1994 when NAFTA took effect (Blecker 1997). The peso lost about 31% of its real, inflation-adjusted value between 1994 and 1995, after the Mexican financial crisis. The peso has gained real value (appreciated) recently because inflation in Mexico has remained well above levels in the U.S. As prices in Mexico rose, its exports became less competitive with goods produced in the U.S. and other countries because the peso's market exchange rate was unchanged between 1998 and 2000. High inflation in Mexico also made imports cheaper, relative to goods purchased in the U.S.

By 2000 the peso's real value had risen to roughly the pre-crisis levels of 1994.[2] Thus, the peso was as overvalued in 2000 as it was when NAFTA took effect. As a result, Mexico's trade and current account balances worsened substantially in 1998–2000, as imports from other countries surged, despite the fact that Mexico's trade surplus with the U.S. continued to improve through 2000. Given Mexico's large overall trade deficits, and the rising value of the peso, pressures are building for another peso crisis in the near future.

The Canadian dollar has depreciated over the past few years. The Canada–U.S. Free Trade Agreement—a precursor to NAFTA—took effect in 1989. Initially, the Canadian dollar rose 4.1% in real terms between 1989 and 1991, as Canada's Central Bank tightened interest rates. During this period, Canada maintained short-term interest rates that averaged 2.25 percentage points above those in the U.S. (1989 to 1994), which caused the initial appreciation in its currency. Canada then began to reduce real interest rates in the mid-1990s. Between 1995 and 2000, short-term interest rates in Canada were 0.75 percentage points *below* U.S. rates, a net swing of 3.0 percentage points. The Canadian dollar began to depreciate in the mid-1990s, as interest rates were reduced, relative to the U.S. Overall, between 1989 and 2000, the Canadian dollar lost 27% of its real value against the U.S. dollar.[3] . . .

NAFTA Costs Jobs in Every State

All 50 states and the District of Columbia have experienced a net loss of jobs under NAFTA (Table 2). Exports from every state have been offset by faster-rising imports. Net job loss figures range from a low of 395 in Alaska to a high of 82,354 in California. Other hard-hit states include Michigan, New York,

Table 2

NAFTA Job Loss by State, 1993–2000

State	Net NAFTA job loss*	State	Net NAFTA job loss*
U.S. total	766,030	Missouri	16,773
Alabama	16,826	Montana	1,730
Alaska	809	Nebraska	4,352
Arizona	8,493	Nevada	4,374
Arkansas	9,615	New Hampshire	2,970
California	82,354	New Jersey	19,169
Colorado	8,172	New Mexico	2,859
Connecticut	9,262	New York	46,210
Delaware	1,355	North Carolina	31,909
District of Columbia	1,635	North Dakota	1,288
Florida	27,631	Ohio	37,694
Georgia	22,918	Oklahoma	7,009
Hawaii	1,565	Oregon	10,986
Idaho	2,768	Pennsylvania	35,262
Illinois	37,422	Rhode Island	7,021
Indiana	31,110	South Carolina	10,835
Iowa	8,378	South Dakota	2,032
Kansas	6,582	Tennessee	25,419
Kentucky	13,128	Texas	41,067
Louisiana	6,613	Utah	5,243
Maine	3,326	Vermont	1,611
Maryland	8,089	Virginia	16,758
Massachusetts	16,998	Washington	14,071
Michigan	46,817	West Virginia	2,624
Minnesota	13,202	Wisconsin	19,362
Mississippi	11,469	Wyoming	864

*Excluding effects on wholesale and retail trade and advertising.

Source: EPI analysis of Bureau of Labor Statistics and Census Bureau data.

Texas, Ohio, Illinois, Pennsylvania, North Carolina, Indiana, Florida, Tennessee, and Georgia, each with more than 20,000 jobs lost. These states all have high concentrations of industries (such as motor vehicles, textiles and apparel, computers, and electrical appliances) where a large number of plants have moved to Mexico. . . .

Long-term Stagnation and Growing Inequality

NAFTA has also contributed to growing income inequality and to the declining wages of U.S. production workers, who make up about 70% of the workforce. NAFTA, however, is but one contributor to a larger globalization process that has led to growing structural trade deficits and has shaped the U.S. economy and society over the last few decades.[4] Rapid growth in U.S. trade and foreign investment, as a share of U.S. gross domestic product, has played a large role in the growth of inequality in income distribution in the last 20 years. NAFTA has continued and accelerated international economic integration, and thus contributed to the growing tradeoffs this integration requires.

The growth in U.S. trade and trade deficits has put downward pressure on the wages of "unskilled" (i.e., non-college-educated) workers in the U.S., especially those with no more than a high school degree. This group represents 72.7% of the total U.S. workforce and includes most middle- and low-wage workers. These U.S. workers bear the brunt of the costs and pressures of globalization (Mishel et al. 2001, 157, 172–79).

A large and growing body of research has demonstrated that expanding trade has reduced the price of import-competing products and thus reduced the real wages of workers engaged in producing those goods. Trade, however, is also expected to increase the wages of the workers producing exports, but growing trade deficits have meant that the number of workers hurt by imports has exceeded the number who have benefited through increased exports. Because the United States tends to import goods that make intensive use of less-skilled and less-educated workers in production, it is not surprising to find that the increasing openness of the U.S. economy to trade has reduced the wages of less-skilled workers relative to other workers in the United States.[5]

Globalization has reduced the wages of "unskilled" workers for at least three reasons. First, the steady growth in U.S. trade deficits over the past two decades has eliminated millions of manufacturing jobs and job opportunities in this country. Most displaced workers find jobs in other sectors where wages are much lower, which in turn leads to lower *average* wages for all U.S. workers. Recent surveys have shown that, even when displaced workers are able to find new jobs in the U.S., they face a reduction in wages, with earnings declining by an average of over 13% (Mishel et al. 2001, 24). These displaced workers' new jobs are likely to be in the service industry, the source of 99% of net new jobs created in the United States since 1989, and a sector in which average compensation is only 77% of the manufacturing sector's average (Mishel et al. 2001, 169). This competition also extends to export sectors, where pressures to cut product prices are often intense.

Second, the effects of growing U.S. trade and trade deficits on wages go beyond just those workers exposed directly to foreign competition. As the trade deficit limits jobs in the manufacturing sector, the new supply of workers to the service sector (displaced workers and new labor market entrants not able to find manufacturing jobs) depresses the wages of those already holding service jobs.

Finally, the increased import competition and capital mobility resulting from globalization has increased the "threat effects" in bargaining between employers and workers, further contributing to stagnant and falling wages in the U.S. (Bronfenbrenner 1997a). Employers' credible threats to relocate plants, to outsource portions of their operations, and to purchase intermediate goods and services directly from foreign producers can have a substantial impact on workers' bargaining positions. The use of these kinds of threats is widespread. A *Wall Street Journal* survey in 1992 reported that one-fourth of almost 500 American corporate executives polled admitted that they were "very likely" or "somewhat likely" to use NAFTA as a bargaining chip to hold down wages (Tonelson 2000, 47). A unique study of union organizing drives in 1993–95 found that over 50% of all employers made threats to close all or part of their plants during organizing drives (Bronfenbrenner 1997b). This study also found that strike threats in National Labor Relations Board union-certification elections nearly doubled following the implementation of the NAFTA agreement, and that threat rates were substantially higher in mobile industries in which employers can credibly threaten to shut down or move their operations in response to union activity. . . .

Bronfenbrenner (2000) described the impact of these threats in testimony to the U.S. Trade Deficit Review Commission:

> Under the cover of NAFTA and other trade agreements, employers use the threat of plant closure and capital flight at the bargaining table, in organizing drives, and in wage negotiations with individual workers. What they say to workers, either directly or indirectly, is if you ask for too much or don't give concessions or try to organize, strike, or fight for good jobs with good benefits, we'll close, we'll move across the border just like other plants have done before.[6]

In the context of ongoing U.S. trade deficits and rising levels of trade liberalization, the pervasiveness of employer threats to close or relocate plants may conceivably have a greater impact on real wage growth for production workers than does actual import competition. There are no empirical studies of the effects of such threats on U.S. wages, so such costs simply have been ignored by other studies of NAFTA.

NAFTA, Globalization, and the U.S. Economy

The U.S. economy created 20.7 million jobs between 1992 and 1999. All of those gains are explained by growth in domestic consumption, investment, and government spending. The growth in the overall U.S. trade deficit eliminated 3.2 million jobs in the same period (Scott 2000). Thus, NAFTA and other sources of growing trade deficits were responsible for a change in the composition of employment, shifting workers from manufacturing to other sectors and, frequently, from good jobs to low-quality, low-pay work.

Trade-displaced workers will not be so lucky during the next economic downturn. If unemployment begins to rise in the U.S., then those who lose their jobs due to globalization and growing trade deficits could face longer unemployment spells, and they will find it much more difficult to get new jobs.

When trying to tease apart the various contributing causes behind trends like the disappearance of manufacturing jobs, the rise in income inequality, and the decline in wages in the U.S., NAFTA and growing trade deficits provide only part of the answer. Other major causes include deregulation and privatization, declining rates of unionization, sustained high levels of unemployment, and technological change. While each of these factors has played some role, a large body of economic research has concluded that trade is responsible for at least 15–25% of the growth in wage inequality in the U.S. (U.S. Trade Deficit Review Commission 2000, 110–18). In addition, trade has also had an indirect effect by contributing to many of these other causes. For example, the decline of the manufacturing sector attributable to increased globalization has resulted in a reduction in unionization rates, since unions represent a larger share of the workforce in this sector than in other sectors of the economy.

So, although NAFTA is not solely responsible for all of the labor market problems discussed in this report, it has made a significant contribution to these problems, both directly and indirectly. Without major changes in the current NAFTA agreement, continued integration of North American markets will threaten the prosperity of a growing share of the U.S. workforce while producing no compensatory benefits to non-U.S. workers. Expansion of a NAFTA-style agreement—such as the proposed Free Trade Area of the Americas—will only worsen these problems. If the U.S. economy enters into a downturn or recession under these conditions, prospects for American workers will be further diminished.

Notes

1. Potential jobs, or job opportunities, are positions that would have been created if the trade deficit with Mexico and Canada had remained constant, in real terms (and holding everything else in the economy constant). The total number of jobs and job opportunities is a measure of what employment in trade-related industries would have been if the U.S. NAFTA trade balance remained constant between 1993 and 2000, holding everything else constant.
2. EPI [Economic Policy Institute] calculations and International Monetary Fund (IMF) (2001).
3. IMF (2001) and EPI calculations. This analysis compares overnight money market rates in Canada (annual averages) with the comparable federal funds rate for the U.S.
4. Globalization includes rapid growth in imports, exports, and the share of trade in the world economy, and even more rapid growth in the international flows of foreign investment around the world. The term is also used to refer to the international convergence of rules, regulations, and even the social structure and role of government in many countries. This process is often viewed as a "race-to-the-bottom" in global environmental standards, wages, and working conditions.
5. See U.S. Trade Deficit Review Commission (2000, 110–18) for more extensive reviews of theoretical models and empirical evidence regarding the impacts of globalization on income inequality in the U.S.
6. Bronfenbrenner (1999).

References

Blecker, Robert A. 1997. *NAFTA and the Peso Collapse—Not Just a Coincidence*. Briefing Paper. Washington, D.C.: Economic Policy Institute.

Bronfenbrenner, Kate. 1997a. "The effects of plant closings and the threat of plant closings on worker rights to organize." *Supplement to Plant Closings and Workers' Rights: A Report to the Council of Ministers by the Secretariat of the Commission for Labor Cooperation*. Lanham, Md.: Bernan Press.

Bronfenbrenner, Kate. 1997b. "We'll close! Plant closings, plant-closing threats, union organizing, and NAFTA." *Multinational Monitor*. Vol. 18, No. 3, pp. 8–13.

Bronfenbrenner, Kate. 1999. "Trade in traditional manufacturing." Testimony before the U.S. Trade Deficit Review Commission. October 29. <http://www.ustdrc.gov/hearings/29oct99/29oct99con.html>

Bronfenbrenner, Kate. 2000. "Uneasy terrain: The impact of capital mobility on workers, wages, and union organizing." Commissioned research paper for the U.S. Trade Deficit Review Commission. <http://www.ustdrc.gov/research/research.html>

Bureau of the Census. 1994. *U.S. Exports of Merchandise on CD-ROM (CDEX, or EX-145)* and *U.S. Imports of Merchandise on CD-ROM (CDIM, or IM-145)*. Preliminary data for December 1993 (month and year to date). Washington, D.C.: U.S. Department of Commerce, Bureau of the Census.

Bureau of the Census. 2001. *U.S. Exports of Merchandise on CD-ROM (CDEX, or EX-145)* and *U.S. Imports of Merchandise on CD-ROM (CDIM, or IM-145)*. Preliminary data for December 2000 (month and year to date). Washington, D.C.: U.S. Department of Commerce, Bureau of the Census.

Bureau of Labor Statistics. 1997. *ES202 Establishment Census*. Washington, D.C.: U.S. Department of Labor.

Bureau of Labor Statistics, Office of Employment Projections. 2001a. *Employment Outlook: 1994–2005 Macroeconomic Data, Demand Time Series and Input Output Tables*. Washington, D.C.: U.S. Department of Labor. <ftp://ftp.bls.gov/pub/special.requests/ep/ind.employment/>

Bureau of Labor Statistics, Office of Employment Projections. 2001b. Private email communication with Mr. James Franklin about 2000 price deflator estimates.

California State World Trade Commission. 1996. *A Preliminary Assessment of the Agreement's Impact on California*. Sacramento, Calif.: California State World Trade Commission.

International Monetary Fund. 2001. *International Financial Statistics*. Database and browser, March.

Mishel, Lawrence, Jared Bernstein, and John Schmitt. 2001. *State of Working America: 2000–01*. An Economic Policy Institute book. Ithaca, N.Y.: ILR Press, an imprint of Cornell University Press.

Rothstein, Jesse and Robert E. Scott. 1997a. *NAFTA's Casualties: Employment Effects on Men, Women, and Minorities*. Issue Brief. Washington, D.C.: Economic Policy Institute.

Rothstein, Jesse, and Robert E. Scott. 1997b. *NAFTA and the States: Job Destruction Is Widespread*. Issue Brief. Washington, D.C.: Economic Policy Institute.

Scott, Robert E. 1996. *North American Trade After NAFTA: Rising Deficits, Disappearing Jobs*. Briefing Paper. Washington, D.C.: Economic Policy Institute.

Scott, Robert E. 2000. *The Facts About Trade and Job Creation*. Issue Brief. Washington, D.C.: Economic Policy Institute.

Tonelson, Alan. 2000. *Race to the Bottom*. New York, N.Y.: Westview Press.

Trade Deficit Review Commission. 2000. *The U.S. Trade Deficit: Causes, Consequences, and Recommendations for Action*. Washington, D.C.: U.S. Trade Deficit Review Commission.

Daniel T. Griswold

NAFTA at 10: An Economic and Foreign Policy Success

Ten years ago . . . , leaders of the United States, Canada, and Mexico signed the historic North American Free Trade Agreement [NAFTA]. Although NAFTA remains a lightning rod for critics of free trade, by any measure it has been a public policy success. As a trade agreement, it delivered its principal objective of more trade. Since 1993, the value of two-way U.S. trade with Mexico has almost tripled, from $81 billion to $232 billion, growing twice as fast as U.S. trade with the rest of the world.[1] Canada and Mexico are now America's number one and two trading partners, respectively, with Japan a distant third.

Exaggerated Impact

One reason NAFTA remains controversial today is that advocates and opponents alike were guilty a decade ago of exaggerating its impact. Advocates claimed it would create hundreds of thousands of jobs in the U.S. economy due to a dramatic rise in exports; opponents claimed far more jobs would be destroyed by a flood of imports entering the United States and a stampede of U.S. companies moving to Mexico to take advantage of cheap labor. During a presidential debate in 1992, H. Ross Perot famously predicted, "You're going to hear a giant sucking sound of jobs being pulled out of this countr y."[2]

In reality, NAFTA was never going to have much of an impact on the U.S. economy. America's GDP [gross domestic product] at the time was almost 20 times larger than Mexico's, and U.S. tariffs against Mexican goods already averaged a low 2 percent.

A Foreign-Policy Triumph

For the United States, NAFTA was more about foreign policy than about the domestic economy. Its biggest payoff for the United States has been to institutionalize our southern neighbor's turn away from centralized protectionism and toward decentralized, democratic capitalism.

By that measure, NAFTA has been a spectacular success. In the decade since signing NAFTA, Mexico has continued along the road of economic and political reform. It has successfully decoupled its economy from the old boomand-bust, high-inflation, debt-ridden model that characterized it and much of Latin America up until the debt crisis of the 1980s. In 2000, Mexico avoided an election-cycle economic crisis for the first time since the 1970s. Today Mexico and Chile are the two most stable and dynamic economies in Latin America—and the two that have reformed most aggressively.

Just as important, the economic competition and decentralization embodied in NAFTA encouraged more political competition in Mexico. It broke the economic grip in which the dominant Institutional Revolutionary Party (PRI) held the country for most of the last century. It is no coincidence that, within seven years of NAFTA's implementation, Vicente Fox became the first opposition-party candidate elected president after 71 years of the PRI's oneparty rule.

"Giant Sucking Sound," Where Art Thou?

With a decade of hindsight, it is difficult to find any evidence of a "giant sucking sound" of jobs, investment, and manufacturing capacity heading south.

American jobs Trade is not about more jobs or fewer jobs but about better jobs, and NAFTA is no exception. Of course, competition from Mexico closed some U.S. factories, but those closures have allowed resources to shift to sectors where American producers enjoy a greater advantage in efficiency. That's the whole idea of trade: we increase production in sectors and industries where we can produce more efficiently and reduce production in sectors where we are less efficient. The result is a shift to better paying jobs. Meanwhile, the overall level of employment is determined by such macroeconomic factors such as monetary policy, labor-market regulations, and the business cycle.

For the record, the U.S. economy created millions of new jobs after passage of NAFTA. Civilian employment in the U.S. economy grew from 120.3 million in 1993 to 135.1 million in 2001, an increase of almost 2 million jobs per year. The unemployment rate fell steadily after the enactment of NAFTA, from an average of 6.9 percent in 1993 to under 4 percent in 2000.[3] The unemployment rate jumped to 6 percent in 2002, but that was because of the recent and relatively mild recession of 2001—a recession brought on not by NAFTA but by rising interest rates and energy prices and a falling stock market.

Foreign investment Despite predictions, NAFTA did not cause anything like an exodus of manufacturing investment to Mexico. U.S. investment in Mexico did increase after NAFTA, along with trade, but those flows are a trickle compared to what we invest domestically. In the eight years after the implementation of NAFTA, from 1994 through 2001, U.S. manufacturing companies invested an average of $2.2 billion a year in factories in Mexico.[4] That is a mere 1 percent of the $200 billion invested in manufacturing each year in the domestic U.S. economy.[5]

The small outflow of direct manufacturing investment to Mexico has been overwhelmed by the net inflow of such investment from the rest of the world—an average of $16 billion a year since 1994, most of it from Europe and Japan.[6] At the end of 2001, the stock of U.S. direct manufacturing investment in Mexico was $19.7 billion, less than one-tenth the stock of U.S. investment in high-wage, high-standard Europe.[7]

U.S. manufacturing Nowhere were the predictions about NAFTA more apocalyptic than in regard to manufacturing. H. Ross Perot accused NAFTA of "deindustrializing our country," and Rep. David Bonior, the soon to be ex-congressman and Democratic Whip from Michigan, predicted flatly that NAFTA "will destroy the auto industry."

In the eight years since the implementation of NAFTA, those predictions have become laughable. Between 1993 and 2001, manufacturing output in the United States, as measured by the U.S. Federal Reserve Board, rose by one-third. Output of motor vehicles and parts rose by 30 percent.[8] In fact, in the first eight years of NAFTA, manufacturing output in the United States rose at an annual average rate of 3.7 percent, 50 percent faster than during the eight years before enactment of NAFTA. (See Figure 1.) Of course, this is not an argument that NAFTA was the primary cause of the acceleration in manufacturing output, but it does knock the wind out of the myth that NAFTA has somehow caused the "deindustrialization" of America.

Manufacturing employment has fallen in the past few years, but that cannot in any plausible way be blamed on NAFTA. In fact, the number of

Figure 1

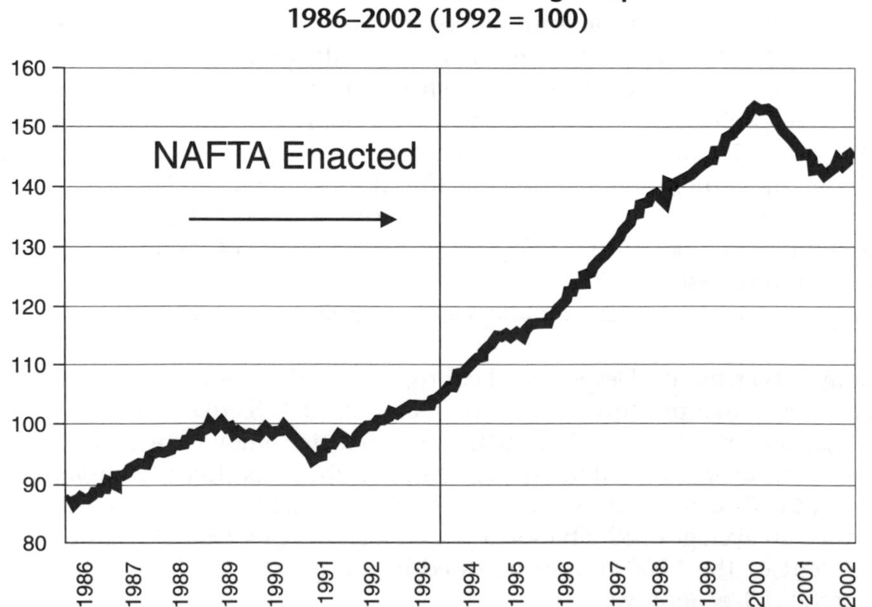

Source: U.S. Federal Reserve Board.

Americans employed in manufacturing grew by 706,000 in the first four years of NAFTA, from January 1994 to January 1998.[9] The decline in manufacturing jobs since 1998 has not occurred because those jobs have gone to Mexico; it has occurred because of (1) collapsing demand for our exports due to the East Asian financial meltdown in 1997–98, (2) our own domestic slowdown in demand due to the 2001 recession, and (3) the ongoing dramatic improvement in manufacturing productivity—fueled by information technology and increased global competition—that has allowed American factories to produce more and better widgets with fewer workers.

Conclusion

By every reasonable measure, NAFTA has been a public policy success in the decade since it was signed. It has deepened and institutionalized Mexico's drive to modernize and liberalize its economy and political system. It has spurred trade, investment, and integration between the United States and Mexico. And in a more modest way it has enhanced American productivity and prosperity—refuting the critics who were wrong 10 years ago and are just as wrong today.

Notes

1. See Bureau of the Census, "FT900—U.S. International Trade in Goods and Services: 1993," www.census.gov/foreign-trade/Press-Release/93_press_releases/Final_Revisions_1993; and "U.S. International Trade in Goods and Services—Annual Revision for 2001," www.census.gov/foreign-trade/Press-Release/2001pr/Final_Revisions_2001.
2. Public Broadcasting System, "Debating Our Destiny: The Third Presidential Debate," *NewsHour,* October 19, 1992, www.pbs.org/newshour/debatingourdestiny/92debates/3prez2.html.
3. Joint Economic Committee of Congress (JEC), *Economic Indicators* (Washington: Government Printing Office), October 2002, p. 11.
4. U.S. Department of Commerce, Bureau of Economic Analysis (BEA) "U.S. Direct Investment Abroad," www.bea.doc.gov/bea/di/di1usdbal.htm.
5. JEC, p. 11.
6. BEA, "Foreign Direct Investment in the U.S.," www.bea.doc.gov/bea/di/di1fdibal.htm.
7. Maria Borga and Daniel R. Yorgason, "Direct Investment Position for 2001: Country and Industry Detail," *Survey of Current Business* (Bureau of Economic Analysis, July 2002), Table 2.2, p. 33.
8. U.S. Federal Reserve Board, "Industrial Production and Capacity Utilization: Data from January 1986 to Present (Tables 1, 2, and 10), Industrial Production, Seasonally Adjusted," Series B00004, www.federalreserve.gov/releases/g17/table1_2.htm.
9. In January 1994, 18,155,000 Americans were employed in manufacturing, compared to 18,861,000 in January 1998. See U.S. Bureau of Labor Statistics, "Employment, Hours, and Earnings from the Current Employment Statistics Survey (National), Manufacturing Employment, Seasonally Adjusted," Series EES30000001, data.bls.gov/cgi-bin/surveymost?ee.

POSTSCRIPT

Has the North American Free Trade Agreement Hurt the American Economy?

Scott sees the most visible negative impact of NAFTA to be increased trade deficits and job losses. With respect to the former, he documents a 378 percent increase in the U.S. trade deficit with Canada and Mexico over the 1993–2000 period. As for job loss, he estimates the number to be over 760,000. He states that the job losses have occurred in all 50 states and the District of Columbia. Scott also addresses the less visible but harmful effects of NAFTA. He argues that the loss of jobs in manufacturing has increased job competition in the service sector; thus, there is downward pressure on wages in both sectors. He also refers to "threat effects"—the credible threats of employers to relocate plants, to outsource portions of their operations, and to purchase intermediate goods and services directly from foreign producers. The threat effects have weakened the ability of workers to bargain for higher wages and improved fringe benefits. The job losses, increased job competition, and threat effects combine to increase income inequality. Scott concludes his analysis by arguing that there needs to be major changes in NAFTA. He also cautions that expansion of a NAFTA-style agreement—such as the proposed FTAA—will only worsen the problems he has identified.

Griswold states that NAFTA has delivered on its principal objective of increased trade, with two-way U.S. trade with Mexico tripling from $81 billion in 1993 to $232 billion. Today Canada and Mexico are America's top trading partners. Griswold also asserts that NAFTA has played an important role in the development of more political competition in Mexico. He takes up the criticisms most frequently directed at NAFTA. As to the criticism of job loss, Griswold cites the increase in U.S. employment over the 1993–2001 period, an increase of almost 2 million jobs per year. He attributes the "mild recession of 2001" to rising interest rates, increasing energy prices, and a falling stock market. As to the criticism that NAFTA redirected investment from the United States to Mexico, Griswold argues that investment in Mexico by American manufacturing is almost trivial—"a mere 1 percent of the $200 billion invested in manufacturing each year in the domestic U.S. economy." As to the contention that NAFTA has led to job losses in manufacturing, Griswold offers two counterarguments. First, manufacturing employment actually increased during the first four years of NAFTA. Second, the loss in manufacturing jobs since 1998 is due to other factors, including an increase in manufacturing productivity. Griswold concludes his evaluation by asserting that "by every reasonable measure, NAFTA has been a public policy success in the decade since it was signed."

Both Scott and Griswold provide references that can be used to obtain more data as well as additional analyses of NAFTA. For a more political critique of NAFTA, see *The Selling of "Free Trade": NAFTA, Washington, and the Subversion of American Democracy* by John R. MacArthur (Hill & Wang, 2000). There are also evaluations that were completed earlier in NAFTA's history. Typical of these are two articles published in the October 1997 issue of *The World & I:* "A Successful Agreement," by Joe Cobb, and "A Failed Approach," by Alan Tonelson. Besides controversy on the macro effects of NAFTA, there is significant debate on various elements within the NAFTA agreement. One good example is NAFTA's Chapter 11, the so-called investor-to-state protections. On this issue see William T. Warren, "NAFTA and State Sovereignty: A Pandora's Box of Property Rights," *Spectrum: The Journal of State Government* (Spring 2002) and "Update on NAFTA Chapter 11 Claim re Methanex," GreenYes Archives, `http://greenyes.grrn.org/2002/11/msg00069.html` (March 2003). For more about FTAA, see "NAFTA Expansion: More About the FTAA," The Sierra Club, `http://www.sierraclub.org/trade/ftaa/more.asp` and the section entitled "Trade Promotion Authority" in chapter 6 of the 2003 *Economic Report of the President.*

ISSUE 18

Is the No Child Left Behind Act Working?

YES: House Education and the Workforce Committee, from "Fact Sheet: No Child Left Behind Is Working," http://edworkforce.house.gov/issues/108th/recess/nclbworks.htm (October 7, 2004)

NO: Gerald W. Bracey, from "The Perfect Law: No Child Left Behind and the Assault on Public Schools," *Dissent* (Fall 2004)

ISSUE SUMMARY

YES: The House Education and the Workforce Committee lists a number of positive results for the No Child Left Behind Act, including higher reading and math test scores in several states as well as improved data and information for teachers and parents.

NO: Professor Gerald W. Bracey believes that the No Child Left Behind Act is, from the perspective of the Republican party, a perfect law because it will ultimately transfer billions from the public sector to the private sector, because it will reduce the size of government, and because it will "wound or kill" a large Democratic party power base.

Elementary and secondary education in the United States is a massive undertaking. First, there is the public school component: during the 2002–03 school year, there were 95,615 public schools with over 48 million students. There is a significant private component as well; the most recent statistics list 27,223 private schools in 1999–00 and over 6 million students in 2003–04. Finally, there is a growing home-school component: 850,000 children in 1999 and about 1.1 million children in 2003.

But the focus in this issue is on public schools. The combined federal, state, and local government spending on elementary and secondary education is currently estimated at slightly more than $500 billion. This is more than the United States spends on national defense. The bulk of this spending is financed by state and local taxes, but there has been an important federal component since the passage of the Elementary and Secondary Education Act (ESEA) in 1965.

Americans are concerned about public education for a variety of reasons. One reason, as just indicated, is that public education absorbs a significant number of tax dollars. But Americans are also concerned because the results of all the spending are less than impressive. This dissatisfaction goes back to at least 1983 when the National Commission on Excellence in Education released its report, entitled *A Nation at Risk*. This report identified a variety of problems in public education. In spite of a number of "reforms" that have been put in place since then, the dissatisfaction with public education continued into the twenty-first century. For example, the U.S. Department of Education reported that in 2003, "Even after four years of public schooling, most students perform below proficiency in both reading and mathematics." And for the year 2000, the Department reported: "Upon graduating from high school, few students have acquired the math and science skills necessary to compete in the knowledge-based economy."

In his presidential campaign in 2000, candidate George W. Bush emphasized education reform. After taking office, he continued to push for educational reform, and the No Child Left Behind Act (NCLBA) was signed into law on January 8, 2002. This is not to say that NCLBA was strictly a Republican effort. In reality, it was a bipartisan effort; it passed the House by a 381–41 margin and the Senate with an 87–10 vote. A leading Democrat, Senator Ted Kennedy (D-MA), was a chief sponsor of the legislation in the Senate.

At this point, it is useful to provide some information regarding the content of NCLBA. As for the broad objectives of the legislation, former Education Secretary Rod Page states that NCLBA "ensures accountability and flexibility as well as increased federal support for education," and that it "continues the legacy of the *Brown v. Board* decision by creating an education system that is more inclusive, responsive, and fair." Turning to more specific provisions, NCLBA mandates that every state set standards for grade-level achievement and develop a system to see if students are reaching those standards. NCLBA rededicates the country to the goal of having a "highly qualified teacher" in every classroom where "highly qualified" means the teacher holds a bachelor's degree, holds a certification or licensure to teach in the state of his or her employment, and has proven knowledge of the subjects he or she teaches.

But just 3 years after its passage, the NCLBA has generated a good deal of controversy. There are those like the House Education and the Workforce Committee who believes the legislation is already beginning to generate positive results. At the same time, there is a significant vocal opposition, represented by critics like Bracey, who believe NCLBA has actually weakened public education.

House Education and the Workforce Committee

Fact Sheet: No Child Left Behind Is Working

As a result of the bipartisan No Child Left Behind education reform law (NCLB) signed two years ago by President George W. Bush, America's public education system is focusing on improving academic achievement for all students like never before.

A short overview of the progress being made under NCLB:

- In exchange for billions in federal education funds, states and local school districts are being held accountable for ensuring every child learns—regardless of race, parents' income, disability, geography, or English proficiency.
- Millions of disadvantaged children who would once have been written off as unteachable are now getting the focus and attention they deserve.
- Reading and math scores in America's large urban schools have improved, and a number of states have reported promising improvement in student achievement.
- Parents and teachers are being empowered with new information to hold schools accountable.
- Parents of children in struggling schools have powerful new options, and they're using them.

Following are a few examples of how NCLB is already making a positive difference for America.

States Are Reporting Increased Reading and Math Test Scores

New test results recently released by several states for 2003–2004 show students are posting high math and reading scores on states tests. Even though No Child Left Behind's reforms have not been completely implemented, parents are already seeing positive results from its call for accountability and high standards for all students.

From the House Education and the Workforce Committee, October 7, 2004.

- **Delaware.** Student test scores in Delaware improved in three out of four grade levels in all three subjects tested—reading, writing and math. Fifth grade reading performance in Delaware climbed to 85 percent, a seven percentage point increase from last year.
- **Ohio.** Fourth grade math scores in Ohio improved dramatically, from 58 percent last year to 66 percent this year. Fourth grade reading test scores in the Dayton increased by 9 percentage points—from 25 percent passing last year to 34 percent passing this year. In math, Dayton fourth graders showed another 9 point gain—going from 22 percent passing on last year's test to 31 percent this year.
- **Maryland.** Seventy-one percent of Maryland's third graders passed the reading exam this year, as compared to 58 percent in 2003. Limited English Proficient (LEP) students posted an impressive 27 point increase in reading scores this year. In Anne Arundel County, 63.8 percent of their third graders scored proficient and advanced on state reading assessments. This year, 78.5 percent of third graders scored proficient and advanced.
- **Illinois.** According to the *Chicago Tribune,* students in every grade level posted increased scores on statewide reading and math tests in the 2003–2004 school year. In large part, these gains were fueled by increased test scores among Hispanic students. On the math test, Hispanic fifth-grade student scores jumped by 11.7 percentage points. Similarly, Hispanic fourth-graders improved by 10.7 percentage points on the reading test.

Teachers Applaud Early Success of No Child Left Behind

More than 3,000 teachers applauded the early success of President Bush's landmark Reading First literacy initiative at a July 2004 national education conference in Minnesota. The conference was the first of its type to bring together teachers who are implementing Reading First in their respective schools, allow them to discuss the program's early successes in raising student achievement and share strategies for continued student success.

Reading First, a cornerstone of the No Child Left Behind Act, is a scientifically based literacy program designed to ensure children have the knowledge base and essential skills needed to learn how to read. States have received more than $3 billion in Reading First grants over the last three years, helping every state ensure all students can read by the time they enter the third grade.

Substantial Gains in Reading and Math in America's Big City Schools

A major new report released in March 2004 concludes America's big city schools are making considerable progress in elevating student achievement, and the No Child Left Behind education law is helping to drive those scores. The report, released by the Council of Great City Schools—a national coalition representing more than 60 of the nation's largest urban school districts—shows students in the nation's major urban schools have posted substantial gains in statewide math and reading assessments since NCLB was enacted. A copy of the report is available online at `http://www.cgcs.org/reports/beat_the_oddsIV.html`.

- **Reading and math scores have climbed in urban schools since NCLB was enacted.** The Great City Schools report shows improvement of fourth and eighth grade public school students in state-developed reading and math tests under NCLB. According to the report, 47.8 percent of urban school students performed at or above proficient in fourth grade reading and 51 percent scored at or above proficient in fourth grade math, a 4.9 and 6.8 percentage point increase respectively compared to 2002 scores. Eighth grade reading and math scores showed increases as well from 2002 to 2003. When compared to 2002, eighth grade reading and math scores increased by 1.1 and 3 percentage points in 2003.
- **Urban school officials credit NCLB with helping teachers and school officials raise student achievement.** "Our most recent report attempted to answer the question, 'Have urban schools improved student achievement since *No Child Left Behind* was enacted?' "The answer appears to be 'yes,'" testified Dr. Michael Casserly before the Education & the Workforce Committee on June 23, 2004. Casserly is the executive director of the Council of the Great City Schools.
- **High standards help teachers succeed.** The Great City Schools report credits the academic standards movement—which culminated in the NCLB law—with sparking real change and improvement in the nation's urban schools. The high standards at the heart of NCLB have helped teachers—not hindered them, as claimed by the National Education Association (NEA) and other reform opponents.

New Independent Report Shows States Are Making Progress in Implementing No Child Left Behind; Better Progress Needed to Ensure There Is a Highly Qualified Teacher in Every Public Classroom

A new independent report by the nonpartisan Education Commission of the States suggests states are making progress in implementing the education reforms included in the No Child Left Behind Act. However, the report's authors say states still have hard work remaining to ensure every classroom has a highly qualified teacher by the 2005–2006 deadline.

According to a recent *Associated Press* article ("Study: States show progress under new school law, but work ahead," Ben Feller, The Associated Press; July 14, 2004), the report's findings include:

- **98% of states are on track to define what constitutes a persistently dangerous school**, a classification which would immediately give parents the option to transfer their children to safer schools.

- **92% of states are on track to publicly report disaggregated student achievement data,** ensuring parents know how all student subgroups are performing, including minority students, poor children, students with disabilities, and English-language learners.
- **53% of states are on track to identify which schools are in need of improvement** before the next school year begins, ensuring parents have time to make knowledgeable decisions on the options available to them to improve their children's educational opportunities.
- **22% of states are on track to place a highly qualified teacher in every classroom.**

A copy of the Education Commission of the States' report, "ECS Report to the Nation: State Implementation of the No Child Left Behind Act," can be found at `www.ecs.org`.

Black & Hispanic School Superintendents Say Weakening NCLB Would 'Turn Back the Clock' on Educating Disadvantaged Students

More than 100 African American and Latino school district superintendents from across the country recently sent a letter to federal leaders—including Sen. John Kerry (D-MA)—expressing their strong support for the No Child Left Behind Act signed by President Bush and warning that weakening the law, as proposed by the NEA and other opponents, would "turn back the clock." These pro-NCLB superintendents are collectively responsible for the education of more than 3 million American students.

- **Weakening NCLB would "pull the rug out from under" dedicated teachers and principals, reform advocates warn.** "Closing achievement gaps is never going to be easy. But it would be next to impossible without the demands and expectations in the federal law," said former urban school principal Paul Ruiz, now an official with the Education Trust (November 18, 2003). "These folks don't have the luxury of thinking they can implement all the changes they need to without the cover of the law. We can't pull the rug out from under them just as they are beginning to get some real traction."

A copy of the "Don't Turn Back the Clock" letter, including a list of signers, is available at: *`http://www2.edtrust.org/NR/exeres/F3232B52-86C1-4792-94A5-13270E4B7D29.frameless.htm?NRMODE=Published`*

Parents & Teachers Have Powerful New Data & Information

No Child Left Behind promised to empower parents and teachers with better information about the education children are receiving, and the law is delivering on that promise in a major way.

- **Report cards for parents and teachers on school performance.** All 50 states are moving to implement accountability plans that include providing report cards for parents on school performance. The light of public scrutiny—"sunshine"—is the primary enforcement mechanism behind the bipartisan NCLB reforms. Contrary to the claims made by the NEA and other education reform opponents, NCLB does not "punish" struggling schools; rather, schools identified by their states as needing improvement qualify for extra help, including additional federal funding and/or technical assistance.
- **Accountability goes online—at no cost to taxpayers.** A nonpartisan website launched by the School Information Partnership—`www.SchoolResults.org`—is providing parents and teachers with up-to-date school, district, and state student achievement data. The website, made possible by the generosity of the Broad Foundation and endorsed by the U.S. Department of Education, is currently up and running for six pilot states—Delaware, Florida, Minnesota, Pennsylvania, Virginia, and Washington. Information from all 50 states, Puerto Rico, and the District of Columbia will be posted in summer 2004 as all of the available and relevant NCLB data is released.
- **New diagnostic tools for teachers, parents, and school leaders.** The new SchoolResults website is giving parents and teachers immediate access to information about the performance of their local schools, neighboring schools and districts, and the entire state. Teachers will be able to use this information as a diagnostic tool to identify areas in need of improvement, as well as identify the methods used by other schools to improve academic achievement. The website will also provide valuable comparative tools and benchmarks to monitor relative progress of local schools and districts within the state.

Parents Have Powerful New Options—and They Like Them

NCLB not only empowers parents with information, but also with choices. If parents are not satisfied with the quality of the education their children are receiving, they can do something about it under NCLB. Millions of children in schools identified by their states as needing improvement have qualified to receive free private tutoring and other supplemental educational services under NCLB. Parents have also been given the right to transfer their children to a higher-achieving or safer public or charter school.

- **Children in struggling schools are getting extra help.** "I'm better with it because I like this school better." That was what nine-year-old Nicole Brittle, a third grade student in southeast Virginia, told a reporter recently to explain the dramatic turnaround in her math scores since her grandmother and guardian exercised her rights under No Child Left Behind and transferred her to a new school. (Kristen King, "Extra Help in New School Turning Things Around for Third Grader," *Virginian-Pilot & Ledger-Star,* 27 May 2003.) "At her old school, Mount Hermon Elementary, she brought home C's and D's," the *Virginian-Pilot* noted. "Now, at Westhaven Elementary, she's earning mostly B's—and math has become her favorite subject."

- **Parents like their new options.** "It felt like a new beginning," said a Pittsburgh-area parent who talked to the *Pittsburgh Post-Gazette* last fall about her decision to transfer her third-grader and kindergartener under NCLB. "I knew they must be doing something up there [at her daughter's new school]. I wanted my kid to get a piece of it. I don't want to wait until she gets to middle school." (Eleanor Chute, "Students not fleeing troubled schools," *Pittsburgh Post-Gazette,* November 24, 2003.)
- **More than 1600 supplemental service providers have been approved.** According to the U.S. Department of Education, more than 1600 supplemental service providers have been approved by the states since NCLB was enacted. With this option, parents can ensure their children get extra help to supplement the education being provided in the schools those children attend.
- **Parents can choose faith-based organizations to help educate their children.** To ensure parents have a wide range of choices, more than $1.7 billion has been made available to faith-based and community-based organizations through NCLB to help these groups provide quality supplemental educational services, according to the Education Department. Such organizations can participate in the Title I supplemental services program, the Early Reading First initiative, and other initiatives authorized under NCLB.

Gerald W. Bracey

The Perfect Law: No Child Left Behind and the Assault on Public Schools

Imagine a law that would transfer hundreds of billions of dollars a year from the public sector to the private sector, reduce the size of government, and wound or kill a large Democratic power base. Impossible, you say. But the law exists. It is Title I of the Elementary and Secondary Education Act of 2001, better known as the No Child Left Behind law (NCLB).

The Bush administration has often been accused of Orwellian doublespeak in naming its programs, and NCLB is a masterpiece of a law to accomplish the opposite of what it apparently intends. While claiming to be the law that—finally!—improves public education, NCLB sets up public schools to fail, setting the stage for private education companies to move in on the $400 billion spent annually on K–12 education ($500 billion according to recent statements by Secretary of Education Rod Paige). The consequent destruction or reduction of public education would shrink government and cripple or eliminate the teachers' unions, nearly five million mostly Democratic voters. It's a law to drool over if you're Karl Rove or Grover Norquist. The Perfect Law, in fact, as in The Perfect Storm.

It doesn't look that way at first glance. Indeed, NCLB appears to fly in the face of all that the Bush administration stands for. That administration has tried to deregulate and outsource virtually everything it touches. Yet from this most deregulatory of administrations comes NCLB laying 1,100 pages of law and reams of regulations on public schools. On closer inspection, those pages are just the law's shiny surface to blind and confuse onlookers.

The principal means to accomplish this amazing end is called Adequate Yearly Progress or AYP. All schools that accept Title I money from the federal government are compelled by the law to show AYP. If they don't, they are labeled "failing schools." The official tag is "in need of improvement" but no one outside of the U.S. Department of Education uses that term.

The concept of AYP in Title I is not new, but NCLB yokes it to sanctions that become increasingly punitive with each consecutive year of failure.

These sanctions alone should have been a clue to Democrats that the law was not what it said it was, for punishment is not an effective means to achieve either individual or institutional change.

NCLB requires not only that each school make AYP, but that each of many subgroups make AYP. For many schools, once test scores are disaggregated by gender, ethnicity, socio-economic status, special education, and English Language Learners, there are thirty-seven separate categories. All categories must make AYP. If one fails, the school fails. Not surprisingly, a study found that more diverse schools were more likely to fail—the odds that one group doesn't make it are against them. Even if all subgroups make AYP, it counts only if 95 percent of the kids in each group showed up on test day. If not, the school fails.

Here's how it works: all schools must test all students every year in grades three through eight in reading and math (and in a couple of years, science as well) and test one high school grade. For these tests, each state establishes a baseline of achievement. Its plan for AYP must be such that by the year 2014, 100 percent of the state's children achieve at the "proficient" level. At the moment, each state defines "proficient," but that will likely change. For some states, the progress from baseline to end state is a straight line. Other states have an accelerating curve with little required initially but a great deal of improvement required as the witching year of 2014 approaches.

How realistic is a goal of 100 percent proficiency? Well, at the 2004 convention of the American Educational Research Association (AERA), the California Department of Education presented projections indicating that by 2014, under AYP, 99 percent of its schools would be failing. In fact, this projection appears to be optimistic. It was predicated on assumptions about how fast test scores will improve. So far, these assumptions are not being met.

A reader might say, "Yes, but that is California. California is so educationally awful that it inspired a John Merrow PBS special, 'From First to Worst: The Rise and Fall of California's Public Schools.'" And it is true that in the National Assessment of Educational Progress's 2003 reading assessment California was at the bottom: forty-ninth at the fourth-grade level and tied with Hawaii for fiftieth at the eighth-grade level.

But consider a 2004 headline in the *St. Paul Pioneer Press:* "All Minnesota Left Behind?" The article beneath the headline described a report from the state's legislative auditor projecting that by 2014 some 80 percent of Minnesota's schools would be failing and that many of them would have failed for five consecutive years, a condition that unleashes the most draconian of NCLB's sanctions.

Academically, Minnesota is not California. In the Third International Mathematics and Science Study (TIMSS), twenty-five of forty-one participating nations outscored California in mathematics and only four (Iran, Kuwait, Colombia, and South Africa) scored lower (the remaining twelve scored about the same). In science, twenty scored higher and six scored lower. For Minnesota, the numbers are quite different. Only six of the forty-one nations outscored Minnesota in math, and only one outscored it in science.

This means that in a few years 80 percent of the schools in a state that outscores virtually the entire world will be labeled as failures.

Why would anyone foist such a no-win system on the public schools? To answer this question we must go back to the original legislation and note that it contained Bush-backed voucher amendments. If passed in this form, students would have been able to use these vouchers at any school that would accept them.

Congress struck the voucher provisions from the law. In the 2000 elections, voucher referenda in California and Michigan had suffered more than two-to-one defeats. The defeats were unusually decisive and not just because of the margins. Milton Friedman had argued that voucher efforts lose because, although the voucher proposals are "well thought out and initially warmly received, the educational establishment—administrators and teachers' unions—then launches an attack that is notable for its mendacity but is backed by much larger financial resources than the proponents can command and succeeds in killing the proposals."

In the 2000 referenda, though, advocates outspent opponents—in California by two to one—and the outcome was still not close. The public at large decisively rejected the concept of vouchers in one liberal and one conservative state. After these referenda, even ardent voucher advocates such as Harvard's Paul Peterson opined that vouchers would be of interest only to a small proportion—perhaps 5 percent—of parents, mostly those with kids in inner-city schools. Congress decided that they had no place in NCLB.

If Bush succeeds in his reelection campaign, vouchers will be back. Actually, they already are. Bush proposed a $75 million voucher program for a half-dozen cities. Congress trimmed it to a $15 million program for only the District of Columbia. The proposal passed the House by a single vote but was repeatedly rejected by the Senate until it was attached to a $328 billion omnibus spending bill. Even Democrats who opposed vouchers thought that law too important to kill just to keep vouchers out of the District. The bill passed sixty-five to twenty-eight. A second-term Bush would no doubt broaden the scope of voucher proposals.

Vouchers, of course, send money to private schools and remove money from public schools. At present, the principal beneficiaries of vouchers are religious schools, especially Catholic schools. In Cleveland, one of two cities with ongoing, tax-funded voucher programs, 96 percent of voucher-using students attend church-affiliated schools and 67 percent attend Catholic schools.

The D.C. program will offer a child up to $7,500 per year, but the elite privates in the D.C. area charge more than $20,000 tuition per year. Independent private schools have also shown no interest in vouchers out of fear that government money will lead to government control.

Catholic schools, on the other hand, charge much less and have been hemorrhaging students. In 1960, Catholic schools accounted for 12.4 percent of all students. In 2000, 4.7 percent. The Catholic connection was made clear when Bush made his strongest pitch for the D.C. voucher proposal in the East Room of the White House to 250 members of the National Catholic Education

Association, in town to mark their 100th anniversary. It could be seen as a cynical ploy to buy the Catholic vote in November. (Democratic presidential nominee John Kerry opposes vouchers. As a presidential candidate, John Edwards voiced similar opposition. Both expressed the position that vouchers help only the few, draw resources away from public schools, and inappropriately send taxpayer dollars to private institutions.)

❧

Thus, after the 2000 elections, even voucher proponents concluded that the middle classes were pretty much satisfied with their schools. To make vouchers attractive to the middle classes, some way would have to be found to drive a wedge between the parents and their public schools and shatter that satisfaction. AYP's impossible standards provide the way. At the AERA convention mentioned earlier, representatives from the Boulder Valley School District, the district that surrounds the University of Colorado at Boulder, reported that parents were surprised when some of their "good" schools failed. It causes, the researchers said, "dissonance" in the parents. One can only wonder how much louder the dissonance will clang as the number of failing schools grows. Already the law appears to be taking its toll. A June 2004 survey by Educational Testing Service found that in 2001, 8 percent of parents gave public schools an "A" and 35 percent gave them a "B." In 2004, the figures had fallen to 2 percent and 20 percent, respectively.

Currently, there are few non-religious schools to receive vouchers, but if the vouchers are there, one can expect the for-profit Educational Management Organizations to expand (currently, there are 53 such companies managing 461 schools). Indeed, the first overbearingly ambitious plan from the largest such company, Edison Schools, Inc., depended on Bush's father and his father's secretary of education, Lamar Alexander. Alexander was once a paid consultant to and board member of Edison's then-parent company, Whittle Communications. Edison's founder, Chris Whittle, had planned to have one thousand private schools by 2000, and that plan hinged on Bush *père* and Alexander's pushing vouchers through Congress (though it was never mentioned in any Edison press releases). When Bush lost to Clinton, the plan came a cropper and left Whittle managing a few schools, not owning a thousand. But Chris Whittle is an ambitious man, and if the vouchers are there, he will come.

One can get some sense of where people think NCLB will lead by looking at what is being said about it by organizations that should, ideologically, oppose it. In 1996, for example, the Heritage Foundation, whose mission statement says it promotes free enterprise and limited government, condemned federal intrusion into education as a "liberal solution." Yet, this organization, once dubbed by *Slate* editor Michael Kinsley as "a right-wing propaganda machine," not only endorses NCLB but also brags that one of its policy analysts, Krista Kafer, "produced two papers that helped define the lines of debate" over NCLB.

The most ardent voucher proponent in academia is Harvard's Paul Peterson, also a senior fellow at the Hoover Institution. Hoover proudly announced that

Peterson, along with Erik Hanushek, another senior fellow, had been named to a Bush-sponsored National Education Panel to evaluate NCLB.

The Eagle Forum's Phyllis Schlafly contended "the tests mandated by NCLB had ripped back the curtain and exposed a major national problem." But, she went on NCLB wouldn't do much about that problem. We need "innovative solutions to introduce competition into the monopoly system." Vouchers, in other words.

With the voucher-touting right solidly lined up in favor of NCLB, shouldn't the center and the left be just a bit suspicious of it?

Even with each state having a unique definition of proficient, most schools fail. The situation will likely get worse. If each state has a unique definition, no two states can be compared. Lack of comparability alone would make some people uncomfortable, but some of the early results seemed, well, anomalous. In the first estimate of how many schools would fail, Michigan projected fifteen hundred, while Arkansas foresaw none. This finding did not produce, so far as is known, a stampede of Michigan parents seeking to educate their children in the Razorback state.

There will be pressure to seek a common yardstick that, in this most normative of nations, will let people compare the states. It exists. It is called the National Assessment of Educational Progress (NAEP). NAEP reports results two ways: in terms of scores on the tests and in terms of what percentage of the students attained its three "achievement levels": basic, proficient (the magic word), and advanced. Secretary Paige has already said that he will use the discrepancy between NAEP and state test results to shame the states into better performance (ironically, the biggest discrepancy turned up in Texas, where Paige had been superintendent of Houston public schools. Texas said 91 percent of its eighth-graders were proficient in math, NAEP said 24 percent).

The result from Texas gives some idea of the problem. The NAEP achievement levels are ridiculously high. In the 2003 math assessment, for instance, only 32 percent of the nation's fourth graders reached the proficient level. Even in high-scoring Minnesota, only 42 percent were designated proficient (for some minorities, nationally, the percentage proficient fell as low as 5 percent). American fourth-graders were well above average on the TIMSS math test and third in the world in science. But only about a third showed up as proficient on NAEP math and science tests administered the same year. Kids who are virtually on top of the world are not proficient? It makes no sense.

And it gets worse. The NAEP levels are not only ridiculously high, they are "fundamentally flawed," to use the words of the National Academy of Sciences. The NAEP achievement levels have been examined and found wanting by the National Center for Research on Evaluation, Standards, and Student Testing; the National Academy of Education; the National Academy of Sciences; the General Accounting Office; and individual psychometricians. The reports say that the process is confusing, internally inconsistent, and lacking in evidence for validity. These conclusions would condemn any proposed commercial test to the trash bin. But NAEP chugs along ignoring the flaws. Having many students score low has political uses.

If NAEP comes to be the common yardstick, the dissonance in people's minds will only increase because the NAEP standards ensure that no one will ever attain 100 percent proficiency for any group. Asian American students score considerably higher than other ethnic groups in math, but on the 2003 NAEP math assessment, their best performance was 48 percent proficient at the eighth grade. In his AERA presidential address in 2003, Robert Linn of the University of Colorado estimated that we could have all twelfth graders proficient in math in 166 years.

Many other problems with NCLB are smaller and of a more technical nature. For instance, the role of summer loss in poor students but not middle class or affluent students, meaning that some schools that do well during the school year will not make AYP because of what happens when they are closed. Then there is the impact of the "choice option." Students in schools that have failed for two consecutive years must be offered the option of choosing another school. This requirement leads to logistical nightmares—currently Chicago must offer the option to two hundred thousand students but has only five hundred spaces—and to peculiar alterations in the schools' test scores. Purportedly, the choice option must be offered first to the "neediest" students, namely those with the lowest test scores. But if these kids leave, the sending school's average score goes up through no merit of its own. At the other end, the receiving school will find it harder to maintain AYP with these incoming hard-core non-achievers.

And no one seems to have thought much about mobility. In some schools, the kids in the building in May are not the kids who were there in September. How, then, can the school be held accountable for their performance?

Although private companies are not yet taking over schools, they are already cashing in on the law. The law makes provisions for "secondary providers"—private firms—to tutor low-scoring students and provide other services. The *Wall Street Journal* estimated that there are some 24.3 billion dollars for companies to lust after in aid to high-poverty schools, reading programs, technology improvements, and building and running charter schools. Educational Testing Service vice president Sharon Robinson is said to have called NCLB a full employment act for test publishers.

The big problem with NCLB, though, remains that its intent is the opposite of what it claims. Former assistant secretary of education, Chester E. Finn, Jr., once said, "The public education system as we know it has proved that it cannot reform itself. It is an ossified government monopoly." As the preordained casualties from NCLB mount, the Chester Finns, George W. Bushes, and the think tanks on the right will intensify their attacks on the "government monopoly" while holding vouchers as the solution. If their attacks on public schools are successful, NCLB will indeed have proved to be The Perfect Law.

POSTSCRIPT

Is the No Child Left Behind Act Working?

The House Education and Workforce Committee claims that NCLBA is working. The Committee divides the arguments and evidence in support of this claim into seven major parts. One part involves reading and math test scores from four states. For example, the Committee attributes a 7 percentage point increase in fifth grade reading performance in Delaware to NCLBA. Another major part concerns progress in big-city schools. Here the Committee relies on data from the Council of Great City Schools, a coalition of more than 60 of the largest urban school districts in the nation. According to the Committee, the Council reports a 4.9 percentage point increase in fourth grade reading and a 6.8 percentage point increase in fourth grade math for urban school students between 2002 and 2003. A third major part involves support for NCLBA from minority school superintendents. Here the Committee reports that more than 100 African and Latino school district superintendents sent a letter to "federal leaders" in which they expressed "strong support" for NCLBA.

Bracey begins his essay by clarifying what he means when he describes NCLBA as a perfect law. From the perspective of Republicans, NCLBA will ultimately achieve three objectives: transfer many dollars from public education to private education, reduce the size of government, and "cripple or eliminate" teachers unions that historically aligned themselves with the Democratic party. Thus the perfect law from the Republican perspective is the perfect storm for Democrats. Bracey states that this is the reason why the Bush administration, which "has tried to deregulate and outsource virtually everything it touches" fought for the NCLBA, legislation that lays "1,100 pages of law and reams of regulations on public schools." Bracey makes his case in terms of the Adequate Yearly Provision of NCLBA. He argues that this provision is such that "in a few years 80 percent of the schools in a state (Minnesota) that outscores virtually the entire world will be labeled as failures." Parents will react to this by demanding a voucher system, something that was supported in the original Bush version of NCLBA but excluded in the final version. The resurrection of a revamped and expanded voucher system becomes the vehicle by which funds get transferred from the public sector to the private sector, reducing the effectiveness of teacher unions and reducing the size of the public sector. Thus, Bracey concludes, the key problem with NCLBA "remains that its intent is the opposite of what it claims"; that is, instead of helping public schools, NCLBA represents an attack on public schools.

The reading from the House Education and the Workforce Committee references a number of Web sites that provide additional information on NCLBA. A wide variety of data on both public and private education is available in

Digest of Education Statistics from the National Center for Education Statistics of the U.S. Department of Education at `http://nces.ed.gov/programs/digest/`. *A Guide to Education and No Child Left Behind* is available from the U.S. Department of Education (October 2004); it provides an overview of NCLBA. More information on private education can be obtained from the Council for American Private Education at `http://www.capenet.org/`. Also of interest are *No Child Left Behind? The Politics and Practice of School Accountability,* edited by Paul E. Peterson and Martin R. West (Brookings Institution, 2004); *Many Children Left Behind: How the No Child Left Behind Act Is Damaging Our Children and Our Schools,* edited by Deborah Meier and George Wood (Beacon, 2004); "U.S. Schools: Underperforming," by William C. Symonds in the January 10, 2005 issue of *Business Week;* "On Leaving No Child Behind," by Chester E. Finn, Jr. and Frederick M. Hess in *Public Interest* (Fall 2004); and "Damage Control for 'No Child Left Behind'" in *National Journal* (June 5, 2004).

Contributors to This Volume

EDITOR

FRANK J. BONELLO was born in Detroit in 1939. He received his B.S. from the University of Detroit in 1961, his M.A. from the University of Detroit in 1963, and his Ph.D. from Michigan State University in 1968. He is currently associate professor of economics at the University of Notre Dame, where he also served as Arts and Letters College Fellow. He writes in the areas of monetary economics and economic education. This is his sixth book. He is the author of *The Formulation of Expected Interest Rates* and coauthor of *Computer-Assisted Instruction in Economic Education*. In addition to *Taking Sides*, he has coedited, with T.R. Swartz, *Alternative Directions in Economic Policy* (Notre Dame Press, 1978); *The Supply Side: Debating Current Economic Policies* (Dushkin, 1983); and *Urban Finance Under Siege* (M.E. Sharpe, 1993).

STAFF

Larry Loeppke	Managing Editor
Jill Peter	Senior Developmental Editor
Nichole Altman	Developmental Editor
Beth Kundert	Production Manager
Jane Mohr	Project Manager
Tara McDermott	Design Coordinator
Bonnie Coakley	Editorial Assistant
Lori Church	Permissions

AUTHORS

ROBERT ALMEDER is a professor of philosophy at Georgia State University. He is the editor of the *American Philosophical Quarterly,* co-editor of the annual book series *Biomedical Ethic Reviews*, and former member of the editorial board of the *Journal of Business Ethics*. He earned his Ph.D. in philosophy at the University of Pennsylvania, and he is the author of *Harmless Naturalism: The Limits of Science and the Nature of Philosophy* (Open Court, 1998).

RICHARD APPLEBAUM is professor of sociology and global and international studies at the University of California at Santa Barbara. He currently serves as director of the Institute for Social, Behavioral, and Economic Research (ISBER) and co-director of the ISBER's Center for Global Studies. He is the founding editor of *Competition and Change: The Journal of Global Business and Political Economy.* He earned his Ph.D. from the University of Chicago.

DEAN BAKER is the co-director of the Center for Economic and Policy Research. His books include *Social Security: The Phony Crisis*, coauthored with Mark Weisbrot, (University of Chicago Press, 1999), *Getting Prices Right: The Battle Over the Consumer Price Index* (M.E. Sharpe Press 1997), and *Globalization and Progressive Economic Policy,* edited with Jerry Epstein and Bob Pollin (Cambridge University Press, 1998). He holds a Ph.D. in economics from the University of Michigan.

LENNY BERNSTEIN has a Ph.D. in chemical engineering from Purdue University. He has authored more than 30 articles on the social, economic, and environmental consequences of climatic change. Currently he heads L.S. Bernstein & Associates, L.L.C., a corporate consulting firm that focuses on the political and scientific developments associated with climate change and other global environmental issues.

GERALD W. BRACEY is an associate professor of education at George Mason University and an associate of the High/Scope Educational Research Foundation. His most recent book is *Setting the Record Straight: Responses to Misconceptions About Public Education in the U.S.*, 2nd ed. (Heinemann, 2004). His prior books include *The War Against America's Public Schools* (Allyn & Bacon, 2002) and *Put to the Test: An Educator's and Consumer's Guide to Standardized Testing* (Phi Delta Kappa, 2002). His education includes a Ph.D. in psychology from Stanford University.

EVELYN Z. BRODKIN is an associate professor at the School of Social Service Administration and lecturer in the Law School of the University of Chicago. She is also a faculty affiliate at the Northwestern University/University of Chicago's Joint Center for Poverty Research. She holds a Ph.D. in political science from the Massachusetts Institute of Technology.

LESTER R. BROWN holds degrees form Rutgers University, the University of Maryland, and Harvard University. In 1974, he founded Worldwatch

Institute, the first research institute devoted to the analysis of global environmental issues. At the Institute, he launched a number of publications, including the annual *State of the World* reports. In 2001, he founded the Earth Policy Institute to "provide a vision and a road map for achieving an environmentally sustainable economy." He has authored or coauthored 49 books including *Eco-Economy: Building an Economy for the Earth* (W.W. Norton, 2001).

PATRICK J. BUCHANAN sought the Republican nomination for the presidency in 1992, 1996, and 2000. He is frequently seen on television, and has served as a cohost on CNN's *Crossfire*. He writes a twice-weekly syndicated column and is the author of *The Great Betrayal: How American Sovereignty and Social Justice Are Being Sacrificed to the Gods of the Global Economy* (Little, Brown, 1998). He holds degrees from Georgetown and Columbia.

CHARLES T. CARLSTROM is a senior economic advisor in the research department at the Federal Reserve Bank of Cleveland. In addition to his interest in organ markets, his principal field of research activity is macroeconomics, concentrating on monetary economics and public finance. His degrees include a Ph.D. in economics, the University of Rochester; an M.A. in economics, the University of Rochester; and an A.B. in economics, the University of Chicago.

ELAINE CHAO is the twenty-forth Secretary of Labor, serving in that capacity since her Senate confirmation on January 29, 2001. She is the first Asian-American woman appointed to a president's cabinet in U.S. history. Her prior positions include, among others, the director of the Peace Corps, president and chief executive officer of United Way of America, and deputy secretary at the U.S. Department of Transportation. She has an undergraduate degree in economics from Mount Holyoke College and an M.B.A. from the Harvard Business School.

CHARLES CRAYPO is a professor emeritus of economics at the University of Notre Dame in Indiana. He is the author of *The Economics of Collective Bargaining: Case Studies in the Private Sector* (BNA, 1986) and coeditor, with Bruce Nissen, of *Grand Designs: The Impact of Corporate Strategies on Workers, Unions, and Communities* (Cornell University Press, 1993). He holds a Ph.D. from Michigan State University.

WILLIAM A. DARITY, JR. is a Research Professor of Public Studies, Africa and African American Studies and Economics at Duke University. He is also the Cary C. Boshamer Professor of Economics at the University of North Carolina. He is coauthor, with Samuel L. Myers, Jr., of *Persistent Disparity: Race and Economic Inequality in the U.S. Since 1945* (Edward Elgar, 1998). He holds a Ph.D. from the Massachusetts Institute of Technology.

DEMOCRATIC STAFF OF THE HOUSE COMMITTEE ON EDUCATION AND THE WORKFORCE. The names of the individuals who serve as members can be found at `http://edworkforce.housegov/democrats/staff.html`.

PETER DREIER is the Dr. E.P. Clapp Distinguished Professor of Politics and the director of the Urban & Environmental Policy Program of the Urban & Environmental Policy Institute at Occidental College in Los Angeles, California. He joined the Occidental faculty in January 1993, after serving 9 years as the director of housing at the Boston Redevelopment Authority and as senior policy advisor to the mayor of Boston. He previously taught at Tufts University. He is the author of *Place Matters: Metropolitics for the twenty-first Century* (University Press of Kansas, 2004) and the forthcoming *The Next LA: The Struggle for a Livable City* (University of California Press).

ROSS EISENBREY is vice president and policy director of the Economic Policy Institute in Washington D.C. He received his J.D. degree from the University of Michigan Law School and is a former commissioner of the U.S. Occupational Safety and Health Review Commission. Between 1999 and 2001, he served as policy director of the Occupational Safety and Health Administration.

JOEL FRIEDMAN joined the staff of the Center on Budget and Policy Priorities in September 2000 as a senior fellow. He divides his time between federal tax and budget issues and the International Budget Project. Immediately prior to coming to the Center, he worked in the South African Ministry of Finance, where he spent nearly 4 years as the U.S. Treasury's resident budget advisor. Before moving to South Africa, he was the director of budget analysis for the Democratic Staff of the House Budget Committee and a financial economist in the Budget Review Division of the Office of Management and Budget. He holds an M.P.A. from the Woodrow Wilson School of Public and International Affairs and a B.A. from Pomona College.

MILTON FRIEDMAN received the 1976 Nobel Prize in Economic Science for his work in consumption analysis and monetary history and theory and for demonstrating stabilization policy complexity. He has been a senior research fellow at the Stanford University Hoover Institution on War, Revolution, and Peace since 1977. In 1998, he received both the Presidential Medal of Freedom and the National Medal of Science. He and his wife, who also writes on economic topics, are coauthors of several publications including *Two Lucky People* (University of Chicago Press, 1998) and *Free to Choose: A Personal Statement* (Harcourt Brace,1990).

ALFREDO GOYBURU is a policy analyst in the Center for Data Analysis at The Heritage Foundation. He previously worked as a regional and energy economist for WEFA, a leader in economic information and forecasting. Before that, he worked as an economist for the New York state legislature, studying the impact of tax policy. Goyburu holds a bachelor's degree in economics from Cornell and an advanced economics degree from the University of Albany.

ROBERT GREENSTEIN is the founder and executive director of the Center on Budget and Policy Priorities. Greenstein is considered an expert on the federal budget and, in particular, the impact of tax and budget proposals on low-income people. Greenstein has written numerous reports, analyses, op-ed pieces, and magazine articles on poverty-related issues. In awarding him a MacArthur Fellowship, the MacArthur Foundation cited Greenstein for making "the Center a model for a non-partisan research and policy organization." In 1994, he was appointed by President Clinton to serve on the Bipartisan Commission on Entitlement and Tax Reform. Prior to founding the Center, Greenstein was administrator of the Food and Nutrition Service at the U.S. Department of Agriculture, where he directed the agency that operates federal food assistance programs, with a staff of 2,500 and a budget of $15 billion.

DANIEL T. GRISWOLD is associate director of the Center for Trade Policy Studies at the Cato Institute. He is the author of *Economic Causalities: How U.S. Foreign Policy Undermines Trade, Growth, and Liberty* (Cato Institute, 1999). He holds degrees from the University of Wisconsin–Madison and the London School of Economics.

ROBERT M. HAYES, an attorney, is president and general counsel of the Medicare Rights Center. Hayes led the national and New York Coalitions for the Homeless from 1979 to 1989. He is a MacArthur Foundation Fellow and has received honorary degrees from 10 colleges and universities. He is a graduate of Georgetown University and the New York University School of Law.

JAMES J. HECKMAN is Henry Schultz Distinguished Service Professor of Economics at the University of Chicago and senior fellow of the American Bar Association. He received the 2000 Nobel Prize in Economic Science for his development of theory and methods for analyzing selective samples. He is coeditor, with Burton Singer, of *Longitudinal Analysis of Labor Market Data* (Cambridge University Press, 1985). He received his Ph.D. in economics from Princeton University.

HOUSE EDUCATION AND THE WORKFORCE COMMITTEE was established on January 7, 1997, and has five subcommittees. It oversees education and workforce programs that affect and support many Americans. Currently, its 49 members include 27 Republicans and 22 Democrats. The chair of the committee is John Boehner (R-OH), and the senior Democrat is George Miller (D-CA).

NICHOLAS D. KRISTOF is a correspondent with *The New York Times* and served for 14 years as one of that newpaper's Asia correspondents. He is coauthor, with Sheryl WuDunn, of *Thunder from the East: Portrait of a Rising Asia*. He received, with Sheryl WuDunn, the 1990 Pulitzer Prize for coverage of the Tiananmen democracy movement in China and its suppression.

LOS ANGELES COUNTY ECONOMIC DEVELOPMENT CORPORATION is a private non-profit organization established in 1981 with the mission to attract, retain, and grow business and jobs in the Los Angeles region.

STEVEN MALANGA is a contributing editor of *City Journal* and a senior fellow at the Manhattan Institute. He previously held the position of executive editor of *Crain's New York Business*. His articles have also appeared in such publications as *The Wall Street Journal, New York Daily News*, and the *New*

York Post. His education includes an M.A. in english literature and language from the University of Maryland.

ROBERT D. MANNING is Caroline Werner Gannett Professor of the Humanities at the Rochester Institute of Technology and research associate of the Center for Comparative Immigration Studies at the University of California, San Diego. He is the author of *Credit Card Nation: The Consequences of America's Addiction to Credit* (Basic Books, 2000). He holds a Ph.D. from Johns Hopkins University.

PATRICK L. MASON is an associate professor of economics at Florida State University and director of African American studies. He is also an associate editor for the Southern Economic Association. He is a past president of the National Economics Association and the co-editor of several books including *Readings in Black Political Economy* (Rowland and Littlefield, 2005).

MICHAEL F. McENENEY is a partner in the law firm of Sidley Austin Brown & Wood L.L.P. and represents the Consumer Bankers Association. He earned his J.D. degree from Boston University School of Law. In his practice, he focuses primarily on regulatory and legislative issues impacting financial institutions with special emphasis on retail banking.

MARK MERRITT has been president and chief executive officer of the Pharmaceutical Care Management Association since March 2003. He previously held positions as senior vice president with the Pharmaceutical Research and Manufacturers of America and senior vice president with the American Association of Heath Plans. In 1996, he was chief spokesman and media strategist for the Republican National Convention. He earned two degrees from Georgetown University.

NORBERT J. MICHEL is a policy analyst with The Heritage Foundation's Center for Data Analysis. His areas of expertise include corporate finance and monetary economics. Before joining The Heritage Foundation, he worked for Entergy, a global energy company. He earned his Ph.D. from the University of New Orleans.

MICHAEL J. NEW received his Ph.D. in political science from Stanford University and is currently an assistant professor at the University of Alabama. He has served as a post-doctoral fellow at the Harvard-MIT data center and as a lecturer at the University of Massachusetts, Boston. His research interests include limitations on government, tax revolts, welfare reform, and campaign finance reform. He is also an adjunct scholar with the Cato Institute.

RALPH A. RECTOR is a research fellow at The Heritage Foundation and is the project manager of its Center for Data Analysis. Before joining The Heritage Foundation, he worked in the Tax Policy Economics Group at Coopers & Lybrand, L.L.P., where he supervised the construction of microsimulation models used to analyze the impact of tax reform on businesses and individuals. He has managed projects involving the use of large-scale relational databases and economic models. He has also served as a tax analyst and revenue estimator at the state and federal levels. He obtained his Ph.D. in economics from George Mason University.

CHRISTY D. ROLLOW, at the time of the writing of her article with Charles T. Carlstrom, was a research associate at the Federal Reserve Bank of Richmond.

MURRAY N. ROTHBARD 1926–1995 was a professor of economics at the University of Nevada, Las Vegas, and the vice president for academic affairs at the Ludwig von Mises Institute. Over his 45-year professional career, he wrote 25 books and thousands of articles, critical of socialism, statism, relativism, and scientism. He was instrumental in reviving an interest in the Austrian school of economics.

THOMAS RUSTICI is an instructor and head of undergraduate development for the economics department at George Mason University. He has published in the *Cato Journal*, *The Free Market*, and *Religion and Liberty*.

NANCY SCHEPER-HUGHES is professor of anthropology at the University of California, Berkeley, where she directs the doctoral program in medical anthropology. She was a member of the international Bellagio task force on transplantation, bodily integrity, and the international traffic in organs and coauthor of the first task force report on the traffic in human organs (*Transplant Proceedings, 29*, 2739–2745). She is currently completing a book entitled *The End of the Body: The Global Traffic in Organs* (Strauss & Giroux). She earned her Ph.D. in anthropology from the University of California, Berkeley.

ROBERT E. SCOTT has a Ph.D. in economics from the University of California, Berkeley, and is director of international programs at the Economic Policy Institute. His research has been published in the *Journal of Policy Analysis and Management*, the *International Review of Applied Economics*, and the *Stanford Law and Policy Review*.

THOMAS R. SWARTZ earned his Ph.D. in economics from Indiana University. He is currently a professor of economics at the University of Notre Dame and Fellow, Institute for Educational Initiatives. He writes in the areas of urban finance and economic education. He served as a coeditor of the first eleven editions of *Taking Sides: Clashing Views on Controversial Economic Issues*. He has also coedited *Alternative Directions in Economic Policy* (Notre Dame Press, 1978); *The Supply Side: Debating Current Economic Policies* (Dushkin Publishing Group, 1983) and *Urban Finance Under Siege* (M.E. Sharpe, 1993). He has also coedited or coauthored three other books. His most recent book is entitled *Working and Poor in Urban America*.

CHRIS TILLY is professor of regional economic and social development at the University of Massachusetts at Lowell and a member of the *Dollars & Sense* collective. His books include *Half a Job: Bad and Good Part-Time Jobs in a Changing Labor Market* (Temple University Press, 1996); *Glass Ceilings and Bottomless Pits: Women's Work, Women's Poverty*, with Randy Albelda (South End Press, 1997); and *American Cities in Transition: The Changing Face of Urban Inequality*, edited with Alice O'Connor and Lawrence Bobo (Russell

Sage Foundation, 2001). He holds a Ph.D. in economics and urban studies and planning from the Massachusetts Institute of Technology.

THE WHITE HOUSE can be reached at `http://wwwwhitehouse.gov/`. At this location is an "Issues" link. Utilizing this link, persons can find prepared statements presenting the position of the Bush administration on a variety of issues including Social Security.

U.S. DEPARTMENT OF HEALTH AND HUMAN RESOURCES is the "U.S. government's principal agency for protecting the health of all Americans and providing essential human services, especially for those who are least able to help themselves." For fiscal year 2005, it has a budget of $581 billion and over 67,000 employees.

JACKSON WILLIAMS, at the time he wrote his essay, was the legal counsel for Public Citizen's Congress Watch concentrating on civil justice issues. Previously, he was manager of public affairs for Defense Research Institute, the bar association of insurance defense counsel, where he also specialized in civil justice policy issues. He is a graduate of Loyola University of Chicago School of Law.

SHERYL WuDUNN is a correspondent with *The New York Times* and served for 14 years as one of that newspaper's Asia correspondents. She is coauthor, with Nicholas Kristof, of *Thunder from the East: Portrait of a Rising Asia*. She received, with Nicholas Kristof, the 1990 Pulitzer Prize for coverage of the Tiananmen democracy movement in China and its suppression.

Index